Not for WEENIES!

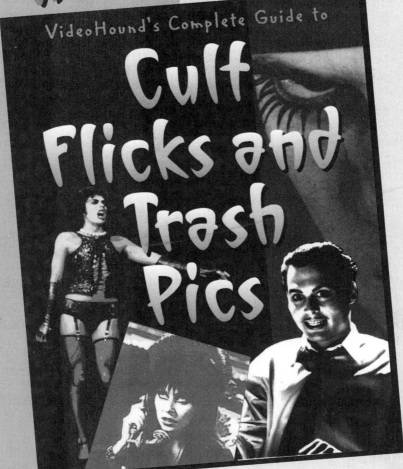

VideoHound's Complete Guide to

Cult Flicks and Trash Pics

Available at your local bookstore

VISIBLE INK PRESS

Also from Visible Ink Press:

VideoHound's Golden Movie Retriever

VideoHound's Complete Guide to
Cult Flicks and Trash Pics

VideoHound's Family Video Guide, Second Edition

The VideoHound & All-Movie Guide StarGazer

VideoHound's Movie LaughLines:
Quips, Quotes, and Clever Comebacks

VideoHound's Idiot's Delight:
The 100 Dumbest Movies of All Time

Toxic Fame: Celebrities Speak on Stardom

VideoHound's

SCI-FI
EXPERIENCE

VideoHound's

SCI-FI EXPERIENCE

Your Quantum Guide to the Video Universe

VISIBLE INK PRESS

Detroit   New York   Toronto   London

VideoHound's®

SCI-FI
EXPERIENCE

CREDITS

DIRECTOR . . . . Carol Schwartz

ASSOCIATE DIRECTOR . . . . Michelle Banks

CAST OF CHARACTERS . . . . Charles Cassady, Jason Rubis, Brian Thomas, Jim Olenski, Mike Mayo, Donald Liebenson, Jason Hirsch, David Massaro, Christine Tomassini, George Stover, Carol Schwartz, Michelle Banks

SUPPORTING CAST . . . . David Kunath, Bryan Lassner, Jim Craddock, Devra Sladics, Brad Morgan, Dean Dauphinais, Christa Brelin, and Dan Bono

RESEARCH CZARINA . . . . Christine Tomassini

ART DIRECTION . . . . Mary Krzewinski

ENGINEERING . . . . Don Dillaman

PRODUCERS . . . . Marty Connors, Julia Furtaw, and Terri Schell

ART SUPERVISION . . . . Cindy Baldwin

PRODUCTION . . . . Mary Beth Trimper, Dorothy Maki, Evi Seoud, and Shanna Heilveil

POST-PRODUCTION . . . . Marco Di Vita/The Graphix Group

SPIN DOCTORS . . . . Susan Stefani, Cyndi Naughton, Lauri Taylor, Jenny Sweetland, and Betsy Revegno

PHOTOGRAPHS . . . . The Kobal Collection

ADDITIONAL PHOTOS . . . . Photo of George Stover being embraced by an alien in *Night Beast* courtesy of Troma, Inc.

PHOTO EDITING . . . . Michelle Banks, Pam Hayes, Randy Bassett, and Barb Yarrow

CAPTIONS . . . . Susan Stefani and Jane Hoehner

TECHNICAL ADVISORS . . . . Al Bogdan, Jim Olenski, Charles Cassady, Jason Rubis, Brian Thomas, Mike Mayo, Donald Liebenson, Jason Hirsch, Peggy Kneffel Daniels, and Christine Tomassini

RESEARCH . . . . Thomas Video, Clawson, MI, the official vid store of *Sci-Fi Experience*, and a handy source for video orders nationwide

Thanks to: the gang at Thomas Video—Jim, Mike, Joel, Rick, Dena, Katie, and Gary—for answering questions and offering opinions (most of which were welcome).

More thanks to: Bob Cosenza at Kobal; George Stover of Baltimore; Marco DiVita, master typesetter; Mary Alice Rattenbury for being Mary Alice; Troma, Inc.; and Donald L-i-e-b-e-n-s-o-n for being so understanding about his name.

Published on location in Detroit, on Planet Earth.

The canine character portrayed in this book considers himself to be purely a hologram; any resemblance to an actual dog, living or dead, is merely an idea that has been subliminally implanted in your brain.

A Cunning Canine™ Production

Visible Ink Press © MCMXCVII

Contents

Introduction **ix**   Instructions for Use **xi**

THE REVIEWS:
A to Z with
photos and quotes **1**

Sidebars

Introduction

All right, already!

Where to cut it off? The Hound just got back from viewing *Independence Day,* and is fighting the urge to stop the presses and slip it in. (So what if the plot was hokey. So what if the president was—how unlikely—a good guy. We kicked alien butt in a big way.) *Star Trek: Deep Space Nine* just came out on video. *Star Trek: First Contact* is about to hit the theatres. *The Outer Limits* is back on TV. I have my order in for the "Star Trek" Barbie (no kiddin'). And I finally got the Sci-Fi Channel on my cable system....

But you gotta draw the line somewhere (so my publisher tells me). For this latest entry in the VideoHound family, we drew that line at nearly 1200 sci-fi features from *The Abyss* to *Zontar, the Thing from Venus,* including 20 TV series that are available on tape (couldn't leave out *The X-Files,* could we?). I've also included some fantasy and a bit of Japanimation (although, again, where to draw the line there? The Hound could do a whole book on that). I also couldn't resist a dozen or so documentaries, in the *Alien Autopsy* tradition, for those of you who know that the truth is out there.

I know, I know, I still left out your favorite movie. I didn't appreciate the subtleties in *Solaris.* I'm too forgiving of Steven Spielberg. As always, write me and tell me what you think—I love to hear from you, my best friends.

Like its predecessor, *VideoHound's Golden Movie Retriever,* each entry in *VideoHound's Sci-Fi Experience* contains such elements as movie title, description/review, alternate titles, bone rating (one to four, including WOOF! for the incomprehensibly bad), year released, MPAA rating, run time in minutes, B&W or color, country the flick was produced in (if other than the U.S.), cast (including voiceovers and cameos), director, writer, cinematographer, music director, awards, format, and distributors. Whew. See the sample entry at the end of this introduction if you need visual aids.

But wait—there's more!

SEE! Sidebars on some of our favorite people and topics in sci fi—including George Lucas, Ray Harryhausen, George Pal, Time Travel, and Mexican Wrestling Superheroes. The Hugos and Godzilla. Bad Science and Mad Scientists.

SEE! Our favorite quotes and tag lines from the movies!

SEE! Over 120 photo stills from the movies!

SEE! "Sci-Fi Connections," an appendix bursting with web sites, 'zines, fan clubs, books, and conventions!

SEE! An Alternate Titles Index!

SEE! Cast and Director Indexes!

SEE! The patented VideoHound Category Index, boasting over 200 classifications ranging from the general ("Comedy," "Fantasy,") to the specific ("Alien Abductions," "Burial at Space"), from "Unexplained Phenomena" to "Conspiracies Involving Unexplained Phenomena."

SEE! A Distributor Guide offering names and addresses for video sources (but beware—many sell only to retail outlets).

And remember...there is nothing wrong with your VCR. Do not attempt to adjust the picture. We are controlling transmission. Sit back, relax, and be entertained. And write the Hound and let 'em know what should be in *VideoHound's Sci-Fi Experience—the Sequel.*

VideoHound's Sci-Fi Experience
Visible Ink Press
835 Penobscot Bldg.
645 Griswold St.
Detroit MI 48226
http://www.thomson.com/videohound.html

Alphabetization

Titles are arranged on a word-by-word basis, including articles and prepositions. Leading articles (A, An, The) are ignored in English-language titles; the equivalent foreign articles are not ignored (because so many people—not you, of course—don't recognize them as articles); thus, *The Abominable Dr. Phibes* appears in the As, but *La Jetee* appears in the Ls. Some other points to keep in mind:

Acronyms appear alphabetically as if regular words. For example, *E.T.* is alphabetized as "ET," *A*P*E* as "APE."

Common abbreviations in titles file as if they were spelled out, so *Dr. Alien* will be alphabetized as "Doctor Alien."

Movie titles with numbers (such as *2001: A Space Odyssey*) are alphabetized as if the number was spelled out—so Kubrick's classic would appear in the Ts as if it were "Two Thousand and One: A Space Odyssey."

Sample Review

Each review contains up to 17 tidbits of information, as enumerated below. Please realize that we faked a bit of info in this review, because we couldn't find one single movie that coincidentally contained every single element that might appear in a review. If anyone out there finds that singular entry, please let us know. And then beam back to the planet you came from.

2001: A Space Odyssey

Director Stanley Kubrick and writer Arthur C. Clarke redefined cinematic science fiction with this masterpiece. Dispensing with many conventional narrative techniques, they told the centuries–spanning story through startling (though sometimes opaque) images. Kubrick succeeded in making space travel seem absolutely real and believable. Who cares if the plot makes no sense? The stately pace, the combination of effects and music, and the core conflict between man and machine have made the film a cultural milestone. Martin Balsam originally recorded the voice of HAL, but was replaced by Douglas Rain. Arthur C. Clarke adapted the script from his novel *The Sentinel*. Followed by a sequel, *2010: The Year We Make Contact*. The laserdisc edition is presented in letterbox format and features a special supplementary section on the making of *2001*, a montage of images from the film, production documents, memos, and photos.

AKA: Stanley Kubrick's 2001. ♫♫♫♫ **1968** **(G)** **139m/C** *GB* Keir Dullea, Gary Lockwood, William Sylvester, Dan Richter, Leonard Rossiter; *V:* Douglas Rain; *D:* Stanley Kubrick; *W:* Stanley Kubrick, Arthur C. Clarke; *C:* Geoffrey Unsworth; *M:* Richard Strauss. Hugos '69: Dramatic Presentation; Academy Awards '68: Best Visual Effects; Nominations: Academy Awards '68: Best Art Direction/Set Direction, Best Director (Kubrick), Best Story & Screenplay. **VHS, Beta, LV** *MGM, CRC, FCT*

---

1. Title (see also Alternate Titles below, and the "Alternate Titles Index")
2. Description/review
3. Alternate titles (we faked it here)
4. One- to four-bone rating (or WOOF!), four bones being the ultimate praise
5. Year released
6. MPAA rating
7. Length in minutes
8. Black and white (B) or Color (C)
9. Country in which produced (if other than the U.S.)
10. Cast, including cameos and voiceovers (V)
11. Director(s)
12. Writer(s)
13. Cinematographer(s)
14. Music (we took some liberties for this one)
15. Awards, including nominations
16. Format, including VHS, Beta, and Laservideo/disk (LV)
17. Distributor code(s) (see also "Distributor List" and "Distributor Guide")

Abbott and Costello Go to Mars

But they don't. Loose-plotted slapstick finds the comedy duo as workmen accidentally launched aboard a rocket ship. First it lands near New Orleans during Mardis Gras, where A&C mistake marching mummers for monstrous Martians. Then they soar into space, hitting not Mars but Venus, where Miss Universe finalists play an Amazon race who haven't seen a man in 400 years. Vintage f/x are surprisingly sharp, and the scriptwriters knew enough about sci fi to dump the term 'positronic brain' in amid all the outdated buffoonery. *♫♫*

1953 77m/B Bud Abbott, Lou Costello, Mari Blanchard, Robert Paige, Martha Hyer, Horace McMahon, Jack Kruschen, Anita Ekberg; *D:* Charles Lamont; *W:* John Grant, D.D. Beauchamp. **VHS** *MCA*

Abbott and Costello Meet the Invisible Man

Abbott and Costello play newly graduated detectives who take on the murder case of a boxer (Arthur Franz) accused of killing his manager. Using a serum that makes people invisible, the boxer helps Costello in a prizefight that will frame the real killers, who killed the manager because the boxer refused to throw a fight. An extra edge is added—this is one of the only invisible man features since the original to make an issue of the drug's mind-altering properties. Some of the invisibility gags are based on a misunderstanding of invisibility—as when Costello splits in two—but this is generally regarded as one of the better A&C comedies. The combination of invisibility and gangsters leads to some truly bizarre sequences, as in the famous boxing match scene, in which Costello faces off against a big bruiser in the ring with some help from his unseen friend. Good supporting cast of familiar faces adds to the fun. Special effects by some of the team that created those used in the original *The Invisible Man* (1932), and are much better than one would expect from a relatively low-budget comedy of the time. *♫♫♫*

1951 82m/B Bud Abbott, Lou Costello, Nancy Guild, Adele Jergens, Sheldon Leonard, William Frawley, Gavin Muir, Arthur Franz, Fred Rinaldo, John Grant; *D:* Charles Lamont; *W:* Robert Lees; *C:* George Robinson. **VHS** *MCA*

The Abominable Dr. Phibes

After being disfigured (and believed dead) in a freak car accident, a twisted genius decides that the members of a surgical team let his wife die and shall each perish by a different Biblical plague. Highly stylish, the murders all have a ceremonial feel to them. Though set in the 1920s, Phibes' equipment seems a bit ahead of its time—and where did he get a Frank Sinatra record? High camp balances gore with plenty of good humor, with the veteran cast of British character actors in top form. Caroline Munro appears only in photographs as the deceased wife, Victoria Regina (which was also the name of the hit play that made Vincent Price a star). Followed in 1972 by *Dr. Phibes Rises Again*. *♫♫♫*

1971 (PG) 90m/C *GB* Vincent Price, Joseph Cotten, Hugh Griffith, Terry-Thomas, Virginia North, Susan Travers, Alex Scott, Caroline Munro; *D:* Robert Fuest. **VHS, Beta, LV** *VES, LIV, ORI*

Abraxas: Guardian of the Universe

Cheapo Canadian production casts World Wrestling Federation vet Jess "The Body" Ven-

"So raise your hand if you think that was a Russian water-tentacle."

—Lindsay (Mary Elizabeth Mastrantonio) in *The Abyss.*

A team of U.S. Navy SEALs try to investigate a downed ship, but who knew the bottom of the ocean would be so dark? *The Abyss.*

tura in the stiff title role, a space cop on Earth to foil his evil ex-partner Secundas, who's inseminated a virgin with the "anti-life equation" that could destroy the universe. There's enough galactic gobbledygook to match *Robot Monster,* but a few camp touches (like James Belushi's cameo) indicate nobody should take it too seriously. Minimal f/x or gore; it's mainly two burly, gravel-voiced bruisers pummeling each other. Also available in an edited PG-13 version. 🎵🎵

1990 (R) 90m/C *CA* Jesse Ventura, Sven Ole-Thorsen, Marjorie Bransfield, Michael Copeman, Francis Mitchell, Jerry Levitan; *Cameos:* James Belushi; *D:* Damien Lee; *W:* Damien Lee; *C:* Curtis Petersen; *M:* Carlos Lopes. **VHS** *PSM*

The Absent-Minded Professor

Classic dumb Disney fantasy of the era is still fun for kids and for adults who remember it with fondness. A professor (Fred MacMurray, at his easy-going likable best) accidentally invents an anti-gravity substance called flubber, causing inanimate objects and people to become airborne. Great sequence of the losing school basketball team taking advantage of flubber during a game, and, of course, the famous "flying flivver" Model T. Also available in a colorized version. Followed by *Son of Flubber.* 🎵🎵🎵

1961 97m/B Fred MacMurray, Nancy Olson, Keenan Wynn, Tommy Kirk, Leon Ames, Ed Wynn; *D:* Robert Stevenson; *C:* Edward Colman; *M:* George Bruns. Nominations: Academy Awards '61: Best Art Direction/Set Decoration (B & W), Best Black and White Cinematography. **VHS, Beta, LV** *DIS, BTV*

The Abyss

When it comes to staging big action scenes involving people and hardware, director James Cameron is as good as anyone in the business. Here, he has created some brilliant underwater set pieces, but the film falls victim to its own excesses: a crippled submarine, dangerous nuclear warheads, the hurricane,

the insane diver, and if those aren't enough, we've also got extraterrestrials who look like tropical fish that have swallowed Tiffany lamps. Fine performances from Ed Harris, Mary Elizabeth Mastrantonio, and Michael Biehn, and even better effects. The laserdisc version contains 27 extra minutes of footage; this director's cut will also be released on VHS. **AKA:** L'Oeuvre au Noir. 🦴🦴🦴

1989 (PG-13) 140m/C Ed Harris, Mary Elizabeth Mastrantonio, Todd Graff, Michael Biehn, John Bedford Lloyd, J.C. Quinn, Leo Burmester, Kidd Brewer Jr., Kimberly Scott, Adam Nelson, George Robert Kirk, Chris Elliott, Jimmie Ray Weeks; **D:** James Cameron; **W:** James Cameron; **C:** Mikael Salomon; **M:** Alan Silvestri. Academy Awards '89: Best Visual Effects; Nominations: Academy Awards '89: Best Cinematography, Best Sound. **VHS, Beta, LV** FXV

Access Code

Government agents attempt to uncover a private organization that has gained control of nuclear weapons for the purpose of world domination. A ragged patchwork of disconnected scenes meant to test the virtue of patience. 🦴

1984 90m/C Martin Landau, Michael Ansara, MacDonald Carey; **D:** Mark Sobel. **VHS, Beta** PSM

The Adventures of Baron Munchausen

Terry Gilliam, director of *Time Bandits, The Fisher King,* and *Brazil* (not to mention the timeshifting *12 Monkeys*), has often tried to blur the line between dreams and reality. With his version of the Munchausen tales, he not only succeeds, he actually takes us right into the adventure. Overstatement and out-and-out lies were the rule for the real life 18th-century raconteur upon whom this ambitious but under-appreciated marvel is based. John Neville's performance as the Baron, Oliver Reed as the god Vulcan, Uma Thurman as Venus, Robin Williams as the King of the Moon, Sarah Polley as Sally Salt, are all splen-

"Yeah, sure, I'll go with you guys. But, uh, I think I forgot my toothbrush." John Lithgow stalls for time in *The Adventures of Buckaroo Bonzai Across the Eighth Dimension.*

did (although all of them at times are overwhelmed by the lush sets, inspired cinematography, and stunning special effects). On the moon, the royally detachable head gives Gilliam the chance to do one of his Pythonesque animations live. Gilliam proves that he knows how to utilize a big budget. Two letterboxed laser versions are available; the Criterion Collection features audio commentary and a large supplemental section, including deleted scenes. 🐾🐾🐾🐾

1989 (PG) 126m/C John Neville, Eric Idle, Sarah Polley, Valentina Cortese, Oliver Reed, Uma Thurman, Sting, Jonathan Pryce, Bill Paterson, Peter Jeffrey, Alison Steadman, Charles McKeown, Dennis Winston, Jack Purvis; *Cameos:* Robin Williams; *D:* Terry Gilliam; *W:* Terry Gilliam; *C:* Giuseppe Rotunno; *M:* Michael Kamen. Nominations: Academy Awards '89: Best Costume Design, Best Makeup. **VHS, Beta, LV, 8mm** *COL, CRC*

The Adventures of Buckaroo Banzai Across the Eighth Dimension

After accidentally opening up a gateway to the eighth dimension, our (and everybody's) hero Buckaroo Banzai (Peter Weller) must call on all of his talents in an interstellar battle for the world. Luckily, he is a multi-skilled genius-expert at everything. Race car driver, top neurosurgeon, rock star, diplomat, comic book hero, martial artist, scientist, last hope of the human race...these all describe Buckaroo. Teaming up with the good Black Lectoids, he and his rock 'n' roll commandos, The Hong Kong Cavaliers, must go head-to-head against the evil Red Lectoids whose leader inhabits the body of Dr. Lizardo (John Lithgow). Offbeat and nutty, campy and culty, this wacky sci fi moves as fast as Buckaroo's jet-propelled fiesta. Ellen Barkin is great as sweetheart Penny Priddy. Implied but never-made sequel is a frequent request at many a "good" video store. **AKA:** Buckaroo Banzai. 🐾🐾🐾🐾

1984 (PG) 100m/C Peter Weller, Ellen Barkin, Jeff Goldblum, Christopher Lloyd, John Lithgow, Lewis Smith, Rosalind Cash, Robert Ito, Pepe Serna, Vincent Schiavelli, Dan Hedaya, Yakov Smirnoff, Jamie Lee Curtis; *D:* W.D. Richter; *W:* Earl Mac Rauch; *C:* Fred W. Koenekamp; *M:* Michael Boddicker. **VHS, Beta, LV** *VES, LIV*

Aelita: Queen of Mars

Now we know how Mars became the Red planet. The title has the stench of turkey about it, but wait; this silent is golden. Director Yakov Protazanov's influential epic concerns a Moscow engineer who, while awake, builds the new Russia, but asleep, dreams of life on Mars and the Martian queen, Aelita. In a machine of his own invention, he blasts off for Mars, where he eventually instigates a revolution amongst the imprisoned Martian slaves. A fascinating curio, with impressive split-screen photography and cubist sets. Based on the novel by Alexi Tolstoi. This Kino on Video edition contains a piano score. **AKA:** Aelita; Aelita: The Revolt of the Robots. 🐾🐾🐾

1924 113m/B *RU* Yulia Solntseva, Igor Illinski, Nikolai Batalov, Nikolai Tseretelli, Vera Orlova; *D:* Yakov Protazanov; *W:* Fedor Ozep, Aleksey Fajko; *C:* Yuri Zhelyabuzhsky, Emil Schoenemann. **VHS, LV** *KIV, FCT, SNC*

After the Fall of New York

Dim-witted post-apocalyptic tale set in New York after the fall of the "Big Bomb." A man, driven to search for the last normal woman, has reason to believe she is frozen alive and kept in the heart of the city. His mission: locate her, thaw her, engage in extremely limited foreplay with her, and repopulate the planet. A poorly dubbed dating allegory. **WOOF!**

1985 (R) 95m/C *IT FR* Michael Sopkiw, Valentine Monnier, Anna Kanakis, Roman Geer, Edmund Purdom, George Eastman; *D:* Martin Dolman. **VHS, Beta** *VES, LIV*

Aftermath

Three astronauts return to Earth to discover the planet ravaged by a nuclear war that has destroyed all semblance of civilization, budget, editing, and acting talent. Lone survivor Steve Barkett helps remaining nice folks combat bikers and fleshy-headed mutants. Watch it only if your scavenger-hunt list requires a cameo by fantasy flick buff/publisher Forrest J. Ackerman, here as a museum curator. **WOOF!**

1985 96m/C Steve Barkett, Larry Latham, Lynne Margulies, Sig Haig; *Cameos:* Forrest J. Ackerman; *D:* Ted V. Mikels. **VHS, Beta** *PSM*

Aftershock

A beautiful alien bimbo beams down to Earth in the mistaken belief that there's intelligent life. Instead, civilization has collapsed, and between the usual *Road Warrior* punks and a repressive government, there are plenty of perils for this mysterious stranger and two kung-fu guys who appoint themselves her guardians. Silly action with a few political slogans thrown in for redeeming social value. 🐰🐰

1988 **(R)** 90m/**C** Jay Roberts Jr., Elizabeth Kaitan, Chris Mitchum, Richard Lynch, John Saxon, Russ Tamblyn, Michael Berryman, Chris De Rose, Chuck Jeffreys; **D:** Frank Harris. **VHS, Beta** *PSM*

Akira

In the future megalopolis of Tokyo, secret government experiments on children with ESP go awry, resulting in an cataclysmic explosion on Tokyo. Akira, the most powerful of the children, is kept in cryogenic suspension under strict security. Some of the city's youth gang members, who may or may not be subjects of the experiment themselves, become involved with the various factions fighting to control the city. When Akira awakes, will he be their savior, or the agent of their destruction? Otomo started his massive, finely detailed manga novel in the early '80s. When it became a gigantic success with Japanese readers, he began to work on the anime feature version, which also became an international hit. Oddly, when he returned to work on the print version of the story, he drastically altered and expanded the storyline. Otomo's obsessive attention to detail shows in every frame—at one time, nearly every animation studio in southeast Asia worked on *Akira*. The work pays off with an exciting, impressive spectacle, although the complex plot is often perplexing. The well-rounded characters are sometimes lost in all the gadgetry. While conceptually it tends to wander at times, it still packs a punch with its awesome visuals. Animated; in Japanese with English subtitles or dubbed. 🐰🐰🐰

1989 124m/**C** *JP* **D:** Katsuhiro Otomo, Sheldon Renan; **W:** Katsuhiro Otomo, Izo Hashimoto; **C:** Katsuji Misawa. **VHS, LV** *WTA, STP, INJ*

Alien

Taught direction by Ridley Scott, stunning sets and special effects, and an excellent ensemble cast make this a suspenseful roller coaster ride in outer space. In the claustrophobic tradition of *The Thing,* an intergalactic freighter is invaded by an unstoppable, carnivorous, acid-spewing alien intent on picking off the crew one by one. While the crew desperately seeks a way to destroy the creature, their numbers and patience dwindle. Sigourney Weaver is exceptional as Ripley, the strong-willed survivor who goes toe to toe with the crew and the Alien. Fantastic futuristic visual design and a horrific creature designed by H. R. Giger create a vivid sense of impending doom, enhanced further by the ominous Jerry Goldsmith score. Oscar-winning special effects include the classic alien "birth," as the creature springs from the chest of its first victim. This scene was said to have movie-goers heading for the bathroom when the film was first released. Successfully followed by *Aliens* and *Alien 3* (with whispers of *Alien 4* still to come). Remember, in space no one can hear you scream. 🐰🐰🐰🐰

1979 **(R)** 116m/**C** Tom Skerritt, Sigourney Weaver, Veronica Cartwright, Yaphet Kotto, Harry Dean Stanton, Ian Holm, John Hurt; **D:** Ridley Scott; **W:** Dan O'Bannon; **C:** Derek Vanlint, Denys Ayling; **M:** Jerry Goldsmith. Hugos '80: Dramatic Presentation; Academy Awards '79: Best Visual Effects; Nominations: Academy Awards '79: Best Art Direction/Set Decoration. **VHS, Beta, LV** *FOX*

Alien 3

This second *Alien* sequel picks up where *Aliens* left off. Survivor Ripley crashlands on Fiorina 161, a planet that serves as a penal colony for sex offenders. Ripley is forced to shave her head because of the planet's lice problem, and she sets out to survive on the cold, unfriendly planet until a rescue ship can come for her. Fending off sexual advances from the men, Ripley soon discovers this is actually the least of her problems. As fate (and sequel writers) would have it, Ripley wasn't the only survivor of the crash—an alien survived too, and has somehow implanted her with a gestating alien of her own. This film attempts to recapture the disturbing claustrophobic tone of the original by focusing more on character conflict and suspense than the unrelenting action of *Aliens*. To a great extent, it succeeds, thanks in large part to another excellent performance by Sigourney Weaver, but the film still goes over the top in a few places, particularly some of the none-too-subtle religious references. Intended as the final installment of the series (but don't you believe it). Though maligned at the time, music video director David Fincher went on to helm the acclaimed 1995 thriller *Seven*. 🦴🦴🦴

1992 (R) 135m/C Sigourney Weaver, Charles S. Dutton, Charles Dance, Paul McGann, Brian Glover, Ralph Brown, Danny Webb, Christopher John Fields, Holt McCallany, Lance Henriksen; **D:** David Fincher; **M:** Elliot Goldenthal. Nominations: Academy Awards '92: Best Visual Effects. **VHS, LV** *FXV*

Alien Autopsy: Fact or Fiction?

Hey, this presentation of some old film footage that may be of the actual autopsy of an alien being, presumably from a saucer crash in 1947 near Roswell, New Mexico, is hosted by Jonathon Frakes (*Star Trek: The Next Generation*). Talk about expert. Other experts interviewed about the authenticity of the footage include special-effects pro Stan ("I don't know how they did this") Winton, New Mexico Congressman Steven Schiff, nuclear physicist Stanton Friedman, Eastman Kodak's Laurence Cate, pathologist Dr. Cyril ("does not appear to be a human being") Wecht, and even the former Roswell coverup, er, public relations officer Walter Haut. Informative to those who already believe and fans of Geraldo. 🦴🦴🦴

1995 70m/C D: Tom McGough; **W:** Robert Kiviat, Tom Seligson; **M:** Robert Wait. **VHS** *VMK*

Alien Contamination

Italian-made tale of two astronauts who return to Earth from an expedition to Mars carrying some deadly bacterial eggs. Controlled by a Martian intent on conquering the world, the eggs squirt a gloppy juice that makes people explode on contact (a special effect). When more and more of the eggs appear, heroes Ian McCulloch and Louise Monroe trace them to a remote colony where a bigger, squishier alien is controlling humans to help grow and harvest the eggs. A cheap and sloppy attempt to cash in on the success of *Alien,* with ideas taken from *Invasion of the Body Snatchers*. From the director of *Starcrash*. Dubbed. **AKA:** Contamination. 🦴

1981 (R) 90m/C *IT* Ian McCulloch, Louise Monroe, Martin Mase, Siegfried Rauch, Lisa Hahn; **D:** Lewis (Luigi Cozzi) Coates; **W:** Lewis (Luigi Cozzi) Coates; **C:** Guiseppe Pinori. **VHS, Beta** *NO*

Alien Dead

Meteorite lands on obnoxious teens, turning them into flesh-eating ghouls. Would you believe flying ace Eddie Rickenbacker is involved? Florida-lensed junk owns its place in history as the first commercially released feature from Fred Olen Ray, shot for only $12,000. Guest star Buster Crabbe—one-time Flash Gordon—looks like he'd rather be somewhere else in this, his last screen appearance. Occasionally amusing dialogue: "She's deader than Mother's Day in an orphanage." **AKA:** It Fell from the Sky. 🦴

1985 (R) 87m/C Buster Crabbe, Linda Lewis, Ray Roberts; **D:** Fred Olen Ray; **W:** Fred Olen Ray. **VHS, Beta** *ACA, GHV*

The Alien Factor

Another low-budget crazed critter from outer space dispatch, this one featuring multiple aliens, one of whom is good, who have the misfortune of crashlanding near Baltimore. The grotesque extraterrestrials jolt a small town out of its sleepy state by wreaking havoc (except for the good one, of course). Decent special effects for a low-budget cheapie, the cast also doubled as the crew. The main focus shifts to the intellectual problem of trying to separate the good alien from his identical evil cronies. Executed with a genuine affection for the genre, this is a fine film for fans of both regional and amateur film making. Worth a view, even if you're not, just to see Baltimorian George Stover wrasslin' with the alien. 🦴🦴🦴

1978 (PG) 82m/C Don Leifert, Tom Griffith, Mary Mertens, Dick Dyszel, George Stover; **D:** Donald M. Dohler. **VHS, Beta** *NO*

George Stover on The Alien Factor

When I was offered a role in *The Alien Factor*, I couldn't believe that my dream of being in a science-fiction film was finally going to come true. However, there were many obstacles to overcome in producing a low-budget 16mm feature, especially one that was ambitious enough to require several different monster costumes, stop-motion animation, and other special-effects scenes.

Not since John Waters started making feature films late in the previous decade had any local fimmaker produced a full-length motion picture in Maryland. Don Dohler—whose background included underground comics and publishing *Cinemagic* magazine—spearheaded the project and was the glue that kept cast and crew together until filming was completed on this story of the crashlanding of a spacecraft transporting several alien creatures.

Considering its minuscule budget and the fact that it was a first-time effort for Dohler and company, *The Alien Factor* enjoyed a surprising amount of success. It was blown up to 35mm and screened in Baltimore theatres, on 42nd Street in New York City, as well as at a film festival in France. Not only was *The Alien Factor* released on prerecorded video, it also enjoyed a long run in TV syndication and was even broadcast on WCBS-TV in New York and shown nationwide on Ted Turner's SuperStation WTBS. Extensive press coverage followed, including a review in *Variety* and an appearance by one of the film's alien creatures on the cover of *Famous Monsters of Filmland* magazine. It could almost be said that *The Alien Factor* is to Baltimore what *Night of the Living Dead* is to Pittsburgh and I'm very proud to have been a part of this local success story.

—George Stover, "Steven Price" in *The Alien Factor.*

Alien from L.A.

A limp comedy about a California girl (Kathy Ireland) who unwittingly stumbles onto the ancient civilization of Atlantis while searching for her lost archaeologist father. She quickly becomes embroiled in a number of rather silly adventures. Much of the alleged humor revolves around the Atlanteans calling Ireland an "alien." Ireland makes an appealing heroine, but that's not enough to save this movie, which is weakly plotted, acted, and filmed. It probably would have been more fun if it had been made in the '70s. 🎞

1987 (PG) 88m/C Kathy Ireland, Thom Mathews, Don Michael Paul, Linda Kerridge, William R. Moses, Richard Haines; **D:** Albert Pyun; **W:** Albert Pyun, Debra Ricci, Regina Davis; **C:** Tom Fraser. **VHS, Beta, LV** *MED*

Alien Intruder

Tracy Scoggins is an evil space demon (or something) in the guise of a beautiful woman, who appears before lustful deep-space astronauts—usually during virtual-reality sex fantasies—and tempts them to kill each other for her affections. Well, it passes the time, anyway, and distracts viewers from the feeble f/x of the spaceship miniatures. Note that all the craft are named after dead rock stars. 🎞

1993 (R) 90m/C Billy Dee Williams, Tracy Scoggins, Maxwell Caulfield, Gary Roberts, Richard Cody, Stephen Davies, Jeff Conaway; **D:** Ricardo Jacques Gale; **W:** Nick Stone; **C:** Michael Pinkey. **VHS, LV** *PMH*

Alien Nation

A few hundred thousand alien slaves in a hijacked saucer find sanctuary on "near-future" 1990s Earth, and face the challenge of any immigrant minority. Some assimilate into American society, others dwell in the ghetto. Mandy Patinkin plays an upscale "newcomer"

"In case you haven't been paying attention to current events, we just got our asses kicked, pal!"

—Private Hudson (Bill Paxton) in *Aliens.*

(renamed—*a la* Ellis Island—after the city of San Francisco) who becomes the first alien LAPD detective and teams with surly, bigoted human cop James Caan to solve murders over an otherworldly narcotic. Transparent script uses science fiction as a lens for examining contemporary racial conflicts and attitudes. Nothing wrong with that, but the filmmakers cuff the plot to every dumb action-buddy-cop cliche since *48 Hrs.,* and the mottle-headed aliens just aren't all that interesting. One expects better from producer Hurd (the force behind *The Terminator* and *Aliens*). The *Alien Nation* universe got a more detailed exploration in a subsequent short-lived TV series and small-screen sequels also on video. 🎞🎞🎞

1988 (R) 89m/C James Caan, Mandy Patinkin, Terence Stamp, Kevyn Major Howard, Peter Jason, Jeff Kober, Leslie Bevins; *D:* Graham Baker; *W:* Rockne S. O'Bannon; *M:* Curt Sobel. **VHS, Beta, LV** *FOX*

Alien Nation: Dark Horizon

The alien Newcomers have successfully adapted to life on Earth but face continuing dangers when a human-supremacy group develops a virus to wipe them out and an alien infiltrator is plotting to return them to slavery on Tencton. Naturally, it's up to detectives Sykes and Francisco to save the day. The first of several TV movies based on the brief series. 🎞🎞

1994 (PG) 90m/C Gary Graham, Eric Pierpont, Scott Patterson, Terri Treas, Michelle Scarabelli, Lee Bryant, Sean Six, Lauren Woodland, Ron Fassier, Jeff Marcus; *D:* Kenneth Johnson; *W:* Diane Frolov, Andrew Schneider; *M:* David Kurtz. **VHS** *FXV*

Alien Predators

Three friends encounter a malevolent alien in this dull reworking of the plot of *The Andromeda Strain* with laughable special effects tossed in for those outwitted by the script. **WOOF!**

1980 (R) 92m/C Dennis Christopher, Martin Hewitt, Lynn-Holly Johnson, Luis Prendes; *D:* Deran Sarafian. **VHS, Beta** *VTR*

Alien Prey

Two lesbians in a dysfunctional relationship induct a wandering simpleton into a *menage a trois*. He's not a lost mental patient, though, but a potentially lethal alien scout. Cult appreciation beckons for this British cheapie originally titled *Prey*. There's something to offend anyone: graphic sex, violence, co-dependence, cross-dressing, and cannibalism. Deadpan, downbeat, and surprisingly well acted, even though in his feral state Barry Stokes gets a leonine makeup job that wouldn't even pass for a production of *Cats*. **AKA:** Prey. 🎞🎞🎞

1983 (R) 85m/C *GB* Barry Stokes, Sally Faulkner; *D:* Norman J. Warren. **VHS, Beta** *NO*

Alien Private Eye

An extraterrestrial detective searches Los Angeles for a missing magic disk while investigating an intergalactic crime ring. **AKA:** Alien P.I. 🎞🎞

1987 90m/C Nikki Fastinetti; *D:* Nik Rubenfeld. **VHS** *NO*

Alien Seed

Aliens kidnap a woman (well played by Heidi Paine) and impregnate her. Erik Estrada is the government scientist hot on her trail. (How far could a woman carrying alien offspring wander?) At best, this goofy B-movie is no more far-fetched than Whitley Strieber's *Communion* or any of the other "alien abduction" tales that some people seem to take seriously. 🎞🎞

1989 88m/C Erik Estrada, Heidi Paine, Steven Blade; *D:* Bob James; *W:* Bob James. **VHS** *AIP*

Alien Space Avenger

After a *Star Wars* space skirmish, four serpentine alien convicts crashland in 1930s' NYC and possess a few mobsters and their molls for fleetingly funny moments when the visitors mistake vintage *Flash Gordon* serials and pulp comics for nonfiction. After 50 years of hibernation, the evil misfits wake up to find that they've inspired the look of the bad guys in the latest *Space Avenger* comic book, and stalk the nosy young artist. Quirky but floundering semi-satire reminiscent of old-time B sci-fi flicks with modern gore and profanity. Writer/director Richard Haines shot this in the

old 3-strip Technicolor method, but cheapo production values made the Hound wonder if that heroic effort was really worth it. **AKA:** Space Avenger. 🦴🦴

1991 88m/C Robert Prichard, Mike McClerie, Charity Staley, Gina Mastrogiacomo, Kick Fairbanks Fogg, Angela Nicholas, Marty Roberts, James Gillis; **D:** Richard W. Haines; **W:** Richard W. Haines, Linwood Sawyer; **M:** Richard Fiocca. **VHS** *AIP*

Alien Warrior

A naive extraterrestrial muscleman (whose predecessor, it's hinted, was Jesus Christ) fights a street pimp to save a crime-ridden Earth neighborhood. Low-brain, high-pain cheapie might have some value as a method to wring confessions from prisoners. **WOOF!**

1985 (R) 92m/C Brett Clark, Pamela Saunders; **D:** Edward Hunt; **W:** Edward Hunt. **VHS, Beta** *VES, LIV*

Alien Women

A soft-core British sci-fi yarn about scantily clad alien babes and the special agent who's trying to uncover their secret. It's all very sketchy, silly, and campy, though pleasantly cast with plenty of lovely British actresses. **AKA:** Zeta One; The Love Factor. 🦴

1969 (R) 86m/C *GB* James Robertson Justice, Charles Hawtrey, Robin Hawdon, Anna Gael, Brigitte Skay, Dawn Addams, Valerie Leon, Yutte Stensgaard, Wendy Lingham, Rita Webb, Caroline Hawkins; **D:** Michael Cort. **VHS, Beta** *PSM, SNC*

Alienator

An intergalactic villain sentenced to execution instead escapes to present-day Earth and terrorizes local nitwits. On his trail is the title Terminator-wannabe, female body-builder Teagan Clive in a cyborg costume with what look like sportscar hubcaps for breasts. Campy, low-budget space junk that recycles costumes, sets, and props from other Fred Olen Ray features. 🦴

1989 (R) 93m/C Jan-Michael Vincent, John Phillip Law, Ross Hagen, Dyana Ortelli, Dawn Wildsmith, P.J. Soles,

Sigourney Weaver and a fashionable female alien take a moment to bond over their 'dos in ***Aliens.***

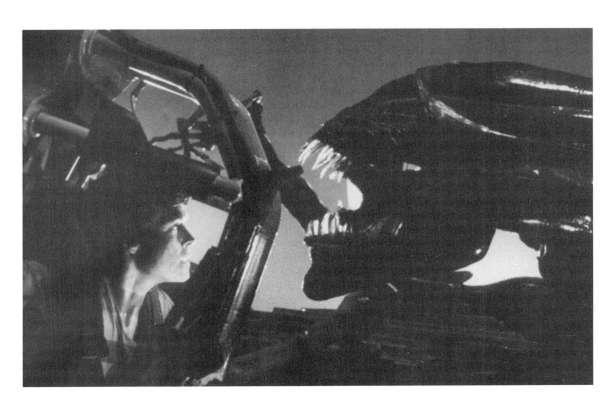

an indistinguishable, foul-mouthed group, the exceptions being *Terminator*'s Michael Biehn, *Mad About You*'s Paul Reiser as a bureaucratic slimeball, and Lance Henrikson as a sympathetic android. But all that is forgotten and forgiven once the mother of all monster battles begins. Young Carrie Henn co-stars as Newt, the lone survivor of the alien-infested colony, who reawakens Ripley's maternal instincts (a hint of the subplot about Ripley's own daughter that was left on the cutting room floor). The special effects won an Academy Award. The *Alien* trilogy is also available as a box set. 🐾🐾🐾🐾

1986 (R) 138m/C Sigourney Weaver, Michael Biehn, Lance Henriksen, Bill Paxton, Paul Reiser, Carrie Henn, Jenette Goldstein; *D:* James Cameron; *W:* James Cameron, Walter Hill; *M:* James Horner. Hugos '87: Dramatic Presentation; Academy Awards '86: Best Sound Effects Editing, Best Visual Effects; Nominations: Academy Awards '86: Best Actress (Weaver), Best Art Direction/Set Decoration, Best Film Editing, Best Sound, Best Original Score. **VHS, Beta, LV** *FOX*

Aliens Are Coming

A spaceship crashlands on Earth, and its devious denizens begin invading human bodies. TV movie that's a dull echo of *Invasion of the Body Snatchers*. 🐾🐾

1980 100m/C Tom Mason, Melinda Fee, Max Gail, Eric (Hans Gudegast) Braeden, Matthew Laborteaux; *D:* Harvey Hart; *M:* William Goldstein. **VHS, Beta** *WOV, GKK*

Aliens from Spaceship Earth

Are strange, celestial forces invading our universe? If they are, is man prepared to defend his planet against threatening aliens of unknown strength? Lame docudrama featuring the Hurdy Gurdy man himself, Donovan. 🐾🐾

1977 107m/C Donovan, Lynda Day George; *D:* Don Como. **VHS, Beta** *GEM*

Alligator

Just when you thought it was safe to go back into the sewers, along comes Ramon. Once a cute little flushable-type alligator, he made the mistake of eating more than just the occasional stray human. When he ingests a dead lab animal chock full o' growth hormones, he begins to swell at an amazing rate. No longer

---

William Hurt takes hydrotherapy to the extreme in *Altered States.*

Teagan Clive, Robert Clarke, Leo Gordon, Robert Quarry, Fox Harris, Hoke Howell, Jay Richardson; *D:* Fred Olen Ray. **VHS, Beta, LV** *PSM*

Aliens

One of those rare sequels that equals, or arguably, surpasses the original. James Cameron fulfilled the promise of *The Terminator* with this state-of-the-art thriller that particularly revitalized the action film. Sigourney Weaver returns as Ripley, who reluctantly agrees to lead an expedition back to Acheron, home of the acid-dripping beast that made mincemeat out of her colleagues way back when (she has been in hyper-sleep for 50 years!). Harry, Yaphet, John, Tom, and Veronica are sorely missed, as her new crew is mostly

content with the Weight Watchers'-approved human-a-day diet, Ramon begins to munch on everything and everyone in sight. So-so special effects and a thrown-in romance between the gator-chasin' cop and lovely-lady scientist aside, a witty (the script is by John Sayles), low-budget eco-monster chiller that's sure to please. 🎬🎬🎬

1980 (R) 94m/C Robert Forster, Jack Carter, Henry Silva, Robin Riker, Dean Jagger, Michael V. Gazzo, Bart Braverman; *D:* Lewis Teague; *W:* John Sayles. **VHS, Beta** *LIV*

The Alpha Incident

Time-worn doomsday drama about an alien organism with the potential to destroy all living things. Government works hard to cover up. 🎬

1976 (PG) 86m/C Ralph Meeker, Stafford Morgan, John Goff, Carol Irene Newell, John Alderman; *D:* Bill Rebane. **VHS, Beta** *MED*

Alphaville

One of Jean-Luc Godard's most accessible films (but still perhaps not quite ready for prime time) stars Eddie Constantine, a B-movie bust in the States, but a star in Paris, where he popularized on film the pulp hero Lemmy Caution. In this sci-fi noir, he is Agent 003, who arrives in Alphaville to search for a scientist who has defected. Contemporary Paris makes an eerie stand-in for the conformist state that is run by a computer, Alpha 60. Now available on video in a digitally remastered, newly subtitled and letterboxed edition. **AKA:** Alphaville, a Strange Case of Lemmy Caution; Alphaville, Une Etrange Aventure de Lemmy Caution. 🎬🎬🎬

1965 100m/B *FR* Eddie Constantine, Anna Karina, Akim Tamiroff, Howard Vernon, Laszlo Szabo; *D:* Jean-Luc Godard; *W:* Jean-Luc Godard; *C:* Raoul Coutard. Berlin International Film Festival '65: Golden Berlin Bear. **VHS, Beta** *HMV, SNC, MRV*

Altered States

Probably everyone who's tried mind-altering substances has believed that the changes in personal perception can also change external reality. That's the idea behind Paddy Chayefsky's (here, AKA Sidney Aaron) tale of a young scientist (William Hurt) who uses psychedelic drugs and sensory deprivation to go back to his evolutionary roots, as it were. Not surprisingly, his wife (Blair Brown) thinks it's a bad idea. Like all of director Ken Russell's best work, the ambitious but unfocused film has some wonderful moments within huge excesses. Hurt's climactic transformation into a nuclear mushroom man—or whatever—is truly nutty. Chayefsky eventually washed his hands of the project after artistic differences with the producers. Others who departed from the film include initial director William Penn and special effects genius John Dykstra (relieved ably by Bran Ferren). 🎬🎬🎬

1980 (R) 103m/C William Hurt, Blair Brown, Bob Balaban, Charles Haid, Dori Brenner, Drew Barrymore, Miguel Godreau; *D:* Ken Russell; *W:* Paddy Chayefsky; *C:* Jordan Cronenweth. Nominations: Academy Awards '80: Best Art Direction/Set Decoration, Best Original Score. **VHS, Beta, LV** *WAR*

Amanda and the Alien

The alien of the title looks like a horseshoe crab but can take over human bodies, killing the host in the process. Bummer. Amanda (Nicole Eggert) is a smart, hip San Francisco girl—tattoos, navel ring, attitude—who takes pity on the creature because...well, because the cops and the feds are after him, or her, or it...whatever. Off these clueless X-Filers go, with Stacy Keach in pursuit. Made for cable and based on a story by Robert Silverberg. 🎬🎬

1995 (R) 94m/C Alex Meneses, Nicole Eggert, Michael Dorn, Stacy Keach, Michael C. Bendetti; *D:* Jon Kroll; *W:* Jon Kroll. **VHS** *REP*

The Amazing Colossal Man

A fairly standard '50s sci-fi film about a monster created by atomic radiation. However, where most similar films of this type were content to use giant insects or rats as the heavies, this flick features a human monster. Gung-ho soldier Colonel Manning is exposed to massive doses of plutonium when an experiment backfires (literally) in his face. When his radiation burns heal practically overnight, the doctors figure something unusual is going on; their suspicions are confirmed when Manning begins growing...and growing...and growing....

"Growing...! GROWING...! **GROWING...!** to a GIANT...! to a MONSTER...! WHEN WILL IT STOP?"

—*The Amazing Colossal Man.*

TV on Tape:
Amazing Stories

When NBC made an unprecedented commitment to Steven Spielberg in 1985 to develop an anthology series, they were no doubt hoping for a ratings bonanza of *E.T.*-like proportions. What they got was closer to *1941*.

Though Spielberg is one of the most commercially successful filmmakers of all time, *Amazing Stories* was an amazing gamble. No anthology series had finished in Nielsen's top 25 since the original *Alfred Hitchcock Presents*. Yet NBC commissioned 44 shows, two season's worth, at a cost of up to $1 million each.

Television, of course, launched Spielberg's career. At the age of 21, he co-directed a pilot episode of Rod Serling's *Night Gallery*. The made-for-TV film *Duel* finally put him in the driver's seat. At the time, Spielberg said that the series would be his "elephant burial ground" for ideas that would not make it to the big screen. He also promised viewers "wonderment, fantasy, irony, and comedy" without the moralizing often associated with *The Twilight Zone*.

Not since Shelley Duvall's *Faerie Tale Theatre* had a series attracted the talents of some of Hollywood's biggest players. In addition to Spielberg himself, episodes were directed by Clint Eastwood, Robert Zemeckis, Martin Scorsese, and Joe Dante. But Spielberg was no match for Angela Lansbury. Whereas *Amazing Stories* finished its first season in 35th place, *Murder She Wrote* finished in third. *Amazing Stories* was moved to Monday nights to be paired with *Alf*.

Amazing Stories is best appreciated on video, free from ratings pressure or the threat of channel surfing. The episodes that are available are a representative cross-section of the show at its whimsical, sentimental, and diabolical best.

"Book 1," appropriately enough, is a good introduction to the series. It includes "The Mission," which was

directed by Spielberg and stars Kevin Costner and Kiefer Sutherland. This claustrophobic episode takes place mostly in a crippled World War II plane, in which an aspiring Disney cartoonist is trapped in gun turret next to the plane's locked wheels. Serling could have pulled this off in an hour. The companion episode is "The Wedding Ring," directed by and starring Danny DeVito and his wife, Rhea Perlman, as a mild-mannered woman who goes homicidal when she puts on a cursed ring.

"Book 2" features "Go to the Head of the Class," directed by Robert Zemeckis and featuring his *Back to the Future* star Christopher Lloyd at full froth as a maniacal teacher who menaces students Scott Coffey and Mary Stuart Masterson. Also on the program is the mean-spirited animated short, "Family Dog," which was designed by Tim Burton and ultimately led to a failed weekly series that *The Simpsons* found time to make fun of.

"Book 4" contains three episodes, including the Scorsese-helmed "Mirror, Mirror," which stars Sam Waterston as a horror film director haunted by his own creations.

1985-86/C VHS, LV *MCA, FCT, MOV*

The former good-guy shoots up to seventy feet and starts taking out his anger on a helpless Las Vegas. Can anything stop his murderous rampages? Maybe a really, really big hypodermic needle....

1957 79m/B Glenn Langan, Cathy Downs, William Hudson, James Seay, Russ Bender, Lyn Osborn; *D:* Bert I. Gordon. **VHS** *COL, FUS*

The Amazing Spider-Man

The Marvel Comics superhero's unique powers are put to the test when he comes to the rescue of the government by preventing an evil scientist from blackmailing the government for big bucks. The wall-walking web-slinger has his origins probed (a grad student bit by a radioactive spider develops super-human powers) in his live-action debut, which was made for television and led to a short-lived series. If you can get past the '70s fashions, television production values, and the fact that Peter Parker is a total dork, enjoyment is possible. As for Marvel-inspired action, this one

doesn't measure up to The Incredible Hulk of the same era. **AKA:** Spider-Man. 🎜 🎜

1977 94m/C Nicholas Hammond, David White, Lisa Eilbacher, Michael Pataki; **D:** E.W. Swackhamer. **VHS, Beta, LV** FOX, IME

The Amazing Transparent Man

A mad scientist is forced to make a crook invisible in order to steal the radioactive materials he needs. A snaky crime boss has them both under his thumb. The crook decides to rob banks instead. Shot at the Texas State Fair in Dallas for that elusive futuristic look. For Ulmer fans only—don't expect another Detour. Aside from some exterior shots that emphasize the barren Texas plains, the direction is merely pedestrian, with little of Edgar Ulmer's usual visual magic. The invisibility transformation effects are great looking—instead of merely fading away, portions of the actor are wiped gradually. Made simultaneously with Beyond the Time Barrier. Marguerite Chapman was also in Charlie Chan at the Wax Museum (1940), Spy Smasher Returns (1942), and Flight to Mars (1952). 🎜 🎜

1960 58m/B Douglas Kennedy, Marguerite Chapman, James Griffith, Ivan Triesault; **D:** Edgar G. Ulmer. **VHS** NOS, SNC

American Cyborg: Steel Warrior

Basic evil-machine-bent-on-mankind's-destruction movie—with a hero bent on rescuing the world. 🎜 🎜 ⌐

1994 (R) 95m/C Joe Lara, John P. Ryan; **D:** Boaz Davidson; **W:** Bill Crounse. **VHS, LV** CAN

The Amphibian Man

What does a scientist do once he's created a young man with gills? Plunge him in the real world of aqua pura to experience life and love, albeit underwater. Trouble is, the protagonist, who's come to be known as the Sea Devil, takes a dive for a young pretty he's snatched from the jaws of death. A '60s Soviet sci-fi romance originally seen on American television. 🎜 🎜

1961 96m/C RU K. Korieniev, M. Virzinskaya; **D:** Y. Kasancki. **VHS** SNC

Android

Mad scientist Klaus Kinski needs a little help producing the now-illegal industrial robots that allow him to get by in the out-of-this-world. Enter human-wanna-be Max 404, an android who wants to help, wants to be human, and thinks he's a mechanized Charlie Chaplin. When Max learns that he is about to be phased out and permanently retired, he takes matters into his own hands, including dealing with a trio of cosmic convicts that have invaded the research lab. Humorous and off-beat science fiction. Another must for Kinski fans, and Don Opper isn't bad either. 🎜 🎜 ⌐

1982 (PG) 80m/C Klaus Kinski, Don Opper, Brie Howard; **D:** Aaron Lipstadt. **VHS, Beta, LV** MED

The Android Affair

Isaac Asimov's name is featured prominently in the credits of this cable-TV feature, though he did little more than provide story material for an early draft. Future doctors practice experimental techniques on lifelike androids. Our surgeon heroine's next patient is William (Griffin Dunne), a handsome and charming android whom she finds all too humanly appealing and helps escape from the research facility. Tale begins promisingly, but eventually settles into a familiar groove of chases and intrigues. 🎜 🎜

1995 (PG-13) 90m/C Harley Jane Kozak, Griffin Dunne, Ossie Davis, Saul Rubinek, Peter Outerbridge, Natalie Radford; **D:** Richard Kletter; **W:** Richard Kletter. **VHS, LV** MCA

The Andromeda Strain

A satellite falls back to Earth carrying a deadly bacteria that must be identified in time to save the population from extermination. A crack team of civilian scientists assemble at a secret underground laboratory to solve the crisis. Unfortunately, the bug keeps on mutating. Though slightly dated technologically, the tension inherent in the bestselling Michael Crichton novel is kept intact due to the precision-paced work of veteran director Robert Wise (The Day the Earth Stood Still). Also available in letterbox format. 🎜 🎜 🎜 ⌐

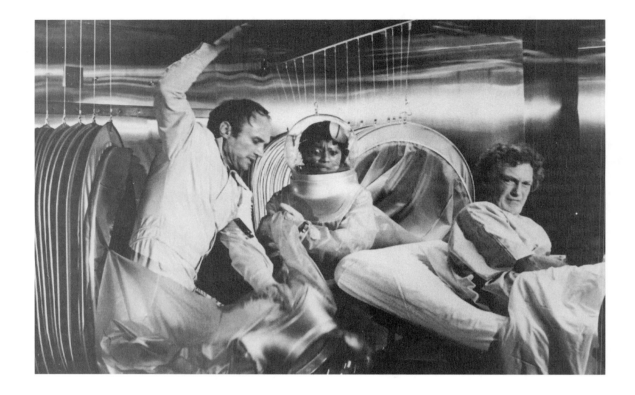

"Hey, put that rubber suit back on. The smell's enough to gag bacteria." George Mitchell pleads with a sweaty James Olson in *The Andromeda Strain*.

1971 (G) 131m/C Arthur Hill, David Wayne, James Olson, Kate Reid, Paula Kelly, George Mitchell; *D:* Robert Wise; *W:* Nelson Gidding; *C:* Richard Kline. Nominations: Academy Awards '71: Best Art Direction/Set Decoration, Best Film Editing. **VHS, Beta, LV** *MCA*

Andy and the Airwave Rangers

Shambling shot-to-tape con aimed at the unwary. After renting a magic videocassette, young Andy and his kid sister are whisked into their TV. You know you've been had when adventures in there—car chases, cosmic battles, and barbarians—are 80% clips inserted from previous Roger Corman productions, like *Deathsport* and *Space Raiders* (especially heinous considering that the latter borrowed footage from Corman's earlier *Battle Beyond the Stars*). Other Corman cut-and-paste jobs to beware of include *Ultra Warrior* and *Futurekick*. **AKA:** Andy Colby's Incredibly Awesome Adventure. **WOOF!**

1989 75m/C Dianne Kay, Vince Edwards, Bo Svenson, Richard Thomas, Erik Estrada, Randy Josselyn, Jessica Puscas, Chuck Kovacic; *D:* Deborah Brock. **VHS, LV** COL

The Angry Red Planet

An unintentionally amusing sci-fi adventure about astronauts on Mars fighting off aliens and giant, ship-swallowing amoebas. Crew comes back infected by cancerous growths, and Nora Hayden must go through the whole story in flashbacks in order to save them. Filmed using bizarre "Cinemagic" process, which turns almost everything pink—it was originally meant to make the actors blend in better with painted backdrops, but it doesn't work very well. Wild effects have earned the film cult status. Romance is added as Jack Kruschen appears to fall in love with his sonic rifle. **AKA:** Invasion of Mars. 🦴🦴

1959 83m/C Gerald Mohr, Les Tremayne, Nora Hayden, Jack Kruschen; *D:* Ib Melchior. **VHS, Beta** NO

Anna to the Infinite Power

Sci fi based on the book of the same name follows a young girl with telepathic powers. When the girl discovers that she has sisters as the result of a strange scientific experiment, she sets out to find them, drawing on her own inner strength. 🐾🐾🐾

1984 101m/C Dina Merrill, Martha Byrne, Mark Patton; **D:** Robert Wiemer. **VHS, Beta** *COL*

A*P*E*

Giant gorilla escapes from a boat, wrestles a rubber shark, faces toy tanks, and generally challenges anything that comes between him and the actress he loves. Allegedly filmed in 3-D; hence the stuff thrown and poked at the camera, but your attention will more likely be riveted to the seams and rips in the cheapo monkey suit. Speaking of suits, Dino De Laurentiis filed one when this stinker, filmed in South Korea, came out at the same time as his remake of *King Kong* to cash in on the free publicity. The leading lady, later known as Joanna Kerns, went on to a more respectable TV acting career. **WOOF!**

1976 (PG) 87m/C Rod Arrants, Joanna DeVarona, Alex Nicol; **D:** Paul Leder; **W:** Paul Leder. **VHS, Beta** *NWV*

The Ape Man

With the aid of a secret potion, a scientist turns himself into a murderous ape. The only way to regain his human side is to ingest human spinal fluid. Undoubtedly inspired by Boris Karloff's 1940 film *The Ape*. **AKA:** Lock Your Doors. 🐾🐾

1943 64m/B Wallace Ford, Bela Lugosi; **D:** William Beaudine. **VHS, Beta** *NOS, MRV, SNC*

A.P.E.X.

Slowly paced shoot-'em-up is set in yet another desolate dystopian future. The plot has to do with time-traveling killer robots and serves mostly to show off visual effects that range from fair to good. The best are reminiscent of *Predator* and *Robocop*. True fans will note other similarities to *Damnation Alley* and *Mad Max*. The script doesn't follow through with all the tricky complications that the subject of time travel entails, and that's a shame because those details can raise so many interesting questions, and that's what the best science fiction is all about. 🐾🐾

1994 (R) 103m/C Richard Keats, Mitchell Cox, Lisa Ann Russell, Marcus Aurelius, Adam Lawson; **D:** Phillip J. Roth; **W:** Phillip J. Roth, Ronald Schmidt; **M:** Jim Goodwin. **VHS, LV** *REP*

Arcade

Kids flock to the amusement hall to play the new virtual-reality video game Arcade, only to disappear if they lose. Seems it can transport you into cyberspace where you really play for your life. Disappointing sci-fi pic from genre producer Charles Band, late with the revelation that murdered human brain cells are secretly wetwired, *Robocop*-style, into Arcade (until that point the Hound thought it was a high-tech demon story). Diehard chipheads may want to fast-forward through the dull stuff to enjoy some so-so computer graphics. 🐾

1993 (R) 85m/C Megan Ward, Peter Billingsley, John de Lancie, Sharon Farrell, Seth Green, Humberto Ortiz, Jonathan Fuller, Norbert Weisser; **D:** Albert Pyun; **W:** David S. Goyer; **C:** George Mooradian; **M:** Alan Howarth. **VHS, Beta** *PAR*

Arena

Remember old boxing melodramas about good-natured palookas, slimy opponents, gangsters, and dames? This Charles Band production puts those cliches in a garish sci-fi setting, with handsome Steve Armstrong battling E.T.s, femme fatales, and the galactic gambling syndicate to be the first human pugilistic champ in decades. A really cute idea (from the screenwriters of *The Rocketeer*), but the plot's sheer predictability makes one feel like throwing in the towel at the halfway point. Worth a look for the creature f/x by John Buechler and Screaming Mad George. Note Armin Shimerman before donning a Ferengi face in *Star Trek: Deep Space 9*. 🐾🐾

1989 (PG-13) 97m/C *IT* Paul Satterfield, Claudia Christian, Hamilton Camp, Marc Alaimo, Armin Shimerman, Shari Shattuck, Jack Carter; **D:** Peter Manoogian; **W:** Danny Bilson, Paul DeMeo; **M:** Richard Band. **VHS, LV** *COL*

"Hey, three eyes! What a crazy peeping tom, huh?"

—Sammy (Jack Kruschen), making light of the alien Dr. Iris Ryan (Nora Hayden) saw peering in the window in *The Angry Red Planet*.

Armageddon: The Final Challenge

After a nuclear holocaust, evil forces rule the Earth in the guise of "The Future Bank." They send out Fear-Permutator Clones to keep order and kill undesirables but naturally there's a rebel ready to do battle. 🦴🦴

1994 ?m/C Todd Jensen, Graham Clarke, Tony Caprari, Joanna Rowlands; **D:** Michael Garcia; **W:** George Garcia, Michael Garcia; **M:** Johan Lass. **VHS**

Army of Darkness

Everyone knows that this is the third *Evil Dead* movie, but Universal Studios thought they could pretend that the more graphic and intense predecessors didn't exist if they changed the name. Bruce Campbell returns as the square-jawed, not-too-bright, thinks-he's-hipper-than-thou hero, Ash, in another Sam Raimi extravaganza. And this one's awfully good, too! Tossed back in time at the end of *Evil Dead 2,* Ash also finds himself transported from the horror genre to fantasy land, where he gets to romance a babe, fight an army of skeletons, and generally cause a lot of grief for all the dark-age bad guys. As usual, Raimi's technical exuberance is apparent, the horror graphic though even more tongue in cheek, and the camera angles all his own. Don't miss this one. The original apocalyptic ending was changed to the more upbeat one at the studio's request. The Japanese laserdisc features the original ending as supplemental material. Both domestic and import discs are letterboxed. **AKA:** Evil Dead 3. 🦴🦴🦴

1992 (R) 77m/C Bruce Campbell, Embeth Davidtz, Marcus Gilbert, Ian Abercrombie, Richard Grove, Michael Earl Reid, Tim Quill, Patricia Tallman, Theodore (Ted) Raimi, Ivan Raimi; **Cameos:** Bridget Fonda; **D:** Sam Raimi; **W:** Ivan Raimi, Sam Raimi; **M:** Danny Elfman, Joseph Lo Duca. **VHS, Beta, LV** *MCA, FCT*

Around the World Under the Sea

Bunch of men and one woman scientist plunge under the ocean in an experiment to predict earthquakes. They plant earthquake detectors along the ocean floor and discover the causes of tidal waves. They have men-women battles. They see big sea critters. 🦴🦴

1965 111m/C David McCallum, Shirley Eaton, Gary Merrill, Keenan Wynn, Brian Kelly, Lloyd Bridges; **D:** Andrew Marton. **VHS, Beta** *MGM*

The Arrival

An never-seen alien parasite turns an old man into a vampiric young stud after female blood. Plot and characterizations never do arrive, as our thirsty antihero tries to keep his secret from a schoolteacher lover. Genre director Stuart Gordon (*Robot Jox*) cameos as a hairy biker. 🦴

1990 (R) 107m/C John Saxon, Joseph Culp, Robert Sampson, Michael J. Pollard; **Cameos:** David Schmoeller, Stuart Gordon; **D:** David Schmoeller; **W:** David Schmoeller; **M:** Richard Band. **VHS, LV** *PSM*

The Asphyx

Clever sf/horror set in the 19th century, where doctor Robert Stephens uses the newly developed invention of photography to detect the Asphyx, an aura that surrounds a person just before death. Trapping one's Asphyx can provide the key to immortality, but it has to be done very carefully, or else.... The briefly glimpsed entity, a hideous puppet in double-exposure, testifies to the low budget of the proceedings; it's the script concepts and fine acting that give this moralistic occult tale its haunting impact. **AKA:** Spirit of the Dead. 🦴🦴🦴

1972 (PG) 98m/C *GB* Robert Stephens, Robert Powell, Jane Lapotaire, Alex Scott, Ralph Arliss, Fiona Walker, John Lawrence; **D:** Peter Newbrook; **C:** Frederick A. (Freddie) Young. **VHS, Beta** *MED*

Assassin

Made-for-TV drama about a mad scientist who creates a bionic killer for a bizarre plot to take over the world. He programs the cyborg to assassinate the President and other key people to help carry out his plan. A retired CIA operative emerges to stop the scientist by trying to destroy the robot. 🦴🦴

1986 (PG-13) 94m/C Robert Conrad, Karen Austin, Richard Young, Jonathan Banks, Robert Webber; **D:** Sandor Stern. **VHS, Beta** *ACA*

TV on Tape:
Astro Boy

If you ask most Americans about Japanese cartoons, it's likely they'll say something about those cartoons where "everybody has those big eyes." It may puzzle them (if they think about it at all), that Asians would draw characters that way. The truth is that the "big eyed" style is but a small indication of how incredible the influence of one man can be on the culture of a nation.

In the 1940s, with Japan suffering a sobering defeat in World War II, a young man named Osamu Tezuka began to contribute cartoons to newspapers and magazines to help support himself through medical school. He drew tales of high adventure, with generous doses of both humor and drama. He drew in a style influenced heavily by artists of the Walt Disney Studios, as Tezuka was a great admirer of Disney. Tezuka's comics (or "manga," as they're known in Japan) became increasingly popular, and he began to produce more and more work to meet the demand.

In 1951 he began a new series he called *Mighty Atom,* a kind of science-fiction version of Pinocchio about a powerful robot boy created by a mad scientist after his real son was killed. Mixing superheroic action, weird science, goofy humor, and heartfelt drama—all rendered in his unique, deceptively simple and cartoony style—the series immediately struck a chord with the public, and

became a sensational hit. He would continue to draw Atom regularly for seventeen years, even while producing a staggering amount of other work.

In the early 1960s, Tezuka began working on plans to animate his work. In 1963, *Mighty Atom* became Japan's first animated television series, eventually running for four years and 193 half-hour episodes. It was so popular that it was also broadcast in the United States on the NBC network under the name *Astro Boy,* where it often reached #1 in the ratings in some areas. However, due to legal complications, after its initial run it rarely appeared in syndication. During the past few years, many of these English-dubbed episodes began to appear on videotape and laserdisc.

When compared to today's ever more popular anime, these old black-and-white shows seem primitive, and indeed, they were produced with a budget far below even the limited-animation television cartoons being made in America at the time.

However, even under these restraints, Tezuka managed to produce a series unlike any other. Though the movement of characters is sometimes very limited, the artwork itself is striking, with stories and characters as charming and entertaining as any series ever produced.

During his lifetime, Tezuka created dozens of comics series (many running concurrently—some estimates say he had published over 150,000 pages), along with many animated and live action films and television series. His success was so overwhelming, and his work so influential, that he became known as the "god of comics." Today, every cartoonist in Japan, and thousands around the world, can point to Tezuka as their prime source of inspiration. Though he's often been called "the Disney of Japan," that description can't even begin to describe his enormous contribution to the culture of the planet. Yet, aside from his most famous creation *Astro Boy* (and to a lesser extent *Kimba, the White Lion*), his work is all but unknown in the U.S. That so much rich entertainment remains ignored is a crime.

Astro Boy is a series that is definitely worth seeking out. If you're old enough to have seen it back in the '60s, you'll experience an unequalled rush of nostalgia along your spine the moment the opening theme begins. If you've never seen an episode, you'll be awed at the incredible treasure you've unearthed.

1963-67/B *JP* **Director:** Osamu Tezuka. **VHS, LV** *WTA, TPV, ING, CPM*

The Astounding She-Monster

How can you not love a movie with a title like this? A bad script and snail-paced plot are a good start. Robert Clarke is a geologist wanting only to be left alone with his rocks and his dog who survives a brush with the kidnappers of a wealthy heiress only to happen upon an alien spacecraft that's crashed nearby. At the helm is a very tall, high-heeled femme alien fatale in an obligatory skintight space outfit and very scary eyebrows. What's not to love? Well, it seems that Miss Galaxy can kill with the slightest touch. With voiced-over narration to help explain the plot. For connoisseurs of truly bad movies; all others should approach with caution! Partially remade by Fred Olen Ray in 1989 as *Alienator*. **AKA:** Mysterious Invader. ✂

1958 60m/B Robert Clarke, Kenne Duncan, Marilyn Harvey, Jeanne Tatum, Shirley Kilpatrick, Ewing Miles Brown; **D:** Ronnie Ashcroft; **W:** Frank Hall. **VHS** *SNC, MRV, CNM*

The Astro-Zombies

One of the schlockiest, most ineptly made, yet compellingly mind-boggling films of all time. John Carradine plays a mad scientist who holes up in his basement lab and cranks out a series of skull-faced zombies who eat people's guts. Yikes! Legendary cult-movie queen Tura Satana (*Faster Pussycat, Kill! Kill!*) stars as the leader of a cadre of foreign agents who try to stop the monsters. Cinematic weirdness of a very high order. This peculiar anti-masterpiece was co-written and co-produced by Wayne Rogers, who played Trapper John on *M*A*S*H*! ✂ ✂

1967 83m/C Tura Satana, Wendell Corey, John Carradine, Tom Pace, Joan Patrick, Rafael Campos; **D:** Ted V. Mikels; **W:** Ted V. Mikels, Wayne Rogers. **VHS, Beta** *NO*

At the Earth's Core

A Victorian scientist (fantasy-film veteran Peter Cushing) invents a giant burrowing machine, intending to market it as a mining tool. During a test run, however, the gizmo goes haywire and digs right down to the center of the Earth, depositing Cushing and his

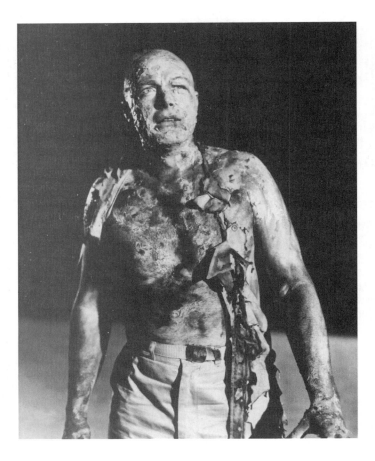

"Honey, quick! Where's the styptic pencil?" *The Atomic Man.*

Assignment Outer Space

A giant spaceship with bytes for brains is on a collision course with Earth. A team of astronauts is sent to save the world from certain peril. Seems they take the task lightly, though, and their mission (and hence the plot) revolves more around saving sexy sultress Farinon from certain celibacy. If you're into stultifying Italian space operas with a gratuitous sex sub-plot then look up this assignment, but don't say we didn't warn you. Narrated by Jack Wallace; director Antonio Margheriti is also known as Anthony Dawson, not to be confused with the actor of the same name. **AKA:** Space Men. ✂

1961 79m/B *IT* Rik von Nutter, Gabriella Farinon, Archie Savage, Dave Montresor, Alan Dijon; **D:** Anthony (Antonio Margheriti) Dawson. **VHS** *NOS, SNC*

assistant in the lost world of Pellucidar. Here they encounter hokey-looking "prehistoric monsters," who look a lot like men in rubber suits. After assorted adventures, they are called upon to rescue Pellucidar's cave-person populace from a society of telepathic pterosaurs and their ape-man slaves. This film isn't much more than a celluloid comic book, but anyone who loves the Edgar Rice Burroughs novel it's based on will probably find it hard to dislike. Peter Cushing is charming as the absent-minded scientist and Caroline Munro is appropriately tough and sexy as Princess Dian the Beautiful. Most of the monsters are laughable, looking more like Godzilla's poor relations than dinosaurs, but the scenes featuring the flying "mahars" and their "sagoth" henchmen are surprisingly eerie. Follow up to *The Land that Time Forgot* and followed by *The People that Time Forgot*. 🦴🦴🦖

1976 (PG) 90m/C *GB* Doug McClure, Peter Cushing, Caroline Munro, Cy Grant, Godfrey James, Keith Barron; **D:** Kevin Connor. **VHS, Beta** *WAR, OM*

The Atomic Brain

An old woman hires a doctor to transplant her brain into the body of a beautiful young girl. Of the three who are abducted, two become homicidal zombies and the third starts to act catty when she's given a feline brain. Oh, and did we mention the hairy monster chained to a tether in the back yard? A serious contender to *Plan 9 from Outer Space*'s title of Worst Film Ever Made, this is a treasure trove of tripe: drunk, horny mad doctors; wheelchair-bound old biddies living in dilapidated gothic mansions; forbidden experiments with atomic power; mutations run amuck; and trampy Euro-dames (with atrocious fake accents). Add screamingly inept dialogue (by FOUR screenwriters!), a droning narrator, and feel your own brainpan go nuclear. A must-see for bad-brain movie devotees; makes a cerebral double bill with *The Brain that Wouldn't Die*. Director Joseph Mascelli provided camera work for Ray Dennis Steckler's *The Incredibly Strange Creatures Who Stopped Living and Became Mixed-Up Zombies* the following year as well as authoring a highly regarded book

on cinematography. Co-producer/writer Jack Pollexfen is an old hand in the bad movie biz, having helmed the Lon Chaney, Jr., electric-psycho flick *The Indestructible Man*. **AKA:** Monstrosity. 🦴

1964 72m/B Frank Gerstle, Erika Peters, Judy Bamber, Marjorie Eaton, Frank Fowler, Margie Fisco; **D:** Joseph Mascelli; **W:** Jack Pollexfen. **VHS** *NOS, SNC*

The Atomic Man

The victim of an accident in a physics lab appears to have lost his mind—until someone notices that he's answering questions before they're asked. Apparently his consciousness now exists several seconds in the future. Naturally, both good and evil forces want to use him for their own purposes. Preposterous but intriguing idea is wasted in this dull, talky British feature. **AKA:** Timeslip. 🦴🦖

1956 78m/B *GB* Gene Nelson, Faith Domergue, Joseph Tomelty, Peter Arne, Vic Perry, Donald Gray; **D:** Ken Hughes; **W:** Charles Eric Maine; **C:** A. T. Dinsdale. **VHS** *NOS, SNC*

Atomic Submarine

Government agents battle alien invaders. The battle, however, is a bit out of the ordinary—it takes place in the ocean beneath the Arctic ice floes and is headed by an atomic-powered submarine clashing with a special alien underwater saucer and its BEM inhabitants. Despite some quarreling among crewmembers, our heroes find a way to win. Brawny cast resembles a B-movie version of a John Wayne feature, with Arthur Franz, Dick Foran, Bob Steele, and Brett Halsey competing to see who has the most granite jaw in the face of death. Sexbomb Joi Lansing, a pin-up favorite, provides inspiration. The entire format was stolen a few years later by Irwin Allen for his silly feature and TV series *Voyage to the Bottom of the Sea*. A better than average '50s sci-fi thriller, more imaginative than most. 🦴🦴🦖

1959 80m/C Arthur Franz, Dick Foran, Bob Steele, Brett Halsey, Joi Lansing, Paul Dubov, Tom Conway; **D:** Spencer Gordon Bennet; **W:** Orville H. Hampton; **C:** Gilbert Warrenton. **VHS, Beta** *SNC*

"A creature from beyond the stars. Evil... Beautiful... Deadly...!"

—*The Astounding She-Monster.*

"He may be a little
frisky, but a guy in
the hand is worth
two in the bush."
***Attack of the
50 Foot Woman***
(1958).

Attack of the 50 Foot Woman

Size matters! The success of *The Incredible Shrinking Man* inspired this inevitable imitation. Allison Hayes stars as a woman recently released from an insane asylum, not the best time for her to tell police and her husband that she witnessed a flying saucer land in the desert. When she is zapped with a ray that transforms her into what the ads hyped as a bikini-clad "female colossus" with "a mountainous torso, skyscraper limbs, giant desires," she tears up the town looking for her two-timing hubby. Written by Mark Hanna, who also wrote *The Amazing Colossal Man*. Too bad no one thought to team those two up for a sequel. Originally released on a double bill with *War of the Satellites*. Recently remade for cable starring Daryl Hannah. Stick with Allison. 🦴🦴🦴

1958 72m/B Allison Hayes, William Hudson, Roy Gordon, Yvette Vickers, George Douglas; **D:** Nathan (Hertz) Juran; **W:** Mark Hanna; **C:** Jacques Marquette. **VHS, Beta, LV** *FOX, FCT*

Attack of the 50 Ft. Woman

A campy remake of the 1958 sci-fi cult classic that tries to expand on the original's subtle humor and feminist overtones. This new version features the statuesque Daryl Hannah in the title role. As Nancy, Hannah's kept in a state of childish dependency by her domineering father (William Windom) and sleazy hubby (Daniel Baldwin). But after a close encounter of the enlarging kind with a flying saucer, Nancy finds that both her physique and self-esteem are steadily growing—like 50 feet worth. After some initial trauma and humiliation, big Nancy decides it's payback time. If you've ever wanted to see Daryl Hannah trash a city, here's your chance. It may not top the original, but it's colorful and amusing, and Hannah makes an attractive and sympathetic heroine. Fun and thrills of gigantic proportions! Originally made for television. 🦴🦴

1993 90m/C Daryl Hannah, Daniel Baldwin, William Windom, Frances Fisher, Cristi Conaway, Paul Benedict, Lewis

Arquette, Xander Berkeley, Hamilton Camp, Richard Edson, Victoria Haas, O'Neal Compton; *D:* Christopher Guest; *W:* Joseph Dougherty; *M:* Nicholas Pike. **VHS, LV** *HBO*

Attack of the Giant Leeches

Typically cheapo Roger Corman monster movie about giant leeches in a murky swamp who suddenly develop a taste for human flesh. A disturbed bartender becomes sympathetic to the leeches' cause when he discovers his wife necking with her lover; he forces them into the murk at gunpoint, much to the leeches' joy. Sometimes tedious, sometimes surprisingly chilling, always low budget and slimy. Although the special effects are fairly crappy (in the tradition of Corman's earlier *Attack of the Crab Monsters,* the "leech" costumes don't quite fit the poor actors), this might be a good choice for a late-night scare/laugh. Just when you thought it was safe to go back in the swamp.... **AKA:** The Giant Leeches; Demons of the Swamp. ♫

1959 62m/B Ken Clark, Yvette Vickers, Gene Roth, Bruno Ve Sota, Michael Emmet; *D:* Bernard L. Kowalski; *W:* Leo Gordon; *C:* John M. Nickolaus Jr. **VHS** *VYY, SNC, NOS*

Attack of the Killer Tomatoes

"I know I'm going to miss her/A tomato ate my sister." This overripe low-budget spoof of low-budget horror and science-fiction films is a staple of worst film festivals, but it is hardly as entertaining as the movies it is supposedly satirizing. Some nice bits though, including the ominous prologue that references Alfred Hitchcock's *The Birds,* a '50s style confrontation between the rampaging tomatoes and the Army, and an unfortunate remark by an incognito human who has infiltrated the tomato forces: "Anybody have some ketchup?" Now available on video in a so-called "director's cut." Inexplicably followed by three direct-to-video sequels. ♫

1977 (PG) 100m/C George Wilson, Jack Riley, Rock Peace, Eric Christmas, Sharon Taylor; *D:* John DeBello; *W:* John DeBello, Costa Dillon; *C:* John K. Culley. **VHS** *TOU*

Attack of the Mushroom People

You might not believe it from the title, but this is actually a well-made and fairly scary monster movie from Toho Studios, home of Godzilla & Co. A group of rich vacationers are stranded on a secluded, fog-bound island. They take up residence in an abandoned ship whose crew has mysteriously vanished, leaving all the mirrors onboard smashed. As time goes by, the castaways get increasingly squirrely and begin turning against one another. Their troubles, however, are only beginning. It seems the ship's original crew aren't dead—after eating the mushrooms plentiful on the island, they've transformed into oversized, killer fungus-creatures and are lurking in the jungle. The rubbery 'shroom-monsters look like something from a five-year-old's nightmare, but some of the scariest moments in this movie come from the paranoia and cruelty that takes over the castaways and makes you wonder who the *real* monsters are. **AKA:** Matango; Fungus of Terror; Curse of the Mushroom People. ♫♫♫

1963 70m/B *JP* Akira Kubo, Kenji Sahara, Yoshio Tsuchiya, Hiroshi Koizumi, Kumi Mizuno, Miki Yashiro; *D:* Inoshiro Honda. **VHS** *SMW*

The Aurora Encounter

Small spaceman lands his flying jalopy in Texas around 1900, befriending Earth kids but panicking authorities (one villain portrayed by the original George "Spanky" McFarland). Warmhearted but hopelessly ragged cheapie claims to be based on a true story, but even UFO buffs disbelieve that bit of regional folklore, and inspiration was *E.T.* all the way. The alien is portrayed by a little boy with a very real genetic disorder that gave him a gnome-like appearance. ♫♪

1985 (PG) 90m/C Jack Elam, Peter Brown, Carol Bagdasarian, Dottie West, George "Spanky" McFarland; *D:* Jim McCullough. **VHS, Beta** *NWV, VTR, HHE*

Automatic

Following his directive to protect and preserve human life, a RobGen "Automatic"-model android Olivier Gruner stops a rape-in-

> "The story of a girl who gets mad, gets big, and gets even."
> —*Attack of the 50 Ft. Woman* (1993).

Time Travel

Time travel stories have always been troubling, since it is a paradox. It's both impossible and very real.

Physicists tell us that time travel is a common phenomenon—but only at one speed and in one direction. For human beings to "travel" into the future at an accelerated pace, or into the past, is as near to a technological impossibility as you're likely to find. This would only be possible by taking the subject outside its relative timeline or dimension, and transporting it to another point on that timeline, or onto a parallel timeline so close to its own as to be indistinguishable, except that the destination timeline began at a different point. So far, the only clue we have as to how to do this is from Einstein's idea that objects traveling near the speed of light decrease in aging relative to the universe around it. But that only works for traveling into the future. Traveling into the past would have to involve sidestepping time altogether.

That leaves us with the hard truth that no scientist of the 19th century, or 22nd century for that matter, can build a working time machine, no matter how many flashing lights and bundles of wires are attached to it. Surely H.G. Wells was aware of this when he wrote his classic novel *The Time Machine* over one hundred years ago. Wells was fascinated by history, both natural and "man made," and used his invention as a device to expound on some of his theories about

where history might eventually take us. Once you accept the fact that time machines are nothing more than tricked-up fantasy elements like the computerized genie of the lamp cooked up by John Hughes in *Weird Science* (1985), you should have no trouble enjoying any good story containing one. Right?

Unfortunately, no. Early science-fiction writers were quick to create, identify, and hammer into dull cliches the classic Time Paradox story, or the familiar "I killed my infant grandfather" plotline. Today, the Time Paradox story, like the Locked Room story of the mystery genre, is looked on affectionately as a nostalgic old chestnut, rarely used by authors once they're out of their teen years. Sadly, movie and TV plots are usually years behind prose fiction—the writing staff of *Star Trek* uses a Time Paradox every time they get lazy. To their credit, the *Back to the Future* and *Bill & Ted* movies did a wonderful job of sending up the whole idea. But the prevalence of the whole paradox theme in modern sci-fi movies can give one a headache. But as an extension of the paradox, time travel movies are among the most popular of all science-fiction films.

In *The Terminator* and its sequel, killer robots are sent back in time to eliminate their enemies from ever existing. But if they succeed in their mission,

their mission becomes unnecessary, and so they are never sent to begin with, which would mean they'd failed. And so on. The story only works if you accept certain conflicting theories about the nature of time—thus, another paradox.

In *Godzilla Vs. King Ghidorah* (1991, but still unfortunately unavailable in the U.S.), characters use their time machine to change events in the past, but those changes only take effect from the point in time they return to—events of the past remain the same, but the changes take effect in the "present."

In *Time Bandits,* Terry Gilliam avoided the Time Paradox by using it as a convenient tool to get his characters from one brilliantly contrived fantasy to the next. But *Twelve Monkeys* ends up making the Time Paradox its platform, from which Gilliam launches dozens of finely tooled concepts, making this his most accessible feature to date.

If the hero of *The Time Machine* had stopped off in 1989 to watch *Bill & Ted's Excellent Adventure*, it may have saved him a lot of trouble. It's been argued that Marty McFly couldn't have met his older self in *Back to the Future 2,* but that's only true if it was an accepted condition of the story. Once you free the genie from the lamp, he can only grant you three wishes—unless he can grant you four.

So next time you watch a movie about time travel, think about what the consequences of time travel would really mean to the story. Or better yet, don't think about it. It will only give you a headache.

progress of employee Daphne Ashbrook, and adequately kills the scumball exec while doing so. Company head John Glover could care less about the near-rape, or the death, but doesn't want the news of a possible "renegade" android leaking out. The solution—KILL THEM BOTH. Easily excited cool-wanna-be mercenary Jeff Kober and crew are called in, leading to explosions, shootings, and chops (karate) galore. Plenty of action but nowhere near the style of Gruner's Woo-ish *Nemesis.* 🦴🦴

1994 (R) 90m/C Olivier Gruner, Daphne Ashbrook, John Glover, Jeff Kober, Dennis Lipscomb; **D:** John Murlowski; **W:** Susan Lambert, Patrick Highsmith. **VHS, LV** *REP*

Baby . . . Secret of the Lost Legend

A sportswriter and his paleontologist wife risk their lives to reunite a hatching brontosaurus with its mother in the African jungle. The story was inspired by actual reports of saurians supposedly surviving in the Congo. A bit simplistic, but kids will enjoy the dinosaurs, even though they're nowhere near the ultra-realistic level of the *Jurassic Park* beasties. Although this Disney film is not lewd in any sense, beware of several scenes displaying frontal nudity and some violence. 🦴🦴🦴

1985 (PG) 95m/C William Katt, Sean Young, Patrick McGoohan, Julian Fellowes, Kyalo Mativo, Hugh Quarshine; **D:** Bill W.L. Norton; **W:** Clifford Green, Ellen Green; **C:** John Alcott. **VHS, Beta, LV** *TOU*

Back to the Future

When neighborhood mad scientist Doc Brown constructs a time machine from a DeLorean, his youthful companion Marty accidentally transports himself to 1955. There, Marty inadvertently alters the events leading up to his own birth, and must do everything he can to bring his parents back together so he can be born on schedule. At the same time, he has to elude the local bully, *and* he's still got to get back to his own time! Solid, fast-paced entertainment is even better due to Christopher Lloyd's wonderful performance as the loony Doc while Michael J. Fox is perfect as the boy

completely out of his element. Followed by two sequels. 🦴🦴🦴

1985 (PG) 116m/C Michael J. Fox, Christopher Lloyd, Lea Thompson, Crispin Glover, Wendie Jo Sperber, Marc McClure, Thomas F. Wilson, James Tolkan, Casey Siemaszko, Billy Zane, George DiCenzo, Courtney Gains, Claudia Wells, Jason Hervey, Harry Waters Jr., Maia Brewton, J.J. Cohen; **Cameos:** Huey Lewis; **D:** Robert Zemeckis; **W:** Robert Zemeckis, Bob Gale; **C:** Dean Cundey; **M:** Alan Silvestri. Hugos '86: Dramatic Presentation; People's Choice Awards '86: Best Film; Nominations: Academy Awards '85: Best Original Screenplay, Best Song ("The Power of Love"), Best Sound. **VHS, Beta, LV** *MCA, FCT, TLF*

Back to the Future, Part 2

Taking up exactly where Part 1 left off, Doc Brown and Marty time-hop into the future (2015 to be exact) to save Marty's kids, then find themselves returning to 1955 to retrieve a sports almanac that causes havoc for the McFly family. Clever editing allows for Marty Part 2 to see Marty Part 1 at the school dance. Most of the cast returns, although Crispin Glover appears only in cuts from the original and Elisabeth Shue steps in as girlfriend Jennifer. It's that rarest of things, a sequel that's as satisfying as the original. Cliffhanger ending sets up Part 3, which was shot simultaneously with Part 2. 🦴🦴🦴

1989 (PG) 107m/C Michael J. Fox, Christopher Lloyd, Lea Thompson, Thomas F. Wilson, Harry Waters Jr., Charles Fleischer, Joe Flaherty, Elisabeth Shue, James Tolkan, Casey Siemaszko, Jeffrey Weissman, Flea, Billy Zane, J.J. Cohen, Darlene Vogel, Jason Scott Lee, Crispin Glover, Ricky Dean Logan; **D:** Robert Zemeckis; **W:** Robert Zemeckis, Bob Gale; **C:** Dean Cundey; **M:** Alan Silvestri. **VHS, Beta, LV** *MCA*

Back to the Future, Part 3

This third and final chapter of Robert Zemeckis' time-travel series picks up where Part 2 climaxed. Stuck once again in 1955, time-traveling hero Marty McFly (Michael J. Fox) frantically searches for Doc Brown so he can return to 1985. Instead, he finds himself in the Wild West circa 1885, trying to save Doc's life and shepherd him through a love-affair with Mary Steenburgen. The plot is closely entwined with those of the earlier movies, so first-time viewers might want to start with Part 1. That way you can appreciate the clever weaving of apparently irreconcilable plot-elements. Near-

"Are you trying to tell me my mom has the hots for me?!"

—Marty McFly (Michael J. Fox) laments the dangers of time travel in *Back to the Future.*

"To the more than 5,000,000 Americans who claim to have all seen UFOs, no explanation is necessary. To all others no explanation is possible."

—prologue to *The Bamboo Saucer.*

ly matches the original for nail-biting excitement and offers some snazzy new special effects. A satisfying conclusion to an excellent trilogy. 🦴🦴🦴

1990 (PG) 118m/C Michael J. Fox, Christopher Lloyd, Mary Steenburgen, Thomas F. Wilson, Lea Thompson, Elisabeth Shue, Matt Clark, Richard Dysart, Pat Buttram, Harry Carey Jr., Dub Taylor, James Tolkan, Marc McClure, Wendie Jo Sperber, J.J. Cohen, Ricky Dean Logan, Jeffrey Weissman; **D:** Robert Zemeckis; **W:** Robert Zemeckis, Bob Gale; **C:** Dean Cundey; **M:** Alan Silvestri. **VHS, Beta, LV** *MCA*

Backlash: Oblivion 2

All of the raucous elements from the original outer-space Western comedy monster flick are back, with the addition of Maxwell Caulfield as a W.C. Fieldsian bounty hunter. Of all the inventive make-up and cosmetic effects, Julie Newmar's stretched-taut face is perhaps the most startling. The hammy overacting is an ensemble effort, as it was in the first film. Though limited, the animation (both stop-motion and morphing) is pretty good. **AKA:** Oblivion 2. 🦴🦴🦴

1995 (PG-13) 82m/C Andrew Divoff, Meg Foster, Isaac Hayes, Julie Newmar, Carel Struycken, George Takei, Musetta Vander, Jimmie F. Skaggs, Irwin Keyes, Maxwell Caulfield; **D:** Sam Irvin; **W:** Peter David; **M:** Pino Donaggio. **VHS, LV** *FLL*

Bad Channels

As the frenzied DJ at nationwide radio station KDUL spins the hits, an alien interloper (accurately described as looking "like a turd in a portable window") shrinks down pretty female listeners to put into specimen jars for transport back to his planet. Grating performances combine with obnoxious music videos; the only thing that semi-saves this is a gag cameo by Full Moon Productions superhero Dollman (Tim Thomerson). Helped set up the sequel *Dollman Vs. the Demonic Toys.* Uninterested viewers need not apply. Features ex-MTV VJ Martha Quinn and a score by Blue Oyster Cult. 🦴

1992 (R) 88m/C Paul Hipp, Martha Quinn, Aaron Lustig, Ian Patrick Williams, Charlie Spradling, Tim Thomerson; **D:** Ted Nicolaou; **W:** Jackson Barr; **C:** Adolfo Bartoli. **VHS, Beta** *PAR*

Bad Girls from Mars

A Z-grade sleaze-o-rama in which everyone is murdered either before, after, or during sex. A director making an sf epic (called, coincidentally, *Bad Girls from Mars*) finds his leading ladies being killed off one by one by a masked maniac. He hires a ditzy but very um, accommodating, actress to play his heroine. Scary big-haired girls run amuck. Tiresome pseudo-thrills directed by direct-to-video sleazemaster Fred Olen Ray. 🦴

1990 (R) 86m/C Edy Williams, Brinke Stevens, Jay Richardson, Oliver Darrow; **D:** Fred Olen Ray; **W:** Sherman Scott, Mark Thomas McGee. **VHS** *VMK*

Bad Taste

Before Peter Jackson made the critically acclaimed gem *Heavenly Creatures,* before he took muppetry out of the kids' room (*Meet the Feebles*), and before he got the government of New Zealand to fund his crowd-pleasing gore-comedy *Dead Alive,* he wrote, directed, and starred in this sick little tale of alien fast-food manufacturers, here on Earth harvesting and processing human munchies. The fate of the world lies in the hands (and chainsaws) of a team of government-type guys trying to stop the rampant gobbling. As one would expect from Jackson, the splatter is fast, funny, and extreme. From the head-cleaving-shovel beginning to the final-alien-chainsaw solution, this ultra-juicy horror-laughfest doesn't stop. The alien on the original VHS packaging came with a removable middle finger so video store owners could choose to flip off or on. 🦴🦴🦴

1988 90m/C *NZ* Peter Jackson, Pete O'Herne, Mike Minett, Terry Potter, Craig Smith, Doug Wren, Dean Lawrie; **D:** Peter Jackson. **VHS, LV** *FCT*

The Bamboo Saucer

Roswell mania has given this relic added interest, but only slightly. After buzzing the USA, a flying disk lands near a village in Maoist China and its (never seen) humanoids perish from Earth germs. Russian and American scientists form an uneasy alliance to secretly investigate the craft. Special f/x and a space odyssey finale are ambitious for the era, but most of

the narrative is talky and static, pushing a Cold War moral typical for the period: Soviets and Americans must learn brotherhood and cooperation—to crush the Red Chinese. Based on the novel *Flight of the Bamboo Saucer* by Gordon Fritz. **AKA:** Collision Course. 🦴🦴

1968 103m/C Dan Duryea, John Ericson, Lois Nettleton, Nan Leslie; ***D:*** Frank Telford. **VHS** *REP*

Barbarella

People change. Before Jane Fonda was a political activist or a serious actress or a workout queen, she was, in the parlance of the times, a sex-kitten starlet. And what was once a boundary-challenging sf romp now carries a tame PG rating. Actually, the film has never been anything more than a tongue-in-cheek comedy, and it has become more than a little dated. It's based on the popular French comic strip drawn by Jean-Claude Forest, and brought to America in the pages of *Evergreen* magazine. The story has Fonda as a sexy bimbo who's sent by Earth's president in search of evil genius Duran Duran (Milo O'Shea), who has invented a new positronic ray weapon and is hiding out in a decadent city that has returned to a barbaric state of "neurotic irresponsibility." In order to complete her mission, she must face biting dolls, leather robots, a blind angel (John Phillip Law), the wicked Black Queen (Anita Pallenberg), a clumsy revolutionary (David Hemmings), and a living labyrinth, all while appearing in (and out of) eight eccentric, sexy outfits. An attention-getting opening features Fonda in her famous zero-G strip tease. **AKA:** Barbarella, Queen of the Galaxy. 🦴🦴🦴

1968 (PG) 98m/C *FR IT* Jane Fonda, John Phillip Law, David Hemmings, Marcel Marceau, Anita Pallenberg, Milo O'Shea; ***D:*** Roger Vadim; ***W:*** Terry Southern; ***C:*** Claude Renoir; ***M:*** Charles Fox. **VHS, Beta, LV** *FUS, PAR*

Baron Munchausen

The German film studio UFA celebrated its 25th anniversary with this lavish version of the Baron Munchausen legend, and until 1981's *Das Boot* this was the most expensive film ever made in Germany (and it was made during the height of World War II). Starring a cast of top-name German performers, and featuring several Munchausen "exaggerations" not used in the later renditions (Terry Gilliam's 1989 *The Adventures of Baron Munchausen* and Karel Zeman's 1961 *The Original Fabulous Adventures of Baron Munchausen*), including a romp of rabid clothing. The film has stunning special effects and even features its own version of the famous cannonball ride. Still thoroughly charming even when compared to the newer films. Filmed in Agfacolor. 🦴🦴🦴

1943 120m/C *GE* Hans Albers, Kaethe Kaack, Hermann Speelmanns, Leo Slezak; ***D:*** Josef von Baky. **VHS, Beta** *INJ, VCD, GLV*

Batman

Tim Burton's dark comic-book epic marked the return of the caped crusader to the big screen and became one of the highest-grossing films ever. Mr. Mom himself, Michael Keaton, dons the cape in this incarnation, and is surprisingly good as the crime fighter and his millionaire alter ego Bruce Wayne. Jack Nicholson as the deranged Joker steals the movie. The story revolves around the Joker's fiendish attempt to take over Gotham City via poisonous make-up as revenge for his own disfigurement. Though the romance between Bruce Wayne and Vicki Vale (Kim Bassinger) is lame, the symbiosis between the two dual personalities of hero and villain is fascinating. Along with the main story, the film traces Batman's origin, and the creation of the Joker. Academy Award winning sets are spectacular, creating a noir Gotham City. Batman's array of gadgets and, of course, the Batmobile, are too cool. The stunning costumes and make-up, along with spectacular action sequences make this a must-see. Jack Palance is menacing as the crime boss Carl Grissom. An appropriately brooding score by Danny Elfman and songs by the artist-formerly-known-as Prince add to the appeal. Look for Billy Dee Williams as District Attorney Harvey Dent, a role later taken by Tommy Lee Jones in *Batman Forever*. Followed in 1992 by *Batman Returns* and in 1995 by *Batman Forever*. 🦴🦴🦴🦴

1989 (PG-13) 126m/C Michael Keaton, Jack Nicholson, Kim Basinger, Robert Wuhl, Tracey Walter, Billy Dee

> "Who strips in space?"
>
> —*Barbarella.*

impossible camera maneuvers. Not as deep as the first, but less muddled and more fun than the second, *Batman Forever* undoubtedly predicts the future of the franchise. ♫♫♫

1995 (PG-13) 121m/C Val Kilmer, Tommy Lee Jones, Jim Carrey, Chris O'Donnell, Nicole Kidman, Drew Barrymore, Debi Mazar, Michael Gough, Pat Hingle; **D:** Joel Schumacher; **W:** Janet Scott Batchler, Akiva Goldsman, Lee Batchler; **C:** Stephen Goldblatt; **M:** Elliot Goldenthal. Blockbuster Entertainment Awards '96: Action Actress, Theatrical (Kidman); Nominations: Academy Awards '95: Best Cinematography, Best Sound; Golden Globe Awards '96: Best Song ("Hold Me, Thrill Me, Kiss Me, Kill Me"). **VHS, LV** *WAR*

Batman Returns

More (actually lots more) of the same from director Tim Burton, with Michael Keaton's Batman remaining the least interesting character. He is again overshadowed by provocative villains. Danny DeVito is the sadly misshapen Penguin who seeks to rule over the city that has tormented him; Michelle Pfeiffer is the exotic and dangerous Catwoman—who has more than a passing purr-sonal interest in Batman; and Christopher Walken is the maniacal tycoon Max Shreck. As the old saying goes, too many cooks spoil the stew; here, too many villains and a muddled plot spoil Batman's return. DeVito is wicked as the Penguin; so wicked, in fact, that he makes mustering any sympathy for this flightless bird awfully difficult. Pfeiffer fares best in her wickedly sexy role and skin-tight costume (complete with bullwhip). The plot is secondary to the special effects and nightmarish settings. Despite a big budget, this bloated sequel is of the love-it-or-leave-it variety. Look for Paul Reubens (Pee Wee Herman) in a cameo. Followed by the improved *Batman Forever* in 1995. ♫♫

1992 (PG-13) 126m/C Michael Keaton, Danny DeVito, Michelle Pfeiffer, Christopher Walken, Michael Gough, Michael Murphy, Cristi Conaway, Pat Hingle, Vincent Schiavelli, Jan Hooks, Paul (Pee Wee Herman) Reubens, Andrew Bryniarski; **D:** Tim Burton; **W:** Daniel Waters; **M:** Danny Elfman. Nominations: Academy Awards '92: Best Makeup, Best Visual Effects. **VHS** *WAR*

*batteries not included

As an evil real estate developer schemes to demolish a New York tenement, the few remaining residents are aided in their struggle

Williams, Pat Hingle, Michael Gough, Jack Palance, Jerry Hall, Lee Wallace; **D:** Tim Burton; **W:** Sam Hamm, Warren Skaaren; **C:** Roger Pratt; **M:** Danny Elfman, Prince. Academy Awards '89: Best Art Direction/Set Decoration; People's Choice Awards '90: Best Film—Drama. **VHS, Beta, LV, 8mm** *FOX, WAR*

Batman Forever

This second sequel considerably lightens up Tim Burton's dark vision. Joel Schumacher steps into the directing boots and delivers a kinder, gentler Caped Crusader. Val Kilmer takes over the cape and cowl, delivering an appropriately deadpan performance. Once again the villains overshadow the hero. An array of bad guys threaten Gotham City in this installment. Tommy Lee Jones shows up as the disfigured (apparently a more common danger in Gotham than elsewhere) "Two-Face" Harvey Dent. Jones' outrageous performance is topped only by Jim Carrey as The Riddler. Chris O'Donnell joins the crime-fighting ranks as Robin, the Boy Wonder, whose quest for revenge for his parents' death parallels Batman's own. Nicole Kidman arrives as psychologist Dr. Chase Meridian, who discovers the perfect subject in Batman/Bruce Wayne. The plot involves a spurned Wayne Industries employee, Edward Nygma (now The Riddler) and his attempt to increase his own intelligence by sucking dry the minds of the citizens of Gotham via a TV-top device. The sets are still awe inspiring, as are the stunts and

The Hound Salutes:
The Science Fiction
of John Sayles

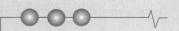

Like many filmmakers, John Sayles got his start in fiction. His first books were *Pride of the Bimbos* (about cross-dressing baseball players) and the well-received *Union Dues.* Then he decided to try his hand at Hollywood, working primarily as a writer but also as a director and actor.

And like many a young filmmaker, he hired on with Roger Corman, and made a name for himself as a writer who could turn out a solid script in a short time. But unlike most, he didn't give in to the pressures and temptations of big money and big studio projects. Such films as *Eight Men Out, Matewan, City of Hope,* and *Return of the Secaucus Seven* may vary in scope, but each is built on believably human characters. Sayles has also been attracted to political themes—the corrupting aspects of capitalism, honest lesbian relationships, racism—and he has treated them with an unapologetically liberal bias. That politi-cal awareness can be seen in the rock videos he has directed for Bruce Springsteen, and also in his science fiction.

Sure, Sayles' early work for Corman was cut to fit the limitations of genre and budget, but over the years, those films have developed strong followings on video. Both *Piranha* and *Alligator* are *Jaws*-style monster movies marked by their strong humor. *The Howling* is a first-rate werewolf tale that has spawned a seemingly endless series of sequels. Perhaps Sayles' best work for Corman is *Battle Beyond the Stars,* a cheerful retelling of *The Seven Samurai/Magnificent Seven* plot set in outer space.

Sayles also wrote scripts for the bigger-budgeted *The Clan of the Cave Bear* and *Wild Thing,* both of which might tangentially be labeled as sf. He also had a supporting role in Joe Dante's wonderful sf appreciation *Matinee.* His most recent film, *The Secret of Roan Inish* deals with Irish magic and mysticism, and he's reported to have written a script for a remake of *The Mummy.*

Perhaps Sayles' most successful work in true science fiction is the ambitious *The Brother from Another Planet.* As the title character, Joe Morton is a mute alien on the run who's retracing the underground railroad used as an escape route by Southern slaves heading north. The story is told with a minimum of special effects and a strong emphasis on social issues and character. Note the scene in a bar where two regulars argue with each other. It's a beautifully observed moment that could grace virtually any film. Like the rest of Sayles' work, it shows how little conventional definitions or expectations of a genre can mean. Good science-fiction films are simply good films.

---

by friendly flying saucers that are only the size of, well, saucers, and these miniature machine-creatures have a talent for home improvement and helping out old folks. Operating on *E.T./Cocoon* autopilot, Steven Spielberg produced this sf reworking of the old elves-and-the-shoemaker fairy tale, with superb f/x from Industrial Light & Magic, awed stares from the human cast, and an overdose of schmaltz. Crusty Hume Cronyn is the only performer who doesn't get carried away by the cutes. 🦴🦴🦴

1987 (PG) 107m/C Hume Cronyn, Jessica Tandy, Frank McRae, Michael Carmine, Elizabeth Pena, Dennis Boutsikaris; *D:* Matthew Robbins; *W:* Matthew Robbins, Brad Bird, Brent Maddock, S.S. Wilson; *C:* John McPherson; *M:* James Horner. **VHS, Beta, LV** *MCA*

Battle Beneath the Earth

The commies try to undermine democracy once again when American scientists discover a Chinese plot to invade the U.S. via a series

of underground tunnels. Perhaps a tad jingoistic. ♫ ♫

1968 112m/C *GB* Kerwin Mathews, Peter Arne, Viviane Ventura, Robert Ayres; **D:** Montgomery Tully. **VHS, Beta** *MGM*

Battle Beyond the Stars

The sf comic book version of *The Magnificent Seven* appeals to the 10-year-old in all of us. Why not? It's a grand plot, and writer John Sayles does his usual innovative work with the material. Richard Thomas is the callow youth who recruits a disreputable gang of adventurers to protect his backwater planet from marauding intergalactic outlaws. The best bits are a sassy spaceship named Nell and Sybil Danning as a sexy Valkyrie in a minimal costume. ♫ ♫ ♫

1980 (PG) 105m/C Richard Thomas, Robert Vaughn, George Peppard, Sybil Danning, Sam Jaffe, John Saxon, Darlanne Fluegel; **D:** Jimmy T. Murakami; **W:** John Sayles; **C:** Daniel Lacambre, George D. Dodge, Dennis Skotak; **M:** James Horner. **VHS, Beta, LV** *VES, LIV*

Battle Beyond the Sun

Francis Ford Coppola was just out of UCLA film school when he was hired as an assistant for $90 a week by Roger Corman. His first assignment was to Americanize (under the pseudonym "Thomas Colchart") what was a blatantly partisan Russian science-fiction adventure called *Niebo Zowiet*. Coppola re-edited, wrote, and re-dubbed English dialogue. The story now takes place on Earth which is divided into two countries, North and South Hemis. One of Coppola's most provocative inserts is a fight between two anatomically correct monsters, one male and the other female. ♫ ♫

1963 75m/C Edd Perry, Arla Powell, Bruce Hunter, Andy Stewart; **D:** Francis Ford Coppola; **W:** Nicholas Colbert, Edwin Palmer; **M:** Les Baxter. **VHS** *NOS, SNC*

Battle for Moon Station Dallos

Confusing but well rendered cartoon feature from *Ghost in the Shell* director Mamoru Oshii about a rebellion waged by slave-like colonists' on the moon against their heartless Earth masters. Dallos is a mysterious (alien?) lunar city the freedom fighters worship as a god. Surprisingly sober-minded (no comic-relief robots, cowboy sidekicks, or talking animals) and somewhat reminiscent of the works of popular Golden Age sf authors like Robert Heinlein and Arthur C. Clarke, pic ends with too many unanswered questions; this was supposed to be chapter one of an ongoing saga, but viewer disinterest stifled any sequels. Despite its relative obscurity, *Dallos* is notable as the very first OVA (original video adaptation), a species of direct-to-video japanimation that has become a booming marketplace for fantastic *anime* artists and enthusiasts—this one was just too ahead of its time. U.S. release is English-dubbed. **AKA:** Dallos. ♫ ♫ ♭

1986 84m/C *JP* **D:** Mamoru Oshii; **W:** Hisayuki Toriumi; **M:** Ichiro Nitta, Hiroyuki Nanba. **VHS, Beta** *JFK, WTA*

Battle for the Planet of the Apes

A tribe of human (well, semi-human) mutants and warlike gorillas make life miserable for the peaceful ape tribe. The story (actually a "prequel" to the series proper) is told primarily in flashback with the opening and closing sequences taking place in the year 2670 A.D, where an old orangutan is telling young chimps the story of ape history, beginning with Cornelius and Zera "descending upon Earth from Earth's own future to bring a savior, Caesar." This was the final film in the five-movie ape saga, and a good thing—the series was getting really tired by 1973—but a regrettable TV show (and still later a Saturday morning cartoon series!) was still waiting in the wings. It's pretty amazing to see Paul Williams and Claude Akins in simian makeup! ♫ ♫

1973 (G) 96m/C Roddy McDowall, Lew Ayres, John Huston, Paul Williams, Claude Akins, Severn Darden, Natalie Trundy; **D:** J. Lee Thompson; **W:** John W. Corrington, Joyce H. Corrington. **VHS, Beta** *FOX*

Battle of the Worlds

Typical low-budget science fiction. A scientist tries to stop an alien planet from destroying the Earth. Even an aging Claude Rains can't help this one. Poorly dubbed in English. **AKA:** Il Pianeta Degli Uomini Spenti; Planet of the Lifeless Men. ♫

1961 84m/C *IT* Claude Rains, Maya Brent, Bill Carter, Marina Orsini, Jacqueline Derval; *D:* Anthony (Antonio Margheriti) Dawson. **VHS** *SNC, MRV*

The Beast from 20,000 Fathoms

One of the first prehistoric-monster-loosed-by-radiation movie of the '50s is still one of the best. When atomic testing defrosts a giant dinosaur in the Arctic, the hungry monster (the fictional "rhedosaurus") proceeds onwards to its former breeding grounds, now New York City. Special effects genius Ray Harryhausen's creature isn't as detailed as some of his later work, but the film is still suspenseful, well constructed, and tons of fun to watch. Based loosely on the Ray Bradbury story "The Foghorn." 🦴🦴🦴

1953 80m/B Paul Christian, Paula Raymond, Cecil Kellaway, Kenneth Tobey, Donald Woods, Lee Van Cleef, Steve Brodie, Mary Hill; *D:* Eugene Lourie; *W:* Fred Freiberger, Louis Morheim. **VHS, Beta, LV** *WAR, FCT, MLB*

The Beast of Yucca Flats

Expecting a giant radioactive dinosaur? Try a radioactive Tor Johnson! In this unbelievably cheap, quasi-nuclear protest film, Tor plays a Russian scientist who's chased by communist agents into a nuclear testing area and is caught in an atomic blast. As a result, he turns into a club-wielding caveman—very like all the "monsters" Tor played in other movies. Droning voice-over narration was used instead of dialogue to keep costs down. Anyone who thinks Tor's roles in *Plan 9 from Outer Space* and *Bride of the Monster* were masterpieces of bad acting needs to check this dog out. Fellow Ed Wood crony Conrad Brooks shows up as a Federal agent. Director/writer/actor Coleman Francis was in lots of B westerns in the '40s and '50s. He later made *The Skydivers* and *Red Zone Cuba,* before ending up doing bit parts in movies for Russ Meyer and Ray Dennis Steckler.

1961 53m/B Tor Johnson, Douglas Mellor, Larry Aten, Barbara Francis, Conrad Brooks, Bing Stafford, Anthony Cardoza; *D:* Coleman Francis; *W:* Coleman Francis; *C:* John Cagle. **VHS** *SNC, CNM, MLB*

Beastmaster

Standard sword-and-sorcery adventure set in a wild and primitive world of magic. The young hero Dar is able to communicate telepathically with animals. He soon becomes involved in an epic battle against the evil priest Maax, who enjoys turning people into murderous zombies by sticking worms in their ears and dressing them in ugly leather costumes. Luckily Dar has his trusty ferrets at his side—goodness knows he'll need them. '70s TV-hounds will recognize John "Good Times" Amos as Maax's assistant and Charlie's Angel Tanya Roberts as Dar's main squeeze. Neither the best nor the worst fantasy film ever made, this is fairly typical of the flicks that emerged during the sword-and-sorcery glut of the early '80s. It could've used a monster or two, but with a little popcorn on a dull Saturday night, it's halfway entertaining. 🦴🦴

1982 (PG) 119m/C Marc Singer, Tanya Roberts, Rip Torn, John Amos, Josh Milrad, Billy Jacoby; *D:* Don A. Coscarelli; *W:* Don A. Coscarelli; *C:* John Alcott. **VHS, Beta, LV** *MGM*

Beastmaster 2: Through the Portal of Time

This time the laughs are intentional as Dar the Beastmaster (Marc Singer) follows an evil monarch through a dimensional gateway to modern-day L.A. Dar finds the shopping is better for both trendy clothes and weapons. It lacks the stupid charm of the first film (that's what happens when you get a different director), but this sequel is still fun for sword-and-sorcery fanatics. The video contains a behind-the-scenes featurette. And there's a tiger! 🦴🐾

1991 (PG-13) 107m/C Marc Singer, Kari Wuhrer, Sarah Douglas, Wings Hauser, James Avery, Robert Fieldsteel, Arthur Malet, Robert Z'Dar, Michael Berryman; *D:* Sylvio Tabet; *M:* Robert Folk. **VHS, LV** *REP*

Beastmaster 3: The Eye of Braxus

You wouldn't think it possible or financially feasible, but heroic hunk Dar the Beastmaster (Marc Singer) has returned once again to battle evil. Lord Agon (David Warner) needs to

obtain a jeweled eye that will bring the demon Braxus back to life, and he'll stop at nothing to reach his terrifying goal, including kidnapping Dar's brother King Tal (Casper Van Dien). But Dar isn't alone; he's got the bewitching sorceress Morgana (Lesley-Anne Down), tempting warrioress Shada (Sandra Hess), and loyal advisor Seth (Tony Todd) to help him out. Perfect for those whose heroic fantasy jones just isn't satisfied by *Hercules: The Legendary Journeys.*

1995 (PG) 92m/C Marc Singer, David Warner, Lesley-Anne Down, Tony Todd, Caspar Van Dien, Keith Coulouris, Sandra Hess, Patrick Kilpatrick; *D:* Gabrielle Beaumont; *W:* David Wise; *C:* Barbara Claman; *M:* Jan Hammer. **VHS, LV** *MCA*

The Bees

Terrible movie. Un-bee-lievably bad. A new strain of killer bees has ransacked South America and are now threatening the rest of the world. "B" movie veterans John Saxon and John Carradine bumble through it, both trying hard to give this flick some class. Unfortunately, it'll just give most viewers hives. It was essentially a cheap, hastily cobbled together steal of *The Swarm*'s killer bee motif. The misleading poster showed a brawny but rather bored-looking hero fending off a gargantuan bee with a torch.

1978 (PG) 93m/C John Saxon, John Carradine, Angel Tompkins, Claudio Brook, Alicia Encinas; *D:* Alfredo Zacharias; *W:* Alfredo Zacharias; *C:* Leon Sanchez. **VHS, Beta** *WAR*

Before I Hang

When a doctor invents a youth serum from the blood of a murderer, he'll stop at nothing to keep his secret. When he tests it on himself, he gets more than restored youth. Boris Karloff gives an amazing performance—one of his best—as the man with the dual personality. In some scenes he transforms before your eyes, without the use of any make-up or camera tricks, from one personality to another. A powerful thriller from the underrated Nick Grinde.

1940 60m/B Boris Karloff, Evelyn Keyes, Bruce (Herman Brix) Bennett, Edward Van Sloan, Pedro de Cordoba; *D:* Nick Grinde. **VHS, Beta** *COL*

Beginning of the End

From the opening shot of a couple necking in a convertible on lovers' lane to the tinny overwrought musical score to the stock footage of soldiers and tanks, this is the archetypal 1950s big-bug B-movie. Huge, radiation-spawned locusts attack Chicago. Peter Graves springs into action and saves the day. Easily the best giant grasshopper film ever made, it's good for giggles but little more. Graves (*It Conquered the World*), Morris Ankrum (*Earth Vs. the Flying Saucers*), and even Peggy Castle (*Target Earth*) were all veterans of cheap sci-fi battles for world domination. The ad campaign stressed the fact that they used "real" grasshoppers in the movie, as opposed to that "phony" stop-motion stuff. Bert I. Gordon would move on to more oversized bugs with *The Spider,* followed by other BIG productions.

1957 73m/B Peggy Castle, Peter Graves, Morris Ankrum, Richard Benedict, James Seay; *D:* Bert I. Gordon; *W:* Fred Freiberger, Lester Gorn; *C:* Jack Marta. **VHS** *NO*

Beneath the Planet of the Apes

In this first sequel to the science-fiction classic, another twentieth-century astronaut, Brent (James Franciscus) arrives in the year 3995 attempting to find his lost colleague Taylor (Charlton Heston). He passes through the same time warp and follows the same path as Taylor did in the original *Planet of the Apes* film. Brent discovers Ape City and travels through the ruins of the post-apocalyptic New York subway system (which looks surprisingly similar to today's New York subway system). In the underground labyrinth, Brent discovers nuclear warhead-worshiping telepathic human mutants. Unfortunately, the militant apes also discover their existence, leading to a violent confrontation. The sequel tries to maintain the allegorical bent of the original, including peace sit-ins and an anti-nuclear message, but falls short of the mark. As with many sequels, the story seems forced and, without the powerful originality of the first film, does not capture the viewer's interest. The makeup and sets remain excellent. Many members of the original cast are back, includ-

ing Kim Hunter as Zira, Maurice Evans as Dr. Zaius, James Gregory as General Ursus, and Charlton Heston as Taylor. Roddy McDowall did not don the makeup for this one, but did provide the voice for his character, Cornelius. The series produced three more sequels. 🎷🎷

1969 (G) 108m/C Charlton Heston, James Franciscus, Kim Hunter, Maurice Evans, James Gregory, Natalie Trundy, Jeff Corey, Linda Harrison, Victor Buono; *D:* Ted Post; *W:* Mort Abrahams, Paul Dehn; *C:* Milton Krasner; *V:* Roddy McDowall. **VHS, Beta, LV** *FOX, FUS*

Beyond the Bermuda Triangle

Don't expect much from this downbeat TV movie in the way of f/x or answers, just a few oblique references to time/space warps as a retired businessman (old pro Fred MacMurray in a nice performance that dignifies the material) suffers friends and family members vanishing in the alleged hoodoo waters off the coast of Florida. He begins a private investigation that leads nowhere—literally. The Hound recommends Lawrence David Kusche's book *The Bermuda Triangle Mystery—Solved* for the scoop on the inspiration for many a lame genre pic. 🎷🎵

1975 78m/C Fred MacMurray, Sam Groom, Donna Mills, Suzanne Reed, Dana Plato, Woody Woodbury; *D:* William A. Graham. **VHS** *NO*

Beyond the Stars

Christian Slater is a problem kid bent on an aerospace career, who befriends reclusive Apollo 11 astronaut Martin Sheen, still bitter over the NASA cover-up of a deadly accident on the moon. Weak drama with sci-fi overtones that come too little too late, though it's a novelty to see a movie that heavily promotes the hobby of model rocketry (Estes rules!). David Saperstein, the original author of *Cocoon,* wrote/directed from a script that turns to Save-the-Whales when it runs out of other messages. Interesting cast. 🎷

1989 94m/C Martin Sheen, Christian Slater, Olivia D'Abo, F. Murray Abraham, Robert Foxworth, Sharon Stone, F. Murray Abraham; *D:* David Saperstein; *W:* David Saperstein; *C:* John Bartley; *M:* Geoff Levin, Chris Many. **VHS, Beta, LV** *LIV*

Beyond the Time Barrier

Air Force test pilot gets more than he bargained for when his high speed plane carries him into the future. There he sees the ravages of an upcoming plague, to which he must return. 🎷🎷🎵

1960 75m/B Robert Clarke, Darlene Tompkins, Arianne Arden, Vladimir Sokoloff; *D:* Edgar G. Ulmer. **VHS, Beta** *SNC, CNM*

Biggles

Generations of English boys thrilled to W.E. Johns' tales of WWI flying ace Bigglesworth, his brave pal Algy, and their Snoopy-style dogfights with the Hun. But when this movie version finally emerged the major influence was *Back to the Future,* as a modern guy—of all things, a bloody Yank—abruptly materializes back in 1917 Europe and helps his "time twin" Biggles in a confrontation with an advanced German superweapon (which, surprisingly, isn't the cause of the time warp after all). Biggles purists will be outraged, but there are some spirited anachronisms and a proper tongue-in-cheek attitude. Beware the '80s disco music though. **AKA:** Biggles: Adventures in Time. 🎷🎷

1986 (PG) 100m/C *GB* Neil Dickson, Alex Hyde-White, Peter Cushing, Fiona Hutchinson, Marcus Gilbert; *D:* John Hough. **VHS, Beta, LV** *VTR, NWV*

Bill & Ted's Bogus Journey

While this big-budget sequel to *Bill & Ted's Excellent Adventure* has better special effects, it doesn't quite capture the charm of the original. It's still fun, though, and to its credit it doesn't simply duplicate the time-travel theme of the first movie. Slain by look-alike robot duplicates from the future, the airhead heroes pass through an impressively visualized heaven and hell before tricking Death into bringing them back for a second duel with their heinous terminators. Non-fans still won't think much of it; phooey on them. If nothing else, this flick will be someday be remembered as Keanu Reeves' last good role. 🎷🎷🎷

1991 (PG) 98m/C Keanu Reeves, Alex Winter, William Sadler, Joss Ackland, Pam Grier, George Carlin, Amy Stock-Poynton, Hal Landon Jr., Annette Azcuy, Sarah Trigger, Chelcie Ross, Taj Mahal, Roy Brocksmith, William

"Once...they made history. Now...they are history."
—Bill & Ted's Bogus Journey.

Shatner; **D:** Pete Hewitt; **W:** Chris Matheson, Edward Solomon; **M:** David Newman. **VHS** *ORI*

Bill & Ted's Excellent Adventure

Many film-goers expected this flick to be nothing more than another brainless teen-comedy, but found themselves pleasantly surprised. When two amiable but intellectually challenged Valley Boys find themselves in danger of failing their history final, they're rescued by Rufus (George Carlin), and his time-traveling telephone booth. It seems that Bill and Ted are destined to become the founders of a future utopia based on heavy metal music (?!). This paradise will never come to pass if they fail their test, so Rufus has come back to give the proto-heroes a chance to brush up on history first-hand. Along the way they meet a host of historical figures and put every time-travel cliche through the wringer. This is a good-natured, wonderfully entertaining film. Too bad the spate of "dumb teen" movies that followed didn't match it in quality. 🦴🦴🦴🦴

1989 (PG) 105m/C Keanu Reeves, Alex Winter, George Carlin, Bernie Casey, Dan Shor, Robert Barron, Amy Stock-Poynton, Terry Camillieri, Rod Loomis, Al Leong; **D:** Stephen Herek; **W:** Chris Matheson, Edward Solomon; **M:** David Newman. **VHS, Beta, LV, 8mm** *COL, SUE, NLC*

Bio Hazard

A government experiment in psychic teleportation somehow beams to Earth a familiarly toothsome monster who goes on a deadly rampage. Pic ends (or more accurately, just stops) with a gag reel of the actors blowing their lines. Low-budget filmmaker Ray further pillaged *Alien* with *Deep Space,* proving that if at first you don't succeed, fail fail again. 🦴🦴

1985 (R) 84m/C Angelique Pettyjohn, Carroll Borland, Richard Hench, Aldo Ray, William Fair, Frank MacDonald; **D:** Fred Olen Ray; **W:** Fred Olen Ray. **VHS, Beta** *MTX*

Biohazard: The Alien Force

Like the original, a 1985 alternative classic, this is a silly little thing about a monster played by a guy in the least-scary rubber suit you ever saw. For fans of bad movies, the quality of ineptitude ranges from just-plain-awful to wonderfully atrocious. After all, ama-

teurish acting, cheap sets, and lots of slime can accomplish only so much. **WOOF!**

1995 (R) 88m/C Steve Zurk, Chris Mitchum, Susan Fronsoe, Tom Ferguson, Patrick Moran, John Maynard; **D:** Steve Latshaw. **VHS** *VMK*

The Birds

Hitchcock's borderline sf chiller is one of the best and most creative Man-versus-Nature shockers. Still wildly original in the way the plot slowly turns from a romantic soap opera—whole first hour details sophisticate Tippi Hedren venturing to a California island community to snare lawyer Rod Taylor despite his disapproving mother—into an environmental nightmare, with bloody, seemingly unmotivated bird attacks poking through the placid narrative until there's nothing else. Only Hitchcock can twist the harmless into the horrific while avoiding the ridiculous; this is perhaps the cinema's purest, most horrifying portrait of the apocalypse. While bluescreen f/x technology has improved considerably since this was made, Hitch's eye for camera placement and editing remains talon-sharp. Based on a short story by Daphne Du Maurier; screenplay by novelist Evan Hunter (AKA Ed McBain), but also inspired by a real-life plague of birds that hit not far from Hitchcock's American home in Santa Cruz (an incident briefly mentioned in the dialogue). 🦴🦴🦴🦴

1963 (PG-13) 120m/C Rod Taylor, Tippi Hedren, Jessica Tandy, Veronica Cartwright, Suzanne Pleshette, Ethel Griffies, Charles McGraw, Ruth McDevitt; **Cameos:** Alfred Hitchcock; **D:** Alfred Hitchcock; **W:** Evan Hunter; **C:** Robert Burks. **VHS, Beta, LV** *MCA*

The Birds 2: Land's End

Unfortunate ripoff of the Hitchcock fright classic. Killer seagulls begin attacking the inhabitants of east coast Gull Island. Seems they're tired of being oil slick victims. Hedren's the town shopkeeper, an in-joke cameo unrelated to her character in the original. Definitely for the birds—even the director refuses to acknowledge it, appearing in the credits using the film industry pseudonym "Alan Smithee." Made for cable TV. **WOOF!**

1994 (R) 87m/C Brad Johnson, Chelsea Field, Tippi Hedren, James Naughton, Jan Rubes, Megan Gallagher; **D:** Alan Smithee, Rick Rosenthal; **W:** Jim Wheat, Ken Wheat; **M:** Ron Ramin. **VHS, LV** *MCA*

The Black Hole

What is mad scientist Maximilian Schell up to as his starship sits at the edge of a black hole? Lots of nasty robots and abominable dialogue provide the answers in this Disney space adventure. Throwback sf recalls *Forbidden Planet* and even the studio's own *20,000 Leagues Under the Sea*. Fine matte paintings by Peter Ellenshaw create a dark, mysterious atmosphere. Despite the glaring flaws in this creaky vehicle, kids will probably enjoy the effects and the good "cute" robots. 🦴🦴

1979 (G) 97m/C Maximilian Schell, Anthony Perkins, Ernest Borgnine, Yvette Mimieux, Joseph Bottoms, Robert Forster; **D:** Gary Nelson; **W:** Jeb Rosebrook, Gerry Day; **C:** Frank Phillips; **M:** John Barry. Nominations: Academy Awards '79: Best Cinematography. **VHS, Beta, LV** *DIS, OM*

The Black Scorpion

King Kong's Willis O'Brien co-designed the effects in this above-average giant insector. Huge and hungry subterranean scorpions get a whiff of human flesh and rush to the surface through pathways created by devastating volcanic eruptions. Once there, are they content to crunch and munch the humans they so crave? Heck no! Wreaking havoc on Mexico City, these larger-than-average arachnids derail a train (an amazing effects sequence requiring 15 different camera set-ups), de-sky a helicopter, and even chomp on one another. Though not as intense as the earlier giant ant thriller *Them*, O'Brien's stop-motion effects place this flick near the top of all '50s big-bug sci-fi thrillers. 🦴🦴🦴

1957 85m/B Richard Denning, Mara Corday, Carlos Rivas, Mario Navarro; **D:** Edward Ludwig; **W:** Robert Blees, David Duncan; **C:** Lionel Linden. **VHS** *WAR, MLB, FRG*

Blade Runner

Moody, beautifully photographed thriller has become better with age. 21st century L.A. is violent, rainy, smoky, and dark; a multi-ethnic, multi-racial place where the wealthy live in

"How come the robot always gets picked for the fun assignments?!" The crew of the *Palamino* complains in *The Black Hole.*

Go ahead, take the assignment, Deckard. That guy looks like he's on the up and up to us! Harrison Ford ponders a job offer in *Blade Runner.*

cool luxury and everyone else fights for a little space and quiet away from the crowd and the constant barrage of advertising. That world is so believable that it gives the action an unusual amount of emotional power. And, by the second or third viewing, the story actually makes sense. World-weary ex-cop tracks down a handful of renegade "replicants" (synthetically produced human slaves who, with only days left of life, search madly for some way to extend their prescribed lifetimes). Based rather loosely on *Do Androids Dream of Electric Sheep,* a novella by Philip K. Dick. On tape, the enduring cult favorite exists in two versions, both different from the original theatrical release. The older 118-minute tape version has a few moments of more violent footage. The 1993 director's cut runs 117 minutes. It eliminates the voice-over narration and has a different ending. 🦴🦴🦴♭

1982 (R) 122m/C Harrison Ford, Rutger Hauer, Sean Young, Daryl Hannah, M. Emmet Walsh, Edward James Olmos, Joe Turkel, Brion James, Joanna Cassidy; **D:** Ridley Scott; **W:**

Hampton Fancher, David Peoples; **C:** Jordan Cronenweth; **M:** Vangelis. Hugos '83: Dramatic Presentation; Los Angeles Film Critics Association Awards '82: Best Cinematography; Nominations: Academy Awards '82: Best Art Direction/Set Decoration. **VHS, Beta, LV, 8mm** COL, WAR, CRC

Blake of Scotland Yard

Blake, the former Scotland Yard inspector, battles against a villain who has constructed a murderous death ray. Condensed version of the 15-episode serial (originally at 180 minutes). 🦴🦴

1936 70m/B Ralph Byrd, Herbert Rawlinson, Joan Barclay, Lloyd Hughes; **D:** Robert F. "Bob" Hill. **VHS, Beta** VYY, DVT, NOS

The Blob

In his first starring role, Steve McQueen is a rebel with a cause: to save his small Pennsylvania town from a gelatinous invader from outer space. Naturally, the adults don't believe him, but they change their tune when

TV on Tape:
Blake's Seven

Key writers behind *Doctor Who* concocted this leaner, meaner sci-fi adventure which might accurately be called the anti-*Star Trek*.

Instead of a touchy-feely crew of super-competent comrades, this has future freedom-fighter Blake in an alliance of convenience with a band of cutthroats and rogues (who threaten to murder one another at least once per episode), piloting the advanced spaceship *Liberator* on raids against an evil empire known as...The Federation. Sure, it's got the impoverished production values of many a BBC serial, and the colossal cosmic clash at the climax of episode 26 looks like something out of *Hardware Wars*. But characters are well conceived, with a surprisingly high mortality rate thanks to actors regularly exiting the series (Gareth Thomas himself departed after two seasons, leaving half of *Blake's Seven* Blakeless).

BBC executives did not like the show, and its unforgettable finale is designed to leave no possibility for revival. Ever. A Vampire Lestat-ish cult following of female sf fans developed a crush on co-star Paul Darrow, who plays the ambitious criminal antihero Avon with Richard III panache. For the guys there's Jacqueline Pearce's vulpine *haute-couture* villainess Servalan. Each volume in the 26-cassette set contains two episodes.

1978-81/C *GB Selected cast:* Gareth Thomas, Sally Knyvette, Paul Darrow, Michael Keating, David Jackson, Jan Chappell, Jaqueline Pearce. ***Directors:*** Michael E. Briant, Vere Lorrimer. **VHS** *VCO, TVC, MOV*

---

this purple people eater engulfs a supermarket, a diner, and most memorably, a movie theatre (where *Daughter of Horror* is playing). McQueen's girlfriend is played by Aneta Corsaut, who is best known as Helen Crump on *The Andy Griffith Show*. One of the most beloved monster movies of the 1950s (it was released the same year as *The Fly*). Producer Jack Harris later made *Mother Goose A Go Go* and the first 3-D adult film, *Paradisio*. Burt Bacharach co-wrote the title tune. The end...question mark? Nope, it was followed by Larry Hagman's 1972 direct-to-drive-in sequel, *Beware! The Blob* (or: *Son of Blob*), and a state-of-the-art remake in 1988. 🦴🦴🦴

1958 83m/C Steve McQueen, Aneta Corsaut, Olin Howlin, Earl Rowe; ***D:*** Irvin S. Yeaworth Jr.; ***W:*** Theodore Simonson, Kate Phillips; ***C:*** Thomas E. Spalding. **VHS, Beta, LV** *COL, GEM, MLB*

The Blob

We will leave it to sociologists to explain why the '80s were a fertile breeding ground for remakes of such beloved '50s sci-fi cult classics as *The Fly, The Thing, Invaders from Mars,* and *The Blob,* which is perhaps best remembered as the film that launched the career of Steve McQueen. But thanks to the advanced art of special effects, the massive glutinous monster is at last, the star. It's a meaner, more ravenous Blob. No longer content just to attack movie theatre projectionists (as in the original), it also slurps dishwashers down the sink and engulfs phone booths. It's probably a sign of the times that the Blob is not an outer-space organism, but a product of the military (and one may or may not read into the Blob's spreading amuck as an AIDS allegory). Beware Del Close, a legend of the Chicago school of improvisational comedy, as Reverend Meeker, whose climactic warnings of the end of the world are given extra urgency by those remnants of the Blob he keeps in a jar.... 🦴🦴🦴

1988 (R) 92m/C Kevin Dillon, Candy Clark, Joe Seneca, Shawnee Smith, Donovan Leitch, Jeffrey DeMunn, Del Close; ***D:*** Chuck Russell; ***W:*** Frank Darabont, Chuck Russell; ***C:*** Mark Irwin. **VHS, Beta, LV** *COL*

"It started out as a little blob, Doc, but it just keeps getting bigger." Steve McQueen and Aneta Corseaut seek medical advice in *The Blob*.

The Blood of Heroes

A post-apocalyptic action flick detailing the adventures of a battered team of "juggers," warriors who challenge small village teams to a brutal sport (involving dogs' heads on sticks) that's a cross between jousting and football. **AKA:** The Salute of the Jugger. 🦴🦴

1989 (R) 97m/C Rutger Hauer, Joan Chen, Vincent D'Onofrio, Anna Katarina; **D:** David Peoples; **W:** David Peoples; **M:** Todd Boekelheide. **VHS, Beta, LV** *HBO*

Blue Flame

Vigilante cop is hired to track down two humanoid aliens who have escaped captivity in futuristic L.A. They evade him by time-traveling through alternate realities, infiltrating the cop's mind, and using his fantasies against him. 🦴🦴

1993 (R) 88m/C Brian Wimmer, Ian Buchanan, Kerri Green, Cecilia Peck, Jad Mager; **D:** Cassian Elwes; **W:** Cassian Elwes. **VHS** *COL*

Blue Monkey

Definitely a cause for blues, this notoriously mistitled mess of creature-feature cliches has a mysterious tropical plant impregnating a man (!), who upchucks a vile insect larva that spreads disease, initiating lockdown quarantine in a huge metro hospital. Thanks to an obnoxious little boy fond of pouring growth serums on things—you know the type—the worm turns into a giant praying mantis and hunts trapped humans to feed upon. "Blue monkey" derives from a throwaway line of dialogue; well, they couldn't very well have called this "Bad Canadian *Alien* Ripoff," right? But we can. **AKA:** Green Monkey. 🦴

1987 (R) 97m/C *CA* Steve Railsback, Susan Anspach, Gwynyth Walsh, John Vernon, Joe Flaherty, Robin Duke; **D:** William Fruet; **W:** George Goldsmith; **C:** Brenton Spencer. **VHS, Beta** *COL*

Blue Thunder

Maverick helicopter pilots Roy Scheider and

Daniel Stern test an experimental high-tech chopper that can see through walls, record a whisper, and destroy a city block. Supposedly the supercopter will ensure security during 1984 Olympics, but the same right-wing ogres who engineered the Vietnam War actually intend to use it to massacre Los Angeles minorities before the assembled worldwide media...huh? Futuristic hardware qualifies this as an sf genre pic, politics classify it as fairy tale. Satisfying aerial combat scenes nearly crash with the much-rewritten script. Inspired a short-lived TV series and a (notably more popular) rival-network imitator, *Airwolf.* Often misidentified as an Apache craft, the Blue Thunder is actually a French-made Aerospatiale Gazelle with design modifications. 🦴🦴

1983 (R) 110m/C Roy Scheider, Daniel Stern, Malcolm McDowell, Candy Clark, Warren Oates; **D:** John Badham; **W:** Dan O'Bannon, Don Jakoby; **C:** John A. Alonzo. Nominations: Academy Awards '83: Best Film Editing. **VHS, Beta, LV** *COL*

Blue Tornado

Mysterious bright light, emitted from a mountain, makes supersonic NATO jets disappear into thin air. A beautiful researcher and a cocky pilot set out to solve the mystery. This Italian UFO opus has better-than-average aerial sequences, but wings are clipped by an ineffective quasi-mystical climax and silly dialogue. **AKA:** Three Tornadoes. 🦴

1992 (PG-13) 96m/C *IT* Dirk Benedict, Patsy Kensit, Ted McGinley, David Warner; **D:** Tony B. Dobb; **W:** Tony B. Dobb. **VHS** *VMK*

Bob Lazar: Excerpts from the Government Bible

The government says that Bob Lazar was never a scientist of any sort for them, much less the chief physicist in charge of "back engineering" alien disc technology at the ultra-secret area known as S4 of area 51 in the Nevada Air Force Range. Nonetheless, this is a pretty convincing presentation. Lazar describes in detail the components necessary for inter-stellar travel, generating a gravitational field, and building a gravity propulsion system. During his stint at the U.S. installation, Lazar claims to have worked on the "Sport Model," only one of nine flying discs that the government was examining and working on. This impressive video may not convince but it will certainly make you think. 🦴🦴🦴

1994 45m/C D: Bob Lazar, Gene Huff; **W:** Bob Lazar, Gene Huff. **VHS** *UFO*

Body Melt

Crazed doctor unleashes a new drug on the unsuspecting citizens of a small New Zealand town, causing both violent insanity, graphic internal blood mutations, and, ultimately, equally graphic total meltdown. The characters are not as interesting (nor the acting as good) as 1987's melting-rotgut epic *Street Trash,* and director Phillip Brophy has a long way to go to match fellow grossout director Peter Jackson in style, humor, or even sickness, but there are enough flashes of gorific fun to appeal to most midnight movie fans. Inbred family, with a horse-faced daughter "hungry" for love, is a killer. 🦴🦴

1993 82m/C *AU* Gerard Kennedy, Andrew Daddo, Ian Smith, Vincent Gil, Regina Gaigalas; **D:** Philip Brophy; **W:** Philip Brophy, Rod Bishop; **M:** Philip Brophy. **VHS, LV** *PSM*

Body Snatchers

"They're out there. They're everywhere. They get you when you sleep, you hear?" The pod people are at it again and who better than *Bad Lieutenant* director Abel Ferrara, who one critic has described as "the poet of the soulless," to bring them to the screen for the third time? This version is set on an army base, a brilliant maneuver as the military's strict code of conduct provides perfect cover for the emotionless pods. Gabrielle Anwar (Al Pacino's tango partner in *Scent of a Woman*) stars as Marti, a teenager whose stepmother, father, and younger brother become victims. The special effects, light years ahead of the 1956 and 1978 versions, literally get under your skin. But after all these years, the paranoia of Jack Finney's original story is still palpable: "Where you gonna go?" asks pod-wife Meg Tilly. "Where you gonna run? Where you gonna

> "Chew, if only you could see what I have seen with your eyes."
>
> —Roy Batty (Rutger Hauer) in *Blade Runner.*

"Get over it," whines a frustrated Meg Tilly. "I've had cramps *way* worse than that." *Body Snatchers.*

hide? Nowhere. Because there is no one...like you...left." 🦴🦴🦴⫰

1993 (R) 87m/C Gabrielle Anwar, Meg Tilly, Terry Kinney, Forest Whitaker, Billy Wirth, R. Lee Ermey; **D:** Abel Ferrara; **W:** Stuart Gordon, Dennis Paoli, Nicholas St. John; **C:** Bojan Bazelli; **M:** Joe Delia. **VHS, LV** *WAR*

Bog

Some leftover stars from sci-fi's Golden Age reunited for this lost cause, filmed in Wisconsin, about a humanoid lake monster who drinks type-A blood and has a more-than-platonic relationship with a rural witch woman (thankfully, we're spared the details). Super-cheap production values and a shoddy creature suit make *Bog* a tough slog. **WOOF!**

1984 (PG) 90m/C Gloria De Haven, Marshall Thompson, Leo Gordon, Aldo Ray, Ed Clark; **D:** Don Keeslar. **VHS, Beta** *PSM*

Boom in the Moon

Buster Keaton fares poorly in this sci-fi come-

dy. He's trapped on a space ship to the moon. Poor production, with uneven direction and acting. **AKA:** A Modern Bluebeard. **WOOF!**

1946 83m/C Buster Keaton, Angel Garasa, Virginia Serret, Fernando Soto, Luis Barreiro; **D:** Jaime Salvador. **VHS** *NO*

The Borrower

An exiled unstable mutant insect alien serial killer (you know the type) must switch heads with human beings regularly to survive. This colorful, garish gorefest has humor and attitude, but never develops behind the basic grossout situation. Director John McNaughton's follow-up to his cult hit debut *Henry, Portrait of a Serial Killer* fails to find the same balance between humor and horror. 🦴🦴

1989 (R) 97m/C Rae Dawn Chong, Don Gordon, Antonio Fargas, Tom Towles; **D:** John McNaughton. **VHS, LV** *WAR, CAN*

Bounty Hunter 2002

An incurable virus kills 98% of the world's

population. A nameless bounty hunter is paid by a psycho preacher to bring him a beautiful survivalist gal, reputedly a virgin and thus uninfected. You've heard the expression 'bottom of the barrel?' Look underneath the barrel and you'll find this low-budget schlock AIDS metaphor. **AKA:** 2002: The Rape of Eden. **WOOF!**

1994 90m/C Phil Nordell, Francine Lapensee, Vernon Wells, Jeff Conaway; **D:** Sam Auster; **W:** Sam Auster. **VHS, LV** *AIP*

A Boy and His Dog

Fetch this cult classic, a "kinky tale of survival," based on Harlan Ellison's novella. In the post-holocaust world of 2014, the essence of humans and animals has been reversed. Don Johnson stars as a dim-witted youth who treks across the barren wilderness foraging for food and women. It is his canine companion, Blood, with whom he communicates telepathically, that is the more cultured, tutored, and civilized. Directed and adapted for the screen by character actor L. Q. Jones. Though Ellison has expressed "enormous appreciation" for Jones's adaptation, he disavows the controversial ending in which Johnson must choose between an ailing Blood and a woman trying to lure him to an underground society that desires his breeding potential. Suffice to say the final pun is not for all tastes. Ellison raised money to re-dub it by hawking clippings from the editing room floor at science-fiction conventions, but Jones prevailed. Produced by Alvy Moore (best remembered as Hank Kimble on *Green Acres*). Blood was played by the late Tiger of *The Brady Bunch*. Tim McIntire supplies the voice. 🦴🦴🦴

1975 (R) 87m/C Don Johnson, Suzanne Benton, Jason Robards Jr., Charles McGraw, Alvy Moore; **D:** L.Q. Jones; **W:** L.Q. Jones; **C:** John Morrill; **V:** Tim McIntire. Hugos '76: Dramatic Presentation. **VHS, Beta, LV** *ICA, MED, MRV*

The Boys from Brazil

With Gregory Peck as an obsessed Nazi hell-bent on cloning a batch of little Adolphs, Laurence Olivier (in an Academy Award-nominated performance) as a Jewish Nazi-hunter, and just a slightly ridiculous plot, Ira Levin's novel is brought to the screen. With numerous "on-location" segments filmed around the world, the movie plays more like a big adventure flick, lacking the intrigue and tension that should appear automatically when someone is attempting to create a "Fourth" Reich. With the brood of young Hitlers needing the proper upbringing, a few murders are definitely called for, both as a plot device and to position the new youth corps into the right environment. Not a bad movie at all, but with Olivier's acting, Heywood Gould's script, and another outstanding score (also Oscar nominated) by composer Jerry Goldsmith, the film could have been much, much more. 🦴🦴🦴

1978 (R) 123m/C Gregory Peck, James Mason, Laurence Olivier, Uta Hagen, Steve Guttenberg, Denholm Elliott, Lilli Palmer; **D:** Franklin J. Schaffner; **W:** Heywood Gould; **M:** Jerry Goldsmith. National Board of Review Awards '78: Best Actor (Olivier); Nominations: Academy Awards '78: Best Actor (Olivier), Best Film Editing, Best Original Score. **VHS, Beta, LV** *FOX*

The Brain

Dr. Blake, host of a popular TV talk show, is in league with a power-hungry alien brain that has a fanged, grimacing face across its frontal lobes. This may be the first time anyone's ever suggested that TV talk shows suffer from too much brains (rimshot). Canadian import, just maybe a satire, is a pain in the pituitary. **WOOF!**

1988 (R) 94m/C Tom Breznahan, Cyndy Preston, David Gale, George Buza, Brett Pearson; **D:** Edward Hunt; **W:** Barry Pearson; **C:** Joe Morhaim. **VHS, Beta** *LIV*

The Brain Eaters

A strange ship from inside the Earth invades a small town, and hairy monsters promptly attach themselves to people's necks in a daring bid to control the planet. The imaginative story compensates somewhat for the cheap special effects. Watch for Leonard Nimoy before he grew pointed ears. 🦴🦴

1958 60m/B Edwin Nelson, Alan Frost, Jack Hill, Joanna Lee, Jody Fair, Leonard Nimoy; **D:** Bruno Ve Sota. **VHS** *NOS, CNM*

"Breeding is an ugly thing."

—Blood the Dog (voice of Tim McIntire) in *A Boy and His Dog*.

Mad Scientists

Both madness and genius are defined somewhat by the fact that both involve a radically different viewpoint than that of the vast majority. Madmen were probably running about declaring that the Earth orbits the Sun for thousands of years before anybody developed the tools necessary to prove them right. After all, Einstein was once laughed at. Of course, he may have had toilet paper stuck on his shoe at the time.

Science is a powerful thing. So, too, is insanity. They are both also somewhat frightening. Somewhere along the line, some mad genius got the brilliant notion that it would be awfully entertaining to get the two together. Just as geniuses often become scientists, they also sometimes become madmen. Why shouldn't a madman become a scientist? All it takes is a crazy idea that just might work.

The first authentic literary mad scientist was no doubt Frankenstein himself, who set the format that's been a surefire hit ever since. A mad scientist; an equally mad laboratory, with bubbling vials of colorful liquids, crackling arcs of electricity, and plenty of big dials and switches; a demented, deformed assistant to do all the dirty work; and the large, destructive monster. Sure, it's all symbolic of mankind's loss of innocence, the dangers of dabbling in the unknown without a license, and a reminder of our own humility in the face of awesome nature. It's also a symbol of purely obnoxious adolescent fun. Give a kid a magnifying glass and what does he do? Does he use it to examine the wonders of nature in all their fascinating detail? Heck no—he starts melting plastic army men in the back yard.

It is a little known fact that the men and women who first began to dabble with nuclear fission were not hoping to find a new source of energy, or even create a horrifying new weapon. They just wanted to see giant grasshoppers try to eat Chicago.

The first authentic cinematic mad scientist was not Frankenstein, but Thomas Edison himself, who stepped before the monster he had created to expose a few frames. Little did he know how much purely obnoxious adolescent fun he was unleashing upon the world.

When *Frankenstein* did make it to the screen, he came equipped with more flashy, noisy gizmos than anyone could have imagined—so impressive were these devices that they became stars in their own right. Kenneth Strickfaden, the mad scientist who provided the laboratory pyrotechnics for the film (and many others) even took them on the road for live shows.

Ever since the movies began, audiences have thrilled to the sight of Colin Clive, Bela Lugosi, John Carradine, Boris Karloff, Peter Lorre, Lionel Atwill, Peter Cushing, Jeffrey Combs, Vincent Price, George Zucco, Whit Bissell, Donald Pleasence, and a host of lesser lights as they toiled away in dank basement laboratories, hoping to invent some kind of really big magnifying glass to burn real soldiers. And usually they think they'll get the girl, too.

VideoHound salutes these brave individuals, who sacrifice so much time and effort just to keep us supplied with plenty of quivering masses of living gelatin and giant hairy beast men to threaten leggy starlets around the world.

The Brain from Planet Arous

Nuclear scientist John Agar is possessed by an evil alien brain named Gor. Gor lusts after Agar's fiancee ("There are some aspects of the life of Earth savages that are appealing and rewarding"), then tries to take over the planet. Rin Tin Tin comes to the rescue in the shapeless shape of Vol, a good alien brain inhabiting the scientist's dog. High camp and misdemeanors, but at least the home-video version bookends the uncut turkey with funny sketches starring Elvira, Mistress of the Dark. 🐾

1957 80m/B John Agar, Joyce Meadows, Robert Fuller, Henry Travis, Thomas B. Henry; *D:* Nathan (Hertz) Juran; *W:* Ray Buffum; *C:* Jacques Marquette. **VHS, Beta, LV** *SNC, CNM, AOV*

The Brain that Wouldn't Die

Love is a many-splattered thing when a brilliant surgeon keeps the decapitated head of his fiancee alive after an auto accident while he searches for a suitably stacked body onto which to transplant the head. Absurd and satiric (head talks so much that Doc tapes her/its mouth shut) adding up to major entry in trash film genre; much of the gore was slashed for the video, however. **AKA:** The Head That Wouldn't Die. 🦴🦴ᵛ

1963 92m/B Herb Evers, Virginia Leith, Adele Lamont; **D:** Joseph Green. **VHS, Beta** SNC, MRV, FCT

Brainstorm

Natalie Wood's last film is far from her best but the good special effects and interesting camera work (not to mention one of the better James Horner scores), make this a well spent couple of hours. Michael and Karen Brace (Christopher Walken and Wood) invent a device that can record dreams, thoughts, and fantasies, like your home VCR, and allow other people to play them back. With their marriage on the rocks, Michael becomes obsessed with perfecting the head-trip machine. Things are going good until fellow scientist Lilian Reynolds (Louise Fletcher) wears the headset while suffering a fatal heart attack. The government, Michael, everybody, wants to see the tape, so for a bit it's a chase and then...PLAY-BACK. The effects really kick in as we get to see her final thoughts and her trip down the famous tunnel of near-death experiences. Helmsman Douglas Trumbull is special effects wiz and it shows. Available letterboxed on the laserdisc version. 🦴🦴ᵛ

1983 (PG) 106m/C Natalie Wood, Christopher Walken, Cliff Robertson, Louise Fletcher; **D:** Douglas Trumbull; **W:** Bruce Joel Rubin; **M:** James Horner. **VHS, Beta, LV** MGM

Brainwaves

A young woman has disturbing flashbacks after her brain is electrically revived following a car accident. Tony Curtis is the demented doctor who jump-starts her. 🦴🦴

1982 (R) 83m/C Suzanna Love, Tony Curtis, Keir Dullea, Vera Miles; **D:** Ulli Lommel; **W:** Ulli Lommel. **VHS, Beta** SUE

Brazil

Relentlessly nightmarish black comedy about an Everyman trying to survive in a paper-choked bureaucratic future society, while at the same time clinging to his hopes and dreams, particularly his dream girl. There are copious references to *1984, The Trial,* and even *A Clockwork Orange,* as well as inspired mergings of glorious fantasy and stark reality intertwined with an astounding visual design. Our story follows the life of a petty bureaucrat (Jonathan Pryce) in a society where the lives of the people are dictated by the paperwork flow of an uncaring government. Early on, he becomes enamored of a young rebel and begins to yearn for freedom. Soon his spirit soars, characterized in his fantasies by a winged man battling the evil forces surrounding him. As he aids the rebels, a combination of government snafus and investigations turn his life into a nightmare. Monty Python alumnus Terry Gilliam, following studio demands, cut his masterpiece from the original 142 minutes down to the 131 minutes released in the U.S. (they also wanted a happier ending, but Gilliam wouldn't give in on that one). As of this printing, a longer cut, or possibly even a new edit by Gilliam himself, is in the works, to be released on a Criterion Collection laserdisc, with commentaries and supplemental materials. 🦴🦴🦴ᵛ

1985 (R) 131m/C GB Jonathan Pryce, Robert De Niro, Michael Palin, Katherine Helmond, Kim Greist, Bob Hoskins, Ian Holm, Peter Vaughan, Ian Richardson; **D:** Terry Gilliam; **W:** Terry Gilliam, Tom Stoppard; **M:** Michael Kamen. Los Angeles Film Critics Association Awards '85: Best Director (Gilliam), Best Film, Best Screenplay; Nominations: Academy Awards '85: Best Art Direction/Set Decoration, Best Original Screenplay. **VHS, Beta, LV** MCA, FCT

The Bride of Frankenstein

The classic sequel to the classic original. When his wife is kidnapped by his old associate Dr. Pretorious (Ernest Thesiger, in a highly amusing role), Dr. Frankenstein (Colin Clive) is forced to help build a mate for his monster. More humor than the first, but also more pathos, including the monster's famous but short-lived friendship with a blind hermit, who teaches the monster to speak. Karloff's monster is once again touching and frightening at

> "I've got the power to make the atom bomb look like a firecracker."
>
> —John Agar speaking as the alien Gor in *The Brain from Planet Arous.*

the same time. The unhappy, neurotic Clive disliked playing in horror films, which may have added to his tortured performances in them. Elsa Lanchester plays both the bride and Mary Shelley in the opening sequence. Una O'Connor contributes standout comedy relief. Features a spectacular score by Franz Waxman. 🦴🦴🦴

1935 75m/B Boris Karloff, Elsa Lanchester, Ernest Thesiger, Colin Clive, Una O'Connor, Valerie Hobson, Dwight Frye, John Carradine, E.E. Clive, O.P. Heggie, Gavin Gordon, Douglas Walton; **D:** James Whale. Nominations: Academy Awards '35: Best Sound. **VHS, Beta, LV** *MCA, MLB*

Bride of the Monster

This bargain-basement epic is a pretty good example of director Ed Wood's ability to cobble together a practically nonexistent budget and skimpy props into a memorable, if not exactly *good* film. Bela Lugosi stars as the mad Dr. Vornoff, a scientist trying to create a race of "atomic supermen" in his laboratory. Bald muscle-man Tor Johnson is "Lobo," one of his failed experiments. Vornoff captures intrepid girl reporter Loretta King, but she awakens Lobo's gentle side, and Vornoff gets a taste of his own atomic medicine. Lugosi's battle with a rubber octopus (a prop left over from *Wake of the Red Witch*) is now the stuff of legend, thanks to Tim Burton's *Ed Wood*, but it was actually a stuntman, not Lugosi, who braved the critter's lifeless tentacles. Bela was in his 70s when *Bride* was filmed, and hardly up to a midnight splash in the swamp. Still, he delivers a remarkable performance, investing Wood's often laughable pulp dialogue with an undefinable style that's pure Lugosi. It's not a great movie by any means, but Wood's desire to tell an exciting story and Lugosi's acting burns through the cliches and occasional inept performance. **AKA:** Bride of the Atom. 🦴🦴

1956 70m/B Bela Lugosi, Tor Johnson, Loretta King, Tony McCoy, Dolores Fuller, Conrad Brooks, Harvey B. Dunn, Don Nagel, George Becwar, Paul Marco; **D:** Edward D. Wood Jr.; **W:** Edward D. Wood Jr., Alex Gordon. **VHS, Beta** *NOS, SNC, VYY*

The Brides of Fu Manchu

Christopher Lee returns in this sequel to *The*

Face of Fu Manchu. This time the supervillain turns up in North Africa, where he's gathered together twelve daughters of various world leaders. Needless to say, the young ladies aren't visiting Fu willingly, especially when the entertainment involves snake-pits and cat-fights. Scotland Yard worthy Nayland Smith hot-foots it to the rescue once again, with the help of several colleagues and one of those blasted death rays. Doesn't pack quite the punch of *Face* but it's still good fun. 🦴🦴🦴

1966 m/C *GB* Christopher Lee, Tsai Chin, Douglas Wilmer, H. Marion Crawford, Heinz Drache, Burt Kwouk, Marie Versini, Rupert Davies; **D:** Don Sharp; **W:** Ernest Steward, Peter Welbeck; **C:** Ernest Steward. **VHS** *NO*

The Bronx Executioner

Android, robot, and human interests clash in futuristic Manhattan and all martial arts hell breaks loose. Special introduction by martial arts star Michael Dudikoff. 🦴

1986 88m/C Rob Robinson, Margie Newton, Chuck Valenti, Gabriel Gori; **D:** Bob Collins. **VHS, Beta** *CAN*

The Brood

An emotionally disturbed woman (Samantha Eggar) falls under the influence of a mad doctor (Oliver Reed). Through his unorthodox treatments, her rage is made manifest in the form of a brood of mutant children. The brood act out her violent emotional states, taking retribution on those who threaten their mother. Director David Cronenberg mixes the traditional mad scientist story with his trademark gross-out special effects, to create a disturbing combination of physical and psychological terror. Remember, mom always said not to make her angry. Look especially for the truly bizarre "birth" scene. Cronenberg's obsession with physical malformities continued with *Videodrome, The Fly, Dead Ringers,* and *Naked Lunch.* 🦴🦴🦴

1979 (R) 92m/C *CA* Samantha Eggar, Oliver Reed; **D:** David Cronenberg; **W:** David Cronenberg; **M:** Howard Shore. **VHS, Beta, LV** *SUE*

The Brother from Another Planet

Written and directed by John Sayles, and char-

acteristic of his work, it is thoughtful, intelligent, and offbeat. But it's not nearly as fun as the genre films (*The Howling, Alligator*) he wrote for Roger Corman. Joe Morton stars as a mute and enigmatic black extraterrestrial recently arrived in Harlem. By all outward appearances he looks human, but he has hidden supernatural powers (he can repair video machines with just the touch of his hand), not to mention clawed, three-toed feet. Like Chance the gardener in *Being There,* he has a profound effect on those he meets, because, as jazz singer Dee Dee Bridgewater tells him, "You could be anybody." She also gets the film's best line. After spending the night with him, she remarks, "You were great in bed last night, but you gonna have to do somethin' about those toenails." Sayles and stock company regular David Strathairn appear as alien bounty hunters. 🎵🎵🎵

1984 109m/C Joe Morton, Dee Dee Bridgewater, Ren Woods, Steve James, Maggie Renzi, David Strathairn, Tom Wright, Herbert Newsome, Leonard Jackson; *Cameos:* John Sayles; *D:* John Sayles; *W:* John Sayles; *C:* Ernest R. Dickerson; *M:* Mason Daring. **VHS, Beta** *FOX, FCT*

Bubblegum Crisis

One of the earliest of the many Japanese anime series set against the backdrop of a future Tokyo, inspired by actual plans for city-wide renovation set to take place over the next 50 years. The nefarious, ever-expanding GENOM corporation unleashes bio-mechanical soldiers called Boomers—originally designed for outer-space projects and foreign wars, but now causing havoc within the city as part of a plot for world domination. The AD Police, a special crimes unit assigned to deal with the Boomers, find their resources stretched to the limit as the Boomers become more and more powerful. Only a group of young women calling themselves the Knight Sabres, using hi-tech suits of armor, pose a threat to GENOM's evil plan. Influenced by *Macross* and *Bladerunner* (the rock singing

"Oh, man. Couldn't they have just sent me to Hell instead?" Joe Morton is *The Brother from Another Planet.*

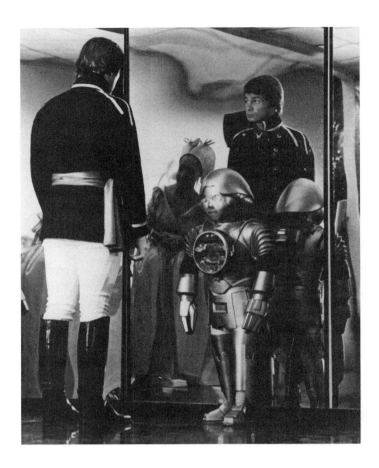

2419 A.D.; Nowlan helped adapt it into the first sf newspaper comic strip. Buck was also the first science-fiction story done in the modern super-hero space genre. Many of the "inventions" seen in this movie have actually come into existence—spaceships, ray guns (lasers), anti-gravity belts—a testament to Nolan's almost psychic farsightedness. 🦴🦴

1939 91m/B Buster Crabbe, Constance Moore, Jackie Moran; **D:** Ford Beebe, Saul Goodkind. **VHS, Beta** *FOX*

Buck Rogers in the 25th Century

An American astronaut (Gil Gerard), preserved in space for 500 years, is brought back to life by a passing Draconian flagship. Outer-space adventures begin when he is accused of being a spy from Earth. There's a sexy princess, a good-girl heroine, and a very, very annoying little robot with voice provided by Mel Blanc. Based on the classic movie serial, this made-for-TV movie is another example of the mad scramble in the late '70s to cash in on the success of *Star Wars*. A fairly popular TV series resulted. The pilot was fairly competent space opera, though nothing to write home about. 🦴🦴

1979 (PG) 90m/C Gil Gerard, Pamela Hensley, Erin Gray, Henry Silva, Tim O'Connor, Joseph Wiseman; **D:** Daniel Haller; **W:** Glen Larson, Leslie Stevens; **C:** Frank Beasoechea; **V:** Mel Blanc. **VHS, Beta, LV** *MCA, MOV*

> "Yes, I think the 38-short is *definitely* the best choice." A helpful saleswoman to Gil Gerard in *Buck Rogers in the 25th Century.*

Knight Saber's name is Priss, and her band is The Replicants), this series was in turn highly influential on other anime series for its Mega-Tokyo setting and sexy girl heroes battling scary monsters, all set to rocking "J-pop" music. This eight-part series was followed by sequel series *Bubblegum Crash* and *AD Police Files*. Available in Japanese with subtitles or dubbed. 🦴🦴🦴

1987 53m/C *JP* **D:** Hayashi Hiroki; **W:** Arii Emu; **V:** Oomori Kinoku, Sakabara Yoshiko, Tomizawa Michie, Hiramatsu Akiko. **VHS, LV** *ANI, WTA, FCT*

Buck Rogers Conquers the Universe

The character of Buck Rogers originated in the 1928 Philip Francis Nowlan novel *Armageddon*

Bug

The city of Riverside is threatened with destruction after a massive Earth tremor unleashes a mob of prehistoric cockroaches that set fires with their butts, attack cats and housewives, and are virtually impervious to Raid. A local biology teacher, not content to leave well enough alone, crosses the critters with the common kitchen-variety roach. The new and improved (and hungry) super-roaches proceed to drive the Riversiders buggy. Based on Thomas Page's novel *The Hephaestus Plague,* this fairly effective creepy-crawler was produced by William "Gimmick King" Castle, who was known in the '50s for publicity stunts like wiring theatre seats to administer mild electric shocks to audiences' bottoms. For *Bug,* Castle wanted to install windshield

wiper-like devices under theatre seats that would brush against the patrons' feet as the cockroaches crawled across the screen. This would have been a nice disco-era follow-up to Castle's previous gimmicks; unfortunately, the idea was squashed flat. ⚗⚗

1975 (PG) 100m/C Bradford Dillman, Joanna Miles, Richard Gilliland, Jamie Smith-Jackson, Alan Fudge, Jesse Vint, William Castle; **D:** Jeannot Szwarc; **W:** William Castle; **M:** Charles Fox. **VHS, Beta** *PAR*

Capricorn One

An Apollo-style mission to Mars stalls because Americans lack the brains to build a decent spacecraft. To ensure continued NASA funds, Hal Holbrook arranges a phony Martian landing for TV cameras in a remote desert soundstage. Astronauts James Brolin, O.J. Simpson, and Sam Waterston learn the scheme calls for their "heroic" demise to ensure silence, and they try to escape. Remarkably, the besmirched space agency cooperated in filming this intriguing but paper-thin conspiracy thriller, mixing a disaster-pic cast with Watergate-era cynicism at its peak (even the Congressional Medal of Honor earns an insult). There's a nice pair of menacing Unmarked Black Helicopters, but half the fun is spotting the mistakes in Peter Hyams' script. Still, you can bet there are paranoiacs in rural compounds who swear this plotline is true. Stirring Jerry Goldsmith musical score. ⚗⚗⚗

1978 (R) 123m/C Elliott Gould, James Brolin, Brenda Vaccaro, O.J. Simpson, Hal Holbrook, Sam Waterston, Karen Black, Telly Savalas; **D:** Peter Hyams; **W:** Peter Hyams; **C:** Bill Butler; **M:** Jerry Goldsmith. **VHS, Beta, LV** *FOX*

Captain America

Marvel Comic character steps into feature film and flounders. The patriotic superhero son of WWII hero fights bad guy with contraband nuclear weapon. Made for television. Followed the same year with *Captain America 2: Death Too Soon.* ⚗⚗

1979 98m/C Reb Brown, Len Birman, Heather Menzies, Steve Forrest, Robin Mattson, Joseph Ruskin, Michael McManus; **D:** Rod Holcomb. **VHS, Beta** *MCA*

Captain America

The Marvel Comics superhero got his own movie in time for his 50th anniversary, but this doesn't make the grade despite the wide-ranging plot. In 1941 a secret Axis serum turns polio-stricken Steve Rogers (Matt Salinger, actor son of author J.D. Salinger) into a super-strong superhero, but he's matched by the Nazis' own superfascist, the Red Skull. Their battle leaves Captain America frozen in the Arctic for 40 years before he thaws to again confront his evil nemesis, now a typical gangster with a nuke. Though a fairly faithful transcription of the comic book's premise, what may have worked ages ago on paper now looks ridiculous. Low-budget production values—and clunky environmentalist themes—don't help. Kids may be amused; adults may note ruefully that this Captain America was made in Yugoslavia. ⚗⚗

1989 (PG-13) 103m/C Matt Salinger, Scott Paulin, Ronny Cox, Ned Beatty, Darren McGavin, Melinda Dillon; **D:** Albert Pyun; **W:** Stephen Tolkin. **VHS, LV** *COL*

Captain America 2: Death Too Soon

Terrorists hit America where it hurts, threatening to use age accelerating drug. Sequelized superhero fights chronic crow lines and series dies slow, painful death. Made for television. ⚗

1979 98m/C Reb Brown, Connie Sellecca, Len Birman, Christopher Lee, Katherine Justice, Lana Wood, Christopher Carey; **D:** Ivan Nagy. **VHS, Beta** *MCA*

Captive Planet

Bargain basement f/x and really atrocious acting hold audience captive in routine Earth-on-the-verge-of-obliteration yarn. ⚗

1978 95m/C Sharon Baker, Chris Auram, Anthony Newcastle; **D:** Al Bradley. **VHS, Beta** *NO*

Carnosaur

Straight from the Corman film factory, this exploitative quickie about dinosaurs harkens back to '50s-style monster epics. The title sequence—some really disgusting stuff apparently filmed in a real chicken processing

Cameron's *Aliens*. The mutant-chicken dinosaurs from the first film are back and they're hungry for more human Happy Meals in a super-secret government installation that's about to blow up. Tick, tick, tick. 🦴🦴

1994 (R) 90m/C John Savage, Cliff DeYoung, Arabella Holzbog, Ryan Thomas Johnson; *D:* Louis Morneau. **VHS, LV** *NHO*

The Carrier

Smalltown Sleepy Rock is ideal family-raising turf until a plague mysteriously blights inhabitants, and townspeople are out to exterminate all potential carriers. The disease is transmitted by touch, so the population has taken to wrapping their bodies in plastic (pre-*Twin Peaks*) to avoid any potential infection from others (sound familiar?). Well orchestrated mob scenes as the town disintegrates into hysteria in their quest to "Kill the Carrier!" Filmed on location in Manchester, Michigan. 🦴🦴

1987 (R) 99m/C Gregory Fortescue, Steve Dixon, Paul Silverman; *D:* Nathan J. White. **VHS, Beta** *NO*

Cast a Deadly Spell

An "elseworld" vision of 1948 Los Angeles where everyone, from bums on the street to master criminals, uses magic for just about everything, from mixing drinks to cutting someone to pieces in a tornado of stolen loot. Everyone, that is, except for gumshoe Harry P. Lovecraft (Fred Ward), although he does use a lucky talisman. Streetsmarts vs. magic. Good vs. evil. Amos Hackshaw (David Warner) has hired Harry to track down a stolen Necronomicon, the key to ultimate-mystical power, in order to prevent a gangster and his zombie sidekick from ending the world as we know it, or at least as they know it. Weird creatures and decent special effects complement this made-for-cable-TV horror-noir comedy thriller. Followed by *Witch Hunt* in 1994, with Dennis Hopper as Lovecraft. 🦴🦴🦴

1991 (R) 93m/C Fred Ward, David Warner, Julianne Moore, Clancy Brown, Alexandra Powers; *D:* Martin Campbell; *W:* Joseph Dougherty, Dave Edison. **VHS, LV** *HBO, FCT*

"One giant step for man ... Oh, shit. There are *dogs* in outer space?"
Capricorn One.

plant—sets the tone for your basic mad-scientist plot with several environmental twists. Dr. Jane Tiptree (Diane Ladd), the mad scientist in question, has been up to nefarious doings out in the Nevada desert, something involving nasty but unseen critters who attack chickens. The film has a wicked sense of humor that gets consistently stronger and more crazed as it goes along. Toward the end, it becomes downright Strangelovian. Followed by a sequel. In true slap-dash Corman style, *Carnosaur* beat Spielberg's *Jurassic Park* to the theatres; while *Carnosaur* was not a box-office rival, it certainly was formidable competition in the video-rental market. And in related casting, Corman used the mother of Spielberg's female lead (Laura Dern). 🦴🦴🦴

1993 (R) 82m/C Diane Ladd, Raphael Sbarge, Jennifer Runyon, Harrison Page, Clint Howard, Ned Bellamy; *D:* Adam Simon; *W:* Adam Simon; *M:* Nigel Holton. **VHS** *NHO*

Carnosaur 2

The real inspiration for this entertaining schlock sequel isn't *Jurassic Park* but James

Cosmostology

The Hound doesn't want to flatly declare that the supposedly genuine UFO occupant dissected in *Alien Autopsy* was a fake. Just that he can name plenty of makeup effects specialists who could have done a better job. Some of them were even active in Hollywood back in 1947. Here are some Golden-Age studio craftsmen who concocted never-before-seen examples of the uncanny and unearthly for the cameras:

JACK PIERCE. Head of Universal's makeup department in the 1930s and '40s, this former projectionist, cameraman, and stuntman designed their classic gothic characters like Frankenstein's creation (and its Bride), the Wolfman, and the Invisible Man. Before Oscars were awarded for makeup achievements, he gained special industry trophies for both *The Mummy* and *Island of Lost Souls*.

LEE GREENWAY. Genre fans (especially Rick Baker partisans) argue over the effectiveness of his best-known creation, the hostile vegetable humanoid in 1951's original *The Thing*. For a look at Greenway's alternative Thing concepts that were never used, see the book *Making a Monster* by Al Taylor and Sue Roy.

WILLIAM TUTTLE. Chief of MGM's makeup department from 1950 to 1969, Tuttle won the Academy of Motion Picture Arts and Science's first-ever makeup Oscar (on behalf of George Pal's fantasy *The Seven Faces of Dr. Lao*) in 1964, and also did memorable work on *The Time Machine* and *Logan's Run*.

THE HOUSE OF WESTMORE. The Westmores are a showbiz dynasty. George Westmore founded cinema's first official makeup department in 1917. Monty Westmore masterminded Fredric March's metamorphosis in 1932's *Dr. Jekyll and Mr. Hyde,* and the Westmore name appears on each *Star Trek* series extant. Bud Westmore presided over the makeup team behind Universal's 1950s

sci-fi cycle beginning with *The Creature from the Black Lagoon* (rumor has it the gill-man was modeled after a Mexican iguana) and continuing with *Tarantula, The Mole People, The Monolith Monsters,* and more. Frank Westmore's memoir *The Westmores of Hollywood,* a fascinating family portrait, cites the Metalunan mutant from *This Island Earth* as Bud's personal fave.

PAUL BLAISDELL. Operating at the low-budget end of the scale, Blaisdell nonetheless fashioned ferocious mutations and aliens (sometimes wearing the suits himself) for Roger Corman and others, in drive-in greats like *It! The Terror from Beyond Space* and *The She Creature*. His grotesque dwarf E.T.s in *Invasion of the Saucer Men* are simultaneously the screen's definitive bug-eyed monsters *and* little green men.

BEN NYE, SR. An apprentice to the Westmores, Nye was appointed to lead 20th Century Fox's makeup department after WWII and invented David Hedison's insect headpiece for 1957's *The Fly*. He retired as *Planet of the Apes* went into production, hiring John Chambers to usher in the modern era of makeup f/x.

The Castle of Fu Manchu

The final film in a series starring Christopher Lee as the ultra-evil Dr. Fu Manchu, directed by the always prolific sleaze-monger Jess Franco. This time, the Doc's plans for world domination involve a gadget which will put the earth into a deep freeze. To fine tune this contraption, he enlists the help of a gifted scientist by abducting him. However, the helper/hostage has a bad ticker, so Fu must abduct a heart surgeon to save his life. Most critics felt this was the weakest installment in the series, and rightly so; it plods on and on with very little action or even interesting dialogue. Apparently the producers had their own doubts about the film, as it was only released several years after completion. Only rabid Christopher Lee fans or those completing masters theses on unfortunate Asian stereotypes

will find this flick interesting. **AKA:** Assignment: Istanbul; Die Folterkammer des Dr. Fu Manchu. ♪

1968 (PG) 92m/C *GE SP IT GB* Christopher Lee, Richard Greene, H. Marion Crawford, Tsai Chin, Gunther Stoll, Rosalba (Sara Bay) Neri, Maria Perschy; **D:** Jess (Jesus) Franco; **W:** Peter Welbeck; **C:** Manuel Merino. **VHS** *MRV*

The Cat from Outer Space

An extraterrestrial cat named Jake crashes his spaceship on Earth and leads a group of people on endless escapades. A cute idea combined with solid scripting and a cast of familiar faces, like Ken (*F-Troop*) Berry, Sandy Duncan as his girlfriend, and Roddy McDowall, who'd apparently gotten tired of monkeying around in the *Planet of the Apes* series. ♪ ♪ ♪

1978 (G) 103m/C Ken Berry, Sandy Duncan, Harry (Henry) Morgan, Roddy McDowall, McLean Stevenson; **D:** Norman Tokar; **W:** Ted Key; **C:** Charles F. Wheeler. **VHS, Beta** *DIS, OM*

Cat Women of the Moon

A team of scientists led by Sonny Tufts land on the moon and encounter a telepathic race of skimpily attired female chauvinists and a giant spider. An aggressively silly picture with romance, excitement, and plenty of unintentional laughs. The "Hollywood Cover Girls" played various cat women. Tufts got his show biz start as an opera singer, then moved on to Broadway musicals (and was sued by showgirls in the '50s for biting them on the thighs). Former Miss Utah Marie Windsor became a star playing bad girls. Director Arthur Hilton was a top editor (*The Killers*) before becoming a B-movie director. *Cat Women* is available on video in its original 3-D format. It was remade (badly) in 1958 as *Missile to the Moon*. **AKA:** Rocket to the Moon. ♪ ♪

1953 65m/B Sonny Tufts, Victor Jory, Marie Windsor, Bill Phipps, Douglas Fowley, Carol Brewster, Suzanne Alexander, Susan Morrow; **D:** Arthur Hilton; **W:** Roy Hamilton; **C:** William F. Whitley; **M:** Elmer Bernstein. **VHS, Beta** *RHI, SNC, MWP*

Charly

In his Oscar-winning performance, Cliff Robertson stars as the original Gump. Charly Gordon is a mentally disabled man who works in a Boston bakery where he is the butt of cruel practical jokes. Experimental brain surgery transforms him into a genius. He turns the tables on his co-workers, lectures to scientists, and has an affair with his therapist (Claire Bloom). But his triumph is fleeting when he learns that he will soon regress. Some of director Ralph Nelson's stylistic flourishes date the film, but it is still a heartbreaker with the courage not to let audiences off the hook with a conventional happy ending. A labor of love for Robertson, who appeared in the original teleplay that was based on Daniel Keyes' novel, *Flowers for Algernon*. He bought the film rights and reportedly spent seven years trying to bring it to the big screen. In a career footnote apropos to this book, Robertson was blacklisted in Hollywood for four years after reporting studio head David Begelman for forging his name on a check. A science-fiction film, *Brainstorm*, marked his return to the screen. ♪ ♪ ♪

1968 103m/C Cliff Robertson, Claire Bloom, Lilia Skala, Leon Janney, Dick Van Patten, William Dwyer; **D:** Ralph Nelson; **W:** Stirling Silliphant. Academy Awards '68: Best Actor (Robertson); Golden Globe Awards '69: Best Screenplay; National Board of Review Awards '68: 10 Best Films of the Year, Best Actor (Robertson). **VHS, Beta, LV** *FOX, BTV*

Cherry 2000

It's 2017. Sam Treadwell has a quick bang on the wet kitchen floor and short-circuits his Cherry 2000, a perfect, always-in-the-mood, man-made woman sex-toy robot. Wishing to avoid the ol' blue balls, Sam enlists the aid of female tracker E. Johnson (Melanie Griffith) and sets off for the treacherous "lawless zone" where replacement parts can still be found. Sam acts as though he's never met, or at least never talked to, a real flesh-and-blood woman, and begins to weigh his options. Does he want a woman who comes with instructions on which buttons to push, or one with her own emotions and thoughts...or maybe just an inflatable? Offbeat, occasionally funny. Score by Basil Poledouris. ♪ ♪

1988 (PG-13) 94m/C Melanie Griffith, David Andrews, Ben Johnson, Tim Thomerson, Michael C. Gwynne, Brion James, Pamela Gidley, Harry Carey Jr.; **D:** Steve DeJarnatt; **W:** Michael Almereyda; **C:** Jacques Haitkin; **M:** Basil Poledouris. **VHS, Beta, LV** *ORI*

Children of the Damned

Six children, living previews of what man will evolve into in a million years, are born all around the world with genius IQs, ray-gun eyes, and murderous dispositions. Two investigators round up the tykes for scientific examination, but before too long they manage to escape. The children hide out in a church, but alas, their destiny is to be destroyed in order to teach modern man a lesson. A fairly good sequel to the classic *Village of the Damned*, based loosely on the novel *The Midwich Cuckoos* by English sf novelist John Wyndham. **AKA:** Horror! 🐾🐾

1963 90m/B *GB* Ian Hendry, Alan Badel, Barbara Ferris, Alfred Burke, Sheila Allen, Clive Powell, Frank Summerscales, Mahdu Mathen, Gerald Delsol, Roberta Rex, Franchesca Lee, Harold Goldblatt; **D:** Anton Leader; **W:** John Briley; **C:** David Boulton. **VHS, LV** *MGM*

The China Syndrome

Jack Lemmon, in an Oscar-nominated role, is supervisor at a nuclear plant who uncovers evidence of an engineering flaw that could cause a devastating meltdown. When his bosses react with a ruthless coverup, he takes drastic steps to get the proof to sympathetic TV journalists Jane Fonda and Michael Douglas. Wiretaut thriller (done without ambient music) was considered sf when it opened; then the Three Mile Island accident occurred, and the script—which coincidentally compares the estimated lethal fallout zone to the size of Pennsylvania—seemed too prophetic for comfort. Note the onscreen thug tactics of the nuclear industry, and ponder that General Electric later bought NBC lock, stock, and news division. Produced by Douglas. 🐾🐾🐾🐾

1979 (PG) 123m/C Jane Fonda, Jack Lemmon, Michael Douglas, Scott Brady, James Hampton, Peter Donat, Wilford Brimley, James Karen; **D:** James Bridges; **W:** Mike Gray, T.S. Cook, James Bridges. British Academy Awards '79: Best Actor (Lemmon), Best Actress (Fonda); National Board of Review Awards '79: 10 Best Films of the Year; Writers Guild of America '79: Best Original Screenplay; Nominations: Academy Awards '78: Best Actress (Fonda), Best Original Screenplay; Academy Awards '79: Best Actor (Lemmon), Best Art Direction/Set Decoration; Cannes Film Festival '79: Best Film. **VHS, Beta, LV** *COL*

A Chinese Ghost Story

This is one of the more famous and certainly among the best of the many fantasy films to come out of Hong Kong in the '80s. A handsome scholar enters a haunted temple in old China and falls in love with a beautiful ghost-lady who's kept imprisoned by an incredible tree-monster. The lovers are aided by a Taoist monk as they battle the gruesome guardian and visit the gates of Hell. Unlike many "fantasy" movies, this is a genuinely magical film with great special effects. It was followed by two equally enchanting sequels. In Cantonese with English subtitles. 🐾🐾🐾🐾

1987 93m/C *HK* Leslie Cheung, Wong Tsu Hsien, Wu Ma; **D:** Ching Siu Tung. **VHS** *FCT*

Chinese Web

Spiderman adventure in which Spidey becomes entwined in international intrigue and corrupt officials. 🐾

1978 95m/C Nicholas Hammond, Robert F. Simon, Rosalind Chao, Ted Danson; **D:** Donald McDougall. **VHS, Beta** *FOX*

Chopping Mall

A freak electric storm unleashes killer security robots on a coed band of teens holding an after-hours slumber party inside the mall (where they can test out the mattresses, wink wink). The robots, created by Robert Short, carry most of the action, and they're pretty good; imagine R2D2 gone bad and you've got the idea. Otherwise this is trivial, low-grade stuff by Roger Corman alumni, laden with B-movie in-jokes (brief cameos by Paul Bartel and Mary Woronov reprise their characters from the cult comedy *Eating Raoul*), gore, and sleaze. **AKA:** Killbots. 🐾🐾

1986 (R) 77m/C Kelli Maroney, Tony O'Dell, Suzee Slater, Russell Todd, Karrie Emerson; **Cameos:** Paul Bartel, Mary Woronov, Dick Miller; **D:** Jim Wynorski; **W:** Steve Mitchell, Jim Wynorski; **C:** Tom Richmond. **VHS, Beta** *LIV*

Chronopolis

Stop-motion animated feature film (a five-year solo effort by Piotr Kamler in his home studio) about the placid, immortal citizens of Chro-

Countdown Halted

Movie history is littered with rumors and wistful assertions of Masterpieces That Never Were. In sf and fantasy genres especially, technical problems, cost overruns, and artistic challenges leave many intriguing projects abandoned on the launch pad. Some might have been immortal classics. Others, well....

CHILDHOOD'S END. Despite the artistic and financial success of *2001: A Space Odyssey,* this Arthur C. Clarke novel of mystical alien contact found no home at Universal Pictures in the early '70s despite screenplays submitted by both Howard W. Koch and Abraham Polonsky. The studio balked at the proposed $13 million price tag, while Polonsky complained "People keep telling me it's too intelligent for a movie."

THE DEMOLISHED MAN. Alfred Bester's 1953 book (the first novel to win a Hugo Award) about a murderer trying to escape justice in a society patrolled and regulated by powerful telepaths, was turned into a script in 1968. By the late '70s it was supposedly ready to roll under *Carrie* director Brian De Palma but never did.

DUNE. A decade before David Lynch's 1984 attempt, filmmaker/illustrator/eccentric Alejandro Jodorowski was tapped to bring Frank Herbert's Hugo-winning saga to the screen, with Orson Welles in a major role and Dan O'Bannon to head special f/x. Prominent fantasy/sf artists H.R. Giger (who later teamed with O'Bannon for *Alien*) and Chris Foss contributed spacecraft, set, and costume designs; their published portfolios contain some amazing paintings of what might have been.

THE FANTASTIC LITTLE GIRL. Success of *The Incredible Shrinking Man* prompted Universal to have writer Richard Math-

eson dash out an encore (while the first film's trick sets still stood available). In it, the Shrinking Man's wife also dwindles and joins him, and they would both return to normal stature in the happy ending, but the studio lost interest.

I, ROBOT. Isaac Asimov's groundbreaking 1950 short-story cycle forever changed how sf literature treated 'mechanical men' and artificial intelligence. In 1978 Harlan Ellison completed a script version that was never filmed. "Harlan was asked to make the robots 'cute' like R2D2," Asimov explained, and when Ellison refused to hack out a *Star Wars* clone, the studio suits aborted the expensive project. Ellison's effort so pleased Asimov, though, that he serialized it in his namesake magazine in 1987. *I, Robot: The Illustrated Screenplay* appeared in book form in 1994.

INTERFACE. Chip Prosler's f/x-crammed original script concerns a wounded pilot on life-support whose body is a shattered shell but whose mind reaches glorious new horizons when he's neurologically linked to high technology. Francis Ford Coppola juggled the property around with other biggies while trying to save his sinking studio. Weak reaction to the soundalike *Innerspace* (another Prosler script) didn't help the cause.

THE ISLAND OF DR. MOREAU. Ray Harryhausen planned a 1970s adaptation of the H.G. Wells novel, in which his famed stop-motion techniques would

animate the half-human "manimals." When other filmmakers commenced the Burt Lancaster version eventually released in 1977 (featuring beast-men in conventional f/x makeup), Harryhausen's remained on the drawing board.

NIGHT SKIES. Long mentioned as Steven Spielberg's *Close Encounters of the Third Kind* followup, this chiller about folks under siege by unfriendly UFO occupants was reportedly influenced by John Ford's settlers-vs.-Indians drama *Drums Along the Mohawk. Night Skies'* pack of unearthly marauders included a less-threatening little being who was always tagging along after the rest. From that seed grew the premise of *E.T.: The Extraterrestrial.*

PUMA. *A Clockwork Orange* author Anthony Burgess scripted this loose reworking of *When Worlds Collide* with a social conscience. It had the backing of the team behind the blockbusters *Jaws* and *The Sting,* but both Paramount and Universal shied at its pre-*Waterworld* budget of $20 million.

STRANGER IN A STRANGE LAND. Robert Heinlein's cult sf novel about a Christ-like alien visitor (somewhat similar thematically to *The Man Who Fell to Earth*) has been bandied about as a screen property for decades, with one script completed in 1971 by Lewis John Carlino. But top movie execs haven't grokked yet.

THE TIME MACHINE II. Throughout the 1970s, George Pal sought to sell uncomprehending studio brass on the idea of a sequel to his 1960 hit that would follow the son of H.G. Wells' Time Traveler onward to more adventures, including a peek at the end of the world. Ray Harryhausen signed on to handle f/x work, but ultimately only the novelization (by Pal and Joe Morhaim) of the screenplay was completed.

nopolis—no relation to the namesake J.G. Ballard novel—who relieve the boredom of perpetual existence by creating time. Except for opening narration (French without subtitles—better have a translator on hand, anglophones), it's a nonverbal spectacle of rhythmic fantastic imagery, visually impressive but too often merely repetitive and opaque. 🎞🎞🎞

1982 70m/C *FR* **D:** Piotr Kamler; **W:** Piotr Kamler; **C:** Piotr Kamler. **VHS** *FCT, WTA*

Cinderella 2000

Soft-core musical version of the classic fairy tale. It's the year 2047 and sex is outlawed, except by computer. Strains of Sugarman's score, including "Doin' Without" and "We All Need Love," set the stage for Catherine Erhardt's Cinderella to meet her Prince Charming at that conventional single prince romance venue, a sex orgy. Trouble is, it wasn't a shoe Cinderella lost before she fled, and the charming one must interface, as it were, with the local pretenders to the throne in order to find his lost princess. Touching. 🎞🎞

1978 (R) 86m/C Catharine Erhardt, Jay B. Larson, Vaughn Armstrong; **D:** Al Adamson; **M:** Sparky Sugarman. **VHS** *NO*

Circuitry Man

In a stylishly bleak post-apocalyptic future that borrows freely from *Blade Runner, Mad Max,* and *Max Headroom,* people have been driven underground by pollution. A tough loner (Dana Wheeler-Nicholson) and an emotional robot (Jim Metzler) are on the run from a group of gonzo bad guys. Plughead (Vernon Wells) likes to experience other people's pain, and Yo-yo (Barbara Alyn Woods) is a tough-talking gangster. The main problems are a leaden pace and apparent ignorance of basic storytelling techniques. But the acting is above average, the characters are interesting, and beneath the gritty surface, there's a strange likable quality to the film. Followed by an unnecessary sequel. 🎞🎞🎞

1990 (R) 85m/C Jim Metzler, Dana Wheeler-Nicholson, Lu Leonard, Vernon Wells, Barbara Alyn Woods, Dennis Christopher; **D:** Steven Lovy; **W:** Steven Lovy; **M:** Deborah Holland. **VHS, LV** *COL*

City Limits

Director Aaron Lipstadt's first film, *Android,* is a precious sleeper. This, his second film, has developed a less welcome cult reputation after being given the *Mystery Science Theater 3000* treatment. In the not-so-distant future, a plague will have wiped out most of the adults, leaving the adolescents to form motorcycle-riding gangs to roam the landscape looking for food, gasoline, and comic books. Loner John Stockwell teams up with L.A. Clippers Rae Dawn Chong, John Diehl, and Darrell Larson (with an assist by James Earl Jones) to take on the sinister Sunya Corporation from violently wresting control of the city from the gangs. Robby Benson, here only for the paycheck, is Sunya's sinister boss. When he is ultimately cornered, he calmly cautions that it would be useless to kill him because he will be replaced by someone even worse. That's doubtful. He spends most of the film glowering behind a desk and glancing at the red light blinking on his telephone. He is finally crushed when a betrayed gang leader rams his motorcycle into his desk (which usually elicits cheers from anyone who has suffered through *Harry and Son*). Written by Don Opper, who also wrote and starred in *Android.* 🎞🎞

1985 (PG-13) 85m/C John Stockwell, Kim Cattrall, Darrell Larson, Rae Dawn Chong, Robby Benson, James Earl Jones, Jennifer Balgobin, John Diehl; **D:** Aaron Lipstadt; **W:** Don Opper. **VHS, Beta, LV** *VES, LIV, HHE*

The City of Lost Children

Weird not-for-the-kiddies fairytale finds crazed inventor Krank (Daniel Emilfork) getting his evil one-eyed minions, the appropriately named 'Cyclops,' to kidnap local children so that he can steal their dreams (because Krank himself is incapable of dreaming). The latest victim is young Denree (Joseph Lucien), the adopted brother of sideshow strongman One (Ron Perlman, TV's *Beauty and the Beast* beast), who single-mindedly pursues a way to get Denree back—aided by 9-year-old feral child Miette (Judith Vittet) and a band of orphan thieves. The visuals are striking, including a bevy of mechanical flies and all-around sharp cinematography. Freaks galore

with avant-garde designer Jean-Paul Gaultier in charge of costumes. **AKA:** La Cite des Enfants Perdus. 🦴🦴🦴

1995 (R) 111m/C *FR* Ron Perlman, Daniel Emilfork, Joseph Lucien, Judith Vittet, Dominique Pinon, Jean Claude Drey-fus, Odile Mallet, Genevieve Brunet, Mireille Mosse; **D:** Jean-Marie Jeunet, Marc Caro; **W:** Jean-Marie Jeunet, Marc Caro, Gilles Adrien; **C:** Darius Khondji; **M:** Angelo Badala-menti; **V:** Jean-Louis Trintignant. Nominations: Cesar Awards '96: Best Art Direction/Set Decoration, Best Cine-matography, Best Costume Design, Best Score; Indepen-dent Spirit Awards '96: Best Foreign Language Film. **VHS**

Clash of the Titans

With a cast that includes Laurence Olivier (Zeus), Claire Bloom (Hera), and Maggie Smith (the sea goddess Thetis), it seems outrageous to suggest that Harry Hamlin (Perseus) does the best job, but it sure looks like the "real" actors took the job just for the bucks. As with any Ray Harryhausen opus (and this was his last), we're really here for his stop-motion effects. Perseus, on a mission from god, must battle some of Ray's best on his way to rescu-ing the adequately beautiful Judi Bowker (Andromeda) from the monstrous and wet Kraken. Well equipped with a helmet of invisi-bility, a tacky sword that will at least cut through anything, and naturally the famous shiny-as-a-mirror, necessary-as-hell god-given shield, Perseus has to deal with Charon the ferryman of the dead, relieve the snake-head-ed gorgon Medusa of her head (Ray's scariest sequence ever), and even gets to mount the winged horse Pegasus. Edit out the constipat-ed acting of the Olympians and the Hound'll double the rating. 🦴🦴

1981 (PG) 118m/C *GB* Laurence Olivier, Maggie Smith, Claire Bloom, Ursula Andress, Burgess Meredith, Harry Hamlin, Sian Phillips, Judi Bowker; **D:** Desmond Davis; **W:** Beverley Cross. **VHS, Beta, LV** *MGM, MLB*

Class of 1999

Actually set in 1997, this loose follow up to Mark L. Lester's non-sf *Class of 1984* shows

teen gangs terrorizing the entire country. A desperate high school principal (Malcolm McDowell) reluctantly installs manlike robot instructors not phased by homeroom punks. But the machines are actually surplus military 'droids (with rocket launchers in their arms), who go into full-combat mode at the flick of a spitball. Result is a violent, frankly amoral spectacle that makes vicious young thugs into heroes by default as they fight for their lives against their Terminator teachers. Undeniably exciting on a crude level. Class dismissed. Available in both R-rated and unrated versions. 🦴🦴

1990 (R) 98m/C Bradley Gregg, Traci Lind, Malcolm McDowell, Stacy Keach, Patrick Kilpatrick, Pam Grier, John P. Ryan, Darren E. Burrows, Joshua Miller; **D:** Mark L. Lester; **W:** C. Courtney Joyner. **VHS, Beta** *VES, LIV*

Class of 1999 2: The Substitute

High school in 1999 is filled with violent gangs who murder at random. Enter substitute teacher John Bolen, who has his own ideas of discipline—leading to an even higher body count. John just doesn't seem human and when a CIA agent starts investigating, school may never be the same. 🦴🦴

1993 (R) 90m/C Sasha Mitchell, Nick Cassavetes, Caitlin Dulany, Jack Knight, Gregory West, Rick Hill; **D:** Spiro Razatos; **W:** Mark Sevi. **VHS, LV** *VMK*

Class of Nuke 'Em High

Following its success in dealing with serious ecological issues in the *Toxic Avenger* series, Team Troma once again experiments with the chemicals, with violent results. Jersey high school becomes a hotbed of mutants, punks, maniacs, and monsters after a nuclear spill occurs. Good teens Chrissy and Warren succumb, the school blows up, life goes on. High camp, low budget, heavy gore, gross special effects, sexy babes. So what else is new? This is a Troma production. You were expecting *Sense and Sensibility*? Followed by sequels. 🦴🦴

Steroids? They'll get you nowhere, man. A member of the graduating **Class of Nuke 'Em High.**

poor taste. Though it was crushed by a giant mutant Godzilla-like squirrel at the end of *Part 2*, Tromaville's state-of-the-art student-run nuclear power facility has reopened, and it's up to Adlai Smith (Brick Bronsky in three roles) to save the town, the school, and his girlfriend Trish (Lisa Star) from the evil Prof. Holt (Lisa Gaye), she of the Marge Simpson hair. Supposedly inspired by Shakespeare's *Comedy of Errors*. Tip: stick to the BBC production for your term paper. *Class of Nuke 'Em High 4: Battle of the Bikini Subhumanoids* is in the works. 🦴🦴🦴

1994 (R) 95m/C Brick Bronsky, Lisa Gaye, Lisa Star; **D:** Eric Louzil; **W:** Lloyd (Samuel Weil) Kaufman. **VHS** *TTV*

1986 (R) 84m/C Janelle Brady, Gilbert Brenton, Robert Prichard; **D:** Richard W. Haines, Lloyd (Samuel Weil) Kaufman. **VHS, Beta** *MED*

Class of Nuke 'Em High 2: Subhumanoid Meltdown

Why are the students at Nuke 'Em High acting so strangely? Where did the Godzilla-sized squirrel come from? What does Professor Holt (Lisa Gaye) have hidden in her Marge Simpson hairdo? What's wrong with Victoria's (Leesa Rowland) navel? Why can't handsome but dumb-as-a-post Roger (Brick Bronsky) get a date? Troma devotees will be delighted; all others will be disgusted. Even judged by the studio's own loose standards, this one is a high watermark in overall cheesiness. Followed by another sequel. 🦴🦴

1991 (R) 96m/C Lisa Gaye, Brick Bronsky, Leesa Rowland; **D:** Eric Louzil. **VHS, Beta, LV** *VTR, MED, FXV*

Class of Nuke 'Em High 3: The Good, the Bad and the Subhumanoid

Arguably the best of the *Nuke 'Em High* series, this irreverent, freewheeling Troma schlock comedy targets environmentalism, political satire, potty jokes, and sex, all in wonderfully

A Clockwork Orange

Droogs don't run and neither does Stanley Kubrick with his head-on punch-you-in-the-face direction of this incredible adaptation of the controversial Anthony Burgess novel. In Britain's near future, a sadistic punk (Malcolm McDowell, fiercely funny and over-the-top throughout), who loves music almost as much as he loves his violence, leads his gang on a nightly spree of rape and "ultra violence." After being caught he is the subject in a grim government experiment to eradicate his violent tendencies using behavior modification (the subject of the classic punk song by Cinecyde). Hard to decide who's the real victim. Many memorable, disturbing sequences, including a rape/beating conducted while assailant McDowell "kicks" out a version of "Singing in the Rain." The language Burgess created for the novel (he did the same for the prehistoric flick *Quest for Fire*) is used in the film, so having the book's glossary handy isn't a bad idea. The score is made up of both classical music and electronic compositions by then-Walter now-Wendy Carlos (get a hold of the album featuring Carlos' renditions of the whole score for the best effect). Originally given an X rating, the film continues to be provocative years later. Sick but fun eye candy for the thinkers among us. 🦴🦴🦴🦴

1971 (R) 137m/C *GB* Malcolm McDowell, Patrick Magee, Adrienne Corri, Michael Bates, Warren Clarke, Aubrey Morris, James Marcus, Steven Berkoff, David Prowse, Miriam Karlin, John Clive, Carl Duering; **D:** Stanley Kubrick; **W:**

Stanley Kubrick; **C:** John Alcott. Hugos '72: Dramatic Pre-sentation; New York Film Critics Awards '71: Best Director (Kubrick), Best Film; Nominations: Academy Awards '71: Best Adapted Screenplay, Best Director (Kubrick), Best Film Editing, Best Picture. **VHS, Beta, LV** *WAR, FCT, FUS*

The Clones

A doctor discovers a government experiment engineered to murder him with a perfect clone. 🦴 🦴

1973 (PG) 90m/C Michael Greene, Gregory Sierra; **D:** Paul Hunt, Lamar Card. **VHS, Beta** *LIV, HHE*

The Clonus Horror

A scientist discovers a government plot to clone the population by freezing bodies alive and using their parts in surgery. **AKA:** Parts: The Clonus Horror. 🦴 🦴

1979 90m/C Tim Donnelly, Keenan Wynn, Peter Graves, Dick Sargent, Paulette Breen; **D:** Robert S. Fiveson. **VHS, Beta** *LIV*

Close Encounters of the Third Kind

Strangers from all over the world become involved in the attempts of benevolent aliens to contact Earthlings. Despite the (intentionally) mundane nature of the characters, this Spielberg epic is a stirring achievement. Studded with classic sequences; the ending is an exhilarating experience of special effects and peace-on-Earth feelings. Richard Dreyfuss and Melinda Dillon excel as friends who are at once bewildered and obsessed by the alien presence, and French filmmaker Francois Truffaut is also strong as the stern, ultimately kind scientist. Departing from the common saucer design for extraterrestrial vehicles, the UFOs appear here as beautiful, multicolored light shows, swooping gracefully about the frame. Released the same year as *Star Wars,* the two features set new standards of special effects spectacle. Steven Spielberg claims he was

"These magnifying make-up mirrors are amazing!" *Close Encounters of the Third Kind.*

rushed to get the picture done for the release date. In 1980, he used his clout to engineer a "special edition" re-release, re-edited to his liking—and sparking an ongoing argument as to which version is better. Deluxe laserdisc includes formerly edited scenes, live interviews with Spielberg, special effects man Douglas Trumbull, and composer John Williams, publicity materials, and over 1000 production photos. 🦴 🦴 🦴 🦴

1977 (PG) 152m/C Richard Dreyfuss, Teri Garr, Melinda Dillon, Francois Truffaut, Bob Balaban, Cary Guffey, J. Patrick McNamara; **D:** Steven Spielberg; **W:** Steven Spielberg; **C:** Vilmos Zsigmond; **M:** John Williams. Academy Awards '77: Best Cinematography, Best Sound Effects Editing; National Board of Review Awards '77: 10 Best Films of the Year; Nominations: Academy Awards '77: Best Art Direction/Set Decoration, Best Director (Spielberg), Best Film Editing, Best Sound, Best Supporting Actress (Dillon), Best Original Score. **VHS, Beta, LV** COL, CRC, FUS

Club Extinction

Claude Chabrol, French filmmaker best known for thrillers in a Hitchcockian vein, pays tribute to vintage German movie ubergangster Dr. Mabuse (sort of a James Bond supervillain long before 007 showed up) in this arcane international coproduction, dumped straight into the American home-video market. Mystery tycoon Dr. Marsfeldt has an artificial heart powered by human suffering. Dwelling in his futuristic hideout beneath an industrial-music club, he employs both media idol Jennifer Beals and a New Age resort in a hypnotism scheme to drive Berlin citizens to commit mass suicide. His explanation: "I am the Wall." Yeah, whatever. **AKA:** Docteur M. 🦴 🦴

1989 (R) 105m/C GE Alan Bates, Andrew McCarthy, Jennifer Beals, Jan Niklas, Hanns Zischler, Benoit Regent, Peter Fitz, Wolfgang Preiss, Isolde Barth; **D:** Claude Chabrol. **VHS, Beta** PSM, FCT

Cocoon

Humanist sci-fi fantasy in which Florida senior citizens discover a watery nest of dormant aliens (from Atlantis, natch) that serves effectively as a Fountain of Youth, restoring their health and vigor. Complications ensue when the cocoons' space cohorts return to check up on them. Warm-hearted and winning, even if

the f/x-crammed finale rips off *Close Encounters of the Third Kind* every which way. An Oscar winner for the visual whammies, but made memorable by screen greats Don Ameche, Wilford Brimley, Jack Gilford, Hume Cronyn, and Jessica Tandy. Based on David Saperstein's then-unpublished novel, which he followed with the literary sequel *Metamorphosis,* essentially unrelated to the inevitable Hollywood encore *Cocoon: The Return.* 🦴 🦴 🦴

1985 (PG-13) 117m/C Wilford Brimley, Brian Dennehy, Steve Guttenberg, Don Ameche, Tahnee Welch, Jack Gilford, Hume Cronyn, Jessica Tandy, Gwen Verdon, Maureen Stapleton, Tyrone Power Jr., Barret Oliver, Linda Harrison, Herta Ware, Clint Howard; **D:** Ron Howard; **W:** Tom Benedek; **C:** Don Peterman; **M:** James Horner. Academy Awards '85: Best Supporting Actor (Ameche), Best Visual Effects. **VHS, Beta, LV** FOX, FCT, BTV

Cocoon: The Return

"Cocoon: the Rerun," as old timers who left with aliens last time revisit Earth and basically go through the same stuff all over again. Filmmakers desperately push familiar emotional buttons in search of the fragile magic of Ron Howard's original. You may find yourself fast-forwarding to the f/x or away from the schmaltz. 🦴

1988 (PG) 116m/C Don Ameche, Wilford Brimley, Steve Guttenberg, Maureen Stapleton, Hume Cronyn, Jessica Tandy, Gwen Verdon, Jack Gilford, Tahnee Welch, Courteney Cox, Brian Dennehy, Barret Oliver; **D:** Daniel Petrie; **W:** Stephen McPherson; **C:** Tak Fujimoto; **M:** James Horner. **VHS, Beta, LV** FOX

Colossus: The Forbin Project

A massive computer designed to manage U.S. defense systems instead merges with its Soviet equal and proceeds to accomplish its prime purpose: to achieve world peace. It does this by the most logical means—world domination. Wire-tight, suspenseful film seems at once dated yet timely—the chattering old computer equipment is used to put a mechanical face on Big Brother concepts, while touching on fears of technology out of control. Based on the novel by D.F. Jones, who also wrote two sequels. The same idea was later expanded in the *Terminator* series, in which a defense computer seeks world peace by

attempting to extinguish the human race altogether. **AKA:** The Forbin Project. ♪♪♪

1970 100m/C Eric (Hans Gudegast) Braeden, Susan Clark, Gordon Pinsent, William Schallert, Georg Stanford Brown; **D:** Joseph Sargent; **W:** James Bridges; **C:** Gene Polito; **M:** Michel Colombier. **VHS, Beta** *MCA*

Communion

A serious adaptation of the purportedly nonfiction bestseller by Whitley Strieber, about his 1985 abduction by dwarf drones under the control of spindly, huge-eyed beings (a breed sometimes referred to by UFO hipsters as "Schwa"). Even skeptics who've met Strieber declare he's sincere, so either the "visitors" are real or he's nuts. Christopher Walken's twitchy Method acting could well support the latter conclusion. The film—produced and written by Strieber—is remarkably candid about the author's eccentricities, right down to the notorious episode in which Strieber claimed a vision of Mr. Peanut (replaced onscreen by a top-hatted toy robot). Philippe Mora's direction, full of strange juxtapositions and hallucination imagery, may be too loose to please all but the very curious and New Age types. Strieber, meanwhile, followed his book with two more vaporous accounts (*Breakthrough* and *Transformation*) and a Strieberesque novelization of the Roswell incident, *Majestic*. ♪♪

1989 (R) 103m/C Christopher Walken, Lindsay Crouse, Frances Sternhagen, Joel Carlson, Andreas Katsulas, Basil Hoffman, Terri Hanauer; **D:** Philippe Mora; **W:** Whitley Strieber; **M:** Eric Clapton. **VHS, Beta, LV** *NO*

The Companion

A 21st-century romance novelist rents remote mountain cabin to write and get over a broken love affair. For assistance and solace she brings a lifelike robot named Geoffrey (Bruce Greenwood). Tinkering with Geoffrey's programming turns him from domestic guardian to devoted lover, but cranked up too high the machine becomes a lethally obsessed Mr. Wrong. Well-acted cable-TV thriller avoids the smirks one might expect, but grows more predictable as it goes along. ♪♪♪

1994 (R) 94m/C Kathryn Harrold, Bruce Greenwood, Talia Balsam, Brion James, Bryan Cranston, Joely Fisher; **D:** Gary Fleder; **W:** Ian Seeberg, Valerie Bennett. **VHS, LV** *MCA*

The Computer Wore Tennis Shoes

Families will want to boot up this post-Walt live-action Disney comedy starring Kurt Russell as Dexter Riley, an underachieving college student who suddenly becomes a genius after the campus computer's memory bank is accidentally downloaded into his brain. Innocuous and dated, but the expert cast keeps this online. Cesar Romero is the local crime boss and the computer's original owner whose clandestine records wind up in Dexter's head. Joe Flynn (Captain Binghamton on *McHale's Navy*) is the fussbudget college dean and Dexter's nemesis. Pat Harrington (Schneider on *One Day at a Time*) hosts the TV quiz show on which Dexter appears. Followed by *Now You See Him, Now You Don't* and *The Strongest Man in the World*. ♪♪♪

1969 (G) 87m/C Kurt Russell, Cesar Romero, Joe Flynn, William Schallert, Alan Hewitt, Richard Bakalayan, Pat Harrington, Debbie Paine; **D:** Robert Butler; **W:** Joseph L. McEveety; **C:** Frank Phillips; **M:** Robert F. Brunner. **VHS, Beta** *DIS, OM*

Conan the Barbarian

The Hyborean age has never been so brutally portrayed as in writer/director John Milius' sword and sorcery epic. Thulsa Doom (James Earl Jones) leads a savage raid on young Conan's home village, both killing Conan's father and stealing the sword bequeathed to him. Doom also kills mom in an eerily beautiful, nearly surrealistic, almost tasteful manner (Milius did have access to an elaborate f/x head with eyes-a-rollin' and tongue-a-flickin', but didn't ruin the scene by showing it). All this makes Conan plenty angry and he has years to stew about it, first on the wheel of pain (where he becomes Arnold Schwarzenegger) and then as a pit fighter. Luckily, what doesn't kill him makes him strong. Freed by his owner, he teams up with a Mongol (Gerry Lopez) and Valeria, the Queen of Thieves (Sandahl Bergman) and sets forth on a quest to get

"Do you want to live forever?"

—Valeria's (Sandahl Bergman) spirit asks Conan (Arnold Schwarzenegger) during a climactic battle in *Conan the Barbarian*.

> "It is as much pleasure as can be obtained with your lower extremities still garbed."
>
> —*Coneheads.*

back his sword, solve "the riddle of steel," and kill Doom, now the leader of the nasty snake-cult of Set. The action is furious and the swordplay violent and incredible. Each character was given their own "swordmaster" and taught a style that both fit their own body style and personalities—Arnold's is a powerful hack and slash, Sandahl's very graceful and dancerlike. Both can disembowel and behead with the best, and boy do they get to! Milius' "warrior spirit" comes across both philosophically and graphically. Based on the character created by Robert E. Howard. Sequel: *Conan the Destroyer.* Rousing score by Basil Poledouris would put some symphonies to shame. 🦴🦴🦴

1982 (R) 115m/C Arnold Schwarzenegger, James Earl Jones, Max von Sydow, Sandahl Bergman, Mako, Ben Davidson, Valerie Quennessen, Cassandra Gaviola, Gerry Lopez, William Smith; *D:* John Milius; *W:* John Milius, Oliver Stone; *M:* Basil Poledouris. **VHS, Beta, LV** *MCA*

Conan the Destroyer

Not as violent or as mythical (although maybe more mythological) as the superior *Conan the Barbarian,* Academy Award-winning director Richard Fleischer's Conan is still good campy fun. This time evil queen Tamaris challenges Conan (Arnold Schwarzenegger) to accompany a beautiful princess in a quest for a magic treasure. If the treasure and the princess's honor return intact, Conan's dead lover Valeria will be brought back to life. Joining Arnold on his quest are singer Grace Jones and hoopster Wilt Chamberlain. Highlights include the evil wizard Thoth-aman, who turns into a giant vulture, and the battle with the dreaming god Dagoth (designed by Carlo Rambaldi, who created E.T.), who wants to turn the entire universe into darkness. 🦴🦴

1984 (PG) 101m/C Arnold Schwarzenegger, Grace Jones, Wilt Chamberlain, Sarah Douglas, Mako, Jeff Corey, Olivia D'Abo; *D:* Richard Fleischer; *C:* Jack Cardiff; *M:* Basil Poledouris. Golden Raspberry Awards '84: Worst New Star (D'Abo). **VHS, Beta, LV** *MCA*

Coneheads

Saturday Night Live skit inflated to feature-length is strangely likable. It can also boast the presence of dozens of *SNL* regulars on both sides of the camera. Dan Aykroyd and Jane Curtin reprise their roles as Beldar and Prymaat, the couple from the planet Remulak who are just trying to fit in on Earth. Laraine Newman, who created the role of teen-aged daughter Connie, appears as Beldar's sister, while Michelle Burke takes over as Connie (toddler Connie is Aykroyd's daughter, in her film debut). The jokes may be thin but the characters are engaging, the effects are inventive, and the film has its heart in the right place. Soundtrack features music by Soft Cell, R.E.M., Red Hot Chili Peppers, k.d. lang, and Barenaked Ladies. 🦴🦴🦴

1993 (PG) 86m/C Dan Aykroyd, Jane Curtin, Laraine Newman, Jason Alexander, Michelle Burke, Chris Farley, Michael Richards, Lisa Jane Persky, Sinbad, Shishir Kurup, Michael McKean, Phil Hartman, David Spade, Dave Thomas, Jan Hooks, Chris Rock, Adam Sandler, Julia Sweeney, Danielle Aykroyd; *D:* Steven Barron; *W:* Dan Aykroyd, Tom Davis, Bonnie Turner, Terry Turner. **VHS, Beta** *PAR, BTV*

Conquest of Space

Would you like a moon crater named after you? That honor was given to the late Chesley Bonestell for being this century's finest astronomical artist. His designs and constructions permeate this film—which is the only conceivable reason to see it. A space commander designs an orbital platform and helps build a moon rocket. When told the craft is to transport him, his son, and select crewman to Mars instead, our leader looks into the Bible and, finding no mention of a Mars expedition, has a nervous breakdown (that Scripture mentions no space platform or moon flight seems to elude this profound thinker!). Endure the melodrama for the stunning Bonestellian visuals; here is a Mars not as we found it but as it should have been. One scene should haunt you forever: the burial-at-space of the dead astronaut, encased in his space suit and floating off into the sun's zodiacal light. Inspired by a speculative nonfiction book *The Mars Project* by Wernher von Braun. 🦴🦴

1955 81m/C Walter Brooke, Eric Fleming, Mickey Shaughnessy, Phil Foster, William Redfield, William Hopper, Benson Fong, Ross Martin; *D:* Byron Haskin; *W:* George O'Hanlon; *C:* Lionel Linden. **VHS** *PAR*

Conquest of the Planet of the Apes

This fourth Apes film picks up where the third left off. After a disease brought from outer space kills all Earth's cats and dogs (the Hound found this aspect particularly frightening), humans begin to keep apes as house pets. Because of their intelligence and adaptability, these pets turn into ill-treated slaves governed by the Gestapo-like Ape Control. Caeser (Roddy McDowall) is the son of the super-intelligent time-traveling apes Cornelius (also previously played by McDowall) and Zira. Because of the threat he poses to the human race, Caeser was left hidden in the care of kind-hearted circus owner Armando (Ricardo Montalban) after his parents were killed. Soon Caeser discovers how his fellow apes are being treated, and leads an armed revolt of the apes against their cruel human masters. The references to American slavery are overt, giving the story a powerful message. Still, the film is not heavy handed, and the story pulls viewers along. McDowall delivers a fine performance, especially difficult behind such heavy makeup. Director J. Lee Thompson does a good job handling the large riot scenes. Followed by the final film, *Battle for the Planet of the Apes*. ♫ ♫ ♫

1972 (PG) 87m/C Roddy McDowall, Don Murray, Ricardo Montalban, Natalie Trundy, Severn Darden, Hari Rhodes; *D:* J. Lee Thompson; *W:* Paul Dehn; *C:* Bruce Surtees. **VHS, Beta, LV** *FOX*

Contact: An Investigation into the Extraterrestrial Experiences of Eduard Meier

Eduard "Billy" Meier at first comes off as sort of an semi-crazy commune-living hippie. For years he has claimed to be in direct contact with extraterrestrial beings from the star system of the Pleiades. This video, narrated by actor David Warner, presents the case with expert testimony on metal samples, sound recordings, scientific theory, and home movie footage of the "beamships" (so called because of the way that they move faster than the camera's shutter) taken by Meier himself. All angles are covered from Billy's eccentricities to computer analysis of the data. A must-see for any UFO buff. ♫ ♫ ♫

19?? 90m/C *D:* Larry Savadone; *W:* Larry Savadone; *M:* Daniel Schwarcz. **VHS** *UFO*

The Cosmic Man

An alien arrives on Earth with a message of peace and restraint. He is regarded with suspicion by us nasty Earthlings. Essentially *The Day the Earth Stood Still* without the budget, but interesting nonetheless. ♫ ♪

1959 72m/B Bruce (Herman Brix) Bennett, John Carradine, Angela Greene, Paul Langton, Scotty Morrow; *D:* Herbert Greene. **VHS, Beta** *SNC*

The Cosmic Monsters

Scientist Forrest Tucker accidentally pops a hole in the ionosphere during a magnetism experiment. As a result, huge, very unfriendly alien insects emerge to plague mankind. Can the intervention of a friendly alien save the world, or is mankind doomed to be bugged to death? Forrest made *The Crawling Eye* that same year, a much creepier tale of alien invasion. **AKA:** The Strange World of Planet X; The Crawling Terror. ♫ ♪

1958 75m/B *GB* Forrest Tucker, Gaby Andre, Alec Mango, Hugh Latimer, Martin Benson; *D:* Gilbert Gunn; *W:* Joe Ambor, Paul Ryder. **VHS, Beta** *MRV, SNC, MWP*

Cosmic Slop

Disappointing anthology done for HBO as sort of a multicultural *Twilight Zone*. The three-eyed floating head of George Clinton emcees three tales, and only the first gives this sf cred: In "Space Traders" (based on a story by Derrick Bell), alien visitors take the form of Ronald Reagan (same diff), offering America wealth and prosperity in exchange for all the African-American citizens, no questions asked. What starts off like a sharp sketch ends up mere agit-prop paranoia. Remaining yarns, about an inner-city Catholic priest bugged by a Santeria goddess, and an abused ghetto wife who gets her revenge when the Revolution comes, offer slightly more food for thought,

"IS IT TRUE? Are Creatures from Space watching us NOW?"

—*The Cosmic Man.*

Faux-Pastronomy

Science fiction by definition requires a certain willing suspension of disbelief. You have to allow for such things as aliens, artificial intelligence, psi, time travel, faster-than-light propulsion, and Slime People; otherwise why bother?

Still, there should be at least some pretense of scientific accuracy; otherwise, why bother? But, even as Mr. Scott in Engineering says you cannot deny the laws of physics, you also cannot deny the autocracy of the producer, the blinkered vision of a director, or the plain old scientific ignorance of a script.

Thus movie sf is replete with factual errors, some big enough to drive a comet through, others just passing absurdities that serve to remind us all why the Nobel Prizes are not handed out at the Dorothy Chandler Pavilion.

Terminal Velocities. The effect of going very, very fast on the human body has been well-documented in sf ever since *Destination Moon* by those tight closeups of astronaut faces grimacing against the pull of inertia during liftoff. One major exception was the classic *Things to Come* in which lunar explorers were fired from the Earth in a giant cannon. Were that to be done, the sudden acceleration would turn the humans into thin protoplasmic jelly against the back of their craft. Similarly, in *Star Trek V* Captain Kirk falls off a mountain peak. Mr. Spock, in flying antigravity boots, snatches him just inches from the ground, saving his life—except that a halt from such a speed to zero would kill a person just as thoroughly as slamming into the soil.

Hollywood Abhors a Vacuum. The nature of interplanetary space itself has given filmmakers plenty of difficulty. "In space no one can hear you scream," went the original ad copy for *Alien,* quite accurately, for sound waves don't travel in space, where no medium exists to carry them. But except for *2001: A Space*

Odyssey and a few other nonconformists, this fact has not been recognized. Explosions generate great roaring sounds, starships and X-Wing fighter craft (which commonly bank and turn exactly like planes in Earth atmosphere) whoosh past, and in some cases passengers inside of a ship can plainly hear things happening outside (except for screams, anyway).

I'm yo' pusher baby. An ancient Greek wise man said that if given a long enough lever and a fulcrum on which to rest it, he could move the world. Too bad he lived several millennia too early to sell that treatment to the movies. Major productions that have dealt with using directed force in making the Earth move include *Gorath* and *Superman: The Movie.* The trouble is, any push strong enough to shove the Earth contrary to its orbit would more likely shatter the globe into a million pieces than ease it along.

Matters of Gravity. Gravitational force is one of the least-understood phenomena in physics. Maybe physicists have been watching too many movies. While *Marooned,* Stanley Kubrick's *2001: A Space Odyssey,* and a few Japanese and Soviet productions made laudable attempts to simulate a zero-G environment, other cosmic flicks have simply ignored the absence of gravity, or included a brief dialogue reference to "artificial gravity" that dispensed with the problem. Astronauts aboard *Rocketship X-M* emphasized how gravity would decrease as they left Earth's influence, and one of their discarded jackets began moving around on cue. But nothing else ever did, and the topic was shelved.

Most inconsistent of all was the non-Kubrick sequel *2010,* in which a ship docking the original movie's *Discovery* must stop spinning its artificial gravity section. Everyone in the movie should be in free fall, but in subsequent scenes cosmonauts are seen walking normally, leaning on chairs and countertops, and the hero casually tosses a prop in the air.

Size Does Count. One of the most frequently violated principles of science, especially in monster movies, is the inverse-square law. Put in biological terms, the bigger an organism is, the more its physiology must adjust to gigantic stature. Therefore, forget the giant bugs on their spindly legs in *Them!, Mothra, Tarantula,* and *The Deadly Mantis.* These are, after all, invertebrates, and without internal skeletons to support them, giant insects and arachnids would squash themselves under their own weight.

Random Noise. Miscellaneous goofs of all sorts... From *The Invisible Man* to *Memoirs of an Invisible Man,* total invisibility means that without opaque retinas the transparent heroes would go blind. In the original motion picture *Voyage to the Bottom of the Sea,* the submarine *Seaview* happens to be underneath a field of unstable icebergs. The ship is pelted by *sinking* boulders of ice. In *Capricorn One* we're told that radio signals from Earth to Mars would make a round trip of 20 minutes (not the accurate figure but it's the spirit that counts); a few scenes later the 'Mars' astronauts are having a real-time transmission conversation with their terrestrial wives. In *TimeCop,* a character casually announces that a sample of gold has been radiocarbon dated, a well-known theoretical impossibility because gold does not undergo atomic decay. Would it surprise you to know that Peter Hyams, who made *TimeCop,* also directed *Capricorn One* and *2010*?

but most viewers will find the 'Magic Eye' videocassette cover more engrossing than the contents. 🦴

1994 (R) 87m/C Robert Guillaume, Jason Bernard, Nicholas Turturro, Richard Herd, Paula Jai Parker, Chi McBride; **D:** Reginald Hudlin, Warrington Hudlin, Kevin Sullivan; **W:** Warrington Hudlin, Trey Ellis, Kyle Baker. **VHS** *HBO*

Cosmos: War of the Planets

The ultimate battle for survival is fought in outer space, though not very well and on a small budget. Dubbed, Italian-made saga cluelessly imitates the *Star Wars* and *Star Trek* formulas, as scrappy-looking toy spaceships shoot down the minions of a planet-ruling tyrant computer, and everyone on the bridge cheers in unison. Beam us up, Scotty. **AKA:** Cosmo 2000: Planet Without a Name; War of the Planets. **WOOF!**

1980 (PG) 90m/C *IT* Katia Christine, West Buchanan, John Richardson, Yanti Somer; **D:** Al Bradley. **VHS, Beta** *NO*

Crash and Burn

Sputtering futurism from Charles Band, wherein the repressive corporate state crushes dissent by banning home computers (an accurate prediction of the Communications Decency Act?). Ralph Waite is an activist broadcaster out in the wastelands whose TV station is infiltrated by the government's *Terminator*-style robot assassins. There's a big build-up to the reactivation of a huge, long-dormant robot (special effects by David Allen) to battle the Establishment androids, but the rusty giant falls to pieces after a few moments of screen time. Low budgets will do that to you. Supporting actor Jack McGee does a barbed Rush Limbaugh impersonation. 🦴🦴

1990 (R) 85m/C Ralph Waite, Paul Ganus, Eva LaRue, Bill Moseley, Jack McGee, Megan Ward; **D:** Charles Band; **W:** J.S. Cardone; **C:** Mac Ahlberg; **M:** Richard Band. **VHS, Beta, LV** *PAR*

The Crawling Eye

Quatermass-like sci-fi with Forrest Tucker as a UN science investigator visiting the Swiss town of Trollenberg, where a strange radioac-

tive cloud hovers on a mountaintop. As the cloud descends and encloses the village, several climbers are discovered decapitated. Tucker teams up with two sisters, one of them a telepath (Janet Munro) who can communicate with aliens, which is very lucky because that darn cloud is chock-full of them. The ensuing battle provides plenty of tension, even tough the effects are so-so at best, and the acting, at most, adequate. At least the aliens themselves don't disappoint with their huge Cyclopean-eyeball-tentacled-creaturoid good looks, and once again a low-budget film is directed and photographed with atmosphere to spare. Adapted by writer Jimmy Sangster from the BBC teleserial by Peter Key. **AKA:** The Trollenberg Terror; The Creature from Another World. 🦴🦴

1958 87m/B *GB* Forrest Tucker, Laurence Payne, Janet Munro, Jennifer Jayne, Warren Mitchell; **D:** Quentin Lawrence; **W:** Jimmy Sangster; **M:** Stanley Black. **VHS, Beta, LV** *SNC, MRV, MED*

The Crawling Hand

An astronaut's hand takes off without him on an unearthly spree of stranglings. Silly stuff is a hands-down loser. **WOOF!**

1963 98m/B Alan Hale Jr., Rod Lauren, Richard Arlen, Peter Breck, Kent Taylor, Arline Judge, Allison Hayes; **D:** Herbert L. Strock. **VHS, Beta, LV** *NOS, RHI, GEM*

The Crazies

When a small Pennsylvania town's water supply is contaminated with an experimental virus, the residents go on a chaotic, murderous rampage. The army is called in to quell the anarchy, and a small war breaks out. This was George A. Romero's second feature, and followed on the heels of his classic *Night of the Living Dead*. Unfortunately, though Romero proved once again it was possible to make an impressive film outside the Hollywood system, *The Crazies*'s overall impact was dulled by its muddled approach to its subject matter. The movie is still disturbing, but it hasn't aged well; today it just seems dated and confused. Romero would go on to make better films, like 1978's vampire thriller *Martin*. **AKA:** Code Name: Trixie. 🦴🦴

"WAITING! WATCHING! WANTON! None can escape this slithering terror spawned from a nuclear hell lusting for another taste of human blood...MAYBE YOURS!"

—The Crawling Eye.

"I'm so glad we waited for our wedding night," says a radiant *Creature from the Black Lagoon.*

Creature

Originally titled *Titan Find,* this low-budget *Alien* rip-off has at least one good thing going for it...Klaus Kinski. The rest of the nondescript cast should have taken some attitudinal hints from K. K. and relaxed, giving this lame material the nonchalant, tongue-in-cheek treatment it deserved. Captain Stan Ivar and crew are on Saturn's moon Titan, investigating a two thousand-year-old alien life form that has been fatally anti-social to the previous spaceketeers. Not enough tension, and definitely not enough Kinski. **AKA:** Titan Find. 🐾 🐾

1985 (R) 97m/C Klaus Kinski, Stan Ivar, Wendy Schaal, Lyman Ward, Annette McCarthy, Diane Salinger; **D:** William Malone; **M:** Tom Chase, Steve Rucker. **VHS, Beta, LV** *MED*

Creature from the Black Lagoon

An anthropological expedition in the Amazon stumbles upon the Gill-Man, a prehistoric humanoid fish monster who supposedly represents a "missing link" between humans and...well, fish. The scaled nasty takes a fancy to the fetching Julie Adams, a coed majoring in "science" (she has brains as well as beauty!), but the menfolk get all riled up (and occasionally bumped off by the monster). Originally filmed in 3-D, this was one of the first movies to sport top-of-the-line underwater photography and remains one of the most enjoyable monster movies ever made. The Gill-Man, at once both utterly alien and strangely sympathetic, is an extraordinary creation. Joseph Gershenson's score became a "Creature Features" standard. Based on a story by Maurice Zimm, the film spawned two sequels: *Revenge of the Creature* and *The Creature Walks Among Us.* 🐾 🐾 🐾

1954 79m/B Richard Carlson, Julie Adams, Richard Denning, Antonio Moreno, Whit Bissell, Nestor Paiva, Ricou Browning, Ben Chapman; **D:** Jack Arnold; **W:** Harry Essex, Arthur Ross; **C:** William E. Snyder; **M:** Hans J. Salter, Joseph Gershenson, Henry Mancini. **VHS, Beta, LV** *MCA, GKK*

1973 (R) 103m/C Lane Carroll, W.G. McMillan, Harold W. Jones, Lloyd Hollar, Lynn Lowry, Richard Liberty; **D:** George A. Romero; **W:** George A. Romero. **Beta** *NO*

The Creation of the Humanoids

Set in the familiar post-holocaust future, this is a tale of humans outnumbered by androids and the resulting struggle for survival. Slow and silly low-budget sets. For some reason, Andy Warhol was reported to love this film. **WOOF!**

1962 84m/C Don Megowan, Frances McCann, Erica Elliot, Don Doolittle, Dudley Manlove; **D:** Wesley E. Barry. **VHS, Beta** *MRV, SNC*

The Creature Walks Among Us

The sequel to *Revenge of the Creature* has the much put-upon Gill-Man captured once more

by scientists bent on "studying" him. During an accidental lab fire, the creature's gills are burned off and the science-boys undertake to save his life with surgery designed to turn him into an air-breather. Sadly, the (ex)Gill-Man remains a fish out of water, lurching around in dingy clothes and once again lusting after one of those faithless human floozies (Leigh Snowden). This final entry in the *Creature from the Black Lagoon* series has little of the original film's magic, but it's a weirdly compelling film in its own right. The altered monster is even more sympathetic here—his being forced to wear human clothes is an especially effective touch. Ricou Browning was back to perform the monster's underwater scenes; Don Megowan played the new and not necessarily improved creature. Like the other films, this flick was shot in 3-D. It's available on laserdisc as part of a special "Encore Edition Double Feature" with *Revenge of the Creature.* 🐟🐟

1956 79m/B Jeff Morrow, Rex Reason, Leigh Snowden, Gregg Palmer, Ricou Browning, Don Megowan; *D:* John Sherwood; *W:* Arthur Ross; *C:* Maury Gertsman; *M:* Joseph Gershenson. **VHS, LV** *MCA, FCT*

Creatures the World Forgot

A British-made yawn-fest about two tribes of cavemen warring over power and a cavewoman. English horror mainstay Hammer Studios apparently reasoned that since all those films featuring animated dinosaurs and scantily clad cavewomen usually did well in the box office, a flick that cut out the expensive dinos to concentrate on cro-magnon cheesecake would be a sure-fire money-maker. Predictably, *Creatures,* which features little or nothing in the way of dinosaurs, special effects, or dialogue, was a bronto-sized flop. Star Julie Ege was once a Miss Norway and had a shot at being a pop singer. She should have tried harder, because this dog did nothing for her career. 🐟

1970 96m/C Julie Ege, Robert John, Tony Bonner, Rosalie Crutchley, Sue Wilson; *D:* Don Chaffey; *W:* Michael Carreras. **VHS, Beta** *COL, MLB*

Creepozoids

In the near future, army deserters hiding out at an abandoned science complex are stalked by a slimy monster. Yet another *Alien* rip-off, substituting extreme, tasteless violence for the original's expert pacing and style. The one semi-effective element is a creepy monster baby, but that's not enough to save this waste of celluloid. 🐟

1987 72m/C Linnea Quigley, Ken Abraham, Michael Aranda, Richard Hawkins, Kim McKamy, Joi Wilson; *D:* David DeCoteau; *W:* David DeCoteau, Burford Hauser; *C:* Thomas Callaway. **Beta, LV** *NO*

Crime Zone

In a totalitarian, repressive, future society, two young lovers try to beat the system and make it on their own. A well-made, if occasionally muddled, low-budget film shot in Peru, of all places. 🐟🐟🐟

1988 (R) 96m/C David Carradine, Peter Nelson, Sherilyn Fenn, Orlando Sacha, Don Manor, Michael Shaner; *D:* Luis Llosa; *W:* Daryl Haney; *M:* Rick Conrad. **VHS** *MGM*

Critters

One of the better *Gremlins* imitations. Hairy, fast-growing, faster-eating little alien "Krites" crash to Earth with a pair of shape-shifting, blast-happy galactic bounty hunters right behind them. Both terrorize a farm family in a small Kansas community. Don Opper (*Android*) is especially fun as a Barney Fife-type deputy who gets on the case. Smart and sarcastic sci-fi action that doesn't push the intrinsic gore to extremes, though the franchise has worn out its welcome with increasingly inferior sequels. Drolly subtitled Krite dialogue culminates in the devouring of an E.T. doll. 🐟🐟🐟

1986 (PG-13) 86m/C Dee Wallace Stone, M. Emmet Walsh, Billy Green Bush, Scott Grimes, Nadine Van Der Velde, Terrence Mann, Billy Zane, Don Opper, Terrence Mann; *D:* Stephen Herek; *W:* Don Opper, Stephen Herek, Dominic Muir; *C:* Tim Suhrstedt; *M:* David Newman. **VHS, Beta, LV** *COL*

Critters 2: The Main Course

First followup to the hit sci-fi-horror comedy, wherein the voracious alien furballs return in

The Hugo Winners

Every year, the World Science Fiction Convention (informally known as "Worldcon") confers the "Hugo" award to novels, short stories, and films judged to be of unusual merit. Named after pioneer science-fiction editor Hugo Gernsback, the Hugo is the most prestigious award that can be bestowed on a work of science fiction—it's the "Oscar" of sf.

In 1960, a dramatic presentation award was added to the list of Hugo categories. Usually given to film, the presentation Hugo has also been awarded to science-fiction TV shows like *Star Trek* and on one occasion news coverage of Apollo XI.

Following is a chronological list of films and shows that have won the Dramatic Presentation Hugo since the its inception. There were several years in which no award was given. These are some of the best science-fiction films and television shows ever made.

The Twilight Zone, 1960, 1961, 1962
"The Menagerie" (*Star Trek*), 1967
"City on the Edge of Forever" (*Star Trek*), 1968
2001: A Space Odyssey, 1969
News coverage of Apollo XI, 1970
A Clockwork Orange, 1972
Slaughterhouse Five, 1973
Sleeper, 1974
Young Frankenstein, 1975
A Boy and His Dog, 1976
Star Wars, 1978
Superman, 1979
Alien, 1980
The Empire Strikes Back, 1981
Raiders of the Lost Ark, 1982
Blade Runner, 1983
Return of the Jedi, 1984
2010, 1985
Back to the Future, 1986
Aliens, 1987
The Princess Bride, 1988
Who Framed Roger Rabbit, 1989
Indiana Jones and the Last Crusade, 1990
Edward Scissorhands, 1991
Terminator 2: Judgment Day, 1992
"The Inner Light" (*Star Trek: The Next Generation*), 1993
Jurassic Park, 1994
"All Good Things" (*Star Trek: The Next Generation*), 1995

full force to Grovers Bend, Kansas, hatching on Easter Sunday from eggs planted two years before. Those memorable alien bounty hunters also return, but considerably less fearsome this time. Occasionally the mayhem is inspired—like when the Krites come together to form an immense, rolling Critterball. Other times the abundant humor is just plain dumb. Better than the other sequels, anyway. 🐾🐾

1988 (PG-13) 93m/C Scott Grimes, Liane Curtis, Don Opper, Barry Corbin, Terrence Mann; *D:* Mick Garris; *W:* Mick Garris, David N. Twohy. **VHS, Beta, LV** *COL*

Critters 3

A family on a picnic return to their seedy city tenement with yet more Krite eggs, which hatch and allow the mini-monsters to spread chaos and terror in an urban environment (translation: they wreck a laundry room). Third time was not the charm for the critters, and Don Opper's act as the bumbling deputy sheriff turned Critterbuster is really wearing thin. Notable early appearance for future Oscar nominee Leonardo DiCaprio. 🐾

1991 (PG-13) 86m/C Francis Bay, Aimee Brooks, Leonardo DiCaprio, Don Opper; *D:* Kristine Peterson; *W:* David J. Schow. **VHS** *COL, NLC*

Critters 4

Direct continuation of *Critters 3* (bet you could hardly wait) is an obvious steal from *Alien,* as the last surviving Krites and their would-be slayer Don Opper arrive on an abandoned space station. Other humanoids show up, mainly to argue with each other and be slain. So uninvolved is this script that the Critters don't even eat their prey anymore, they just kill pointlessly, and likeable alien bounty-hunter Ug (Terrence Mann) has arbitrarily turned into a bad guy (and ceased his shapeshifting). Notable early appearance for future Oscar nominee Angela Bassett. 🐾🐾

1991 (PG-13) 94m/C Don Opper, Paul Whitthorne, Angela Bassett, Brad Dourif, Terrence Mann; *D:* Rupert Harvey; *W:* Joseph Lyle, David J. Schow; *C:* Thomas Callaway. **VHS, LV** *NLC, COL*

The Curse of Frankenstein

It's 1957 and England's Hammer Studios decides to take the classic Mary Shelley mad-scientist-makes-a-monster-and-boy-does-it-cause-trouble novel *Frankenstein* and give it some new Technicolor blood, and suddenly gothic horror is in again. Pairing up Peter Cushing (as Baron Frankenstein) and Christopher Lee (as the monster) for the first time, they created a scream-team that would last for decades. Also for the first time, the audience is treated to body parts and make-up job by Jack Pierce (who also created the famous make-up for Universal's Frankenstein monster) that actually looks like a stitched-together man might look. Same as before, the kinda-insane Baron gathers pieces of the freshly dead to assemble his experiment, with the one fatal flaw...a bad brain. Said brain, and a little disorientation, cause the dead-alive one to wreak havoc, spread destruction, and, of course, kill. When a gunshot takes off part of the creature's head in a swelter of blood, audiences—and censors—worldwide (except in Japan where they have always loved their violence) were aghast! Don't worry, you can take it. Worth it for the atmosphere alone. 🐾🐾🐾

1957 83m/C *GB* Peter Cushing, Christopher Lee, Hazel Court, Robert Urquhart, Valerie Gaunt, Noel Hood; *D:* Terence Fisher; *W:* Jimmy Sangster; *C:* Jack Asher; *M:* James Bernard. **VHS, Beta** *WAR, MLB*

Curse of the Swamp Creature

A mad scientist in the Everglades with some weird ideas about evolution attempts to create half-human/half-reptilian monsters. He succeeds (more or less), producing a series of clawed, rubbery-skinned varmints that look like low-rent versions of the Creature from the Black Lagoon. Most of these things go to Lizard-man Heaven in fairly short order, but his final experiment lives...though it's none too happy about that fact, having previously been quite happy as the doc's wife, thank you. Before long a geological expeditionary force, headed by B-movie hero extraordinaire John Agar, arrives and attempts to stop the good doctor's tamperings with Forbidden Knowledge. Ah, but will they be

"In space, they love to hear you scream."
—*Critters 4.*

Giant Japanese Monsters-a-Go-Go

In Japanese they're called *kaiju eiga*—literally, "monster movies." By now virtually everyone has been exposed to these gems at some point in their development and had the basic plot implanted in their brains: a giant, rubbery monster is somehow unleashed on Japan and destroys Tokyo simply by walking through it and roaring. At the last minute, a handsome young scientist finds the solution, and the monster is dispatched—until the sequel.

To most people, Godzilla is the epitome of the *kaiju eiga,* but there *are* other monsters in Tokyo's history. Success inevitably breeds competition, and Japan's Daiei Studios, noticing the success of Toho's Godzilla movies, decided that they'd give the genre a shot. The result was 1965's *Gamera, the Invincible,* a film featuring a giant, flying, fire-breathing prehistoric turtle. Like Godzilla, Gamera was released on the world by ill-advised experiments with atomic energy. Also like Godzilla, Gamera's first movie spawned a number of increasingly juvenile sequels, in which the one-time villain became a force for good. Gamera, now "friend to children everywhere," teamed up in each film with a parade of annoying little kids to battle monsters like Gaos, Guiron, Zigra, and Jiger, all of whom looked even weirder than their nemesis.

In fact, if you think about it, most Japanese monsters are pretty unlikely from a zoological point of view. Guiron, for instance, seemed to be built more along the lines of a kitchen knife than any known animal. *The X from Outer Space* looked kind of like a big cartoon chicken. And when you think about it, who would ever think to cast a giant *moth* in the role of a monster? As the '70s progressed, the critters in *kaiju eiga* became more and more outlandish, like "King Seesar" in *Godzilla Vs. the Bionic Monster,* who resembled a cross between a dinosaur and a cocker spaniel, or "Gaigan" in *Godzilla Vs. Megalon,* a metallic, bird-like thing with a buzz-saw in its stomach. By comparison, the gigantic yeti-like monsters of *War of the Gargantuas* looked pretty plausible.

Tokyo's days of peril are far from over, however. The early '90s saw a series of "new look" Godzilla movies being produced in Japan, like *Godzilla Vs. Mothra,* which introduced a new "evil" Mothra named "Battra," or *Godzilla Vs. King Ghidorah,* which explained the origins of both Godzilla and his chief nemesis. Even Gamera is back, in 1995's *Gamera, Guardian of the Universe.* Most of these films haven't yet made their way to U.S. video stores, but it's only a matter of time.

too late? Low-budget but atmospheric thrills courtesy of Larry Buchanan, the man who also brought you *The Eye Creatures*. 🎬📼

1966 80m/C John Agar, Francine York, Shirley McLine, Bill Thurman, Jeff Alexander; **D:** Larry Buchanan. **VHS** *MOV, VDM*

Cyber Bandits

Written by comic book author James Robinson, this low-budget cyber-noir film holds it own against its bigger brothers. Jack Morris (Spandau Ballet's Martin Kemp) has just sailed a wealthy Morgan Wells' hi-tech expensive-as-hell yacht into the island city of Pacifica. The millionaire (Robert Hays) has developed a deadly virtual-reality weapon capable of sending his victims deep into cyberspace. Wells' mistress Rebecca (*Baywatch*'s Alexandra Paul) steals the plans and seduces Jack, convincing him to have the data digitally tattooed onto his back. Rebecca disappears and suddenly Jack's hide becomes very valuable. Entertaining view of the future. Also stars rockers Grace Jones and Adam Ant. Available as a "cyber double feature" with *Circuitry Man II* on laserdisc. 🎬📼

1994 (R) 86m/C Martin Kemp, Alexandra Paul, Robert Hays, Adam Ant, Grace Jones; **D:** Erik Fleming; **W:** James Robinson, Winston Beard. **VHS, LV** *COL*

Cyber Ninja

Action-oriented mix of samurais and science fiction should please most fans. Warrior princess Saki (no slouch herself) is captured by the Dark Overlord, who needs a sacrifice to increase his already overwhelming power. Enter the title character, with the usual exaggerated talents and moves of most ninja-kung fu-samurai-karate superheroes, to find both glory and romance. This genre is owned by the Japanese, they kick them out by the dozen, but for non-stop, lightweight fun, this one should do it for you. 🦴🦴ᵇ

1994 80m/C *JP* Hanbel Kawai, Hiroki Ida. **VHS** *FXL*

Cyber-Tracker

Eric Phillips (Don Wilson) is on Senator Dilly's security team. But the evil lawmaker is ready to turn the California legal system over to computers that establish guilt or innocence without trials and robot "trackers" to dispense instant justice. Two things set the *Terminator* knock-off apart from other action flicks. First, the story has some concerns for civil liberties, as opposed to the kneejerk fascist authoritarianism so common to the genre. Second, it benefits considerably from Wilson's always welcome presence. 🦴🦴ᵇ

1993 (R) ?m/C Don "The Dragon" Wilson, Richard Norton, Joseph Ruskin, Abby Dalton, John Aprea; **D:** Richard Pepin. **VHS, LV** *PMH*

Cyber-Tracker 2

Sequel finds that Don "The Dragon" Wilson is now a cop in near-future L.A. where the police are aided by virtually indestructible armed robot "trackers." The bad guys have created their own outlaw trackers that can assume any identity. (Shades of *T2.*) Villainous versions of our hero and heroine (Stacie Foster) are committing dastardly acts, and something blows up or crashes or is shot about every five minutes. All the action and gun violence is handled with such cartoonish energy that it's nei-

ther offensive nor sadistic. But you do have to wonder why everybody spends so much time shooting at these robots when they know that bullets can't hurt them. 🦴🦴ᵇ

1995 (R) 97m/C Don "The Dragon" Wilson, Stacie Foster, Stephen Burton; **D:** Richard Pepin. **VHS** *PMH*

Cyborg

Plague reduces Earth to a deathly, dirty, urban ruin patrolled by pumped-up punks. A lady cyborg transporting the disease cure must be protected by wandering avenger Van Damme, in a non-plot full of caricatured creeps howling like animals and breaking each others' bones. If it all seems made up on the spot, it largely was; this was planned as a sequel to the He-Man movie *Masters of the Universe* but mutated into a kickboxer apocalypse instead. 🦴

1989 (R) 85m/C Jean-Claude Van Damme, Deborah Richter, Vincent Klyn, Dayle Haddon, Alex Daniels, Rolf Muller; **D:** Albert Pyun; **W:** Kitty Chalmers; **C:** Philip Alan Waters; **M:** Kevin Bassinson. **VHS, Beta, LV** *MGM*

Cyborg 2

In the year 2074, a devious company that manufactures cyborgs plans to off the competition by sending them an advanced female creation (Angelina Jolie, daughter of actor Jon Voigt) filled with explosives. But a human technician is infatuated with the deadly doll, and the pair turns fugitive with help from mysterious freedom-fighter Jack Palance. There's no real link with the original *Cyborg,* and fine actors bring some juice to a B-movie pursuit-around-the-ruins plot. 🦴🦴

1993 (R) 99m/C Angelina Jolie, Elias Koteas, Jack Palance, Billy Drago, Allen (Goorwitz) Garfield; **D:** Michael Schroeder; **W:** Michael Schroeder, Ron Yanover, Mark Geldman; **C:** Jamie Thompson; **M:** Peter Allen. **VHS, LV** *VMK*

Cyborg Cop

DEA agent Phillip (Todd Jensen) is captured during a foreign drug raid and is turned into a half-man, half-machine by mad scientist Kessel (John Rhys-Davies), who wants to sell his cyborgs as unstoppable hitmen. Phillip's brother Jack (David Bradley) tries to come to his rescue. Lots of stunts and car chases and

even a minor romantic subplot with Jack and a tough reporter (Alonna Shaw). 🦴🦴

1993 (R) 97m/C David Bradley, John Rhys-Davies, Todd Jensen, Alonna Shaw; **W:** Glenn A. Bruce. **VHS, LV** *VMK*

Cyborg Soldier

Loose cannon cop Jack Ryan (David Bradley) is up against psycho killer Starkraven (Morgan Hunter), who gets turned into a new-model cyborg by your basic suspicious government agency. But when the cyborg decides to go on an unplanned human killing spree, Ryan gets to break out the heavy artillery to mow him down. Also available in an unrated version. **AKA:** Cyborg Cop 2. 🦴🦴🦴

1994 (R) 96m/C David Bradley, Morgan Hunter, Jill Pierce; **D:** Sam Firstenberg; **W:** Jon Stevens. **VHS, LV** *NLC*

Dagora, the Space Monster

Gangsters with incredibly silly voices tangle with a giant, slimy, pulsating whatsit from space that eats diamonds. Meanwhile, a group of scientists with slightly less silly voices join together in a massive effort to destroy the critter. This really isn't the best Japanese monster movie ever made, and the voices dubbed in for the U.S. version are particularly bad—coming from the grim-faced villains, they sound more like second-rate cartoon-characters than hardened criminals. Nonetheless, the movie's unusual blending of the gangster and monster genres makes it rather memorable. From Inoshiro Honda, director of the Godzilla films. **AKA:** Dagora; Space Monster Dagora; Uchudai Dogora; Uchu Daikaiiju Dogora. 🦴🦴

1965 80m/C *JP* Yosuke Natsuki, Yoko Fujiyama, Akiko Wakabayashi, Hiroshi Koizumi; **D:** Inoshiro Honda; **W:** Shinichi Sekizawa; **C:** Hajime Koizumi. **VHS, Beta** *VYY*

Daleks—Invasion Earth 2150 A.D.

A slightly more ambitious sequel to *Dr. Who and the Daleks.* Peter Cushing is back as the befuddled Doctor, once again accidentally transported into the future to do battle with the robotic mutants known as the Daleks. In this one the Daleks have taken over the Earth's population with mind control, and plot to blow out the Earth's core and use the whole planet as a titanic spaceship. Slicker and more interesting than the first movie, it will still be a bit of a shock to U.S. fans used to the British TV series. **AKA:** Invasion Earth 2150 A.D. 🦴🦴🦴

1966 81m/C *GB* Peter Cushing, Bernard Cribbins, Ray Brooks, Andrew Keir, Jill Curzon, Roberta Tovey; **D:** Gordon Flemyng; **W:** Milton Subotsky; **C:** John Wilcox. **VHS, Beta** *NO*

Damnation Alley

After a chilling World War III introduction, this post-Apocalypse film slides downhill quickly. Several disposable characters led by George Peppard and Jan-Michael Vincent set off across America in a huge "landmaster," in search of Albany. They have a series of improbable adventures, culminating in an ending that is so ridiculous it makes the rest of the film seem almost reasonable. Poorly adapted from Roger Zelazny's fine novel. 🦴🦴

1977 (PG) 87m/C George Peppard, Jan-Michael Vincent, Paul Winfield, Dominique Sanda, Jackie Earle Haley, Kip Niven; **D:** Jack Smight; **W:** Alan Sharp, Lukas Heller; **C:** Harry Strandling Jr.; **M:** Jerry Goldsmith. **VHS, Beta** *FOX*

Danger: Diabolik

Supercool '60s-style tongue-in-cheek thriller with loads of psychedelia, as many toys as a James Bond flick, fast cars, mini skirts, and more. But, unlike Bond, Diabolik is on the wrong side of the law. The title character even has a underground lair equipped with computers, an enormous rotating circular bed, and the coolest see-through showers ever. Diabolik (John Phillip Law) and his superbabe cohort (Marisa Mell) plan and execute one elaborate heist after another, each time managing to make government officials and the police look dumber and dumber. While the laughing gas press conference inspires as much confidence (and as many laughs) as most real life briefings, something must be done to stop Diabolik. How about melting all the gold left in the treasury into one enormous twenty-ton bar that would be impossible for any supercrimi-

nal to steal...except? Italy's Mario Bava, best known for his atmospheric horror films, changes genres with ease and even manages to pull off an explosive climax with a final image that parodies some of his more horrific closings. **AKA:** Diabolik. 🦴🦴🦴

1968 (PG-13) 99m/C *IT* John Phillip Law, Marisa Mell, Michel Piccoli, Terry-Thomas, Adolfo Celi; *D:* Mario Bava; *W:* Mario Bava, Dino Maiuri, Adriano Barracio; *C:* Antonio Rinaldi; *M:* Ennio Morricone. **VHS** *PAR*

The Dark

The titular bogeyman from outer space looks a little like James Arness' killer carrot in *The Thing,* with long hair and turn-signal eyes that emit laser beams. He kills people at night by yanking their heads off. The murders are accompanied by a soundtrack that includes loud voice-over whispers saying "The Dark." A competent cast is saddled with lots of unintentional laughs and zero scares. **AKA:** The Mutilator. 🦴🦴

1979 (R) 92m/C William Devane, Cathy Lee Crosby, Richard Jaeckel, Keenan Wynn, Vivian Blaine, Jacquelyn Hyde, Warren Kemmerling, Biff Elliot; *D:* John Cardos; *W:* Stanford Whitmore; *C:* John Morrill. **VHS, Beta** *MED*

The Dark Backward

Marty Malt (Judd Nelson) is having a bad day; in fact he's having a bad life. He's a garbage man and a desperate wanna-be stand-up comedian. On the good side, he doesn't feel the need to nurse on dead-girl breasts at the dump as his pal does. When he grows a third arm, the sheer grotesqueness finally gets him the laughs, the agent (Wayne Newton), and the girl that he needs. First-time director Adam Rifkin creates a darkly subversive alternate world *a la* David Lynch. The critics hated it. But so what! Humorous fat-woman sex and great casting of Newton and James Caan just add to the sick, sick fun. Reminiscent of *Brazil* and *Eraserhead,* and as urbanely weird as Jeunet and Caro's *Delicatessen.* 🦴🦴🦴

1991 (R) 97m/C Judd Nelson, Bill Paxton, Wayne Newton, Lara Flynn Boyle, James Caan, Rob Lowe, Claudia Christian; *D:* Adam Rifkin; *W:* Adam Rifkin. **VHS, LV** *COL*

The Dark Crystal

The Muppets go Tolkien in this ambitious epic from Jim Henson. Jen and Kira, the two last surviving Gelflings, journey to the castle of the cruel, vulture-like Skeksis to return a lost piece to the damaged Dark Crystal and thus heal an ancient wrong. Along the way, they encounter a multitude of strange beings both good and evil. The intricately detailed alien world was designed by children's book illustrator Brian Froud. The abundance of bizarre creatures make up for the familiar plot and make this a film that can be enjoyed over many repeated viewings. 🦴🦴🦴

1982 (PG) 93m/C *D:* Jim Henson, Frank Oz; *W:* David Odell; *C:* Oswald Morris; *M:* Trevor Jones, Trevor Jones; *V:* Dave Goelz, Kathryn Mullen, Jim Henson, Frank Oz. **VHS, Beta, LV** *TOU*

Dark Side of the Moon

Astronauts aboard a space shuttle on a routine mission to the far side of Earth's moon are bedeviled by a force that feeds on human emotion and consumes the soul. Could it be...SATAN?!! Hey, the Hound got it right on the first guess. Not to be confused with Pink Floyd, this turgid brew of sf and horror, set in the year 2022, even throws the Bermuda Triangle into the mix. 🦴🦴

1990 (R) 96m/C William Bledsoe, Alan Blumenfeld, John Diehl, Robert Sampson, Wendy MacDonald, Camilla More, Joe Turkel; *D:* D.J. Webster; *W:* Carey Hayes, Chad Hayes; *C:* Russ T. Alsobrook; *M:* Mark Ryder, Phil Davies. **VHS, LV** *VMK*

Dark Star

John Carpenter's directorial debut is a low-budget, sci-fi satire that focuses on a group of scientists whose mission is to destroy unstable planets. During their journey, they battle their alien mascot (who closely resembles a walking beach ball), as well as a "sensitive" and intelligent bombing device which starts to question the meaning of its existence. Faced with all these problems, the former captain is consulted—even though he's dead. Enjoyable early feature from John (*Halloween*) Carpenter and Dan (*Alien*) O'Bannon. Fun, weird, and

left for dead by gangsters, uses his invention of short-duration synthetic flesh to alter his charred visage and become Darkman, chameleon-like scourge of the criminal underworld. Kinetic camerawork, exquisite violence, and comic-book kitsch add up to a movie that's impossible to take seriously but fun while it lasts. Music by Danny Elfman. ♫ ♫ ♫

1990 (R) 96m/C Liam Neeson, Frances McDormand, Larry Drake, Colin Friels, Nelson Mashita, Jenny Agutter, Rafael H. Robledo; *D:* Sam Raimi; *W:* Chuck Pfarrer, Daniel Goldin, Joshua Goldin, Sam Raimi, Ivan Raimi; *M:* Danny Elfman. **VHS, Beta, LV** *MCA, CCB*

Darkman 2: The Return of Durant

The first direct-to-video sequel continues the adventures of disfigured scientist Peyton Westlake (now played by Arnold Vosloo), still conducting liquid-skin research in hopes of permanently repairing his hideous exterior. Old nemesis crime boss Robert G. Durant (Larry Drake) comes out of a coma and into the business of peddling ray guns, and Darkman has to once again confound the villain with disguises and sabotage. Sam Raimi, who directed the original film, served as one of the producers, and this limp follow up sorely misses his wizardry behind the camera lens. ♫ ♫

1994 (R) 93m/C Arnold Vosloo, Larry Drake, Kim Delaney, Renee O'Connor, Rod Wilson; *D:* Bradford May; *W:* Steven McKay, Chuck Pfarrer; *M:* Randy Miller. **VHS, LV** *MCA*

unpredictable—except for the cut-rate special effects it's a film ahead of its time. ♫ ♫ ♫

1974 (G) 95m/C Dan O'Bannon, Brian Narelle, Drew Pahich, Cal Kuniholm, Joe Saunders, Miles Watkins; *D:* John Carpenter; *W:* John Carpenter, Dan O'Bannon; *C:* Douglas Knapp; *M:* John Carpenter. **VHS, Beta, LV** *HHT, IME, VCI*

Dark Universe

An alien terror wants to conquer the Earth and make its inhabitants their new food source. ♫ ♪

1993 (R) 83m/C Blake Pickett, Cherie Scott, Bently Tittle, John Maynard, Paul Austin Saunders, Tom Ferguson, Steve Barkett, Joe Estevez, Patrick Moran; *D:* Steve Latshaw; *W:* Patrick Moran. **VHS, Beta** *PSM*

Darkman

Campy horror filmmaker Sam Raimi took the traditional gothic disfigured-man-seeks-revenge premise, mixed it with high-tech details, and turned the monster into a superhero. Mild-mannered scientist Peyton Westlake (Liam Neeson), gruesomely burned and

Darkman 3: Die Darkman Die

Peyton Westlake, the Darkman, is one unhappy scientist, made miserable through two previous films by his scarred, skull-like visage and spiritual agony. A steroid pusher, wanting to market the adrenaline that gives Westlake the strength of ten men, lures the hero with a promise of synthetic flesh equipment that will restore his features permanently, but in a struggle the villain's little daughter is facially disfigured too. Does anyone doubt whose face Darkman chooses to restore to pristine beauty? Viewers will find a premise grown tiresome through repetition. ♫ ♫

1995 (R) 87m/C Arnold Vosloo, Jeff Fahey, Darlanne Fluegel, Roxann Biggs-Dawson; *D:* Bradford May; *W:* Mike Werb, Michael Colleary; *C:* Bradford May; *M:* Randy Miller. **VHS, LV** *MCA*

D.A.R.Y.L.

Boy found by the side of the road is too polite, too honest, and too smart. Taken in by a childless couple, Daryl is told by a kid pal the necessity of imperfection (if you don't want the grown-ups to bother you too much) and he becomes more like a real child. But he's actually a lost American military project ("Data Analyzing Robot Youth Lifeform"), a computer brain in a cloned body. Intriguing parental *Twilight Zone* situation, aimed at family audiences, concentrating on characterizations rather than f/x hardware. Doesn't quite hold up to the finale; compare with the more effective TV pic *Prototype* with its grownup android. 🦴🦴🦴

1985 (PG) 100m/C Mary Beth Hurt, Michael McKean, Barret Oliver, Colleen Camp, Danny Corkill, Kathryn Walker, Josef Sommer; *D:* Simon Wincer; *W:* David Ambrose, Allan Scott, Jeffrey Ellis; *C:* Frank Watts; *M:* Marvin Hamlisch. **VHS, Beta, LV** *PAR*

The Day After

A powerful drama which graphically depicts the nuclear bombing of a Midwestern city and the after-effects on the survivors. A talented cast made the most of the then very topical and frightening material. Originally made for television, this film was the subject of enormous controversy when it aired in 1983. In the tradition of the best science-fiction horror films, it allowed a nation for whom nuclear war seemed a daily possibility to live out its worst nightmare, gathering huge ratings and vast media coverage in the process. 🦴🦴🦴

1983 122m/C Jason Robards Jr., JoBeth Williams, John Lithgow, Steve Guttenberg; *D:* Nicholas Meyer. **VHS, Beta, LV** *PAR*

The Day It Came to Earth

Completely silly and unbelievable sci-fi flick has meteor crashing into the watery grave of a mobster. The decomposed corpse is revived by the radiation and plots to take revenge on those who fitted him with cement shoes. **WOOF!**

1977 (PG) 89m/C Roger Manning, Wink Roberts, Bob Ginnaven, Rita Wilson, Delight de Bruine; *D:* Harry Z. Thomason. **VHS, Beta** *NO*

Day of the Triffids

The majority of Earth's population is blinded by a meteor shower. As if this isn't bad enough, it also causes plant spores to mutate into giant mobile carnivores. The plants look like big shaggy cornstalks, with poisonous whip-like tentacles. Howard Keel, who managed to retain his sight, fights to survive in a hostile new world. Well-done entry in the World Apocalypse category, adapted from John Wyndham's (*The Midwich Cuckoos*) classic novel. 🦴🦴🦴

1963 94m/C Howard Keel, Janet Scott, Nicole Maurey, Kieron Moore, Mervyn Johns, Ian Wilson, Alison Leggatt, Janina Faye, John Tate, Arthur Gross, Ewan Roberts; *D:* Steve Sekely; *W:* Philip Yordan; *C:* Ted Moore; *M:* Ron Goodwin. **VHS, Beta, LV** *MED, MRV, PSM*

You plant 'em, you prune 'em, and then they turn on you. Janet Scott in *Day of the Triffids.*

And What a Day It Was

> "In nature's scheme of things, there are certain plants which are carnivorous—or eating plants. The Venus Fly Trap is one of the best known of these plants. A fly, drawn to the plant by a sweet syrup, brushes against trigger bristles. Just how these plants digest their prey has yet to be explained. There is much still to learn about these fascinating eating plants. This is a newcomer: Triffidus Cellesus, brought to Earth on the meteorite during...THE DAY OF THE TRIFFIDS."

—introduction to *Day of the Triffids.*

> "There are
> several
> thousand
> questions I'd
> like to ask you."
>
> —The professor (Sam Jaffee) to
> Klaatu (Michael Rennie) in *The
> Day the Earth Stood Still.*

The Day the Earth Caught Fire

"World saved." "World doomed." Which headline will be correct after the Earth is knocked out of its orbit and hurtles toward the sun? Leo McKern stars as the gruff science reporter who discovers the catastrophe after investigating the sudden floods, cyclones, and mysterious mists that arise in the wake of simultaneous nuclear testing at the North and South Poles by the Americans and Russians. A literate script and played-for-realism newsroom setting will keep you sweating as the world's powers unite to try and get the planet back on track.

1961 95m/B Janet Munro, Edward Judd, Leo McKern, Michael Goodliffe, Bernard Braden; **D:** Val Guest; **W:** Val Guest, Wolf Mankowitz. British Academy Awards '61: Best Screenplay. **VHS, Beta** *REP, KAR*

The Day the Earth Stood Still

The first big-budget sf feature of the '50s has aged gracefully. Michael Rennie stars as the alien Klaatu, who arrives in D.C. to warn Earth's leaders that our planet faces obliteration should they not halt atomic testing. His invitation to live in peace with "the other planets" is met with fear and hysteria. He escapes hospital confinement and takes a room in a boarding house among us. Patricia Neal co-stars as the woman with whom he entrusts his secret identity. If the effects are a tad simple, Gort is still one of the screen's great robots. The story is involving, and the sight of tanks and howitzers in the midst of Washington's monuments and memorials is more frightening than any flying saucer. It's a film about fear with strong Christian influences, first-rate performances in all of the leads, and one of Bernard Herrmann's better scores. Based on the Harry Bates story, "Farewell to the Master." Among the greatest science-fiction films of all time, well worth a third or fourth look. "Klaatu barada nikto!" 🗡🗡🗡🗡

1951 92m/B Michael Rennie, Patricia Neal, Hugh Marlowe, Sam Jaffe, Frances Bavier, Lock Martin, Billy Gray; **D:** Robert Wise; **W:** Edmund H. North; **C:** Leo Tover; **M:** Bernard Herrmann. **VHS, Beta, LV** *FOX, FCT, MLB*

The Day the Sky Exploded

Sci-fi disaster drama doesn't live up to the grandiose title, as a runaway rocket ship hits the sun, unleashing an asteroid shower that threatens Earth with tidal waves, earthquakes, heat waves, and terrible dialogue. The highlight of this Franco-Italian effort is the cinematography by horror director Mario Bava. **AKA:** Death from Outer Space; La Morte Viene Dalla Spazio; Le Danger Vient de l'Escape. 🗡

1957 80m/B *FR IT* Paul Hubschmid, Madeleine Fischer, Fiorella Mari, Ivo Garrani, Dario Michaelis; **D:** Richard Benson. **VHS** *NOS, FCT*

Day the World Ended

This was exploitation film guru Roger Corman's first science-fiction movie. Five survivors of a nuclear holocaust stumble onto a desert ranch house fortress owned by a survivalist (Paul Birch) and his daughter (Lori Nelson). Animosity quickly develops between the "good" survivors (Birch, Nelson, and wholesome Richard Denning) and the "bad" survivors—a tough-talking gangster (Mike "Mannix" Connors) and his moll (Adele Jergens). Eventually another survivor—this one disfigured and wasting away from radiation poisoning, stumbles into their refuge. The radiation

is slowly changing him into something even less pleasant, and it seems he's got friends waiting in the hills around the house. The one monster we get to see isn't particularly convincing, and the heroes' '50s-macho posturings will inspire more laughter than admiration from today's audiences. Still, the film holds up pretty well today, and paved the way for countless other radiated monster epics during the '50s. 🎞️🎞️

1955 79m/B Paul Birch, Lori Nelson, Adele Jergens, Raymond Hatton, Paul Dubov, Richard Denning, Mike Connors; **D:** Roger Corman; **W:** Lou Rusoff; **C:** Jock Feindel. **VHS** *COL*

Day Time Ended

Glowing UFOs streaking across the sky, an alien mechanical device with long menacing appendages, and dinosaurs battling in the front yard are only some of the bizarre phenomena witnessed by a family whose desert dream home slips around in the time continuum. Moral: always get an expert to check the foundation. Good special effects are the only reason this undercooked Charles Band production exists—it could have been called "The Day the Scriptwriter Stood Still." **AKA:** Vortex; Timewarp. 🎞️🕊️

1978 80m/C Chris Mitchum, Jim Davis, Dorothy Malone, Marcey Lafferty, Natasha Ryan, Scott Kolden; **D:** John Cardos; **W:** David Schmoeller, J. Larry Carroll, Wayne Schmidt; **C:** John Morrill; **M:** Richard Band. **VHS, Beta, LV** *MED, MRV*

Dead End Drive-In

In a surreal, grim future a man is trapped at a drive-in theatre-cum-concentration camp, where the government incarcerates undesirables. Fueled by an original concept and good acting, this dystopian drama has enough strangeness and dark thrills to make it memorable. 🎞️🎞️🕊️

1986 (R) 92m/C *AU* Ned Manning, Natalie McCurry, Peter Whitford; **D:** Brian Trenchard-Smith; **W:** Peter Smalley; **C:** Paul Murphy; **M:** Frank Strangio. **VHS, Beta** *NWV*

Dead Man Walking

In a post-holocaust future, half the population has been stricken with a deadly disease

(whose exact nature remains undescribed) and so-what attitudes abound. Thus Wings Hauser, an infected mercenary, plunges heedlessly into danger when he's hired to rescue a rich girl kidnaped by Brion James and held in the plague zone. Interesting premise yields standard post-apocalypse action, done with little finesse by moonlighting porn filmmakers. 🎞️

1988 (R) 90m/C Wings Hauser, Brion James, Pamela Ludwig, Sy Richardson, Leland Crooke, Jeffrey Combs; **D:** Gregory Brown; **W:** R.J. Marx. **VHS** *REP*

Dead Space

Dead space lay between the ears of whoever thought we needed this remake of 1982's *Forbidden World*. At a lab on a hostile planet an experimental vaccine mutates into a prickly

Who knew? Future Devo alumni make their film debut in *The Day the Earth Stood Still*.

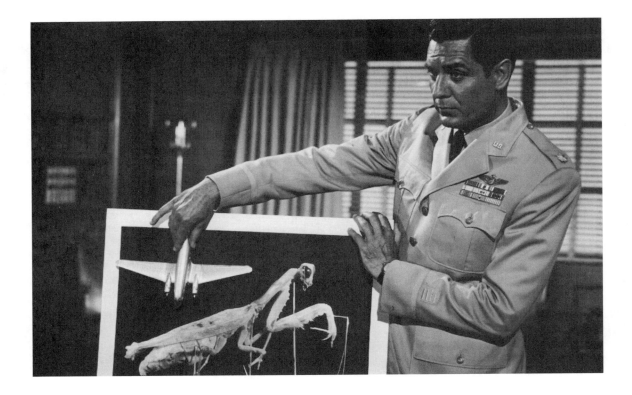

"Look at it this way. Compared to this 747 the mantis is way bigger. And deadlier." Defense spending at work in ***The Deadly Mantis.***

puppet monster who menaces the medicos. What humanity is really clamoring for is a vaccine against cheapo *Alien* ripoffs. 🗡

1990 (R) 72m/C Marc Singer, Laura Tate, Bryan Cranston, Judith Chapman; *D:* Fred Gallo; *W:* Catherine Cyran; *C:* Jonathan Winfrey; *M:* Daniel May. **VHS, LV** *COL*

Dead Weekend

Alien is detected in town, so the government's psycho paramilitary riot squad clears out citizens and begins enthusiastically shooting whoever's left. Lucky soldier Stephen Baldwin has close encounters of the closest kind with the visitor, a hot space babe who needs sex to survive and regularly transforms into an entirely different, seductive woman. With no f/x worth mentioning, this airhead mixture of sleaze and pseudohip social commentary made its debut on Showtime Cable (or did you guess that already?). **WOOF!**

1995 (R) 82m/C Stephen Baldwin, David Rasche, Damian Jones; *D:* Amos Poe; *W:* Joel Rose; *M:* Steve Hunter. **VHS** *PAR*

Dead Zone

With the exception of a few sequences, this one at first seems like director David Cronenberg selling out in order to make a movie for a big studio. But who cares? This is a great adaptation of the Stephen King thriller. Christopher Walken is given the gift of psychic powers following a near-fatal (and quite spectacular) accident and subsequent five-year-long coma. Regaining consciousness, he finds that he has lost his bride-to-be (the now-married Brooke Adams) and acquired the ability to see the personal future of anyone he touches, and a damned scary thing it is. Good performances all around, particularly Walken and Martin Sheen as a psychotic, let-me-push-the-button politician. Plenty of tension, philosophical dilemmas, a patently Cronenberg use of

scissors...the "mainstream" finally got to see what Cronenberg could do. 🐾🐾🐾

1983 (R) 104m/C Christopher Walken, Brooke Adams, Tom Skerritt, Martin Sheen, Herbert Lom, Anthony Zerbe, Colleen Dewhurst; **D:** David Cronenberg; **W:** Jeffrey Boam; **M:** Michael Kamen. **VHS, Beta, LV** PAR

Deadlock

Rutger Hauer and Mimi Rogers star as inmates in a prison of the future. This prison has no walls, no fences and no guards—and no one EVER escapes. Each prisoner wears an explosive collar that is tuned to the same frequency as one of the other prisoner's. Should the two separate by more than 100 yards, the collars explode. When Rogers convinces Hauer that they are on the same frequency, the two escape. Trouble is, they are being pursued not only by the police, but by Hauer's former partners in crime as well. Can the two find the freedom they are looking for—without losing their heads? Originally made for cable television. 🐾🐾🐾

1991 (R) 103m/C Rutger Hauer, Mimi Rogers, Joan Chen, James Remar, Stephen Tobolowsky, Basil Wallace; **D:** Lewis Teague. **VHS, Beta, LV** VTR, FXV, MED

Deadlock 2

Same basic plot as in the first TV movie. Tony Archer (Esai Morales) and Allie Thompson (Nia Peeples), two strangers who have been set up by the same corrupt businessman, are being held in a violent correctional facility. Inmates wear electronic collars programmed to explode if they venture too far apart. But Tony figures a way around this trap only to discover he and Allie are caught in another. **AKA:** Deadlocked: Escape from Zone 14. 🐾🐾

1994 (R) 120m/C Esai Morales, Nia Peeples, Stephen McHattie, Jon Cuthbert; **D:** Graeme Campbell. **VHS** HMK

Deadly Harvest

Scientists' worst fears have been realized—due to ecological abuse and over-development of the land, food has become extremely scarce. This in turn has caused people to become a bit savage. They are particularly nasty to a farmer and his family. Not a bad plot, but a poorly acted film. 🐾

1972 (PG) 86m/C Clint Walker, Nehemiah Persoff, Kim Cattrall, David G. Brown, Gary Davies; **D:** Timothy Bond. **VHS, Beta** VTR, NWV

The Deadly Mantis

After an opening explains the U.S. military's Distant Early Warning Line in the manner of a government training film, that hardware tracks a giant prehistoric praying mantis released from an iceberg via volcanic eruption (hey, it could happen). Roaring like a bear, the insect bugs Washington, D.C., and New York City until humans fumigate. Typically silly '50s sci fi with awful comedy relief, decent monster f/x. Tape includes the original coming-attractions trailer. **AKA:** The Incredible Praying Mantis. 🐾🐾

1957 79m/B Craig Stevens, William Hopper, Alix Talton, Pat Conway, Donald Randolph; **D:** Nathan (Hertz) Juran; **W:** Martin Berkeley. **VHS** MCA

Deadly Weapon

Producer Charles Band raided his own *Laserblast* from 10 years earlier for this rather nerdish wish fulfillment, when 15-year-old geek Rodney Eastman finds a secret anti-matter weapon conveniently fallen off a military transport. He uses the way-cool death ray to threaten bullies, parents, a preacher, and other nasty authority figures. You'll hardly like the kid any more than the grownups, even with the ultimately tragic script taking his side. Good but brief f/x. 🐾🐾

1988 (PG-13) 89m/C Rodney Eastman, Gary Frank, Michael Horse, Ed Nelson, Kim Walker; **D:** Michael Miner; **W:** Michael Miner. **VHS** TWE, HHE

Death Machine

Exec uncovers questionable scientific project at weapons technology company and the scientist in charge decides to get even by testing his death machine, which works by sensing fear, in corporate headquarters. 🐾🐾

1995 (R) 99m/C Brad Dourif, Ely Pouget, William Hootkins; **D:** Stephen Norrington. **VHS, LV** VMK

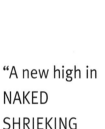

> "A new high in NAKED SHRIEKING TERROR!"
>
> —*Day the World Ended.*

Death Race 2000.
Gee! How do I
enter?!

followed by *Deathsport*. Made for television.
♬ ♬ ▷

1975 (R) 80m/C David Carradine, Simone Griffeth, Sylvester Stallone, Mary Woronov, Roberta Collins; **D:** Paul Bartel; **W:** Charles B. Griffith, Robert Thom. **VHS, Beta** *VDM, MRV*

Death Sport

This followup to Roger Corman's *Death Race 2000* could have used more of that film's freewheeling spirit and black humor. David Carradine and former Playboy Playmate of the Year and legendary B-movie queen Claudia Jennings star as "Ranger Guides" who are pursued across the post-nuclear wilderness by motorcycle-riding "Statesmen" who want them for gladiatorial contests, and cannibal mutants. Jennings was killed in a car crash shortly after this was released. Much more interesting than the film is the rivalry between Carradine and director Nicholas Niciphor (who for this film used the pseudonym Henry Suso), which was revealed in a series of amazing letters printed in *Psychotronic* magazine (issues 7, 9, and 12). ♬ ♬ ▷

1978 (R) 83m/C David Carradine, Claudia Jennings, Richard Lynch, William Smithers, Will Walker, David McLean, Jesse Vint; **D:** Henry Suso, Allan Arkush; **W:** Donald Stewart, Henry Suso; **C:** Gary Graver. **VHS, Beta** *WAR, OM*

Death of the Incredible Hulk

Scientist David Banner's new job just may provide the clues for stopping his transformation into the monstrous Incredible Hulk. But first there are terrorists after the Hulk who need to be defeated and Banner's new romance to contend with. Made for television. ♬ ▷

1990 96m/C Bill Bixby, Lou Ferrigno, Elizabeth Gracen, Philip Sterling; **D:** Bill Bixby. **VHS** *RHI*

Death Watch

This provocative drama unwittingly anticipated the abuses of today's tabloid talk shows. In a future where science has banished disease and people die of old age, a terminal illness is big news. Romy Schneider stars as the doomed Katharine, who is courted by TV producer Harry Dean Stanton. He wants to give the morbid public what it wants—death—so he signs her to a contract allowing him to film her last days. When she flees, he hires Harvey Keitel to pursue her and gain her confidence. Keitel has had a miniature camera implanted in his brain which beams back to the station all that he sees. "Art house" science fiction, brooding, thoughtful, and deliberately paced. ♬ ♬ ♬

1980 (R) 128m/C *FR GE* Romy Schneider, Harvey Keitel, Harry Dean Stanton, Max von Sydow; **D:** Bertrand Tavernier; **W:** Bertrand Tavernier, David Rayfiel. **VHS, LV** *SUE*

Death Race 2000

In the 21st century, a leather-suited David Carradine is the defending champion of the nationally televised Transcontinental Death Race, in which participants score points for running over pedestrians. His challengers include Sylvester Stallone as Machine Gun Joe Viterbo, Mary Woronov as Calamity Jane, and Roberta Collins as Mathilda the Hun. A year later, Stallone would become a Hollywood contender with the Oscar-winning *Rocky*. Based on the 1956 story by Ib Melchior, and

Temporal Anomalies

It's a good idea to stamp expiration dates on food, medicine, and unexposed film—but not so prudent with sf. Even well-told genre tales tend to lose their luster if their predictions are tied down to a specific year that has come and gone.

The big exception is George Orwell's *1984*, which, although meant as a commentary on society in 1948, even today remains a potent warning, probably more so than had Orwell gone with an early working title, "The Last Man in Europe." However, scattered across screen sci fi are less fortunate examples of portentious prognostications by camera-wielding Cassandras....

1980 in JUST IMAGINE (1930): *Just Imagine* is an oddball, unwieldy mixture of vaudeville gags, banal musical numbers, and satirical speculation in which jokester El Brendel (a then-popular comical Swede) is struck by lightning in 1930 and resurrected by the super-science of 1980, when numbers have replaced names, pills are food, and test-tube infants can be bought at sidewalk vending machines. Pic concludes with a 'rocket plane' journey to a Mars inhabited by pretty alien girls and evil twins. Its elaborate futuristic Manhattan skyline contributed to a budget that helped make this a massive financial flop, which reportedly gave epic-scale sf a reputation as box-office poison in Hollywood for years afterwords. Though not yet released on video, footage from *Just Imagine* resurfaced in *Buck Rogers* and other fantasies.

1970 in THINGS TO COME (1936): Spanning 100 years, this H.G. Wells-inspired classic of sf prophecy starts out with an uncanny (but at the time, not uncommon) forecast of World War in 1940, complete with a Pearl-Harbor style sneak bombardment of a placid England. The ensuing battle and plague-tainted aftermath lasts though the 1960s. In 1970 a feudal gangster rules the rubble through brute force until technologically advanced airmen from an authoritarian Utopia crush his ragtag militia. The pic ends with the first attempt at a lunar expedition—in 2036.

1970 in PROJECT MOON BASE (1953): Master sf author Robert Heinlein contributed to this screen cheapie (conceived as a TV pilot but released to theatres) that hits close to the calendar with an orbital moon shot in 1970. When the ship crashes on the lunar surface the crew erect an ersatz shelter, and the infamous finale has a matronly lady U.S. president performing the long-distance marriage ceremony via radio of the two male and female survivors, thus preserving 1970s American moral decency.

1973 in IT! THE TERROR FROM BEYOND SPACE (1958): Minor classic of the alien-monster genre undercuts its serious tone a tad with the opening statement that it takes place in 1973, in the aftermath of the first successful human voyage to Mars.

1980s in QUEEN OF OUTER SPACE (1958) and CONQUEST OF SPACE (1955): Former is a camp-classic B-picture (whose script simply reversed the digits of its year of release *a la* George Orwell); latter is a ponderous, high-minded epic that drew from the latest scientific sources. But both followed the widely accepted doctrine that permanent, manned space colonies, shuttlecraft, and giant zero-G launch platforms would have to be exist as a precondition before anyone dared attempt a landing on any other planets or moons.

1965 in BATTLE OF THE WORLDS (1959): This Japanese War-of- the-Worlds type saga envisions the first space station, of traditional doughnut shape, activated in 1965. This draws the attention of nasty dwarf aliens on the moon, who destroy it and provoke interplanetary war with the united and resourceful nations of Earth.

1979 in GORATH (1962): Similar in concept to *Battle of the Worlds,* this Japanese disaster epic depicts the nations of the world as seasoned spacefarers in the near future, who together accomplish incredible and improbable engineering feats to fight an external menace; in this case a wandering star on a collision course.

1990 in 1990 (1977): Orwellian BBC TV series (not available on video in the U.S.) depicting life in tomorrow's dismal England dominated by left-wing welfare-state bureaucracy. Heroic reporter Edward Woodward regularly leads dissidents to that free-market paradise, the USA. The program only lasted a year, but it must have done its job; ruling conservatives have won elections over there ever since.

1993 in PRIMAL SCREAM (1987): This low-budget sf detective tale gets the Hound's acceleration-evolution award for foreseeing aerial cars in every garage and deep-space colonies only six years around the corner.

1994 in ALIEN NATION (1988): Short-dating the arrival of thousands of aliens in the very near future mainly gave filmmakers an excuse to use footage of President Ronald Reagan out of context, apparently welcoming the 'Newcomers.'

> "The price of admission...is the rest of your life!"
>
> —*Dead End Drive-In.*

Deep Red

The clever opening toys with perceptions of scale, revealing that an incredible alien spaceship zooming to Earth is about the size of a splinter. When it lodges in the body of a little girl, her altered blood chemistry can confer immortality, indestructibility, shape-shifting, and other superpowers. Good guy Michael Biehn (*The Terminator*) has to protect the child from ruthless scientist John de Lancie and his goons. Made-for-cable TV movie soon turns into standard action despite the offbeat curtain-raiser. 🎞🎞

1994 (R) 85m/C Michael Biehn, Joanna Pacula, John de Lancie; **D:** Craig R. Baxley; **W:** D. Brent Mote. **VHS, LV** *MCA*

Deep Space

"A UFO? What's that, some kind of foreign car?" says the exceptionally stupid cop hero of this *Alien* ripoff. He's intent on nailing the lawbreaker who devoured his partner, a flesh-eating, fanged, and tentacled horror from a crashed space probe. Some humorous moments try to keep one from thinking too hard about how much the monster resembles H.R. Giger's bigger-budget creation. 🎞🎞

1987 90m/C Charles Napier, Ann Turkel, Ron Glass, Bo Svenson, Julie Newmar, James Booth, Anthony Eisley; **D:** Fred Olen Ray. **VHS, Beta** *TWE*

Deepstar Six

While James Cameron's epic *The Abyss* was still in production, various cheapo filmmakers raced to have their own undersea sci-fi creature features in cinemas first. In this triumph of speed over quality, scientists in a submarine lab suffer a bad case of the crabs. Make that one crab: a giant, hungry crustacean out to avenge countless boiled lobster tails. Silly stuff shows its low budget when the monster surfaces, though there is a standout human performance by Miguel Ferrer. 🎞🎞

1989 (R) 97m/C Taurean Blacque, Nancy Everhard, Greg Evigan, Miguel Ferrer, Matt McCoy, Nia Peeples, Cindy Pickett, Marius Weyers; **D:** Sean S. Cunningham; **W:** Geof Miller, Lewis Abernathy; **C:** Mac Ahlberg; **M:** Harry Manfredini. **VHS, Beta, LV** *NO*

Def-Con 4

Three astronauts watch helplessly as a nuclear holocaust devastates Earth below, then return to the planet's surface to try to start civilization again. In the way are the usual *Road Warrior* slimeballs (led by a young military brat), who don't want to give up their dominance. Canadian postnuke hijinks with streak of sadism unusually strong even for this genre. 🎞🎞

1985 (R) 85m/C *CA* Maury Chaykin, Kate Lynch, Tim Choate, Lenore Zann, Kevin King, John Walsch; **D:** Paul Donovan; **W:** Paul Donovan; **C:** Doug Connell, Les Kriszan; **M:** Christopher Young. **VHS, Beta** *NWV, VTR*

Delicatessen

Set in post-apocalyptic 21st-century Paris, this hilarious debut from directors Jean-Marie Jeunot and Marc Caro focuses on the lives of the oddball tenants over a butcher shop. Although there is a famine, the butcher shop is always stocked with fresh meat...and the building does seem to go through quite a few tenants. Part comedy, part horror, part romance, this film merges a cacophony of sights and sounds with intriguing results. Watch for the scene involving a symphony of creaking bed springs, a squeaky bicycle pump, a cello, and clicking knitting needles. Shot almost entirely in browns and whites, you'll be hard pressed to find another film with such unique visuals, so unique that Terry Gilliam, a master of movie images himself, presented it worldwide. In French with English subtitles. 🎞🎞🎞

1992 (R) 95m/C *FR* Marie-Laure Dougnac, Dominique Pinon, Karin Viard, Jean Claude Dreyfus, Ticky Holgado, Anne Marie Pisani, Edith Ker, Patrick Paroux, Jean-Luc Caron; **D:** Jean-Marie Jeunet, Marc Caro; **W:** Gilles Adrien; **M:** Carlos D'Alessi. Cesar Awards '92: Best Art Direction/Set Decoration, Best Writing. **VHS, Beta, LV** *PAR, INJ, BTV*

Deluge

Tidal waves causd by earthquakes have destroyed most of New York (though some may think this is no great loss) in this early sci-fi pic. 🎞🎞

1933 72m/B Edward Van Sloan, Peggy Shannon, Sidney Blackmer, Fred Kohler Sr., Matt Moore, Samuel S. Hinds, Lane Chandler; **D:** Felix Feist. **VHS, Beta** *MWP*

Demolition Man

Sf shoot-'em-up meets all the demands of the genre—lots of fights and macho posturing, gunfire and/or shattering glass at least every seven minutes, an explosion or two in between, car chases and cartoon characterizations—and those are all plugged into a script that has surprisingly witty moments. As a cop and a criminal transported to the near future, Stallone and Snipes (under ugly blond hair!) deliver nice tongue-in-cheek performances. The film borrows liberally from several sources. The most obvious are H.G. Wells' *The Time Machine,* the film *Total Recall,* and Kurt Vonnegut's apocalyptic creation, Ice Nine. The best parts of the script are the satiric digs it takes at all forms of polite behavior that new Puritans of both the right and left are demanding these days. 🎬🎬

1993 (R) 115m/C Sylvester Stallone, Wesley Snipes, Sandra Bullock, Nigel Hawthorne, Benjamin Bratt, Bob Gunton, Glenn Shadix; *D:* Marco Brambilla; *W:* Daniel Waters, Robert Reneau, Peter M. Lenkov; *M:* Elliot Goldenthal. Nominations: MTV Movie Awards '94: Best Villain (Snipes). **VHS, Beta, LV, 8mm** *WAR*

Demon City Shinjuku

In the near future the evil Levih Rah has created a "Demon City" surrounded by a moat in the heart of Tokyo, where he commands his army of thugs and monsters. Sayama Rama and the streetwise Kyoya venture into Shinjuku in search of Sayama's kidnapped father. They encounter the cynical Mephisto, an aging mystic whose strange healing powers may be able to help them. They'd better hurry—Levih Rah is scheduled to destroy the entire planet in three days! An impressive example of Japanese animation. In Japanese with English subtitles. 🎬🎬🎬

1993 82m/C *JP* **VHS, LV** *CPM*

Demon of Paradise

Dynamite fishing off the coast of Hawaii unleashes a homicidal marine lizard-man on a resort island. Belated and tedious Filipino *Creature from the Black Lagoon* ripoff ambles

as clumsily as the Godzillian monster costume. **WOOF!**

1987 (R) 84m/C Kathryn Witt, William Steis, Leslie Huntly, Laura Banks, Frederick Bailey; *D:* Cirio H. Santiago; *W:* Frederick Bailey. **VHS, Beta** *WAR*

Demon Seed

Early entry in the computer-gone-nuts subgenre, based on a Dean R. Koontz novel, is surprisingly watchable and tense. The world's most sophisticated computer, Proteus IV, puts the moves on his creator's estranged wife (Julie Christie) when it takes over the running of her house. The second half of the film is much stronger than the beginning. 🎬🎬🎬

1977 (R) 97m/C Julie Christie, Fritz Weaver, Gerrit Graham, Berry Kroeger, Ron Hays, Lisa Lu; *D:* Donald Cammell; *W:* Robert Jaffe, Roger O. Hirson; *C:* Bill Butler; *V:* Robert Vaughn. **VHS, Beta, LV** *MGM*

Destination Moon

American scientists and engineers finance their own moon rocket, despite government interference. Story of man's first lunar voyage was so influential that it not only set the format for almost every space travel film for the next 15 years (for example, one crew member must be from Brooklyn), but it also probably gave NASA a few ideas. Contains Chesley Bonstell's famous astronomical artwork and a cartoon in which Woody Woodpecker helps explain how the mission will work to potential investors (and the audience). Includes previews of coming attractions from classic science-fiction films. 🎬🎬🎬

1950 91m/C Warner Anderson, Tom Powers, Dick Wesson, Erin O'Brien Moore, John Archer, Ted Warde; *D:* Irving Pichel; *W:* Robert Heinlein, Rip Van Ronkel, James O'Hanlon; *C:* Lionel Linden. Academy Awards '50: Best Special Effects; Nominations: Academy Awards '50: Best Art Direction/Set Decoration (Color). **VHS, Beta, LV** *SNC, MED*

Destination Moonbase Alpha

In the 21st century, an explosion has destroyed half the moon, causing it to break away from the Earth's orbit. The moon is cast far away, but the 311 people manning Alpha, a research station on the moon, must continue their search for other life forms in outer space.

> "This was the day that engulfed the world in terror!"
> —*The Deadly Mantis.*

A thankless task. Pilot for the television series *Space: 1999.* 🎵🎵

1975 93m/C Martin Landau, Barbara Bain, Barry Morse. **VHS, Beta** *FOX*

Destination Saturn

Buck Rogers awakens from suspended animation in the twenty-fifth century. **AKA:** Buck Rogers. 🎵🎵

1939 90m/B Buster Crabbe, Constance Moore; **D:** Ford Beebe. **VHS, Beta** *NOS, CAB, VYY*

Destroy All Monsters

The ultimate Japanese monster bash! Aliens from the planet Kilaak take control of Godzilla and his monstrous colleagues, who've been incarcerated on a remote island. Various monsters are dispatched to destroy different Earth cities (Godzilla is sent to New York, apparently to give Tokyo a rest). Adding insult to injury, the Kilaakians send three-headed Ghidrah in to take care of the loose ends. Can the planet possibly survive this madness? In addition to Godzilla, this classic Toho flick stars the Son of Godzilla, Mothra, Rodan, Angilas, Varan, Baragon, Spigas, and others. If you're wondering why relative unknown Gorosaurus (from *King Kong Escapes*) is featured so prominently—the reason has to do with the condition of the monster suits, some of which were in bad shape and not vital enough to the plot to be rebuilt. Old Angilas (from *Godzilla Raids Again*) picked up some admirers with this film, as a result of his courage shown in the scrap with Ghidrah. This was director Inoshiro Honda's second-to-last Godzilla pic, and the last really good one for nearly two decades. Dubbing is better than usual. U.S. video TV version is cropped and slightly edited. **AKA:** Kaiju Soshingeki; Operation Monsterland. 🎵🎵🎵

1968 (G) 88m/C *JP* Akira Kubo, Jun Tazaki, Yoshio Tsuchiya, Kyoko Ai, Yukiko Kobayashi, Kenji Sahara, Andrew Hughes, Emi Ito, Yumi Ito; **D:** Inoshiro Honda; **W:** Kaoru Mabuchi, Inoshiro Honda; **C:** Taiichi Kankura. **VHS** *FRG*

Destroy All Planets

Aliens whose spaceships turn into giant flying squids are attacking Earth. Once again Gamera, the flying, fire-breathing space-turtle must bust his shell to save the day. He's assisted in his task by two rather annoying little boys with a miniature submarine. This silly but amusing film was the fourth in the Gamera series, and padded out with a turtle soup of footage from the big guy's previous adventures. Anyone who thinks all heroic turtles are teenage ninjas should find this film very enlightening. 🎵🎵

1968 ?m/C *JP* Peter Williams, Kojiro Hongo, Toru Takatsuka, Carl Crane, Michiko Yaegaki; **D:** Noriaki Yuasa. **VHS** *SNC*

Devil Girl from Mars

Sexy female from Mars, clad in a black vinyl skirt, arrives at a small Scottish inn with her very large, clumsy robot to announce that a Martian feminist revolution has occurred. But Mars needs men! The distaff aliens are in search of healthy Earth males for breeding purposes. Believe it or not, the red-blooded Earth males don't want to go and therein lies the rub. An enjoyably ridiculous space farce. Based on a stage play, the characters seem to be as equally concerned with their soap opera problems as they are with the Martian invasion, and always take time for a cup of tea before planning their defenses. 🎵🎵

1954 76m/B *GB* Hugh McDermott, Hazel Court, Patricia Laffan, Peter Reynolds, Adrienne Corri, Joseph Tomelty, Sophie Stewart, John Laurie, Anthony Richmond; **D:** David MacDonald; **W:** John C. Mather, James Eastwood. **VHS, Beta** *NOS, MRV, SNC*

Die, Monster, Die!

A young man (Nick Adams) visits his fiancee's family home, even though everyone in the neighboring village advises him against it. He finds his prospective father-in-law is a reclusive, wheelchair-bound scientist (Boris Karloff) who's been fooling around with a radioactive meteorite in his laboratory. As a result, he's got a greenhouse full of mutant animals and his disfigured wife runs around the estate in a veil scaring people. Eventually

the meteorite gives Karloff back his ability to walk, but in the process changes him into a glowing, metallic monster. This adaptation of H.P. Lovecraft's classic "The Color Out of Space" is pretty pale compared to the original, but Karloff (in one of his last roles and beginning to look a bit peaked) still delivers a great performance, investing every line with quiet menace. **AKA:** Monster of Terror. 🦴🦴ᵇ

1965 80m/C *GB* Boris Karloff, Nick Adams, Suzan Farmer, Patrick Magee; *D:* Daniel Haller; *M:* Don Banks. **VHS, LV** *NO*

Digital Man

Umpteenth post-apocalyptic sf action movie is about an army patrol composed of humans and cyborgs (who think they are human) on the trail of the titular Matthias Hues, a super-cyborg who totes a quintuple-barreled rocket gun. The main attractions are effective use of desert locations, fairly good effects, and a little cornball humor. 🦴🦴

1994 (R) 95m/C Ken Olandt, Adam Baldwin, Ed Lauter, Matthias Hues, Kristen Dalton, Paul Gleason; *D:* Phillip J. Roth; *W:* Phillip J. Roth, Ronald Schmidt. **VHS** *REP*

Dinosaur Island

Five U.S. soldiers survive a plane crash on an island where huge-breasted ladies dwell without males and, despite their Amazonian ferocity, remain at the mercy of hungry prehistoric dinosaurs that roam the place. Will the military men score?—against the monsters, we mean (no we don't). Dinos, including the big reptile prop left over from *Carnosaur,* are outrageously fake rubber constructions and stop-motion puppets. Some shooting on this campy Roger Corman sexploitation comedy-fantasy took place on David Carradine's ranch, Bronson Canyon, and over a hill near where *The Flintstones* was in production. **WOOF!**

1993 (R) 85m/C Ross Hagen, Richard Gabai, Antonia Dorian, Peter Spellos, Tom Shell, Griffin Drew, Steve Barkett, Toni Naples; *D:* Jim Wynorski, Fred Olen Ray; *W:* Bob Sheridan, Christopher Wooden. **VHS** *NHO, HVL*

"Those pants are to die for," says the fashion-conscious Boris Karloff to his lion pal in *Die, Monster, Die!*

Dinosaurus!

A nasty Tyrannosaurus Rex and a gentle brontosaurus and apeman appear for some reason on an island. The bronto and apeman befriend a little boy. Guess who the villain is? This film is really aimed at dinosaur-crazy kids, and they'll probably enjoy it. Adults lassooed into watching it will find it harmless fun. Oh, and the T. Rex fights a steam-shovel, prefiguring a scene that would later turn up in *Carnosaur 2*(!). This only goes to show that prehistory repeats itself. 🦴

1960 85m/C Ward Ramsey, Kristina Hanson, Paul Lukather, Alan Roberts, Gregg Martell; **D:** Irvin S. Yeaworth Jr. **VHS, Beta** *NWV, SNC*

Disaster at Silo 7

When the engine of a Titan missile goes on the fritz, the Air Force tries to prevent a nuclear disaster. Based on an actual Titan II missile incident near Little Rock, Arkansas. Made for television. 🦴🦴

1988 92m/C Peter Boyle, Patricia Charbonneau, Perry King, Michael O'Keefe, Joe Spano, Dennis Weaver; **D:** Larry Elikann; **W:** Douglas Lloyd McIntosh; **C:** Roy Wagner. **VHS** *TRI*

Doc Savage

Dr. Clark Savage, Jr., and "The Amazing Five" fight a murderous villain who plans to take over the world. Based on the long series of pulp novels by Kenneth Robeson, the plotline loosely follows the initial entry *The Man of Bronze*, while incorporating several ideas from other stories. This is almost sure to disappoint fans of the pulp series, as a camp approach is taken, but most of the comedy falls flat and some of the performances are poor. Also disappointing for fans of producer George Pal, who may expect something more spectacular from the man who gave us *The War of the Worlds* and *The Time Machine*. Ron Ely, despite his years as Tarzan, serves as only a passable Doc. May prove to be a revelation for comic-book fans—Doc Savage, raised from infancy by a group of scientists to be a perfect mental and physical specimen, began his war on crime about the same time as The Shadow.

Many aspects of the series were later appropriated by the creators of Superman, Batman, and even Buckaroo Banzai. 🦴🦴

1975 (PG) 100m/C Ron Ely, Pamela Hensley, Paul Gleason, William Lucking, Paul Wexler; **D:** Michael Anderson Sr.; **W:** George Pal, Joe Morhaim; **C:** Fred W. Koenekamp. **VHS, Beta** *WAR*

Dr. Alien

A 1950s-style bulbous-headed alien assumes the delectable form of Judy Landers and, posing as an Earth scientist, turns a dorky college freshman into a sex-addicted stud whose skull sprouts a wriggly, phallic stalk of flesh whenever he gets aroused by the ubiquitous large-bosomed coeds. Trashy, overacted comedy. **AKA:** I Was a Teenage Sex Mutant. **WOOF!**

1988 (R) 90m/C Billy Jacoby, Olivia Barash, Stuart Fratkin, Troy Donahue, Arlene Golonka, Judy Landers; **D:** David DeCoteau; **W:** Kenneth J. Hall; **C:** Nicholas Von Sternberg. **VHS, Beta, LV** *PAR*

Dr. Cyclops

The famous early Technicolor fantasia about a mad scientist miniaturizing a group of explorers who happen upon his jungle lab. Landmark f/x still hold up, while the slow-moving story occasionally takes on aspects of a fairy story. Albert Dekker makes for a fine mad scientist, his bald pate and thick glasses immediately recalling Eric von Stroheim. Ripped off in the 1970s by the producers of the *Dr. Shrinker* television series. 🦴🦴🦴

1940 76m/C Albert Dekker, Janice Logan, Victor Kilian, Thomas Coley, Charles Halton, Frank Yaconelli; **D:** Ernest B. Schoedsack; **W:** Tom Kilpatrick; **C:** Winton C. Hoch, Henry Sharp. **VHS, Beta, LV** *MCA, FCT, MLB*

Doctor Faustus

Christopher Marlowe's 16th-century morality play, brilliantly rendered and filmed. Aged scholar Faustus bargains away his soul to the Devil for youth, adventure, and a meeting with Helen of Troy ("Was this the face that launched a thousand ships...?"). Richard Burton's stentorian tones provide oratorical fireworks, whilst among the spectacle is an enjoyable sequence of invisible Faustus tormenting the Pope and his counselors. All good things

must come to an end, and Faustus is dragged off to Hell, with Helen (played by Burton's then-wife Elizabeth Taylor) revealed as an infernal demon from the nether regions, pulling him down. Archetypal fantasy-fable received a very mixed reception from late-'60s critics no doubt due to the famously wedded leads. Now divorced (no pun intended) from tabloid notoriety, it's worth rediscovering on home video. 🦴🦴🦴🦴

1968 93m/C Richard Burton, Andreas Teuber, Elizabeth Taylor, Ian Marter; *D:* Richard Burton, Nevill Coghill. **VHS, Beta** *COL*

Dr. Goldfoot and the Bikini Machine

Price spoofs his image for the umpteenth time as a San Francisco mad scientist who uses gorgeous female robots to seduce the wealthy and powerful in a scheme to take over the world. Opposing him is Frankie Avalon, Secret

Agent oo 1/2, later demoted to oo 1/4. Harmlessly dumb drive-in fun from Roger Corman, with a great title sequence (theme song by the Supremes). Great cameos by Annette and fellow beach-movie cohort Harvey Lembeck. Italian-made sequel, *Dr. Goldfoot and the Girl Bombs,* is not yet on video. 🦴🦴

1965 90m/C Vincent Price, Frankie Avalon, Dwayne Hickman, Annette Funicello, Susan Hart, Kay Elkhardt, Fred Clark, Deanna Lund, Deborah Walley, Harvey Lembeck; *D:* Norman Taurog; *W:* Robert Kaufman, Elwood Ullman; *C:* Sam Leavitt; *M:* Les Baxter. **VHS** *AIP*

Doctor Mordrid: Master of the Unknown

Two immensely powerful sorcerers from the 4th dimension cross over into our world with very different missions—one wants to destroy the Earth, one wants to save it. Star Jeffrey Combs wandered into this from Lovecraftian horror movies like *Re-Animator* and *From Beyond.* Not a bad film for when you're in

"You're going to wear *that* when *Dr. Goldfoot and the Bikini Machine* open for the Beach Boys?" asks a prudish Vincent Price.

After the untimely demise of Doctors What, When, Where, and How, a single victor remains. **Dr. Who.**

those powerful sorcerer movie moods. Hardcore Arthurian buffs, who know who the original "Mordrid" was, will probably be irritated by this flick. ♫♫

1990 (R) 102m/C Jeffrey Combs, Yvette Nipar, Jay Acovone, Brian Thompson; **D:** Albert Band, Charles Band; **M:** Richard Band. **VHS, Beta** *PAR*

Doctor Satan's Robot

Art is long and life is short, and if you haven't time to watch the 15-episode Republic serial *Mysterious Doctor Satan* in full-length video reissue, this feature condensation will do. Deranged Dr. Satan chews up the scenery as he cavorts with his metallic robot, and the superhero known as Copperhead (Robert Wilcox) makes his most sensational escape

from an entrapped flaming coffin. Yes, that bit of business shows up again in the James Bond film *Diamonds Are Forever*; where did you think they got the idea? Check out 007's original inspiration for more excitement. ♫♫♫

1940 100m/B Eduardo Ciannelli, Robert Wilcox, William Newell, Ella Neal; **D:** William Whitney, John English. **VHS** *VCN*

Dr. Strange

A made-for-television pilot based upon the Marvel Comics character who, with the help of a sorcerer, practices witchcraft in order to fight evil. ♫♫

1978 94m/C Peter Hooten, Clyde Kusatsu, Jessica Walter, Eddie Benton, John Mills; **D:** Philip DeGuere. **VHS, Beta** *MCA*

Dr. Strangelove, or: How I Learned to Stop Worrying and Love the Bomb

It's the end of the world as we know it in Stanley Kubrick's classic black comedy that is undimmed by the collapse of the "evil empire." Sterling Hayden stars as cigar-chomping General Jack Ripper, who is convinced of a Communist conspiracy to sap "our precious bodily fluids" and orders American bombers to attack Russia. George C. Scott is in his element as military hawk General Buck Turgidson, but it's Peter Sellers' show all the way. In a bravura triple role, he portrays the befuddled American president Merkin Muffley, British officer Mandrake, and the wheelchair-bound former Nazi Dr. Strangelove. Aboard the plane racing toward its target are James Earl Jones and Slim Pickens as gung-ho pilot Major Kong. Keenan Wynn is Colonel "Bat" Guano, who has a memorable Coke machine encounter with "prevert" Sellers. Not to be missed. Pickens riding down the bomb to oblivion is one of the movies' most indelible images. Kubrick wisely decided to delete a climactic pie fight. As Muffley admonishes at one point, "Gentleman, you can't fight in here. This is the war room." ♫♫♫♫

1964 93m/B *GB* Peter Sellers, George C. Scott, Sterling Hayden, Keenan Wynn, Slim Pickens, James Earl Jones,

TV on Tape:
Doctor Who

In the late '70s, American science-fiction fans began hearing a lot about a strange British television show called *Doctor Who*. Pictures in sf magazines showed a tall man with a mop of curly hair and an apparently endless scarf, usually standing beside what looked like a blue telephone booth.

This fellow was pretty far removed from the conventional American science-fiction hero, who, from Captain Video to Captain Kirk, has usually been military. But plenty of fans were intrigued and began tuning in when the show appeared on their local channels. The man in the scarf was Tom Baker, and for many he was the first glimpse of a most unusual hero known only as the Doctor.

The show's history had quite a bit more to it than Tom Baker, however. It was the oldest-running science-fiction show in the world, having begun broadcasting in England in 1963 and ended (perhaps) in 1989. The show was originally conceived by the BBC as an "adventure in time and space" and in fact is still regarded in its native country as a children's show, though certainly a remarkable one. The Doctor, as originally played by British character actor William Hartnell, was an elderly, slightly crotchety scientific genius who traveled the cosmos in an enormous time-and-space machine that was somehow contained within an ordinary "police call-box." This was the TARDIS ("Time and Relative Dimensions in Space"), probably the show's most recognizable icon. *Doctor Who* quickly became a beloved fixture of British culture. The TARDIS allowed the Doctor and his companions (and he had a total of 33 over the course of the series) to travel anywhere from Aztec Mexico to alien planets thousands of years in the future. The stories were always fast-moving and imaginative, and over time the show developed an internal mythology that was as far-ranging as it was colorful.

At first the Doctor's identity (and that of his "granddaughter" Susan) was left vague. But by the time the aging Hartnell was ready to leave the show in 1966, things had firmed up somewhat. The Doctor was not a human being at all, but a rebel "Time Lord," one of an immensely advanced race of beings from the planet Gallifrey. Time Lords have two hearts and also the enviable ability to "regenerate" their bodies when critically injured. Hartnell was thus able to relinquish the role of the Doctor to the younger Patrick Troughton, who gave the role a gentler, more humorous touch. In 1970, the tall, imposing Jon Pertwee took over, playing the Doctor as a theatrical dandy. Most of the shows in the Pertwee years were set on Earth, with the Doctor collaborating with a paramilitary organization called UNIT. 1974 saw the advent of Tom Baker, who with his slightly off-kilter humor is still THE Doctor to many fans. In 1982, Peter Davidson, the youngest man to play the Doctor, took the role. He was followed by the burlier, slightly more acerbic Colin Baker in 1984, and then in 1987 by Sylvester McCoy, who seemed to echo Troughton's whimsical approach.

The Doctor in all his incarnations fought a galaxy of monsters and villains from all time and space. Probably the most famous were the Daleks, mutant creatures encased in robot shells, who were intent on conquering the universe. Fans who didn't find the Daleks frightening enough could take their pick of the Cybermen, the Ice Warriors, the Sontarans, the Draconians, and a host of others.

Doctor Who ended in 1989 with McCoy facing his old nemesis and fellow Time-Lord the Master one last time. But by the time this book hits the shelves a new *Doctor Who* movie will have aired on Fox Television, featuring Paul McGann as the eighth Doctor. If the movie does well, the series may be revived. The Doctor's adventures, it would seem, are far from over.

1963-89/C *GB Selected cast:* William Hartnell, Patrick Troughton, Jon Pertwee, Tom Baker, Peter Davison, Colin Baker, Sylvester McCoy. **VHS** *FOX, MOV*

Peter Bull; **D:** Stanley Kubrick; **W:** Terry Southern, Peter George, Stanley Kubrick; **M:** Laurie Johnson. British Academy Awards '64: Best Film; New York Film Critics Awards '64: Best Director (Kubrick); Nominations: Academy Awards '64: Best Actor (Sellers), Best Adapted Screenplay, Best Director (Kubrick), Best Picture. **VHS, Beta, LV, 8mm** COL, HMV

Doctor Who and the Daleks

A silly feature adapted from the popular BBC series, with Peter Cushing playing the Doctor as an absent-minded old (human) inventor. The Doctor, his two granddaughters, and the older girl's boyfriend accidentally transport themselves to a barren planet inhabited by the Daleks, mutant creatures in protective robotic suits. The travelers must help the friendly, pacifistic Thals throw off the threat of Dalek tyranny. Obviously aimed at children, this is a good-natured but rather simple-minded film that will leave fans of the TV series disappointed or bewildered. Followed by the superior *Daleks—Invasion Earth 2150 A.D.* 🦴🦴

1965 78m/C GB Peter Cushing, Roy Castle, Jennie Linden, Michael Coles, Roberta Tovey, Geoffrey Toone; **D:** Gordon Flemyng; **W:** Milton Subotsky; **C:** John Wilcox. **VHS, Beta** REP

Doctor Who: Cybermen—The Early Years

Baker, the 6th Doctor, hosts this look at one of the Time Lord's favorite enemies, the robotic and ruthless Cybermen from their first appearance in "The Tenth Planet" to "Tomb of the Cyberman" and "The Invasion." 🦴🦴

1992 120m/C GB **VHS** FXV, MOV

Doctor X

Something weird is going on at Dr. Xavier's research labs—and murder is the least of it. A classic horror oldie, famous for its very early use of two-color Technicolor, as well as the wonderful sets designed by director Michael Curtiz (*Things to Come*). Lee Tracy was an engaging personality in films of the time, but he grates on the nerves a bit here. Made a name for Lionel Atwill in horror films, not to mention some pre-Kong screams from Fay Wray. The who-done-it is easy to guess—but the how-done-it is a real mind blower. 🦴🦴🦴

1932 77m/C Lionel Atwill, Fay Wray, Lee Tracy, Preston Foster; **D:** Michael Curtiz. **VHS, Beta, LV** MGM, MLB

Dog Soldier: Shadows of the Past

The CIA has discovered a cure for AIDS in this animated Japanese feature. The problem is, a bevy of other organizations want the antidote for themselves, including smugglers and Japan's own intelligence service. Ex-Green Beret John Kyosuke Hiba is recruited to recover the cure, but finds himself facing a conflict of interest. This Japanimated attempt at a U.S.-style action flick is surprisingly lifeless, and in fact tops many anime fans' "worst of" lists. Hiba is an embarrassing Rambo-clone, the kind of hero most American viewers got tired of in the mid-'80s. In Japanese with English subtitles, but it makes more sense if you don't read them. 🦴

1989 45m/C JP **D:** Hiroyuki Ebata; **W:** Shou Aikawa. **VHS, LV** INJ, CPM, WTA

Doin' Time on Planet Earth

Adolescent boy feels out of place amid his obnoxious family and tacky suburban community. Two UFO nuts (Adam West and Candice Azzara) suddenly pop up and provide an explanation: the kid is descended from a long-marooned race of spacemen—teenage alienation, get it? If he can recall the coordinates, he and other outcasts can blast off this lousy world for their true home planet. One suspects that this comedy captures the wistful secret hopes of many an sf fan, but it ultimately cops out on the extraterrestrial premise. Too bad. Directed by the son of Walter Matthau. 🦴🦴🦴

1988 (PG-13) 83m/C Adam West, Candice Azzara, Hugh O'Brian, Matt Adler, Timothy Patrick Murphy, Roddy McDowall, Maureen Stapleton, Nicholas Strouse, Andrea Thompson, Hugh Gillin, Gloria Henry; **D:** Charles Matthau. **VHS, Beta** WAR

Donovan's Brain

Curt Siodmak's novel is the basis for this McCarthy-era brain-control thriller. Jerk mil-

lionaire W. H. Donovan is killed in a plane crash. So far, so good. Genius-type Patrick Cory (Lew Ayres) takes Donovan's brain and keeps it alive in his lab. Cory becomes obsessed with the brain...or is it possessed? Gradually he is changed by the more and more powerful brain. No more Mister Nice Guy; in fact, he is doing the Jekyll/Hyde flip-flop, turning into the not-so-"Mellow Yellow" Donovan. Some of the subtleties of the book are gone, but overall a fine adaptation featuring future first lady Nancy (Reagan) Davis. 🦴🦴🦴

1953 85m/B Lew Ayres, Gene Evans, Nancy Davis, Steve Brodie; **D:** Felix Feist. **VHS, Beta, LV** *MGM, IME, MLB*

Dragon Fury

Evil dictator tries to conquer what remains of America in the year 2099—a world peopled by barbarians and victims of a deadly plague. Naturally, there's a martial arts hero around to stop him. 🦴🦴

1995 80m/C Robert Chapin, Richard Lynch, Chona Jason, Deborah Stamble; **D:** David Heavener. **VHS** *MNC*

Dragonfight

In the near future, multinational corporations rule the world and vie for supremacy through gladiator combat (apparently execs go to business school to be Masters of Barbarian Administration). Fights are to the death in the wastelands, and when the disillusioned champ refuses a new challenger, the corporate honchos, watching omnipotently via remote cameras, try to provoke him into battle by having the psycho opponent slaughter innocent bystanders. Weak scenario, cheapie production values make this one a writeoff. 🦴

1992 (R) 84m/C Robert Z'Dar, Michael Pare, Paul Coufos, Charles Napier, James Hong, Alexa Hamilton, Fawna MacLaren. **VHS, Beta** *WAR*

Dragonslayer

An excellent medieval fantasy about a sorcerer's apprentice who suddenly finds himself called upon to save his country from a fire-breathing, virgin-eating dragon named Vermithrax. Unlike many fantasy movies, *Dragonslayer* never gets too cute. There are no comic-relief goblins or baby unicorns, but there are some very nasty baby dragons, a corrupt king, and heroes who are as human as they are valorous. Caitlin Clarke is especially good as the heroine and Ralph Richardson is wonderful as the wizard. The special effects are quite impressive, even by today's standards; Vermithrax was an early triumph of computer-aided animation, and still looks remarkably real. 🦴🦴🦴

1981 (PG) 110m/C Peter MacNicol, Caitlin Clarke, Ralph Richardson, John Hallam, Albert Salmi, Chloe Salaman, Peter Eyre; **D:** Matthew Robbins; **W:** Matthew Robbins, Hal Barwood; **M:** Alex North. Nominations: Academy Awards '81: Best Original Score. **VHS, Beta, LV** *PAR, COL*

Dreamscape

A doctor teaches a young psychic Dennis Quaid how to enter into other people's dreams in order to end their nightmares—but what if a rival psychic is causing those nightmares? The President of the United States (Eddie Albert) is the victim, suffering visions of nuclear holocaust designed to push him over the edge, and the hero enters the sleeping chief executive's dreams to try and undo the damage. Wild and remarkable premise peaks with a clash of mental titans within a White House bedroom silent except for the Presidential snoring. Worthwhile f/x include a stop-motion reptile man. 🦴🦴🦴

1984 (PG-13) 99m/C Dennis Quaid, Max von Sydow, Christopher Plummer, Eddie Albert, Kate Capshaw, David Patrick Kelly, George Wendt, Jana Taylor; **D:** Joseph Ruben; **W:** Chuck Russell; **M:** Maurice Jarre. **VHS, Beta, LV** *IME*

Dune

Auteur of the bizarre David Lynch directed this science-fiction epic based on the Frank Herbert novel of the same name. A stellar cast, good special effects, and sweeping desert vistas lift the film above a somewhat muddled script. In the year 10,991, a group of noble houses struggle for control of the universe. Among political and religious intrigue, the key to absolute power is control of the mind-enhancing drug Spice, found only the desert planet Arrakis (which also happens to be inhabited by giant worms). Paul, heir to House Atreides, leads the lowly but fierce Freemen in

revolt against the evil Harkonens and the Emperor, who have seized control of Arrakis and attempted to destroy House Atreides. Lynch creates a totally unique and complex world, with its own culture and mythos, inhabited by staple Lynch weirdos and grotesque images. Though far from perfect, the film strives to deliver intelligent science fiction, a rarity in film. Look for director Lynch in a cameo. An extended version has been disowned by Lynch, and directing credit goes to the eponymous Alan Smithee. Stick with the original—just be sure to pay close attention (and reading the book sure couldn't hurt). Makes a great bookend to *Waterworld*. 🦴🦴🦴

1984 (PG-13) 137m/C Kyle MacLachlan, Francesca Annis, Jose Ferrer, Sting, Max von Sydow, Juergen Prochnow, Linda Hunt, Freddie Jones, Dean Stockwell, Virginia Madsen, Brad Dourif, Kenneth McMillan, Silvana Mangano, Jack Nance, Sian Phillips, Paul Smith, Richard Jordan, Everett McGill, Sean Young, Patrick Stewart; *Cameos:* David Lynch; *D:* David Lynch; *W:* David Lynch; *C:* Freddie Francis; *M:* Brian Eno. Nominations: Academy Awards '84: Best Sound. **VHS, Beta, LV** *MCA, FCT*

Dune Warriors

Future Earth is a parched planet, where civilized people are terrorized by water-seeking bandits. A peasant girl gathers five brave warriors to defend her family's imperiled commune against the thirsty barbarians, in a postnuke premise inspired by (and marked down from) Kurosawa's classic *The Seven Samurai*. Good action and stunts, if the dummy plot doesn't get you first. Filmed in the Philippines. 🦴

1991 (R) 77m/C David Carradine, Richard Hill, Luke Askew, Jillian McWhirter, Blake Boyd, Val Garay; *D:* Cirio H. Santiago; *W:* T. C. McKelvey; *C:* Joe Batac. **VHS, LV** *COL*

Dungeonmaster

You can't fault low-budget fantasy producer Charles Band for lack of ambition: this omnibus from his Italy-based Empire studio consists of seven segments, each by a different director in a different genre. Plot concerns a jealous Devil (Richard Moll) deciding to pit

his occult powers against computer jock Jeffrey Byron and his portable micro XCALIBR8. Thus, in a series of contests, our hero must rescue his girlfriend from *Road Warrior* mutants, rotting zombies, a Harryhausenesque stop-motion idol, and the rock band W.A.S.P. It all looks like a slick demo reel for potential investors, but don't phone your broker; Empire went belly-up a few years later. Stirring (but endlessly rerun) musical score by Charles Band's brother Richard. **AKA:** Ragewar; Digital Dreams. 🦴🦴

1983 (PG-13) 80m/C Jeffrey Byron, Richard Moll, Leslie Wing, Danny Dick; **D:** John Carl Buechler, Charles Band, David Allen, Stephen Ford, Peter Manoogian, Ted Nicolaou, Rosemarie Turko; **W:** Allen Actor; **C:** Mac Ahlberg; **M:** Richard Band. **VHS, Beta, LV** *LIV*

Duplicates

Gregory Harrison and Kim Greist are a married couple whose young son has disappeared. When the boy is found, he has no memory of his former life or parents, and the couple discover he's the victim of secret experiments which transfer human memories into computer banks. Will they become the next targets? 🦴🦴

1992 (PG-13) 92m/C Gregory Harrison, Kim Greist, Cicely Tyson, Lane Smith, William Lucking, Kevin McCarthy; **D:** Sandor Stern. **VHS, Beta** *PAR, PMS*

Dust Devil

Three travelers find themselves in Africa's vast Namibia desert: a policeman (Zakes Mokae), a woman on the run (Chelsea Field), and her abusive husband. They all have the misfortune of meeting up with an evil spirit trapped in human form. This supernatural being, known as the "Dust Devil" (Robert Burke), must kill, stealing as many souls as he can, in order to re-enter the spiritual realm. Well acted and stylized, this one puts some good quirky twists on the serial killer theme. 🦴🦴

1993 (R) 87m/C Robert Burke, Chelsea Field, Zakes Mokae, Rufus Swart, John Matshikiza, William Hootkins, Marianne Sagebrecht; **D:** Richard Stanley; **W:** Richard Stanley; **M:** Simon Boswell. **VHS, Beta** *PAR*

Earth Girls Are Easy

Valley girl Valerie (Geena Davis) is having a bad week: first she catches her fiance with another woman, then she breaks a nail, then furry aliens land in her swimming pool. What more could go wrong? When the aliens are temporarily stranded, she decides to make amends by giving them a head-to-toe makeover with the help of her hairdresser, Julie "I Like 'Em Big and Stupid" Brown. Devoid of their excessive hairiness, the handsome trio of fun-loving extraterrestrials (Jeff Goldblum, Jim Carrey, and Damon Wayons) set out to experience the Southern California lifestyle, with the help of surfer dude cum pool cleaner Michael McKean. Stupid, stupid, story that actually works, thanks to a colorful and energetic cast. Sometimes hilarious sci-fi/musical, featuring bouncy shtick, Julie Brown's music, and a gleeful dismantling of modern culture. 🦴🦴🦴

1989 (PG) 100m/C Geena Davis, Jeff Goldblum, Charles Rocket, Julie Brown, Jim Carrey, Damon Wayans, Michael McKean, Angelyne, Larry Linville, Rick Overton; **D:** Julien Temple; **W:** Julie Brown, Charlie Coffey, Terrance McNally; **M:** Nile Rodgers. **VHS, Beta, LV** *LIV, VES*

Earth Vs. the Flying Saucers

"If it lands in our nation's capital uninvited, we don't meet it with tea and cookies." Hugh Marlowe, the jerk who turned in Klaatu in *The Day the Earth Stood Still,* is a scientist who establishes contact with the survivors of a dying race of aliens looking to colonize our planet. The real star of this '50s classic is, of course, special effects master Ray Harryhausen, whose peerless flying saucers crash into Washington, D.C.'s most treasured landmarks. Rent this after seeing the big-budget pyrotechnics of *Independence Day.* **AKA:** Invasion of the Flying Saucers. 🦴🦴🦴

1956 83m/B Hugh Marlowe, Joan Taylor, Donald Curtis, Morris Ankrum; **D:** Fred F. Sears; **W:** George Worthing Yates, Raymond T. Marcus; **C:** Fred Jackman. **VHS, Beta, LV** *COL, MLB*

Earth Vs. the Spider

Man-eating giant mutant...well, if you can't tell what it is from the title, there's no hope for you. It's discovered in a cave, eats alcoholics, and makes life miserable for a small town in general and high school partiers in particular. Exterminators are called in to kill the beast,

than would most new kids on the block, and he struggles with being different and lonely in a cardboard-cutout world. Visually captivating fairy tale full of splash and color, however predictable the Hollywood-prefab denouement. Director Tim Burton created the character of the Inventor specifically for his idol, Price. 🐾🐾🐾

1990 (PG-13) 100m/C Johnny Depp, Winona Ryder, Dianne Wiest, Vincent Price, Anthony Michael Hall, Alan Arkin, Kathy Baker, Conchata Ferrell, Caroline Aaron, Dick Anthony Williams, Robert Oliveri, John Davidson; **D:** Tim Burton; **W:** Caroline Thompson, Tim Burton; **M:** Danny Elfman. Hugos '91: Dramatic Presentation; Nominations: Academy Awards '90: Best Makeup. **VHS, Beta, LV** *FOX, FCT*

Electric Dreams

Despite its terminal-ly cute ending, this "fairy tale for computers" manages to generate a mild paranoid buzz for anyone who has ever been on the down side of a mainframe. Lenny Von Dohlen stars as Miles, an architect whose life is gradually taken over by Edgar, his home computer which (don't ask) develops feelings of its own and tries to sabotage Miles' budding romance with Madeline, his cello-playing upstairs neighbor (Virginia Madsen). Edgar is no HAL (from *2001*) or even Joshua (*War Games*), but he/it is still more interesting than his bland B-movie co-stars, thanks to the voice of Bud Cort, who manages to make this newly plugged-in being both menacing (he cancels Miles' credit cards and rigs his apartment's security system) and sympathetic (he woos Madeline with a poem composed of words gleaned from TV commercials). Steve Barron was among the first generation of music video directors (Michael Jackson's "Billie Jean") who brought the MTV aesthetic to the big screen. He has since made *Teenage Mutant Ninja Turtles: The Movie* and *The Coneheads*. 🐾🐾🐾

1984 (PG) 95m/C Lenny Von Dohlen, Virginia Madsen, Maxwell Caulfield, Bud Cort, Koo Stark; **D:** Steven Barron. **VHS, Beta, LV** *MGM*

The Electronic Monster

Insurance claims investigator Rod Cameron looks into the death of a Hollywood starlet and discovers an exclusive therapy center

---

"If this isn't an argument against the dumping of nuclear waste, I'll eat your head."
Giant ant to Robert Pine in *Empire of the Ants*.

after which it's hauled into the high school gym. But wouldn't you know it—the monster is revived by rock and roll. The laconic Midwesterners don't seem particularly surprised to find gigantic arachnids running loose. Silly old drive-in fare is agony for many, camp treasure for a precious few. Retitled to cash in on the success of *Earth Vs. the Flying Saucers*. Bert I. Gordon made many films that were much worse than this one. **AKA:** The Spider. 🐾🐾

1958 72m/B Edward Kemmer, June Kennedy, Gene Persson, Gene Roth, Hal Torey, Mickey Finn; **D:** Bert I. Gordon; **W:** Laszlo Gorog, George Worthing Yates; **C:** Jack Marta. **VHS** *COL, MLB*

Edward Scissorhands

Edward's (Johnny Depp) a young man created by a loony scientist (Vincent Price), who dies before he can attach hands to his boy-creature. Then the boy is rescued from his lonely existence outside of suburbia by an ingratiating Avon lady. With scissors in place of hands, Edward has more trouble fitting into suburbia

dedicated to hypnotism. At the facility, people vacation for weeks in morgue-like body drawers, while evil Dr. Illing uses an electronic device to control the sleeper's dreams and actions. Eerie, but falls victim to static handling and dull acting that wastes the premise's potential. Intriguingly, it is one of the first films to explore the possibilities of brainwashing and mind control. **AKA:** Escapement; The Electric Monster. 🎬 🎬

1957 72m/B *GB* Rod Cameron, Mary Murphy, Meredith Edwards, Peter Illing; *D:* Montgomery Tully; *W:* Charles Eric Maine, J. Maclaren-Ross; *C:* Bert Mason. **VHS** *SNC*

The Element of Crime

In a monochromatic, post-holocaust future, a detective tracks down a serial killer of young girls. Made in Denmark, this minor festival favorite features an impressive directional debut and awaits cult status. Filmed in Sepiatone. **AKA:** Forbrydelsens Element. 🎬 🎬 🎬

1984 104m/C *DK* Michael Elphick, Esmond Knight, Jerold Wells, Meme Lei, Astrid Henning-Jensen, Preben Leerdorff-Rye, Gotha Andersen; *D:* Lars von Trier. Nominations: Cannes Film Festival '84: Best Film. **VHS, Beta** *UNI, INJ, TPV*

The Eliminators

Cyborg escapes from the evil scientist who created him, then recruits a handful of adventurers for an assault on the madman's fortress before he can take over the world via time travel. Roy Dotrice makes a memorable villain, on screen intermittently but transformed a bit more each time. Comic-book level action and drama prevails; producer Charles Band later borrowed the lead avenger's moniker, 'Mandroid,' for another action romp of that title. 🎬 🎬

1986 (PG) 95m/C Roy Dotrice, Patrick Reynolds, Denise Crosby, Andrew Prine, Conan Lee; *D:* Peter Manoogian; *W:* Danny Bilson, Paul DeMeo; *M:* Richard Band. **VHS, Beta** *FOX*

Embryo

Rock Hudson looks uncomfortable as a scientist who salvages a human fetus, treating it with genetic serum that creates a fully mature, intelligent, beautiful test-tube woman (Barbara Carrera) in a matter of days. After her 'birth,' things look upbeat for the happy couple—until the side effects. An average sci-fi drama with roots in the Frankenstein story (and Germany's *Alraune* tales of lab-created femme fatales), this plods along predictably until a finale that's truly shocking and ghastly compared with the blandness that preceded it. **AKA:** Created to Kill. 🎬 🎬

1976 (PG) 108m/C Rock Hudson, Barbara Carrera, Diane Ladd, Roddy McDowall, Ann Schedeen, John Elerick; *Cameos:* Dr. Joyce Brothers; *D:* Ralph Nelson; *W:* Anita Doohan, Jack W. Thomas; *C:* Fred W. Koenekamp. **VHS, Beta** *VTR, LIV*

Empire of the Ants

A group of enormous, nuclear, unfriendly ants stalk a real estate dealer and prospective buyers of undeveloped oceanfront property. They flee down a river in boats, only to reach the safety of a neighboring town. Or do they? Fun for fans of inept cinema that occasionally slips into mind-bending surrealism. Seventies fashions will make you think you happened upon a very odd episode of *The Love Boat*. Story originated by master science-fiction storyteller H. G. Wells, but only for marquee value. 🎬

1977 (PG) 90m/C Joan Collins, Robert Lansing, John David Carson, Albert Salmi, Jacqueline Scott, Robert Pine; *D:* Bert I. Gordon; *W:* Bert I. Gordon; *C:* Reginald Morris. **VHS, Beta** *SUE*

The Empire Strikes Back

In the second film of George Lucas' trilogy, the characters become more firmly set. Luke continues his training—now with the wonderful Yoda (created by Frank Oz); Han and Leia begin to sort things out; Lando Calrissian enters the story; Darth Vader becomes creepier and more important. The stop-motion and creature effects are terrific, but the real key is the never-a-dull-moment script from veterans Leigh Brackett (her last work) and Lawrence Kasdan. Despite the fact that the film is a second act, it stands on its own and has a terrific conclusion. The remastered tape released in 1995 looks great. Followed by *Return of the Jedi*. Also available on laserdisc with *The Making of 'Star Wars'*. 🎬 🎬 🎬 🎬

1980 (PG) 124m/C Mark Hamill, Carrie Fisher, Harrison Ford, Billy Dee Williams, Alec Guinness, David Prowse,

"Dad! If you'll just put the laser away, I promise I'll go to Sunday School!" Luke Skywalker (Mark Hamill) finds that being Darth Vader's son takes some getting used to in *The Empire Strikes Back.*

Kenny Baker, Frank Oz, Anthony Daniels, Peter Mayhew, Clive Revill, Julian Glover, John Ratzenberger; **D:** Irvin Kershner; **W:** Leigh Brackett, Lawrence Kasdan; **C:** Peter Suschitzsky; **M:** John Williams; **V:** James Earl Jones. Hugos '81: Dramatic Presentation; Academy Awards '80: Best Sound, Best Visual Effects; People's Choice Awards '81: Best Film; Nominations: Academy Awards '80: Best Art Direction/Set Decoration, Best Original Score. **VHS, Beta, LV** *FOX, FCT, RDG*

Encounter at Raven's Gate

Life on an unhappy Australian farm is made even more miserable by sudden, deadly flyovers by (unseen) extraterrestrials. In lieu of a Spielberg-sized budget, director Rolf de Heer goes for sheer suspense and terror of the unknown, incomprehensible visitors. Some of it works, but the aimless plot gets tangled up in tangents about misunderstood punk rockers and brutal cops. A nice try. **AKA:** Incident at Raven's Gate. 🐺🐺

1988 (R) 85m/C Steven Vidler, Ritchie Singer; **D:** Rolf de Heer; **W:** Rolf de Heer, Marc Rosenberg; **C:** Richard Michalak; **M:** Graham Tardiff. **VHS, Beta, LV** *IME*

End of the World

A coffee machine explodes, sending a man through a window and into a neon sign, where he is electrocuted. A priest witnesses this and retreats to a convent where he meets his alien double and heads for more trouble with outer space invaders. Interesting premise. **WOOF!**

1976 (PG) 88m/C Christopher Lee, Sue Lyon, Lew Ayres, MacDonald Carey, Dean Jagger, Kirk Scott; **D:** John Hayes; **M:** Andrew Belling. **VHS, Beta** *MED*

Endless Descent

Made at the height of the none-too-brief underwater monster fad that Hollywood went through, this one's actually not bad. The sub Siren II is sent to investigate the disappearance of the original Siren and, to nobody's surprise, they find something evil lurking on the ocean floor. R. Lee Ermey is the by-the-book commanding officer; Jack Scalia is the ship's designer; Deborah Adair is his estranged wife.

Several others are on hand, too, but few make it to the last reel. The pace is brisk and the critter is fun. A Spanish film, shot in English, by director J. P. Simon, whose other works of art include *Pieces* and *Slugs*. **AKA:** La Grieta. 🦴🦴

1990 (R) 79m/C *SP* Jack Scalia, R. Lee Ermey, Ray Wise, Deborah Adair, Ely Pouget, John Toyles-Bey; *D:* J. Piquer Simon; *W:* David Coleman. **VHS, Beta, LV** *LIV*

Enemy Mine

A moralistic space opera in which two pilots from warring planets, one an Earthling, the other an asexual reptilian "Drac," crashland on a barren planet and are forced to work together to survive. Eventually a strange friendship develops between them. The message gets a bit heavy handed at times, but fortunately never slows down the compelling story. Plus, Louis Gossett, Jr., makes one of the most effectively "alien" aliens ever seen in a sci-fi flick. His drac purrs, hisses, and warbles in a language that seems more feline than reptilian; it's fascinating, a bit scary, and mercifully (considering what many aliens were like in the '80s) not the least bit cutesy. This is fast-moving adventure that's also a thoughtful meditation on cooperation and friendship. 🦴🦴🦴

1985 (PG-13) 108m/C Dennis Quaid, Louis Gossett Jr., Brion James, Richard Marcus, Lance Kerwin, Carolyn McCormick, Bumper Robinson; *D:* Wolfgang Petersen; *W:* Edward Khmara; *C:* Tony Imi; *M:* Maurice Jarre. **VHS, Beta, LV** *FOX*

Equalizer 2000

Nothing new here. A warrior in a post-nuclear holocaust future plots to overthrow a dictatorship that seizes all available oil and water. Hero's main ally is the title character, a high-powered gun, and indeed it turns in the best performance. 🦴

1986 (R) 85m/C Richard Norton, Corinne Wahl, William Steis; *D:* Cirio H. Santiago. **VHS, Beta** *MGM*

"It's not because you're of a different race. Not even that you're asexual. I've just never been comfortable dating reptiles." Dennis Quaid lays it on the line for Lou Gossett, Jr. in *Enemy Mine*.

"Trust me, a little chin tuck is all you need." Kurt Russell gives cosmetic advice to Lee Van Cleef in *Escape from New York.*

Equinox

Young archaeologists uncover horror in a state forest. The ranger, questing for a book of spells that the scientists have found, threatens them with wonderful special effects, including winged beasts, huge apes, and Satan. Though originally an amateur film, it stands up well to most exploitation features of its day, mainly due to the good f/x. Director Jack Woods later became a feature editor. **AKA:** The Beast. 🦴🦴

1971 (PG) 80m/C Edward Connell, Barbara Hewitt, Frank Bonner, Robin Christopher, Jack Woods; *Cameos:* Fritz Leiber; *D:* Jack Woods. **VHS** *NO*

Escape from Galaxy Three

Two lovers flee galactic villain Auriclon (most likely his glitter-filled beard scared them). The couple land on a planet that has been reduced to stone-age state by atomic war and honeymoon during the local tribe's fertility festival.

Ridiculous, Italian variation on the Adam-and-Eve-were-aliens theme, crudely dubbed. Claims a G-rating despite sex and nudity. **WOOF!**

1976 (G) 90m/C James Milton, Cheryl Buchanan. **VHS, Beta** *PSM*

Escape from New York

Once you accept the premise—that Manhattan, one of the most expensive pieces of real estate on the planet, would be turned into a big jail—you've got a fine sf shoot-'em-up. In fact, this one established the formula that so many others would copy in the '80s and '90s. When convicts hold the President hostage, a disgraced war hero (Kurt Russell at his best) unwillingly attempts an impossible rescue mission. The pace is quick, the characters are colorful, and the evocation of a desolate urban landscape is effective. Followed by a sequel in 1996. 🦴🦴🦴

1981 (R) 99m/C Kurt Russell, Lee Van Cleef, Ernest Borgnine, Donald Pleasence, Isaac Hayes, Adrienne Barbeau, Harry Dean Stanton, Season Hubley; **D:** John Carpenter; **W:** John Carpenter, Nick Castle; **C:** Dean Cundey; **M:** John Carpenter. **VHS, Beta, LV** SUE, NLC, FUS

Escape from Planet Earth

As Red Chinese blow up Earth (probably with a bicycle pump; such is the budget), a co-ed crew of astronauts rocket toward an uncertain future in deep space. Soon petty rivalries and claustrophobia take their toll. Lousy f/x take their own toll on a quaint cast—dig song-and-dance man Bobby Van as a hep-cat survivor—and the abrupt ending came about because the clueless production ran out of money. Later, doubles in spacesuits were posed for a quickie epilogue. **AKA:** The Doomsday Machine. **WOOF!**

1967 91m/B Grant Williams, Bobby Van, Ruta Lee, Henry Wilcoxon, Mala Powers, Casey Kasem, Mike Farrell, Harry Hope; **D:** Lee Sholem. **VHS** ACA

Escape from Safehaven

Give the makers of this cheapie Z-movie a bone for having the chutzpah to set their *Mad Max* variant almost entirely within the confines of one crummy apartment building! Brutal slimeballs rule a mad, sadistic world in the post-apocalyptic future. A family pays dearly to enter a supposedly crime-free community but learns it's just a protection racket run by yet another freakish street gang. Violent retribution ensues. 𝄞

1988 (R) 87m/C Rick Gianasi, Mollie O'Mara, John Wittenbauer, Roy MacArthur, William Beckwith; **D:** Brian Thomas Jones, James McCalmont. **VHS, Beta** NO

Escape from the Planet of the Apes

Reprising their roles as intelligent, English-speaking apes from a future Earth society, Roddy McDowall and Kim Hunter flee their world before it's destroyed, and travel back in time to present-day America. In L.A. they become the subjects of a relentless search by the fearful population, much like humans

Charlton Heston and James Franciscus were targeted for experimentation and destruction in simian society in the earlier *Planet of the Apes* and *Beneath the Planet of the Apes.* Although the "fish out of water" scenes of the apes reacting to our civilization are great fun, the heavy-handed messages drag down the latter half. Probably the least expensive of the series, since only three actors wear ape make-up, and there was no need for the extensive sets built for the previous entries. Sequelled by *Conquest of the Planet of the Apes, Battle for the Planet of the Apes,* and two television series. 𝄞 𝄞 𝄞

1971 (G) 98m/C Roddy McDowall, Kim Hunter, Sal Mineo, Ricardo Montalban, William Windom, Bradford Dillman, Natalie Trundy, Eric (Hans Gudegast) Braeden; **D:** Don Taylor; **W:** Paul Dehn; **C:** Joseph Biroc; **M:** Jerry Goldsmith. **VHS, Beta, LV** FOX, FUS

Escapes

In the tradition of *The Twilight Zone,* Vincent Price introduces five short thrillers featuring time travel, aliens, and telepathy. Produced with computer assistance for sharper, more contrasted images. 𝄞 𝄞

1986 72m/C Vincent Price, Jerry Grisham, Lee Canfield, John Mitchum, Gil Reade; **D:** David Steensland. **VHS, Beta** PSM

E.S.P.

A young man is given the amazing power of extra-sensory perception. 𝄞 𝄞

1983 96m/C Jim Stafford, George Deaton. **VHS, Beta** BFV

E.T.: The Extra-Terrestrial

Spielberg's exquisite enchantment, one of the most popular films in history, portrays a limpid-eyed alien stranded on Earth and his special bonding relationship with the young children who find and try to conceal him from grownup authorities. A modern fairy tale providing warmth, humor, and sheer wonder, this was conceived as a second chapter for "Night Skies," a much-discussed but never-filmed thriller about close encounters of an unfriendly kind. That was scrapped, and *E.T.* went into production under the smokescreen title "A

> "They sent in their best man, and when we roam out on the 69th Street bridge tomorrow, on our way to freedom, we're going to have their best man leading the way...from the neck up!"
>
> —The Duke (Isaac Hayes) in *Escape from New York.*

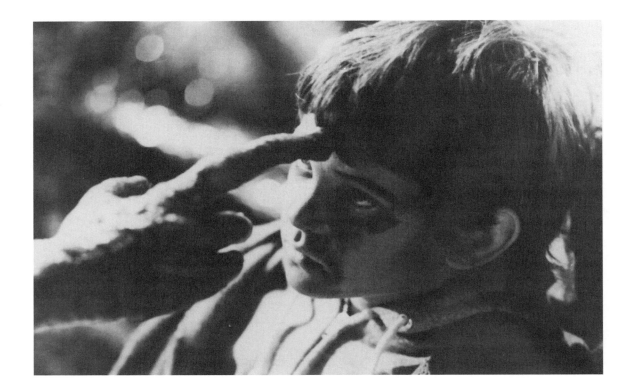

Boy's Life." An immediate smash and cultural phenomenon, it held the first-place spot as the highest grossing movie ever. At least until a later Spielberg hit replaced it—*Jurassic Park.* Steven Spielberg has declared he will never sequelize this (more power to him), but an authorized followup did appear in print, *E.T.—The Storybook of the Green Planet,* by William Kotzwinkle. Creature design by Carlo Rambaldi; Debra Winger contributed to the throaty voice of E.T. 🐾🐾🐾🐾

1982 (PG) 115m/C Henry Thomas, Dee Wallace Stone, Drew Barrymore, Robert MacNaughton, Peter Coyote, C. Thomas Howell, Sean Frye, K.C. Martel; **D:** Steven Spielberg; **W:** Melissa Mathison; **C:** Allen Daviau; **M:** John Williams; **V:** Debra Winger. Academy Awards '82: Best Sound, Best Visual Effects, Best Original Score; Golden Globe Awards '83: Best Film—Drama, Best Score; Los Angeles Film Critics Association Awards '82: Best Director (Spielberg), Best Film; National Society of Film Critics Awards '82: Best Director (Spielberg); People's Choice Awards '83: Best Film; Writers Guild of America '82: Best Original Screenplay; Nominations: Academy Awards '81: Best Film Editing; Academy Awards '82: Best Cinematography, Best Director (Spielberg), Best Picture, Best Sound. **VHS, Beta, LV** *MCA, APD, RDG*

Eve of Destruction

Hell knows no fury like a cutting-edge android-girl on the warpath. Modeled after her creator, Dr. Eve Simmons, Eve VII has android-babe good looks and a raging nuclear capability. Wouldn't you know, something goes haywire during her trial run, and debutante Eve turns into a PMS nightmare machine, blasting all the good Doctor's previous beaux. That's where military agent Gregory Hines comes in, though you wonder why. Dutch actress Renee Soutendijk does well playing the dual Eves in her first American film. 🐾🐾

1990 (R) 101m/C Gregory Hines, Renee Soutendijk, Kevin McCarthy, Ross Malinger; **D:** Duncan Gibbins; **W:** Duncan Gibbins. **VHS, Beta, LV** *COL, NLC, SUE*

The Evil of Frankenstein

Peter Cushing returns as Baron Frankenstein in the third Hammer Frankenstein film. Not dead (just chilling), the monster-man is found by the

mad doctor, and who decides that even a cold monster is better than no monster. Back in the lab, the Baron puts the beast on defrost. Unfortunately, the ice-ing on the cake is that being frozen alive made the monster-brain dormant. Enter a supposedly mystical and definitely sleazy hypnotist who is able to make contact and control the monster...and knows how to use him to the best advantage. Director Freddie Francis supplies enough atmosphere but has to work with a far too predictable script. The monster make-up is very reminiscent of the Universal Frankenstein films. Preceded by *Revenge of Frankenstein* and followed by *Frankenstein Created Woman*. 🦴🦴

1964 84m/C *GB* Peter Cushing, Duncan Lamont, Peter Woodthorpe, Sandor Eles, Kiwi Kingston, Katy Wild; *D:* Freddie Francis; *W:* John Elder; *C:* John Wilcox; *M:* Don Banks. **VHS, Beta** *MCA, MLB*

Evil Spawn

Fading movie queen takes an experimental drug to restore her youthful beauty, but side effects turn her into a giant silverfish, or something. Watch for a quick cameo by Forrest J. Ackerman as a pool cleaner. Sleazy 16mm semi-remake of *The Wasp Woman* (with better makeup f/x) opens with a John Carradine scene shot for a never-completed Frankenstein project. Released under several alternate titles with varying running times, *Evil Spawn* was later itself re-assembled into the Fred Olen Ray production *The Alien Within*. Ray's book *The New Poverty Row* tells a making-of account that's more fun than anything happening onscreen. **AKA:** Deadly Sting; Alive by Night; Alien Within. **WOOF!**

1987 70m/C Bobbie Bresee, John Carradine, Drew Godderis, John Terrance, Dawn Wildsmith, Jerry Fox; *Cameos:* Forrest J. Ackerman; *D:* Kenneth J. Hall; *W:* Kenneth J. Hall; *C:* Christopher Condon. **VHS, Beta** *NO*

Excalibur

Stylized, brooding vision of the life of King Arthur and his knights of the roundtable as seen by director John Boorman. This one is all Boorman; in fact, it's the best Boorman. When Arthur removes the sword Excalibur from the stone, he fulfills a prophecy and becomes the "boy king." His goal, to unite the land, will not be easy, particularly in his early dimwit state. But never fear, Merlin is here to help Arthur. Years ago, Merlin also assisted Arthur's dad, Uther Pendragon, but with a less honorable goal: horny for another warlord's wife (Morgana the temptress), some mystical wizard-type deception gave daddy the appearance of the murdered-as-we-speak husband, allowing copulation no recognizo (indeed an amazing Boorman touch as Uther in tank-like armor makes love to the nude Morgana). Conceived during this liaison is Mordred, who'll be the death of Arthur, and who lives only to avenge the murder of his father and rape his mother. Seems like sex is the main cause of the Roundtable's decay into drunkenness and squabbling. Even superknight Lancelot succumbed and gave a lancing to Arthur's beloved Guinevere. In an attempt to restore honor, Arthur sends the boys out on a quest for the Holy Grail. The soundtrack is a mix of original incidental and classical music with Carl Orff's "Carmina Burana" sending the knights galloping off into a once-upon-a-time glory that has never been done better. 🦴🦴🦴🦴

1981 (R) 140m/C Nigel Terry, Nicol Williamson, Nicholas Clay, Helen Mirren, Cherie Lunghi, Paul Geoffrey, Gabriel Byrne, Liam Neeson, Patrick Stewart, Charley Boorman, Corin Redgrave; *D:* John Boorman; *W:* John Boorman, Rospo Pallenberg; *M:* Trevor Jones. Nominations: Academy Awards '81: Best Cinematography; Cannes Film Festival '81: Best Film. **VHS, Beta, LV** *WAR, TVC*

Explorers

What if, in the middle of *E.T.,* Spielberg's classic alien suddenly took off his mask and revealed...Mork from Ork? That's more or less what happens to this delicate, promising sci-fi tale that takes a galactic detour into gonzo comedy. In a reworking of *This Island Earth,* three boys are prompted by mysterious dreams to build a circuit that turns a scrapped carnival ride into real spaceship (a tad crude; the control console is an Apple IIC). Zooming into space, the heroes discover who invited them, and that's where the picture either charms or falls apart, take your choice. Recommended for kid viewers who may better appreciate/forgive the punchline. Creature f/x by Rob Bottin. 🦴🦴🦴

1985 (PG) 107m/C Ethan Hawke, River Phoenix, Jason Presson, Amanda Peterson, Mary Kay Place, Dick Miller, Robert Picardo, Dana Ivey, Meshach Taylor, Brooke Bundy; **D:** Joe Dante; **W:** Eric Luke; **C:** John Hora; **M:** Jerry Goldsmith. **VHS, Beta, LV** *PAR*

Exterminators of the Year 3000

The Exterminator and his mercenary girlfriend battle with nuclear mutants over the last remaining tanks of purified water on Earth. Low-budget *Road Warrior* rip-off. **WOOF!**
1983 (R) 101m/C *IT SP* Robert Jannucci, Alicia Moro, Alan Collins, Fred Harris; **D:** Jules Harrison. **VHS, Beta** *NO*

The Eye Creatures

John Ashley stars in this gory uncredited remake of the 1957 low-budget sci-fi *Invasion of the Saucermen.* Following the same basic plot, multi-eyed aliens are fought off by an overaged teenager and his girlfriend, this time without any of the humor or energy of the first one. Even the rubber suits aren't as good. 🦴
1965 80m/B John Ashley, Cynthia Hull, Warren Hammack, Chet Davis, Bill Peck; **D:** Larry Buchanan. **VHS** *NOS, SNC*

Eyes Behind the Stars

Long before *The X-Files,* Italian filmmakers spread the gospel of paranoia to flying saucer believers with this low-budget yarn of a photographer who gets pictures of a UFO as his model is abducted (she returns as a basket case). Our hero teams with a reporter to expose an international shadow conspiracy of paramilitary Men in Black determined cover up the presence the E.T.'s, who are seemingly non-corporeal and couldn't care less anyway. Torrid and downbeat. 🦴🦴
1972 95m/C *IT* Martin Balsam, Robert Hoffman, Nathalie Delon, Sherry Buchanan; **D:** Roy Garrett. **VHS, Beta** *NO*

The Face of Fu Manchu

Christopher Lee is novelist Sax Rohmer's nefarious Chinese arch-villain Fu Manchu, holed up in England in a secret laboratory under the Thames. With the help of his daughter and an imprisoned German scientist, Fu is after a deadly gas that will allow him to take over the world. It's the very proper Sir Nayland Smith to

the rescue, along with enough dynamite to blow the Fu-ster's hiding place sky high. Will goodness prevail? Or will Fu triumph? This somewhat silly but enjoyable flick was the first of Lee's Fu Manchu films, followed in 1966 by *The Brides of Fu Manchu.* 🦴🦴🦴
1965 96m/C *GB* Christopher Lee, Nigel Green, James Robertson Justice, H. Marion Crawford, Tsai Chin, Walter Rilla; **D:** Don Sharp; **W:** Peter Welbeck; **C:** Ernest Steward. **VHS**

Fahrenheit 451

French auteur Francois Truffaut adapts Ray Bradbury's classic novel about an oppressive future where books are burned. Firemen are responsible for eliminating all books by burning them—Fahrenheit 451 is the temperature at which paper begins to burn. Recollections of firemen putting out fires have become ancient myths. The story follows Montag, a fireman, content and unquestioning in his work, until he meets a book-loving subversive played by Julie Christie (who also plays Montag's pill-popping, TV-addicted wife). Montag begins to question the morality of his actions, and actually begins to read the books he is supposed to burn. Enthralled by the words of Dickens, Montag too becomes a rebel from the police state. Though heavy handed in its portrayal of a society where free thought has been outlawed, the film does succeed in capturing the essence of the novel (the credits are spoken, instead of displayed on screen), if not the subtleties. A haunting ending helps make up for slow going early on. Oskar Werner gives a solid performance as the hero who begins the question the system, and Cyril Cusack is splendid as his evil boss. Bernard Herrmann provides the dramatic score. This was Truffaut's first color and only English-language film. 🦴🦴🦴
1966 112m/C Oskar Werner, Julie Christie, Cyril Cusack, Anton Diffring, Jeremy Spenser; **D:** Francois Truffaut; **W:** Francois Truffaut, Jean-Louis Richard; **C:** Nicolas Roeg; **M:** Bernard Herrmann. **VHS, Beta, LV** *MCA, MLB, INJ*

Fail-Safe

A nail-biting nuclear age nightmare, in which American planes have been erroneously sent to nuke Moscow with no way to recall them.

"The medieval philosophers were right. Man is the center of the universe. We stand in the middle of infinity between outer and inner space, and there's no limit to either."

—Dr. Peter Duval (Arthur Kennedy) in *Fantastic Voyage.*

This straight-faced flipside to *Dr. Strangelove* has absolutely no comic relief, and is high-tension all the way through. The all-star cast impels the drama as the heads of the Russian and United States governments try to end the crisis as time runs out. Henry Fonda is impressive as the U.S. president forced to offer an eye for an eye. Fine black-and-white cinematography and an intelligent script top off this great adaptation of the Eugene Burdick/Harvey Wheeler novel. 🦴🦴🦴🦴

1964 111m/B Henry Fonda, Dan O'Herlihy, Walter Matthau, Larry Hagman, Fritz Weaver, Dom DeLuise; **D:** Sidney Lumet; **W:** Walter Bernstein. **VHS, Beta, LV** *COL*

Fantastic Planet

A critically acclaimed, animated French sci-fi epic based on the drawings of Roland Topor. A race of small humanoids are enslaved and exploited by a race of telepathic blue giants on a savage planet. The film follows one of the small creatures on his quest to unite his people and win them equality with their captors. This film has a haunting, alien quality that makes it stand out even today; there's little dialogue, and the backgrounds and character designs are delicate with a dreamlike strangeness. The film is full of inventive, startling images: the hero is in one scene forced to fight another of his race with vicious, snapping reptiles strapped to their chests. And the blue giants, with their staring, emotionless faces, are particularly haunting. The story, however, is humanistic and gently satirical. A memorable, eerie film that'll stay with you for some time. **AKA:** La Planete Sauvage. 🦴🦴🦴🦴

1973 (PG) 68m/C *FR* **D:** Rene Laloux; **V:** Barry Bostwick. Nominations: Cannes Film Festival '73: Best Film. **VHS, Beta** *VYY, MRV, SNC*

Fantastic Voyage

An important scientist, rescued from behind the Iron Curtain, is wounded by enemy agents. A tiny clot within his brain means that tradi-

"How's that for science! We can get into a man's bloodstream to perform surgery from the inside, but we can't grow Ralph, here, any hair or stop Vinnie's sweat glands from workin' overtime!" Raquel Welch finds irony in the *Fantastic Voyage.*

tional surgery is impossible. After being shrunk to microscopic size, a medical team uses a hi-tech submarine to journey inside his body where they find themselves threatened by the patient's natural defenses, as well as a sabotaging spy who has made his way aboard. Great action, award-winning special effects. The weird "inner space" settings depicting a microbes'-eye-view of the human body sometimes recall Jules Verne films, especially *Journey to the Center of the Earth*. The performances are generally bland—except for Donald Pleasence, who gives us one of his trademark twitchy, nervous characterizations. Richard Fleischer also directed *20,000 Leagues Under the Sea* and *Soylent Green*. Later adapted into a Saturday morning cartoon series. **AKA:** Microscopia; Strange Journey. 𝄞 𝄞 𝄞

1966 100m/C Stephen Boyd, Edmond O'Brien, Raquel Welch, Arthur Kennedy, Donald Pleasence, Arthur O'Connell, William Redfield, James Brolin; **D:** Richard Fleischer; **W:** Harry Kleiner; **C:** Ernest Laszlo. Academy Awards '66: Best Art Direction/Set Decoration (Color), Best Visual Effects; Nominations: Academy Awards '66: Best Color Cinematography, Best Film Editing. **VHS, Beta, LV** FOX, CCB

Fiend Without a Face

This early attempt at gore cinema works quite well, addressing the problems of nuclear power, while promising—and delivering—a real bloodbath. A paranormal atomic scientist's thoughts materialize as invisible creatures who slurp human brains right out of the skull. When the nearby reactor's power is increased, the creatures become visible, revealing themselves to be replicas of brains with spinal cords. Now they can be chopped, sliced, and shot, all on camera, allowing enormous amounts of blood to be spilled. The sound effects are also quite disgusting for both the brain-drainings and -splatterings. Great fun and lots of silliness for '50s sci-fi/horror fans. 𝄞 𝄞

1958 77m/B Marshall Thompson, Kim Parker, Terence Kilburn, Michael Balfour, Gil Winfield, Shane Cordell; **D:** Arthur Crabtree. **VHS, LV** CCB, REP, MLB

The Fiendish Plot of Dr. Fu Manchu

Peter Sellers' last film stood the whole Fu Manchu series on its head with gentle, occa-

sionally surreal humor. Sellers portrays both the evil Doctor Fu and Nayland Smith, his heroic Scotland Yard nemesis. In Sellers' version, Smith is getting slightly dotty with old age and insists on pushing around a lawnmower everywhere he goes, while Fu recalls studying at Eton in his youth. All of this is incidental to the plot, which as usual involves Fu's quest for immortality—but with some very unusual twists. 𝄞 𝄞 𝄞

1980 (PG) 100m/C GB Peter Sellers, David Tomlinson, Sid Caesar, Helen Mirren, Simon Williams; **D:** Piers Haggard. **VHS, Beta, LV** WAR, FCT

Final Approach

U.S. Air Force stealth pilot Jason Halsey (James B. Sikking) crashes in the desert and awakens in the office of ominous psychiatrist Dio Gottlieb (Hector Elizondo). Remembering nothing of his past, and not even recognizing his own face, Halsey begins to work with Gottlieb while the commander of the covert stealth operation, General Geller (Kevin McCarthy), tries to debrief him on the crash. Although the video packaging suggests that this might be an aerial shoot-'em-up, it's really a well acted, fairly intense drama with plenty of plot twists. Scenes of the SR71, the spy plane that could fly so fast and high that it was nearly impossible to shoot down, are pretty incredible, and the computer display effects give the feel of being in the cockpit. The letterboxed version, available on VHS and laserdisc, is the only way to see it. Notable as the first film made with a totally digital soundtrack, and claims over 18,000 digital sound effects. 𝄞 𝄞 ♪

1991 (R) 100m/C James B. Sikking, Hector Elizondo, Madolyn Smith, Kevin McCarthy, Cameo Kneuer, Wayne Duvall; **D:** Eric Steven Stahl. **VHS, LV** VMK

The Final Combat

When the French tried a post-apocalyptic action flick, filmmaker Luc Besson went mad to the max and created a black-and-white nightmare world of deserts, ruins, and bleached wreckage, with no dialogue (possible explanation: poison gas has burned out everyone's vocal cords) and weird weather phenomena. The 'Man,' a spear-carrying everybarbarian,

tires of life in the parched wastelands and pilots his homebuilt aircraft to a devastated city where he befriends a doctor (who does caveman-style paintings on the walls) and fights a running duel with relentless brute Reno. Good luck puzzling through some of the grunting mime "dialogue," and the ending feels like a bit of a cheat. But as a glimpse at what lies beyond the fall of civilization this will stick in your mind a lot longer than all those low-octane *Road Warrior* wannabes. 🎞️🎞️🎞️

1984 (R) 93m/B *FR* Pierre Joviet, Fritz Wepper, Jean Bouise, Jean Reno; *D:* Luc Besson. **VHS** *FOX*

The Final Countdown

On December 7, 1980, the nuclear carrier USS Nimitz is caught in a time warp and transported back in time to Pearl Harbor, December 7, 1941, just hours before the Japanese bombing attack that crippled the U.S. and propelled the country into WWII. The commanders are faced with the ultimate decision—leave history intact or stop the incident and maybe the war itself. Making the decision are the captain (Kirk Douglas), his first mate (James Farentino), and a civilian observer (Martin Sheen). The real star of the movie is the Nimitz itself; the footage taken aboard it offered a look at the magnitude of power available and adds to the realistic feel of the film. Excellent cinematography and a surprise ending wrap things up nicely. 🎞️🎞️🎞️

1980 (PG) 92m/C Kirk Douglas, Martin Sheen, Katharine Ross, James Farentino, Charles Durning, Ron O'Neal; *D:* Don Taylor; *W:* Thomas Hunter, David Ambrose, Gerry Davis, Peter Powell; *C:* Victor Kemper. **VHS, Beta, LV** *VES*

The Final Executioner

A valiant man finds a way to stop the slaughter of innocent people in a post-nuclear world. **AKA:** The Last Warrior. 🎞️

1983 95m/C William Mang, Marina Costa, Harrison Muller, Woody Strode; *D:* Romolo Guerrieri. **VHS, Beta** *MGM*

The Final Programme

In this futuristic story, a man must rescue his sister—and the world—from their brother, who holds a microfilmed plan for global domination. Meanwhile, he must shield himself from the advances of a bisexual computer programmer who wants to make him father to a new, all-purpose human being. Based on the Michael Moorcock "Jerry Cornelius" stories, the film has gained a cult following. **AKA:** The Last Days of Man on Earth. 🎞️🎞️🎞️

1973 85m/C *GB* Hugh Griffith, Harry Andrews, Jon Finch, Jenny Runacre, Sterling Hayden, Patrick Magee, Sarah Douglas; *D:* Robert Fuest. **VHS, Beta** *SUE*

Fire in the Sky

The mysterious disappearance of logger Travis Wilson (D. B. Sweeney) sparks a criminal investigation of his drinking buddies. Then Travis returns, telling a frightening story of alien abduction. Though everyone in town doubts his story, viewers won't, since the alleged aliens have already made an appearance, shifting the focus to Sweeney and friends as he tries to convince skeptics that his trauma is genuine. Sweeney is sympathetic and believable as the abductee, as is Robert Patrick as the unjustly accused friend. James Garner is great as the incredulous hard-nosed investigator. Still, the movie does a better job of making viewers feel sorry for everyone than turning them into believers. A weekly episode of *The X-Files* is better than this. Spooky and captivating special effects of the alien abduction and alien experiments are some of the few bright spots. Based on a story that might be true. 🎞️🎞️🎞️

1993 (PG-13) 98m/C D.B. Sweeney, Robert Patrick, Craig Sheffer, Peter Berg, James Garner, Henry Thomas, Kathleen Wilhoite, Bradley Gregg, Noble Willingham; *D:* Robert Lieberman; *W:* Tracy Torme; *M:* Mark Isham. **VHS, Beta, LV** *PAR*

Fire Maidens from Outer Space

Fire maidens prove to be true to the space opera code that dictates that all alien women be in desperate need of male company. Astronauts on an expedition to Jupiter's thirteenth moon discover the lost civilization of Atlantis, which, as luck would have it, is inhabited only by women (except for one busy old man). An unexplained beast man prowls around looking to carry off fire maidens (can you blame him?).

What with *Cat Women on the Moon, Queen of Outer Space, Abbott & Costello Go to Mars, Invasion of the Star Creatures,* and *Missile to the Moon,* one might get the impression that outer space was swarming with scantily clad beauty queens. Was this part of a secret government plot to recruit volunteers for the space program? 🎞

1956 80m/B *GB* Anthony Dexter, Susan Shaw, Paul Carpenter, Harry Fowler, Jacqueline Curtiss, Sydney Tafler, Maya Koumani, Jan Holden, Kim Parker, Owen Barry, Ian Struthers; **D:** Cy Roth; **W:** Cy Roth. **VHS** *CNM, MLB*

The Fire Next Time

In the year 2017, the United States is being ravaged by an ecological holocaust caused by a deadly combination of pollution and global warming. Craig T. Nelson, Bonnie Bedelia, and their children are forced from their Louisiana home by a natural disaster and decide to head for better times in Canada. Their travels aren't easy. Made for television. 🎞🎞◗

1993 195m/C Craig T. Nelson, Bonnie Bedelia, Juergen Prochnow, Richard Farnsworth, Justin Whalin, Charles Haid, Sal Lopez, Shawn Toovey, Ashley Jones; **Cameos:** Odetta; **D:** Tom McLoughlin; **W:** James Henerson. **VHS** *CAF*

Firebird 2015 A.D.

A dreary action adventure set in a 21st-Century society where automobile use is banned because of an extreme oil shortage. Private cars are hunted down for destruction by the Department of Vehicular Control. One overzealous enforcer decides to make it a package deal by throwing in the owners as well. Red and Indie (Darren McGavin and George Touliatos) are rebels who refuse to give up the pleasures of driving. They manage to avoid capture for a while, but eventually the DVC abduct Indie's daughter and it's time for a show-down. Everyone connected with this effort should have had their license revoked. 🎞

1981 (PG) 97m/C Darren McGavin, George Touliatos, Doug McClure; **D:** David Robertson. **VHS, Beta** *SUE*

Firestarter

Don't make her angry. You wouldn't like her when she's angry. A C.I.A.-like organization is after a little girl who has the ability to set any-thing on fire with her mind, courtesy of Mom and Dad's participation in a drug study while in college. Future vixen Drew Barrymore steps outside E.T.'s shadow with solid work in the title role. George C. Scott is eminently creepy as a tracker who has mysterious reasons for finding her. Script faithfully follows Stephen King away from the horror and gore and onto the road with what, until the last twenty minutes, is basically a chase movie. If you like seeing things blow up, good special effects help a silly plot. 🎞🎞

1984 (R) 115m/C David Keith, Drew Barrymore, Freddie Jones, Martin Sheen, George C. Scott, Heather Locklear, Louise Fletcher, Moses Gunn, Art Carney, Antonio Fargas, Drew Snyder; **D:** Mark L. Lester; **M:** Tangerine Dream. **VHS, Beta, LV** *MCA*

First Man into Space

An astronaut returns to Earth covered with a crust of strange space dust and with an organism feeding inside him (shades of *Alien*). The alien needs human blood to survive and starts killing in order to get it. Prototypical "astronaut turns into monster" plotline sets down the plodding formula used for years afterward (see *Monster A Go-Go* and *Incredible Melting Man* for more of the same) until the climax, which creates a great deal of sympathy for the helpless man within the monster. May have served as partial inspiration for Marvel Comics' *Fantastic Four* series. **AKA:** Satellite of Blood. 🎞🎞◗

1959 78m/B *GB* Marshall Thompson, Marla Landi, Bill Edwards, Robert Ayres, Bill Nagy, Carl Jaffe; **D:** Robert Day; **W:** John C. Cooper, Lance Z. Hargreaves; **C:** Geoffrey Faithfull. **VHS, Beta** *DVT, RHI, HEG*

First Men in the Moon

A fun, special effects-laden adaptation of the H. G. Wells novel about an Edwardian civilian spacecraft visiting the moon and the creatures found there. Wells' vision of space travel has a unique twist—the vehicle is a globe covered with an anti-gravity substance, controlled by a shutter system. The explorers hang in webbed hammocks for protection during the rough landing, stretching credibility even beyond the light tone of the film, and they quickly discover a breathable atmosphere below the Moon's

The Hound Salutes:
Ray Harryhausen

Perhaps the best introduction to the work of special effects pioneer Ray Harryhausen is the videotape (and disc) *Aliens, Dragons, Monsters & Me* (Midwich Entertainment, Lumivision, 1992). This celebration of Harryhausen's long career in stop-motion animation is based on an exhibit of his work at the Museum of the Moving Image in London. Also included are an affectionate analysis of Harryhausen's appeal by his friend Ray Bradbury and highlights of the best moments from his films.

The story is told in rough chronological order, beginning when a Los Angeles teenager saw *King Kong* and knew that his life had been changed. He started making home movies with models, and then short films. When World War II came along, he continued his work with Frank Capra's film unit and even made a propaganda film entitled *Guadalcanal*.

After the war, Harryhausen moved to features and found that his tastes in fantasy and science fiction weren't shared by the larger movie-going public. Though much of his black and white work is respected and studied today, such films as *Mighty Joe Young, The Beast from 20,000 Fathoms, Earth Vs. the Flying Saucers, It Came from Beneath the Sea,* and *20 Million Miles to Earth* were relegated to drive-ins and double features in the 1940s and '50s.

But then he and his long-time producer Charles H. Schneer made the bold leap to color and myth, and *The Seventh Voyage of Sinbad* became the sleeper hit of 1958. After it came *The Three Worlds of Gulliver, Mysterious Island, Valley of Gwangi, The Golden Voyage of Sinbad,* and several others, including everybody's favorite, *Jason and the Argonauts*.

Some were commercial hits; some weren't. All contain Harryhausen's wonderful creations—cyclops and griffins, metal giants and moon men, sword-waving skeletons and flying horses, and perhaps best of all, dinosaurs and dragons.

If they lack the crystalline clarity and intricate detail of more expensive computer-generated creatures that fill screens these days, they can still inspire gasps of wonder. Take a look at a kid watching Talos, the bronze giant, come to life in *Jason* and you'll see pure amazement. That's movie magic at its timeless best.

Harryhausen's work stands up to repeated viewings because even the worst of it—with silly plots and thin characters—contains visual surprises and flair. Ray Harryhausen has always pushed the limits of his craft while imbuing his creations with strong, recognizable personalities that equal their human co-stars. He made characters we care about, and that's the secret of all good films.

---

surface. However, the insectoid "sellenites" inhabiting the lunar caverns are genuinely unsettling. Lionel Jeffries' performance as the outlandish inventor is an easy scene stealer—at times too much so. Visual effects by Ray Harryhausen. Peter Finch makes a brief appearance. Nathan Juran often used the "Hertz" pseudonym for films he was less than proud of, but it was unwarranted in this case. 🦴🦴🦴

1964 103m/C *GB* Martha Hyer, Edward Judd, Lionel Jeffries, Erik Chitty, Peter Finch, Miles Malleson; *D:* Nathan (Hertz) Juran; *W:* Nigel Kneale, Jan Read; *C:* Wilkie Cooper, Harry Gillam. **VHS, Beta, LV** *COL, MLB*

First Spaceship on Venus

Eight international scientists set foot on Venus, but what they find is as downbeat as it was a decade earlier on Mars in *Rocketship X-M*, which showed structures of a dead civilization standing silent as blind Martians staggered about. The cause: atomic war, but here the nukes have also done in the natives; the only

identifiable life form is a gray organic ooze that spurts out with such menacing force that the entire Earth expedition retreats and goes home. Pic is worth one viewing just to drink in the bizarre architecture of the Venusian ruins. It's like being caught in a Yves Tanguy painting; elongated, twisted, curvy shapes cast forth by alien minds who knew different laws of time and space. Antinuke sci-fi effort was made with German and Polish backing and originally released at 130 minutes. **AKA:** Der Schweigende Stern; Milczaca Gwiazda. 🎬🎬

1960 78m/C GE PL Yoko Tani, Oldrich Lukes, Ignacy Machowski, Julius Ongewe, Michal Postnikow, Kurt Rackelmann, Gunther Simon, Tang-Hua-Ta, Lucyna Winnicka; **D:** Kurt Maetzig; **W:** Jan Fethke, Wolfgang Kohlaase, Guenther Reisch, Guenther Ruecker; **C:** Joachim Hasler. **VHS, Beta** NOS, MRV, SNC

Flash Gordon

A campy, updated version of the classic adventures of the blonde, spacefaring hero. The bones of the story are the same: Flash and his gal-pal Dale Arden are forced by nutty Dr. Zarkov to accompany him on a mission to far-off planet Mongo. It seems Mongo's head bad-guy, one Ming the Merciless, is threatening to destroy the Earth, and they Must Stop Him. Sam Jones makes a pretty unconvincing Flash, but if you can overlook his leaden performance, this flick is fast moving, cheerfully sleazy, and a lot of fun. Max von Sydow does a fine job of rehashing Charles Middleton's classic performance as Ming and Brian Blessed is great as Vultan, the blowhard king of the hawkmen. Queen did the soundtrack. 🎬🎬🎬

1980 (PG) 111m/C Sam Jones, Melody Anderson, Chaim Topol, Max von Sydow, Ornella Muti, Timothy Dalton, Brian Blessed; **D:** Mike Hodges; **W:** Lorenzo Semple Jr.; **M:** Howard Blake. **VHS, Beta, LV** MCA

Flash Gordon Conquers the Universe

Third and last Flash Gordon serial works well as both a 12-chapter play and a feature-length condensation (both have the same title). Ming the Merciless of Mongo is dusting the Earth with toxic spores, the Purple Death. Naturally Flash, Dale Arden, and Dr. Zarkov visit Mongo to frustrate the Emperor; assisting them are the running characters Prince Barin of Arboria and Aura, Ming's daughter now married to Barin. Considered by serial authorities as weakest of the three F.G.'s, it's nonetheless the most elegant looking because filmmakers had the sense to copy clothing and set designs predominant in Alex Raymond's source comic strip (Raymond was greatly influenced by Cecil B. DeMille's 1935 epic The Crusades and turned medieval soap opera into space opera when drafting his costumes and textures). In the concluding chapter Flash unleashes an out-of-control rocketship against Ming's castle battlement, and the latter was actually part of the set for Universal's 1939 Tower of London. Whence came the title of this serial? Ming, in his egotistical blindness, calls himself "The Universe," and because Flash so thoroughly quells him at the conclusion, Flash is entitled, according to Dr. Zarkov, to say that he has conquered the universe. Sheesh! **AKA:** Purple Death from Outer Space. 🎬🎬🎬

1940 240m/B Buster Crabbe, Carol Hughes, Charles Middleton, Frank Shannon; **D:** Ford Beebe, Ray Taylor; **W:** George Plympton; **C:** Jerome Ash. **VHS, Beta** VYY, MRV, SNC

Flash Gordon: Mars Attacks the World

This feature condensation of the second Flash Gordon serial (*Flash Gordon's Trip to Mars*) was supposed to take place on Mongo, but all the characters and the locale switched to Mars after Orson Welle's famed War of the Worlds Halloween broadcast of 1938. So Azura, Queen of the Blue Caverns on Mongo in the Alex Raymond comic strip, became Azura, Queen of Mars. And so on. Plot concerns Ming the Merciless, planet-hopping, aiming a death ray at Earth in revenge for what Flash did to him in the first serial. Mongo's Prince Barin of Arboria also drops in to help his old friend Flash, and there are some put-upon Martian citizens called the Clay People to lend a muddy hand. Besides their eerie language (actually normal English played backwards!) and great entrance scene, literally oozing out of their cave walls (simple but effective double exposure f/x), the

Clay People also benefit from some great Franz Waxman music borrowed from *The Bride of Frankenstein*. Overall, this serial is not as good as the first *Flash Gordon* but is worth a look. **AKA:** The Deadly Rays from Mars; Flash Gordon's Trip to Mars. 🦴🦴🦴ᵇ

1938 87m/B Buster Crabbe, Jean Rogers, Charles Middleton; *D:* Robert F. "Bob" Hill, Ford Beebe; *W:* Ray Trampe; *C:* Jerome Ash. **VHS, Beta** *CAB*

Flash Gordon: Rocketship

Re-edited from the original Flash Gordon serial in which Flash and company must prevent the planet Mongo from colliding with Earth. Its ruler, Ming the Merciless (impeccably played by Charles Middleton), is hurling his world into Earth orbit to crush all terrestrial life, but the human adventurers, united with rebel citizens of Mongo, stop his despotic schemes. Buster Crabbe is a perfect Flash Gordon, Frank Shannon his brainy scientist sidekick Hans Zarkov, and Jean Rogers a demure blonde Dale Arden. She turned into a brunette in the succeeding serial, more accurate to the classic Alex Raymond comics (which this otherwise follows with great fidelity). Yes, much was cut out in this condensation, but the smooth story progression will amaze you, as will the production values; this is considered the most expensive serial ever lensed. Condensed feature version has something the original (also available on video) lacks, Franz Waxman's stirring music excerpted from *The Bride of Frankenstein*. **AKA:** Spaceship to the Unknown; Perils from Planet Mongo; Space Soldiers; Atomic Rocketship. 🦴🦴🦴ᵇ

1936 97m/B Buster Crabbe, Jean Rogers, Frank Shannon, Charles Middleton, Priscilla Lawson, Jack Lipson; *D:* Frederick Stephani; *W:* George Plympton; *C:* Jerome Ash. **VHS, Beta** *VYY, PSM, CAB*

Flatliners

A group of medical students begin after-hours experimentation with death, taking turns being "killed" and brought back to life with CPR techniques. Some start to see frightening visions afterwards—is a part of them still connected to the afterlife? Plot is weak, but visuals are striking and spooky. Julia Roberts and Kiefer Sutherland create an energy that makes it worth watching. 🦴🦴

1990 (R) 111m/C Kiefer Sutherland, Julia Roberts, William Baldwin, Oliver Platt, Kevin Bacon, Kimberly Scott, Joshua Rudoy; *D:* Joel Schumacher; *M:* James Newton Howard. **VHS, Beta, LV, 8mm** *COL*

The Flesh Eaters

This crudely effective shocker stars Rita Morley as an alcoholic film star who, with her secretary, crashlands on an island inhabited by—what else—a Nazi scientist (Martin Kosleck, a Universal contract player who, by one count, portrayed Joseph Goebbels three times). He is experimenting with sea creatures to develop a solvent for human flesh. The swarming critters were achieved by scratching the film with pins. This one, with its grisly effects and surprising shock ending, just might get under your skin. Director Jack Curtis also directed *We Are All Naked*. Editor Randy Metzger is also best known for adult films, including *I, a Woman, Camille 2000,* and *The Lickerish Quartet*. Restored video release restores the more gruesome footage as well as Nazi experiment flashbacks that were cut from TV prints. Reportedly, Curtis died during production and his widow/co-producer had to scramble to finish shooting. 🦴🦴🦴

1964 87m/C Martin Kosleck, Rita Morley, Byron Sanders, Barbara Wilkin, Ray Tudor; *D:* Jack Curtis; *W:* Arnold Drake; *C:* Carson Davidson. **VHS, Beta** *SNC*

Flesh Gordon

Meanwhile, back on the planet Porno, the evil Emperor Wang is bombarding the Earth with his insidious sex ray. The streets are teeming with the bodies of coupling citizens unable to control their rampant desires. Is there no one who can save our planet from total carnal chaos? This 1974 relic from the Golden Age of midnight movies was originally conceived as a hard-core spoof on the sci-fi serial hero Flash Gordon. Seen today, the sex is perfunctory and the humor sophomoric with smutty, silly wordplay. But its cult status is assured as the launching pad for a group of artists who would later revolutionize the art of special effects and make up, including Dennis Muren (*E.T.*), Rick

"I'm not really Robin Hood, but I do know a little john...." *Flesh Gordon.*

Baker (*An American Werewolf in London*),and Greg Jein (*Close Encounters of the Third Kind*). Craig T. Nelson, at the time a stand-up comedian, provides the voice of the scene-stealing, stop-motion animated beast ("A monster's work is never done"). Available in its original 90-minute uncut and unrated version. This "Collector's Edition" also features the original theatrical preview. The R-rated, 72-minute version is also available. 🦴🦴🦴

1972 90m/C Jason Williams, Suzanne Fields, Joseph Hudgins, John Hoyt, Howard Zieff, William Hunt; *Cameos:* Candy Samples; *D:* Michael Benveniste, Howard Ziehm; *W:* Michael Benveniste; *C:* Howard Ziehm; *V:* Craig T. Nelson. **VHS, LV** *HTV, IME, MED*

Flesh Gordon 2: Flesh Gordon Meets the Cosmic Cheerleaders

The evil and perverted Emperor Wang (William Dennis Hunt) once again threatens the Universe—this time with his powerful Impotence Ray—in this long-awaited sequel to the (in)famous sf parody. Flesh (Vince Murdocco), along with Dale (Robyn Kelly) and Dr. Flexi Jerkoff (Tony Travis), do battle with a belt of farting "assteroids" and other weirdos, including a race of adult babies. Director Howard Ziehm delivers this one on a shoestring of under $1 million, and from a technical standpoint, at least, tops the original. The sex scenes however, are considerably more watered down, apparently in an attempt to gain a wider audience. That's all well and good, but it tends to make the film as a whole seem a little pointless. The humor tends to be scatological rather than sexual; the parade of bathroom references are amusing at first, but they get old real fast. Fans of the original will be sorely disappointed. 🦴

1990 98m/C *CA* Vince Murdocco, Tony Travis, William Dennis Hunt, Robyn Kelly; *D:* Howard Ziehm. **VHS** *NHO*

Flight of the Navigator

A 12-year-old comes back from a walk in the woods to learn that eight years have passed

for his family and the rest of the world. Meanwhile NASA finds a parked UFO nearby but can't open it. The bewildered boy is the key and has an incredible adventure in time and space. Disney sf starts with a genuine sense of mystery and wonder, later largely abandoned in favor of comedy as Paul Reubens, in his Pee Wee Herman character, provides the voice of the alien intelligence. Good fun nonetheless, with some cool computer-generated f/x. 🎵🎵🎵

1986 (PG) 90m/C Joey Cramer, Veronica Cartwright, Cliff DeYoung, Sarah Jessica Parker, Matt Adler, Howard Hesseman; *D:* Randal Kleiser; *W:* Michael Burton, Matt MacManus; *M:* Alan Silvestri; *V:* Paul (Pee Wee Herman) Reubens. **VHS, Beta, LV** *DIS*

Flight to Mars

Interplanetary explorers crashland on Mars and find an advanced underground society that looks and acts just like humans, except they've never heard of uranium. Mars leaders help fix the rocket, while secretly scheming to copy its atom-powered design for an invasion fleet. Notable as the first color movie of this genre (two-strip Technicolor), it's still static and uninvolving—Flash Gordon with no flash. Turn down your TV brightness and this talky opus could pass for a vintage radio play. Nice touch: Marguerite Chapman plays a Martian maiden named Alita, in reference to the 1924 expressionist Soviet fantasy *Aelita, Queen of Mars*. 🎵🎵

1951 72m/C Cameron Mitchell, Marguerite Chapman, Arthur Franz, Virginia Huston, John Litel, Richard Gaines; *D:* Lesley Selander; *W:* Arthur Strawn; *C:* Harry Neumann. **VHS, Beta, LV** *MED, IME*

The Fly

The original sci-fi tale about a hapless scientist Hedison, experimenting with teleportation, who accidentally gets anatomically mixed with a housefly. Now, how to tell the wife? No matter how repellently fascinating the premise, an earnest, wordy script (by novelist James Clavell) and direction better suited to domestic-crisis drama lend this a campy air even the actors couldn't ignore—rumor has it Vincent Price and Herbert Marshall had to sti-

fle giggles while shooting the notorious "... help me ... help meeeeeee!" climax. Required viewing nonetheless. Mediocre sequel *Return of the Fly* is also on video; the British-made *Curse of the Fly* (1965) is not. While this stays close to source material of George Langelaan's short story, David Cronenberg's 1986 remake took a boldly different approach. 🎵🎵🎵

1958 94m/C Vincent Price, David Hedison, Herbert Marshall, Patricia Owens; *D:* Kurt Neumann; *W:* James Clavell. **VHS, Beta, LV** *FOX*

The Fly

This may be director David Cronenberg's ultimate study of the decay of the flesh in this remake of the 1958 classic. Jeff Goldblum is perfect as the eccentric scientist Seth Brundle, whose genes and molecules are intermixed with those of a housefly via his experimental teleportation device. As he begins to change, Seth at first becomes stronger, more agile, and virile as hell. But girlfriend Geena Davis watches in horror as genetic mutation kicks into high gear and Seth's body literally begins to fall apart. Cronenberg sets things up with some lighthearted humor during the degeneration, only to lead into one of the most brutally emotional conclusions ever filmed. A thoughtful, sensitive, and ultimately shocking horror film with amazing special effects by Chris Walas, who went on to direct *The Fly 2* in 1989. 🎵🎵🎵🎵

1986 (R) 96m/C Jeff Goldblum, Geena Davis, John Getz, Joy Boushel; *D:* David Cronenberg; *W:* David Cronenberg, Charles Edward Pogue; *M:* Howard Shore. Academy Awards '86: Best Makeup. **VHS, Beta, LV** *FOX*

The Fly 2

Although inferior to Cronenberg's opus, this sequel continues the study of the decay of the flesh and how it affects the mental and emotional as well as the physical. Martin (Eric Stoltz), son of fly/man Seth Brundle, achieves full genius maturity in five years. Machiavellian industrialist Anton Bartok (Lee Richardson) cares about his ward about as much as he cares for his other experimental animals, but the sheltered Martin loves him as a father. Computer operator Beth (Daphne Zuniga) awakens Martin's human desires and makes

"Fifty years into the future...the most fantastic expedition ever conceived by man!"

—*Flight to Mars.*

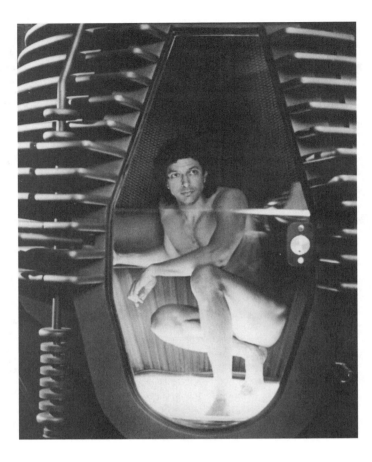

Monster Strikes. There they could barely get down to Earth and back without tapping human ingenuity. Now they know all about atomic power and weapons so powerful only a handful of Martians can rule the globe with their mighty flying discs. Alas, Republic had little money for a sally into sci fi, so there is only one disc and only one Martian, a certain Professor Mota (atom spelled backwards). As for the saucer, it's a squat cigar-shaped structure built over an automobile and first appeared in the 1942 serial *Spy Smasher* (and in miniature for 1942's *King of the Mounties*). Naturally the studio reused this earlier footage wherever it could and filmed no new flying scenes at all for this lower-berth effort. All Republic serials are worth seeing, but put this one on the back burner until you've found all the others you can lay hands on. 🦴🦴

1951 167m/B VHS *REP, MLB*

The Flying Saucer

U.S. and Russian scientists clash over their search for a huge flying saucer that is hidden under a glacier. The first movie to deal with flying saucers. The cassette includes animated opening and closing sequences plus previews of coming attractions. 🦴🦴

1950 120m/B Mikel Conrad, Pat Garrison, Hanz von Teuffen; *D:* Mikel Conrad. **VHS, Beta** *MWP, SNC*

Food of the Gods

A husband and wife on a secluded island discover some bubbling, seething *stuff* oozing out of their property. When fed to animals, the unappetizing glop creates giant offspring. The pious couple think that this is the Lord's way of ending world hunger, since it makes for some mighty big chickens. Inevitably, though, some less pleasant critters get hold of it and as a result the wife, a couple of young folks, and a corrupt businessman are trapped on the island by a platoon of giant rats and wasps. This updated version of the H. G. Wells novel was a '70s comeback for '50s giant-radioactive-monster auteur Bert I. Gordon. The performances are nothing special—in fact, they're lousy. But the film does have some sur-

him long for a life outside the confines of his laboratory. Continuing his father's work to perfect the teleportation device, Martin's insect genes (note title of film) begin to transform him into a powerful if pathetic son-of fly/man. Like father like son. Director Chris Walas handled the special effects and won the Academy Award for Best Makeup for the 1986 *The Fly.* 🦴🦴

1989 (R) 105m/C Eric Stoltz, Daphne Zuniga, Lee Richardson, John Getz, Harley Cross; *D:* Chris Walas; *W:* Mick Garris, Jim Wheat, Ken Wheat, Frank Darabont. **VHS, Beta, LV** *FOX, CCB*

Flying Discman from Mars

Martians are greatly advanced in this 12-episode Republic chapter play compared to where they were in Republic's 1945 *The Purple*

prisingly effective visual moments; the giant rats (regular-sized vermin swarming over model cars) look much better than you'd have any reason to suspect. On the other hand, the giant fake rooster-head that attacks the hero is pretty lame. 🦴🦴

1976 (PG) 88m/C Marjoe Gortner, Pamela Franklin, Ralph Meeker, Ida Lupino, Jon Cypher, Belinda Balaski; **D:** Bert I. Gordon; **W:** Bert I. Gordon; **C:** Reginald Morris. **VHS, Beta** *LIV, VES*

Food of the Gods: Part 2

A knock-off sequel to Bert I. Gordon's 1976 giant-animals-run-amok epic. The killer animals of the first film strike again...and again...and.... The emphasis here is on the always-entertaining spectacle of gigantic rats maiming young girls. This confused mess actually makes the original flick look pretty good. By the way, that sound you hear is original *Food* author H.G. Wells turning over in his grave. **AKA:** *Gnaw: Food of the Gods 2.* 🦴

1988 (R) 93m/C *CA* Paul Coufos, Lisa Schrage, Colin Fox, Jackie Burroughs; **D:** Damian Lee; **W:** E. Kim Brewster. **VHS, Beta, LV** *NO*

Forbidden Planet

"Prepare your minds for a new scale of scientific values, gentlemen." MGM's first foray into the genre is Must-See sci fi. Following Disney's lead in the wake of the success of *20,000 Leagues Under the Sea,* the studio lavished its considerable resources on this adventure that was loosely based on William Shakespeare's *The Tempest.* In the 23rd century, Leslie Nielsen leads an expedition to Altair-4 to discover the fate of a previous mission to colonize the planet. They are warned away by Morbius (Walter Pidgeon), who claims to be the only survivor, and states that he needs no help and cannot be responsible for the consequences if Nielsen and company land. Turns out Morbius, who lives in automated luxury, is not alone. He has a beautiful daughter (Anne Francis) who greets the visitors with, "What beautiful men!" They are tended to by Robby the Robot (the film's breakout star and an icon of science-fiction movies). More malevolent is the Monster from the Id, a beast unwittingly summoned from Morbius's subconscious after his daughter hooks up with Nielsen. Arguably the best sci-fi film of the '50s. Now available on video in a preferred letterbox edition. 🦴🦴🦴🦴

1956 98m/C Walter Pidgeon, Anne Francis, Leslie Nielsen, Warren Stevens, Jack Kelly, Richard Anderson, Earl Holliman, George Wallace; **D:** Fred M. Wilcox; **W:** Cyril Hume; **C:** George Folsey; **M:** Bebe Barron, Louis Barron. **VHS, Beta, LV** *MGM, CRC*

Forbidden World

Space scientists on a remote planet are stalked by their own creation, a hostile organism capable of changing its genetic structure as it grows and matures (though it merely looks like a giant rubber spider). Roger Corman-produced quickie followup to *Galaxy of Terror* is a graphically violent ripoff of *Alien* that almost received an X rating for gore. One plus: the cramped, effectively claustrophobic set design. Remade unmemorably in 1990 as *Dead Space.* **AKA:** *Mutant.* 🦴

1982 (R) 82m/C Jesse Vint, Dawn Dunlap, June Chadwick, Linden Chiles; **D:** Allan Holzman; **W:** Jim Wynorski, R.J. Robertson, Tim Curnen. **VHS, Beta, LV** *SUE*

Forbidden Zone

Members of a strange family journey to an underground sixth dimension kingdom ruled by the midget, King Fausto (Herve Villechaize), and inhabited by dancing frogs, bikini-clad tootsies, robot boxers, and degraded beings of all kinds. A very odd black-and-white concoction with many musical numbers, some of which are lip-synched to old records, a la *Pennies from Heaven.* Sets were designed to look like Max Fleischer cartoons. Original music by Oingo Boingo, and directed by Richard Elfman, brother of founding member Danny Elfman. Richard would eventually go on to direct *Shrunken Heads,* which is nearly as bizarre as this one. Danny, who also plays the Devil, would compose the soundtracks for *Batman, Pee Wee's Big Adventure, Edward Scissorhands,* and many others. 🦴🦴

1980 (R) 75m/B Herve Villechaize, Susan Tyrrell, Viva, Danny Elfman; **D:** Richard Elfman; **W:** Matthew Bright, Richard Elfman; **M:** Danny Elfman. **VHS, Beta** *MED*

"Sorry, miss, I was giving myself an oil job."

—Robby the Robot in *Forbidden Planet.*

"Wait just a minute, boys. I'm picking up the Sci-Fi Channel!" Leslie Nielsen and cohorts pirate cable in **Forbidden Planet**.

young Elijah Wood turns out to be the most authentic and endearing love in the film. 🦴🦴🦴🕊

1992 (PG) 102m/C Mel Gibson, Jamie Lee Curtis, Elijah Wood, Isabel Glasser, George Wendt, Joe Morton, Nicolas Surovy, David Marshall Grant, Art LaFleur; **D:** Steve Miner; **W:** Jeffrey Abrams; **M:** Jerry Goldsmith. **VHS, LV, 8mm** *WAR, BTV*

Fortress

When John and Karen Bennick (Christopher Lambert and Loryn Locklin) are caught trying to have a second child (in the future it will be illegal even if the first pregnancy resulted in a miscarriage), they are shipped to the Fortress, a miles-deep underground desert prison, run not by the government but by a huge corporation with designs on the yet-to-be-born child. Act up in this slammer and you'll get a jolt on the "intestinator," a device implanted in each new prisoner allowing instantaneous and excruciating indigestible pain. Act up too often and face instant laser disembowelment. The sick fantasies of the cyber-warden (character actor Kurtwood Smith) add to the merriment of this good-but-could-be-better, depressing-but-not-as-much-as-*Soylent Green* depiction of our wonderful future. 🦴🦴

1993 (R) 91m/C Christopher Lambert, Kurtwood Smith, Loryn Locklin, Lincoln Kilpatrick; **D:** Stuart Gordon; **W:** Steve Feinberg, Troy Neighbors, Terry Curtis Fox. **VHS, LV** *LIV*

Fortress of Amerikka

In the not-too-distant future, mercenaries get their hands on a secret weapon that could allow them to take over the USA. 🦴🕊

1989 ?m/C Gene Le Brock, Kellee Bradley. **VHS** *IMP*

Four Sided Triangle

Two mad scientists find their friendship threatened when they discover that they are both in love with the same woman. So they do what anyone would do in this situation—they invent a machine and duplicate her. 🦴

1953 81m/B *GB* James Hayter, Barbara Payton, Stephen Murray, John Van Eyssen, Percy Marmont; **D:** Terence Fisher; **M:** Malcolm Arnold. **VHS** *NOS, SNC, MLB*

Force on Thunder Mountain

A father and son go camping and encounter peculiar stuff, the work of an old man from a flying saucer (it's the Jupiter II, in stolen clips from TV's *Lost in Space*). Benign but dull mess of a family-oriented sf flick that sometimes spontaneously turns into a nature documentary. 🦴

1977 93m/C Christopher Cain, Todd Dutson. **VHS, Beta** *VCI*

Forever Young

When test pilot Mel Gibson's girlfriend is hit by a car and goes into a coma, he volunteers to be cryogenically frozen for one year. Oops!—he's left frozen for fifty years, until he is accidentally thawed out by a couple of kids. Predictable, designed to be a tearjerker, though it serves mostly as a star vehicle for Gibson who bumbles with '90s technology, finds his true love, and escapes from government heavies, adorable as ever. Through all the schmaltz, the relationship Gibson develops with the

The 4D Man

A physicist makes two fateful discoveries while working on a special project that gets out of control, leaving him able to pass through matter and see around corners. He also finds that his touch brings instant death. Cheap but effective sci-fier. A young Patty Duke has a small part. 🦴🦴🦴

1959 85m/C Robert Lansing, Lee Meriwether, James Congdon, Guy Raymond, Robert Strauss, Patty Duke; **D:** Irvin S. Yeaworth Jr. **VHS, Beta, LV** NWV, MLB

Frankenstein

The definitive expressionistic Gothic horror classic that set the mold. Adapted from the Mary Shelley novel about Dr. Henry Frankenstein (Colin Clive), the mad scientist who creates life from the death. He accidentally installs a criminal brain, making for a terrifying, yet strangely sympathetic monster. Great performances by Clive as the ultimate mad doctor, and Boris Karloff as the creation, which made him a monster star. Several powerful scenes, excised from the original version, have been restored. Side two of the laserdisc version contains the original theatrical trailer, plus a collection of photos and scenes replayed for study purposes. 🦴🦴🦴🦴

1931 71m/B Boris Karloff, Colin Clive, Mae Clarke, John Boles, Dwight Frye, Edward Van Sloan, Frederick Kerr, Lionel Belman; **D:** James Whale; **W:** Francis Edwards Faragoh, Garrett Fort, John Balderston, Robert Florey; **M:** David Broeckman. **VHS, Beta, LV** MCA, TLF, HMV

Frankenstein Meets the Space Monster

Proclaimed by its writers—English professors at the University of Virginia!—as the worst sf/horror movie ever made, this wonder actually lives up (or down, as the case may be) to its billing. When a human-looking NASA android goes berserk after crashlanding in Puerto Rico, James Karen and Nancy Marshall are sent to track it down, but they instead run across weird-looking aliens intent on kidnapping poolside go-go girls for breeding purposes. They fix up their android buddy enough to try to stop the invaders, but the aliens counter-attack with their watchdog space monster, Mull. It was once shown at a drive-in with the reels out of order and no one noticed, or at least no one bothered to honk a horn. Required viewing for alternative aficionados. **AKA:** Mars Invades Puerto Rico; Frankenstein Meets the Spacemen; Duel of the Space Monsters. 🦴🦴

1965 80m/B James Karen, Nancy Marshall, Marilyn Hanold, David Kerman, Robert Reilly, Lou Cutell; **D:** Robert Gaffney; **W:** George Garret; **C:** Saul Midwall. **VHS, Beta** PSM

Frankenstein Unbound

It took Roger Corman 19 years to decide to make a comeback, and he did it Corman style, completing the shooting in seven weeks, writing the screenplay himself, and making a better-than-B "B" movie. It's 2031 and Dr. Joseph Buchanan is about to perfect the ultimate humanitarian weapon. No splattering, no charring, just instantaneous, implosionary, vaporization. How kind...poof! You're gone. Unfortunately, the experiment ruptures the time continuum and lands the Doc in Geneva, 1817. Fortunately, he runs in to fellow scientist Victor Frankenstein (Raul Julia), whose experiment has also gone haywire. Seems that, in trying to create life, Victor has constructed a monster who (although cool enough to wear eyeballs with stitches) ultimately kills Victor's six-year-old brother. Promising to cut out the doin' in if he has someone to do, the monster bullies the bad doctor into making him a mate. Buchanan gets to rub elbows with poet Percy Shelley, Lord Byron, and falls for future *Frankenstein* authoress Mary Shelley. The monster is a surprisingly touching sort of brute and the climatic, apocalyptic time trip is sure to grab you. The atmosphere is striking, the effects are fun, the actors have fun, and the plot twists fly. Corman is back! Based on a novel by Brian Aldiss. **AKA:** Roger Corman's Frankenstein Unbound. 🦴🦴🦴

1990 (R) 86m/C John Hurt, Raul Julia, Bridget Fonda, Jason Patric, Michael Hutchence, Catherine Rabett, Nick Brimble, Catherine Corman, Mickey Knox; **D:** Roger Corman; **W:** Roger Corman, F.X. Feeney; **C:** Armando Nannuzzi, Michael Scott; **M:** Carl Davis; **V:** Terri Treas. **VHS, Beta, LV** FOX

> "He walks through walls of solid steel and stone...INTO THE 4TH DIMENSION."
>
> —The 4D Man.

Freejack

There is a $15 million bounty on Emilio Estevez's head, placed not by outraged *Men at Work* viewers, but by a tycoon who wants to achieve immortality by transplanting his deranged mind into Estevez's body. The year is 2009, when such "psychic surgery" is possible. Except that in the polluted future, uncontaminated host bodies are scarce. So scientists reach back to 1991, snatching race car driver Alex Furlong just before a fatal crash. Furlong escapes and the chase is on. Mick Jagger, as the chief bounty-hunting "bone-jacker," chose an ill-fated vehicle with which to return to the screen after two decades. Rene Russo also stars as the woman Alex left behind, but who 18 years later (she hasn't aged a bit) works for the very corporation hunting him down. A post-Lector Anthony Hopkins lends his freshly minted Oscar stature to the brief role of the tycoon who wants Estevez's body. Amanda Plummer (Honey Bunny in *Pulp Fiction*) gives another characteristically quirky performance as a groin-kneeing nun: "Our savior never really had to deal with **** like you," she states. Geoff Murphy also directed *This Quiet Earth* (not to mention *Young Guns 2*). Adapted from Robert Sheckley's more highly regarded novel, *Immortality Inc.* 🦴 🦴 🦴

1992 (R) 110m/C Emilio Estevez, Mick Jagger, Rene Russo, Anthony Hopkins, Jonathan Banks, David Johansen, Amanda Plummer, Grand Bush, Frankie Faison, Esai Morales, John Shea; **D:** Geoff Murphy; **W:** Dan Gilroy, Ronald Shusett, Steven Pressfield; **M:** Trevor Jones, Michael Boddicker. **VHS, Beta, LV** *WAR*

From Beyond

A gruesome, tongue-in-cheek flick based on a story by H.P. Lovecraft that goes *way* beyond its source material with highly original, occasionally shocking special effects. Two scientists discover a way to tap into another dimension by fooling around a vibrating whatchamacallit that stimulates the human pineal gland. One of them turns into a rather

amazing monster. Another guy is devoured by bees and gigantic worm-like beasties turn up in the basement. Hero Jeffrey Combs must battle his transformed colleague, who in addition to a grotesque new body now has an unpleasant array of super-powers. From the makers of *Re-Animator,* and just as funny and unpredictable. An amazing rollercoaster-ride that never lets up for a single ghoulish second. 🎞🎞🎞

1986 (R) 90m/C Jeffrey Combs, Barbara Crampton, Ted Sorel, Ken Foree, Carolyn Purdy-Gordon, Bunny Summers, Bruce McGuire; **D:** Stuart Gordon; **W:** Dennis Paoli, Brian Yuzna; **M:** Richard Band. **VHS, Beta, LV** *LIV, VES*

From "Star Wars" to "Jedi": The Making of a Saga

In Earth years, *Star Wars* is nearly 20 years old. But in Hollywood years, it is timeless, a pop-culture classic that revitalized science-fiction films and revolutionized the art of special effects. But you knew that. What you perhaps didn't know is how George Lucas and his cast and crew of artisans brought this space saga to life. Mark Hamill, Luke Skywalker himself, narrates this behind-the-scenes look at the making of *Star Wars, The Empire Strikes Back,* and *Return of the Jedi.* Lots of clips, special-effects footage, and even an inside look at Jabba the Hut. With the series recently re-released on video, a reworked theatrical release in the offing, and plans for a new trilogy in the works, this program will be of great interest to old fans and a new generation who wasn't around "a long time ago in a galaxy far, far away." 🎞🎞🎞

1983 65m/C David Prowse, Harrison Ford, Carrie Fisher, Billy Dee Williams, Alec Guinness; **D:** George Lucas. **VHS, Beta** *FOX, FLI*

From the Earth to the Moon

Is this trip really necessary? George Sanders and Joseph Cotten, members of the Gun Club, launch themselves (as well as Debra Paget) on the title voyage. Despite a top-flight cast, this never gets off the ground. Jules Verne has been served better on the screen with *The War of the Worlds,* Disney's *20,000 Leagues Under the Sea, The Fabulous World of Jules Verne,* and *First Men in the Moon.* 🎞🎞

1958 100m/C George Sanders, Joseph Cotten, Debra Paget, Don Dubbins, Patric Knowles, Morris Ankrum; **D:** Byron Haskin; **W:** Robert Blees, James Leicester; **C:** Edwin DuPar. **VHS, Beta, LV** *NO*

Frozen Alive

A scientist experiments with suspended animation but, wouldn't you know, someone murders his wife while he's on ice. Apparently being frozen stiff does not an alibi make, and he becomes the prime suspect. Much unanimated suspense. 🎞

1964 80m/B *GB GE* Mark Stevens, Marianne Koch, Delphi Lawrence, Joachim Hansen, Walter Rilla, Wolfgang Lukschy; **D:** Bernard Knowles. **VHS** *MOV*

Fugitive Alien

Alien invaders from Valnastar and Earth forces battle it out. Ken, an enemy soldier with superhuman strength, deserts and becomes a hero for the home team. Dubbed and re-edited from Japanese, this is a condensation of part of a TV series from Tsuburaya Studios called *Sutaurufu* ("Starwolf"). As a result, the plot is rushed, episodic, and confusing. Joe Shishido, the chipmunk-cheeked star of flashy gangster films in the '60s, turns up as hard-drinking Captain Joe. Followed by *Star Force: Fugitive Alien 2.* 🎞

1986 103m/C *JP* Tatsuya Azuma, Miyuki Tanigawa, Joe Shishido, Choei Takahashi, Akihiko Hirata; **D:** Kiyosumi Kukazawa, Minoru Kanaya; **M:** Norio Maeda. **VHS, Beta** *CEL*

Future Force

In the crime-filled future cops can't maintain order. They rely on civilian bounty-hunters to clean up the streets. When a snoopy TV reporter points out flaws in the system, free-lance gunslinger David Carradine uses his skills to protect her from his own evil superiors. The action hero's casual tough-guy bit is the only reason to watch this cheapo *Mad Max* mimicry. Unnecessary sequel: *Future Zone.* 🎞

1989 (R) 90m/C David Carradine, Robert Tessier, Anna Rapagna, William Zipp. **VHS, Beta** *AIP*

SEE!

"SEE: The deadly cave of forbidden moon-gold! SEE: The lost city of love-starved cat-women! SEE: The bloodthirsty battle of moon monsters!"

—Cat Women of the Moon.

"SEE strangest of all rites in the temple of love! SEE supersonic excitement as you hurtle through space to a lost planet! SEE fire maidens...dedicated to the purpose of creating a new race of supermen!"

—Fire Maidens of Outer Space.

"SEE teenagers vs. the saucer men! SEE a disembodied hand that crawls...! SEE the night the world nearly ended...! SEE Earth attacked by flying saucers!"

—Invasion of the Saucer Men.

"SEE the space killers plan to wipe out the human race! SEE strange monsters, flying saucers, giant creatures... SENSATIONAL!"

—Killers from Space.

"SEE: 8 ft. spiders! SEE: Super women!"

—Mesa of Lost Women.

"SEE: A fiery meteor hurtle from outer space! SEE: People turned into stone! SEE: The monsters feeding upon water!"

—The Monolith Monsters.

"SEE! SEE! SEE! A 6 ft. astronaut shrink to 6 inches before your very eyes! The moon maidens! The attack of the fire people!"

—The Phantom Planet.

"SEE! The first contact between Earth and Mars!"

—Red Planet Mars.

"SEE a sixty foot giant destroyed...IN COLOR!"

—War of the Colossal Beast.

Future Hunters

In the *Road Warrior* postnuke-holocaust opening, the fabled Spear of Longinus (that pierced Christ's side and now has mighty powers) is sent back through time to the present day for safekeeping. That's all as far as sf; the rest of the Philippines-made spectacle has to do with a heroic young couple battling neo-Nazis for possession of the artifact. One of many cheapo actioners Robert Patrick did before (and after) his role as the lethal T-1000 in *Terminator 2: Judgment Day.* ⚰

1988 96m/C Robert Patrick, Linda Carol, Ed Crick, Bob Schott; **D:** Cirio H. Santiago. **VHS, Beta, LV** *LIV, VES*

Future Shock

A psychiatrist uses "virtual reality" computer technology (which looks like plain ol' hypnotism to the Hound) as therapy. He confronts patients with their deepest fears: a paranoid lady is trapped in her heavily fortified mansion, a nerd gets victimized by a greaser roommate, and a comatose guy backtracks the events that stranded him between life and death. This is really three separate short subjects, strung together with a feeble sf gimmick. Three strikes and it's out. ⚰

1993 (PG-13) 93m/C Bill Paxton, Vivian Schilling, Brion James, Martin Kove, Scott Thompson; **D:** Eric Parkinson, Matt Reeves, Oley Sassone; **C:** Gerry Lively; **M:** John McCallum. **VHS** *HMD*

Future Zone

Tedious sequel to *Future Force* has even fewer sf trappings than its predecessor, at least initially. Crime-fighter David Carradine battles numerous urban punks, and he's assisted in his efforts by a mystery muscleman. The Big Secret: the interloper is the hero's unborn son, sallying back in time to save his father from being betrayed and murdered. ⚰

1990 (R) 88m/C David Carradine, Charles Napier, Ted Prior; **D:** David A. Prior. **VHS, LV** *AIP*

FutureKick

One of those movies that annoys you completely, then serves up a marvelously devious trick ending in its final moment. You don't know whether to applaud or throw things. In the slum-like New Los Angeles of the next century, a murder victim's wife hangs around ubiquitous topless bars (the future's industrial base, apparently) in search of her husband's murderer. Available to help is a kickboxing cyborg bounty-hunter played by martial-arts champ Wilson. On second thought, throw things; much of this post-apocalyptic Roger Corman quickie is padded with footage lifted from previous post-apocalyptic Roger Corman quickies. 🐟🐟

1991 (R) 80m/C Don "The Dragon" Wilson, Meg Foster, Christopher Penn, Eb Lottimer; **D:** Damian Klaus; **W:** Damian Klaus. **VHS** *NHO*

Futureworld

In this competent sequel to Michael Crichton's *Westworld*, two reporters (Peter Fonda and Blythe Danner), one cynical, one enthusiastic, cover the grand reopening of the Delos theme park, closed since the disaster chronicled in the first film. The super-expensive park offers visitors experiences in different worlds, populated by robots who meet guests' every need. The exclusive park draws guests from the highest echelon of society. Once again, however, Delos is the center of trouble as its head scientist and chief executive are up to no good. Convincing performances from Danner and Fonda and an intriguing premise help overcome the predictability of the story. Yul Brynner makes a cameo appearance as his memorable Gunslinger character from *Westworld*. Includes footage shot at NASA locations. 🐟🐟🐟

1976 (PG) 107m/C Peter Fonda, Blythe Danner, Arthur Hill, Yul Brynner, Stuart Margolin, John P. Ryan; **D:** Richard T. Heffron; **W:** Mayo Simon, George Schenck; **C:** Howard Schwartz, Gene Polito. **VHS, Beta, LV** *WAR, OM*

Futuropolis

Fearless Lieutenant Cosmo fights off a ragged group of space invaders in this animated sci-fi/action-adventure parody. Combines a litany of sf gags and a range of low-budget f/x methods to create an amusing spoof of the genre. 🐟🐟

1990 30m/C VHS *WTA, EXP, TPV*

Galactic Gigolo

An alien broccoli (star/co-writer Carmine Capobianco, in a Fruit-of-the-Loom costume) wins a game show prize to assume the portly form of an irresistible Elvis dressalike and visit Prospect, Connecticut, "the horniest town in the galaxy," to get it on with Earth women. Cartoon sound effects, sex, heavy profanity, and ethnic slurs try to pass for wit in this amateurish satire. Watch it along with *The Pink Chiquitas* and Amnesty International will class your VCR as an instrument of torture. **WOOF!**

1987 (R) 80m/C Carmine Capobianco, Debi Thibeault, Ruth Collins, Angela Nicholas, Frank Stewart; **D:** Gorman Bechard; **W:** Carmine Capobianco. **Beta** *AFE*

Galaxina

This well-meaning but ultimately rather dull sf flick features *Playboy* Playmate Dorothy Stratten as Galaxina, a beautiful androidette capable of human feelings. The film features parodies of *Alien* and *Star Wars,* which today gives it a rather dated feel. Avery Schreiber is always fun to watch, though (here portraying Capt. Butt, which gives you a good idea of the humor), and Stratten looks terrific in her space-suit. Sadly, Stratten was murdered the day of the film's premiere. 🐟🐟

1980 (R) 95m/C Dorothy Stratten, Avery Schreiber, Stephen Macht, James David Hilton; **D:** William Sachs; **W:** William Sachs; **C:** Dean Cundey. **VHS, Beta, LV** *MCA*

Galaxis

In a *Star Wars* opening, space tyrant Kila (Richard Moll) wipes out a planetful of rebels and seizes their magic crystal. A second crystal is hidden on present-day Earth and Kyla time-warps here after it. The physically impressive Brigitte Nielsen stars as freedom fighter Ladera, who beams down to battle the hammy villain. Derivative and joyless, it's an example of what happens when an f/x expert (William Mesa, who worked on Sam Raimi's *Army of Darkness*) turns director and gives visuals top priority. Even they're not so hot. 🐟🐟

1995 (R) 91m/C Brigitte Nielsen, Richard Moll, Craig Fairbrass; **D:** William Mesa. **VHS** *TTC*

"He squashes cities, squishes people...and those are his *good* points."

—*Gamera, the Invincible.*

Galaxy Invader

Grotesque lizard man isn't really a bad guy, but after his spaceship crashes on Earth, jerk-water humans try to kill him and he naturally fights back. The slob leading the lynch mob is portrayed by genre fan/publisher George Stover, Maryland's equivalent of Forrest J. Ackerman. No-budget, no-brainer plea for interplanetary tolerance, with substandard f/x. **WOOF!**

1985 (PG) 90m/C Richard Ruxton, Faye Tilles, Don Leifert, George Stover; **D:** Donald M. Dohler. **VHS, Beta** *NO*

Galaxy of Terror

Astronauts sent to rescue a stranded spaceship find themselves with a new mission: find the hidden alien leader in a mysterious pyramid (which contains a gauntlet of weird death traps) before they all get killed by vicious aliens. Big first: Erin Moran (Joanie on *Happy Days*) explodes. The entertaining cast also includes Sid Haig (*Spider Baby*). Inferior Corman-produced *Alien* imitation still manages to shock and displays generous gore and nudity, and the low budget f/x are well done. Zalman King (*Blue Sunshine*) later became a producer/director and churned out loads of well photographed erotic nonsense such as *Wild Orchid*. Followed by *Forbidden World*. **AKA:** Mindwarp: An Infinity of Terror; Planet of Horrors. 🦴🐾

1981 (R) 85m/C Erin Moran, Edward Albert, Ray Walston, Grace Zabriskie, Zalman King; **D:** B.D. Clark; **W:** Mark Siegler, B.D. Clark. **VHS, Beta, LV** *SUE*

Game of Survival

Amusement-hungry masters of the planet Xenon teleport seven of the galaxy's most brutal warriors to an unsuspecting Earth to fight barbarian blood matches over a ball. The token good alien gets help from Los Angeleans against these non-American gladiators. Amateurish, badly photographed excuse for stunts and stupid dialogue. **WOOF!**

1989 85m/C Nikki Hill, Cindy Coatman, Roosevelt Miller Jr.; **D:** Armand Gazarian. **VHS, Beta** *NO*

Gamera, the Invincible

This fun monster flick was Japanese Daiei Studio's answer to *Godzilla*. Gamera, a monstrous prehistoric turtle with huge tusks, is released from his arctic tomb by an ill-timed atomic explosion. Able to breathe fire and fly (presumably a side-effect of that pesky ol' radiation), the Shelled Wonder zooms around destroying things and generally causing panic. The first and probably the best of the Gamera series, this one is in black and white and portrays the mighty turtle as a villain. A turtle-obsessed little boy named Kenny, however, foreshadows Gamera's later role as "Friend to Children Everywhere." Dubbed in English. Like *Godzilla*, the American theatrical version of *Gamera* was altered to include added scenes featuring Anglo actors—in this case, Brian Donlevy and Albert Dekker as U.S. military men. This version has almost completely disappeared in favor of the current, more straightforward video incarnation. After this initial outing, director Noriaki Yuasa stepped down to concentrate on only the special effects. The giant turtle returned for seven silly sequels full of juvenile hijinks aimed at children (which also succeeded in dragging the Godzilla series down to the same level), before returning for a surprisingly good semi-remake in 1985. **AKA:** Gamera; Gammera; Daikaiju Gamera. 🦴🦴

1966 86m/B *JP* Eiji Funakoshi, Harumi Kiritachi, Junichiro Yamashiko, Yoshiro Uchida, Brian Donlevy, Albert Dekker, Diane Findlay, John Baragrey, Dick O'Neill, Yoshiro Kitahara; **D:** Noriaki Yuasa; **W:** Fumi Takahashi; **C:** Nobuo Munekawa. **VHS, LV** *JFK, SNC*

Gamera Vs. Barugon

The monstrous turtle returns to Earth after being freed from his outer-space prison by a passing meteor, and battles with 130-foot lizard Barugon, who comes equipped with a rainbow melting ray and a freeze gas shooting tongue. This strange beast hatched from an egg smuggled to Japan from New Guinea, and has been raising hell ever since. Tokyo and Osaka get melted and/or frozen in the process. The first sequel to *Gamera, the Invin-*

Japanimation: Big-Eyed Girls Kick Butt!

Japanese animation, or "anime" as it's known in its home country, has become remarkably well represented in U.S. video stores these days. A lot of people who have never heard the word "anime" are surprised to find that they grew up on it; in the '60s, '70s, and '80s, Japanese-produced series like *Speed Racer, Kimba the White Lion, Battle of the Planets,* and *Starblazers* were very popular on American TV.

The distinctive style of these shows, with their emphasis on high-tech gadgets and characters with very large eyes, stayed with most of the people who watched them. But up until the early '90s, actual anime fandom was comparatively small; a network of fans produced 'zines and met to trade videos of the new shows and movies being produced in Japan. By the late '80s, anime epics like *Akira* and *Fist of the North Star* began to attract widespread notice; sophisticated and violent, these were anything but children's films. As the '90s began, those

big-eyed girls were back in a big way, as numerous video companies began acquiring rights to more recent series. Cognoscenti and casual video-shop browsers alike suddenly had access to a whole new world.

"Anime" is a Japanese adaptation of "animation," and trying to define anime by one particular style is about as futile as defining all U.S. animation by *The Smurfs.* Still, there are a few basic themes that tend to recur. There are visually stunning, often very violent science-fiction epics like *Appleseed* and *Wings of*

Honnemaise and the recent *Ghost in the Shell.* There are eerie horror-stories like *Laughing Target* and *Vampire Princess Miyu,* and sword-and-sorcery epics like the *Records of the Lodoss Wars* series. There are also a couple of subgenres that are peculiar to anime, romantic comedies set in contemporary Japan that focus on the problems involved in having a girlfriend who might be an alien, an android, or merely psychic. *Kimagure Orange Road, Urusei Yatsura, Ranma 1/2,* and the delightfully named *All-Purpose Cultural Cat-Girl Nuku-Nuku* would be good examples.

It should be pointed out that while anime girls are cute, they're hardly cream puffs; a lot of them have super strength and are quite capable of making short work of villains or oversexed menfolk. It should also be mentioned that a lot of anime contains a wealth of sexual scenes and innuendo that might seem a little much to some American viewers. But parents looking for family fare won't be disappointed by charming fantasies like *My Neighbor Totoro* and *Miss China's Ring.*

---

cible (the first in color) is not quite as silly as those that came later, and the battle scenes even achieve a sort of goofy grandeur. This Barugon is not to be confused with the monster Baragon, featured in Toho's *Frankenstein Conquers the World.* Star Kojiro Hongo returned for two more Gamera films. Noriyaki Yuasa, who'd done a competent job directing the initial entry in the series, stepped down to concentrate on only the special effects. **AKA:** Gamera Tai Barugon; Gambara Vs. Barugon; The War of the Monsters. 🦴🦴

1966 101m/C *JP* Kojiro Hongo, Kyoko Enami, Akira Natsuki, Koji Fujiyama, Ichiro Sugai; **D:** Shigeo Tanaka; **W:** Fumi Takahashi; **C:** Michio Takahashi. **VHS, Beta** *JFK*

Gamera Vs. Gaos

Now fully the good guy, giant flying turtle Gamera slugs it out with a bloodthirsty batlike critter named Gaos, who has been gobbling up folks. Gaos is also able to generate ultra-powerful sound waves from his throat in the form of a cutting beam, which neatly slices

"Winged monster from 17,000,000 B.C.! Big as a battleship! Flies 4 times the speed of sound! Atomic weapons can't hurt it!"

—*The Giant Claw.*

a few vehicles in half. With Gamera recovering from injuries sustained from his first clash with Gaos, heroic scientists come up with an outrageous idea (even for the Gamera series) to defeat the bat-creature. Hundreds of gallons of blood are used to lure Gaos atop a revolving tower restaurant, in the hope that the beast will become too dizzy to escape until dawn, when the sunlight will destroy him. If only they'd used that idea on Dracula! A subplot about road construction and a boy named Eiichi (which sounds like "Itchy" to Western ears) serves as filler. More weird fun from the increasingly silly Gamera series. **AKA:** The Return of the Giant Monsters; Gamera Vs. Gyaos; Boyichi and the Supermonster; Gamera Tai Gaos. *♫♫*

1967 87m/C *JP* Kojiro Hongo, Kichijiro Ueda, Naoyuki Abe, Reiko Kasahara; **D:** Noriaki Yuasa; **W:** Fumi Takahashi. **VHS, Beta, LV** *JFK*

Gamera Vs. Guiron

Sexy, leotard-clad aliens take two boys on a ride to a distant planet. They have fun playing with hi-tech equipment, until they find out the aliens really want to eat their brains! They call on the monster Gamera, who is Friend to All Children, to come rescue them, but the alien headquarters is guarded by the evil, cleaver-headed monster Guiron. Meanwhile, little sister tries to tell disbelieving adults about the abduction. Many Gamera films have been released in more than one English-dubbed version. The currently available version of *Gamera Vs. Guiron* is the most complete, and the most fun—the kooky alien girls have Southern accents, and in one scene we get to see Guiron slice up guest star Gaos like a sausage. An intentionally funny monster movie that provides plenty of mind-twisting fun, especially for youngsters. **AKA:** Attack of the Monsters; Gamera Tai Guiron. *♫♫*

1969 88m/C *JP* Nobuhiro Kashima, Christopher Murphy, Miyuki Akiyama, Yuko Hamada, Eiji Funakoshi; **D:** Noriaki Yuasa; **W:** Fumi Takahashi; **C:** Akira Kitazaki. **VHS, Beta** *JFK*

Gamera Vs. Zigra

Gamera the flying turtle visits Sea World to battle a cheap, shoddy-looking monster and

hand out some cheap morality. The alien Zigrans come to Earth to wrest the planet from the hands of the polluting humans who have nearly destroyed it. The alien monster Zigra nearly kills the staunch turtle, but some of his human friends revive him that he may defend Earth once more. Not nearly as much fun as previous entries in this crazy series, as the producers increasingly padded out running time with stock footage from the earlier films. Probably the only novelty is that Zigra can talk. Though this one's incredibly bad, the following entry, *Gamera, Super Monster,* is even worse, remarkable only for killing off the heroic monster until the 1995 reworking of the series, beginning with the surprisingly good *Gamera, Guardian of the Universe.* **AKA:** Gamera Tai Shinkai Kaiju Jigara; Gamera Vs. the Deep Sea Monster Zigra. *♫*

1971 91m/C *JP* Reiko Kasahara, Mikiko Tsubouchi, Koji Fujiyama, Arlene Zoellner, Gloria Zoellner, Isamu Saeki, Yasushi Sakagami; **D:** Noriaki Yuasa; **W:** Fumi Takahashi; **C:** Akira Uehara. **VHS, Beta, LV** *JFK*

The Gamma People

Cold War sci-fi in which two journalists in Eastern Europe stumble into the obscure socialist state of Gudavia, where no-goodnik doctor uses gamma rays to turn kids into fanatical geniuses or adults into brainless zombies. Bland relic has very weak *Village of the Damned* vibes; the Hound thinks they should have given the radioactive kids a crack at the script. *♫*

1956 83m/B *GB* Walter Rilla, Paul Douglas, Eva Bartok; **D:** John Gilling. **VHS, Beta** *NO*

Gappa the Trifibian Monster

Journalists and scientists visiting a tropical island find a giant egg. It hatches a baby monster and they take it back to Tokyo with them, dismaying the baby's giant monster parents. The birdlike pair come to town to rescue baby, leaving a wake of destruction. Nearly a direct remake of the British film *Gorgo,* and a weak one at that. Dubbed. **AKA:** Daikyoju Gappa; Monster from a Prehistoric Planet. *♫♭*

1967 (PG) 90m/C *JP* Tamio Kawaji, Yoko Yamamoto, Yuji Okada, Koji Wada; **D:** Haruyasu Hoguchi; **W:** Iwao Yamazaki, Ryuzo Nakanishi; **C:** Muneo Keda. **VHS, Beta** *ORI*

Geisha Girl

Forgotten sci-fi film about a mad scientist and his Japanese cohorts who develop small explosive pills that are more powerful than nuclear bombs. Their plans of world conquest are thwarted when the pills inadvertently fall into the hands of two American G.I.s. 🦴🦴

1952 67m/B Martha Hyer, William Andrews, Archer MacDonald, Kekao Yokoo, Teddy Nakamura; **D:** George Breakston, C. Ray Stahl; **W:** C. Ray Stahl. **VHS** *SNC*

Ghidrah the Three Headed Monster

This fun all-star monster fight is a more-or-less direct sequel to *Godzilla Vs. Mothra.* When a three-headed monster from outer space threatens the world, hapless humans are forced to appeal to the (comparatively) friendly Mothra, Rodan, and Godzilla. Mothra's tiny priestesses are back (guests on a TV talk-show, no less!). Ghidrah (who would appear in several more movies, including *Godzilla Vs. Monster Zero* the next year) is an impressive monster, materializing out of a flaming meteorite. It's rock 'em-sock 'em giant monster action as poor Tokyo once again is threatened with the trampling of a lifetime. The 1966 U.S. version was heavily re-edited, damaging continuity. **AKA:** Ghidorah Sandai Kaiju Chikyu Saidai No Kessan; Ghidora, the Three-Headed Monster; Ghidrah; The Greatest Battle on Earth; The Biggest Fight on Earth; Monster of Monsters. 🦴🦴🦴

1965 85m/C *JP* Akiko Wakabayashi, Yosuke Natsuki, Yuriko Hoshi, Hiroshi Koizumi, Takashi Shimura, Emi Ito, Yumi Ito, Kenji Sahara, Eiji Okada; **D:** Inoshiro Honda; **W:** Shinichi Sekizawa; **C:** Hajime Koizumi; **M:** Akira Ifukube. **VHS, Beta** *HHT, VCN, VHE*

Ghost Patrol

A cowboy duo kidnaps the inventor of a ray gun in order to hijack mail planes, but they're stopped by G-Man Tim McCoy and friends. An odd hybrid of science fiction and western, to say the least. 🦴🦴

1936 57m/B Tim McCoy, Walter Miller, Wheeler Oakman; **D:** Sam Newfield. **VHS, Beta** *GPV, VCI, VCN*

The Giant Claw

Hilarious '50s giant-monster flick, featuring a buzzard-like bird, which not only arrives from outer space to hatch an egg, but is also surrounded by an anti-matter shield that makes it radar invisible, and prevents conventional weapons from doing any damage. South-of-the-border special effects ensure that the taco, er, big bird will wreak a little havoc, and have a lot of fun before the inevitable down-in-flameless plunge, which will probably save the world for a little while longer. Scientist Mara Corday was *Playboy*'s Miss October, 1958. What a goofy bird. What a goofy movie (not to be confused with *The Goofy Movie*). You gotta love it! 🦴🦴

1957 76m/B Jeff Morrow, Mara Corday, Morris Ankrum, Louis D. Merrill, Edgar Barrier, Robert Shayne, Morgan Jones, Clark Howat; **D:** Fred F. Sears. **VHS** *MOV*

The Giant Gila Monster

Through the magic of rear-projection film techniques, a giant lizard (yes, a gila monster) terrorizes the plucky teens of a small southwestern town. You'd think from that description that the cheesy special effects of the monster would be the worst thing about this movie, but you'd be wrong—the acting is far worse! One young couple has a run in with the lizard while "talking" (nudge, nudge, wink, wink) out in the boondocks, and that good ol' 1950s moral is hard to miss—if you're going to be sexually promiscuous, you're going to pay the price. All in all, the film provides many unintentional laughs. 🦴🦴

1959 74m/B Don Sullivan, Lisa Simone, Shug Fisher, Jerry Cortwright, Beverly Thurman, Don Flourney, Pat Simmons; **D:** Ray Kellogg. **VHS** *NOS, RHI, SNC*

The Giant Spider Invasion

A notoriously bad film from the '70s with some of the worst special effects of all time. A small town is attacked by extraterrestrial spiders of various sizes. The little rascals get into blenders and showers and generally cause a panic. The largest of them are simply Volkswagens covered with fake fur (the eyes are headlights, get it?) with a few legs tacked on. The

Glen and Randa

Two young people experience the world after it has been destroyed by nuclear war. Early Jim McBride, before the hired-gun success of *The Big Easy.* 🦴🦴🦴

1971 (R) 94m/C Steven Curry, Shelley Plimpton; **D:** Jim McBride; **W:** Rudy Wurlitzer, Jim McBride. **VHS, Beta, LV** *VCI, IME*

God Told Me To

When this Larry Cohen-directed opus hit the screens, many TV stations refused to run the original trailer, fearing its nature too offensive. Religious New York cop (Tony LoBianco) is investigating a series of grisly murders. In each case when the murderers are questioned for their motives, they simply state "God told me to." In true Cohen fashion, this is no ordinary murder thriller. LoBianco quickly becomes embroiled in the occult, finding his belief systems challenged by a "religious" cult composed of not-so-ordinary worshipers and a not-so-traditional "god." One of Cohen's best. **AKA:** Demon. 🦴🦴🦴

1976 (R) 89m/C Tony LoBianco, Deborah Raffin, Sylvia Sidney, Sandy Dennis, Richard Lynch, Andy Kaufman; **D:** Larry Cohen; **W:** Larry Cohen. **VHS, Beta, LV** *NLC*

"I prefer the waxed floss, damn it!"
Godzilla, King of the Monsters.

B-movie veteran cast includes Alan Hale, Jr. (the Skipper from *Gilligan's Island,* whose first line is "Hi, little buddy!"). 🦴

1975 (PG) 76m/C Steve Brodie, Barbara Hale, Leslie Parrish, Robert Easton, Alan Hale Jr., Dianne Lee Hart, Bill Williams, Christianne Schmidtmer, Kevin Brodie; **D:** Bill Rebane; **W:** Richard L. Huff, Robert Easton; **C:** Jack Willoughby. **VHS** *MOV*

The Gladiators

Televised gladiatorial bouts are designed to subdue man's violent tendencies in a futuristic society until a computer makes a fatal error. **AKA:** The Peace Game; Gladiatorerna. 🦴

1970 90m/C Arthur Pentelow, Frederick Danner; **D:** Peter Watkins. **VHS, Beta** *NO*

Godzilla, King of the Monsters

A monstrous prehistoric reptile emerges from the depths to terrorize Tokyo after being awakened by atomic testing. Godzilla is finally foiled by means of a heroic scientist's "oxygen destroyer," though as we all know, he would survive to menace Japan again and again. Scenes featuring Raymond Burr were added in the 1956 American version (directed by Terry Morse), where he serves as a narrator telling the monster's tale in flashbacks. In addition, the scenes in which the scientist sacrifices himself to destroy Godzilla with his invention were downplayed in the U.S. release. Unlike many of the later sequels, the original *Godzilla* was a grim, serious movie that helped give voice to the world's collective fears about nuclear weapons. Significantly, it was one of the first post-WWII Japanese films to break

through commercially in the U.S. Followed by 21(!) sequels to date. **AKA:** Gojira.

1954 80m/B *JP* Takashi Shimura, Raymond Burr, Akira Takarada, Akihiko Hirata, Momoko Kochi, Sachio Sakai; **D:** Inoshiro Honda, Terry Morse; **W:** Takeo Murata, Inoshiro Honda; **C:** Masao Tamai; **M:** Akira Ifukube. **VHS, Beta, LV** PAR, VES

Godzilla 1985

A latter-day sequel released to coincide with the 30th anniversary of the original *Godzilla, King of the Monsters.* The Great Green One is (once again) awakened from underwater slumber by trolling nuclear submarines belonging to the superpowers near Japan. The giant monster's newly acquired appetite for nuclear energy inadvertently precipitates an international incident. Steve Martin (no, not *that* Steve Martin—this one is actually Raymond Burr) is called in to help mediate the conflict, being the only living American witness to Godzilla's destructive 1955 outburst. Sadly, the film doesn't quite make it; it's talky and lacks the original's urgency. G-fans will probably still want to see it, though.

1985 (PG) 91m/C *JP* Keiju Kobayashi, Ken Tanaka, Raymond Burr, Yasuka Sawaguchi, Shin Takumaa; **D:** Kohji Hashimoto, Robert J. Kizer. **VHS, Beta, LV** NWV, VTR

Godzilla on Monster Island

Aliens from Nebula Spacehunter M conduct their nefarious schemes from the cover of Godzilla Tower in the World Children's Land amusement park. When they're discovered by an unemployed cartoonist and his friends, they summon the giant three-headed dragon Ghidrah (last seen taking a beating in *Destroy All Monsters*) and giant cyborg monster from space Gigan to destroy Earth civilization. Godzilla and Angilas slip past the laughable security of Monster Island to defend Japan from the invaders. Though perhaps not the very worst of the Godzilla series, this one's not a big favorite even among fans. The script is a disjointed mess and the special effects are either poorly executed, or lifted from other films. An embarrassing highlight comes when Godzilla and Angilas actually speak to each other—the original Japanese version wasn't

much better, having the monsters' growls translated within little cartoon speech balloons. **AKA:** Godzilla Vs. Gigan.

1972 89m/C *JP* Hiroshi Ichikawa, Tomoko Umeda, Yuriko Hishimi, Minoru Takashima, Zan Fujita, Kunio Murai, Toshiaki Nishizawa; **D:** Jun Fukuda; **W:** Shinichi Sekizawa; **C:** Kiyoshi Hasegawa. **VHS** SNC, MRV, NWV

Godzilla Raids Again

Warner Bros. had a problem securing rights to Godzilla's name, and opted to release this theatrically using a monster pseudonym ("Gigantis"), doing some heavy editing while they're at it. In this first Godzilla sequel of the original series, a second Godzilla appears to cause trouble, while another monster—the spiny Angilas—also appears to threaten mankind. They battle to the death while trashing Osaka. Although the monster scenes are fun, with Godzilla facing off against another creature for the first time, too much of the story centers around a fishing industry troubled by the behemoths. The special effects fail to match the power of the original's. However, the climax shows a lot of imagination. The U.S. release in 1959 was directed by Hugo Grimaldi and produced by Paul Schreibman. **AKA:** Gigantis, the Fire Monster; Godzilla's Counter Attack.

1955 78m/B *JP* Hiroshi Koizumi, Setsuko Wakayama, Minoru Chiaki; **D:** Motoyoshi Oda; **W:** Takeo Murata; **C:** Seichi Endo. **VHS** VTR

Godzilla Vs. Biollante

In this sequel to *Godzilla 1985*, Doctor Surigama's secret plant formula could free the industrialized world from oil dependency. He also runs his pet Godzilla experiment from the same laboratory. When terrorist thieves attempt to steal the plant formula, a petri dish mixup unleashes Biollante, a titanic rose-monster. Yes, that was *rose*-monster. As if a gigantic rosebush wasn't enough, Godzilla soon arrives to do some more Tokyo sight-seeing. The world's only hope may lie in the tendrils of Biollante. This film may come as a surprise to long-time fans of the Godzilla series; it's visually lush and the tone is considerably moodier and more poetic than earlier entries. Biollante is a memorable, startling monster. First

"God told me to."

—every single killer in *God Told Me To.*

The Hound Salutes: Godzilla

Ten things you probably don't know about Godzilla:

1. He's not a dinosaur. Most folks think that Godzilla is a prehistoric creature revived by the A-bomb. Actually, he was once a Godzillasaurus, a species dying out during the 1940s on a small Pacific island. Nuclear energy from weapons tests mutated him into an entirely new and different life form.

2. At last measure, he was over 100 meters tall. Although not completely impervious, his tough hide can quickly heal itself due to the properties of the G-cell, of which Godzilla is composed. The G-cell's regenerative properties, powered by atomic energy, give Godzilla incredible strength and endurance.

3. Despite claims presented in *King Kong Vs. Godzilla,* he has a much larger brain than any reptile of proportionate size, and also has an additional brain at the base of his spine. His atomic breath is produced by igniting nuclear fuel discharged into his throat while exhaling, and can produce a beam of varying levels of power. The same energy can also be discharged throughout his entire system at once, to quickly heal and re-energize his body.

4. He can eat normal foods such as fish, but prefers to absorb nuclear energy whenever he can (although the furnaces within his body can produce this energy without an outside source).

5. He is constantly mutating, which is why he sometimes looks very different from one film to the next.

6. He's not the last of his kind. The original Godzilla was dissolved by the Oxygen Destroyer in *Godzilla.* The monster that appeared in *Godzilla Raids Again* was supposedly another of the same species. This Godzilla appeared in 14 features, most or perhaps all set in the future (at least the future from the time of their release). In *Godzilla 1985,* which ignores all 14 of those movies to present a *second* direct sequel to the original (got that), yet another Godzilla appears. Or perhaps Godzilla actually survived the Oxygen Destroyer in one or both series. In both the original and the modern series, a mutated Godzillasaurus egg hatches *Son of Godzilla* (1969), *Godzilla Vs. MechaGodzilla* (1993) . There have been 22 Godzilla features to date.

7. In 1996, Godzilla received a lifetime achievement award at the annual MTV Movie Awards.

8. He really is the King of the Monsters. Unlike Frankenstein, Dracula, King Kong, or any other critter, he's not misunderstood. He doesn't want our love. Although he occasionally appears to be mankind's protector facing a greater menace, he's usually just protecting his own turf. He's never been seen stepping gingerly around a building to avoid killing some puny human. He is a true monster, an aberration outside of nature and beyond good and evil.

9. He's still around. Even though the last Godzilla film released in the U.S. was *Godzilla Vs. Biollante,* there have been five more made since then. Toho has so far refused all offers to release them in the U.S., because of the poor treatment they usually receive from American distributors. These films are quite unlike the cheap ones made during the 1970s that are so familiar to Americans—they have much better production values, with f/x that rival and often surpass those created for Hollywood product. There is an American-made Godzilla film in the works, scheduled for release in 1998.

10. He's dead. In his latest film, *Godzilla Vs. Destroyah,* Godzilla is consumed by the energy of his own body, while the efforts of the G-Force make sure he doesn't take the rest of the planet with him. He is, however, survived by Godzilla, Jr., who may be friendlier towards mankind, having spent his first few weeks in the company of caring humans.

---

appearance by psychic girl Miki Saegusa (Megumi Odaka), who became a series regular. The same team returned in 1991 for the even-better *Godzilla Vs. King Ghidorah,* which awaits a U.S. release. Viewers received an unexpected bonus when HBO "accidentally" transferred this to video in widescreen format. 🦴🦴🦴

1989 (PG) 104m/C *JP* Koji Takahashi, Yoshiko Tanaka, Megumi Odaka, Kunihiko Mitamura; **D:** Kazuki Ohmori; **W:** Kazuki Ohmori. **VHS** *NO*

Godzilla Vs. Megalon

Godzilla is once again a good guy in this '70s outing, considered by many to be one of the

worst in the series. This time, the villainous "Seatopians" unleash two giant monsters to conquer the world: Megalon, a giant cockroach with drills for arms, and Gigan, a flying metal creature with a buzz-saw in its stomach. Fortunately, cyborg hero Jet Jaguar (sort of a low-rent Ultraman) is on hand to slug it out side by side with Tokyo's ultimate defender. Oh yes, and there's also an annoying little boy to round things out. Filled with clumsily used stock footage and laughable dialogue, this film was obviously aimed at children. A low mark in monster history. Adding insult to injury, NBC cut out half the footage and aired it in 1977 with campy segments hosted by John Belushi in a shoddy Godzilla costume. **AKA:** Gojira Tai Megalon. 🎵🎵

1973 (G) 80m/C *JP* Katsuhiko Sasakai, Hiroyuki Kawase, Yutaka Hayashi, Robert Dunham, Kotaro Tomita; *D:* Jun Fukuda; *W:* Jun Fukuda, Shinichi Sekizawa; *C:* Yuzuru Aizawa; *M:* Richiro Manabe. **VHS** *NOS, MRV, NWV*

Godzilla Vs. Monster Zero

Novel Godzilla adventure with the big guy and Rodan in outer space! Suspicious denizens of Planet X (who wear some truly suspicious goggles) require the help of Godzilla and Rodan to rid themselves of "Monster Zero," who's been menacing their world. Earth agrees to "lend" the Xians the monsters (they're transported through space in giant, levitating bubbles) and once on Planet X, we learn that "Monster Zero" is none other than Godzilla's old foe Ghidrah, the three-headed superdragon! Will Godzilla and Rodan defeat Ghidrah? Will the men from Planet X help Earth in return for the favor, or is this just one big, fat double cross? Despite the shaky logic of the plot, this direct sequel to *Ghidrah the Three-Headed Monster* remains one of the more entertaining entries in Toho's monster series. The addition of Nick Adams as the hipster astronaut (at the suggestion of producer Henry Saperstein) provides as much amusement from his daddy-o dialogue and manner as it does the intended Anglo identification. Released in the U.S. in 1970 on a twin bill with *War of the Guargantuas*. **AKA:** Monster Zero; Battle of the Astros; Invasion of the Astro-Monsters; Invasion of the Astros; Invasion of Planet X; Kaiju Daisenso. 🎵🎵🎵

1965 (G) 93m/C *JP* Akira Takarada, Nick Adams, Kumi Mizuno, Jun Tazaki, Akira Kubo, Keiko Sawai; *D:* Inoshiro Honda; *W:* Shinichi Sekizawa; *C:* Hajime Koizumi; *M:* Akira Ifukube. **VHS, Beta** *PAR, FUS*

Godzilla Vs. Mothra

A gigantic egg washes ashore in Japan via a hurricane. Despite warnings from a pair of tiny girls (the fairy priestesses of Mothra from the earlier movies), a wealthy industrialist plans to build an amusement park around it. Before too long, however, Godzilla shows up, hungry to do some city-stompin'. The fairies convince Mothra to come to Tokyo's aid. Though the huge flying critter fares badly against the Big G, two junior Mothras hatch from the giant egg in the nick of time and join the fray. This is one of the better entries in the series; wonderful entertainment for monster-fans. Except for a sequence added at the request of American International, in which Godzilla is attacked by U.S. Navy missiles, the U.S. version is nearly the same as the original, and the dubbing was done decently. Unfortunately, half the image is lost in the video release. **AKA:** Godzilla Vs. the Thing; Godzilla Vs. the Giant Moth; Godzilla Fights the Giant Moth; Mothra Vs. Godzilla; Mosura Tai Gojira; Godzilla Tai Mosura; Godzilla Fights the Giant Moth. 🎵🎵🎵

1964 88m/C *JP* Akira Takarada, Yuriko Hoshi, Hiroshi Koizumi, Emi Ito, Yumi Ito; *D:* Inoshiro Honda; *W:* Shinichi Sekizawa; *C:* Hajime Koizumi. **VHS, Beta** *PAR, FUS*

Godzilla Vs. the Cosmic Monster

Godzilla appears once again to ravage the Japanese countryside. Nothing new about that—until he beats up on his ol' pal Angilas. Then, a *second* Godzilla shows up to battle the first! The first monster's skin is torn away to reveal a robot version of Godzilla, which is under the control of evil apes from the black hole nebula (swiping an idea from the then-popular *Planet of the Apes* series). The apes don't seem like much of a threat—instead of just marching in to take over, they needed to enlist an Earth scientist to build Mechagodzilla. Why do they disguise the robot as Godzil-

> "Nature has a way of reminding man just how puny we are, whether it tells us in the form of a tornado, an earthquake, or a Godzilla."
>
> *—Godzilla 1985.*

la? Why do they disguise themselves as humans? Since Mechagodzilla is such a match for Godzilla, why not build *two* robots just to be sure? Stop asking intelligent questions and just enjoy the fireworks, as the giant monsters wage war across a crumbling cityscape. Originally released by AIP as *Godzilla Vs. the Bionic Monster* in an attempt to cash in on *The Six Million Dollar Man* television series, the prints and ad campaign had to be quickly altered when a lawsuit was threatened. Not to be confused with the much superior *Godzilla Vs. MechaGodzilla* (1993), which has yet to be released in the U.S. **AKA:** Godzilla Vs. the Bionic Monster; Godzilla Vs. Mechagodzilla; Gojira Tai Meka-Gojira. 🧦🧦

1974 (G) 80m/C *JP* Masaki Daimon, Kazuya Aoyama, Reiko Tajima, Hiroshi Koizumi, Akihiko Hirata, Kenji Sahara; **D:** Jun Fukuda; **W:** Jun Fukuda, Hiroyasu Yamamura; **C:** Yuzuru Aizawa. **VHS** *NWV, MRV, VYY*

Godzilla Vs. the Sea Monster

A young man and his friends steal aboard a sailboat, hoping to use it to find his brother, who was lost at sea. The "owner" of the boat turns out to be a thief, who happened to be hiding out on board. They all end up on an island guarded by a gigantic monster crustacean. The island is also the secret headquarters of a group of criminals bent on world domination. In a desperate gamble for survival they decide to awaken Godzilla, found sleeping in a cave, and the monster mayhem begins. This engaging adventure film was originally planned as a King Kong film, but Toho Studios substituted Godzilla when rights to the big ape proved too expensive. The first of a trio of cost-cutting Godzilla adventures set on South Pacific islands, where no miniature cities were required. Also the first Godzilla film for director Jun Fukuda, who would go on to helm four others, although none would turn out quite as well as this one. **AKA:** Nankai No Daiketto; Ebirah, Terror of the Deep; Big Duel in the North Sea. 🧦🧦🧦

1966 80m/C *JP* Akira Takarada, Toru Watanabe, Hideo Sunazuka, Kumi Mizuno, Jun Tazaki; **D:** Jun Fukuda; **W:** Shinichi Sekizawa; **C:** Kazuo Yamada. **VHS, Beta** *DVT, MRV, HHT*

Godzilla Vs. the Smog Monster

Godzilla battles a creature borne of pollution, an ever-growing sludge blob named Hedora. Godzilla fans expecting another apocalyptic science-fiction adventure of mythical proportions may be disappointed. Avante-garde director Yoshimitu Banno tried to take this Godzilla film further into surrealism, with mixed results. Some scenes are illustrated with animated children's drawings. Japanese teenagers marshal their dancing talents to combat the threat amid the hypnotic swirl of disco lighting. Great opening song: "Save the Earth." Hedora is seen flying over crowds of people as they drop in their tracks, dead from poison gas—and yet, at one point the monster spares a little kitten. The relevant anti-pollution message occasionally becomes heavy handed, at other times things are just plain weird. **AKA:** Gojira Tai Hedora; Godzilla Vs. Hedora. 🧦🧦

1972 (G) 87m/C *JP* Akira Yamauchi, Hiroyuki Kawase, Toshie Kimura; **D:** Yoshimitu Banno; **W:** Kaoru Mabuchi, Yoshimitu Banno; **C:** Yoichi Manoda. **VHS, Beta** *ORI*

Godzilla's Revenge

Not really a monster movie at all, but actually a strange juvenile drama. A young boy who is having problems with school, family, and local bullies, dreams of going to Monster Island to learn from Minya, son of the boy's hero, Godzilla, who is having similar problems. Using the lessons in real life, the boy captures some bandits and beats up the tough kid who's been bothering him (and even gets the girl). The scenes depicting the boy's bleak urban environment, as well as the harsh lessons he must learn in order to survive there, are more than a little depressing—somewhat at odds with the fantasy-filled adventure that was intended. Shamelessly recycles footage from *Godzilla Vs. the Sea Monster* and *Son of Godzilla* for battle scenes. Certainly the oddest Godzilla movie of all. **AKA:** Oru Kaiju Daishingeki. 🧦🧦

1969 70m/C *JP* Kenji Sahara, Tomonori Yazaki, Machiko Naka, Sachio Sakai, Chotaro Togin, Yoshibumi Tajima; **D:** Inoshiro Honda; **W:** Shinichi Sekizawa; **C:** Mototaka Tomioka. **VHS** *NO*

Golden Voyage of Sinbad

Sinbad (the *Danger*ously *Diabolik*al John Phillip Law) travels to Lemuria, a legendary pre-Atlantean continent that allegedly connected Africa to Australia. The Black Prince Koura (Tom Baker of *Dr. Who* fame) will stop at nothing to beat Sinbad to the Fountain of Destiny and to claim the beautiful slave girl Margiana (Hammer queen Caroline Munro) as his own. With symbolism and mysticism based on the Middle Eastern view of destiny, there may be more meat and subtleties than the usual Harryhausen adventure, but there's still loads of mythical creatures. Koura even gets to build a living homunculus for spying, brings a ship's figurehead to life for killing, and invisibly duels Sinbad with effects reminiscent of the rain sequence in *The Invisible Man Returns*. While the battle between the Griffin (good) and the one-eyed centaur (evil), with each being assisted by their human counterparts, seems to come out of nowhere, it somehow fits. The elaborate fight between Sinbad's men and the six-armed Kali is masterpiece of choreography. Of course, Miklos Rozsa's score doesn't hurt the flow at all. 🦴 🦴 🦴

1973 (G) 105m/C John Phillip Law, Caroline Munro, Tom Baker, Douglas Wilmer, Martin Shaw, John David Garfield, Gregoire Aslan; *D:* Gordon Hessler; *W:* Brian Clemens; *M:* Miklos Rozsa. **VHS, Beta, LV** *COL, MLB*

Gorath

One of the few Japanese sci-fi flicks you'll see with a display at the Smithsonian Air and Space Museum. Title refers to a collapsed star on a collision course with Earth. Top scientists of 1979 cooperate internationally to construct huge nuclear jet engines in the Antarctic to literally shove Earth out of Gorath's path. Imaginative details (*a la* Immanuel Velikovsky) show disasters spawned by Gorath's gravity, like the sucking away of Saturn's rings. Because Toho Studios specialized in giant monster movies, a last-minute cast addition was 'Magma,' a pre-

"Hold on, I'm almost there!" A breathless *Gorgo.*

historic walrus awakened by the heat. He's been cut from the print on U.S. home video—no great loss—but the re-edits and clumsy dubbing (half the actors speak with distinct pipes of voiceover artist Paul Frees) lend a tacky feel to this elaborate space-disaster drama. **AKA:** Yosei Gorasu. 🎵🎵

1964 77m/C *JP* Ryo Ikebe, Akihiko Hirata, Jun Tazaki, Yumi Shirakawa, Takashi Shimura, Kumi Mizuno; **D:** Inoshiro Honda; **W:** Takeshi Kimura; **C:** Hajime Koizumi. **VHS, Beta** *GEM, PSM*

Gorgo

An undersea explosion off the coast of Ireland brings to the surface a prehistoric sea monster, which is captured and brought to a London circus. All seems well, until scientists learn that Gorgo is but an infant. Its irate (and much larger) mother appears looking for her baby, creating havoc in her wake. Though London had been used as a setting for monster rampages before (director Eugene Lourie had done so just two years before in *The Giant Behemoth*), never has the destruction been quite as spectacular—although the monsters are portrayed by stiff costumes, the miniatures and matte work are impressive. Commonly mistaken by critics as the only monster movie where "the monster wins"—giant movie monsters seem to get away with their rampages quite often, even as far back as 1925's *The Lost World.* 🎵🎵♭

1961 76m/C *GB* Bill Travers, William Sylvester, Vincent Winter, Bruce Seton, Christopher Rhodes, Joseph O'Conor; **D:** Eugene Lourie; **W:** John Loring, Daniel Hyatt; **C:** Frederick A. (Freddie) Young. **VHS, Beta, LV** *NOS, MRV, VCI*

Grampa's Sci-Fi Hits

Sequel to *Grampa's Monster Movies*, this one carries some of the more fantastic of sci-fi creatures from beyond. An entertaining collection of movie trailers, including *The Day the Earth Stood Still, The Fabulous World of Jules Verne, Earth Vs. The Flying Saucers,* and many more, frequently broken up by corny skits featuring Al Lewis as the "Grampa" character he portrayed on TV's *The Munsters* back in the '60s. 🎵🎵♭

1990 65m/C VHS, Beta *NO*

Grand Tour: Disaster in Time

"Grand, simply grand." The aliens visiting Jeff Daniels' midwestern inn are among the most terrifying ever put on film. They have no superpowers. They do not wish to rule our planet. Worse, they are tourists so bored with their perfect world that they have become disaster junkies, time-traveling to catch such cataclysmic events as the 1906 San Francisco earthquake, the Hindenberg crash, and the eruption of Mt. St. Helens. Starts off slow, but things pick up after Daniels is given some friendly words of advice: "Leave. Today. Take your family and do not come back until you're absolutely certain it is safe." David Twohy went on to direct *The Arrival.* **AKA:** Disaster in Time. 🎵🎵🎵

1992 (PG-13) 98m/C Jeff Daniels, Ariana Richards, Emilia Crow, Jim Haynie, Nicholas Guest, Marilyn Lightstone, George Murdock; **D:** David N. Twohy; **W:** David N. Twohy. **VHS, LV** *ACA*

The Green Slime

Ah, they just don't make 'em like this anymore! It's danger and romance and slime-monsters galore as a spaceship assigned to intercept an oncoming asteroid inadvertently brings aboard malevolent alien creatures that proceed to menace the whole crew. The one-eyed "Green Slime" are among the, uh, *shortest* monsters in cinema history. They look more grumpy than vicious, and have the annoying habit of multiplying when the astro-boys plug 'em with their space-guns. Watching this ultra-cheap, U.S./Japanese co-production is kind of like eating a big, greasy hamburger. It'll leave you satisfied, but come dawn you'll feel guilty as heck you didn't consume something more nutritious. Then again, who cares? What could be healthier, after all, than the guffaws inspired by this glorious piece of crap? You can rent that Miramax thing next time. The title song, like that of *The Blob*, is legendary among aficionados of this particular brand of madness. **AKA:** Gamma Sango Uchu Daisakusen; Battle Beyond the Stars; Death and the Green Slime. 🎵🎵

1968 (G) 90m/C *JP* Robert Horton, Richard Jaeckel, Luciana Paluzzi, Bud Widom, Ted Gunther, Robert Dun-

ham, Charles Sinclair, William Finger; **D:** Kinji Fukasaku; **W:** Tom Rowe; **C:** Yoshikazu Yamasawa. **VHS, Beta** *MGM*

Gremlins

An appealing comedy/horror tale with a far sharper satiric edge than you'd expect from a movie about fuzzy gnomes who turn into murderous goblins. Produced by Spielberg, who seemed to be riding some kind of wave at the time. A fumbling gadget salesman named Rand Peltzer (Hoyt Axton) is looking for something really special to get his son Billy for Christmas. He finds it in a dingy little store run by a wise Chinese shopkeeper. The shopkeeper is reluctant to sell him the adorable, bulgy-eyed, furry, lisping, sweet-natured, not at all revolting "mogwai." He eventually relents, but not before laying down the three commandments of mogwai ownership: "Don't expose him to bright light, don't get him wet, and don't ever, ever feed him after midnight." Naturally, the rules are soundly broken and the result is a gang of nasty, reptilian gremlins who decide to tear up the town on Christmas Eve. The film is a wild, good-natured romp, but there's a decidedly dark side to its humor. That might make it all the more appealing to some; others might prefer the lighter laughs of *Gremlins 2*. 𝄢𝄢𝄢

1984 (PG) 106m/C Zach Galligan, Phoebe Cates, Hoyt Axton, Polly Holliday, Frances Lee McCain, Keye Luke, Dick Miller, Corey Feldman, Judge Reinhold, Glynn Turman; **D:** Joe Dante; **W:** Chris Columbus; **M:** Jerry Goldsmith. **VHS, Beta, LV, 8mm** *WAR, TLF*

Gremlins 2: The New Batch

This sequel to *Gremlins* is superior to the original, which was quite good. Here, director Joe Dante presents a less violent but far campier tale of critters on the rampage. This time the gremlins take Manhattan, getting into a research lab housed in a skyscraper with disastrous results. The film pays surreal tribute to classic movies, including *The Wizard of Oz*, and musical extravaganzas of the past (the gremlins' version of "New York, New York" is not to be missed). Tony Randall is splendid as

the voice of "the Brain," a gremlin inadvertently given super intelligence. The film on the whole is so good you almost wish there'd been a third movie. 𝄢𝄢𝄢𝄢

1990 (PG-13) 107m/C Phoebe Cates, Christopher Lee, John Glover, Zach Galligan, Robert Prosky, Richard Picardo; **Cameos:** Jerry Goldsmith; **D:** Joe Dante; **W:** Charles Haas; **M:** Jerry Goldsmith; **V:** Tony Randall. **VHS, Beta, LV, 8mm** *WAR, HHE*

The Groundstar Conspiracy

Spy thriller brings to life L.P. Davies' novel, *The Alien*. After an explosion kills all but one space project scientist, George Peppard is sent to investigate suspicions of a cover-up. Meanwhile, the surviving scientist (Michael Sarrazin) suffers from disfigurement and amnesia. He pursues his identity while Peppard accuses him of being a spy. Splendid direction by Lamont Johnson. Sarrazin's best role. 𝄢𝄢𝄢

1972 (PG) 96m/C *CA* George Peppard, Michael Sarrazin, Christine Belford, Cliff Potts, James Olson, Tim O'Connor, James McEachin, Alan Oppenheimer; **D:** Lamont Johnson. **VHS** *MCA*

GUY: Awakening of the Devil

Guy and Raina, two intergalactic vagabonds, travel to the prison-planet Geo in search of a youth drug. What they find is an evil female warden and a plague that turns people into hideous monsters. Guy turns into a giant blue critter that (barely) retains his human memory and scruples. Can Guy control his transformations? Can Raina keep all her clothes on for five consecutive seconds? This Japanimated adventure is fast-moving and exciting, but also sexually explicit and extremely violent. It's available in general release and uncut versions, but parents and those with weak stomachs should approach even the former with caution. In Japanese with English subtitles. Followed by *GUY II: Second Target*. 𝄢𝄢

1993 ?m/C *JP* **D:** Yorihisa Uchida; **M:** Nobuhiko Kashihara. **VHS** *CPM, WTA*

The Guyver

Wimp college student is transformed into a chitinous superhero thanks to his discovery of an organic alien battle suit, the "Guyver," and helps CIA agent Mark Hamill keep the device from falling into the claws of Zoanoids, evil mutants guiding the evolution of mankind. Based on a popular Japanese comic book (and resulting cartoons), this rather predictable series of creature wrestling matches has its roots in Ultraman, Infra-Man, and other futuristic good guys who combat guest-starring monstrosities. F/x artist Screaming Mad George endows each Zoanoid with a different grotesque look, and thus the whole thing feels like an excuse for the collectible trading cards. 🦴🦴

1991 92m/C Mark Hamill, Vivian Wu, David Gale, Jeffrey Combs, Michael Berryman, Jack Armstrong, Jimmie Walker; *D:* Steve Wang, Screaming Mad George; *W:* Jon Purdy; *C:* Levie Isaacks; *M:* Matthew Morse. **VHS** *COL, NLC*

Guyver 2: Dark Hero

Director Steve Wang gets more bucks, an R rating, and just an overall more gutsy feel to this sequel also based on the popular Japanese comic books and anime. Both the Guyver and the ever-so-nasty evil mutant morphing Zoanoids are on location at the site of an archaeological dig where many alien secrets and weapons are ready to be used for good or evil, to save or destroy the world. This time around we are spared the talents of Jimmie Walker (Lisker in the first film) and get to see a much more graphic "suiting up" of the Guyver by his biologically imbedded alien armor. The sets are bigger, the rubber suits are better, and the violence juicier, making this far superior to the original. Should even be enjoyable to fans of the more highly regarded animated versions. 🦴🦴

1994 (R) 127m/C David Hayter, Kathy Christopherson, Christopher Michael; *D:* Steve Wang; *W:* Nathan Long. **VHS, LV** *COL*

H-Man

Police are stumped when a gangster disappears in the middle of a busy Tokyo street, leaving only his clothes. While they investigate, more people disappear in the same fashion. A young scientist doing research into the effects of radioactivity comes forth with an

incredible theory: the victims are being dissolved by formerly human creatures who have been turned into protoplasmic monsters by exposure to H-bomb radiation. His theory turns out to be true, and the sewers beneath the city are infested with the oozing, ghostly monsters. Genuinely creepy f/x highlight this mixture of two commonly underrated genres of Japanese cinema—science fiction and gangster drama. Though Inoshiro Honda was famous for his giant monster sagas (*Godzilla, War of the Gargantuas,* and many others), he was also adept at these less-epic chillers. **AKA:** Bijo to Ekitai Nigen. 🦴🦴🦴

1959 79m/C *JP* Koreya Senda, Kenji Sahara, Yumi Shirakawa, Akihiko Hirata, Mitsuru Sato; *D:* Inoshiro Honda; *W:* Takeshi Kimura; *C:* Hajime Koizumi. **VHS, Beta** *COL*

Hackers

In another poor attempt to capitalize on the Internet craze, a group of teenage computer hackers surf their way into the wrong system. When Dade (Jonny Lee Miller) breaks into the computer system at Ellingson Oil, he becomes the perfect scapegoat for the industrial espionage being conducted by security chief Fisher Stevens. The underground hackers band together in an effort to clear their good names, and buy better hardware. Unfortunately, without the techno gadgets, the plot is mundane. Miller and Angelina Jolie both have charisma, and manage to generate some chemistry between them, but Fisher Stevens as the corporate security chief is about as scary as a kitten with a ball of yarn. Director Iain Softley, despite taking drastic liberties with the technology, does a good job with the visuals, taking viewers inside the minds of the hackers, rather than just watching geeks type on keyboards. A snappy techno soundtrack adds spice to this otherwise flavorless thriller. Jolie (hacker Acid Burn) is the daughter of actor Jon Voight. Look for magician Penn Jillette (of Penn & Teller) in a small role. 🦴

1995 (PG-13) 105m/C Jonny Lee Miller, Angelina Jolie, Fisher Stevens, Lorraine Bracco, Jesse Bradford, Wendell Pierce, Alberta Watson, Laurence Mason, Renoly Santiago, Matthew Lillard, Penn Jillette; *D:* Iain Softley; *W:* Rafael Moreu; *C:* Andrzej Sekula; *M:* Simon Boswell. **VHS, LV** *MGM*

Half Human

A strange little Yeti picture from Japan, badly mishandled by the U.S. distributor. An expedition discovers an adult and child hairy bi-ped creatures in the mountains. A circus captures the creatures, but when the young one is killed, the adult goes on a rampage. When released in the U.S., more than half of the original film was cut out, while cheap scenes with John Carradine and Morris Ankrum were added. Most of the film plays without subtitles or dubbing, just Carradine's narration. The bigfoot monsters are most unusual looking. Director Inoshiro Honda made better movies before and after, with Godzilla and Rodan—although it's unfair to judge this one on the basis of the U.S. version. 🐾🐾

1958 78m/B *JP* Akira Takarada, Kenji Sahara, Momoko Kochi, Robert Karnes, Russ Thorson, Morris Ankrum; *D:* Inoshiro Honda. **VHS** *SNC, MLB*

The Handmaid's Tale

Set in "the recent future" when "a country went wrong," this fundamentally sterile adaptation of Margaret Atwood's bestselling novel still manages to be chilling thanks to its not so inconceivable premise. Militant fundamentalists seize control of the United States (now known as Gilead). The written word, except for the Bible, is replaced by television, photographs and bar codes. Smoking, drinking, and sex are officially outlawed. Abortion is punishable by hanging. An ecological disaster has left most of the population infertile. The women who can still reproduce are packed off for indoctrination before they are assigned to the homes of infertile couples as surrogate "handmaids." Natasha Richardson stars as a fertile woman whose escape attempt lands her in the home of Commander Robert Duvall and his increasingly resentful wife, Faye Dunaway, who, in a ceremony inspired by the Old Testament, is present in bed while her husband tries to conceive with Richardson. Elizabeth McGovern energizes her scenes as a "gender-traitor," who recruits her to join the rebels and assassinate the Commander. 🐾🐾🐾

1990 (R) 109m/C Natasha Richardson, Robert Duvall, Faye Dunaway, Aidan Quinn, Elizabeth McGovern, Victoria Tennant, Blanche Baker, Traci Lind; *D:* Volker Schlondorff; *W:* Harold Pinter; *C:* Igor Luther. **VHS, Beta, LV** *HBO, FCT, IME*

Hands of Steel

Italian *Terminator* takeoff in which an indestructible cyborg carries out government assassinations, until a mission against an environmentalist scientist changes his mind. The bionic brute turns against his own masters with little change of expression. Pretty terrible acting, but stunts and sadism enough to keep action fans sedated and happy. 🐾🐾

1986 (R) 94m/C *IT* Daniel Greene, John Saxon, Janet Agren, Claudio Cassinelli, George Eastman; *D:* Martin Dolman. **VHS, Beta** *LIV*

Hangar 18

Somewhat silly and cynical (and what's wrong with that?) UFO coverup story, with a plot similar to *Capricorn One*. Two astronauts are scapegoated for the loss of a shuttle that has actually collided with a UFO. When they learn that the government is hiding the evidence in the title hangar (think it's in area 51, boys?), they set out to blow the lid of off things. Robert Vaughn delivers as a typically sleazy and very sneaky politician who will do anything to prevent the news from leaking out. Directed by James L. Conway, who made some of the "fine" Sunn Classic pseudo-documentaries. The ending should satisfy most conspiracy freaks who will probably shout "I told you so" out loud. Shown on TV as *Invasion Force* with a different ending. **AKA:** Invasion Force. 🐾🐾

1980 (PG) 97m/C Darren McGavin, Robert Vaughn, Gary Collins, James Hampton, Philip Abbott, Pamela Bellwood, Tom Hallick, Cliff Osmond, Joseph Campanella; *D:* James L. Conway; *W:* David O'Malley. **VHS, Beta** *WOV*

Hardware

Post-apocalyptic ragpicker gives artist Stacy Travis some robot remains he collected (ours is not to ask why). The skeletal 'droid she reassembles turns out to be a government-spawned population controller programmed to destroy warm bodies—though from it looks more like a rock band drummer, thanks to Boswell's MTV-delirium camerawork. With more attitude than originality (and some carnage excised to avoid an X rating), this holds one's attention only briefly. Due to a plagiarism lawsuit, the tape now carries a tacked-on end credit attributing the story to *SHOK!*, a piece in the cult comic book *2000 A.D.* Iggy Pop is heard in voiceover only, while former Sex Pistol John Lydon performs the punk theme song. 🦴🦴

1990 (R) 94m/C *GB* Dylan McDermott, Stacy Travis, John Lynch, William Hootkins; *D:* Richard Stanley; *W:* Richard Stanley; *C:* Steven Chivers; *M:* Simon Boswell; *V:* Iggy Pop. **VHS, Beta, LV** *HBO, WAR*

Hardware Wars and Other Film Farces

Indie filmmaker/actor Ernie Fosselius created one of most successful short subjects ever with his 1977 parody of *Star Wars* starring a vacuum cleaner as R2D2, an "Oz"-style tin man as C3PO, and a general emphasis on common household appliances for Lucasfilm-scale starships and special effects. The homemade effort packs more laughs than *Spaceballs* into a fraction of the running time. This tape compilation also includes Fosselius' *Apocalypse Now* spoof centered on a deli, *Porklips Now*; the self-explanatory *Closet Cases of the Nerd Kind*; and Marv Newland's infamous cartoon snippet *Bambi Meets Godzilla*. 🦴🦴🦴

1978 51m/C *D:* Ernie Fosselius. **VHS, Beta** *PYR*

Have Rocket Will Travel

Three janitors (named Moe, Larry, and Curly Joe—sound familiar?) help a scientist who is about to lose her job if she can't send a rocket to Venus. They accidentally initiate the launch while still on board and introduce their brand of slapstick to a whole new planet. While on Venus (which looks a lot more like Colorado), the boys encounter a unicorn who speaks archaic English, a giant spider, and clones of themselves. This feature-length film gave the Stooges' careers a jump-start and led to five more movies, including *The Three Stooges Go Around the World in a Daze* and *The Three Stooges Meet Hercules*(!). They're all good fun for Stooge fans. Lesser humans just won't understand.... 🦴🦴

1959 76m/B Moe Howard, Larry Fine, Joe DeRita, Anna-Lisa, Jerome Cowan, Bob Colbert; *D:* David Lowell Rich; *W:* Raphael Hayes; *C:* Ray Cory. **VHS** *COL*

The Head

Mad scientist (whose lab-enhanced genius has driven out all conscience) keeps the head of an old surgeon alive when the guy's heart fails. The unhappy cranium reluctantly assists the villain in his personal project to transfer the head of a hunchbacked nurse to the body of a beautiful stripper. Moody cinematography and production design is reminiscent of German Expressionism from the great days of silent cinema, but we're not in *Metropolis* any more, Toto. Lurid, tacky cheapie. 🦴🦴

1959 92m/B *GE* Horst Frank, Michel Simon, Paul Dahlke, Karin Kernke, Helmut Schmidt, Christiane Maybach, Dieter Eppler; *D:* Victor Trivas; *W:* Victor Trivas. **VHS** *SNC*

Heartbeeps

In a 1995 very different from what *we* experienced, two domestic robot-servants fall in love and run off together. This weird sf romance isn't without its charms, and Andy Kaufman and Bernadette Peters tackle their robotic parts gamely enough. Kids might well enjoy the funny voices and off-key humor. Most viewers, however, will think the film has a few loose screws too many. Director Alan Arkush also made the noted teen epic *Rock 'n' Roll High School*. 🦴🦴

1981 (PG) 79m/C Andy Kaufman, Bernadette Peters, Randy Quaid, Kenneth McMillan, Christopher Guest, Melanie Mayron, Jack Carter; *D:* Allan Arkush; *W:* John Hill; *C:* Charles Rosher Jr.; *M:* John Williams. Nominations: Academy Awards '81: Best Makeup. **VHS, Beta** *MCA*

Hearts & Armour

Based on Ludovico Ariosto's *Orlando Furioso*, this medieval mini-epic is a far more lavish spectacle than its budget should have allowed. Knights and knightesses in armor as stylized as *Excalibur*'s viciously have at it in a passionate tale of magic, honor, and "holy" war. Tanya Roberts, in her pre-softcore days, plays a Moorish princess whose kidnapping incites war to erupt between the Moors and Christians. Combatants such as Mongol, the Human Weapon, and the Black Warrior clash in violent battles to the death inspired by loyalty, love, religion, or maybe just to fulfill some wild prophecy...hey, sounds like the real world. With the use of a cool, atmospheric, electronic soundtrack, and a cast that looks like (and in many cases is) Supermodels Inc., you hardly notice that all the battles involve no more than four warriors! 🦴🦴🦴

1983 101m/C *IT* Tanya Roberts, Leigh McCloskey, Ron Moss, Rick Edwards, Giovanni Visentin; **D:** Giacomo Battiato. **VHS, Beta** *WAR*

Heatseeker

Corporations use mechanical fighters to participate in brutal kickboxing contests in 2019 New America. Human Chance (Keith Cooke) must battle cyborg opponent Xao if he wants to save his kidnapped trainer. Lots of action and even some intentional humor. 🦴🦴

1995 (R) 91m/C Keith Cooke, Gary Daniels, Norbert Weisser, Thom Mathews; **D:** Albert Pyun. **VHS** *VMK*

Heavy Metal

"Louder and nastier than ever!" proclaims the vid box of this midnight movie staple, long unavailable on video until Columbia Home Video rereleased it in June 1996, THX digitally mastered, and with three extra minutes of never-before-seen footage. It's a collection of

"Alas poor Yorick...I knew him well." Dylan McDermott in **Hardware.**

tle thin after a while. SCTV regulars John Candy and Eugene Levy provided some of the voices. Based on original art and stories by Richard Corben, Angus McKie, Dan O'Bannon, Thomas Warkentin, and Berni Wrightson. 🦴🦴🦴

1981 (R) 90m/C *CA* Rodger Bumpass, Jackie Burroughs; **D:** Gerald Potterton; **W:** Dan Goldberg, Len Baum; **M:** Elmer Bernstein; **V:** John Candy, Joe Flaherty, Eugene Levy, Don Francks. **VHS, LV** *COL*

Hell Comes to Frogtown

When you're running with the *Mad Max* ripoff pack you need gimmicks to stand out, and this sure has a few. In post-nuclear holocaust land, hostile mutant frog people abduct some precious, fertile human women. Sam Hell (thesped by "Rowdy" Roddy Piper, of pro wrestling fame), being one of the few fertile males left, is a government-sanctioned stud and must rescue the ladies to impregnate them. Fitfully fun sci-fi spoof has some good frog getups despite the extreme low-budget. Sorry guys, sex and sleaze are mainly just talk. Filmmaker Donald G. Jackson did the even sillier post-nuke cheapie *Roller Blade,* as well as an unfortunate *Frogtown* sequel. 🦴🦴

1987 (R) 88m/C Roddy Piper, Sandahl Bergman, Rory Calhoun, Cec Verrell; **D:** Donald G. Jackson, Robert J. Kizer; **W:** Randall Frakes; **C:** Donald G. Jackson. **VHS, Beta, LV** *VTR, NWV*

The Henderson Monster

Don't be fooled by the P.T. Barnum title or sf/horror packaging; there's no monster at all in this talky TV drama. Potentially hazardous experiments by a genetic scientist wind up the subject of courtroom debate. But each character has his or her own hidden agenda divorced from the facts (like Nehemiah Persoff as an old pal of Einstein's who opposes gene-splicing to expunge his own guilt over helping build the atom bomb). Interesting, if overstated primer in science ethics, reviewed here for the record. 🦴🦴

1980 105m/C Jason Miller, Christine Lahti, Stephen Collins, David Spielberg, Nehemiah Persoff, Larry Gates; **D:** Waris Hussein. **VHS, Beta** *LIV*

The original **Heavy Metal** groupie, Taarna.

animated tales loosely derived from the "adult comics" mag of the same name. The stories are all vaguely connected by the presence of a malevolent green globe that somehow represents Ultimate Evil. Best of the tales is "Den": in a fluke happening a teenage boy finds his mind transferred across space and time to the body of a mighty warrior. The man-child Den is thrust into an ages-old fight between religious cults, rescues bare-breasted babes, and has a general, all-around good time. The animation is in some cases impressive, and there's a plethora of metal music on the soundtrack (featuring such bands as Black Sabbath, Blue Oyster Cult, Cheap Trick, Devo, Grand Funk Railroad, Journey, Nazareth, and others), but depending on your tolerance for T&A and forced drug humor, it might begin to wear a lit-

Sword and Sorcery Movies

There's something about a man with a big sword...particularly if he's up against the forces of darkness in a primeval world. Tales of heroic warriors are of course among the oldest stories told. Later on, in the boring old 20th Century, writers like Robert E. Howard would appropriate the best elements of the old sagas for stories set in magical worlds that never existed. Countless pulp stories and paperback novels established the barbarian hero as an archetype of modern fantasy.

It took the movies a while to catch up, though. Before the '80s, U.S. and British directors had made impressive use of the legends of King Arthur and the *Arabian Nights*. Many of these, like Ray Harryhausen's Sinbad movies, are still wonderful. Russian director Alexander Ptushko drew on the myths of his homeland to create the truly epic *The Sword and the Dragon*. Hercules movies were all the rage in Italy in the '60s, and a number of Asian films of the same era also drew on heroic legendry.

But it wasn't until fantasy role-playing games began getting press in the late '70s that budget-strapped filmmakers started to take notice. The success of fantasy films like *Dragonslayer* and John Milius' long-awaited film version of *Conan the Barbarian* in 1982 made a sword-and-sorcery boom seem inevitable. Why not make some movies to take advantage of this latest fad? Any local forest would do for a set; clothe your actors in fake-fur loincloths, rent some swords from a costume shop, some low-rent special effects and you got yourself a modest blockbuster, right?

Well, in theory maybe, but the results could be less than overwhelming. Take *Sorceress*, for instance, the tale of a young warrior queen in a pseudo-medieval kingdom. This film by cult-film legend Jack (*Spider Baby*) Hill is so bad it's been known to make grown Conan fans weep. *Sorceress'* Neanderthal cheesecake look, however, became a staple of the new genre, as witness such low-rent wonders as *Barbarian Queen* and *Amazons*. Love those chainmail-and-rabbitskin bikinis! Italian director Luigi Fulci, best known for his zombie movies, contributed *Conquest*, whose villainess wears little more than a metal mask. Other films of this type at least tried to tell a good story. *The Sword and the Sorcerer* in 1982 featured a high-tech flying sword that looked like something from a medieval James Bond's private arsenal. *Beastmaster* spawned two sequels with its appealing use of friendly animals as plot-devices. *Deathstalker*, with former Playboy Bunnie Barbie Benton as the heroine, also inspired sequels, but was far hokier.

Entertainingly cheap sword-and-sorcery films have become a little less popular these days, but the success of TV shows like *Hercules, The Legendary Journeys,* and *Xena, Warrior Princess* suggest that quest for the perfect fantasy is likely to continue for some time.

Hercules

The one that started it all. This Italian-import prototype sword-and-sandaleer features Steve Reeves as the mythical strongman who encounters love, bad guys, monsters, and of course the Labors of Hercules, in this retelling of the story of "Jason and the Golden Fleece." Fine cinematography by Mario Bava helped make this a far bigger hit than expected, and encouraged an onslaught of spaghetti-adventures to be shipped to the U.S. **AKA:** La Tatiche de Ercole. 🦴🦴🦴
1958 107m/C *IT* Steve Reeves, Sylva Koscina, Fabrizio Mioni, Gianna Maria Canale, Arturo Dominici; **D:** Pietro Francisci. **VHS, Beta, LV** *MRV, IME, VDM*

Hercules

Lackluster remake of 1957 original finds legendary muscle guy Hercules in the person of

Hercules Against the Moon Men

This is one of the more visually striking of the '60s Hercules movies. Actually, the hero was called Maciste in his native Italy, but American audiences didn't care; they just wanted more sword-and-sandal epicry, and boy, did they get it here! The big guy is summoned to an isolated kingdom in the shadow of the Mountain of Death, wherein live a race of beings from the moon, brought to Earth by a prehistoric meteorite. The moon-men themselves are groovy-looking humanoids made of jagged rock and led by an really tall guy with an impressive metallic skull-mask. They promise the kingdom's evil queen immortality in return for a human sacrifice every year. Young lovers are separated, oppressed peasants plot revolution, and time is drawing near to revive the moon-men's dead queen Selena! Can Herc triumph?? Not even fun to make fun of (although those wacky folks at *Mystery Science Theater* gave it their best shot), it's really just kind of painful to watch. **AKA:** Maciste la Regina di Samar. *♪*

1965 88m/C *IT FR* Alan Steel, Jany Clair, Anna Maria Polani, Nando Tamberlani; **D:** Giacomo Gentilomo; **W:** Arpad De Riso, Nino Scolaro, Angelo Sangarmano, Giacomo Gentilomo. **VHS, Beta** *SNC, MRV*

"Damn, I was supposed to point it away from me!" Naive alien Kyle MacLachlan in *The Hidden.*

Lou Ferrigno's Hulkster fighting against the evil King Minos for his own survival and the love of Cassiopeia, a rival king's daughter. *♪*

1983 (PG) 100m/C *IT* Lou Ferrigno, Sybil Danning, William Berger, Brad Harris, Ingrid Anderson; **D:** Lewis (Luigi Cozzi) Coates; **W:** Lewis (Luigi Cozzi) Coates; **M:** Pino Donaggio. Golden Raspberry Awards '83: Worst Supporting Actress (Danning), Worst New Star (Ferrigno). **VHS, Beta, LV** *MGM, IME*

Hercules 2

The muscle-bound demi-god returns to do battle with more evil foes amidst the same stunningly cheap special effects. **AKA:** The Adventures of Hercules. *♪*

1985 (PG) 90m/C *IT* Lou Ferrigno, Claudio Cassinelli, Milly Carlucci, Sonia Viviani, William Berger, Carlotta Green; **D:** Lewis (Luigi Cozzi) Coates; **M:** Pino Donaggio. **VHS** *MGM*

Hercules and the Captive Women

Hercules' son is kidnapped by the Queen of Atlantis, and the bare-chested warrior goes on an all-out rampage to save the boy. Directed by sometimes-lauded Vittorio Cottafavi. **AKA:** Hercules and the Haunted Women; Hercules and the Conquest of Atlantis; Ercole Alla Conquista di Atlantide. *♪ ♪*

1963 93m/C *IT* Reg Park, Fay Spain, Ettore Manni; **D:** Vittorio Cottafavi. **VHS, Beta** *RHI, MRV, CCB*

Hercules and the Princess of Troy

Hercules is up to his pecs in trouble as he battles a hungry sea monster in order to save a

beautiful maiden. Originally a pilot for a prospective television series, and shot in English, not Italian, with Hercules played by erstwhile Tarzan Gordon Scott. Highlights are special effects and color cinematography. 🎬🎬🎬

1965 ?m/C *IT* Gordon Scott, Diana Hyland, Paul Stevens, Everett Sloane. **VHS, Beta** *SNC, MLB*

Hercules in New York

This is it! You've heard about it, you've wondered about it, you've very wisely avoided it! This was Arnold Schwarzenegger's motion-picture debut; as the muscle-bound son of Zeus, Ahnold is transported through time by his deity dad to 20th-Century Manhattan. Schwarzenegger (his voice is dubbed) and his geeky friend Arnold Stang have all kinds of fun in the Big Apple, including driving a chariot up Broadway. Wouldn't you, if you had the chance? Eventually the muscle-bound future star becomes a professional wrestling superstar. Two hundred and fifty pounds of stupid, lighthearted fun. **AKA:** Hercules: The Movie; Hercules Goes Bananas. 🎬🎬

1970 (G) 93m/C Arnold Schwarzenegger, Arnold Stang, Deborah Loomis, James Karen, Ernest Graves; **D:** Arthur Seidelman. **VHS, Beta** *MPI*

Hercules in the Haunted World

Another good Italian fantasy-adventure featuring the mighty Hercules—played yet again by Reg Park, who must have been genetically engineered to look exactly like former series star Steve Reeves. Here the son of Zeus must journey into the depths of Hell in order to find a plant that will cure a poisoned princess. There are stone men and fiery perils a-plenty, plus Christopher Lee as a servant of Pluto, King of Hades. Far more interesting and atmospheric than other Herc-fests, thanks largely to Mario Bava's inspired direction. **AKA:** Ercole al Centro Della Terra. 🎬🎬🎬

1964 91m/C *IT* Reg Park, Leonora Ruffo, Christopher Lee, George Ardisson; **D:** Mario Bava. **VHS, Beta** *CCB, RHI, MRV*

Hercules, Prisoner of Evil

Spaghetti myth-opera in which Hercules battles a witch who is turning men into werewolves. Made for Italian television by director Anthony Dawson (the nom-de-cinema of Antonio Margheriti). 🎬

1964 ?m/C *IT* Reg Park; **D:** Anthony (Antonio Margheriti) Dawson. **VHS** *SNC*

Hercules Unchained

Sequel to *Hercules* finds the muscleman (Steve Reeves) and his princess bride (Sylva Koscina) setting off for the city of Thebes, trying to prevent a war. Along the way he drinks from the "waters of forgetfulness" and is captured by a beautiful evil queen intent on making him hard (seems she collects famous warriors and turns them into statues). More campy fun and still better than most of the imitations. **AKA:** Ercole e la Regina de Lidia. 🎬🎬🎬

1959 101m/C *IT* Steve Reeves, Sylva Koscina, Silvia Lopel, Primo Carnera; **D:** Pietro Francisci. **VHS, Beta, LV** *VDM, SUE, MRV*

The Hidden

A seasoned cop (Michael Nouri) and a benign alien posing as an FBI agent (Kyle MacLachlan) team up to track down and destroy a hyper-violent alien lifeform that lives for fast cars and loud rock music and survives by invading the bodies of humans, causing them to go on murderous rampages. In its initial release, the film was coolly received by many as a *Terminator/Robocop* ripoff. It's still violent, but the humor, high-velocity action, and fine performances all around have earned the film a substantial cult following. On laserdisc, the widescreen transfer captures the image and sound with sharp clarity, and director Jack Sholder provides commentary on a secondary audio track. Followed by a sequel. 🎬🎬🎬

1987 (R) 98m/C Kyle MacLachlan, Michael Nouri, Clu Gulager, Ed O'Ross, Claudia Christian, Clarence Felder, Richard Brooks, William Boyett; **D:** Jack Sholder; **W:** Bob Hunt; **C:** Jacques Haitkin; **M:** Michael Convertino. **VHS, Beta, LV** *MED, CDV, VTR*

Lips; Terror from the Sun; The Sun Demon. 🦴🦴ᵇ

1959 75m/B Robert Clarke, Patricia Manning, Nan Peterson; *D:* Robert Clarke. **VHS, Beta** *NOS, MRV, RHI*

High Desert Kill

Pals on a hunting trip in the New Mexico desert find strange phenomena and begin behaving irrationally. Turns out a tentacled alien in the neighborhood is playing with their heads. Cable TV-movie is the sort of premise Rod Serling could have done better in one-third the time on any given *Twilight Zone.* 🦴🦴

1990 (PG) 93m/C Chuck Connors, Marc Singer, Anthony Geary, Micah Grant; *D:* Harry Falk; *W:* T.S. Cook. **VHS, Beta** *MCA*

Highlander

Action-fantasy about 'immortals,' a race of, well, immortals (spontaneously born to ordinary folk) who must meet in battle down through the centuries, decapitating each other—the only way to kill one—until the last survivor inherits their accumulated power. Christopher Lambert is 16th-century Scotsman Connor MacLeod, whose feud with an equally ageless foe comes to blows in modern Manhattan. Sean Connery makes a memorable appearance as MacLeod's mentor, but the real energy comes from spectacular swordfights and death scenes, plus a glam-rock lyricism thanks to musical inserts by Queen. A cult fave for Russell Mulcahy's flashy visual style, this spawned weak sequels (which more or less jettisoned the already loose logic of the original), and inspired both animated live-action TV spinoffs (bits of the TV series were re-edited into the feature *Highlander: The Gathering*). Different versions of the original exist on laserdisc imports, with more extensive flashbacks throughout world history. 🦴🦴🦴

1986 (R) 110m/C Christopher Lambert, Sean Connery, Clancy Brown, Roxanne Hart, Beatie Edney, Alan North, Sheila Gish, Jon Polito; *D:* Russell Mulcahy; *W:* Gregory Widen, Peter Bellwood, Larry Ferguson; *M:* Michael Kamen. **VHS, Beta, LV** *REP*

Heads up! It's the *Highlander,* starring Christopher Lambert.

The Hidden 2

The hyper-violent alien of the 1987 movie returns. With its love of fast cars, high-caliber weapons, and heavy metal music, this body-possessing creature appears to be unstoppable. 🦴🦴ᵇ

1994 (R) 91m/C Raphael Sbarge, Kate Hodge, Michael Nouri; *D:* Seth Pinsker; *W:* Seth Pinsker; *M:* David McHugh. **VHS, LV** *NLC, IME*

Hideous Sun Demon

A physicist exposed to radiation must stay out of sunlight or he will turn into a scaly, lizard-like creature. Although commonly lumped in with most other '50s monster pictures, this one can also be taken as an allegory for alcoholism. Star/director Robert Clarke hides from the Sun all day, but stays out all night in saloons, eventually alienating his friends as the monster within him gradually takes control. The scene of the maddened Clarke eating a rat was excised from most TV prints, but has been restored on video. **AKA:** Blood on His

Highlander 2: The Quickening

Even Christopher Lambert disowned this second chapter in the saga of Connor MacLeod, which tries retroactively to explain everything that happened in the first movie in a sci-fi context. Now we learn that immortals are political exiles from the planet Zeist, whose psycho tyrant (Michael Ironside), not satisfied to let MacLeod die old in the year 2024, sends flying porcupine men to Earth to restore the Highlander to youth so they can kill him...Huh? There's a sense the filmmakers were seriously drunk when they made this; in any case, Connery looks like he's having fun. Visual f/x are extremely iffy. A "Renegade Director's Cut" is available at 108 minutes. **WOOF!**

1991 (R) 90m/C Christopher Lambert, Sean Connery, Virginia Madsen, Michael Ironside, John C. McGinley; **D:** Russell Mulcahy; **W:** Peter Bellwood; **C:** Phil Meheux; **M:** Stewart Copeland. **VHS, LV, 8mm** *COL*

Highlander: The Final Dimension

The third *Highlander* pointedly ignores what went on in the second *Highlander* but can't claim much of an improvement. Immortal Connor MacLeod battles sadistic master illusionist Kane (Mario Van Peebles, hamming it up laughably amid computer-generated f/x), who seeks to rule the world. MacLeod returns to his old Scottish stomping grounds to prepare for battle, giving armchair tourists something to look at, anyway. Original theatrical release was PG-13 and 94 minutes; the director's cut has been re-edited and footage added. **AKA:** Highlander 3: The Magician; Highlander 3: The Sorcerer. 🐕

1994 (R) 99m/C Christopher Lambert, Mario Van Peebles, Deborah Unger, Mako; **D:** Andrew Morahan; **W:** Paul Ohl; **M:** J. Peter Robinson. **VHS, LV** *TOU*

The Hitchhiker's Guide to the Galaxy

BBC-TV adaptation of Douglas Adams' hilarious radio serial (better known to many as a series of best-selling books), done with many of the original audio cast members and positing a riotous universe of adventure, absurdity, and really wild things, of which Earth is completely ignorant, yet of momentous importance. Thus typical Englishman Arthur Dent survives the sudden demolition of his planet (by a hyperspace road crew) thanks to hitchhiking skills of his best friend, secretly an alien travel writer updating the latest edition of the eminent Hitchhiker's Guide. Together they ricochet through time and space, meeting an odd assortment of creatures like the infamous Marvin the Paranoid Android and mod master criminal/entrepreneur/galactic president Zaphod Beebelbrox. Viewers will also learn the answer to the question of life, which certainly makes this worth a rental despite cut-rate computer graphics and low-budget f/x that are a painful distraction half the time (dig Zaphod's inanimate, superfluous second head). Adams' crafty intellect makes this not just first-rate comedy but splendidly imaginative sf. David Prowse—the big guy who was really inside Darth Vader's costume—cameos as an intergalactic rock star's thug bodyguard. Available in both single-cassette and double-cassette versions; the latter "special edition" includes a copy of the first book in the series and a mock dedication from Adams at the beginning. 🐕🐕🐕

1981 194m/C *GB* Simon Jones, David Dixon, Sandra Dickinson, Mark Wing-Davey; **Cameos:** David Prowse; **D:** Alan Bell. **VHS, LV** *FOX, MOV, FUS*

Hollywood Boulevard 2

A "B" movie studio finds its top actresses being killed off and terror reigns supreme as the mystery grows more intense. Could that psycho-bimbo from outer space have something to do with it? 🐕

1989 (R) 82m/C Ginger Lynn Allen, Kelly Monteith, Eddie Deezen, Ken Wright, Steve Vinovich; **D:** Steve Barnett. **VHS, Beta** *MGM*

Hologram Man

Unapologetic rip-off of Stallone/Snipes' *Demolition Man* is almost as much guilty fun. California becomes a warzone where the corporate bosses at Cal Corp. aren't much better

> "Why does the sun come up, or are the stars just pinholes in the curtain of night?"
>
> —Ramirez (Sean Connery) *in Highlander.*

than the gangs. Thug Evan Lurie (who also co-wrote and -produced) is sentenced to "holo-gramatic reprogramming," i.e., they separate his personality from his physical body. But his henchman William Sanderson (the veteran sf B-movie character actor who specializes in henchmen) hot wires the computer. Lurie is reborn as an indestructible electronic "virtual" villain. Actually, he looks like a grainy late-'50s color TV broadcast, but that's O.K. 🎜🎜

1995 (R) 96m/C Joe Lara, Evan Lurie, William Sanderson, Tiny Lister, Michael Nouri, John Amos; **D:** Richard Pepin; **W:** Evan Lurie; **M:** John Gonzalez. **VHS, LV** PMH

Homewrecker

Robby Benson stars as a scientist who invents a computer, with a female voice, as the ulti-mate domestic worker. Only the computer turns possessive and against Benson's estranged wife. 🎜🎜

1992 (PG-13) 88m/C Robby Benson, Sydney Walsh, Sarah Rose Karr; **D:** Fred Walton; **W:** Eric Harlacher; **V:** Kate Jack-son. **VHS, Beta** PAR

Honey, I Blew Up the Kid

To parents, it is the ultimate nightmare: the Terrible Twos magnified 100 times. To children, it is the ultimate fantasy: to tower above adults and have the world (or in this case, Las Vegas) as your playground. Rick Moranis returns as Wayne Szalinski, the screwball inventor who shrunk his kids in the first *Honey, I....* misadventure. It's a *Son of Flubber* for the '90s, with awesome special effects its '60s counterpart could not even imagine. Cherubic twins Daniel and Joshua Shalikar steal their scenes (not hard for a 100-foot tod-dler) as the rampaging Adam. A third *Honey* has been produced for the direct-to-video market. 🎜🎜🎜

1992 (PG) 89m/C Rick Moranis, Marcia Strassman, Robert Oliveri, Daniel Shalikar, Joshua Shalikar, Lloyd Bridges, John Shea, Keri Russell, Gregory Sierra, Julia Sweeney, Kenneth Tobey; **D:** Randal Kleiser; **W:** Thom Eberhardt, Peter Elbling, Garry Goodrow; **M:** Bruce Broughton. **VHS, Beta, LV** DIS

Honey, I Shrunk the Kids

The popular Disney fantasy about a suburban inventor (Rick Moranis), who is probably the son of Fred MacMurray's character in *The Absent-Minded Professor*. His shrinking device accidentally reduces his kids to 1/4 inch tall, and he subsequently throws them out with the garbage. Now they must journey back to the house through the jungle that was once the back lawn, overcoming the dangers of insects, sprinklers, and the like. A fine comic script that takes things in stride, plus outstanding effects make this one worthwhile. Matt Frewer steals scenes as Moranis' annoy-ing neighbor. Accompanied by "Tummy Trou-ble," the first of a projected series of Roger Rabbit Maroon Cartoons. Followed by *Honey, I Blew Up the Kid*. 🎜🎜🎜

1989 (G) 101m/C Rick Moranis, Matt Frewer, Marcia Strassman, Kristine Sutherland, Thomas Wilson Brown, Jared Rushton, Amy O'Neill, Robert Oliveri; **D:** Joe John-ston, Rob Minkoff; **W:** Ed Naha, Tom Schulman, Stuart Gordon; **M:** James Horner; **V:** Charles Fleischer, Kathleen Turner, Lou Hirsch, April Winchell. **VHS, Beta, LV** DIS, MOV, RDG

Horror of the Blood Monsters

John Carradine made a career out of being in bad movies, and this one competes as one of the worst. This is an editor's nightmare, made up of black & white film from a bizarre Filipino fantasy picture about battling tribes of mutants, spliced together and tinted. Added footage shows vampires attacking people, while Carradine spouts nonsense about the bloodsuckers being from outer space. Robert Dix and Vicki Volante lead an expedition to another world to track down the source of the vampire plague—or do they? There's so much mix-and-match editing, with plenty of "action" taking place off screen (while the on-screen imported antics remain unexplained), that it's difficult to tell whether this can actually be called a movie or not. A milestone in the auda-cious career of Al Adamson, who made a bun-dle from this assemblage of film stock by releasing it over and over under different titles, even touting the tinted scenes as a rev-olutionary new process. No doubt many of you caught a piece of this on late night TV, and

Planet Mirth

"There is a legend that sf and humor do not mix, but it is false," conclusively declares Peter Nicholls' *Science Fiction Encyclopedia*. Even casual video viewers recognize genre spoofs like Mel Brooks' *Spaceballs* and Woody Allen's Hugo Award-winning *Sleeper*. The Hound would like to spotlight some shorter sci-fi parodies and futuristic satires for the true connoisseur:

HARDWARE WARS. "You'll laugh! You'll cry! You'll kiss three bucks goodbye!" Actually this is the most successful short parody on record, a hilarious *Star Wars* goof with an emphasis on common household appliances (R2D2 is a vacuum cleaner), cranked out cheaply in 1978 by actor/sound editor Ernie Fosselius. What the Wookie Monster's many fans don't know is that the title is available on tape, part of a one-hour compilation of Fosseliusizations entitled *Hardware Wars and Other Film Farces,* with a bonus inclusion of Marv Newland's notorious cartoon snippet *Bambi Meets Godzilla.*

FUTUROPOLIS. A brave but fatality-prone team of "Space Rangers" go up against evil Lord Egghead in this 1984 short done in Richmond, Virginia, that claims to be the biggest low-budget movie ever. It's crammed with genre gags and nonstop cheapo f/x of every variety, stumbling the gamut from stop-motion pixillation to computer graphics (on a Commodore 64, natch) to drawing directly on the film emulsion with a magic marker. Beware the Chamber of Nameless Dread!

ARISE! Anarchic recruitment video of the Church of the SubGenius, a Dallas-based gag flying-saucer cult that's even funnier than Scientology and wields the technique of "media barrage" to get incomprehensible doctrines across. This means a mind-breaking collage of clips culled from vintage sci-fi, monster, religious, and instructional films, all pushing New Age mantras of personal growth and alien-borne doom on July 5, 1998, for all who have not paid their SubGenius membership dues.

THE FIRESIGN THEATRE. Future-shock sf and cyberpunk themes dominate the cosmology of this freeform West Coast audio comedy troupe. Their few videos include *Nick Danger and the Case of the Missing Yolks,* that pits America's Only Detective against an automated house holding hillbillies hostage, while *Eat or Be Eaten* details the deeds of a voracious plant. Their *Hot Shorts* compilation includes farcical redubs of the vintage TV sci-fi *Commander Cody.* The Firesigners made a movie out of their UFO pseudo-science parody album *Everything You Know Is Wrong* but thus far refuse to release it.

THE STARSHIP PIDDLEY-SHITS. Disgusted by jargon-laden space operas, Clevelander Jason Lukianowicz made this dirt-cheap trilogy of black-and-white spoofs (images from which wound up in Pink Floyd's concert show) centering on a couple of galactic pizza-delivery buttheads and their adventures with flatulent aliens, an Evil Factory, and molecular instability. The unexpurgated climax of episode three is one of the cinema's great moments of scatology and should not be viewed by anyone under any circumstances whatsoever.

---

woke up the next morning convinced you dreamed it all. **AKA:** Vampire Men of the Lost Planet; Horror Creatures of the Prehistoric Planet; Creatures of the Prehistoric Planet; Creatures of the Red Planet; Flesh Creatures of the Red Planet; The Flesh Creatures; Space Mission of the Lost Planet.

1970 (PG) 85m/C *PH* John Carradine, Robert Dix, Vicki Volante, Jennifer Bishop, Joey Benson, Bruce Powers; *D:* Al Adamson; *W:* Sue McNair; *C:* William G. Troiano, William Zsigmond. **VHS, Beta** *REP*

Horror Planet

Cheapie takeoff on *Alien.* In the catacombs of a dead planet, a female member of an Earth research team meets one of the not-quite-extinct natives, who impregnates her. Now

endowed with superhuman strength, the mother-to-be goes on a crazed cannibal rampage among her former comrades. Monster-happy viewers must wait until the grisly end to get a clear look at the alien creatures. Graphic and sensationalistic stuff wastes a classy cast (in every sense of the word). **AKA:** Inseminoid. **WOOF!**

1980 (R) 93m/C *GB* Robin Clarke, Jennifer Ashley, Stephanie Beacham, Judy Geeson, Stephen Grives, Victoria Tennant, Barry Houghton; **D:** Norman J. Warren; **W:** Nick Maley, Gloria Maley; **M:** John Scott. **VHS, Beta, LV** *SUE*

Horrors of the Red Planet

Cheapo epic sees astronauts crash on Mars, meet its Wizard, and stumble into a few Oz-like creatures. Technically advised by Forrest J. Ackerman. **AKA:** The Wizard of Mars. 🦴

1964 81m/C John Carradine, Roger Gentry, Vic McGee; **D:** David L. Hewitt. **VHS, Beta** *GHV, MRV, REP*

Howard the Duck

A megabucks megaflop from Lucasfilm, an adaptation of the short-lived, cult Marvel Comics superhero spoof. Alien from a parallel world where everything is ducky, literally, accidentally beams to Earth (to Cleveland, in fact, which is badly portrayed by Marin County, California). First half has Howard trying to fit into human society, amid birdbrained sex and drug jokes. When those fowl gags run dry, the filmmakers give him space demons to fight in a climactic f/x barrage. Despite the fancy visuals, this one's a real turkey. The hero's creature costume looks stiff and lifeless enough to be a decoy. 🦴

1986 (PG) 111m/C Lea Thompson, Jeffrey Jones, Tim Robbins; **D:** Willard Huyck; **W:** Willard Huyck, Gloria Katz; **M:** John Barry, Sylvester Levay; **V:** Chip Zien. Golden Raspberry Awards '86: Worst Picture, Worst Screenplay. **VHS, Beta, LV** *MCA*

The Human Duplicators

Kiel is an alien who has come to Earth to make androids out of important folk, thus allowing the "galaxy beings" to take over. When the androids are used steal valuable scientific equipment, FBI chief Hugh Beaumont puts George Nader on the case. Cheap stuff (the FBI headquarters looks like a seedy motel), but earnest performances make this more fun than it should be. It helps that some of the invaders are sexy women. Director Hugo Grimaldi also gave us the mediocre *Mutiny in Outer Space.* **AKA:** Spaziale K.1. 🦴🦴

1964 82m/C George Nader, Barbara Nichols, George Macready, Dolores Faith, Hugh Beaumont, Richard Kiel, Richard Arlen; **D:** Hugo Grimaldi; **W:** Arthur C. Pierce; **C:** Monroe Askins. **VHS, Beta** *LIV*

Humanoid Defender

A made-for-television film about a scientist and an android rebelling against the government that wants to use the android as a warfare prototype. 🦴🦴

1985 94m/C Terence Knox, Gary Kasper, Aimee Eccles, William Lucking; **D:** William Lucking. **VHS, Beta** *MCA*

Hyper-Sapien: People from Another Star

Two alien kids (humanlike except for their massive Don King hairstyles) sneak away from the family saucer accompanied by a space pal who looks like a big furry starfish. They befriend a Wyoming farmboy and get mistaken for terrorists, but never fear, there's a happy—and quite illogical—ending. Haphazard pic, dedicated "to the young in spirit throughout the Universe," had a problem-plagued production history and it shows. Keenan Wynn's last film. 🦴

1986 (PG) 93m/C Sydney Penny, Keenan Wynn, Gail Strickland, Ricky Paull Goldin, Peter Jason, Talia Shire; **D:** Peter Hunt; **W:** Christopher Adcock, Christopher Blue; **C:** John Coquillon; **M:** Arthur B. Rubinstein. **VHS, Beta, LV** *WAR*

I Come in Peace

A tough, maverick Texas cop (Dolph Lundgren) embarks on a one-way ride to Nosebleed City when he attempts to track down a malevolent alien drug czar who kills his victims by sucking their brains. Highlights include the big alien's main weapon, a device that shoots laser-sharp CDs, and his title greeting, which he uses every time he meets someone to catch them

off guard (just before the mayhem begins again). Brian Benben (of TV's *Dream On*) provides limited comic relief as a nervous FBI agent teamed with Lundgren to track down the malevolent visitor. Good for some mindless thrills, but nothing out of the ordinary. Another routine action epic from former stuntman Craig Baxley. **AKA:** Dark Angel. 🗡️🗡️
1990 (R) 92m/C Dolph Lundgren, Brian Benben, Betsy Brantley, Jesse Vint, Michael J. Pollard, Matthias Hues, Jay Bilas, Sherman Howard; **D:** Craig R. Baxley; **W:** Leonard Mass Jr., Jonathan Tydor; **M:** Jan Hammer. **VHS, Beta, LV** *MED, VTR*

I Married a Monster from Outer Space

A vintage thriller about a race of monstrous aliens who try to conquer Earth by turning themselves into duplicates of human beings. One of them marries Gloria Talbott. The poor woman soon learns the horrible truth (on their wedding night, no less!), but nobody will believe that her good-looking, clean-cut hubby is really a thing from another world. Ignore the hokey title; this is a highly effective '50s sci-fi creeper with truly frightening monsters. Newlyweds, however, should approach with caution; it might make for a rather unpleasant honeymoon. 🗡️🗡️❄️
1958 78m/B Tom Tryon, Gloria Talbott, Maxie "Slapsie" Rosenbloom, Mary Treen, Ty Hardin, Ken Lynch, John Eldridge, Valerie Allen; **D:** Gene Fowler Jr.; **W:** Louis Vittes; **C:** Haskell Boggs. **VHS, Beta** *PAR, MLB*

I Was a Zombie for the FBI

Aliens who look just like old-fashioned gangsters land near Pleasantville, USA, and make a deal with a couple of human criminals to rule the world. Their extraterrestrial super-science hypnotizes victims "clinically in what is known as a zomboid state," while just-the-facts-ma'am federal agents combat the un-American menace and their badly animated reptile monster. Black-and-white production by Memphis State University students is a dry, deadpan recreation of McCarthy-era sci-fi quickies, so close to the real thing that the mirth turns to tedium under an interminable running time. Still, some kind of achievement. 🗡️🗡️

1982 105m/B James Raspberry, Larry Raspberry, John Gillick, Christina Wellford, Anthony Isbell, Laurence Hall, Rick Crowe; **D:** Maurice Penczner; **W:** Maurice Penczner; **C:** Rick Dupree. **VHS, Beta** *NO*

Ice Pirates

Space pirates in the far future steal blocks of ice to fill the needs of a thirsty galaxy. With its cast of goofy characters and crazy situations, this is nearly the *Airplane* of space operas. Time warping finale may have taken things too far—then again maybe not. Much funnier than Mel Brooks' *Spaceballs*. Director Stewart Raffill may have peaked in 1984, making this film and the surprisingly charming *The Philadelphia Experiment*. 🗡️🗡️❄️
1984 (PG) 91m/C Robert Urich, Mary Crosby, Michael D. Roberts, John Matuszak, Anjelica Huston, Ron Perlman, John Carradine, Robert Symonds; **D:** Stewart Raffill; **W:** Stewart Raffill; **M:** Bruce Broughton. **VHS, Beta, LV** *MGM*

Iceman

A frozen caveman is brought back to life, and proceeds to experience some rather severe culture shock. Gentle scientist Timothy Hutton tries to befriend him, even though his colleagues seem intent on dissecting the befuddled Neanderthal. The film is a little sparse plotwise, but has some nice acting. John Lone is especially effective as the lost, bewildered "Iceman." The film manages to be poignant without being sickly sweet or going for cheap laughs, as did most of the "alien being in a strange land" type films that followed in the wake of *E.T.: The Extraterrestrial*. It's also somewhat more uplifting than *Quest for Fire*. 🗡️🗡️🗡️
1984 (PG) 101m/C CA Timothy Hutton, Lindsay Crouse, John Lone, David Strathairn, Josef Sommer, Danny Glover; **D:** Fred Schepisi; **W:** Chip Proser, John Drimmer; **M:** Bruce Smeaton. **VHS, Beta, LV** *MCA*

Idaho Transfer

Director Peter Fonda's sober-sided cautionary tale is about time travel, government repression, and ecological disaster. It was made on a minuscule budget with modest effects and a mostly non-professional cast. Before Fonda arrives at a leaden downbeat ending, he presents the future as a post-apocalyptic camping trip taken by obnoxious teens to Idaho in the year 2044. (By the way, the last words of the film, "Esto Perpetua," are the state motto of Idaho: "May she endure forever.") Keith Carradine's first screen appearance. **AKA:** Deranged. 🦴

1973 (PG) 90m/C Keith Carradine, Kelley Bohanan; **D:** Peter Fonda. **VHS, Beta** *MPI, FCT*

The Illustrated Man

Ambitious but ultimately limited attempt at dramatizing the famous short-story anthology by Ray Bradbury. Young drifter meets obsessed wanderer Rod Steiger, searching for a mystery woman (Claire Bloom, at the time Steiger's wife) who, before dematerializing, tattooed him head to foot. Uncanny tattoo designs inspire three narratives with the same three actors: "The Veldt" concerns a children's holographic-type playroom that becomes all too real; "The Long Rains," probably the most effective of the lot, details astronauts on Venus struggling to survive the planet's eternal downpour that makes it a true Waterworld; "The Last Night of the World" botches a Bradbury mood piece about, well, the last night of the world. The skin-art framing story tries too hard to be weird. Conversely, the short segments aren't halfway weird or imaginative enough. 🦴 🦴

1969 (PG) 103m/C Rod Steiger, Claire Bloom, Robert Drivas, Don Dubbins, Tim Weldon, Christine Matchet, Jason Evers; **D:** Jack Smight; **W:** Howard B. Kreitsek; **C:** Philip Lathrop; **M:** Jerry Goldsmith. **VHS, Beta** *WAR, FCT, MLB*

In the Aftermath: Angels Never Sleep

Mix of animation and live-action in this post-nuclear wasteland tale never quite works. 🦴 🦴

1987 85m/C Tony Markes, Rainbow Dolan; **D:** Carl Colpaert. **VHS, Beta** *VTR, NWV*

In the Cold of the Night

A photographer with a vivid imagination dreams he murders a woman he doesn't know, and when that very same dream girl enters his life (and bed), the stud shutterbug faces an etiquette quandary: haven't they met before? The ultimate solution qualifies this as a sci-fi pic, though it's generally a drowsy erotic thriller. Star cameos include Tippi Hedren (Hitchcock's *The Birds* and Melanie Griffith's mother). 🦴

1989 (R) 112m/C Jeff Lester, Adrienne Sachs, Shannon Tweed, David Soul, John Beck, Marc Singer; **Cameos:** Tippi Hedren; **D:** Nico Mastorakis. **VHS, LV** *REP*

The Incredible Hulk

Bill Bixby is a scientist who achieves superhuman strength after he is exposed to a massive dose of gamma rays. But his personal life suffers, as does his wardrobe. Lou Ferrigno is the Hulkster. The pilot for the television series is based on the Marvel Comics character. 🦴 🦴 🦴

1977 94m/C Bill Bixby, Susan Sullivan, Lou Ferrigno, Jack Colvin; **D:** Kenneth Johnson. **VHS, Beta, LV** *MCA*

The Incredible Hulk Returns

The beefy green mutant is back and this time he wages war against a Viking named Thor. Very little substance in this made for television flick, so be prepared to park your brain at the door. Followed by *The Trial of the Incredible Hulk.* 🦴 🦴

1988 100m/C Bill Bixby, Lou Ferrigno, Jack Colvin, Lee Purcell, Charles Napier, Steve Levitt; **D:** Nick Corea. **VHS, LV** *VTR, NWV*

Incredible Melting Man

Two transformations change an astronaut's life after his return to Earth. First, his skin starts to melt, then he displays cannibalistic tendencies. Hard to swallow. An intended tribute to '50s sci-fi shockers like *First Man into Space* and *The Amazing Colossal Man,* this one misses a prime opportunity for some campy, over-the-top gory fun by instead sticking to a dull plot, with most of the running time devoted to the messy monster Rebar plodding around the desert, while the rest of the cast searches for him. Some decent yucky special effects makeup by future Oscar winner Rick Baker. Look for director Jonathan Demme in a bit part. Cheryl Smith (who used the name "Rainbeaux" mostly in porn films) went from this to the only-slightly better *Laserblast.*

William Sachs went on to direct *Galaxina,* which at least had a sense of fun. 🦴

1977 (R) 85m/C Alex Rebar, Burr de Benning, Cheryl "Rainbeaux" Smith, Myron Healey, Michael Aldredge, Ann Sweeney, Lisle Wilson; *Cameos:* Jonathan Demme; *D:* William Sachs; *W:* William Sachs. **VHS, Beta** *LIV, VES*

The Incredible Petrified World

Divers are trapped in an underwater cave when volcanic eruptions begin. Suffocating nonsense. **WOOF!**

1958 78m/B John Carradine, Allen Windsor, Phyllis Coates, Lloyd Nelson, George Skaff; *D:* Jerry Warren. **VHS** *NOS, SNC*

The Incredible Shrinking Man

By any standard, an sf masterpiece. Adapted by Richard Matheson from his own novel, the film is a philosophical thriller about Robert Scott Carey (Grant Williams) who is exposed to a radioactive mist and begins to slowly shrink. Why? That's not really the question. Each new size means that everyday objects take on sinister meaning, and he must fight for his life in an increasingly hostile, absurd environment. If some of the effects are dated, few sf films contain more psychological truths, particularly in regard to men and matters of size. Surreal, suspenseful allegory also has a serious intellectual dimension that's almost never seen in American popular movies. It's also endowed with the tension usually reserved for Hitchcock films. Williams, a familiar figure in sf films of the era, was never more effective. The idea was spoofed in the less-than-satisfactory *Incredible Shrinking Woman.* 🦴🦴🦴

1957 81m/B Grant Williams, Randy Stuart, April Kent, Paul Langton, Raymond Bailey, William Schallert; *D:* Jack Arnold; *W:* Richard Matheson; *C:* Ellis W. Carter. **VHS, Beta, LV** *MCA, MLB*

The Incredible Shrinking Woman

A good-natured spoof of *The Incredible Shrinking Man,* with some inoffensive social

"Quick! I'll hold it down and you stab it!" Big Spider and *The Incredible Shrinking Man* team up against a killer spool of thread.

satire. Various environmental toxins combine to slowly shrink homemaker Lily Tomlin down to doll-house size. Everyday chores suddenly become "big" challenges, and just as she starts getting comfortable with her new size, she's snatched by a cabal of scientists who want to similarly down-size (er, right-size?) the rest of the world. Suddenly the tiny Tomlin must become a hero. The cuteness starts shrinking a bit itself towards the end, but Tomlin is charming, and the satire still works today. That's makeup wizard Rick Baker in the gorilla suit, by the way. 🦴🦴🦴

1981 (PG) 89m/C Lily Tomlin, Charles Grodin, Ned Beatty, Henry Gibson, Elizabeth Wilson; *Cameos:* Rick Baker; *D:* Joel Schumacher; *W:* Jane Wagner; *C:* Bruce Logan. **VHS, Beta, LV** *MCA*

The Indestructible Man

Lon Chaney, electrocuted for murder and bank robbery, is brought back to life by a scientist. Naturally, he seeks revenge on those who sentenced him to death. Chaney does the best he can with the material. 🦴

1956 70m/B Lon Chaney Jr., Marian Carr, Casey Adams; *D:* Jack Pollexfen. **VHS** *NOS, MRV, SNC*

Indiana Jones and the Last Crusade

In this, the third and last (?) Indiana Jones adventure, the fearless archaeologist is once again up against the Nazis in a race to find the Holy Grail. Sean Connery is perfectly cast as Indy's father; opening sequence features River Phoenix as a teenage Indy and explains his fear of snakes and the origins of the infamous fedora. Returns to the look and feel of the original with more adventures, exotic places, dastardly villains, and daring escapes than ever before; a must for Indy fans. 🦴🦴🦴

1989 (PG) 126m/C Harrison Ford, Sean Connery, Denholm Elliott, Alison Doody, Julian Glover, John Rhys-Davies, River Phoenix, Michael Byrne, Alex Hyde-White; *D:* Steven Spielberg; *W:* Jeffrey Boam; *M:* John Williams. Hugos '90: Dramatic Presentation; Nominations: Academy Awards '89: Best Sound, Best Original Score. **VHS, Beta, LV, 8mm** *PAR, TLF*

Indiana Jones and the Temple of Doom

Daredevil archaeologist Indiana Jones is back. This time he's on the trail of the legendary Ankara Stone and a ruthless cult that has enslaved hundreds of children. More gore (this is the one where the cult leader gets his kicks pulling beating hearts out of living bodies) and violence than the original; Kate Capshaw's whining character is an irritant, lacking the fresh quality that Karen Allen added to the original. Enough action for ten movies, special effects galore, and the usual booming John Williams' score make it a cinematic roller coaster ride, but with less regard for plot and pacing than the original. Though second in the series, it's actually a prequel to *Raiders of the Lost Ark.* Followed by *Indiana Jones and the Last Crusade.* 🦴🦴🦴

1984 (PG) 118m/C Harrison Ford, Kate Capshaw, Ke Huy Quan, Amrish Puri; *D:* Steven Spielberg; *W:* Willard Huyck, Gloria Katz; *M:* John Williams. Academy Awards '84: Best Visual Effects; Nominations: Academy Awards '84: Best Original Score. **VHS, Beta, LV, 8mm** *PAR, APD*

Infra-Man

The Mighty Morphin Power Rangers TV show, with its cheesy monsters and hyper-kinetic fight sequences, owes a lot to this outrageous Hong Kong production. Ancient Princess Dragon Mom unleashes an incredible array of creatures (including Octopus Man and Beetle Man) on the Earth. She wreaks such apocalyptic havoc that a scientist is forced to tell the world's leaders, "This situation is so bad that it is the worst that has ever been." It's Infra-Man, a bionic superhero, to the rescue. Tremendous fun for all ages, with non-stop martial arts action and priceless corny English-dubbed dialogue ("Drop the Earthling to her doom"). It's "infratastic." **AKA:** The Super Inframan; The Infra Superman. 🦴🦴🦴

1976 (PG) 92m/C *HK* Li Hsiu-hsien, Wang Hsieh, Yuan Man-tzu, Terry Liu, Tsen Shu-yi, Huang Chien-lung, Lu Sheng; *D:* Hua-Shan; *W:* Peter Fernandez. **VHS, Beta** *PSM*

Innerspace

A space pilot (Dennis Quaid) is miniaturized for an experimental journey through the body of a

TV on Tape:
The Invaders

The old sci-fi premise—aliens in our midst—was briefly brought to life in this ABC series, which has endured with cult status and a recent TV movie update. January 1967 saw the Quinn Martin-produced series debut, as architect David Vincent (Roy Thinnes) made a wrong turn down an empty country road and witnessed the landing of an alien spacecraft.

At least, he *thinks* so, since his later return to the scene provides no clues, but something weird is happening.... Soon Vincent learns aliens have indeed landed—a vanguard from a dying planet who want to make Earth their new home (and don't want to share) and can assume human form.

Alien Detection 101: Some have a mutated little finger; they have no emotions; they have no hearts—so no heartbeat or pulse; sometimes they glow (a warning of the need to regenerate); pure oxygen is fatal and they disintegrate to dust when killed.

Much like the boy who cries wolf, Vincent tries to alert a disbelieving populace, stave off incipient paranoia, and elude the clutches of his alien foes. Tired of battling alone, the second season saw David Vincent finally getting a small group of allies to assist him.

The two-part 1995 TV movie found David Vincent (briefly reprised by Thinnes) turning over his alien-hunting duties to Nolan Wood (Scott Bakula), who uncovers a plot to cause total ecological destruction so that the carbon monoxide-feeding invaders can have the planet for themselves. And this time, the aliens don't merely assume human form—they take over otherwise-occupied human bodies (the fiends!).

The original series' 43 episodes have been shown on the Sci Fi Channel and are available on tape.

1967-68/C *Selected cast:* Roy Thinnes, Kent Smith, Diane Baker, J. D. Cannon, James Daly, John Milford, Ellen Corby, Vaughn Taylor. *Director:* Joseph Sargent. **VHS** *GKK, MOV*

---

lab rabbit (a la *Fantastic Voyage*) and is accidentally injected into a nebbishy supermarket clerk (Martin Short), and together they nab some bad guys and get the girl. Although Short's brand of physical slapstick gets a little tiresome, he and the exasperated Quaid make an effective, unusual comedy team. The Award-winning special effects support some funny moments, including a scene in which Short manages to off a miniature villain by getting an upset stomach. Meg Ryan supplies the slightly confused romantic interest. 🕹🕹✌

1987 (PG) 120m/C Dennis Quaid, Martin Short, Meg Ryan, Kevin McCarthy, Fiona Lewis, Henry Gibson, Robert Picardo, John Hora, Wendy Schaal, Orson Bean, Chuck Jones, William Schallert, Dick Miller, Vernon Wells, Harold Sylvester, Kevin Hooks, Kathleen Freeman, Kenneth Tobey; *W:* Jeffrey Boam, Chip Proser; *C:* Andrew Laszlo; *M:* Jerry Goldsmith. Academy Awards '87: Best Visual Effects. **VHS, Beta, LV, 8mm** *WAR*

Interzone

A heroic adventurer battles mutant punks in post-apocalyptic world to keep the unsullied 'Interzone' region free from despoiling. Despite the title, there's no connection to William S. Burroughs or *Naked Lunch*. Too bad; anything could have helped. **WOOF!**

1988 97m/C Bruce Abbott; *D:* Deran Sarafian. **VHS, Beta** *MED*

Intruder Within

Half-baked thriller about crew on an isolated oil rig in Antarctica who, while drilling, unearth a nasty creature that goes around terrorizing the frost-bitten men and occasional stray woman. Made for television. 🕹

1981 91m/C Chad Everett, Joseph Bottoms, Jennifer Warren; *D:* Peter Carter. **VHS, Beta** *TWE*

tigator find that there is something to the nutty theory. In some respects, this is a B-movie that could have been made in the '50s. It's an imaginative story with a strong streak of humor, often tongue in cheek. At the same time, the script has rough spots, the acting isn't all that it might be, and the special effects aren't consistent. Still, as any fan knows, those come with the territory. The important effects involving a Stealth fighter and stop-motion models are fine. 🎵🎵 ᵇ

1991 (R) 95m/C Hans Bachman, A. Thomas Smith, Rich Foucheux, John Cooke, Robert Diedermann, Allison Sheehy, Ralph Bluemke, George Stover; **D:** Phillip Cook. **VHS, LV** *VMK*

Invaders from Mars

Famous but dated sci-fi fave about a little boy who sees a flying saucer bury itself behind his house. He can't convince grownups, though, and parents and playmates are systematically brainwashed by the green meanies. Though the cheapo budget shows (note the balloons bobbing on the walls of the Martians' glass cave stronghold), this can be enjoyed both as a basic juvie adventure and on a deeper level, as the camera and production design conveys a child's-eye-view of grownup society—dominant, threatening, and sometimes hostile as any space invader. Originally released in 3-D; remade in 1986 by Tobe Hooper. 🎵🎵 ᵇ

1953 78m/C Helena Carter, Arthur Franz, Jimmy Hunt, Leif Erickson, Hillary Brooke, Morris Ankrum; **D:** William Cameron Menzies; **W:** Richard Blake; **C:** John Seitz. **VHS, Beta** *MED, MLB*

Invaders from Mars

Adequate but pointless remake of Menzies' 1953 semi-classic about a body-snatching Martian invasion perceived only by one young boy and a sympathetic school nurse (played by mother and son Karen Black and Hunter Carson). Jimmy Hunt, child star of the first flick, cameos here as an adult cop, and even the fishbowl-headed 1953 Martian leader prop can be glimpsed in the background of his big scene. Otherwise Stan Winston's colorful creature f/x are the main attractions. 🎵🎵

1986 (PG) 102m/C Hunter Carson, Karen Black, Louise Fletcher, Laraine Newman, Timothy Bottoms, Bud Cort,

"Put me down NOW, or I'm telling Mom who stole her workout suit!" Jimmy Hunt to the velveteen Martian in *Invaders from Mars* (1953).

Intruders

Follows the story of three people who have unexplained lapses of time in their lives which they eventually believe are connected to visits by aliens. The three are brought together by a skeptical psychiatrist. The aliens are your typical bugged-eyed, white-faced spooks but part of the film is genuinely unsettling. 🎵🎵

1992 162m/C Richard Crenna, Mare Winningham, Susan Blakely, Ben Vereen, Steven Berkoff, Daphne Ashbrook; **D:** Dan Curtis. **VHS** *FXV*

Invader

When one group of soldiers inexplicably massacres another, a reporter for a sleazy tabloid is sent to uncover (or to invent) a story about UFOs and Martians. But he and an army inves-

James Karen; **Cameos:** Jimmy Hunt; **D:** Tobe Hooper; **W:** Dan O'Bannon, Don Jakoby; **C:** Daniel Pearl; **M:** Christopher Young. **VHS, Beta, LV** *MED, IME*

Invasion

A hospital opens its doors to an accident victim, and his attractive female visitors don't seem sympathetic to the idea of a long hospital stay. Turns out he's an escaped alien prisoner, and the alien babes, intent on intergalactic extradition, place a force field around the hospital and demand his return. Early effort of director Alan Bridges, who later did *The Shooting Party.* Interesting, creepy, atmospheric, with very cool camera moves. 🐾🐾🐾

1965 82m/B *GB* Edward Judd, Yoko Tani, Valerie Gearon, Lyndon Brook, Tsai Chin, Barrie Ingham; **D:** Alan Bridges. **VHS** *MOV*

Invasion Earth: The Aliens Are Here!

A cheap spoof of monster movies, as an insectoid projectionist takes over the minds of a movie audience. Clips of Godzilla, Mothra, and other beasts are interpolated. 🐾

1987 84m/C Janice Fabian, Christian Lee; **D:** George Maitland. **VHS, Beta, LV** *VTR, NWV*

Invasion of the Animal People

Hairy monster from outer space attacks Lapland. Narrated by John Carradine, the only American in the cast. Pretty silly. **AKA:** Terror in the Midnight Sun; Space Invasion of Lapland; Horror in the Midnight Sun; Space Invasion from Lapland. **WOOF!**

1962 73m/C *SW* Robert Burton, Barbara Wilson, John Carradine; **D:** Virgil W. Vogel, Jerry Warren. **VHS** *VMK, SNC, NOS*

Invasion of the Bee Girls

Early in their television career, critics Gene Siskel and Roger Ebert declared this to be one of their favorite "guilty pleasures" and its reputation was set. Add in the presence of Playmate Victoria Vetri, who has a dedicated following of her own, Anitra "Big Bird Cage" Ford, and a gloriously wacky plot involving the "Queen Bee" and her conquests, and you've got prime Bee-movie camp fun. The murky audio sounds as if it were coming from a drive-in speaker, which ideally is the best way to experience this compellingly quirky and perversely comic thriller. Written by Nicholas Meyer, who later directed *Star Trek II: The Wrath of Khan.* **AKA:** Graveyard Tramps. 🐾🐾🐾

1973 85m/C Victoria Vetri, William Smith, Anitra Ford, Cliff Osmond, Wright King, Ben Hammer; **D:** Denis Sanders; **W:** Nicholas Meyer; **M:** Charles Bernstein. **VHS** *SUE*

Invasion of the Body Snatchers

Based on Jack Finney's novel, the definitive take on '50s American paranoia and conformity is still one of the most frightening sf movies ever made, a chilling exercise in nightmare dislocation. The infamous "pod people" are just like you and me...only they're not. Everything about the film works right from the small town setting of Santa Mira to the flawless acting and the tight script. Director Donald Siegel's solid craftsmanship was seldom applied to a better story. Yes, that's Sam Peckinpah as the meter reader in the cellar. He also worked on the screenplay. The laserdisc version contains commentary by Maurice Yacowar, the text of an interview with Siegel, and the original theatrical trailer. The film itself is presented in its original widescreen format. Remade twice to date. 🐾🐾🐾🐾

1956 80m/B Kevin McCarthy, Dana Wynter, Carolyn Jones, King Donovan, Donald Siegel, Larry Gates, Jean Willes, Whit Bissell; **Cameos:** Sam Peckinpah; **D:** Donald Siegel; **W:** Sam Peckinpah, Daniel Mainwaring; **C:** Ellsworth Fredericks. **VHS, LV** *REP, CRC, MLB*

Invasion of the Body Snatchers

The subtlety of Donald Siegel's original gives way to gaudy special effects and self-consciously artsy camera work from director Philip Kaufman. The film is indulgently overlong, too, though it certainly has some shocking moments. In the leads, Donald Sutherland and Brooke Adams are excellent, and they get solid support from Leonard Nimoy and Jeff Goldblum. The change in setting from small town to big city (San Francisco) provides more

> "Creeping horror...from the depths of time and space!"
>
> —*Invasion of the Saucer Men.*

"Who's there??" Claude Rains is *The Invisible Man.*

must convince the authorities that the creatures exist before said aliens can multiply and take over the world. Designer Paul Blaisdell's aliens are the best part, but the atmosphere is great considering the budget. Remade with John Ashley and more gore as *The Eye Creatures* in 1965. 🧦🦴

1957 69m/B Steven Terrell, Gloria Castillo, Frank Gorshin, Lyn Osborn, Ed Nelson, Angelo Rossitto; **D:** Edward L. Cahn; **M:** Ronald Stein. **VHS** *COL*

Invasion of the Space Preachers

A wrong-headed attempt to make a sf satire on crooked evangelists. Two sub-moronic yuppies take off for a weekend in the boondocks; they encounter the usual inbred backwoods stereotypes and a crashed alien who transforms into a gorgeous blonde named Nova. As if that weren't enough, Nova (who downs cans of beer with one gulp) informs them that the local preacher, Reverend Lash, is actually a fellow extraterrestrial bent on world domination. The sneeringly charismatic Lash controls his flock by means of a whip and tiny radio-implants that can control behavior or make believers' heads explode. This flick tries hard to please, and there's some good music lurking around in it, but the acting is pretty lifeless and the humor never rises above the level of T&A and outhouse jokes. Yee-haw! 🧦

1990 100m/C Jim Wolfe, Guy Nelson, Eliska Hahn, Gary Brown, Jesse Johnson, John Riggs; **D:** Daniel Boyd; **W:** Daniel Boyd. **VHS, Beta** *RHI*

complications and striking visuals, but it doesn't really add to the atmosphere of dread created in the first film. 🧦🧦🧦

1978 (PG) 115m/C Donald Sutherland, Brooke Adams, Veronica Cartwright, Leonard Nimoy, Jeff Goldblum, Kevin McCarthy, Art Hindle; **Cameos:** Donald Siegel; **D:** Philip Kaufman; **W:** W.D. Richter; **C:** Michael Chapman. **VHS, Beta, LV** *MGM*

Invasion of the Body Stealers

Aliens are thought to be the captors when skydivers begin vanishing in mid-air. Uneven sci fi with nothing going for it. **AKA:** Thin Air; The Body Stealers. **WOOF!**

1969 (PG) 115m/C *GB* George Sanders, Maurice Evans, Patrick Allen; **D:** Gerry Levy. **VHS, Beta** *LIV*

Invasion of the Saucer Men

Frank Gorshin (*Batman*'s Riddler) plays the town drunk in this kinda slow sci-fi comedy about bulbous-headed long-fingered aliens who are hassling teenagers at the local lovers lane. Suspected of murder, the teenagers

Invisible Adversaries

A photographer uncovers an extra terrestrial plot to cause excessive aggression in humans. She and her lover attempt to hold on to their crumbling humanity. Movies like this make you mad enough to tear something up. Enjoyed a meek cult following. In German with English subtitles. 🧦🧦

1977 112m/C *GE* Susanne Widl, Peter Weibel; **D:** Valie Export. **VHS, Beta** *FCT*

The Invisible Boy

A mathematically challenged little boy ("Three? Seventeen? Forty four? A hundred?" he responds to his father's quizzing him on how many 24ths there are in one quarter) is a disappointment to his father, keeper of the super-computer at the Stoneman Mathematical Institute. Dad takes the problem to the massive computer ("He's ten and can't even play a decent game of chess."); said computer hypnotizes ten-year-old Timmy and teaches him the ins and outs of the game, so Timmy subsequently sandbags Dad at chess and wrangles a wish—he wants to play with Robby (*Forbidden Planet*) the Robot. Timmy quickly finds many uses for his new-found friend, including ordering the Robot to build him the biggest kite ever—which Timmy climbs upon for a flight above the trees. When Mom objects to this play, Timmy complains to Robby: "I wish there was some way she couldn't see me when I was having fun." And the fun really begins when Robby makes it so. Timmy plays childish pranks on the adults (giggling while his parents smooch in bed, giving himself away) and whacking "that nasty Sidney," a bigger boy who'd socked Timmy. The whole adventure turns devious when the super-computer uses Robby for evil purposes, with Timmy as a hostage. Charming boy-and-his-robot story with amusing dialogue and campy '50s computer plot; anything with Robby in it has to be a winner. Based on a story by Edmund Cooper. 🦴🦴🦴

1957 (G) 89m/C Richard Eyer, Diane Brewster, Philip Abbott, Harold J. Stone, Robert Harris; **D:** Herman Hoffman; **W:** Cyril Hume; **M:** Les Baxter. **VHS** *MGM, FCT*

Invisible Invaders

Short, cheap, and silly aliens-try-to-take-over-the-Earth flick. This time they're moonmen who use the bodies of dead Earthlings (ugh) to attack the living until John Agar can save the day. He and Robert Hutton seem so bored with this script one can hardly pick them out among the zombies. John Carradine has a brief role as a formerly dead scientist. Though this film's lack of vision wasted the idea, ten years later George Romero would pick up their fum-ble and run it in for a touchdown with his *Night of the Living Dead*. 🦴🦴

1959 67m/B John Agar, Robert Hutton, Hal Torey, Jean Byron, Philip Tonge, John Carradine; **D:** Edward L. Cahn; **W:** Samuel Newman; **C:** Maury Gertsman. **VHS** *MGM*

The Invisible Man

The vintage horror-fest based on H. G. Wells' novella about a scientist whose formula for invisibility slowly drives him insane. His mind definitely wandering, he plans plans to use his recipe to rule the world. Claude Rains' first role; though his body doesn't appear until the final scene, his voice characterization is magnificent. The visual detail is excellent, setting standards that are imitated because they are difficult to surpass; with special effects by John P. Fulton. 🦴🦴🦴🦴

1933 71m/B Claude Rains, Gloria Stuart, Dudley Digges, William Harrigan, Una O'Connor, E.E. Clive, Dwight Frye; **D:** James Whale; **W:** R.C. Sherriff. **VHS, Beta, LV** *MCA, MLB*

The Invisible Man Returns

Vincent Price stars as the original invisible man's brother. Using the same invisibility formula, Price tries to clear himself after being charged with murder. He reappears at the worst times, and you gotta love that floating gun. Fun sequel to 1933's classic *The Invisible Man*. 🦴🦴🦴

1940 81m/B Cedric Hardwicke, Vincent Price, John Sutton, Nan Grey; **D:** Joe May. **VHS** *MCA, MLB*

The Invisible Man's Revenge

Left for dead on a safari five years before, Jon Hall seeks revenge against Gale Sondergaard and Lester Matthews, aided by scientist John Carradine who renders Hall invisible. Only problem is Hall doesn't stay that way. Fifth in Universal's *Invisible Man* film series. 🦴🦴🦴

1944 78m/B Jon Hall, John Carradine, Gale Sondergaard, Lester Matthews, Evelyn Ankers, Alan Curtis, Leon Errol, Doris Lloyd; **D:** Ford Beebe; **W:** Bertram Millhauser. **VHS** *MCA*

The Invisible Ray

For a change, this horror film features Bela Lugosi as the hero, fighting Boris Karloff, a sci-

> "I wish there was some way she couldn't see me when I was having fun."
>
> —Timmy (Richard Eyer) gets more than he hoped for in *The Invisible Boy*.

...A Theory Whispered in the Cloisters of Science

" **E**very scientific fact accepted today once burned as a fantastic find in the mind of someone called mad. Who are we on this youngest and smallest of planets to say that the Invisible Ray is impossible to science? That which you are now to see is a theory whispered in the cloisters of science. Tomorrow these theories may startle the universe as a fact."

— prologue to *The Invisible Ray*
(which proceeds to have Boris Karloff demonstrate Einsteinian relativity, not bad for 1936!).

entist who locates a meteor that contains a powerful substance. Karloff is poisoned and becomes a murdering megalomaniac. Watching Karloff and Lugosi interact, and the great special effects—including a hot scene where a scientist bursts into flames—helps you ignore a generally hokey script. 🦴🦴🦴

1936 82m/B Boris Karloff, Bela Lugosi, Frances Drake, Frank Lawton, Beulah Bondi, Walter Kingsford; *D:* Lambert Hillyer. **VHS, Beta, LV** *MCA, MLB*

The Invisible Terror

A maniac steals a mad scientist's invisibility formula and uses it on a number of innocent victims. 🦴🦴

1963 ?m/C Herbert Stass, Ellen Scheirs. **VHS** *SNC*

Invisible: The Chronicles of Benjamin Knight

Continuation of the storyline from the direct-to-video opus *Mandroid,* and it's starting to look like the Fantastic Four minus two. Benjamin Knight, rendered invisible by a splash of the secret chemical Supercon, joins with fellow good guy Mandroid against both Romanian government spies and mad scientist Drago

(who persists in wearing a metal Dr. Doom mask even though his scarred face has healed since the last movie!). Lively but hopelessly lowbrow. 🦴🦴

1993 (R) 80m/C Brian Cousins, Jennifer Nash, Michael DellaFemina, Curt Lowens, David Kaufman, Alan Oppenheimer, Aharon Ipale; *D:* Jack Ersgard; *W:* Earl Kenton; *C:* Cristiano Pogany; *M:* David Arkenstone. **VHS, Beta** *PAR*

The Invisible Woman

Above average comedy about zany professor John Barrymore discovering the secret of invisibility and making luscious model Virginia Bruce transparent. Great cast makes this a very likeable movie. Based on a story by Curt Siodmak and Joe May, the same team that wrote *The Invisible Man Returns*. 🦴🦴🦴

1940 73m/B John Barrymore, Virginia Bruce, John Howard, Charlie Ruggles, Oscar Homolka, Margaret Hamilton, Donald MacBride, Edward Brophy, Shemp Howard, Charles Lane, Thurston Hall; *D:* Edward Sutherland; *W:* Robert Lees, Fred Rinaldo, Gertrude Purcell. **VHS** *MCA, FCT*

Island of Dr. Moreau

A wrong-headed remake of the 1933 classic *Island of Lost Souls*. Burt Lancaster is Dr. Moreau, a scientist who has isolated himself on a Pacific island in order to continue his chromosome research. He can transform animals into near-humans and humans into animals. He imprisons Michael York and nearly turns him into an animal. Barbara Carrera is a panther converted into a woman. The beastman makeup is more impressive here than in the original movie, but the final product is too slick. Another regrettable adaptation of a classic H.G. Wells novel. 🦴🦴

1977 (PG) 99m/C Burt Lancaster, Michael York, Nigel Davenport, Barbara Carrera, Richard Basehart, Nick Cravat; *D:* Don Taylor; *W:* John Herman Shaner, Al Ramus; *C:* Gerry Fisher. **VHS, Beta** *WAR, OM*

Island of Lost Souls

A horrifying, highly effective adaptation of H.G. Wells' *The Island of Dr. Moreau*, initially banned in parts of the U.S. because of its disturbing content. Charles Laughton is a mad scientist on a remote tropical island, obsessed with making men out of jungle animals

through extensive, painful surgery. The jungle is full of Laughton's half-finished experiments, all of whom are kept in line by a rigid code of behavior ("the Law") and threats of a return to the laboratory where they were created (the aptly named "House of Pain"). When a ship-wreck survivor is stranded on the island, Laughton plots to mate him with Lota, a young woman who was originally a panther. The film is as unsettling today as it was in the '30s. Kathleen Burke beat out more than 60,000 young women in a nationwide search to play Lota the Panther Woman; she won the role with her "feline" looks. Bela Lugosi has a small but unforgettable role as the Sayer of the Law. Remade in 1977 as *The Island of Dr. Moreau*; plans for another big-budget remake are in the works for 1996. 🦴🦴🦴⁰

1932 71m/B Charles Laughton, Bela Lugosi, Richard Arlen, Leila Hyams, Kathleen Burke, Stanley Fields, Robert F. (Bob) Kortman, Arthur Hohl; *Cameos:* Alan Ladd, Randolph Scott, Buster Crabbe; *D:* Erle C. Kenton; *W:* Philip Wylie, Waldemar Young; *C:* Karl Struss. **VHS** *MCA, FCT, BTV*

Island of Terror

First-rate science-fiction chiller about a British island overrun by single-celled creatures with protective shells that suck the bones out of their living prey with slimy tentacles. Good performances and interesting twists make for prickles up the spine. Another British sci-fi feature in the tried and true tradition of the *Quatermass* series: a remote community is slowly overrun by a creeping terror from beyond, while a tough scientist is called in to battle it. Terence Fisher is much more well known for his Hammer horror films (*Horror of Dracula, Curse of Frankenstein, The Mummy,* etc.), but he also could deliver solid science fiction when called upon. **AKA:** Night of the Silicates; The Creepers. 🦴🦴🦴

1966 90m/C *GB* Peter Cushing, Edward Judd, Carole Gray, Sam Kydd, Niall MacGinnis, Eddie Byrne; *D:* Terence Fisher; *W:* Alan Ramsen, Edward Andrew Mann; *C:* Reg Wyer. **VHS** *MCA, SNC, MLB*

Island of the Burning Doomed

Director Terence Fisher's atmospheric style worked for his Hammer Studio gothic horror films, but when it comes to this attempt at sci-

fi, a little more punch was needed. Based on the John Lymington novel *Night of the Big Heat,* this story concerns an alien protoplasm that takes over a British island, and somehow causes a bizarre winter heatwave intense enough to burn most of the inhabitants to death. Peter Cushing and Christopher Lee (without whom this film would rate a solo boner) survive to do battle with the egg-like blobacious creatures who are desperate for any heat source. **AKA:** Island of the Burning Damned; Night of the Big Heat. 🦴🦴

1967 94m/C *GB* Christopher Lee, Peter Cushing, Patrick Allen, Sarah Lawson, Jane Merrow; *D:* Terence Fisher. **VHS** *NO*

It Came from Beneath the Sea

A giant octopus arises from the depths of the sea to scour San Francisco for human food. Ray Harryhausen effects are special, but more suspense is generated by the unusual soap-opera triangle among the three leads than by any plans to deal with the menacing behe-moth. Faced with the problem of having an aquatic beast ravaging a city, Harryhausen inventively designed scenes in which its tenta-cles invade the city streets like serpents, and the sight of the octopus breaking apart the Golden Gate bridge is especially inspired. All this with only five tentacles, which is all the budget would allow. Kenneth Tobey's affable charm was used to better effect battling *The Thing from Another World,* but beautiful Faith Domergue fared less well in *This Island Earth.* 🦴🦴⁰

1955 80m/B Kenneth Tobey, Faith Domergue, Ian Keith, Donald Curtis, Dean Maddox; *D:* Robert Gordon; *W:* George Worthing Yates, Hal Smith; *C:* Henry Freulich. **VHS, Beta, LV** *GKK, MLB*

It Came from Outer Space

Non-humanoid aliens crash in the Arizona desert and take the form of captured local res-idents to repair their spacecraft and get away before Earth authorities move in. Good perfor-mances and outstanding direction by genre specialist Jack Arnold enhance an unusually sympathetic portrayal—for the time period—of cosmic visitors (compare this with *Invaders*

"The natives... they are restless tonight."

—Dr. Moreau (Charles Laughton) in *Island of Lost Souls.*

Variations on the Heimlich maneuver. *It! The Terror from Beyond Space.*

It Conquered the World

Eccentric scientist Lee Van Cleef makes radio contact with a dying race of intelligent creatures on Venus and, believing he'd be saving mankind from itself, aids the aliens in their invasion of Earth. By the time he finds out that their plans are less than benevolent, it's too late, and only his buddy Peter Graves can stop the invaders. The largely immobile (and goofy looking) Venusian invader hides out in a cave giving birth to creepy bat-like creatures, which fly to their specified human targets and implant stingers in the backs of their necks, bringing them under telepathic control. Shares many of the same attributes of *Invasion of the Body Snatchers* (released several months earlier), but with all the subtlety removed for the target drive-in crowd. Much like the work of Ed Wood during the same years, Corman's early-vintage zero-budget exploitation pictures are hilariously bad, but with an intellectual subtext. The difference is that Corman, the better-educated man, was always much more self aware. This one's hip-deep in anti-fascist rhetoric, especially in its handling of Van Cleef's character, who has the only working appliances in town as a reward for his treason. Graves brings the message home with a huge thud by making a closing speech. Remade for television as *Zontar, the Thing from Venus.* 🐾 🐾 🐾

1956 68m/B Peter Graves, Beverly Garland, Lee Van Cleef, Sally Fraser, Russ Bender, Jonathan Haze, Dick Miller, Karen Kadler, Paul Blaisdell; *D:* Roger Corman; *W:* Charles B. Griffith, Lou Rusoff; *C:* Frederick E. West. **VHS** *COL, FCT, MLB*

from Mars that same year). Based on the story "The Meteor" by Ray Bradbury, though Hollywood vet Harry Essex (*The Creature from the Black Lagoon*) insisted he rather than Bradbury authored the shooting script. Originally filmed in 3-D. 🐾 🐾 🐾

1953 81m/B Richard Carlson, Barbara Rush, Charles Drake, Russell Johnson, Morey Amsterdam, Joseph Sawyer; *D:* Jack Arnold; *W:* Harry Essex; *C:* Clifford Stine; *M:* Herman Stein, Henry Mancini. **VHS** *MCA, MLB, GKK*

It Came from Outer Space 2

Poorly updated cable version of the sci-fi film finds desert dwellers temporarily possessed by shape-shifting aliens, who need the human bodies to rebuild their crashed space ship. 🐾 🐾

1995 (PG-13) m/C Elizabeth Pena, Brian Kerwin, Lauren Tewes. **VHS**

It!
The Terror from Beyond Space

Sole survivor of a Mars expedition is arrested for the mass slaughter of his colleagues. As he protests his innocence, the real culprit, a big, hungry Martian, stows away aboard the Earthbound rocket and begins killing crew members en route. An obvious inspiration for Ridley Scott's *Alien,* though suspense here is more claustrophobic, as the brute pounds its way through hatch after hatch, backing the desperate survivors up into the nose cone.

Jerome Bixby's commendably sober script ends with the warning "Another name for Mars is Death!," and Paul Blaisdell contributed a fearsome lizard man costume. Tape includes the original theatrical trailer ("See IT! Don't miss IT!"). **AKA:** It! The Vampire from Beyond Space. 🌀🌀🌀

1958 68m/B Marshall Thompson, Shawn Smith, Kim Spalding, Ann Doran, Dabbs Greer, Paul Langton, Ray Corrigan, Robert Bice; *D:* Edward L. Cahn; *W:* Jerome Bixby; *C:* Kenneth Peach Sr. **VHS, Beta** *MGM, MLB*

It's Alive

A memorable cult film about a mutant baby born to a normal Los Angeles couple. The clawed, fanged infant wrecks havoc in the delivery room, then escapes the hospital and goes on a bloodthirsty, murderous rampage. In one grimly amusing scene, Junior goes after a milk-truck. The concept is ingenious, the gore kept at a minimum, and the monster tot all the more effective for being rarely glimpsed. This nasty little gem was followed by two sequels. Prospective parents should probably avoid them, though. 🌀🌀🌀

1974 (PG) 91m/C John P. Ryan, Sharon Farrell, Andrew Duggan, Guy Stockwell, James Dixon, Michael Ansara; *D:* Larry Cohen; *W:* Larry Cohen; *C:* Fenton Hamilton; *M:* Bernard Herrmann. **VHS, Beta** *WAR, FCT*

It's Dead——Let's Touch It!

A twisted satire about the fight between good and evil, as a pleasant little alien crash lands and is repeatedly abused by the motley assortment of degenerates he encounters. The Earthlings pay for their sins when the baby powder that the dead alien's carcass emits turns them into sickeningly nice pod-type people, culminating in an explosive ending. Slicker follow-up to Bogdan's *The Weasel that Dripped Blood.* 🌀🌀🌀

1992 27m/C Cheri Roberts, Randy Thomas, Larc Levy; *Cameos:* Marty Smith, Steve Bogdan, Al Bogdan; *D:* Al Bogdan; *W:* Al Bogdan. **VHS** *NO*

Jabberwocky

Pythonesque chaos prevails in the cartoonish medieval kingdom of King Bruno the Questionable, who rules with cruelty and stupidity.

Jabberwocky is a dragon who threatens the kingdom's questionable peace until hero Michael Palin decides to take it on. Not one of Terry Gilliam's better films, it usually resembles a misguided effort to duplicate the medieval comedy of *Holy Grail*. Still, Eric Idle and Michael Palin's presence helps a little, and there are some genuinely funny moments. 🌀🌀🌀

1977 (PG) 104m/C *GB* Michael Palin, Eric Idle, Max Wall, Deborah Fallender, Terry Jones, John Le Mesurier; *D:* Terry Gilliam; *W:* Terry Gilliam. **VHS, Beta, LV** *COL*

Jack the Giant Killer

A young farmer joins a medieval princess on a journey to a distant convent. Along the way, they combat an evil wizard, dragons, sea monsters, and other mystical creatures, and are assisted by leprechauns, a dog, and a chimp. Generally considered a blatant rip-off of *The Seventh Voyage of Sinbad*—right down to the hiring of Nathan Juran, Kerwin Mathews, and Torin Thatcher—the film nonetheless delivers plenty of fun and excitement of its own. A young Jim Danforth of "Gumby" fame provided the stop-motion animation. 🌀🌀🌀

1962 (G) 95m/C Kerwin Mathews, Judi Meredith, Torin Thatcher, Walter Burke, Roger Mobley, Barry Kelley, Don Beddoe, Anna Lee, Robert Gist; *D:* Nathan (Hertz) Juran. **VHS, Beta, LV** *MGM, FCT*

Jason and the Argonauts

Many of Ray Harryhausen's fans consider this to be his finest moment. His stop-motion special effects are the real stars in the mythological tale of Jason, son of King of Thessaly, who sails on the Argo to the land of Colchis, where the Golden Fleece is guarded by a seven-headed hydra. The best moments are the flying harpies, the bronze giant Talos, and the sword-wielding skeleton warriors. The script is one of the most elegant ever written for a fantasy, and the acting is equally good. The Criterion laserdisc is a superbly remastered transfer. It also includes supplemental material. Recommended for all ages. 🌀🌀🌀🌀

1963 (G) 104m/C *GB* Todd Armstrong, Nancy Kovack, Gary Raymond, Laurence Naismith, Nigel Green, Michael Gwynn, Honor Blackman; *D:* Don Chaffey; *W:* Jan Read,

> "Every man
> its prisoner...
> every woman
> its slave!"
>
> —It Conquered the World.

Keanu Reeves
models the latest in
rollerblade
protective gear.
Johnny Mnemonic.

Beverley Cross; *C:* Wilkie Cooper; *M:* Bernard Herrmann.
VHS, Beta, LV, 8mm *COL, MLB, FUS*

Jet Benny Show

Steve Norman doesn't look much like comedy legend Jack Benny, but he indeed wears glasses and says "Wellllll...." a lot during this obscure parody of the original *Star Wars* trilogy, in which Benny, his robot Rochester, and the spaceship The Maxwell assume the Han Solo/Chewbacca/ Millennium Falcon roles, respectively. Dimestore f/x include the airborne chase through the forests of Endor recreated using what appear to be G.I. Joe dolls. 🦴 🐾

1986 76m/C Steve Norman, Kevin Dees, Polly MacIntyre, Ted Luedemann; *D:* Roger Evans. **VHS, Beta** *NLC*

Johnny Mnemonic

Based on a screenplay by cyberpunk godfather William Gibson (author of cult favorite

Neuromancer) and directed by artist Robert Longo (in his first film), this flick could more aptly be called *Johnny Moronic*. Keanu Reeves plays a high-tech courier of the future, whose brain has been technologically enhanced, allowing him to carry a huge amount of computer information in his head. Only problem is, he can only store the information for a limited amount of time before his brain turns to mush (even in the future they can't fix that). Johnny takes one last mission to earn enough money to restore memories he gave up for added cyber storage. Of course, things go badly as Johnny is hunted by the Japanese Yakuza and various other unsavory characters who want his head (literally). Johnny is aided by an implant-enhanced bodyguard (Dina Meyer), a group of underground hackers called the LoTeks (get the subtle anti-technology message in a technology-laden flick), and a former doctor (Henry Rollins) who is trying to cure a technology-induced plague. Keanu

TV on Tape: Johnny Sokko and His Giant Robot

Of the various Japanese science-fiction series imported for American television in the '60s and '70s, few are more beloved than *Johnny Sokko and His Giant Robot*. Toei Studio's live-action series premiered in the U.S. in 1967, the same year as its Japanese debut, courtesy of AIP-Television. The series consisted of only 26 episodes, repeated over and over on UHF channels until the kids who loved the show practically had them memorized.

The first episode set the tone for the entire series: a flying saucer containing the evil space-emperor Guillotine (a clawed, octopus-headed being) appears in Earth's skies, and, after shooting down some Japanese planes, disappears under the ocean. Later, Johnny Sokko, a young boy traveling (apparently alone) on a ship, meets Jerry Mano, who is actually a secret agent for a world defense organization known as Unicorn. Their ship is sunk by Dracolon, a giant fish-monster who's apparently part of Guillotine's plans for taking over the world. Jerry and Johnny are washed up on an island, actually the headquarters of the Gargoyle Gang, Guillotine's human henchmen. Imprisoned by the Gargoyles, Jerry and Johnny meet super-scientist Lucius Guardian, who's been ordered to construct a gigantic robot for Guillotine's evil purposes. Johnny accidentally activates the robot's control device, and when an atomic bomb Guardian planted to destroy the Gargoyles' headquarters inadvertently activates the robot, the powers of good gain a powerful new ally.

Johnny joins Unicorn as a full-fledged agent, and proceeds to have a wonderful time fighting a parade of colorful monsters and alien spies. *Johnny Sokko*'s menagerie of rubber-suited beasties rivaled anything in the Godzilla movies. They included a giant ambulatory eye-ball, a huge flying robot head, a monster bull able to swallow an entire train, and a dinosaur with the power to conjure up blizzards. The expressionless Giant Robot (who for some reason wore what appeared to be an Egyptian head-dress) didn't have much personality compared to, say, Ultraman, but millions of kids loved the fantasy of being in control of a mountain-sized being of limitless strength.

In 1970, several of the *Johnny Sokko* episodes were edited (rather badly) into a feature-length movie called *Voyage into Space*. Like the series proper, it was sold directly to American television, where it delighted children and bewildered their parents. More recently, Japanese director Yasuhiro Imagawa created an animated series, *Giant Robo*, based (very vaguely) on *Johnny Sokko*. Although *Giant Robo* is vastly more sophisticated than its predecessor and contains some wonderful characters (like a modern-day samurai who can breathe fire), most fans are likely to have a special place in their hearts for the original series.

1967/C JP *Director:* Yasuhiro Imagawa. **VHS** *ORI*

gives an even more dead-pan performance than usual, perhaps because he is missing part of his brain (what's his excuse for *Dracula* then?). The effects are appropriately engaging, but any flick that ends with a tele-pathic dolphin has to be all wet. Look for an almost-unrecognizable Dolph Lundgren as the Preacher. 🦴🦴

1995 (R) 98m/C Keanu Reeves, Dina Meyer, Ice-T, Takeshi, Dolph Lundgren, Henry Rollins, Udo Kier, Barbara Sukowa, Denis Akiyama; *D:* Robert Longo; *W:* William Gibson; *C:* Francois Protat; *M:* Brad Fiedel. **VHS, LV, 8mm** *COL*

Journey Beneath the Desert

Three engineers discover the lost-but-always-found-in-the-movies kingdom of Atlantis when

big-budget studio work. James Mason and Arlene Dahl are fine in the leads and Pat Boone doesn't embarrass himself either. The limitations of the effects are overcome, at least in part, by a strong sense of wonder and a grand plot, based on the Jules Verne novel, that includes dinosaurs, disasters, treachery, and the lost city of Atlantis. Bernard Herrmann's superb guttural music is marred only by Boone's singing. 🎵🎵🎵

1959 132m/C James Mason, Pat Boone, Arlene Dahl, Diane Baker, Thayer David, Alan Napier, Peter Ronson; **D:** Henry Levin; **W:** Charles Brackett, Walter Reisch; **C:** Leo Tover; **M:** Bernard Herrmann. Nominations: Academy Awards '59: Best Art Direction/Set Decoration (Color), Best Sound. **VHS, Beta, LV** *FXV, FCT, FUS*

Journey to the Center of the Earth

Aired in TV syndication as a "Famous Classic Tales" special, this generic cartoon stays faithful to Jules Verne's 1864 narrative of subterranean exploration and adventure but is otherwise singularly workmanlike and unimaginative. Other titles in the "Famous Classic Tales" series that burn Verne on video include *Master of the World* and *20,000 Leagues Under the Sea*. 🎵

1976 50m/C VHS, Beta *MGM, WTA*

"Let me at 'em. Nobody calls *me* a mimbo and get's away with it!" Pat Boone, a cheesed-off Peter Ronson, James Mason, and Arlene Dahl face peril number 434 on their *Journey to the Center of the Earth* (1959).

their helicopter's forced down in the sunny Sahara. A poor hostess with a rotten disposition, the mean sub-saharan queen doesn't roll out the welcome mat for her grounded guests, so a beautiful slave babe helps them make a hasty exit. Dawdling Euro production with adequate visuals. **AKA:** Antinea, l'Amante Della Citta Sepolta. 🎵🎵

1961 105m/C *FR IT* Haya Harareet, Jean-Louis Trintignant, Brad Fulton, Amedeo Nazzari, George Riviere, Giulia Rubini, Gabriele Tinti, Gian Marie Volonte; **D:** Edgar G. Ulmer, Giuseppe Masini, Frank Borzage. **VHS, Beta** *SNC*

Journey to the Center of the Earth

Slowly paced adventure may seem a little clunky today but it's a nicely done piece of

Journey to the Center of the Earth

Below 'C' level bastardization of Jules Verne. A young nanny and two teenage boys explore a cave beneath an obvious matte painting of a volcano. They discover a campy underground civilization of leather punks, black-clad stormtroopers, and silly monsters, like detritus from a music video. There's no ending, just a random collection of clips; the film crew found their funding cut off, and director Rusty Lemorande completed this mess with inserts from the Kathy Ireland comedy *Alien from L.A.* Be warned. **WOOF!**

1988 (PG) 83m/C Nicola Cowper, Paul Carafotes, Ilan Mitchell-Smith; **D:** Rusty Lemorande; **W:** Rusty Lemorande, Kitty Chalmers. **VHS, Beta, LV** *CAN*

Journey to the Far Side of the Sun

From the creators of the classic TV puppet shows *Supercar* and *Thunderbirds* comes this unjustly neglected adventure that, like the new planet that inspires the title journey, is worthy of discovery. Roy Thinnes (of *The Invaders*) stars as an astronaut who is sent to the heretofore hidden planet that lies, as the title indicates, on the far side of the sun with an orbit parallel to the Earth. Needlessly overplotted, but neat special effects and an ending worthy of *The Twilight Zone*. **AKA:** Doppelganger. 🦴🦴🦴

1969 (G) 92m/C *GB* Roy Thinnes, Ian Hendry, Lynn Loring, Patrick Wymark, Loni von Friedl, Herbert Lom, Ed Bishop; **D:** Robert Parrish; **W:** Gerry Anderson. **VHS, Beta, LV** *MCA*

Journey to the Seventh Planet

Uranus is controlled by a wicked entity in the year 2001. The UN space team sent to explore the planet discovers that on Uranus their thoughts become reality. Can they overcome their nightmares and stop the alien from his reign of terror? 🦴🦴

1961 83m/C *DK* John Agar, Greta Thyssen, Ann Smyrner, Mimi Heinrich, Carl Ottosen; **D:** Sidney Pink. **VHS, LV**

Judge Dredd

A cop who acts as judge, jury, and executioner? Admittedly, they should have let John Milius write and direct, but hell, overall this is a fine film version of the famous cult comic *2000 AD* that retains all the spirit of the British strip. Stallone even looks the square-jawed part, and once you get over his slurring of Dredd's most noted line—"I am the law!"—he ain't so bad at all. Dredd is framed for murder by ex-judge/arch-criminal Rico (Armand Assante), who loves to kill and knows some dark, Dredded family secret. Banished from Mega City One with nothing but comic relief in the form of Rob Schneider, Dredd must face

"No shave today, thanks, just a haircut." Sylvester Stallone keeps his mad barber at bay in *Judge Dredd.*

1995 (R) 96m/C Sylvester Stallone, Armand Assante, Diane Lane, Rob Schneider, Joan Chen, Juergen Prochnow, Max von Sydow; **D:** Danny Cannon; **W:** Steven E. de Souza, Michael De Luca, William Wisher; **M:** Alan Silvestri. Nominations: Golden Raspberry Awards '95: Worst Actor (Stallone). **VHS, LV** *TOU*

Jurassic Park

Michael Crichton's spine-tingling thriller translates well (but not entirely faithfully) to the big screen due to its main attraction: realistic, rampaging dinosaurs. A rich industrialist (Richard Attenborough) plans to open a theme park whose attraction is genetically cloned dinosaurs hatched from prehistoric DNA. When an unscrupulous technician (*Seinfeld*'s Wayne Knight) shuts down the computer system in an attempt to steal the dinosaur DNA, all hell breaks loose. The dinosaurs escape from their pens, smarter and less predictable than expected, and change this park from Disneyland to Tokyo in a *Godzilla* movie. Though the plot is recycled from *Frankenstein,* and even Crichton's own *Westworld,* the movie is still tremendously entertaining. The characters are the typical mix of scientists (Laura Dern, Sam Neill, and, most interestingly, Jeff Goldblum), some engaged by the majesty of the dinosaurs, others more incredulous, worried about the implications of man playing God, and of course, the millionaire's grandchildren, who are awestruck by the creatures but end up being terrorized by them. The real stars are the dinos, an incredible combination of models and computer animation, both totally convincing. Violent, suspenseful, and realistic with gory attack scenes. Not for small kids, though much of the marketing is aimed at them. Super director Steven Spielberg knocked his own *E.T.* out of first place as *JP* became the highest-grossing movie of all time. Also available in a letterboxed version. 🎞🎞🎞

1993 (PG-13) 127m/C Sam Neill, Laura Dern, Jeff Goldblum, Richard Attenborough, Bob Peck, Martin Ferrero, B.D. Wong, Joseph Mazzello, Ariana Richards, Samuel L. Jackson, Wayne Knight; **D:** Steven Spielberg; **W:** David Koepp, Michael Crichton; **C:** Dean Cundey; **M:** John Williams; **V:** Richard Kiley. Hugos '94: Dramatic Presentation; Academy Awards '93: Best Sound, Best Sound Effects Editing, Best Visual Effects; Nominations: MTV Movie Awards '94: Best Film, Best Villain (T-Rex), Best Action Sequence. **VHS, LV** *MCA*

"What? I've got goat flesh in my teeth again, don't I?" The giant T-Rex frets over his dental hygiene in *Jurassic Park.*

the more-likely-than-not inbred Angel family, most notably the hacked-up, cyber-enhanced, ugly-as-hell, psychotic-mental misfit Mean Machine, who just happens to have a dial on his head to crank up the ol' nastiness. Add to this lady judge Diane Lane, an opening aerial tour of Mega City One that goes one up on *Blade Runner,* a high-speed, high-altitude motorcycle chase with lots-o'-bullets and tons-o'-neon, dialogue intensely delivered with the acting-be-damned attitude required, and you've got one great piece of comic book celluloid. *Robocop* obviously owes Dredd-the-comic book a lot. Dredd-the-movie took so long to get to the screen that they made *Robocop* into three movies, a TV show, and a cartoon series, before the real mechanized hero hit the theatres. 🎞🎞🎞

Kamikaze '89

German director Fassbinder has the lead acting role (his last) in this offbeat story of a police lieutenant in Berlin, circa 1989, who investigates a puzzling series of bombings. In German with English subtitles. 🦴🦴🦴

1983 90m/C *GE* Rainer Werner Fassbinder, Gunther Kaufman, Boy Gobert; **D:** Wolf Gremm; **M:** Tangerine Dream. **VHS, Beta** *MGM, FCT, GLV*

The Killer Shrews

This certified "golden turkey" stars Baruch Lumet (father of famed director Sidney of *Serpico* and *Network* fame) as Dr. Craigis, who creates a serum that transforms tiny shrews into rabid beasts (actually dogs in make-up). Producer and co-star Ken Curtis is better known as Festus on the classic TV series *Gunsmoke*. Ingrid Goude was Miss Universe of 1957. From the people who brought you *The Giant Gila Monster*. Director Ray Kellogg would later co-direct with John Wayne *The Green Berets,* the pro-Vietnam War epic in which the sun inexplicably sets in the East. 🦴🦴

1959 70m/B James Best, Ingrid Goude, Baruch Lumet, Ken Curtis; **D:** Ray Kellogg. **VHS** *SNC, MRV, HHT*

Killers from Space

Cheap flick in which big-eyed men from beyond Earth bring scientist Peter Graves back to life and force him to assist them with their evil plan for world domination. Some atmospheric photography makes this almost worthwhile as an entry in the newborn genre of early '50s sci-fi noir. But some incredibly shoddy special effects involving enlarged shots of bugs and lizards, along with a lethargic pace, put this one deep in the trash barrel. The same year W. Lee Wilder made this and *The Snow Creature,* brother Billy was making *Sabrina.* 🦴

1954 80m/B Peter Graves, Barbara Bestar, James Seay, Frank Gerstle, Steve Pendleton, John Merrick; **D:** W. Lee Wilder; **C:** William Clothier. **VHS, Beta** *NOS, MRV, RHI*

The Killing Edge

In post-nuclear holocaust Earth, a lone warrior seeks justice, and his family, in a lawless land. 🦴🕊️

1986 85m/C Bill French, Marv Spencer; **D:** Lindsay Shonteff. **VHS** *VCD, HHE*

Killings at Outpost Zeta

Earthmen investigate a barren planet where previous expeditions have disappeared, and find hordes of aliens. 🦴

1980 92m/C Gordon Devol, Jackie Ray, James A. Watson Jr. **VHS, Beta** *VCI*

King Dinosaur

There's a new planet in the solar system! It's called Nova, and it's full of really big lizards. A scientific expedition zips up to check out the action on Nova and gets chased by one of the lizards and (just for good measure) a giant armadillo. Director Bert I. Gordon really liked giant things (check out his initials). He did giant grasshoppers, giant rats, even a giant man, but a giant armadillo was definitely a cinematic first. There are some mushy lovescenes for the girls (who, as we all know, aren't that big on armadillos), a narrator to help us keep things straight, and even an atom bomb to round things out. In case you don't get the message, Gordon's is one of the more audacious '50s monster-fests. 🦴🕊️

1955 63m/B Bill Bryant, Wanda Curtis, Patti Gallagher, Douglas Henderson; **D:** Bert I. Gordon; **W:** Tom Gries. **VHS, Beta, LV** *MLB*

King Kong

The original beauty and the beast film classic tells the story of Kong, a giant ape captured on Skull Island (a lost world where dinosaurs still thrive) and brought to New York as a Broadway attraction. Kong falls for Fay Wray, escapes from his captors, and rampages through the city, ending up on top of the newly built Empire State Building. Moody Max Steiner score adds color, and Willis O'Brien's stop-motion animation and other special effects still hold up well. Available in a muddy colorized version. The laserdisc, produced from a superior negative, features extensive liner

"I saw her first!" *King Kong* and a testy pterodactyl fight over Fay Wray.

notes and running commentary by film historian Ronald Haver. 🦴🦴🦴🦴

1933 105m/B Fay Wray, Bruce Cabot, Robert Armstrong, Frank Reicher, Noble Johnson, Sam Hardy, James Flavin; **D:** Ernest B. Schoedsack; **W:** James A. Creelman, Ruth Rose; **M:** Max Steiner. **VHS, Beta, LV, 8mm** *TTC, MED, FUS*

King Kong

Oil company official travels to a remote island to discover it inhabited by a huge gorilla. The transplanted beast suffers unrequited love in classic fashion: monkey meets girl, monkey gets girl and brandishes her while atop the World Trade Center. An updated remake of the 1933 movie classic that also marks the screen debut of Jessica Lange. Jeff Bridges is too self-righteously annoying to make an acceptable hero, but Charles Grodin is fine as the greedy exec. Impressive sets and a believable King Kong (played by make-up wizard Rick Baker in his own creation) romp around New York City in this film. Limited use of a stiff full-scale model of Kong, heavily promoted by the producer—plus comparison with the classic original—did much to damage critical opinion of this remake, but it's really a fine film in its own way, especially in John Guillermin's direction and a superb soundtrack from John Barry. Watch for Joe Piscopo, and quickly for Corbin Bernsen as a reporter. 🦴🦴🦴

1976 (PG) 135m/C Jeff Bridges, Charles Grodin, Jessica Lange, Rene Auberjonois, John Randolph, Ed Lauter, Jack O'Halloran, Joe Piscopo, Corbin Bernsen; **D:** John Guillermin; **M:** John Barry. Academy Awards '76: Best Visual Effects; Nominations: Academy Awards '76: Best Cinematography, Best Sound. **VHS, Beta, LV, 8mm** *PAR, HMV*

King Kong Lives

Unnecessary sequel to the 1976 remake of *King Kong* in which two scientists revive the big ape with a big artificial heart. They plan to get him together with a female of his kind and take them back to his island home, but their plans go astray, and Kong ends up tragically fighting for his life against an army. There are

some good ideas in the script, but there were obviously too few of them, and the story goes astray. ♫ ♫

1986 (PG-13) 105m/C Brian Kerwin, Linda Hamilton, John Ashton, Peter Michael Goetz; **D:** John Guillermin; **W:** Steven Pressfield. **VHS, Beta, LV** *MED, WAR*

King Kong Vs. Godzilla

An entrepreneur captures a giant ape on a South Pacific island, names him King Kong (after the classic movie), and plans to bring him back to Japan to star on the TV show he sponsors. Unfortunately, the beast escapes. Meanwhile, Godzilla breaks out of an iceberg and begins another campaign of destruction. The government figures that if they get the two monsters to fight, maybe they'll finish each other off. The planet issues a collective shudder as the two mightiest monsters slug it out. Humankind can only stand by and watch in impotent horror as the tide of the battle sways to and fro. For Godzilla's third appearance, Toho went for a more whimsical atmosphere, spicing their outlandish story with doses of satire. Godzilla appears positively nasty and looking for trouble—while the Kong costume is, sadly, rather shoddy looking, and the actor inside fails to act like an ape. For the U.S. version, Universal altered the film drastically, deleting and rearranging scenes while adding bland sequences from the viewpoint of a TV anchor desk. Even Akira Ifukube's powerful score was thrown out in favor of stock library music. In any case, *King Kong Vs. Godzilla* became a monster hit at the box office all over the world, and is still a mighty entertaining monster mash. **AKA:** King Kong Tai Gojira. ♫ ♫ ♫

1963 105m/C *JP* Tadao Takashima, Mie Hama, Kenji Sahara, Akihiko Hirata, Michael Keith; **D:** Inoshiro Honda; **W:** Shinichi Sekizawa; **C:** Hajime Koizumi; **M:** Akira Ifukube. **VHS** *GKK*

King of the Rocketmen

Mystery villain Dr. Vulcan is knocking off eminent scientists, so researcher Jeff King (Tristam Coffin, a mustachioed actor often seen in bad-guy roles) fights back in disguise, using a newly invented jet backpack and metal mask to become the flying hero Rocket Man. Twelve-chapter Republic serial created the simple but way-cool Rocket Man costume later reused in non-sequel serials *Radar Men from the Moon* and *Zombies of the Stratosphere,* and, of course, inspired *The Rocketeer.* Action is lively, if a bit on the low-budget side (Dr. Vulcan's lavish death-ray mayhem is actually composed of clips from the vintage disaster flick *Deluge*), but flying scenes, done using a mannequin on cables, are pretty good for the era. Later released as a feature titled *Lost Planet Airmen.* ♫ ♫ ♭

1949 156m/B Tristram Coffin, Mae Clarke, I. Stanford Jolley; **D:** Fred Brannon. **VHS, LV** *MED, VCN, REP*

The Kirlian Witness

A woman uses the power of telepathic communication with house plants to solve her sister's murder. **AKA:** The Plants Are Watching. ♫

1978 (PG) 88m/C Nancy Snyder, Joel Colodner, Ted Leplat; **D:** Jonathan Sarno. **VHS, Beta** *NO*

Kiss and Kill

Christopher Lee returns in his fourth outing as Fu Manchu. This time the evil one has set up housekeeping in Brazil, where he's injected ten beautiful girls with a deadly poison that is activated when the lovelies smooch an unsuspecting victim. They are then sent out to seduce world leaders and give a new meaning to the phrase "kiss of death." While not quite on a par with the previous movies, this is still enjoyable, and certainly far superior to *The Castle of Fu Manchu,* which would end the series. **AKA:** Blood of Fu Manchu; Against All Odds; Fu Manchu and the Kiss of Death. ♫ ♫

1968 (R) 91m/C *GB* Christopher Lee, Richard Greene, Shirley Eaton, Tsai Chin, Maria Rohm, H. Marion Crawford, Goetz George; **D:** Jess (Jesus) Franco; **W:** Peter Welbeck; **C:** Manuel Merino. **VHS** *MRV*

Kiss Me Deadly

Director Robert Aldrich's adaptation of Mickey Spillane's private eye tale takes pulp literature high concept. Ralph Meeker, as Mike Hammer, is a self-interested, rough and tumble all American dick (detective, that is). When a woman to whom he happened to give a ride is found murdered, he follows the mystery straight into a nuclear conspiracy. Aldrich, with tongue deftly in cheek, styles a message through the medium; topsy turvy camerawork and rat-a-tat-tat pacing tell volumes about Hammer, the world he orbits, and that special '50s kind of paranoia. Now a cult fave, it's considered to be the American grandaddy to French New Wave. Cinematography by Ernest Laszlo. 🦴🦴🦴🦴

1955 105m/B Ralph Meeker, Albert Dekker, Paul Stewart, Wesley Addy, Cloris Leachman, Strother Martin, Marjorie Bennett, Jack Elam; **D:** Robert Aldrich; **C:** Ernest Laszlo. **VHS, Beta, LV** *MGM, FCT*

Knights

In a futuristic wasteland a young martial-arts warrior (Kathy Long) and a cyborg (Kris Kristofferson) team up to battle rebel cyborgs that have discovered a new source of fuel— human blood. 🦴🦴

1993 (R) 89m/C Kathy Long, Kris Kristofferson, Lance Henriksen, Scott Paulin, Gary Daniels; **D:** Albert Pyun; **W:** Albert Pyun. **VHS, Beta** *PAR*

Kronos

Energy-hungry aliens send an 'accumulator,' a giant robot resembling a piston, to drain the Earth of all power sources. Scientists and their computer SUSIE (Synchro Unifying Sinometric Integrating Equitensor) sweat out a solution. Offbeat '50s space-invader saga is hopelessly hobbled by a low budget; whenever Kronos is on the move it turns into a cartoon so obviously hand-drawn that Wile E. Coyote could order it from Acme to use on the Roadrunner. 🦴🦴

1957 78m/B Jeff Morrow, Barbara Lawrence, John Emery, George O'Hanlon, Morris Ankrum; **D:** Kurt Neumann; **W:** Lawrence Louis Goldman; **C:** Karl Struss. **VHS, Beta, LV** *MED, MLB*

Krull

Though set on the distant world of Krull, filled with fantasy creatures of myth and magic, there's a labored sense of familiarity all over this costly dud, in which a Kong-sized invader called the Beast lands his starship/fortress in a peaceful kingdom and sends hordes of insec-

toid stormtroopers to ravage the land. Handsome prince embarks on a quest to find the Glaive (a sort of buzzsaw-boomerang weapon) and joins with Merrie Men types to save his Beastnapped bride. Actors unfortunately treat this material like Shakespeare; in truth, it's yet another pompous '80s try at the Ultimate Fairy Tale, never mind that one had already been done in 1977—*Star Wars*. Special effects by Derek Meddings (*Batman*). 🦴🦴

1983 (PG) 121m/C *GB* Ken Marshall, Lysette Anthony, Freddie Jones, Francesca Annis, Liam Neeson, Alun Armstrong; **D:** Peter Yates; **C:** Peter Suschitzsky; **M:** James Horner. **VHS, Beta, LV** *GKK*

Kurt Vonnegut's Harrison Bergeron

In the year 2053 the American government has gone to absurd lengths to ensure equality. Mediocrity is championed and everyone is forced to wear metallic headbands that stifle intellect through electronic impulses. All of which is too bad for Harrison Bergeron (Sean Astin), a smart young man being punished for his intelligence. A secret underground elite offers Harrison the chance to think freely, but naturally this power comes with a price. An adaptation of Kurt Vonnegut's 1961 short story, originally made for cable TV. Much of Vonnegut's dry humor is lost here, but the excellent cast makes it worth watching. **AKA:** Harrison Bergeron. 🦴🦴🦴

1995 (R) 99m/C Sean Astin, Christopher Plummer, Miranda de Pencier, Nigel Bennett, Buck Henry, Eugene Levy, Howie Mandel, Andrea Martin; **D:** Bruce Pittman; **W:** Arthur Crimm; **C:** Michael Storey; **M:** Lou Natale. **VHS** *REP*

La Jetee

One of the greatest film shorts of all time, and the inspiration for the 1995 Terry Gilliam sci-fi thriller *12 Monkeys*. Told almost completely through still photographs with narration, this post WWIII tale takes place in a future Paris where survivors now live in subterranean vaults. Repeating image of a woman's face and a childhood experience at an airport provide impetus for time travel through memory

projection. Director Chris Marker, also a novelist and photographer, makes use of all his talents and delivers a totally unique and completely spellbinding photo-novel-movie with such a deep philosophical paradox that it better make you think a little. Available on VHS with *An Occurrence at Owl Creek Bridge,* an Oscar-winning French short (based on the Ambrose Bierce story) that was aired as an episode of TV's *The Twilight Zone.* 🎬🎬🎬📼

1964 60m/B *FR D:* Chris Marker. **VHS, Beta** *FCT*

Land of Doom

Amazon chick named Harmony teams up reluctantly with a warrior in battle against minions of a punk muscleman in a metallic mask—as if one of the villains of the World Wrestling Federation survived the nuclear holocaust. Dumb *Road Warrior* ripoff, though the mountainous Turkish scenery makes a change of pace from the usual diesel 'n' dust highway settings. 🎬

1984 87m/C Deborah Rennard, Garrick Dowhen; *D:* Peter Maris. **VHS, Beta** *LIV*

The Land that Time Forgot

WWI veteran Bowen Tyler, a beautiful woman, and their German enemies are stranded in the land of Caprona, which is filled with phoney-looking dinosaurs and cave-people. If you enjoy hokey dinosaur movies, you'll probably find this amusing, but more discerning viewers will probably want to skip it and just watch *Jurassic Park* for the sixth time. Better still, take the dough you would have laid out renting this turkey and hunt up Edgar Rice Burroughs' original novel in a good used bookstore. This dubious epic was for some reason followed by a sequel in 1977, *The People that Time Forgot,* itself also best left forgotten. 🎬📼

"Wait a minute! I'm only doing 20 reps. You added weight!" Doug McClure does the ultimate clean and jerk in *The Land that Time Forgot.*

"Merge! Merge!" Dan O'Herlihy gives Lance Guest a Driver's Ed lesson that's out of this world in *The Last Starfighter*.

Laserblast

Prolific low-budget producer Charles Band first gained genre attention (little of it positive) with this drive-in hybrid of *Carrie* and *Close Encounters* in which an abused wimp gets revenge when he finds a powerful laser gun dropped by dinosaur-like aliens. The more our antihero wields the death ray, the more mutated he becomes, though his tiny-budget rampage mainly zaps just an empty street, few parked cars, a mailbox, and a crudely hand-made billboard for *Star Wars* (dream on!). Stop-motion f/x by David Allen. Later remade as *Deadly Weapon*. 🦴🦴

1978 (PG) 87m/C Kim Milford, Cheryl "Rainbeaux" Smith, Keenan Wynn, Roddy McDowall; **D:** Michael Rae; **W:** Franne Schacht, Frank Ray Perilli; **M:** Richard Band, Joel Goldsmith. **VHS, Beta, LV** *MED*

Last Chase

Famed race car driver becomes a vocal dissenter against the sterile society that has emerged, in this drama set in the near future. Made for television. Screenplay written by Christopher Crowe under the pseudonym C.R. O'Cristopher. 🦴🦴

1981 (PG) 106m/C *CA* Lee Majors, Burgess Meredith, Chris Makepeace, Alexandra Stewart; **D:** Martyn Burke; **W:** Christopher Crowe, Martyn Burke. **VHS, Beta** *VES*

1975 (PG) 90m/C *GB* Doug McClure, John McEnery, Susan Penhaligon; **D:** Kevin Connor; **W:** James Cawthorn, Michael Moorcock. **VHS, Beta** *LIV, VES*

The Land Unknown

A Naval helicopter is forced down in a tropical land of prehistoric terror, complete with ferocious creatures from the Mesozoic Era. While trying to make repairs, the crew discovers the sole survivor of a previous expedition who was driven to madness by life in the primordial jungle. Good performances from cast, although monsters aren't that believable. Based on a story by Charles Palmer. 🦴🦴🦴

1957 78m/B Jock Mahoney, Shawn Smith, William Reynolds, Henry Brandon, Douglas Kennedy; **D:** Virgil W. Vogel; **W:** Laszlo Gorog; **M:** Henry Mancini. **VHS** *MCA*

Last Days of Planet Earth

More interesting as a societal symptom than entertainment, this Japanese doomsday movie focuses on scientists and their families who witness a build-up of pollution responsible for giant mutant slugs, marauding bats, freak weather conditions, birth defects, and other environmental calamities. Positively gleeful in describing how bad things could possibly get, it inserts footage from previous Toho disaster flicks like *The Last War* and *The Submersion of Japan,* then abandons pretense of narrative to become a documentary about the prophecies of Nostradamus! Join our doomsday cult, listen to our leader, be saved. Where have you heard that one before, reader-san? Dubbed in English. **AKA:** Prophe-

cies of Nostradamus; Catastrophe 1999; Nostradamus No Daiyogen.

1974 88m/C *JP* Tetsuro Tamba, So Yamamura, Takashi Shimura; *D:* Toshio Masuda. **VHS** *PAR*

The Last Man on Earth

Richard Matheson's compelling novel *I Am Legend* has been the uncredited inspiration for many zombie/plague/end-of-the-world films and sort-of actually made into two movies: this one, and the 1971 *The Omega Man.* Vincent Price plays *The Last Man on Earth,* lone survivor of a plague which first kills, and then zombifies its victims. On one of his daytime zombie hunts, Price comes across a group who, through injections, are not as zombied-out as the rest of the neighbors, but still have a bit of the ol' pasty face and resent his total aliveness. Where as *Omega Man* replaced the paranoia of the novel with Chuck Heston's machismo, this one fills in with poorly done repetitive violence and a hero who is pretty much too tired to go on. Matheson himself was so dissatisfied with the project that he used the fictitious name Logan Swanson for his co-scripting credit. **AKA:** L'Ultimo Uomo Della Terra.

1964 86m/B *IT* Vincent Price, Franca Bettoya, Giacomo "Jack" Rossi-Stuart, Emma Danieli; *D:* Ubaldo Ragona, Sidney Salkow; *W:* Richard Matheson. **VHS** *SNC, MRV*

The Last Starfighter

The outer-space scenes in this warm-hearted adventure aren't nearly as interesting as the Starlight Starbright Trailer Court where the beginning is set. As a young man whose talent at video games turns him into the title character, Lance Guest is an engaging hero. The film is almost stolen by veteran character actors Robert Preston and Dan O'Herlihy, even though his face is completely hidden behind a lizard mask.

1984 (PG) 100m/C Lance Guest, Robert Preston, Barbara Bosson, Dan O'Herlihy, Catherine Mary Stewart, Cameron Dye, Kimberly Ross, Wil Wheaton, Norman Snow; *D:* Nick Castle; *W:* Jonathan Betuel. **VHS, Beta, LV** *MCA*

Last War

After World War III, continued tensions between the United States and Russia triggers Armageddon. Made by Toho Studios in 1961 during a period in which several films were made dealing with global destruction via atomic weapons, but not released in the U.S. (directly to TV) until '68. The difference in this one is in its viewpoint from the unique perspective of the only country (so far) to have actually been a victim of nuclear warfare. As such, it's a sad tale of helpless victims resigned to destruction, as things continue to get worse around the globe. Awfully depressing stuff, enlivened only by the spectacle of Eiji Tsuburaya's masterful f/x work. The U.S. distributor tacked on the familiar song "It's a Small World" and an excerpt from President Kennedy's anti-arms race speech in an attempt to Americanize the production. Often confused with the rarely seen and reportedly similar *The Final War,* produced by Toei the year before.

1968 79m/C Frankie Sakai, Nobuko Otowa, Akira Takarada, Yuriko Hoshi, Yumi Shirakawa; *D:* Shue Matsubayashi; *W:* Takeshi Kimura; *C:* Rokuro Nishigaki. **VHS, Beta** *GEM*

The Last Woman on Earth

Two men vie for the affections of the sole surviving woman after a vague and unexplained disaster of vast proportions. Robert Towne, who appears herein under the pseudonym Edward Wain, wrote the script (his first screenwriting effort). You might want to watch this if it were the last movie on earth, although Corman fans will probably love it. **WOOF!**

1961 71m/C Antony Carbone, Edward Wain, Betsy Jones-Moreland; *D:* Roger Corman; *W:* Robert Towne. **VHS** *NOS, MRV, SNC*

Lathe of Heaven

In a near-future world, young George Orr visits a psychologist complaining that his dreams can alter and mold the real world. The ambitious shrink tries hypnosis to use the awesome superpower on a grand scale and cure mankind's many ills. Unfortunately, Orr's dreams have disastrous consequences—a

Blue Lagoon meets *The Hobbit*. Tom Cruise and Mia Sara in **Legend**.

Chile), executed in the belief that a cattle skull mounted on the grill of a car is all you need to enter *Mad Max* territory. 🦴

1988 (R) 81m/C Leon Berkeley, Xander Berkeley, Nick Corri, Amanda Peterson; **D:** Jon Hess; **W:** Tony Cinciripini, Larry Leahy. **VHS, Beta** *MGM*

The Lawnmower Man

Scientist Pierce Brosnan uses a dim-witted gardener named Jobe (Jeff Fahey, in a fright wig) to test his virtual-reality computer techniques for enhancing intelligence. He's able to increase Jobe's mental powers beyond human measure, and not necessarily for the better, as the simple groundsman becomes a wrathful superbeing. So minimally based on a non-sf short story by Stephen King that the author successfully sued to remove his precious name from the credits. Instead this is the premise of *Charly* crossbred with tired Frankenstein cliches and pumped up with trendy computer graphics f/x (including a memorable cybersex scene). Available in an unrated version with additional footage. 🦴🦴

1992 (R) 108m/C Jeff Fahey, Pierce Brosnan, Jenny Wright, Mark Bringleson, Geoffrey Lewis, Jeremy Slate, Dean Norris; **D:** Brett Leonard; **W:** Brett Leonard, Gimel Everett; **C:** Russell Carpenter. **VHS, LV** *COL, FCT, MOV*

Lawnmower Man 2: Jobe's War

Since just about everything and everyone had been blown up at end of the first film, this one's less a sequel than a cinematic videogame. As such, it's a good sf adventure for teen audiences with a quick pace and whiz-bang computer effects. In all other respects, it's not nearly interesting as the original. Corporate baddie Walker (Kevin Conway) enlists Jobe to (what else?) take over the world using virtual reality. To the rescue come one burned-out computer expert (Patrick Bergin) and a group of VR-addicted kids living in an abandoned subway. Techno-babble abounds but nothing interesting ever happens. **AKA:** Lawnmover Man 2: Beyond Cyberspace. 🦴

1995 (PG-13) 93m/C Patrick Bergin, Matt Frewer, Austin O'Brien, Kevin Conway, Ely Pouget, Camille Cooper; **D:** Farhad Mann; **W:** Farhad Mann; **C:** Ward Russell; **M:** Robert Folk. **VHS** *NLC*

demand for peace between all nations is realized via alien invasion—and much-redreamt reality, not to mention the plot, starts to fall apart. Promoted as the first made-for-TV movie done by Public Television, this adaptation of Ursula K. LeGuin's novel gets points for striving to be a highly cerebral affair (in an era when the commercial networks, not to mention major studios, mainly brainstormed over how to best rip off *Star Wars*). Suffers from an opaque finale, not helped by a PBS-level budget, but maintains a strong cult of admirers even though the videocassette release is notoriously difficult to find. 🦴🦴

1980 120m/C Bruce Davison, Kevin Conway, Margaret Avery; **D:** David Loxton. **VHS, Beta** *WNE*

The Lawless Land

Post-holocaust America is ruled by a tyrant. Two young lovers who can't take it anymore try to escape his despotic rule, with a punk bounty-hunter in pursuit. Minimal sf elements in this Roger Corman chase flick (shot in

Legend

A colorful, unabashedly Tolkienesque fantasy full of unicorns, magic swamps, bumbling dwarves, and rainbows. Tom Cruise, who in the same year would try to save America in *Top Gun,* here attempts to save an innocent waif from the Prince of Darkness, a Satanic critter with really big horns (Tim *Rocky Horror Picture Show* Curry). Rather more original and certainly more attractive than the usual '80s fantasy-flick, which more often tended to emphasize musclebound heroes in skimpy loincloths. Produced in Great Britain. 🦴🦴

1986 (PG) 89m/C *GB* Tom Cruise, Mia Sara, Tim Curry, David Bennent, Billy Barty, Alice Playten; **D:** Ridley Scott; **M:** Jerry Goldsmith. Nominations: Academy Awards '86: Best Makeup. **VHS, Beta, LV** *MCA*

Leviathan

A motley crew of ocean-floor miners unwarily open a scuttled Soviet sub and are exposed to a failed genetic experiment that turns humans into insatiable, regenerating fish-creatures. Inspired by *The Abyss* but ripped off from *Alien,* this one sinks instead of swims, leaving a good cast all wet. Toothy monster f/x by Stan Winston. 🦴🎵

1989 (R) 98m/C Peter Weller, Ernie Hudson, Hector Elizondo, Amanda Pays, Richard Crenna, Daniel Stern, Lisa Eilbacher, Michael Carmine, Meg Foster; **D:** George P. Cosmatos; **W:** David Peoples, Jeb Stuart; **C:** Alex Thompson; **M:** Jerry Goldsmith. **VHS, Beta, LV** *MGM*

Lifeforce

The most common complaint about this Tobe Hooper effort used to be that it moved too fast. The recent release of the European cut solves that problem (if it was one) by delivering 20 more minutes of story. Everything you'd ever want in a sci-fi/horror film is here. Haley's comet, the space shuttle, a gigantic spaceship, exploding bodies, apocalyptic zombie mob scenes, oversized batlike creatures,

"Anyone for a giant, studded Twinkie?" Astronaut explorers stop for a quick snack in *Lifeforce.*

weird sex featuring Mathilda May showing herself off in her first film, and Steve "Manson" Railsback ranting and raving as only he can. May and two pals are brought to Earth from a ship found following a comet. Things take a nasty turn when the three are found to be soul-draining vampires, channeling their goodies back up to the vessel which has now parked itself in orbit around Earth and has unfolded a gigantic umbrella as a collector. Railsback, having gotten very close to May on the shuttle trip, finds himself psychically linked to her and is hot on her trail as she moves from body to body, spreading her plague of soulless zombies across Great Britain. *The Next Generation*'s Patrick Stewart appears as an asylum's head shrink in one of the niftiest effects scenes involving an incredibly tense "conversation." Score by Henry Mancini ends with quirky march during the credits and is exhilarating on its own. Script by Dan O'Bannon was originally titled *They Bite*. 🦴🦴

1985 (R) 100m/C *GB* Steve Railsback, Peter Firth, Frank Finlay, Patrick Stewart, Michael Gothard, Nicholas Ball, Aubrey Morris, Nancy Paul, Mathilda May, John Hallam; **D:** Tobe Hooper; **W:** Dan O'Bannon, Don Jakoby; **C:** Alan Hume; **M:** Henry Mancini, Michael Kamen. **VHS, Beta, LV** *FHE, LIV, VES*

Lifepod

A group of intergalactic travelers is forced to evacuate a luxury space liner when a mad computer sabotages the ship. 🦴

1980 94m/C Joe Penny, Jordan Michaels, Kristine DeBell. **VHS, Beta** *VCI*

Lifepod

Loose adaptation of Hitchcock's 1944 *Lifeboat* begins at a full run with the explosion of an interplanetary cruise ship. A few survivors manage to escape in a poorly equipped lifepod, and are beset by a series of disasters. Who's the saboteur? Actor Ron Silver, making a credible debut behind the camera, keeps the action moving at a good clip, and the ensemble cast does solid professional work. The effects, while not up to *Star Wars* standards, are remarkably good. For a stay-at-home evening's entertainment, this one's a good bet. Made for television. 🦴🦴🦴

1993 120m/C Ron Silver, Robert Loggia, CCH Pounder, Stan Shaw, Adam Storke, Jessica Tuck, Kelli Williams, Ed Gate; **D:** Ron Silver; **W:** M. Jay Roach, Jim Densham. **VHS, LV** *CAF*

Light Years

Garish animated fantasy epic about an idyllic land suddenly beset by evil mutations and death rays. Based on the novel *Robots Against Gondohar* by Jean-Pierre Andrevan. 🦴🦴

1988 (PG) 83m/C **D:** Harvey Weinstein; **W:** Isaac Asimov, Raphael Cluzel; **M:** Gabriel Yared; **V:** Glenn Close, Jennifer Grey, Christopher Plummer, Penn Jillette, John Shea, David Johansen, Bridget Fonda, Paul Shaffer, Terrence Mann, Teller. **VHS, Beta, LV** *VMK, WTA, FUS*

Link

Primatologist Terence Stamp conducts his behavioral experiments in the remote English countryside assisted by Link, an ex-circus chimp (played by an orangutan) trained to act just like a butler. When the old ape suspects his days of employment—and living, for that matter—are numbered, he mimics another humanlike trait: premeditated murder. The borderline-sf suspense plot works well until a carload of typically stupid movie teens show up, just asking to be turned into monkey chow, and nubile Elisabeth Shue's acting sure wasn't Oscar caliber until later. But this critically undervalued chiller is well worth rediscovering on video, especially for Jerry Goldsmith's witty and menacing soundtrack. 🦴🦴

1986 (R) 103m/C *GB* Elisabeth Shue, Terence Stamp; **D:** Richard Franklin; **W:** Everett DeRoche; **M:** Jerry Goldsmith. **VHS, Beta** *REP*

Liquid Sky

Androgynous bisexual model (Anne Carlisle) living in Manhattan attracts a miniature UFO, which lands atop her penthouse. Its tiny, invisible occupant is in search of the chemical high it can only get by killing her sex partners in the throes of ecstasy, and a weird symbiotic relationship develops. Viewers either adore or

despise this talky, one-of-a-kind weirdness directed by Russian expatriate Slava Tsukerman, but the Hound found it five times more creative than many mainstream astro-budget Hollywood productions, and despite the bizarre premise (perhaps because of it) the film succeeds in making its seedy punk environment completely real and believable. Look for Carlisle also playing a gay male. Title is slang for heroin. ♫ ♫ ♫

1983 (R) 112m/C Anne Carlisle, Paula Sheppard, Bob Brady, Susan Doukas, Otto von Wernherr; **D:** Slava Tsukerman; **W:** Anne Carlisle; **C:** Yuri Neyman. **VHS, Beta, LV** *MED*

Lobster Man from Mars

When a rich movie producer (Tony Curtis) learns from his accountant that he must produce a flop as a tax writeoff, he buys and promotes the titular homemade sci-fi movie from a young Ed Wood type. The film takes up most of the narrative, a cross between Corman's *It*

Conquered the World, Robot Monster, and other notorious turkeys, about an invading lobster man, a screaming damsel, and a metaphor-spouting detective (stand-up comic Tommy Sledge). Not strictly an sf film (and not too original either, having borrowed the premise of Mel Brooks' *The Producers,*) but enough knowing spoofs of the genre warrant its inclusion here. Narration by radio's Dr. Demento. ♫ ♫

1989 (PG) 84m/C Tony Curtis, Deborah Foreman, Patrick Macnee, Tommy Sledge, Billy Barty, Phil Proctor, Anthony Hickox; **D:** Stanley Shiff; **W:** Bob Greenberg; **C:** Gerry Lively. **VHS, Beta, LV** *LIV*

Lock 'n' Load

Colorado production rises above its shoe-string budget. Far-fetched tale of veterans and mind control recalls *The Manchurian Candidate* and *Jacob's Ladder*. It's slow in the unwinding—people spend far too much time on such simple business as getting in and out

"Ex*cuse* me, but that look went out in 1982." Paula Sheppard and Anne Carlisle in ***Liquid Sky***.

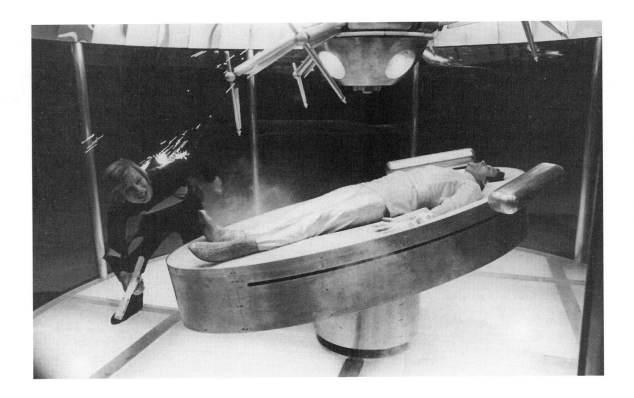

"The Barcalounger works in this room, but that lighting has *got* to go." Michael York is burned by the decor in *Logan's Run*.

of cars—and sometimes predictable. But the characters are realistic, flawed, and multi-dimensional. One good character is worth a hundred effects and this movie has several. If the young cast is inconsistent, they're believable in the important scenes. 🦴🦴🦴⁰

1990 (R) ?m/C Jack Vogel, Renee Cline, Jeffrey Smith, William Hathaway-Clark, Perry Roberts; **D:** David A. Prior. **VHS, LV** *AIP*

Logan's Run

In the 23rd century, a hedonistic society exists in a huge bubble and people are only allowed to live to the age of 30, at which point they are expected to participate in ritual public suicide. Michael York plays a "Sandman," a sort of cop assigned to track down and assassinate "Runners"—those that try to escape and live past 30. The central government sends him on a mission to track down a rumored Runner enclave beyond the city, and turn him into a Runner himself to do so. Intriguing concepts

and great futuristic sets prevail here, but the plot tends to wander all over the place. The special effects, thought impressive at the time, were made instantly obsolete with the release of *Star Wars* the following year. Roscoe Lee Browne provides the voice of a rather clumsy looking robot named Box, while Peter Ustinov shows up late in the game as the oldest man in the world. Based on the novel by William Nolan and George Clayton Johnson. 🦴🦴

1976 120m/C Michael York, Jenny Agutter, Richard Jordan, Roscoe Lee Browne, Farrah Fawcett, Peter Ustinov, Camilla Carr, Ann Ford; **D:** Michael Anderson Sr.; **W:** David Zelag Goodman; **C:** Ernest Laszlo; **M:** Jerry Goldsmith. Academy Awards '76: Best Visual Effects; Nominations: Academy Awards '76: Best Art Direction/Set Decoration, Best Cinematography. **VHS, Beta, LV** *MGM*

Looker

Models being digitized for computer-generated TV commercials are systematically murdered. Albert Finney (looking understandably

TV on Tape: Lost in Space

One of the golden rules of storytelling is that a good yarn is a good yarn, no matter how the storyteller might change or update it. For *Lost in Space,* producer Irwin Allen took *Swiss Family Robinson* to the space age, thrilling '60s TV audiences with the adventures of a futuristic but all-American family marooned on an alien planet.

Guy Williams and perpetual TV-mom June Lockhart were the perfect parents, Marta Kristen was their perfect teenage daughter Judy, and Angela Cartwright and Billy Mumy played the perfectly mischievous kids Penny and Will. There was even a Nice Young Man for Judy in the person of Don West (Mark Goddard).

Another thing about storytelling is that characters sometimes evolve into something the storyteller didn't anticipate. In *Lost in Space*'s 1965 pilot, "The Reluctant Stowaway," Dr. Zachary Smith (Jonathan Harris) was a villain, pure and simple. A spy representing an unnamed foreign power, Smith sabotages the Robinson family's spaceship, the "Jupiter 2," but unexpectedly becomes trapped aboard with his intended victims. By the time the Jupiter 2 settled on the planet where the better part of the series would take place, Smith had changed from a cold, heartless spy to a lazy, greedy, lovable scoundrel. Likewise, the Jupiter 2's robot (always known simply as "the Robot" in the series), originally a vaguely menacing machine with little personality, became Smith's chief flunky and foil. Although many episodes focused on the problems of growing up in outer space, or the constant problem of trying to get back to Earth, most fans fondly remember the show as a series of misadventures instigated by Dr. Smith and played out by him, the Robot, and Will.

The show's bright colors, cheesy special effects, and increasingly juvenile tone over its three-year run have led many fans to regard the show as nothing more than a campy period piece. Still, the show had humor, occasional pathos, and an impressive menagerie of rubbery monsters (including a blob-like creature which for some reason screamed like a mountain-lion). Rumors of a *Lost in Space* movie have been floating around since the early '80s, but remain unconfirmed as of this writing.

1965-67/B&C *Selected cast:* Guy Williams, June Lockhart, Mark Goddard, Marta Kristen, Billy Mumy, Jonathan Harris. **VHS** *VRS, WTA*

---

confused) plays their Beverly Hills plastic surgeon, who investigates and discovers a subliminal-ad conspiracy. Though subject matter was ahead of its time, a half-baked plot by the normally reliable Michael Crichton ultimately makes no sense, and offers only mild distractions through semi-satirical potshots at the media, virtual reality, and mind control. Title refers to Light Ocular Oriented Kinetic Energetic Responsers. And some nude bimbos. 🦴🦴

1981 (PG) 94m/C Albert Finney, James Coburn, Susan Dey, Leigh Taylor-Young, Dorian Harewood, Darryl Hickman; *D:* Michael Crichton; *W:* Michael Crichton; *C:* Paul Lohmann. **VHS, Beta, LV** *WAR*

Lords of the Deep

Producer Roger Corman puts in a cameo appearance (as a treacherous company boss, of all things) in this cheapie about underwater technicians trapped on the ocean floor with a menacing race of manta-like aliens. Low-budget, low-yield film was all wet when rushed out to capitalize in anticipation of undersea sci-fi adventures like *The Abyss.* Cinematic small fry, you might say. 🦴🦴

1989 (PG-13) 95m/C Bradford Dillman, Priscilla Barnes, Melody Ryane, Eb Lottimer, Daryl Haney; *Cameos:* Roger Corman; *D:* Mary Ann Fisher; *W:* Howard R. Cohen, Daryl Haney. **VHS, Beta** *MGM*

171

Sci-Fi Experience

The Lost Missile

A lost, alien missile circles the Earth, causing overheating and destruction on the planet's surface. A scientist works to find a way to save the planet before it explodes into a gigantic fireball. Director William Berke's last film. 🦴🦴

1958 70m/B Robert Loggia, Ellen Parker, Larry Kerr, Phillip Pine, Marilee Earle; **D:** William (Lester Williams) Berke. **VHS** *FRG*

Lost Planet Airmen

The planet is Earth, so it's not lost; and there's only one airman, a scientist in a jet backpack and metal mask who fights the evil genius killing eminent scientists. Mistitled, feature-length distillation of the 12-part Republic serial *King of the Rocket Men* (also available complete on tape). Useful as a quick intro to the iconographic Rocket Man character, who has come to epitomize vintage sci-fi serials. 🦴🦴

1949 65m/B Tristram Coffin, Mae Clarke, Dale Van Sickel; **D:** Fred Brannon. **VHS, Beta** *AOV, DVT, RXM*

Lost Was the Key

This is gotta be the most in-depth video on a single alien abduction. In this case, the subject, Leah Haley, is no dummy at all. She is both a CPA and an author of several books, including *Lost Was the Key*. While the story sounds fairly fantastic, abductions by both aliens and the military, the downing of an alien spacecraft while Haley was aboard, and communication with several different types of entities, the discussion is presented intelligently and will hold your interest throughout. 🦴🦴🦴

19?? 95m/C D: Thomas Tulien; **M:** Thomas Dougherty. **VHS** *UFO*

"Spare my life and I'll show you a really great skin softener." Victim-to-be pleads in *The Lost World*.

The Lost Continent

An expedition searching for a lost rocket on a jungle island discovers dinosaurs and other extinct creatures. Are you ready for this? The dinosaurs are animated cartoons, the hero is Cesar Romero (who'd go on to play the Joker in the '60s *Batman* series), and the director previously did the classic "all-midget western" *The Terror of Tiny Town*. A cast of dependable faces from '50s sf rounds things out. Not precisely a "must-see," the sheer audacity of this flick makes it worth a look. 🦴🦴

1951 82m/B Cesar Romero, Hillary Brooke, Chick Chandler, John Hoyt, Acquanetta, Sid Melton, Whit Bissell, Hugh Beaumont; **D:** Sam Newfield; **W:** Richard H. Landau; **C:** Jack Greenhalgh. **VHS, Beta, LV** *MRV, MLB*

The Lost Empire

Three bountiful and powerful women team up to battle the evil Dr. Syn Do. 🦴

1983 (R) 86m/C Melanie Vincz, Raven De La Croix, Angela Aames, Paul Coufos, Robert Tessier, Angus Scrimm, Angelique Pettyjohn, Kenneth Tobey; **D:** Jim Wynorski; **W:** Jim Wynorski. **VHS, Beta** *LIV*

The Lost World

A zoology professor (Wallace Beery) leads a group on a South American expedition in search of the "lost world," an inaccessible plateau where dinosaurs roam in this silent film. Once there, they encounter many adventures. They return to London with a captured apatosaurus, which breaks loose and causes a

riot in the streets. Based on a story by Sir Arthur Conan Doyle. Special effects by Willis O'Brien led directly to his work on *King Kong*. A 90-minute version includes the film's original trailer and a recreation of some of the missing footage (the film was released at 108 minutes). ⚔️⚔️⚔️

1925 62m/B Wallace Beery, Lewis Stone, Bessie Love, Lloyd Hughes; *D:* Harry Hoyt; *W:* Marion Fairfax. **VHS, Beta, LV** *NOS, MIL, VYY*

The Lost World

Land of the Lost/Jurassic Park themes, based on the story by Sir Arthur Conan Doyle. A scientific team ventures deep into uncharted African jungles where they find themselves confronted by dinosaurs and other dangers. ⚔️⚔️🕊️

1992 99m/C John Rhys-Davies, David Warner; *D:* Timothy Bond. **VHS** *WOV*

The Lucifer Complex

Nazi doctors are cloning exact duplicates of such world leaders as the Pope and the President of the United States on a remote South American island in the year 1996. ⚔️

1978 91m/C Robert Vaughn, Merrie Lynn Ross, Keenan Wynn, Aldo Ray; *D:* David L. Hewitt, Kenneth Hartford. **VHS, Beta** *VCI*

Mac and Me

Heavy backing by McDonalds created a merchandising opportunity that turns into a sub-plot-for-subplot ripoff of *E.T.* Here a whole family of Chaplinesque aliens are hauled to Earth by a Mars probe. 'Mac,' the smallest, escapes government captivity and befriends a handicapped boy. Apparently feeling he had nothing to lose critic-wise, director Stewart Raffill (of *Wilderness Family* fame) takes the plot into directions that Spielberg wouldn't have dared; dig that wild final scene. Sure to please younger kids, and it might even break down the resistance of adult viewers. Maybe. ⚔️⚔️

1988 (PG) 94m/C Christine Ebersole, Jonathan Ward, Katrina Caspary, Lauren Stanley, Jade Calegory; *D:* Stewart Raffill; *W:* Stewart Raffill; *M:* Alan Silvestri. Golden Raspberry Awards '88: Worst Director (Raffill). **VHS, Beta, LV** *ORI*

Mad Doctor of Blood Island

The second of the Philippine-made Blood Island Trilogy. In this sequel to *Brides of Blood*, former teen idol John Ashley (*Frankenstein's Daughter, Beach Party*) returns to Blood Island and encounters an ugly chlorophyll monster created by Dr. Lorca (Ronald Remy), which survived for *Beast of Blood*. After Ashley's acting and recording career in the U.S. wound down, he came to the Philippines to star in the Blood Island pictures, then stayed to act in and produce a string of exploitation features. Costar Angelique Pettyjohn was a Playboy centerfold and acted in several features (*Biohazard, Repo Man*), as well as starring in porn under the name Heaven St. John. Audiences were given vials of "green blood" as a gimmick/souvenir/snack. **AKA:** Tomb of the Living Dead; Blood Doctor. ⚔️⚔️🕊️

1969 110m/C John Ashley, Angelique Pettyjohn, Ronald Remy; *D:* Gerardo (Gerry) De Leon. **VHS, Beta** *NO*

Mad Max

First entry in the post-nuclear supercharged George Miller-directed trilogy which features Mel Gibson as the gung-ho super-cop Max. Leather-punk rebel bikers have nothing better to do than roam the desolate wasteland, chasing and being chased by police who are guarding the remnants of civilization. When his best-buddy fellow cop is killed, Max calls it quits and takes off cross country with the family. But boozin', brawlin', brain-bustin' punks with really fast vehicles are hard to lose, even if they're born to lose, and the wife and kid get it. Now Max is Mad and out for revenge using the last of the big engine squad cars in vicious, savage-energy death chases and violent crashes. Those crazy stunt guys. Followed by *The Road Warrior* (also known as *Mad Max 2*) in 1981, and *Mad Max: Beyond Thunderdome* in 1985. American release has dubbed voices because of the Australian accents, although the newer letterboxed laserdisc has at least Gibson's voice back in place. Spectacular chase scenes and excellent stunt work make this an exceptionally entertaining action adventure. ⚔️⚔️⚔️🕊️

"People don't believe in heroes anymore."

—Fifi Macaffee (Roger Ward) in *Mad Max.*

(George Ogilvie is listed as co-director) and Gibson reportedly wanted a "much more human story" and not a "reworking of *The Road Warrior*." Therefore, dumped-in-the-desert Max is rescued by a band of feral orphans who have survived the dimly remembered nuclear holocaust and believe that Max is their prophesized savior. Interesting concept, but not enough killer cars or Millerian high-energy sped-up death chases. 🦴🦴🐾

1985 (PG-13) 107m/C *AU* Mel Gibson, Tina Turner, Helen Buday, Frank Thring Jr., Bruce Spence, Robert Grubb, Angelo Rossitto, Angry Anderson, George Spartels, Rod Zuanic; *D:* George Miller, George Ogilvie; *W:* George Miller, Terry Hayes; *C:* Dean Semler; *M:* Maurice Jarre. **VHS, Beta, LV, 8mm** *WAR*

Magic Serpent

A fantasy set in medieval Japan about an abducted prince who must regain his throne from a treacherous sorcerer. Fortunately, the prince was raised by a good wizard, who taught him neat tricks like how to confuse enemies by separating his head from his body. The tale climaxes with a grand duel of magic between the heroic prince and the sorcerer, who transform into a dragon and a giant frog-monster for a battle royal. The heroine helps out with a magic brooch that turns into a gigantic flying spider. The film drags a bit in the middle, but otherwise is an excellent fantasy adventure, especially fun for samurai-film buffs. George Lucas claimed that this movie was a major influence on *Star Wars*. 🦴🦴🦴🐾

1966 ?m/C Hiroki Matsukata, Tomoko Ogawa, Ryutaro Otomo, Bin Amatsu; *D:* Tetsuya Yamauchi. **VHS** *SMW*

Making Contact

Oddball German production is one long tribute/ripoff of the imagery of George Lucas and Steven Spielberg. Joey (pic's original title), a sci-fi obsessed small boy with a pet R2D2 robot, is assailed by poltergeists—something to do with his deceased father and a malevolent ventriloquist's dummy. Can his souvenir Jedi window curtains save him? How about his E.T. drinking glass? Harmless but annoying unoriginal, this celluloid fan letter is a telling footnote in the career of Roland Emmerich,

Mel Gibson struggles to maintain eye contact with the gifted Tina Turner in *Mad Max: Beyond Thunderdome.*

1980 (R) 93m/C *AU* Mel Gibson, Joanne Samuel, Hugh Keays-Byrne, Steve Bisley, Tim Burns, Roger Ward; *D:* George Miller; *W:* James McCausland, George Miller; *C:* David Eggby. **VHS, Beta, LV** *LIV, VES*

Mad Max: Beyond Thunderdome

Third and final episode in the Mad Max trilogy has Max (Mel Gibson) drifting into a nasty methane-fueled Bartertown (pig slop abounds) ruled by Auntie Entity (Tina Turner), an evil over-sexed dominatrix type lookin' for love and more power from Max. Disputes are settled in the Thunderdome, gladiator style, and Max has a go-at-it with the Blaster, an iron-clad behemoth with the required more-brawn-than-brains ratio needed for the smaller Max's victory to be believable. Spears, maces, spikes, and even chainsaws are all used while the opponents are tethered from the top of the Thunderdome. Oh, the only rule is: "Two men enter. One man leaves." All this makes for a pretty exciting, gritty, violent fight. After leaving the Thunderdome the movie goes downhill as both director George Miller

who later indeed reached Hollywood and helmed genre blockbusters like *StarGate* and *Independence Day.* 🎬🎬

1986 (PG) 83m/C Joshua Morrell, Eve Kryll; ***D:*** Roland Emmerich; ***W:*** Hans J. Haller, Thomas Lechner, Roland Emmerich; ***M:*** Paul Gilreath. **VHS, Beta** *NWV, VTR*

Making Mr. Right

Despite an inspired performance from Ann Magnuson as an "image consultant," Susan Seidelman's off-beat satire is never as funny or as enjoyable as it ought to be. The most promising elements of the plot aren't developed while the most irritating run amok. John Malkovich plays the dual role of a scientist and his innocent robot creation. The unbalanced film begins as *Splash* with the sexes reversed, wanders into social satire for a time, and almost becomes a bedroom farce before it sputters to an unconvincing conclusion. 🎬🎬

1986 (PG-13) 95m/C John Malkovich, Ann Magnuson, Glenne Headly, Ben Masters, Laurie Metcalf, Polly Bergen, Hart Bochner, Polly Draper, Susan Anton; ***D:*** Susan Seidelman; ***W:*** Laurie Frank, Floyd Byars; ***C:*** Edward Lachman. **VHS, Beta, LV** *HBO*

A Man Called Rage

Rage is the only man capable of safely escorting a group of pioneers through a nuclear wasteland infested with mutants and cannibals. **WOOF!**

1984 90m/C *IT* Stelio Candelli, Conrad Nichols; ***D:*** Anthony Richmond. **VHS, Beta** *LIV*

The Man from Atlantis

Patrick Duffy stars as the water-breathing alien who emerges from his undersea home, the Lost City of Atlantis. The made-for-TV movie led to a brief television series. 🎬🎬

1977 60m/C Patrick Duffy, Belinda J. Montgomery, Victor Buono; ***D:*** Lee H. Katzin. **VHS, Beta** *WOV*

Man Made Monster

Lon Chaney stars as carnival performer "Dynamo" Dan McCormick, whose act has caused Dan to build up an immunity to electrical charges. Dan falls prey to the mad Dr. Rigas (Lionel Atwill) who seeks to create a race of electro-men who'll do his bidding. Experiments on the hapless Dan turn him into a glowing monster whose very touch can kill. Lackluster script is pepped up by good handling of atmosphere by director George Waggner. Chaney's first role in the horror genre led to Universal's casting him in *The Wolf Man* and *The Ghost of Frankenstein*. At first attempting to avoid comparison with his superstar father, Chaney originally appeared using his real name, Creighton. But it seemed inevitable that Universal would cash in on the connection for the revival of their popular horror film series. 🎬🎬🎬

1941 61m/B Lon Chaney Jr., Lionel Atwill, Anne Nagel, Frank Albertson, Samuel S. Hinds; ***D:*** George Waggner; ***W:*** Joseph West. **VHS** *MCA*

The Man They Could Not Hang

A good doctor tinkering with artificial hearts is caught by police while experimenting on a willing student. When the doctor is convicted and hanged for a murder, his assistant uses the heart to bring him back to life. No longer a nice guy, he vows revenge against the jurors that sentenced him. Boris Karloff repeated the same story line in several films (three of them directed by Nick Grinde), and this one is representative of the type. 🎬🎬🎬

1939 70m/B Boris Karloff, Lorna Gray, Roger Pryor, Robert Wilcox, Don Beddoe, Ann Doran; ***D:*** Nick Grinde; ***W:*** Karl Brown; ***C:*** Benjamin Kline. **VHS, Beta** *GKK*

The Man Who Fell to Earth

Enigmatic, visionary cult pic about a man from another planet (David Bowie, in a bit of typecasting) who ventures to Earth in hopes of finding water to save his drought-stricken planet. Instead he becomes a successful American inventor and businessman, discovering the human vices of booze, sex, TV, and apathy. Full of eccentric performances and odd moments that seem to portend non-linear timelines and parallel universes. Based on the relatively straightforward Walter Tevis novel, but with an apparent influence from Robert Heinlein's *Stranger in a Strange Land* (an oft-discussed and oft-aborted film project itself). Also available in a considerably better

> "You know, it's a curious fact that ever since my earliest experiments with rabbits and guinea pigs, I always found the female of the species was more sensitive to electrical impulse than the male."
>
> —Lionel Atwill's pickup line to Anne Nagel in *Man Made Monster.*

images of Lincoln are repeated in the background.) The attitudes on sex and race are equally avant-garde. It's also a bitter satire on the naivete and machinations of the left and right. Excellent performances by an all-star cast, with Angela Lansbury, James Gregory, Henry Silva, and Khigh Deigh particularly delicious as the villains. But Laurence Harvey is the real star, and his performance becomes more impressive with repeated viewings. He gives his Raymond Shaw character the emotional depth of a true tragic hero and easily overshadows co-star Frank Sinatra. In many ways, this film was the high-water mark for everyone involved—the cast, director John Frankenheimer, writer/producer George Axelrod, even novelist Richard Condon. Though they've all done fine work since, none has approached this level. Tape features a special interview with Sinatra and Frankenheimer in which Sinatra is deified. 🦴🦴🦴🦴

1962 126m/B Frank Sinatra, Laurence Harvey, Angela Lansbury, Janet Leigh, James Gregory, Leslie Parrish, John McGiver, Henry Silva, Khigh Deigh; **D:** John Frankenheimer; **W:** George Axelrod, John Frankenheimer; **M:** David Amram. Golden Globe Awards '63: Best Supporting Actress (Lansbury); National Board of Review Awards '62: Best Supporting Actress (Lansbury); Nominations: Academy Awards '62: Best Film Editing, Best Supporting Actress (Lansbury). **VHS, Beta, LV** *MGM*

Mandroid

An uneasy coalition of East- and West-Bloc scientists use a mighty remote-controlled robot, Mandroid, to handle Supercon, a powerful new element they've discovered. Sinister Dr. Drago steals Mandroid to put his evil plans for power into action, but becomes horribly disfigured and insane. Comic-bookish diversion from producer Charles Band, shot on location in Romania. Okay if you don't expect profundities. Sequelized by *Invisible: The Chronicles of Benjamin Knight.* 🦴🦴

1993 (R) 81m/C Brian Cousins, Jane Caldwell, Michael DellaFemina, Curt Lowens, Patrick Ersgard, Robert Symonds; **D:** Joakim Ersgard; **W:** Jackson Barr, Earl Kenton. **VHS, Beta** *PAR*

The Manhattan Project

For a science fair, a high-school genius builds a functional nuclear bomb, complete with plu-

"Are you sure you can swim the race in those snug trunks?" A skeptical Pat Morita to the pre-*Dallas* Patrick Duffy in **The Man from Atlantis.**

restored version at 138 minutes. Remade for television in 1987. 🦴🦴🦴

1976 (R) 118m/C *GB* David Bowie, Candy Clark, Rip Torn, Buck Henry, Bernie Casey; **D:** Nicolas Roeg. **VHS, Beta, LV** *COL*

The Manchurian Candidate

Perhaps the best political thriller of the 1960s is still sharp and shocking today, and tons of fun to watch. Tells the story of an American Korean War vet who suspects that he and his platoon may have been brainwashed during the war, with his highly decorated, heroic friend programmed by commies to be an operational assassin. The film was years ahead of its time in the amount of visual information that's packed into the screen. (Notice the way

tonium swiped from a government lab, and a manhunt (or kidhunt) begins. John Lithgow is excellent as a flippant weapons scientist who belatedly realizes the destructive power held by a mere boy—and, by extension, anyone with nukes. Teen technothriller has a splendid concept (far better than *My Science Project*) but after raising viewer expectations, is disarmed by way too many plot implausibilities. Director Marshall Brickman co-wrote Woody Allen's similarly titled but ever-so-unrelated *Manhattan*. **AKA:** Manhattan Project: The Deadly Game. 🦴🦴

1985 (PG-13) 112m/C John Lithgow, Christopher Collet, Cynthia Nixon, Jill Eikenberry, John Mahoney, Sully Boyer, Richard Council, Robert Schenkkan, Paul Austin; **D:** Marshall Brickman; **W:** Marshall Brickman, Thomas Baum; **C:** Billy Williams; **M:** Philippe Sarde. **VHS, Beta, LV** REP

Manhunt of Mystery Island

Serial about the super-powered Captain Mephisto. **AKA:** Captain Mephisto and the Transformation Machine. 🦴🦴

1945 100m/C Linda Stirling, Roy Barcroft, Richard Bailey, Kenne Duncan; **D:** Spencer Gordon Bennet. **VHS, Beta, LV** MED, MLB

Maniac Warriors

A nuclear apocalypse has caused some strange changes in the population—and not for the better. Blood-crazed mutants attack the heavily armed inhabitants of New State Idaho and there's lots of mayhem in store. 🦴

199? 91m/C Tom Schioler, John Wood, Melanie Kilgour. **VHS** AIP, MOV

The Manster

Another masterpiece from the director who brought us *Monster from Green Hell*. An American journalist (Peter Dyneley) is sent to interview an eccentric scientist in Japan. Unfortunately, his host's work is not likely to receive the Nobel Peace Prize; his former wife is now a gibbering monster locked in a cage and he had to shoot a former patient after the poor guy went ape—literally. Undaunted by these past failures, the doc gives the journalist a mysterious potion that causes him to begin giving in to his animal desires—he neglects his wife, fools around with geisha after geisha, and begins drinking heavily. After a while it gets worse; he sprouts unsightly hair and an extra head that looks like a mutant coconut. Driven by his less-than-better half, he goes on a murderous rampage until, in a rather startling scene he literally splits in two and has to confront his savage alter ego. Fans of Japanese monster-films might be surprised to find the characters' lips moving in synch with the dialogue in this under-rated specimen. **AKA:** The Manster—Half Man, Half Monster; The Split. 🦴🦴

1959 72m/B JP Peter Dyneley, Jane Hylton, Satoshi Nakamura, Terri Zimmern; **D:** Kenneth Crane, George Breakston. **VHS** SNC, MRV

Marooned

Three-man team of American astronauts are stranded in orbit 200 miles above Earth when their ship engines fail, but it's a deadly 200 miles if Yankee ingenuity cannot launch a rescue mission in time. Try desperately to care in this overlong film when James Franciscus looks out a spaceport at a rather fetching painting of Mother Earth and announces "So beautiful...so beautiful" in a quavering voice as his oxygen fails. Enjoy the Oscar-winning special f/x. 🦴🦴

1969 (G) 134m/C Gregory Peck, David Janssen, Richard Crenna, James Franciscus, Gene Hackman, Lee Grant; **D:** John Sturges; **W:** Mayo Simon. Academy Awards '69: Best Visual Effects; Nominations: Academy Awards '69: Best Cinematography, Best Sound. **VHS, Beta, LV** GKK

Mars Needs Women

So, who doesn't? From the director of *Zontar, the Thing from Venus* comes one of the classic golden turkeys of all time. Former Disney kid Tommy Kirk virtually reprises his character from *Pajama Party* as Dop, the leader of a Martian advance team looking for Earth women with whom to repopulate their planet. Yvonne Craig, best known as Batgirl, stars as Pulitzer Prize-winner Dr. Marjorie Bolen, our foremost expert on extraterrestrial reproduction. A Martian fashion tip: they "abandoned neckties 50 years ago as foolish vanity." What did you expect from the title; *2001*? 🦴

1966 80m/C Tommy Kirk, Yvonne Craig, Byron Lord, Roger Ready, Warren Hammack; **D:** Larry Buchanan; **W:** Larry Buchanan; **C:** Robert C. Jessup. **VHS** SNC

"They could lock you in a room...and throw the room away."

—John Lithgow to Christopher Collet in *The Manhattan Project*.

Mars: Planet Hollywood?

Abbott and Costello Go to Mars

Aelita: Queen of Mars

Angry Red Planet

Bad Girls from Mars

D-Day on Mars

Devil Girl from Mars

Flash Gordon: Mars Attacks the World

Flying Discman from Mars

Horrors of the Red Planet

Invaders from Mars

Lobster Man from Mars

Mars Needs Women

The Martian Chronicles

Mission Mars

Oversexed Rugsuckers from Mars

Planet of Blood

Red Planet Mars

Robinson Crusoe on Mars

Santa Claus Conquers the Martians

The Martian Chronicles: Part 1

Hollywood had long planned to film Ray Bradbury's 1950 collection of interlinked vignettes about mankind's exploration and tentative conquest of the planet Mars, but this limping network TV miniseries (marketed on tape as three separate 90-minute episodes) is a disappointment, with flimsy f/x, weak dialogue, and very sparse doses of Bradbury's trademark lyricism surviving Richard Matheson's script. First cassette, "The Expeditions," depicts first three manned NASA expeditions to Mars, and the humans' often fatal reception at the hands of the placidly mystical Martians.

As in the book, Mars—here impersonated by the islands of Malta and Lanzarote—is less a scientific reality than a place of dreams, yearning and nostalgia. Maybe that's why production values are on par with *Fantasy Island*. 🦴🦴

1979 120m/C Rock Hudson, Bernie Casey, Nicholas Hammond, Darren McGavin; **D:** Michael Anderson Sr.; **W:** Richard Matheson. **VHS, Beta** *FRH*

The Martian Chronicles: Part 2

Middle installment of the weak network TV miniseries based on Ray Bradbury's book. In a segment called "The Settlers," humans flock from a strife-torn Earth to Mars in droves after disease apparently wipes out the ancient and inscrutable Martian civilization. Some colonists still wish to meet the creatures, like NASA colonel Rock Hudson and priest Fritz Weaver, the latter in a very clunky adaptation of "The Fire Balloons" (a Bradbury story actually from his *Illustrated Man* collection, but published in a few editions of *The Martian Chronicles* as well). The drama improves considerably with the introduction of a shape-shifting Martian whose unfortunate fate is to conform to human brain waves, like it or not. 🦴🦴

1979 97m/C Rock Hudson, Fritz Weaver, Roddy McDowall, Bernie Casey, Darren McGavin, Gayle Hunnicutt, Barry Morse, Bernadette Peters; **D:** Michael Anderson Sr.; **W:** Richard Matheson. **VHS, Beta** *FRH*

The Martian Chronicles: Part 3

Subtitled "The Martians," this final chapter of the Ray Bradbury adaptation manages to pull various story threads together, but purists will still simmer at the liberties taken with a classic book—like casting luscious Bernadette Peters as a character who on paper was grossly fat and unattractive. After one of Hollywood's cheaper nuclear holocausts engulfs Earth, a handful of lonely human remnants languish on an abandoned Mars, until Rock Hudson and his family finally figure out how the planet holds the secret of mankind's destiny. 🦴🦴

1979 97m/C Rock Hudson, Bernadette Peters, Christopher Connelly, Fritz Weaver, Roddy McDowall, Bernie Casey, Nicholas Hammond, Darren McGavin, Gayle Hunnicutt, Barry Morse; **D:** Michael Anderson Sr.; **W:** Richard Matheson. **VHS, Beta** *FRH*

TV on Tape:
Max Headroom

In 1984 Britain's Channel 4 wanted to create an innovative music video/interview program and came up with the idea of TV's first cyberpunk, with a computer-generated head-with-an-attitude as its host.

A pilot, "Rebus: The Max Headroom Story," explained the character's background; although computer graphics were heavily featured, "Max" was not an actual computer image but heavily made-up actor Matt Frewer.

In 1987, Lorimar acquired the U.S. rights, redid the pilot, and premiered the series (for one season). The series' tagline, "twenty minutes into the future," found a world where TV ruled (in fact, it was illegal to turn it off) and ratings and advertisers were in control. The show's hero was intrepid Network 23 reporter Edison Carter (Matt Frewer), who exposed corruption thanks to a minicam and simultaneous live, global network coverage.

When Carter is seriously injured for getting too close to network secrets, his memories are downloaded by teenaged computer nerd/genius and network R&D head, Bryce Lynch (Chris Young), into a special program that has "people trans-lated as data." Naturally, Edison Carter survives and now has a computer alter ego. But Bryce only had enough memory to generate a head, and Max (who took his name from the last thing Carter saw—a sign reading "Max Headroom") is born—complete with maniacal stutter and sarcasm to spare.

Max wanders, uncontrollable, throughout Network 23's vast computer system, popping up unexpectedly to insult advertisers, interrupt program-ming, and garner great ratings.

Unfortunately, the quirky series didn't do the same, and lasted but 14 episodes—although Max did became a successful huckster for Coca-Cola. Only the pilot episode is currently available on video.

1987-88/C *Selected cast:* Matt Frewer, Chris Lynch, Nickolas Grace, Hilary Tindall, Amanda Pays, Rocky Morton, Annabel Jankel. **VHS, LV** *LHV, WAR*

Martians Go Home!

Joke-loving Martians come to Earth and pester a nerdy composer. 🦴🦴
1990 (PG-13) 89m/C Randy Quaid, Margaret Colin, Anita Morris, John Philbin, Ronny Cox, Gerrit Graham, Barry Sobel, Vic Dunlop; **D:** David Odell. **VHS, Beta, LV** *NO*

The Mask of Fu Manchu

The original, and many feel the best Fu Manchu movie. The evil Dr. Fu (played here by Boris Karloff) and his equally evil daughter (Myrna Loy) set out to capture the scimitar and golden mask of Genghis Khan. With them (and the help of a somewhat more up-to-date death ray) they will be able to destroy the white race and rule the world. Although Scotland Yard detective Nayland Smith tries his best to stop them, the pair get the treasures and several prisoners in their evil clutches. Tortures follow. Can Fu be stopped before he carries out his evil plans? Can the world be made safe for the white race? Even though its portrayal of Asians seems offensive today, this is still an exciting, creepy movie with killer performances by Karloff and Loy. Like the '60s Fu movies, which starred Christopher Lee, this film was based on the series of novels by Sax Rohmer. 🦴🦴🦴🦴
1932 72m/B Boris Karloff, Lewis Stone, Karen Morley, Charles Starrett, Myrna Loy, Jean Hersholt, Lawrence Grant, David Torrence; **D:** Charles Brabin, Charles Vidor; **W:** Irene Kuhn, Edgar Allen Woolf; **C:** Gaetano Antonio "Tony" Gaudio. **VHS** *MGM*

Master of the World

This charming aerial version of *20,000*

"Are you even *listening?* Rock Hudson and an earless alien in *The Martian Chronicles.*

1961 95m/**C** Vincent Price, Charles Bronson, Henry Hull; **D:** William Witney; **W:** Richard Matheson; **M:** Les Baxter. **VHS, Beta** *ORI, WAR*

Masters of the Universe

A big-budget live-action version of the cartoon character's adventures, with He-Man battling Skeletor for the sake of the universe. Though audiences were ready to laugh off this feature based on characters that originally appeared as toys, contributions by the talented cast and crew managed to turn things in their favor, resulting in a fairly decent fantasy adventure film. The saving grace was probably the idea of bringing the fantasy characters into our world, sustaining audience interest in watching the two worlds react to each other. 🦴🦴

1987 (PG) 109m/**C** Dolph Lundgren, Frank Langella, Billy Barty, Courteney Cox, Meg Foster; **D:** Gary Goddard; **M:** Bill Conti. **VHS, Beta, LV** *WAR*

Meet the Hollowheads

Futuristic sitcom-style family have Dad's boss over for dinner in hopes of securing that promotion that he so richly deserves. Slicing off a chunk of some prime-tentacle from the kitchen's living food supply, Mom cooks up a sickly gourmet delight, but the guest of honor has something else of her's in mind. Juliette Lewis starts to show her one-sided acting talents as the dysfunctional daughter. Trying to be one of those entertainingly weird alternative-world grossout comedies, it almost succeeds, but most of the cast seems a little uncomfortable, and the whole thing has been done better (*The Dark Backward* for example). 🦴🦴

1989 (PG-13) 89m/**C** John Glover, Nancy Mette, Richard Portnow, Matt Shakman, Juliette Lewis, Anne Ramsey; **D:** Tom Burman; **W:** Tom Burman. **VHS, LV** *MED, IME*

Leagues Under the Sea is actually based on two Jules Verne novels, *Clipper of the Clouds* (known in America as *Robur the Conqueror*), and *Master of the World.* Vincent Price plays Robur, a fanatical-but-genius-type 19th-century inventor who flies his incredible fortress, the Albatross, around the world attacking only men and weapons of war, unless someone else gets in the way. Charles Bronson, whose began his career in Price's horror classic *House of Wax,* is the government agent trying to stop the moral(?) killing. American International spent a lot on this one and it shows. Richard Matheson's entertaining screenplay cohesively merges the two novels and Lex Baxter's score is what adventure music should be. Also available letterboxed on laserdisc. 🦴🦴🦴

Megaforce

Futuristic thriller directed by stuntman Hal Needham follows the adventures of the military task force, Megaforce, on its mission to save a small democratic nation from attack. Barry Bostwick leads the attack. 'Nuff said. **WOOF!**

1982 (PG) 99m/C Barry Bostwick, Persis Khambatta, Edward Mulhare, Henry Silva, Michael Beck, Ralph Wilcox; **D:** Hal Needham. **VHS, Beta** *FOX*

Megaville

Unfairly ignored cyberpunk noir, set in an Orwellian not-too-distant future. Decrepit dictator Daniel J. Travanti dispatches a hitman with a defective memory chip in his head to Megaville, ostensibly to stop the smuggling of the virtual-reality drug "Dream-a-Life." But there's something fishy about the mission that our brainwashed protagonist isn't being told. Count yourself lucky if you can follow all of the plot in one sitting, but the knowing references to genre faves, from *Alphaville* to *Total Recall* and beyond, make this an undiscovered (if downbeat) treat for buffs. 🦴🦴🦴

1991 (R) 96m/C Billy Zane, Daniel J. Travanti, J.C. Quinn, Grace Zabriskie, Kristen Cloke, Stefan Gierasch; **D:** Peter Lehner; **W:** Peter Lehner; **C:** Zoltan David; **M:** Stacy Widelitz. **VHS** *LIV*

Memoirs of an Invisible Man

Nick Halloway (Chevy Chase), a slick and shallow stock analyst, is rendered invisible by a freak accident. When he is pursued by a CIA agent/hit man who wants to exploit him, Nick turns for help to Alice (Daryl Hannah), a documentary filmmaker he has just met. Naturally, they fall in love along the way. There are some effective sight gags, but the hardworking cast can't overcome pitfalls in the script, which indecisively meanders between comedy and thrills. Entertaining for a dull Saturday night, but it lacks the focus of director John Carpenter's much better horror films. 🦴🦴

1992 (PG-13) 99m/C Chevy Chase, Daryl Hannah, Sam Neill, Michael McKean, Stephen Tobolowsky, Jim Norton, Patricia Heaton, Rosalind Chao; **D:** John Carpenter; **W:** Robert Collector. **VHS, LV** *WAR*

Mesa of Lost Women

A madder-than-usual mad scientist, played by none other than *Addams Family* regular Jackie "Uncle Fester" Coogan, cloisters himself on a remote Mexican mesa. Here he creates a giant tarantula and a brave new race of vicious women with long fingernails...and that's pretty much it. This is one of those "bad" films that's SO bad it can't even properly be called a B picture; a "wanna-B" is more like it. Trailers for the film showed one of the "Lost Women" glowering with psychotic sultriness at the camera, while a voice asks the puzzling question "Have you ever been kissed by a woman like this"? **AKA:** Lost Women; Lost Women of Zarpa.

1952 70m/B Jackie Coogan, Richard Travis, Allan Nixon, Mary Hill, Robert Knapp, Tandra Quinn, Lyle Talbot, Katherine Victor, Angelo Rossitto; **D:** Herbert Tevos, Ron Ormond; **W:** Herbert Tevos; **C:** Gilbert Warrenton, Karl Struss. **VHS** *NOS, MRV, SNC*

Messengers of Destiny

UFOlogists know the significance of July 11, 1991. The solar eclipsed prophesied by Mayan priests in 755 C.E. ushered in a wave of UFO sightings over Mexico City that were videotaped by so many people that even *A Current Affair* has covered it. The sightings continue to the point of being considered normal and everyday occurrences by the residents. In addition to the video footage, this tape also follows an international team of UFO investigators as they track the sightings and attempt to correlate the event(s) to the ancient prophecies. Aren't we all ready for the coming Earth changes and cosmic awareness? Watch it! 🦴🦴🦴🦴

1992 75m/C W: Brit Elders, Lee Elders; **M:** Devi De Lavie. **VHS** *UFO*

Metallica

Alien warmongers endeavor to conquer Earth and scientists try to stop them. Been there, done that, on to next video. 🦴

1985 90m/C Anthony Newcastle, Sharon Baker; **D:** Al Bradley. **VHS, Beta** *NO*

Metalstorm: The Destruction of Jared Syn

The last time we saw Lemuria it was a legendary continent between Australia and Africa, populated by creatures of myth and Ray Harryhausen's Sinbad. Well, it didn't do the Atlantean sink thing, it became a stark

> "It's lonely,
> isn't it, when
> you're a freak?"
>
> —CIA agent (Sam Neill) to Nick
> Halloway (Chevy Chase) in
> *Memoirs of an Invisible Man.*

"This is not the beginning of the end...it is the end of the beginning."

—Sherman the Robot (Robert Joy) in *Millenium*.

desert island planet, controlled by the evil intergalactic magician Jared Syn. Syn and his army of Cyclops have created deadly forbidden zones, killing and enslaving for the purpose of sacrifice to their life-giving crystal. Enter Dogen, a peacekeeping ranger, who enlists the aid of Rhodes (Tim Thomerson—*Trancers*'s Jack Deth) and the ex-enemy cyclopean warlord Hurok (Richard Moll). Strange combination of sorcery and space jockeys is actually quite entertaining with more than adequate special effects. Sacrifice-wanna-be Dhyanais is played by Kelly Preston, in her first billed role. 🦴🦴

1983 (PG) 84m/C Jeffrey Byron, Mike Preston, Tim Thomerson, Kelly Preston, Richard Moll; ***D:*** Charles Band; ***W:*** Alan J. Adler; ***M:*** Richard Band. **VHS, Beta, LV** *MCA*

Metamorphosis

Italian-made familiarity about a novice scientist using himself as the guinea pig for his anti-aging experiments (injecting in the eyeball, for your viewing pleasure). He suffers monster side-effects of a serum brewed from reptile DNA, though there's a cute twist ending if you can last that long. Loses half a bone for the agony inflicted on helpless video-store clerks by the original cassette box, which had an annoying electronic buzzer emitting a spooky "woo-woo" tremolo whenever customers pressed the button. Good luck finding a copy today—undamaged. 🦴

1990 (R) 90m/C Gene Le Brock, Catherine Baranov, Stephen Brown, Harry Cason, Jason Arnold; ***D:*** G.L. Eastman. **VHS, Beta** *IMP, VMK*

Meteor

American and Soviet scientists attempt to save the Earth from a fast-approaching barrage of meteors from space (with their big daddy on its way) in this disaster dud. Destruction ravages parts of Hong Kong, the Big Apple, and other areas of the world, allowing producer Irwin Allen to incorporate scenes from other movies. Big-name actors do their professional best, but they all seem rather embarrassed by the big flooding of New York climax, which was included for no other reason than to get them personally involved in the crisis. Good for a laugh, and for a few nice effects scenes. 🦴

1979 (PG) 107m/C Sean Connery, Natalie Wood, Karl Malden, Brian Keith, Martin Landau, Trevor Howard, Henry Fonda, Joseph Campanella, Richard Dysart; ***D:*** Ronald Neame. Nominations: Academy Awards '79: Best Sound. **VHS, Beta, LV** *WAR, OM*

The Meteor Man

Robert Townsend is a school teacher who becomes a reluctant superhero after being socked in the gut by a meteor. As "Meteor Man," Townsend flies only four feet off the ground (he's afraid of heights) and wears costumes fashioned for him by his mother. An excellent, good-natured satire on superhero movies with a strong pro-community message. James Earl Jones has what may be the most unusual role of his career as Townsend's eccentric neighbor (who's constantly changing his hairstyle). Includes some fine cameos by Sinbad, Luther Vandross, Lawanda Page, and Bill Cosby as a wise street-person. 🦴🦴🦴

1993 (PG) 100m/C Robert Townsend, Robert Guillaume, Marla Gibbs, James Earl Jones, Frank Gorshin; ***Cameos:*** Bill Cosby, Sinbad, Luther Vandross, LaWanda Page; ***D:*** Robert Townsend; ***W:*** Robert Townsend; ***C:*** John A. Alonzo. **VHS, LV** *MGM*

Meteor Monster

A young boy is hit by a meteor and grows up to be a raving, hair-covered maniac. His mom tries to keep him a secret, but has little success. One of those movies that feels like it was built purely around budget. Since Western sets and costumes were available, they made it a Western. Even though the "monster" is just a big ugly guy with mental problems, they threw in a meteor and sold it as science fiction, which was hot at the box office at the time. Director Jacques Marquette was better known as a cinematographer, notably for Corman's *A Bucket of Blood*. Probably the last leading role for Anne Gwynne, a familiar face in Universal horror films of the '40s. She was last seen in a small role in *Adam at 6 A.M.* (1970). **AKA:** Teenage Monster.

1957 73m/C Anne Gwynne, Stuart Wade, Gloria Castillo, Chuck Courtney; ***D:*** Jacques Marquette. **VHS, Beta** *SNC*

Metropolis

Classic meditation on technology and mass mentality, about the mechanized society of 2000 A.D. where workers are trudging drones on constant duty underground, as upper classes dwell in splendor and decadence on the surface. Then the son of an elite leader falls for a prominent worker chick. Disapproving dad commissions an evil android duplicate of the girl to incite the workers into doomed revolt. Part fairy tale, part allegory of Capital and Labor, so politically simplistic it had admirers simultaneously in the Reichstag and the Kremlin; all inspired by German director Fritz Lang's awestruck first sight of Manhattan by night. Outstanding set designs, colossal crowd shots, and still-striking f/x made this innovative and influential, though the silent-mime style of acting badly dates the material. True landmark of the genre, and generally held to be the first sf screen epic. Certainly set a trend by nearly ruining the German UFA studios, who spent about six million marks on its cost (and the red ink continues: a recent British stage musical version was a mammoth flop). Foreign export re-edits and the loss of the original negative in WWII means that various versions circulate on video and laserdisc. The 1984 re-release features some color tinting, partial reconstructions of long-lost sequences, sound effects, and a controversial rock score with songs by Pat Benatar, Bonnie Tyler, Giorgio Moroder, and Queen. A special treat for completists: the little-known, recently republished novelization by Lang's then-wife and screenwriter Thea von Harbou, which fills in the gaps between title-cards. 🎭🎭🎭🎭

1926 115m/B *GE* Brigitte Helm, Alfred Abel, Gustav Froehlich, Rudolf Klein-Rogge, Fritz Rasp, Heinrich George; *D:* Fritz Lang; *W:* Fritz Lang, Thea von Harbou; *C:* Gunther Rittau, Karl Freund. **VHS, Beta, LV** *SNC, NOS, MRV*

Midnight Movie Massacre

Retro splatterama has really gross alien land outside a movie theater in 1956, and the really weird movie patrons try to terminate it. 🎭🎭🎭

1988 86m/C Robert Clarke, Ann Robinson; *D:* Mark Stock. **VHS** *NO*

Mighty Joe Young

Tongue-in-cheek King Kong variation features giant ape brought to civilization and exploited in a nightclub act, whereupon things get darned ugly. Bullied and given the key to the liquor cabinet, mild-mannered Joe goes on a drunken rampage, but eventually redeems himself by rescuing orphans from a fire. Robert Armstrong recreates his *Kong* persona as the hard-nosed promoter—it may be that audiences were expected to think he may have been the same guy with a new name. Special effects (courtesy of Willis O'Brien and the great Ray Harryhausen) are probably the film's greatest asset. Newly restored prints recreate the tinting used in the films fiery climax. Also available colorized. 🎭🎭🎭

1949 94m/B Terry Moore, Ben Johnson, Robert Armstrong, Frank McHugh; *D:* Ernest B. Schoedsack. Academy Awards '49: Best Special Effects. **VHS, Beta, LV** *TTC*

Millenium

A Federal Aviation Agency investigator finds temporal anomalies at plane crashes and is haunted by mystery woman Cheryl Ladd. It seems Earth's people 1,000 years from now are sterile and rotting. To keep humanity alive they send time-travel squads back to yank fresh, untainted people off doomed airliners, thus skirting apocalyptic time paradoxes—until Kris Kristofferson and Daniel J. Travanti begin putting the pieces together. John Varley's source novel (an expansion of his superior short story "Air Raid") was so frazzled it required a cameo by God to sort things out. This Canadian adaptation has no such luck, and warps unsteadily between the serious premise and mere camp (much of the latter provided by a sarcastic robot). Good special effects. 🎭🎭

1989 (PG-13) 108m/C *CA* Kris Kristofferson, Cheryl Ladd, Daniel J. Travanti, Lloyd Bochner, Robert Joy, Brent Carver, Maury Chaykin, David McIlwraith, Al Waxman; *D:* Michael Anderson Sr.; *W:* John Varley; *C:* Rene Ohashi; *M:* Eric N. Robertson. **VHS, Beta, LV** *CCB*

Mind Snatchers

An American G.I. becomes involved in U.S. Army experimental psychological brain opera-

> "It's too bad you're so pretty...but you won't be pretty for long."
>
> —Cornelia (Elizabeth Kent) to Judy (Marta Alicia) in *Mindwarp*.

tions when he is brought into a western European hospital for treatment. **AKA:** The Happiness Cage. 🐾🐾📼

1972 (PG) 94m/C Christopher Walken, Ronny Cox, Ralph Meeker, Joss Ackland; **D:** Bernard Girard. **VHS, Beta** *PSM*

Mindwarp

When Judy (Marta Alicia) rebels against the Sysop and goes offline from the "The Happiness System" (brought to us by Infinisynth), she actually uses the line "There's no place like home" when she teams up with Stover (Bruce Campbell) to battle the mutant monsters (who all look like the Toxic Avenger but with a lot less imagination) of the outside world. Campbell plays the straight hero he consistently spoofs in all of his better parts (*Thou Shalt Not Kill...Except, Army of Darkness, Evil Dead 1 & 2*); it's hard to watch him try to be serious—the Hound hoped for some tongue-in-cheek mugging for the camera that makes the man o' one brow one of the Hound's faves. Not to be confused with 1972's *Mind Warp.* 🐾🐾

1991 (R) 91m/C Marta Alicia, Bruce Campbell, Angus Scrimm, Elizabeth Kent, Mary Becker, Wendy Sandow, Gene McGarr; **D:** Steve Barnett; **W:** Henry Dominick; **C:** Peter Fernberger; **M:** Mark Governor. **VHS, LV** *COL*

Misfits of Science

A seriously uninspired pilot for an even worse '80s television series about a group of teens with standard-issue "super-powers" who fight to save the world. One guy has blue skin and can freeze things (like the plot, apparently). The series, which was about on a par with other '80s schlock like *Manimal,* was mercifully short lived. 🐾

1985 96m/C Dean Paul Martin, Kevin Peter Hall, Mark Thomas Miller, Kenneth Mars, Courteney Cox; **D:** Philip DeGuere. **VHS, Beta** *MCA*

Missile to the Moon

First expedition to the moon encounters not acres of dead rock but a race of gorgeous women in lingerie and high heels. Take one cheap, silly sci-fi groaner, then remove the name stars and the 3-D effects, and there you have it—a bad but entertaining remake of *Cat Women of the Moon,* featuring a bevy of beauty contest winners from New Hampshire to Yugoslavia. Cast is not quite as accomplished as the original's. Gary Clarke (who took over Michael Landon's Teenage Werewolf role in *How to Make a Monster*) is pretty good, but he's no Sonny Tufts. Laurie Mitchell no doubt put this on her resume right next to *Queen of Outer Space.* Cathy Downs was also in *The Amazing Colossal Man* and *She Creature.* K. T. Stevens was the daughter of famed comedy director Sam Wood. Tommy Cook was in Arch Obeler's *Strange Holiday* and played Little Beaver in the "Red Ryder" series. Director Richard Cunha churned out this quickie to fill out a bill with *Frankenstein's Daughter.* 🐾🐾📼

1959 78m/B Gary Clarke, Cathy Downs, K.T. Stevens, Laurie Mitchell, Michael Whalen, Nina Bara, Richard Travis, Tommy Cook, Marjorie Hellen; **D:** Richard Cunha. **VHS, Beta** *RHI, SNC, CNM*

Mission Mars

American astronauts Darren McGavin and Nick Adams, on a mission to the red planet, discover the bodies of two cosmonauts floating in space. After landing on the planet's surface, they find a third cosmonaut, this one in a state of suspended animation. While putting the

viewer to sleep, they proceed to revive the third cosmonaut and have at it with the sinister alien force responsible for all the trouble. 🎵

1967 87m/C Darren McGavin, Nick Adams, George DeVries; *D:* Nicholas Webster. **VHS, Beta** *UNI*

Mission Stardust

An internationally produced but thoroughly unambitious adaptation of the once-popular Perry Rhodan sci-fi serial, in which Rhodan and his team bring ill aliens back to Earth and defend them against evil spies. Dubbed. **AKA:** 4...3...2...1...Morte. 🎵🎵

1968 90m/C *GE IT SP* Essy Persson, Gianni Rizzo, Lang Jeffries, Pinkas Braun; *D:* Primo Zeglio. **VHS, Beta** *RHI*

Mistress of the World

A scientist, aided by Swedish Intelligence agent Ventura, works to protect his gravity-altering invention from Chinese agents. Partly based on a German serial from the silent film era, but not up to director William Dieterle's usual fare. A must-see for Lino Ventura fans and Mabuse mavens. 🎵🎵

1959 107m/C Martha Hyer, Micheline Presle, Gino Cervi, Lino Ventura, Sabu, Wolfgang Preiss; *D:* William Dieterle. **VHS, Beta** *VMK*

Modern Problems

Chevy gets splashed with nuclear waste and develops some rather tasteless telekinetic powers, including the ability to vacuum up cocaine through his nostrils like a Hoover. Ah, the magic that was Hollywood in the early 1980s. Slapstick takeoff on psy-pics like *The Fury* and *Scanners* was done with a fine comic cast at low points in their personal lives, and their distraction shows in this unsuccessful fission trip. **WOOF!**

1981 (PG) 93m/C Chevy Chase, Patti D'Arbanville, Mary Kay Place, Brian Doyle-Murray, Nell Carter, Dabney Coleman; *D:* Ken Shapiro. **VHS, Beta** *FOX*

Melanoma, or just a few moles?? You decide. *The Mole People.*

> "From a lost age...Horror crawls from the depths of the Earth!"
>
> —*The Mole People.*

The Mole People

A really bad '50s creature feature which finds two archeologists accidentally discovering an underground civilization of albinos who shun all forms of light. They've also enslaved the local populace of half-human, half-mole creatures who decide to help the good guys escape by rising up in a revolt against their evil masters. When the weapon of choice is a flashlight you know not to expect much. *♪*

1956 78m/B John Agar, Cynthia Patrick, Hugh Beaumont, Alan Napier, Nestor Paiva, Phil Chambers; *D:* Virgil W. Vogel; *W:* Laszlo Gorog. **VHS** *MCA*

Mom and Dad Save the World

Planet Spengo, populated entirely by idiots, plans to destroy Earth. But nasty King Tod spies through his telescope an average suburban housewife (Teri Garr) and falls in love. He teleports both Mr. and Mrs. to Spengo and postpones death-raying their world until he can marry Mom, dispose of Dad. Highlights are the goofy playpen sets, mixing vintage *Flash Gordon* style with *Romper Room*. Lowlight is the misuse of a gifted cast in an attempt to do a picture that's so dumb it's funny, but only gets the dumb aspect correct. Very young viewers might be amused. *♪*

1992 (PG) 87m/C Teri Garr, Jeffrey Jones, Jon Lovitz, Eric Idle, Wallace Shawn, Dwier Brown, Kathy Ireland, Thalmus Rasulala; *D:* Greg Beeman; *M:* Jerry Goldsmith. **VHS, LV** *HBO*

Monkey Boy

Decent sci-fi horror from Britain, about a cunning human-ape hybrid that escapes from a genetics lab after massacring the staff. Not excessively gruesome or vulgar, and some sympathy is aroused for the killer mutant. A condensation of a TV miniseries; original author Stephen Gallagher adapted and sharpened his own novel *Chimera*. *♪ ♪ ♭*

1990 104m/C John Lynch, Christine Kavanagh, Kenneth Cranham; *D:* Lawrence Gordon Clark. **VHS, Beta** *PSM*

Monolith

A coed team of squabbling LAPD officers check out a senseless murder and learn that a secret government agency has an ancient, captured UFO in their vaults. Its troublesome occupant, a hostile alien life force, can possess any living creature, throw out heat rays, and generally behave like a cut-rate ripoff of Carpenter's *The Thing*. Low-grade alloy of buddy-cop comedy, stunt-crazy f/x infernos, and a hand-me-down sf premise. *♪*

1993 (R) 96m/C Bill Paxton, Lindsay Frost, John Hurt, Louis Gossett Jr.; *D:* John Eyres; *W:* Stephen Lister; *C:* Alan M. Trow; *M:* Frank Becker. **VHS, LV** *MCA*

The Monolith Monsters

Despite the title and goofy premise (killer rocks), this is one of the more enjoyable '50s B-movies. A meteor, described by the orotund narrator as "another strange calling card from the limitless reaches of space," is the source. Geologist Grant Williams discovers strange crystals that absorb silicon from people and objects, killing the humans and growing to towering heights in the process. The effects aren't bad and the plot is so inventively put together that the film is fun all the way through. *♪ ♪ ♪*

1957 76m/B Grant Williams, Lola Albright, Les Tremayne, Trevor Bardette; *D:* John Sherwood; *W:* Norman Jolley, Robert M. Fresco; *C:* Ellis W. Carter; *M:* Joseph Gershenson. **VHS** *MCA, MLB, FRG*

Monster a Go-Go!

A team of go-go dancers battle a ten-foot monster from outer space who's actually a mutated astronaut. Herschell Gordon Lewis, director of *Blood Feast* and other timeless trash/gore movies, acquired this flick (then titled *Terror at Halfday*) in an unfinished state, threw in a couple of new scenes, and released it as a co-feature with his hillbilly movie *Moonshine Mountain*. That may seem like an unlikely combo, but hey, monsters and hillbilly music were a big draw in the '60s (see Lee Frost's 1961 girly/monster epic *House on Bare Mountain* for a perfect example). The fellow who played the Frankenstein-looking monster was a genuine giant. Too bad he couldn't dance.

1965 70m/B Phil Morton, June Travis, Bill Rebane, Sheldon Seymour; *D:* Herschell Gordon Lewis. **VHS, Beta** *VCI*

Monster from Green Hell

An experimental rocket containing radiation-contaminated wasps crashes in Africa, making giant killer wasps that run amok. Stinging big bug horror. 🦴

1958 71m/B Jim Davis, Robert Griffin, Barbara Turner, Eduardo Ciannelli; **D:** Kenneth Crane. **VHS, Beta** *NOS, MRV, SNC*

Monster from the Ocean Floor

Roger Corman's first production was shot in six days for $12,000. The comely Anne Kimball stars as a tourist vacationing in a Mexican village that is being terrorized by an octopus-type sea monster (actually, a puppet shot from behind a cloudy fishtank—but no matter, you don't get to see it until the end of the movie). Stuart Wade costars as a marine biologist who dismisses the monster talk as superstition, until he is forced to go mano-a-monster in his mini-sub. Director Wyott Ordung also appears in the film and later wrote the immortal *Robot Monster*. Making his film debut is Jonathan Haze, who was discovered pumping gas on Santa Monica Boulevard, and became a part of Corman's ensemble. His finest hour is, of course, *The Little Shop of Horrors*. **AKA:** It Stalked the Ocean Floor; Monster Maker. 🦴🦴

1954 66m/C Wyott Ordung, Anne Kimball, Stuart Wade, Jonathan Haze, Dick Pinner, Jack Hayes; **D:** Wyott Ordung; **W:** William Danch; **C:** Floyd Crosby. **VHS, Beta** *VMK*

The Monster Maker

A low-budget monster-fest with an interesting concept: a deranged scientist (J. Carrol Naish) develops a serum that inflates heads, feet, and hands (if anyone cares, this is an actual medical condition called acromegaly). He recklessly inflicts others with this potion, then must contend with his deformed victims. On top of all these shenanigans, he's trying to court the pretty daughter of one of his "experiments." 🦴🦴

1944 65m/B J. Carrol Naish, Ralph Morgan, Wanda McKay, Terry Frost; **D:** Sam Newfield. **VHS, Beta** *NOS, MRV, SNC*

The Monster of Piedras Blancas

During a seaside festival, two fisherman are killed by a bloodthirsty oceanic critter with no respect for holidays. The fishing village is determined to find it and kill it. Low-budget, with amateurish effects and poor acting. **WOOF!**

1957 72m/B Les Tremayne, Jeanne Carmen, Forrest Lewis; **D:** Irvin Berwick. **VHS** *VDM, MRV, REP*

Monster on the Campus

A forerunner to *Animal House*? One of Jack Arnold's more mediocre science-fiction thrillers is a workaday Jekyll-and-Hyde story about a college professor who turns into a hairy Neanderthal guy when he accidentally smokes (!) the blood of a prehistoric fish. At least it's true to life. 🦴🦴

1959 76m/B Arthur Franz, Joanna Moore, Judson Pratt, Nancy Walters, Troy Donahue; **D:** Jack Arnold; **W:** David Duncan; **C:** Russell Metty. **VHS** *MCA*

The Monster that Challenged the World

Huge, ancient eggs are discovered in the Salton Sea and eventually hatch into killer, crustaceous caterpillars. Superior monster action. 🦴🦴🦴

1957 83m/B Tim Holt, Audrey Dalton, Hans Conried, Harlen Ward, Casey Adams, Mimi Gibson, Gordon Jones; **D:** Arnold Laven. **VHS** *MGM, FRG, MLB*

Moon 44

One of German filmmaker Roland Emmerich's Hollywood-style B movies before he had a mainstream commercial hit with *Stargate*. Filching largely from *Outland*, it's mediocre mayhem about cop Michael Pare going undercover as a cosmic convict. His mission: thwart corporate marauders planning to attack a giant space prison that doubles as a mining colony. Some impressive f/x are largely lost on the small screen. 🦴🦴

1990 (R) 102m/C *GE* Malcolm McDowell, Lisa Eichhorn, Michael Pare, Stephen Geoffreys, Roscoe Lee Browne, Brian Thompson, Dean Devlin, Mechmed Yilmaz, Leon Rippy; **D:** Roland Emmerich; **W:** Dean Heyde, Oliver Eberle. **VHS, LV** *LIV, IME, BTV*

"Living skyscrapers of stone thundering across the Earth! ...crushing ALL that stand in their path!"
—The Monolith Monsters.

with Earth next on their agenda. Made-in-Detroit feature has ambitions far beyond its low budget. 🦴🦴

1989 92m/C Walter Koenig, Bruce Campbell, Leigh Lombardi, Robert Kurcz, John J. Saunders, Revis Graham, Tom Case; **D:** Robert Dyke; **W:** Tex Ragsdale; **C:** Peter Klein; **M:** Joseph Loduca. **VHS, LV** *MOV, IME*

Mosquito

An alien spaceship crashlands on earth and a hungry mosquito snacks on one of the dead pilots. The extraterrestrial blood transforms the annoying insects into turkey-sized monsters able and very willing to suck their victims dry. A bunch of misfits do battle with the killer bugs at an isolated campground. Not what you'd call a *good* film, *Mosquito* does manage to deliver some laughs and a storyline that feels more like a homage to old monsters than a blatant rip-off. 🦴🦴🦴

1995 (R) 92m/C Gunnar Hansen, Ron Asheton, Steve Dixon, Rachel Loiselle, Tim Loveface; **D:** Gary Jones; **W:** Gary Jones, Steve Hodge, Tom Chaney; **C:** Tom Chaney; **M:** Allen Lynch, Randall Lynch. **VHS** *HMD*

Mothra

Classic Japanese monster shenanigans about an enraged giant caterpillar that invades Tokyo while searching for the Alilenas, a pair of tiny twin princesses who've been kidnapped by an evil nightclub owner in the pursuit of big profits. After tiring of crushing buildings and wreaking incidental havoc, the enormous creepy-crawler zips up into a cocoon and emerges as Mothra, a moth distinguished by both its size and bad attitude. Mothra and the wee babes make appearances in a number of later Godzilla epics. The Alilenas were played by Emi and Yumi Ito, who had a singing career in Japan as "the Peanuts." *Mothra* was one of the best of the '60s Japanese giant monster epics, a colorful, fast-moving fantasy with an unforgettable monster. **AKA:** Mosura. 🦴🦴🦴

1961 101m/C *JP* Frankie Sakai, Hiroshi Koizumi, Kyoko Katawa, Yumi Ito, Emi Ito; **D:** Inoshiro Honda, Lee Kresel; **W:** Shinichi Sekizawa; **C:** Hajime Koizumi. **VHS, Beta** *GKK*

Al Gore: The Early Years? Nah, it's just Michael Pare in *Moon 44*.

Moon Pilot

First astronaut scheduled to orbit the moon is followed prior to the launch by an enticing mystery woman. She turns out to be a (French-accented?) alien from the planet Beta Lyrae, who's only trying to be helpful. But government security forces panic and chase them both. Outdated, frankly dull comedy from Walt Disney productions, more of a romantic farce than sci fi. No f/x whatsoever. 🦴🦴

1962 98m/C Tom Tryon, Brian Keith, Edmond O'Brien, Dany Saval, Tommy Kirk, Bob Sweeney, Kent Smith; **D:** James Neilson; **W:** Maurice Tombragel; **C:** William E. Snyder. **VHS, Beta** *DIS*

Moontrap

USS Enterprise icon Walter Koenig, reputedly the member of the Classic 'Trek' cast most seriously into sf, takes a rare lead role here as an Apollo astronaut who returns to the moon to investigate evidence of ancient alien habitations. He and comrade Bruce Campbell find a killer race of evolving, self-replicating robots

Murder by Moonlight

Rival agents investigate a mysterious murder in a prosperous mining colony on the moon. Not only do they discover a dastardly trail that leads all the way back to Earth, but a strange romantic attraction for each other. Originally broadcast on British TV. 🦴🦴

1991 (PG-13) 94m/C *GB* Julian Sands, Brigitte Nielsen, Gerald McRaney, Jane Lapotaire, Brian Cox; **D:** Michael Lindsay-Hogg; **M:** Trevor Jones. **VHS** *VMK*

Murder in Space

Nine multinational astronauts are stranded aboard a space station when they discover one of them is a murderer. This creates anxiety, particularly since the killer's identity is unknown. Oatmeal salesman Wilford Brimley is the Earth-bound mission control chief trying desperately to finger a spaceman while the bodies pile up. Made for television. 🦴🕊

1985 95m/C Wilford Brimley, Martin Balsam, Michael Ironside; **D:** Steven Hilliard Stern. **VHS, Beta** *VMK*

Mutant Hunt

NYC-made direct-to-video production about manlike robots gone haywire on a sexual stimulant called Euphoron. Mutated and mutilated, they rampage through Manhattan and must be eliminated by an all-American hero of flesh and blood. Cheap and lurid. **AKA:** Matt Riker. **WOOF!**

1987 90m/C Rick Gianasi, Mary-Anne Fahey; **D:** Tim Kincaid; **W:** Tim Kincaid. **VHS, Beta** *NO*

Mutant on the Bounty

Jazz musician, lost in space as a beam of light for 23 years, is materialized aboard a spaceship alive but with a face that looks like he's been "bobbing for french fries." As if that's not enough (and it isn't), the motley crew then must fight a couple of thugs who are trying to steal a vial of serum. Good f/x go to waste in a galactic spoof whose biggest laff is the pun in the title. 🦴🕊

1989 93m/C John Roarke, Deborah Benson, John Furey, Victoria Catlin, John Fleck, Kyle T. Heffner; **D:** Robert Torrance. **VHS** *HMD*

Mutant Species

Soldier is accidentally exposed to altered DNA and begins to mutate into a remorseless and terrifying killer. **AKA:** Bio-Force I. 🦴

1995 (R) 100m/C Leo Rossi, Ted Prior, Grant Gelt, Denise Crosby, Powers Boothe, Wilford Brimley; **D:** David A. Prior; **W:** David A. Prior, William Vigil; **C:** Carlos Gonzalez. **VHS, LV** *LIV*

Mutator

A corporation makes a tiny genetic mistake and winds up creating a new life form—brawny, humanoid pussycats who prey on humans. The laughable monsters are displayed only briefly, but that's all it takes. Hopefully these South African filmmakers will never get their claws into any dramatizations of Larry Niven's *Man-Kzin Wars*. **AKA:** Time of the Beast. 🦴

1990 (R) 91m/C Brion James, Carolyn Ann Clark, Milton Raphiel Murrill; **D:** John R. Bowey; **W:** Lynn Rose Higgins. **VHS, Beta** *PSM*

My Stepmother Is an Alien

Eccentric physicist Steve Mills (Dan Aykroyd) sends a beam out to a galaxy far, far away and gets a visit from the beautiful and sexy (although from some angles she does look like Mick Jagger) Celeste (Kim Basinger). Fortunately for the plot, and the ensuing slapstick comedy, this gorgeous blonde is an alien with a mission: seduce the recently widowed Steve and get the details of his experiments which could save her planet. Despite her rather odd (and sometimes funny) habits, romance commences, love and marriage follow. Celeste's fellow alien on the mission comes off as a living Felix-the-Cattish bag and supplies some great comic moments—the kissing scene is a classic. Jon Lovitz is fun as the pervert-playboy brother. Fast forward through the Durante imitations. Otherwise it's good fluff. 🦴🦴🕊

1988 (PG-13) 108m/C Dan Aykroyd, Kim Basinger, Jon Lovitz, Alyson Hannigan, Joseph Maher, Seth Green, Wesley Mann, Adrian Sparks, Juliette Lewis, Tanya Fenmore; **D:** Richard Benjamin; **W:** Herschel Weingrod, Timothy Harris, Jonathan Reynolds; **M:** Alan Silvestri. **VHS, Beta, LV** *COL*

"We don't take no shit from a machine!"

—Ray Tanner (Bruce Campbell), and reiterated by Jason Grant (Walter Koenig), in *Moontrap*.

What woman can resist an expensive French perfume? Kim Basinger in **My Stepmother Is an Alien.**

Mysterious Doctor Satan

This 15-episode chapter play is the second and last Republic serial to give the actor playing the villain top billing, and rightly so, for Edward (Eduardo) Ciannelli, best known for his role as a crazed high priest in the 1939 *Gunga Din,* is quite wonderful as the snarling madman planning to conquer the world with an army of robots (although Doctor Satan only manages to get one built and employed for the entire running time!). Originally based on a script called "The Adventures of Superman," it had to be rewritten when legal rights to the Man of Steel couldn't be obtained. Reporter Lois Lane was turned into columnist Lois Scott, and Superman/Clark Kent transforms into the very mortal Bob Wayne (Robert Wilcox) who dons a chain-mail head mask to become the Copperhead and gets into one predicament after another as each episode reaches its climactic scene. Dorothy Herbert, a trick circus horseback rider, acts as a secretary and does some amazing stunts in episodes 1 and 8. 🦴🦴🦴

1940 250m/B Eduardo Ciannelli, Robert Wilcox, Ella Neal, Dorothy Herbert; **D:** William Witney. **VHS** *REP, VCN, MLB*

Mysterious Island

Solid and often-overlooked adventure combines the talents of three proven crowd-pleasers—author Jules Verne, special effects pioneer Ray Harryhausen, and composer Bernard Herrmann—each at the top of his game. The story continues the saga of Captain Nemo, and concerns escaped Civil War prisoners who fly a balloon to a remote island filled with wondrous giant beasts and a new surprise around every corner. One of stop-motion animation's finest hours. 🦴🦴🦴⁄

1961 101m/C *GB* Michael Craig, Joan Greenwood, Michael Callan, Gary Merrill, Herbert Lom, Beth Rogan, Percy Herbert, Dan Jackson, Nigel Green; **D:** Cy Endfield; **W:** Daniel Ullman, John Prebble, Crane Wilbur; **C:** Wilkie Cooper; **M:** Bernard Herrmann. **VHS, Beta, LV** *COL, MLB*

The Mysterians

Caped aliens land their saucers on Earth and release the giant death-ray-shooting robot bird Mogella, hoping to find some fresh tail to replenish their race after the home planet was destroyed by a nuclear explosion. Even though alien, this "big monster" was also a result of the misuse of nuclear power (the aliens only need to be here because of the nuclear disaster), so once again Japan is portrayed as the victim. Directed by Inoshiro Honda, who also directed the original *Godzilla,* with music supplied by the Japanese classical composer Akira Ifukube. **AKA:** Earth Defense Forces; Chikyu Boelgun. 🦴🦴⁄

1958 85m/C *JP* Kenji Sahara, Yumi Shirakawa, Takashi Shimura; **D:** Inoshiro Honda; **M:** Akira Ifukube. **VHS, Beta** *MLB*

Mysterious Two

Eerie atmosphere is everything in this network TV movie about a beatific, middle-aged couple

TV on Tape:
Mystery Science Theater 3000

Mystery Science Theater 3000 may well be the funniest sci-fi show on cable television. Weathering some major cast and crew changes, it maintained its originality for several years and moved from the small screen to home video to motion picture theatres.

"**M**ST3K," as it's abbreviated by fans, was created in 1988 at a small UHF station in Minneapolis, MN, by comedian Joel Hodgson and producer-writer-director Jim Mallon. Their idea was to poke fun at bad B-movies, and to use those films as a springboard for more wide-ranging humor. Here's the premise:

A worker (first played by Hodgson and then by Michael Nelson when Hodgson left the show) at the Gizmonic Institute angered his bosses, the proverbial mad scientists (played variously by Trace Beaulieu, Josh Weinstein, and Frank Conniff), who shot him into space and marooned him on the Satellite of Love. To ease his loneliness, Joel created robot companions, the puppets Crow, Gypsy, and Tom Servo (the voices of Beaulieu,

Mallon, and co-writer Kevin Murphy). At the beginning of each show, Joel and the 'bots exchange goofy inventions with the scientists. After that, the scientists send them a "cheesy movie, the worst ever made," as the theme song puts it.

Then Joel or Mike, the 'bots, and the TV audience settle down to watch. You can see their silhouettes in the lower right-hand corner of your screen, as if you were in a theatre and they were three cut-ups in the first row. Their comments on the movies—plus some terrific skits and songs—are the real point.

Those wisecracks cover the full spectrum of popular and serious culture. Movies like *Robot Monster* and *It Conquered the World* provoke rapidfire references to everything from C.S. Lewis to

Vidal Sassoon, free will, God, artist Mark Rothko, Bill Keene's "Family Circus" comic strip, playwright Tom Stoppard, Robert Ludlum novels, dumb fish puns, *The Wizard of Oz,* and *The Dirty Dozen.* When Joel remarks that a character on screen looks like a cross between Jerry Mathers and James Dean, one of the 'bots cracks, "Beaver Without a Cause."

In terms of the sets and props, they take a defiantly low-tech approach. Tom Servo was obviously a gumball machine in a previous life, and Crow's beak is made from a bowling pin. According to Mallon, that part of the show deliberately recalls the kids' shows on local stations during the early years of television. Hodgson has cited Jay Ward's work with "Rocky and Bullwinkle" as another source of inspiration.

Recently, the series has moved from the Comedy Central cable channel, which has devoted entire Thanksgivings to "Turkey Day" MST3K marathons, to the Sci-Fi Channel. The series' best efforts are showing up on tape from Rhino Home Video, and in 1996, *Mystery Science Theater 3000: The Movie* played in theatres.

1988-95/C *Selected cast:* Joel Hodgson, Michael Nelson, Trace Beaulieu, Josh Weinstein, Frank Conniff. **VHS** *RHI*

---

called He and She, who entice a cult-like following of plain folks toward a desert rendezvous point where the space brothers will supposedly take them to a cosmic paradise. Based on actual events—except the real He and She led their dazed rabble to a New Age commune in the woods. This production cops out with the strong suggestion that they were aliens after all. Talk about hedging your bets. 🦴🦴🦴

1982 100m/C John Forsythe, Priscilla Pointer, Noah Beery Jr., Vic Tayback, James Stephens, Karen Werner, Robert Englund, Robert Pine; *D:* Gary Sherman. **VHS, Beta** *LIV*

Navy Vs. the Night Monsters

When Antarctic plant specimens collected by the Navy turn out to be horrible, acid-secreting monsters out to take over the world,

blonde bombshell Mamie Van Doren and her pals have to come to the rescue. Most of the action takes place in a South Pole military base that looks remarkably like southern California. Way too much of this flick is taken up with dated, tiresome jokes about the rigors of Navy life. Mamie looks good, but the monsters and acting are nothing special. It was supposedly based on a novel by classic sf writer Murray Leinster. **AKA:** The Night Crawlers. 🦴

1966 87m/C Mamie Van Doren, Anthony Eisley, Pamela Mason, Bobby Van, Russ Bender, Walter Sande; *D:* Michael Hoey; *W:* Michael Hoey; *C:* Stanley Cortez. **VHS, Beta** *NO*

Nemesis

Kung-fu cyborgs clash in the post-nuke future in this tribute to John Woo. Olivier Gruner plays a human crime fighter (although he's mostly composed of mechanical replacement parts) in a world overrun with terrorists, sexy gangsters, and Terminatoresque android cops intent on conquering their own creators. The extremely confusing script plugs him into gory fight gymnastics in exotic locations, with far more visual style than attempts at logic. Special f/x are good despite the obviously low budget. 🦴🦴🦴

1993 (R) 95m/C Olivier Gruner, Tim Thomerson, Cary-Hiroyuki Tagawa, Merele Kennedy, Yuji Okumoto, Marjorie Monaghan, Nicholas Guest, Vincent Klyn, Deborah Shelton, Brion James; *D:* Albert Pyun; *W:* Rebecca Charles; *C:* George Mooradian; *M:* Michael Rubini. **VHS, LV** *IMP, UND*

Nemesis 2: Nebula

Sequel to *Nemesis* utterly writes off the Oliver Gruner character in opening narration to tell the *Terminator*-dependent tale of an infant sent back through time to the African veldt, so she can later lead humanity as a freedom-fighter against the cyborg onslaught. Grown to maturity as bodybuilder Sue Price (a female Schwarzenegger in a leather tribal bikini), she must fight Nebula, a time-traveling machine-creature of the future, revealed in all his armored splendor only bit by bit. Kitschy action, f/x slams, and Price's superstructure may hold viewer attention despite common sense. 🦴🦴

1994 (R) ?m/C Sue Price, Tina Cote, Earl White, Chad Stakelski; *D:* Albert Pyun. *IMP*

Neo-Tokyo

A collection of three short animated films from Japan. "The Order to Stop Construction" finds an anal-retentive bureaucrat sent to inspect an automated mining city in a remote jungle. The resident robots imprison him and show him how meaningless the policies that run his life are. "Labyrinth" follows a young girl and her pet cat into a strange wonderland, and "The Running Man" is a startling tale of a futuristic racer. The films are visually stunning, but "Order to Stop Construction," with its wry satire, is probably the most readily accessible. 🦴🦴🦴

1986 50m/C *D:* Rin Taro, Yoshiaki Kawajiri, Katsuhiro Otomo; *W:* Rin Taro, Yoshiaki Kawajiri, Katsuhiro Otomo. **VHS**

Neon City

Critics keep repeating the inaccurate dictum that sci-fi movies merely reinvent the western. That generalization only really applies to the subgenre of *Mad Max/Road Warrior* imitations like this Canadian post-apocalypse actioner clearly patterned after John Ford's *Stagecoach,* set in the year 2053. Eight travelers in an armored transport truck seek safety from the Earth's toxic environment via an overland trek to the title settlement. Mutants and highway bandits take the place of the traditional marauding Indians. 🦴🦴

1991 (R) 99m/C Michael Ironside, Vanity, Lyle Alzado, Valerie Wildman, Nick Klar, Juliet Landau, Arsenio "Sonny" Trinidad, Richard Sanders; *D:* Monte Markham. **VHS** *VMK*

The Nest

Killer mutant cockroaches that take over a small resort island. That's the plot, but the overall Yuck! factor is high with lots of icky special effects, assorted creepy crawly critters, and the cast is better than you'd expect, especially Terri Treas, as the scientist who turns out to be a little kinky for her bugs. The story gets funnier and grosser as it goes along, and so gives fans everything they could ask for. 🦴🦴🦴

1988 (R) 89m/C Robert Lansing, Lisa Langlois, Franc Luz, Terri Treas, Stephen Davies, Diana Bellamy, Nancy Mor-

gan; **D:** Terence H. Winkless; **W:** Robert King; **M:** Rick Conrad. **VHS, Beta** *MGM*

The Net

The ever-spunky Sandra Bullock gets stuck behind a computer screen rather than the wheel of a bus as reclusive computer systems analyst Angela Bennett. After a tip from a friend she has met only via the Internet, Angela investigates a Web page linked to top-secret government information. Soon after her discovery, Angela's friend dies in a suspicious plane crash just as they are to meet face to face. Angela decides to take a much-needed vacation, where she meets the suave man of her dreams, Jeremy Devlin (Jeremy Northam). All is perfect, until he tries to kill her for a computer disk. Angela discovers her identity has been erased, and she is on the run from the conspirators who want to eliminate her. She turns to her ex-boyfriend Dennis Miller for help. This high-tech update of the traditional Hitchcockian thriller works well, mostly thanks to Bullock. Director Irwin Winkler smoothly weaves the high-tech aspects into the plot, demonstrating just how technology dependent society has become. That makes this bit of techno paranoia engaging and effective. 🦴🦴🦴

1995 (PG-13) **114m/C** Sandra Bullock, Jeremy Northam, Dennis Miller, Diane Baker, Ken Howard, Wendy Gazelle, Ray McKinnon; **D:** Irwin Winkler; **W:** John Brancato, Michael Ferris; **C:** Jack N. Green; **M:** Mark Isham. **VHS, LV, 8mm** *COL*

Neutron and the Black Mask

It's Neutron, the ultimate wrestling super hero! Well, actually, Santos was the ultimate wrestling superhero, but don't tell that to this masked dynamo. He's trying to save the world from the evil Dr. Caronte, for heaven's sake! You know, the one with the neutron bomb? The bomb that'll keep coming back in sequel after sequel? Just like Neutron himself? This was only the first of a number of Mexican-made movies featuring the man with the lightning-bolt mask. Many were hastily dubbed into English and sold to American TV stations in the '60s to delight hordes of fans. Well, several, anyway. 🦴🦴

1961 **80m/B** *MX* Wolf Ruvinskis, Julio Aleman, Armando Silvestre, Rosita Arenas, Claudio Brook; **D:** Frederick Curiel. **VHS** *SNC*

Neutron Vs. the Amazing Dr. Caronte

The evil Dr. Caronte from *Neutron and the Black Mask* is back and he just won't give up that neutron bomb! This time Caronte intimidates a corpulent fellow villain (a sort of Latin Sydney Greenstreet with a passion for Beethoven) and uses black magic to take over the body of a respected scientist. The mysterious (and at least modestly amazing) Doctor is aided by his dwarf assistant, "Nick" (who sounds like Grover on *Sesame Street*), and an army of zombies whose faces look like partially melted gorilla masks. Fortunately for freedom-loving people everywhere, the wrestling hero Neutron (Wolf Ruvinskis) is once again on hand to foil his schemes. More badly dubbed Mexican wrestling superhero insanity. 🦴🦴

1961 **80m/B** *MX* Wolf Ruvinskis, Julio Aleman, Armando Silvestre, Rosita Arenas, Rodolfo Landa; **D:** Frederick Curiel. **VHS** *SNC*

Neutron Vs. the Death Robots

A masked wrestling superhero's work is never done. In this flick, Neutron takes on a giant blood-drinking brain, an army of killer robots, and (yes, *again*!), that pesky neutron bomb to protect the world. Another Neutron adventure guaranteed to bemuse red-blooded insomniacs and those perpetually in search of fodder for bad-movie parties. 🦴🦴

1962 **80m/B** *MX* Wolf Ruvinskis, Julio Aleman, Armando Silvestre, Rosita Arenas; **D:** Frederick Curiel. **VHS** *SNC*

New Crime City: Los Angeles 2020

Futuristic action flick borrows blatantly from *The Road Warrior* and *Escape from New York*. Hero Rick Rossovich is an ex-cop named Ricks who's got a date with the gas chamber. Seems he ran afoul of the totalitarian authorities in 2020 for helping out the criminal inhabitants of New Crime City, a portion of L.A. that's been walled off from the rest. A delightfully evil military type (Stacy Keach) sends Ricks and the gutsy Darla (Sherrie Rose) into the place to fetch a virus that's been developed by a local warlord (Rick Dean). The pace is pokey and, with the exception of Keach, the acting is no better than so-so. The film does have enough unusual quirks, including an aggressive anti-organized religion streak, to keep your finger away from the fast-forward button. 🦴🦴

1994 (R) 95m/C Rick Rossovich, Stacy Keach, Sherrie Rose, Rick Dean; **D:** Jonathan Winfrey; **W:** Rick Rossovich. **VHS, LV** *NHO*

New Eden

Setting is an arid prison planet in 2237, where an Earth political dissident winds up in charge of a peaceful refugee settlement. Meanwhile his old cellblock pal fights his way to leadership of the barbaric Sand Pirates. It's a case of old wine in new genres, taking the old western/gangster plot of the two buddies who walk different paths and wind up confronting each other from opposite sides of the law. The only thing not utterly predictable is that Pat O'Brien ain't in it. Made for cable TV. 🦴🎵

1994 (R) 89m/C Stephen Baldwin, Lisa Bonet, Tobin Bell, Michael Bowen, Janet Hubert-Whitten; **D:** Alan Metzger; **W:** Dan Gordon; **C:** Geoffrey Erb. **VHS, LV** *MCA*

The New Gladiators

In the future, criminals try to kill each other on television for public entertainment. Two such gladiators discover that the network's computer is using the games in order to take over mankind, and they attempt to stop it. Even if the special effects were any good, they couldn't save this one. **WOOF!**

1987 90m/C *IT* Jared Martin, Fred Williamson, Eleanor Gold, Howard Ross, Claudio Cassinelli; **D:** Lucio Fulci. **VHS, Beta** *MED*

The New Invisible Man

A so-so Mexican adaptation of the popular H.G. Wells novel has a prisoner receiving a vanishing drug from his brother, who created it—perhaps to aid an escape attempt. **AKA:** H.G. Wells' New Invisible Man. 🦴🦴

1958 95m/B *MX* Arturo de Cordova, Ana Luisa Peluffo, Jorge Mondragon; **D:** Alfredo B. Crevenna. **VHS** *SNC*

Next One

A mysterious visitor from another time, with miraculous powers and no memory winds up on an isolated Greek island, as the result of a magnetic storm, and is taken in by astronaut's-widow Adrienne Barbeau. Oh, and you may have heard of this guy's brother, if you were hanging around Galilee 2,000 years ago. Quasi-mystical sci-fi, moody but pretentious and generally uneventful. 🦴🎵

1984 105m/C Keir Dullea, Adrienne Barbeau, Jeremy Licht, Peter Hobbs; **D:** Nico Mastorakis. **VHS, Beta** *VES*

Night Beast

Alien creature lands his spaceship near a small town and begins a bloody killing spree, in a plot that goes all the way from Point A to Point A. Made in Maryland, and except for the monster suit, amateur nite. **WOOF!**

1983 90m/C Tom Griffith, Dick Dyszel, Jaimie Zemarel, George Stover; **D:** Donald M. Dohler. **VHS, Beta** *NO*

Night Caller from Outer Space

When a woman-hunting alien arrives in London, women begin to disappear. At first, incredibly, no one makes the connection, but then the horrible truth comes to light. **AKA:** Blood Beast from Outer Space; The Night Caller. 🦴🎵

1966 84m/B *GB* John Saxon, Maurice Denham, Patricia Haines, Alfred Burke, Jack Watson, Aubrey Morris; **D:** John Gilling. **VHS, Beta, LV** *COL*

Night of the Blood Beast

An astronaut comes back from space, only to find that he's been impregnated by an alien creature, and a mass of extraterrestrial larvae is growing within him. Adding to his problem: his parental instincts are kicking in. Creepy venereal horror, decades before Cronenberg and *Alien*. The low-budget, most apparent when the rubber monster waddles out of Bronson Canyon cave, defeats a valiant attempt at a story. **AKA:** Creature from Galaxy 27. 🦴🦴

1958 65m/B Michael Emmet, Angela Greene, John Baer, Ed Nelson; **D:** Bernard L. Kowalski. **VHS** *SNC, MRV*

Night of the Bloody Apes

When a doctor transplants an ape's heart into his dying son's body (shown in actual surgical footage), the son turns into an ape man and goes berserk. Police race to end the bloody rampage. Gory Mexican-made horror is a color remake of director Rene Cardona's *Doctor of Doom* (1962, AKA: *Wrestling Women Vs. the Aztec Ape*), but with a lot of added blood and nudity. **AKA:** Gomar the Human Gorilla; La Horriplante Bestia Humana. 🦴🦴

1968 (R) 84m/C *MX* Jose Elias Moreno, Carlos Lopez Monctezuma, Armando Silvestre, Norma Lazarendo, Augustin Martinez Solares, Gina Moret, Noelia Noel, Gerard Zepeda; **D:** Rene Cardona Jr. **VHS, Beta** *MPI*

Night of the Comet

After surviving the explosion of a deadly comet, two California girls discover that they are the last people on Earth. What do they do? Go shopping of course! When zombies and other nasty folks begin to chase them, things begin to lose their charm. Luckily, Daddy taught them how to shoot machine guns. Cute and funny, this is probably the most charming End of the World movie since *Dr. Strangelove*. Oddly, director Thom Eberhardt made award-winning documentaries about serious social issues before moving on to features, which have been mostly as light hearted as this one. 🦴🦴🦴

1984 (PG-13) 90m/C Catherine Mary Stewart, Kelli Maroney, Robert Beltran, Geoffrey Lewis, Mary Woronov, Sharon Farrell, Michael Bowen; **D:** Thom Eberhardt; **W:** Thom Eberhardt; **C:** Arthur Albert. **VHS, Beta** *FOX*

Night of the Creeps

In 1958 alien meanies crashland on Earth and assume the form of parasitic slugs. The man they infect is cryogenically frozen, then thawed out thirty years later on the campus of Corman (homage to Roger) University, where he staggers about as a moldering zombie, spreading the living-dead contagion throughout the town.

"Which dial is for the front right burner, again?" Scientist Geoffrey Lewis cooks up another caper in *Night of the Comet*.

Good-looking B-movie satire plays around with every schlock-horror cliche there is, yet manages to avoid the sleaze factor itself. Contains numerous nods to B-movie folks, including cameos by such regulars as Dick Miller. Director Fred Dekker's first film. 🦴🦴🕊

1986 (R) 89m/C Jason Lively, Jill Whitlow, Tom Atkins, Dick Miller, Steve Marshall; *D:* Fred Dekker; *W:* Fred Dekker. **VHS, Beta, LV** *NO*

Night Siege Project: Shadowchaser 2

Smooth actioner finds a terrorist android taking over a nuclear arsenal and threatening to make Washington, D.C., a mushroom cloud. Naturally, there's a hero (and a heroine) to take care of the evildoers. **AKA:** Project Shadowchaser 2. 🦴🦴🕊

1994 (R) 97m/C Bryan Genesse, Frank Zagarino, Beth Toussaint; *D:* John Eyres; *W:* Nick Davis; *M:* Steve Edwards. **VHS, LV** *TTC, NLC*

Nightfall

Television adaptation of a classic Isaac Asimov short story can make a legitimate claim for Worst Sf Movie of All Time. A planet that has two suns (and therefore no night) experiences an eclipse and its inhabitants go mad. So will viewers! The plot makes no sense. The actors ham it up shamelessly, but given their idiotic costumes and dialogue that no one could read without giggling, why shouldn't they ham it up? **WOOF!**

1988 (PG-13) 87m/C David Birney, Sarah Douglas, Alexis Kanner, Andra Millian, Starr Andreeff, Charlie Hayward, Jonathon Emerson, Susie Lindemann; *D:* Paul Mayersberg; *W:* Paul Mayersberg. **VHS, Beta** *MGM*

Nightflyers

From its strained premise involving a half-baked mission to find an extraterrestrial entity to the sets that make a spaceship look like a living room straight from the pages of *Architectural Digest,* this one's a mistake, a silly mistake. Colored light and haze are used to hide the limited effects, though they become better in the second half. From a novella by George R.R. Martin; the original director, Fritz

Kiersch, was replaced by Robert Collector, here using the pseudonym T. C. Blake. 🦴

1987 (R) 88m/C Michael Praed, Michael Des Barres, Catherine Mary Stewart, John Standing, Lisa Blount, Glenn Withrow, James Avery, Helene Udy; *D:* T.C. Blake; *W:* Robert Jaffe. **VHS, Beta, LV** *NO*

984: Prisoner of the Future

In an Orwellian future society, a former member of the ruling elite undergoes various interrogations and flashbacks in a high-tech fortress, and plots his escape. You can see the ending coming miles away, but the Canadian filmmakers concocted a few striking effects on an ultra-low budget (dig the robot guards on roller skates!). **AKA:** The Tomorrow Man. 🦴🕊

1984 70m/C *CA* Don Francks, Stephen Markle; *D:* Tibor Takacs. **VHS, Beta** *NO*

1984

A timely (note the release date) and very impressive adaptation of George Orwell's famous novel. This version differs from the overly simplistic and cautionary 1954 film in its fine casting and production design. John Hurt delivers an excellent performance as Winston Smith, a government official in an ultra-totalitarian future who falls into an illegal love affair that inspires him to defy the crushing inhumanity of his world. Filmed in London, it skillfully visualizes our time's most central prophetic nightmare. Bleak but hauntingly beautiful, this is a film you won't soon forget. 🦴🦴🦴🦴

1984 (R) 117m/C *GB* John Hurt, Richard Burton, Suzanna Hamilton, Cyril Cusack, Gregory Fisher, Andrew Wilde, Rupert Baderman; *D:* Michael Radford; *C:* Roger Deakins. **VHS, Beta, LV** *LIV*

No Escape

This is another dreadful prison-of-the-future flick. In 2022, Captain Robbins (Ray Liotta) has been banished (unjustly, of course) to a prison-colony island called Absalom by a sadistic prison warden (Michael Lerner). The island, which looks more like it should be inhabited by Ewoks than the world's most dangerous criminals, is without walls and guards, leaving the prisoners free to kill each other. Robbins discovers a relatively peaceful

community of prisoners known as the Insiders, led by The Father (Lance Henriksen). The Insiders help each other and build a sort of medieval community. These guys are poster boys for prison reformation. They are predictably plagued by the Outsiders, the bad guys who live on the other side of the island. This cross between *Lord of the Flies* and *Escape from New York* becomes a redundant series of clashes between the good guys and bad guys, and fruitless attempts to escape. The action sequences are well done, but the story is empty. Adapted from the book *The Penal Colony* by Richard Herley. 🦴

1994 (R) 118m/C Ray Liotta, Lance Henriksen, Stuart Wilson, Kevin Dillon, Kevin J. O'Connor, Michael Lerner, Ernie Hudson, Ian McNeice, Jack Shepherd; *D:* Martin Campbell; *W:* Joel Gross; *M:* Graeme Revell. **VHS, LV** *HBO*

No Survivors, Please

Aliens from Orion take over politicians in order to rule the Earth. Bizarre, obscure, based on true story. **AKA:** Der Chef Wuenscht Keine Zeugen; The Chief Wants No Survivors. 🦴🦴

1963 92m/B *GE* Maria Perschy, Uwe Friedrichsen, Robert Cunningham, Karen Blanguernon, Gustavo Rojo; *D:* Hans Albin, Peter Berneis. **VHS** *MOV*

Non-Stop New York

Mystery tale with interesting twist. A wealthy woman can give an alibi for a murder suspect, but no one will listen, and she is subsequently framed. Pays homage to Hitchcock with its photography and humor. Quick and charming. 🦴🦴🦴

1937 71m/B Anna Lee, John Loder, Francis L. Sullivan, Frank Cellier; *D:* Robert Stevenson. **VHS** *NOS, SNC*

Not of this Earth

Jim Wynorski's remake of Roger Corman's original has virtually everything that a B-movie fan could ask for: total lack of seriousness, a silly plot that zips right along, cheesy special

M*A*S*H enters the space age...but the food still sucks in *1984.*

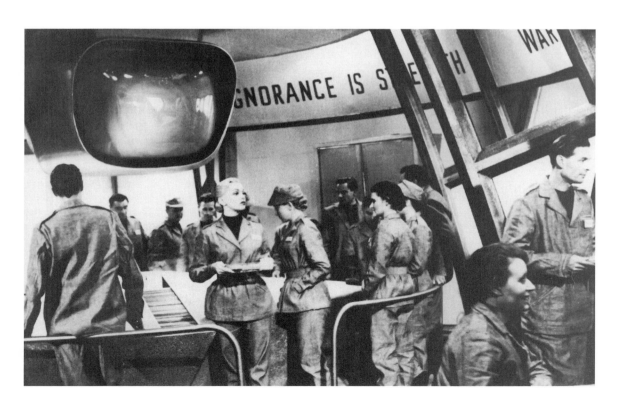

effects, and oodles of gratuitous nudity. Vampire from the planet Davonna is here to send blood to the folks back home. Traci Lords is the nurse who unwittingly helps him by providing transfusions. But before long, she and her policeman beau realize that something untoward is going on down in the basement. Why is there smoke coming from the furnace when the temperature is close to 100 outside? Is someone getting rid of the remains of an unlucky door-to-door vacuum cleaner salesman? Corman executive-produced this remake of his 1957 piece. 🦴🦴🦴

1988 (R) 92m/C Traci Lords, Arthur Roberts, Lenny Juliano, Rebecca Perle, Ace Mask, Roger Lodge; **D:** Jim Wynorski; **W:** Jim Wynorski, R.J. Robertson. **VHS, Beta** *MGM*

Now You See Him, Now You Don't

Light Disney comedy involving a gang of crooks who want to use a college student's invisibility formula to rob a local bank. Sequel to Disney's *The Computer Wore Tennis Shoes.* 🦴🦴

1972 (G) 85m/C Kurt Russell, Joe Flynn, Cesar Romero, Jim Backus; **D:** Robert Butler; **M:** Robert F. Brunner. **VHS, Beta** *DIS*

Nude on the Moon

Lunar expedition discovers moon inhabited by people who bare skin as hobby. Groovy theme song, "I'm Mooning Over You, My Little Moon Doll." Part of Joe Bob Brigg's "Sleaziest Movies in the History of the World" series. **WOOF!**

1961 83m/C D: Doris Wishman. **VHS** *VTR*

The Nutty Professor

A mild-mannered (but nutty) chemistry professor creates a potion that turns him into a suave, debonair, playboy type with an irresistible attraction to women. Jerry Lewis has repeatedly denied the slick character is a Dean Martin parody, but the evidence is quite strong. Easily Lewis's best film, with many great bits of comedy and substantial contributions from the supporting cast. Remade in 1996 as a vehicle for Eddie Murphy. 🦴🦴🦴

1963 107m/C Jerry Lewis, Stella Stevens, Howard Morris, Kathleen Freeman, Del Moore; **D:** Jerry Lewis; **W:** Bill Richmond, Jerry Lewis; **C:** Wallace Kelley. **VHS, Beta, LV** *PAR*

Oblivion

It's cowboys versus aliens in this Charles Band production, not the first sci-fi western by a long shot but pretty much the only one that doesn't make the mistake of taking itself seriously. On a frontier planet the sheriff of Oblivion is murdered by outlaws led by reptilian desperado Redeye. The lawman's peace-loving son (genetically unable to do violence, unless it's convenient to the script) reluctantly returns to the settlement to face the bad guys. Pic has fun with the cliches instead of merely slouching through them, and a droll gallery of characters includes *Star Trek*'s George Takei as a drunken doctor, Carel Struycken as a giant psychic undertaker, and Julie Newmar spoofing her *Batman* Catwoman persona as the overtly feline town madame. Like other Full Moon productions, this was shot back-to-back with its own sequel, *Backlash.* 🦴🦴🦴

1994 (PG-13) 94m/C Richard Joseph Paul, Andrew Divoff, Jackie Swanson, Meg Foster, Isaac Hayes, Julie Newmar, Carel Struycken, George Takei; **D:** Sam Irvin; **W:** Peter David; **M:** Pino Donaggio. **VHS, Beta** *PAR*

Octaman

This film is very nearly as bad as the title suggests. A hideously non-threatening octopusman is discovered by scientists in Mexico, who are also occupied with a tiresome love triangle. This is basically a rip-off of the classic *Creature from the Black Lagoon,* which coincidentally was written by *Octaman*'s director Harry Essex. A young makeup wiz named Rick Baker designed the octopus man before going on to do swell work in *American Werewolf in London,* while female lead Pier Angeli died of a drug overdose during filming. As big a mess as this film is, those who love monsters will likely find a place in their hearts for the shambling, rubbery Octaman. They don't make monsters like him anymore (well, hardly ever). 🦴🦴

1971 79m/C Kerwin Mathews, Pier Angeli, Harry Guardino, David Essex, Jeff Morrow, Norman Fields; **D:** Harry Essex. **VHS, Beta** *GEM, CNG, PSM*

Odin: Photon Space Sailor Starlight

In the year 2099 the spaceship Starlight is off

on an adventurous mission to unexplored galaxies. When the crew rescues a mysterious girl she lures them on a trip to the planet Odin, which may be the birthplace of humanity, but they're sidetracked by a power-mad computer. Hardware-crazed Japanimation for devotees only, insufficiently exploiting Norse mythology themes. Open ending leading into further chapters (not yet available on U.S. home video) is followed by a live rock-music video. In Japanese with English subtitles. A dubbed version is also available. 🦴🦴

1985 139m/C *JP* **D:** Takeshi Shirado, Eiichi Yamamoto, Toshio Masuda; **W:** Eiichi Yamamoto, Kazuo Kasahara, Toshio Masuda. **VHS** *CPM, WTA*

Official Denial

Cable TV-movie follows one of the more interesting alien-abduction theories from Whitley Strieber's book *Communion*. Average joe has been repeatedly seized and examined by 'Schwa'-type humanoids. The Air Force—

whose bedside manner is hardly any warmer—are watching, however, and shoot down the saucer with a Reagan "Star Wars" satellite (ah, so that's what they were really for!). The one surviving little grey man won't talk, however, so our victimized hero is brought in for a face-to-face confrontation. Pic's ultimate revelation may actually please UFO skeptics more than believers; add half a bone if applicable. Mediocre f/x. 🦴🦴🦴

1993 86m/C Parker Stevenson, Erin Gray, Dirk Benedict, Chad Everett; **D:** Brian Trenchard-Smith; **W:** Bruce Zabel; **M:** Garry McDonald, Laurie Stone. **VHS, Beta** *PAR*

Omega Cop

In a post-apocalyptic future when solar flares have spread madness and death, John Travis is the only beat patrolman keeping peace in the ruins. He uses his martial arts skills and tons of ammo to rescue three women from slave-trading freaks. Fans of TV's *Batman* might enjoy (?) this for West's mock-serious

"Okay! So maybe all of them *weren't* business dinners." Worried guy, Charlton Heston, faces a mean tax-audit team in *The Omega Man.*

presence as the hero's chief. Otherwise, move along. 🦴

1990 (R) 89m/C Ron Marchini, Adam West, Stuart Whitman, Troy Donahue, Meg Thayer, Jennifer Jostyn, Chrysti Jimenez, D.W. Landingham, Chuck Katzakian; **D:** Paul Kyriazi. **VHS** *HMD*

The Omega Man

In post-holocaust Los Angeles, Charleton Heston is immune to the effects of a biologically engineered plague and battles those who aren't—an army of albino victims bent on destroying what's left of the world. Strong suspense with considerable violence, despite the PG rating. Based on the science-fiction thriller "I Am Legend" by Richard Matheson, which is also the basis for the film *The Last Man on Earth*. 🦴 🦴 🦴 🦴

1971 (PG) 98m/C Charlton Heston, Anthony Zerbe, Rosalind Cash, Paul Koslo; **D:** Boris Sagal. **VHS, Beta, LV** *WAR*

On the Beach

A group of survivors attempt to live normal lives in post-apocalyptic Australia, waiting for the inevitable arrival of killer radiation. At times they're all so stoic and good natured about it all that you want to smack them. Fred Astaire is strong in his first dramatic role. Though scientifically implausible, still a good anti-war vehicle. Based on the best-selling novel by Nevil Shute, this was one of the first films to be heavily advertised as an Important Event by a Hollywood studio (rightfully worried at the reception a film would receive in which all of the characters are doomed from the start). It paid off big at the box office. 🦴 🦴 🦴

1959 135m/B Gregory Peck, Anthony Perkins, Donna Anderson, Ava Gardner, Fred Astaire, Guy Doleman; **D:** Stanley Kramer; **W:** John Paxton; **C:** Giuseppe Rotunno; **M:** Ernest Gold. Golden Globe Awards '60: Best Score; National Board of Review Awards '59: 10 Best Films of the Year; Nominations: Academy Awards '59: Best Film Editing, Best Original Score. **VHS, Beta, LV** *FOX, FCT*

On the Comet

Lesser-known sci-fi fantasy by Jules Verne brought to life by Czech animator Karel Zeman. Wandering planetoid brushes past 19th-century Earth and takes part of the Mediterranean coast with it. Drifting through the solar system, assorted Europeans, Arabs, dinosaurs (?), soldiers, lovers, and scalawags realize their old nationalist squabbles are pointless now that they're completely alone, and there are some satirical jabs at human nature. Zeman's signature animation whimsies, combining live-action, stop-motion, and life-size cutouts, put the viewer in a storybook universe where anything seems possible. If conventional Hollywood studios tried to film this yarn straight the f/x budget would be higher than that comet. Not the easiest tape to locate, but a real treasure if you do. Dubbed in English. **AKA:** Na Komete; Hector Servadac's Ark. 🦴 🦴 🦴

1968 76m/C *CZ* Emil Horvath Jr., Magda Vasarykova, Frantisek Filipovsky; **D:** Karel Zeman. **VHS, Beta** *FCT, MRV*

One Million B.C.

The strange saga of the struggle of primitive cavemen and their battle against dinosaurs and other monsters. Curiously told in flashbacks, this film provided stock footage for countless dinosaur movies that followed. Portions of film rumored to be directed by cinematic pioneer D. W. Griffith. **AKA:** The Cave Dwellers; Cave Man; Man and His Mate. 🦴 🦴 🦴

1940 80m/B Victor Mature, Carole Landis, Lon Chaney Jr.; **D:** Hal Roach, Hal Roach Jr. Nominations: Academy Awards '40: Best Original Score. **VHS, Beta** *MED, RXM*

The Original Fabulous Adventures of Baron Munchausen

Easily the most surrealistic screen telling of the life and times of history's most famous liar. Director Karel Zeman utilizes a unique blend of live action, art, animation, special effects, and his lyrical eye for the not-quite-real to create a world all its own. When a modern day astronaut is stranded on the moon, he is amazed enough just to meet the Baron, let alone return to Earth in Munchausen's sailing ship pulled by winged horses. Back on Earth,

he is witness to some amazing adventures in a world not quite the same as the one he left. The lovable liar rescues a princess from a evil sultan, gets swallowed by a giant sea creature who has swallowed many ships whole, is carried off by a mythical Roc, and is desired and wooed by a mermaid before escaping on a giant sea horse. A fantasy masterpiece of big and little adventures. You'll wish that flowers could bloom as mystically in real life. **AKA:** The Fabulous Baron Munchausen. 🎵🎵🎵♭

1961 84m/C *CZ* Milos Kopecky, Jana Brejchova, Rudolph Jelinek, Jan Werich; *D:* Karel Zeman. **VHS, LV** *NO*

Out There

Unemployed photojournalist buys obsolete camera at a yard sale and discovers the 25-year-old film shows pictures of a flying saucer encounter and abduction by 'Schwa' aliens. Attempts to verify the photos plunges him into an underground of crackpots, Hollywood has-beens, tabloid reporters, and insane conspira-cies. Gag topics in this cable-made farce touch on such arcane matters as the Ada computer compiler, Nixon's hidden heroism, and *THX-1138,* but during the film shoot there must have been a humor-dampening field switched on; amazingly little of it is funny despite the promising cast. 🎵♭

1995 (PG-13) 98m/C Bill Campbell, Wendy Schaal, Julie Brown, David Rasche, Paul Dooley, Bill Cobbs, Bob(cat) Goldthwait, Rod Steiger, June Lockhart, Jill St. John, Carel Struycken, Billy Bob Thornton, P.J. Soles; *D:* Sam Irvin; *W:* Thomas Strelich, Alison Nigh; *C:* Gary Tieche; *M:* Deborah Holland, Frankie Blue. **VHS, Beta** *PAR*

Outbreak

Director Wolfgang Petersen (*Shattered, In the Line of Fire*), an expert in the thriller genre, stumbles badly here, along with star Dustin Hoffman. An animal smuggler (Patrick Dempsey) sneaks a rare African monkey into the U.S. Unfortunately, the monkey carries a deadly virus, which infects the smuggler, and those with whom he comes into contact. The

Periodontal treatment, c. ***One Million B.C.***

Outland

On Io, a volcanic moon of Jupiter, miners begin suffering from spells of insanity (stepping out into the vacuum without their suits, for your viewing pleasure). Sean Connery, by far the best thing in the movie, is the planet's lone federal marshal who begins an investigation that bad guys try to stop. Essentially a western in space, with some of Peter Hyams' typically poor science, so-so f/x, and some spectacular exits for the villains. Might make an interesting double feature with *High Noon,* though, and it even sired its own blatant imitator, *Moon 44.* 🎗🎗🎗

1981 (R) 109m/C Sean Connery, Peter Boyle, Frances Sternhagen, James B. Sikking, Kika Markham, Clarke Peters; *D:* Peter Hyams; *W:* Peter Hyams; *C:* Stephen Goldblatt; *M:* Jerry Goldsmith. Nominations: Academy Awards '81: Best Sound. **VHS, Beta, LV** *WAR*

Overdrawn at the Memory Bank

Like *The Lathe of Heaven,* this shot-on-tape cerebral sf was done for Public Television and remains one of the better (and least-known) screen translations of cyberpunk. Complicated setup finds a nonconformist in the sterile future separated from his body due to a bureaucratic snafu. For safekeeping, his mind is stored inside the giant HX368 Novicorp computer that more or less runs the world; there he manipulates virtual reality to simulate his favorite flick *Casablanca,* and tries to access software controls to the outside to work some serious mischief. Raul Julia plays both the hacker hero and Humphrey Bogart, and the whole thing is a delicious lark even if you're scratching your head by the end. Based on a short story by John Varley. 🎗🎗🎗

1983 84m/C Raul Julia, Linda Griffiths; *D:* Douglas Williams. **VHS, Beta** *VTR, NWV*

Panic in the Year Zero!

Ray Milland doubled as actor/director on this one, generally considered to be the best of his five efforts. Milland and family luck out(?) and miss getting nuked in Los Angeles when an urge for fishing comes up. Continuing out into the wilderness for safety, the family finds a

"Your reflexes are just *not* as sharp with that nitrous oxide pumping!" Renee Russo chides Dustin Hoffman in **Outbreak.**

plague begins to spread through a California suburb, requiring the help of military disease-expert Hoffman, and his ex-wife (Rene Russo), a scientist with the Centers for Disease Control. They search for an antidote as the virus continues to mutate, and they uncover a secret government plot to exterminate the victims to prevent the spread of the disease. Despite scientific pretensions, the film ends with the traditional chase scene, this time in a military helicopter. Hoffman looks ridiculous wandering around in his bright yellow airtight suit and is hardly a threat to Arnold or Sylvester as the next action hero. Both Morgan Freeman and Donald Sutherland give solid performances as military higher-ups at odds with each other. Based on two books: Richard Preston's *The Hot Zone* and Laurie Garrett's *The Coming Plague.* 🎗🎗

1994 (R) 128m/C Dustin Hoffman, Rene Russo, Morgan Freeman, Donald Sutherland, Cuba Gooding Jr., Kevin Spacey, Patrick Dempsey; *D:* Wolfgang Petersen; *W:* Laurence Dworet, Robert Roy Pool, Laurence Dworet, Robert Roy Pool; *C:* Michael Ballhaus; *M:* James Newton Howard. New York Film Critics Awards '95: Best Supporting Actor (Spacey). **VHS, LV** *WAR*

TV on Tape:
The Outer Limits

They called it "The Control Voice." The racket coming from your television set became suddenly stilled, the picture reduced to a wavering line, while a matter-of-fact voice icily informed you that "We are taking control of your television set." At that instant, the thought that you might have the ability to change the channel were instantly erased. You really had no choice—unknown hypnotic entities had indeed taken control, and for the next 60 minutes, there was nothing you could do about it.

And you wouldn't have it any other way.

Though rare today, anthology shows were once very popular on television. Although mostly dramas and comedies, there was an occasional short-lived science-fiction series such as *Tales of Tomorrow*. Frustrated by the network censors, writer/producer Rod Serling turned to fantasy and science fiction to sneak his ideas on the air, creating a series called *The Twilight Zone* as his vehicle. Excellently written and directed, episodes of *The Twilight Zone* were intellectually stimulating, sometimes whimsical, and often downright preachy. As host, Serling was always on hand to reassure us with his wry commentary.

For *The Outer Limits*, producer Leslie Stevens had something quite different in mind. While Serling invited us to enter "another dimension," *The Outer Limits* reached right out and grabbed you. While *The Twilight Zone* had always brought you to the edge of imagination, the Control Voice (Vic Paren) leaped out from beyond that edge and commanded, "You are about to experience the awe and mystery that reaches from the inner mind to... *The Outer Limits*!"

And they weren't kidding. The stories had more to do with sensation than speculation. Every story had some sort of fantastic monster or weird alien visitor (affectionately termed "the Bear" by insiders), courtesy of the best make-up and f/x that television had to offer. One week an energy being from beyond the stars would invade a radio station. The next, swarms of tiny alien criminals would be set loose in your neighborhood. They weren't above starting the show with a scene in which a weird, ugly mutant creature would jump out of the shadows straight at the camera.

Not that the show could be called lowbrow. On the contrary, a lot of episodes were based on excellent stories by some of science fiction's finest talents. As long as there was some kind of monster in it. Even if the aliens or mutants were benign, they were always presented in such a way that you'd get a few thrills out of them. *The Outer Limits* probably caused more nightmares for little kids than any other show. Even if you were sent to bed at the start of the show, it was too late—the Control Voice already had you.

Recently, the Showtime cable channel revived the series. The new series has excellent production values, and follows the tradition of basing stories on solid stories (sometimes remaking classic episodes), still with the required "Bear," and some of them have been quite good. But it's just not the same. With 60 cable channels available via your remote control, there's no way to reproduce the chilling effect of the Control Voice.

But in 1963, when an unknown force from *The Outer Limits* seized control of your television in a darkened room, who would dare get up and defy the authority of the Control Voice? They were controlling transmission. You really didn't have any choice.

1963-65/B VHS *MGM, MOV*
1995-present/C VHS *MGM*

"Look, I'll pay you a million bucks if you'll spend just one night with the 3-D *Parasite*!" James Davison makes an early indecent proposal to Demi Moore.

survivalist's dream come true in an every-man-for-himself world. An intriguing plot and very competent cast (even Frankie Avalon does the job) make this an above average '60s end-of-the-world thriller. **AKA:** End of the World. 🦴🦴🐾

1962 92m/B Ray Milland, Jean Hagen, Frankie Avalon, Mary Mitchell, Joan Freeman, Richard Garland, Rex Holman; **D:** Ray Milland; **M:** Les Baxter. **VHS** *FRG*

Parasite

A small town is beset by gross parasites that infest human hosts. This effort is notable today mostly as an early screen credit for a young Demi Moore. Genuinely revolting stuff about sluglike critters invading human bodies is undone by budgetary limitations and a dark, dirty look. In 3-D, no less, during the technique's brief return in the early '80s. 🦴🐾

1982 (R) 90m/C Bob Glaudini, Demi Moore, Luca Bercovici, Cherie Currie, Gale Robbins, James Davidson, Al Fann, Cheryl "Rainbeaux" Smith, Vivian Blaine; **D:** Charles

Band; **W:** Michael Shoob, Frank Levering, Alan J. Adler; **C:** Mac Ahlberg; **M:** Richard Band. **VHS, Beta, LV** *PAR*

Peacemaker

Two manlike, virtually indestructible aliens rampage through the city. Each claims to be an interstellar cop hunting a galactic serial killer. Which one is lying? Fun, completely overlooked genre entry, a diverting action slam with only as much sci-fi trappings as it needs to keep things in motion. The tricky script does keep you off-balance regarding the bad guy's true identity. Great stunts, solid performances. 🦴🦴🦴

1990 (R) 90m/C Robert Forster, Lance Edwards, Hilary Shepard, Bert Remsen, Robert Davi; **D:** Kevin S. Tenney; **W:** Kevin S. Tenney; **C:** Thomas Jewett. **VHS, Beta, LV** *FRH*

The People

A young teacher takes a job in a small town and finds out that her students have telepath-

ic powers and other strange qualities. Adapted from a novel by Zenna Henderson. Good atmosphere, especially for a TV movie. 🐟🐟🦤

1971 74m/C Kim Darby, Dan O'Herlihy, Diane Varsi, William Shatner; **D:** John Korty; **M:** Carmine Coppola. **VHS, Beta** *PSM*

The People that Time Forgot

A totally unnecessary sequel to *The Land that Time Forgot,* based, once again, on an Edgar Rice Burroughs novel. Compared to this adaptation, Burroughs' no-frills pulp fiction reads like Tolstoy. A rescue team returns to the lost land of Caprona to rescue Bowen Tyler, who was abandoned the end of *The Land that Time Forgot.* This time, in addition to the rubbery, unconvincing dinosaurs and frantically overacting cavemen, they encounter a lost race of samurai who are holding Tyler captive. Their leader is a fat bald guy looks like Tor Johnson with big eyebrows. The heroes consist of various tiresome stereotypes: an absent-minded scientist, a drunken pilot, a couple of spunky heroines, and an outspokenly chauvinistic hero. The film is not without a chuckle or two—watch for the remarkably lifeless pterodactyls. 🐟🦤

1977 (PG) 90m/C *GB* Doug McClure, Patrick Wayne, Sarah Douglas, Dana Gillespie, Thorley Walters, Shane Rimmer; **D:** Kevin Connor; **W:** Patrick Tilley. **VHS, Beta** *SUE*

People Who Own the Dark

A group of wealthy men and a coterie of call girls are having an orgy in the basement of an old home when a nuclear war breaks out. Everyone outside is blinded by the blast but some survivors manage to make their way to the house where they try to attack the inhabitants. Don't bother. **WOOF!**

1975 (R) 87m/C Paul Naschy, Tony Kendall, Maria Perschy, Terry Kemper, Tom Weyland, Anita Brock, Paul Mackey; **D:** Armando de Ossorio; **W:** Armando de Ossorio. **VHS** *SUN, MRV*

The Phantom Creeps

Evil Dr. Zorka (Bela Lugosi), armed with a meteorite chunk which can bring an army to a standstill, provides the impetus for this enjoyable serial in 12 episodes. Lugosi also employs an invisibility belt in his evil schemes, as well as what is possibly the strangest looking robot in cinema history. Though standard serial plotting tries to keep things from rising above mediocrity, Lugosi's spirited performance and a series of weird plot twists keep this one humming along. 🐟🐟

1939 235m/B Bela Lugosi, Dorothy Arnold, Robert Kent, Regis Toomey, Roy Barcroft, Edward Van Sloan; **D:** Ford Beebe, Saul Goodkind; **W:** George Plympton, Basil Dickey, Mildred Barish; **C:** Jerome Ash, William Sickner. **VHS, Beta** *NOS, SNC, VCN*

The Phantom Empire

So you think you've seen it all with computer-generated dinosaurs and liquid-metal Terminators? Bah! No true fan should turn down a chance to watch truly one of the weirdest of the vintage serials. Bad guys want to force singing cowboy Gene Autry off his ranch so they can mine a secret radium depost. Meanwhile 25,000 feet underground, the 'Scientific City' of Murania, an advanced, ancient civilization driven beneath the surface by glaciers, wants to avoid discovery, and dispatches oxygen-masked 'Thunder Riders' to the surface to ward off nosy cowboys. Autry is framed for murder, beaten up, slain, and resurrected (!) throughout the 12 episodes; but no matter what happens he always gets back to a microphone, often with the help of his kiddie fan club, in time to croon another number for his radio program. Dig the cheesy robots in their metal stetsons, and the Muranian production design, impressive despite Rhino Home Video's scratchy print. Studio publicity of the era claimed that the writer dreamt up the plot while doped with anesthesia in a dentist's chair (that should classify this as a "head" movie 30 years before *2001*), but a definite influence were the hollow-Earth theories of assorted crackpot authors, whom had among their adherents Adolf Hitler. Meanwhile the script lifts lines from such far-flung sources as Shakespeare's *Henry V* and Ripley's Believe It or Not. Also available in an edited theatrical version at 80 minutes. Avoid like the plague Fred Olen Ray's recent soundalike feature *Phantom Empire.* **AKA:** Radio Ranch. 🐟🐟🐟

"His secret power menaced the world! He came from a billion miles of space to meet the strangest destiny every told!"

—*Phantom from Space.*

"Captives
of a power...
far, far out!"

— *The Phantom Planet.*

1935 245m/B Gene Autry, Frankie Darro, Betsy King Ross, Smiley Burnette; **D:** B. Reeves Eason, Otto Brower. **VHS, Beta** *NOS, SNC, VYY*

Phantom from Space

An invisible alien lands on Earth, begins killing people, and is pursued by a pair of scientists. 🐾🐾

1953 72m/B Ted Cooper, Rudolph Anders, Noreen Nash, James Seay, Harry Landers; **D:** W. Lee Wilder. **VHS, Beta** *VYY, SNC, NOS*

The Phantom from 10,000 Leagues

Slimy sea monster attacks swimmers and fishermen; investigating oceanographer pretends not to notice monster is hand puppet. Early AIP release, when still named American Releasing Company. 🐾

1956 80m/B Kent Taylor, Cathy Downs, Michael Whalen, Helene Stanton, Phillip Pine; **D:** Dan Milner. **VHS** *VYY, SNC, MLB*

The Phantom Planet

An astronaut crashlands on an asteroid and discovers a race of tiny people living there. Having breathed the atmosphere, he shrinks to their dimunitive size and aids them in their war against brutal invaders. Infamously peculiar. 🐾🐾

1961 82m/B Dean Fredericks, Coleen Gray, Tony Dexter, Dolores Faith, Francis X. Bushman, Richard Kiel; **D:** William Marshall. **VHS, Beta** *NOS, SNC*

Phase 4

Sole directorial effort from Saul Bass (eminent screen title designer who helped bring off the shower scene in *Psycho*) is a bizarre, visionary chiller of common ants suddenly endowed by extraterrestrial force with mass-intelligence. When they conquer a patch of Arizona countryside, a pair of scientists in a high-tech domed lab try to destroy the environmental menace. The humans have pesticides, grenades, and their own fierce cunning. The ants have adaptive mutation, Archimedean engineering talents, and their own fierce cun-

ning. It's not a fair fight... The six-legged thespians turn in a remarkable performance (sorry animal-rights fanatics, bugs *were* harmed in the production of this film, you betcha!), and half the pic occurs from their minute point of view. Inspired by *2001: A Space Odyssey,* Bass planned a cosmic f/x sequence at the end that had to be scrapped for budget reasons; thus the finale seems truncated, but this is still an offbeat genre flick deserving of greater attention. 🐾🐾🐾

1974 (PG) 84m/C Nigel Davenport, Michael Murphy, Lynne Frederick, Alan Gifford, Helen Horton, Robert Henderson; **D:** Saul Bass; **W:** Mayo Simon; **C:** Dick Bush. **VHS, Beta, LV** *PAR*

The Philadelphia Experiment

If you're into conspiracies, this one really happened (at least the first part of the story). In 1943, the U.S. destroyer Eldridge was involved in a WWII experiment to make it radar invisible. Not only did the Eldridge disappear from the radar screens, it completely vanished! Now for the second part: two of the sailors from the vessel reappear in the year 1984 and as they try to figure out where they are, one of them has trouble holding it all (his molecules, that is) together and vanishes. The other (Michael Pare) is captured by the military, escapes, finds romance and an old friend or two, and discovers that they are trying to duplicate the 1943 experiment in 1984. All this leads to trouble with his molecules, the discovery of a rip in the very fabric of time, and the revealing of the horrible consequences of the first experiment. Nancy Allen as Allison Hayes (a tribute to the actress who played 1958's *50 Foot Woman*) energetically tries to help Pare and shipmate Bobby DiCicco adjust to their new home. Based on the book by William I. Moore and Charles Berlitz. A pet project of John Carpenter, who didn't direct but became executive producer. 🐾🐾🐾

1984 (PG) 101m/C Michael Pare, Nancy Allen, Eric Christmas, Bobby DiCicco, Michael Currie, Louise Latham; **D:** Stewart Raffill; **W:** William Grey, Michael Janover; **C:** Dick Bush. **VHS, Beta, LV** *VTR*

Philadelphia Experiment 2

David Herdeg, the surviving time-transplanted sailor from the original *Philadelphia Experiment,* is alive and well in 1993 until he begins to experience the same molecular displacement that had destroyed his fellow tar ten years ago. In a nearby top-secret military lab, a mad scientist (Gerritt Graham) is conducting another experiment. Unknown to everyone, the goal of this experiment is to transport a Stealth Fighter back to 1943 in order to bomb Washington, D.C., thus ensuring Germany's victory in WWII. Seems said mad scientist's dad (also Graham) was a cohort of Adolph's, and his son wants to fertilize his Nazi roots. Consequently, Herdeg (Brad Johnson) must risk life and molecular stabilization to travel back to 1943, prevent the bombing, thusly saving his son, the world, life, liberty, justice for all, and all those sorts of good-type things. 🦴🦴

1993 (PG-13) 98m/C Brad Johnson, Gerrit Graham, Marjean Holden, James Greene, Geoffrey Blake, John Christian Grass, Cyril O'Reilly; *D:* Stephen Cornwell; *W:* Kevin Rock, Nick Paine; *M:* Gerald Gouriet. **VHS, LV** *VMK*

Phoenix the Warrior

Sometime in the future, female savages battle each other for control of the now ravaged Earth, and take long nude showers under waterfalls. Phoenix (Kathleen Kinmont), who acts like Clint Eastwood and talks like a Valley girl, is a newcomer on whose aerobicised shoulders rests the fates of the last few males on the planet. Cheap junk. Persis Khambatta is better remembered from *Star Trek: The Motion Picture.* **WOOF!**

1988 90m/C Persis Khambatta, James H. Emery, Peggy Sands, Kathleen Kinmont; *D:* Robert Hayes. **VHS** *NO*

The Pink Chiquitas

Abysmal Canadian sci-fi spoof about a tough detective arriving in the town of Beamsville, where a living meteorite (its purring vocals

"At the count of three, you will be my lover." Fiendish ant gives post-hypnotic suggestion in *Phase IV.*

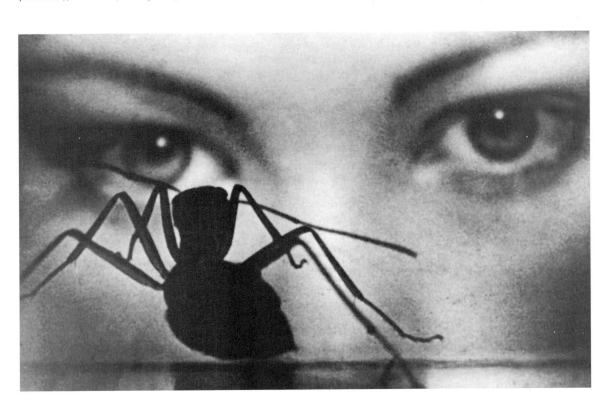

Charlton Heston makes a bold fashion statement by introducing the loin cloth to Simian society. *Planet of the Apes.*

about this movie is true: Bela Lugosi died a few days after production on this film began. Wood supplemented the few minutes of footage he had by substituting a stand-in (a chiropractor noticeable taller than Lugosi) to walk through the film with a cape over his face. The sets are pitiful (cardboard gravestones, shower curtain cockpit, Cadillac hubcaps for UFOs) and the stupefying dialogue ludicrous. Tell your friends. By the way, Plan 9 deals with the resurrection of the dead. "Can you prove it didn't happen?" **AKA:** Grave Robbers from Outer Space. **WOOF!**

1956 78m/B Bela Lugosi, Tor Johnson, Lyle Talbot, Vampira, Gregory Walcott, Duke Moore, Tom Keene; **D:** Edward D. Wood Jr.; **W:** Edward D. Wood Jr.; **C:** William C. Thompson. **VHS, Beta, LV** *NOS, SNC, MED*

Planet Earth

One of Gene Roddenberry's numerous aborted projects after cancellation of the classic *Star Trek,* this postnuke feature-length TV pilot is a remake of 1973's *Genesis II* and was itself redone later as *Strange New World.* By the year 2133, John Saxon, in suspended animation since 1979, is revived and working for Pax, the city that survived the 'Great Conflict' unscathed and now explores the world (thanks to conveniently intact global subway system) trying to rehab an anarchic planet. Here the hero and his team (Ted Cassidy as an intriguing Spock equivalent, even Majel Barrett in cameo) infiltrate a fiercely feminist tribe that keeps males drugged as docile 'dinks.' Regrettably campy curio, of interest mainly to Trekkers welcome to sift through the limp dialogue in search of Roddenberrian profundities. 🐾🐾

1974 78m/C John Saxon, Janet Margolin, Ted Cassidy, Diana Muldaur, Johana DeWinter, Christopher Gary; **D:** Marc Daniels; **W:** Gene Roddenberry; **C:** Arch R. Dalzell. **VHS** *UNI*

courtesy of Eartha Kitt, who never appears onscreen) has transformed the local women into glam-bitch harlots. Prominent among the actors/casualties is Sylvester Stallone's brother. **WOOF!**

1986 (PG-13) 86m/C *CA* Frank Stallone, Eartha Kitt, Bruce Pirrie, McKinlay Robinson, Elizabeth Edwards, Claudia Udy; **D:** Anthony Currie. **VHS, Beta** *PSM*

Plan 9 from Outer Space

You are interested in the unknown, the mysterious, the unexplainable. That is why you are reading this book. And that is why *Plan 9 from Outer Space* has over the years become the unanimous choice as "the worst film of all time." It is one of two films that secured Ed Wood's "reputation." Everything you've heard

Planet of Blood

Space opera about an female alien vampire (Florence Marly) discovered in a derelict spaceship on Mars by a rescue team. If you've ever seen the Soviet film *Niebo Zowiet,* don't be surprised if some scenes look familiar; the

script was written around f/x segments cut from that film. Surprisingly effective nonetheless; director Curtis Harrington wrings suspense within the limited confines of the low-budget sets, and Marly (*Sealed Verdict*) makes for a sexy/creepy monster. Yet another inspiration for *Alien*. Basil Rathbone is mainly seen standing around mission control barking orders via radio. Dennis Hopper and Curtis Harrington had collaborated previously on the atmospheric *Night Tide* (1963). **AKA:** Queen of Blood. 🦴🦴🦴

1966 81m/C John Saxon, Basil Rathbone, Judi Meredith, Dennis Hopper, Florence Marly, Forrest J. Ackerman; **D:** Curtis Harrington. **VHS** SNC, NOS, MRV

Planet of Dinosaurs

Spaceship crashes on an uncharted, prehistoric planet, and the human survivors must put aside their considerable squabbles about what to do next to fight for their lives against hungry, Earth-style dinosaurs. Good stop-motion f/x done on a minuscule budget; it's acting and dialogue that seem fossilized. Will they really be telling farmer's-daughter jokes in the far future? Horror genre fans may be amused to see James Whitworth, memorable as a cannibal mutant in Wes Craven's *The Hills Have Eyes*. 🦴🦴

1980 (PG) 85m/C James Whitworth; **D:** James K. Shea. **VHS, Beta** AHV, VTR

Planet of the Apes

Astronaut Charleton Heston crashlands on a planet in the future (3978 A.D.) where apes are masters and humans are merely brute animals. Superior science fiction with sociological implications. Heston delivers one of his more plausible performances, and superb ape makeup creates realistic pseudo-simians of Roddy McDowall, Kim Hunter, Maurice Evans, James Whitmore, and James Daly. The story is slightly reminiscent of the *Twilight Zone* episode in which astronauts end up inhabitants in an alien zoo; in fact, Rod Serling co-wrote the screenplay for *Planet of the Apes*, adapted from Pierre Boulle's novel *Monkey Planet*. Followed by four sequels (some of which are pretty good), including *Beneath...*,

Escape from..., *Conquest of...*, and *Battle for...*, and two television series. 🦴🦴🦴🦴

1968 (G) 112m/C Charlton Heston, Roddy McDowall, Kim Hunter, Maurice Evans, Linda Harrison, James Whitmore, James Daly; **D:** Franklin J. Schaffner; **W:** Rod Serling, Michael G. Wilson; **M:** Jerry Goldsmith. National Board of Review Awards '68: 10 Best Films of the Year; Nominations: Academy Awards '68: Best Costume Design, Best Original Score. **VHS, Beta, LV** FOX, FUS

Planet of the Vampires

Atmospheric, low-budget, sci-fi horror at its best. Dan O'Bannon has admitted that this Mario Bava gem was one of his main influences while writing *Alien*. Responding to a SOS from the planet Aura, the spaceship Argos crashlands on a set previously used for a Italian sword-and-sandal not-quite epic. The landscape is loaded with other wrecked space hulks including the SOSer. The bodies inside make it clear that the crew have violently offed each other and to confirm that, a hologram of the ship's commander appears and tells the story of madness and killing. Faced with new murders and disappearances, the captain of the Argos (Barry Sullivan) finds he is dealing with dastardly mind-possessing space vampires who manifest themselves as dots that can only be seen peripherally. To make matters worse, the minds of all the dead astronauts can also be controlled, leading to an outer space Zombie revival with the newly resurrected shedding their cellophane shrouds in Bavaesque style and flair. **AKA:** Terror in Space; Terreur dans l'Espace; Space Mutants; The Demon Planet; Terrore nello Spazio. 🦴🦴🦴

1965 86m/C IT SP Barry Sullivan, Norman Bengell, Angel Aranda, Evi Marandi, Fernando Villena; **D:** Mario Bava; **W:** Mario Bava, Callisto Cosulich, Antonio Roman; **C:** Antonio Rinaldi. **VHS, Beta** ORI

Planet on the Prowl

A fiery planet causes earthly disasters, so a troop of wily astronauts try to destroy it with the latest technology. They fail, leading one sacrificial soul to do it himself. **AKA:** War Between the Planets. 🦴

1965 80m/C IT Giacomo "Jack" Rossi-Stuart, Amber Collins, Peter Martell, John Bartha, Halina Zalewska, James Weaver; **D:** Anthony (Antonio Margheriti) Dawson. **VHS, Beta** NO

P

"They opened up a hole...and it stayed open!"
—*The Philadelphia Experiment.*

"If it bleeds, then we can kill it."

—Dutch Schaefer (Arnold Schwarzenegger) in *Predator*.

Planeta Burg

A classic Soviet sci-fi flick about a space exploration team landing on Venus. Their job becomes a rescue mission when one of the crew is stranded. Along the way, they are threatened by volcanic eruptions, hostile plant life, monstrous animals, and other dangers. Although there are some silly moments, some good plot twists and acting make up for them. The robot "John" they take with them could easily rival *Forbidden Planet*'s Robby in personality—his final scene of self-sacrifice is truly touching. In Russian with English subtitles. Much footage from this was reused by American International and turned into *Journey to a Prehistoric Planet* (1965). **AKA:** Cosmonauts on Venus; Storm Planet; Planet of Storms.

1962 90m/C *RU* Vladimir Temelianov, Gennadi Vernov, Kyunna Ignatova, Georgi Zhonov; **D:** Pavel Klushantsev; **W:** Pavel Klushantsev, Alexander Kazantsev. **VHS, Beta** *SNC*

Planets Against Us

Science-fiction tale of escaped alien humanoid robots who take refuge on Earth, but whose touch is fatal. Good special effects. **AKA:** I Pianeti Contro di Noi; The Man with the Yellow Eyes; Hands of a Killer; The Monster with Green Eyes.

1961 85m/B *IT FR* Michel Lemoine, Maria Pia Luzi, Jany Clair; **D:** Romano Ferrara. **VHS** *SNC*

Plughead Rewired: Circuitry Man 2

Like most sequels, this one's about half as good as the original. It tells essentially the same futuristic story about a romantic robot (Jim Metzler), a tough woman (Deborah Shelton), and the villainous Plughead (Vernon Wells) who lives to share other people's pain and terror directly. It shares most of the first film's strengths and weaknesses, too, but has a stronger emphasis on comedy, much of it broad and hammy, with two supporting characters whose appearance and shtick could have come straight from the mad scientists on

Mystery Science Theater 3000. Recommended for fans of the original only. **AKA:** Circuitry Man 2.

1994 (R) 97m/C Vernon Wells, Deborah Shelton, Jim Metzler, Dennis Christopher, Nicholas Worth, Traci Lords; **D:** Steven Lovy, Robert Lovy; **W:** Steven Lovy, Robert Lovy. **VHS** *COL*

The Power Within

An electrified stuntman finds he can send electrical shocks from his hands and becomes the victim of a kidnapping plot.

1979 90m/C Eric (Hans Gudegast) Braeden, David Hedison, Susan Howard, Art Hindle; **D:** John Llewellyn Moxey. **VHS, Beta** *PSM*

Prayer of the Rollerboys

Violent, futuristic, funky action as Corey Haim infiltrates a criminal militia of syncopated roller-blading neo-Nazi youth (references to *The Turner Diaries* abound) with plans for nationwide domination via narco-terrorism. Though routinely plotted and predictable, it's got great skating stunts and a wry vision of tomorrow's shattered USA—broke, drug-soaked, homeless, foreign owned; even sharper when you realize this is a Japanese-American co-production.

1991 (R) 94m/C *JP* Corey Haim, Patricia Arquette, Christopher Collet, Julius W. Harris, J.C. Quinn, Jake Dengel, Devin Clark, Mark Pellegrino, Morgan Weisser; **D:** Rick King; **W:** W. Peter Iliff; **C:** Phedon Papamichael. **VHS, LV** *ACA*

Predator

Schwarzenegger leads a team of soldier-of-fortune types with big muscles and big weapons into the Central American jungles to rescue hostages. They encounter an alien force that attacks them one by one. Soon it's just Arnold and the Beast. Yes, it's all just as silly as it can be, but some really inventive special effects and a break-neck pace make this one loads of fun. It's a pivotal film for both its star and director John McTiernan. Followed by a sequel.

1987 (R) 107m/C Arnold Schwarzenegger, Jesse Ventura, Sonny Landham, Bill Duke, Elpidia Carrillo, Carl Weathers, R.G. Armstrong, Richard Chaves, Shane Black, Kevin Peter Hall; **D:** John McTiernan; **W:** Jim Thomas, John Thomas; **C:** Donald McAlpine; **M:** Alan Silvestri. **VHS, Beta, LV** *FXV*

Predator 2

Tough cop Danny Glover takes time away from battling drug dealers to deal with malicious extraterrestrial who exterminated Arnold's band of commandos in the original. Shifting the scene from the Central American jungle to the urban jungle of L.A. is a plus. So are the inspired casting, the inventive effects, and the fast pace. The action is ultraviolent, gory, and illogical but still exciting. The spooky introduction, a long subway sequence, and the big finish are all corkers. Overall, a more-than-worthy sequel. 🦴🦴🦴

1990 (R) 105m/C Danny Glover, Gary Busey, Ruben Blades, Maria Conchita Alonso, Bill Paxton, Robert Davi, Adam Baldwin, Kent McCord, Morton Downey Jr., Calvin Lockhart, Teri Weigel, Kevin Peter Hall; **D:** Stephen Hopkins; **W:** John Thomas, Jim Thomas; **C:** Peter Levy. **VHS, Beta, LV** *FXV, CCB*

Prehistoric Women

A tribe of prehistoric women look for hus-bands the old-fashioned way—they drag them back to their caves from the jungle. So bad it's almost good. **AKA:** Slave Girls. **WOOF!**

1950 74m/C Laurette Luez, Allan Nixon, Mara Lynn, Joan Shawlee, Judy Landon; **D:** Greg Tallas. **VHS, Beta** *FHE, NOS, RHI*

Primal Impulse

An astronaut, stranded on the moon because of a sinister experimental double-cross, unleashes a mental scream which possesses a young woman's mind back on Earth. 🦴🦴

1974 90m/C Klaus Kinski. **VHS, Beta** *NO*

Primal Scream

Valiant but utterly disjointed attempt to do a hard-boiled sci-fi detective tale like *Blade Runner* on a budget that wouldn't buy birdseed for the *Maltese Falcon*. After a giant research lab on Saturn explodes in 1993 (!), a world-weary gumshoe investigates hideous

"I don't want her. Come on, YOU take her!" Arnold Schwarzenegger, Carl Weathers, and Bill Duke battle it out over the girl in *Predator*.

TV on Tape:
The Prisoner

The Prisoner was a very special kind of science-fiction show. Although it took place in a strange, otherworldly place that sometimes seems to be in the future, it wasn't about aliens or spaceships or time machines. It owed more to Kafka than Heinlein. The story of a secret agent who resigns his post and is abducted to a strange place called the Village, it created a cult following still going strong today.

Actor Patrick McGoohan played "Number 6" for the show's 17 hour-long episodes. The show began in 1967, when the world was in love with spies. McGoohan had already turned down the role of Ian Fleming's super-agent James Bond, having been offered it before Sean Connery. He had created and starred in *Danger Man* (also known as *Secret Agent Man*), an unorthodox "spy series" about an agent who relies on his intellect rather than gadgets and fists. The filming of one *Danger Man* episode took McGoohan to the grounds of a hotel in Portmeirion, Wales. A strange, whimsical-looking place that looked like it belonged in Lewis Carroll's Wonderland, it got McGoohan thinking. Two years later he'd sold networks on *The Prisoner*.

For *The Prisoner*, McGoohan also played a secret agent who disdains his profession. As "Number 6," McGoohan resigns against his superiors' wishes, and is abducted to the weird, surreal Village, which seems to have no other pur-

pose than to crush Number 6's individuality. Escape is rendered difficult by "rovers," strange bouncing bubble-creatures that can envelope straying Villagers. McGoohan revealed in interviews that the rovers were originally conceived as hovercraft-like vehicles, but this idea was scrapped when the prototype sank in Portmeirion's harbor. A handy weather-balloon provided a substitute, and the infinitely weirder bubble-rovers were created on the spur of the moment.

The 17 episodes of *The Prisoner* took on questions of identity and authority with a characteristically British sense of humor. The final episode saw Number 6 finally uncover the identity of the mysterious "Number 1," with a typically unexpected twist. There's never been a show quite like *The Prisoner*, and its possible there never will again. Fortunately, the magic of video has preserved its unique charms for posterity.

1968-69 (in the U.S)/C *GB Selected cast:* Patrick McGoohan, Virginia Maskell, Guy Doleman, Paul Eddington, George Baker, Angelo Muscat. **VHS, LV** *MPI, MOV, TVC*

---

deaths connected with a revolutionary new energy source (whose chemical formula spells out 'hellfire') managed by a corrupt corporation. Filmed in Philadelphia and New Jersey, looking just as seedy as ever with rusty spaceships poking out of suburban garages. **AKA:** Hellfire. 🦴🦴

1987 (R) 95m/C Kenneth John McGregor, Sharon Mason, Julie Miller, Jon Maurice, Mickey Shaughnessy; **D:** William Murray. **VHS** *NO*

The Princess Bride

Director Rob Reiner scores again with this take on the basic fairy tale formula that masterfully works as both a spoof and the real thing. Crammed wittily with all the cliches, this adventurously irreverent love story centers around a beautiful maiden and her young swain as they battle the evils of the mythical kingdom of Florin. Great dueling scenes, scary beasts (especially the "Rodents of Unusual Size"), and offbeat satire of the genre make this perhaps even more fun for adults than for children. Inspired cast, including Andre the Giant as, well, a giant; Mandy Patinkin as a Spanish swordsman; Christopher Guest as a five-fingered villain; and cameos by Billy Crys-

tal and Carol Kane as too-cute wizards. You don't have to even like fairy tales to love this film; like the reluctant little boy (*Wonder Year*'s Fred Savage) who's being read this tale by his Grandfather (Peter Falk), you will be drawn to the story and it's humor—we promise. Based on William Goldman's cult novel. 🦴🦴🦴🦴

1987 (PG) 98m/C Cary Elwes, Mandy Patinkin, Robin Wright, Wallace Shawn, Peter Falk, Andre the Giant, Chris Sarandon, Christopher Guest, Billy Crystal, Carol Kane, Fred Savage, Peter Cook, Mel Smith; **D:** Rob Reiner; **W:** William Goldman; **M:** Mark Knopfler. Hugos '88: Dramatic Presentation; Nominations: Academy Awards '87: Best Song ("Storybook Love"). **VHS, Beta, LV, 8mm** *COL, SUE, HMV*

Prison Planet

Political rebel of the future gets himself arrested and sent to the infamous Prison Planet, in search of a rightful ruler exiled there long before. But *Road Warrior* goons patrol the deserts, and our hero has some low-budget fights ahead of him. The script casually mentions some prominent names in screen sci fi; names are just about the only things the basement-level budget could afford. **WOOF!**

1992 (R) 90m/C James Phillips, Jack Willcox, Michael Foley, Deborah Thompson-Carlin; **D:** Armand Gazarian; **W:** Armand Gazarian. **VHS** *COL*

Prisoners of the Lost Universe

Talk-show hostess and her buddy are transported to a hostile universe by a renegade scientist. The two terrified humans search desperately for the dimensional door that is their only hope of escape. Made for television. 🦴🦴

1984 94m/C Richard Hatch, Kay Lenz, John Saxon; **D:** Terry Marcel. **VHS, Beta** *NO*

The Professor

Rare sci-fi thriller featuring a werewolf, an eccentric scientist, and a communist plot. Also includes several werewolf-oriented movie trailers. 🦴🦴

1958 30m/C Doug Hobart, John Copeland, Irene Barr. **VHS** *SNC*

Programmed to Kill

A beautiful terrorist is killed by the CIA and transformed on the operating table into a cyborg assassin, to infiltrate and slay her former comrades. She does, but vestigial memories compel the bionic babe to turn against her creators with equal fury. Sandahl Bergman goes the *Terminator* career route in imitation of her leading man from *Conan the Barbarian*. Action and violence galore, but ultimately average. **AKA:** Retaliator. 🦴🦴

1986 (R) 91m/C Robert Ginty, Sandahl Bergman, James Booth, Louise Caire Clark; **D:** Allan Holzman. **VHS, Beta** *MED*

Project A-ko

Set in the near future, this Japanese animated feature, which is intended for adults, concerns teenagers with strange powers, an alien spaceship, and lots of action. Seventeen year-old A-ko possesses superhuman strength and a ditzy sidekick, C-ko. B-ko, the spoiled and rich daughter of a business tycoon, decides to fight A-ko for C-ko's companionship. Meanwhile, an alien spaceship is headed toward Earth with unknown intentions. Somehow, everything ties together—watch and see how. In Japanese with English subtitles. 🦴🦴🦴

1986 86m/C *JP* **VHS, LV** *CPM, INJ, WTA*

Project: Alien

Cattle mutilations, scary abductions, and sightings of strange figures in spacesuits—it's enough to send rival reporters off on a race to blow open a government coverup of what seems like attacks by beings from space. What's actually happening revolves around tests of deadly biological weapons. Sf fans in search of a good extraterrestrial flick may feel let down by this teaser, shot in Yugoslavia (under the title *No Cause for Alarm*) as more of a breezy romantic caper. 🦴🦴

1989 (R) 92m/C Michael Nouri, Darlanne Fluegel, Maxwell Caulfield, Charles Durning; **D:** Frank Shields; **W:** Anthony Able. **VHS, LV** *VMK*

"This word 'inconceivable.' I do not think it means what you think it means."

—Inigo Montoya (Mandy Pantinkin) doubts his boss (Wallace Shawn) in *The Princess Bride*.

Project: Genesis

Stagebound, indecipherable low-budget sf from Canada involves a drug-smuggling star pilot shot down on an uninhabited planet. He, his CO, and a smart-aleck computer philosophize at length, as spaceships that look like homemade Christmas ornaments clash in the skies above. Gets a consolation bone just for being different. 🦴

1993 79m/C *CA* David Ferry, Olga Prokhorova; **D:** Philip Jackson; **W:** Philip Jackson; **M:** Andy McNeill. **VHS, LV** *PSM*

Project Metalbeast: DNA Overload

A CIA agent, cryogenically frozen for 10 years, becomes the guinea pig when a group of scientists decide to unthaw him for a DNA experiment involving living metallic skin. Too bad he turns into a metal beast by the light of the full moon. Sci-fi take on the werewolf saga. 🦴🦴🦴

1994 (R) 92m/C Kim Delaney, Barry Bostwick; **D:** Alessandro DeGaetano; **W:** Timothy E. Sabo; **M:** Conrad Pope. **VHS** *PSM*

Project Moon Base

Espionage runs rampant on a spaceship headed by a female officer. Eventually the ship is stranded on the moon. Actually filmed for a television series titled *Ring Around the Moon*. A cold-war sexist relic. 🦴🦴

1953 64m/C Donna Martell, Hayden Rourke; **D:** Richard Talmadge. **VHS, Beta** *VMK*

Project: Nightmare

Project Touchstone, to test the endurance of astronauts in space flights, is run by a HAL-9000 style computer that naturally goes haywire and takes over a patch of the countryside. A couple of heroic air-conditioning contractors blunder into the hazard zone and fight an onslaught of low budget f/x, in a chintzy cheapie that should prove inspirational to air-conditioning contractors everywhere. Dialogue must be heard to be disbelieved. 🦴

1985 75m/C Elly Koslo, Lance Dickson; **D:** Donald M. Jones. **VHS** *ACA, MOV*

Project Shadowchaser 3000

Derelict craft suddenly collides with a Mars-orbiting space station, forcing the crew of overacting idiots to contend with a visitor, an evil, shape-changing, deformed robot. No real connection to earlier *Project Shadowchaser* pics except for the same ripoff-happy production team, here so intent on aping *Alien* that they appear to have scrounged the original *Nostromo* space helmets. Watch with the sound turned off and you'll enjoy some cool f/x untroubled by the semicoherent plot and dimwit dialogue. Inclusion of a nauseatingly cute little dog, obviously meant to curry favor with the Hound, almost cost this loser its one bone. 🦴

1995 (R) 99m/C Frank Zagarino, Sam Bottoms, Christopher Atkins, Musetta Vander, Christopher Neame; **D:** John Eyres; **W:** Nick Davis; **M:** Steve Edwards. **VHS, LV** *TTC, NLC*

Project X

Bemused Air Force pilot gets a strange assignment—training lab chimpanzees to pilot planes in a computerized flight simulator. He grows close to the appealing apes and is shocked to learn the true, cruel purpose of the experiments. High-tech tale falls somewhere between science-fiction drama and animal-rights fable, but some scenes possess the "sense of wonder" that sf at its finest is meant to evoke. Great performances by the primates, somewhat soured by persistent allegations by activists of real-life animal abuse on the set. 🦴🦴🦴

1987 (PG) 107m/C Matthew Broderick, Helen Hunt, William Sadler, Johnny Rae McGhee, Jonathan Stark, Robin Gammell, Stephen Lang, Jean Smart, Dick Miller; **D:** Jonathan Kaplan; **W:** Stanley Weiser, Lawrence Lasker; **C:** Dean Cundey; **M:** James Horner. **VHS, Beta, LV** *FOX*

Prototype

Intelligent TV pic is the kinder, gentler side of the Frankenstein legend. Scientist Christopher Plummer perfects an inquisitive, ultra-logical android (David Morse) but learns that the military intends to train the prototype as a super-soldier. He and his discovery go on the lam together, but don't expect action chases or *Terminator* f/x blowouts; the drama centers on

American Giant Monsters

The 1950s were, among other things, the decade of technology. The fledgling science of nuclear energy was seen as mankind's savior; magazines of the period looked forward to a day when every household would be virtually run by the friendly atom. But there was a darker side to this dream, and the science-fiction movies popular at the time helped visualize it.

The '50s were a golden age for giant monster movies, just as the '60s saw an explosion of "demonic possession" movies and the late '70s were the era of the slasher movie. Some of these monsters were from outer space, like the "Ymir" of *20 Million Miles to Earth,* but a surprising number hailed from Earth. Many were survivors from the prehistoric past, like the giant insects of *The Black Scorpion* and *The Deadly Mantis,* the titanic ocean-dwelling monstrosities of *It Came from Beneath the Sea* and *The Monster that Challenged the World* or the reptiles of *The Beast from 20,000 Fathoms* and *The Giant Gila Monster.* As every child knows, there's something strangely satisfying about the idea of a gigantic whatsit smashing down buildings.

But a number of these critters were a direct result of man's monkeying with things better left alone. The question implied by many of these films was, "Suppose we create something we can't control? Suppose that something destroys us"? Take for example the 1955 classic *Tarantula.* All the elements of the '50s monster film are in evidence: a scientist experimenting with a substance that causes growth in animals accidentally unleashes one of his less pleasant experiments—a colossal tarantula that begins killing everything in sight.

It's interesting that so many of the '50s monster brigade were tiny pests in their original forms; there were no films about giant mutant horses, for instance. Of course, from the filmmakers' perspective, this had the advantage of making for cheap monsters. Impressive effects could be had by superimposing shots of screaming people over footage of live critters ambling harmlessly around little model cities. This could be overdone, however. *The Beginning of the End,* a film about giant radioactive grasshoppers (!) used footage of real grasshoppers crawling over PICTURES of buildings for key scenes. Other giant mutant monster movies, however, used impressive full-size mechanical monsters or animated models, like the giant ants of *Them.* The majority of these varmints, however, were more on the level of *The Killer Shrews,* who were simply dogs with papier-mache snouts and fangs.

After the '50s, really good monster films got harder to come by. The legacy continued well into the '70s in Japan of course, with Godzilla, Gamera, and friends, but the rest of the world became fascinated with vampires, witches, zombies, and serial killers. Or maybe it was only the shape of the monsters that changed. Maybe under the skin, monsters and the fears that inspire them are fundamentally the same.

---

the warm father-son relationship between creator and creation. Script by the award-winning team of tube veterans Richard Levinson and William Link. 🦴🦴🦴

1983 100m/C Christopher Plummer, David Morse, Frances Sternhagen, James Sutorius; *D:* David Greene; *M:* Billy Goldenberg. **VHS, LV** *LIV*

Prototype X29A

In 2057's desolate, lawless Los Angeles, a research scientist conducting experiments on a crippled ex-soldier uses an embargoed cyborg suit to enable her patient to walk again. Pre-programmed into the X29A armor, however, are assassination orders that turn the clomping creature into a mindless killing machine. So much for the health care system. *Terminator/Robocop* takeoff goes about its business in ultra-serious, doom-laden fashion that only points out how lame the whole thing is. 🦴🦴

1992 (R) 98m/C Brenda Swanson, Robert Tossberg, Lane Lenhart, Paul Coulj, Mitchell Cox; *D:* Phillip J. Roth; *W:* Phillip J. Roth. **VHS, LV** *VMK*

PSI Factor

Civilian NASA researcher observes and records signals from planet Sirius B. Subsequently he and his spouse are dogged by glowing UFOs and nosy government goons. There's some unexpected spark in the two leads and a heavy dose of Good Vibes at the end, but the real rationale for this cheapie might have been a wish that box-office lightning would strike twice, what with Steven Spielberg's sister Anne listed as one of the producers, when *Close Encounters of the Third Kind* was still a hot topic. 🦴🦴

1980 91m/C Peter Mark Richman, Gretchen Corbett, Tommy Martin; **D:** Bryan Trizers; **W:** Quentin Masters. **VHS** *NO*

The Psychotronic Man

An innocent man suddenly finds he possesses amazing and dangerous powers, enabling him to control outside events with a thought. 🦴🖐

1991 88m/C Peter Spelson, Christopher Carbis, Curt Colbert, Robin Newton, Paul Marvel; **D:** Jack M. Sell. **VHS** *UNI*

Pulse

Fear of technology pervades this low-voltage thriller in which electricity goes awry, causing common appliances and other household devices to super-charge, malfunction, and threaten their owners. Genre fans who enjoy the sight of glowing circuits and melting insulation should find *Pulse* friction a minor turn-on. 🦴🦴

1988 (PG-13) 90m/C Cliff DeYoung, Roxanne Hart, Joey Lawrence, Charles Tyner, Dennis Redfield, Robert Romanus, Myron Healey; **D:** Paul Golding; **M:** Jay Michael Ferguson. **VHS, Beta, LV** *COL*

The Puma Man

Alton inherits his family's ancient Incan UFO power to become Puma Man, a superdork in a peasant frock who makes catlike swatting motions as he pounces on the flunkies of bad guy Dr. Kobras (Donald Pleasence), who wants to rule the world. Unreleased theatrically in the U.S., this cheapo Italian *Superman* takeoff has some of the worst flying f/x ever. That's got to count for something, no? **WOOF!**

1980 80m/C *IT* Donald Pleasence, Walter George Alton, Sydne Rome, Miguel Angel Fuentes; **D:** Alvin J. Neitz, Alberto De Martino. **VHS, Beta** *PSM*

The Punisher

Marvel Comics anti-hero The Punisher is brought to life in this filmed-in-Australia tale of both justice and revenge. This is what a comic-book inspired movie should look like. Dolph Lundgren does the job as Frank Castle, who, inspired by the mob killing of his family, sets his sights on any and all bad guy types to be found. No shortage of bullets or explosives as one thug after another is judged, juried, and splattered. The Punisher's killing rituals take on a mystical quality as he lashes out from his subterranean sewer headquarters, and the unique "Punisher" skull (normally a part of his costume in the comics) even makes an appearance framed by the stubble of his facial hair. Stan Lee should be proud. 🦴🦴🦴

1990 (R) 92m/C Dolph Lundgren, Louis Gossett Jr., Jeroen Krabbe, Kim Miyori; **D:** Mark Goldblatt; **W:** Boaz Yakin; **C:** Ian Baker; **M:** Dennis Dreith. **VHS, Beta, LV** *LIV*

The Puppet Masters

Government official (Donald Sutherland) discovers that aliens are taking over the bodies of humans and if he doesn't find a way to stop the parasites they'll soon rule the Earth. The parasites are sufficiently yucky but, unfortunately, this adaptation is mediocre and generally wastes a talented cast. The filmmakers are fairly faithful to Heinlein's 1951 novel, but they missed the atmosphere of paranoia that he created. In that regard, the film doesn't measure up to the original 1956 *Invasion of the Body Snatchers* or, to take a more modern comparison, a really good episode of TV's *The X-Files*. **AKA:** Robert A. Heinlein's The Puppet Masters. 🦴🦴

1994 (R) 109m/C Donald Sutherland, Eric Thal, Julie Warner, Keith David, Will Patton, Richard Belzer, Yaphet Kotto; **D:** Stuart Orme; **W:** Terry Rossio, David S. Goyer, Ted Elliott; **M:** Colin Towns. **VHS, LV** *HPH*

The Purple Monster Strikes

Serial authority Donald F. Glut declares *The Purple Monster Strikes* as the last great

Republic serial and he's right; it was all downhill after this, the first and best of Republic's three Martian-invasion chapter plays. The red planet's emissary, a humanoid in a purple-colored scaly suit and played by cowboy star Roy Barcroft, comes to Earth to kill the human inventor of a reusable rocketship. All the poor Martians are capable of launching is a one-way capsule, and after Barcroft completes his assignment, he continues construction of the craft (with the help of Earth criminals). If he can get back home with the technology we will soon have a Mars invasion fleet in our backyard. The Purple Monster is also able to reanimate and possess the corpse of the late inventor (shades of *Invasion of the Body Snatchers* a decade ahead of time) but pops out for fistfights with a heroic lawyer attempting to foil him throughout the 15 cliffhanger episodes. These choreographed punchouts, so beloved by serial buffs, are the last good ones Republic would ever film. The studio's subsequent *Flying Discmen from Mars* and *Zombies of the Stratosphere* are pale imitations of what had gone before. 🦴🦴🦴

1945 188m/B Dennis Moore, Linda Stirling, Roy Barcroft; **D:** Spencer Gordon Bennet. **VHS** *REP, VCN, MLB*

Purple People Eater

The alien of the title descends to earth to mix with young girls and rock 'n' roll. Based on the song of the same name whose performer, Sheb Wooley, appears in the film. Harmless, stupid fun for the whole family. 🦴

1988 (PG) 91m/C Ned Beatty, Shelley Winters, Neil Patrick Harris, Kareem Abdul-Jabbar, Little Richard, Chubby Checker, Peggy Lipton; **D:** Linda Shayne. **VHS, Beta, LV** *MED, VTR*

Q (The Winged Serpent)

Aztec flying serpent god Quetzlcoatl is summoned to Manhattan by a modern-day high priest expert in the art of flaying human beings. Small-time crook and barroom pianist

"The Swiss Alps was a great choice for our honeymoon, Dear. If only our transportation hadn't failed us." Roy Barcroff in ***The Purple Monster Strikes.***

Cover your heads! It's *Q, The Winged Serpent,* and he just had lunch!

wanna-be Michael Moriarty stumbles across the beast's nest and becomes the unwilling teammate of copper David Carradine, trying both to stop the eating habits of the aforementioned, and at the same time not give up some recently acquired loot. The effects could have been better, but who cares? The winged thing gives great headless, devours a sunbather or two, drops a few body parts around town, and causes mayhem throughout. Witty script by director Larry Cohen avoids most cliches, delivers the gore, and actually gives this monster movie's cast plenty to say (and/or eat). As with most of Cohen's films, *Q* has developed a cult following. 🦴🦴🦴

1982 (R) 92m/C Michael Moriarty, Candy Clark, David Carradine, Richard Roundtree; *D:* Larry Cohen; *W:* Larry Cohen. **VHS, Beta** *MCA*

Quarantine

"Declare war on bacteria!" is one of the slogans during an ill-defined plague epidemic, during which a power-mad senator (Jerry Wasserman, a look alike for Roy Cohn) seizes control of the government and holds HUAC-style hearings to determine which citizens are "healthy" and which get forcibly ejected into the lawless quarantine zones. Overlooked Orwellian sf from Canada, part AIDS metaphor, part satire of McCarthyism. Not all of it works, and some is downright looney, but this takes a fresh approach to oft-bungled material. 🦴🦴🦴

1989 (R) 92m/C *CA* Beatrice Boepple, Garwin Sanford, Jerry Wasserman, Charles Wilkinson; *D:* Charles Wilkinson; *W:* Charles Wilkinson. **VHS** *REP*

Quatermass 2

Second film based on Nigel Kneale's critically acclaimed 1953 BBC series *Quatermass*. British egghead Professor Quatermass is sent to investigate some abnormalities in a rural area. Soldiers and government officials in the area are behaving like brainwashed zombies.

Meteorites are far too plentiful and tend to erupt and injure when approached. A large "food" processing plant has been set up with too much security for the professor's liking. When a friend is covered by, eaten away by, and killed by the food, the professor knows what must be done. Extremely well written (by Kneale and director Val Guest), *Quatermass 2* can also be taken as an allegory for the dangers of an authoritarian government. Preceded by *The Quatermass Experiment,* and followed by *Quatermass and the Pit.* **AKA:** Enemy from Space. ♫ ♫ ♫

1957 84m/B *GB* Brian Donlevy, John Longden, Sidney James, Bryan Forbes, William Franklyn, Vera Day, John Van Eyssen, Michael Ripper, Michael Balfour, Tom Chatto, Percy Herbert; *D:* Val Guest; *W:* Val Guest, Nigel Kneale; *C:* Gerald Gibbs; *M:* James Bernard. **VHS, Beta, LV** *FCT, CTH, SNC*

Quatermass and the Pit

While constructing a new subway, British workers unearth a Martian spaceship and insect-like alien remains. Professor Quatermass is called in, and through a telepathic link, is able to learn the history of the craft, the Martians, and mankind itself. Writer Nigel Kneale supplies speculation of the third, fourth, and occult kind, and in fact at one point, the dear professor refers to the "satanic" Martians. May have a little too much plot for the allotted time, but this is a fine example of good storytelling and grand-concept fllm-making done on a sparse budget. Based on Kneale's 1958 BBC serial and released in the U.S. as *Five Million Miles to Earth.* ♫ ♫ ♪

1968 180m/B *GB* Andre Morell, Cec Linder, James Donald, Barbara Shelley, Julian Glover; *D:* Roy Ward Baker. **VHS** *SNC, MRV*

Quatermass Conclusion

Elderly and eccentric, Professor Bernard Quatermass is called out of retirement when a death ray from outer space begins to zap youths around the world. Adding to the problems, the super-powers aren't so super anymore and anarchy has taken over the streets, and it appears that Armageddon is just around the corner. Once again the screenplay is by Nigel Kneale and this is actually an edited-down version of the BBC miniseries. Poorly produced, and only slightly better acted, the story is still terrific, and as the other Quatermass films entertaining and thought provoking. ♫ ♫ ♪

1979 105m/C *GB* John Mills, Simon MacCorkindale, Barbara Kellerman, Margaret Tyzack; *D:* Piers Haggard; *W:* Nigel Kneale. **VHS, Beta** *NO*

The Quatermass Experiment

Preceding *The Blob* by two years, this excellent British production (from the Hammer Studio) is the story of an astronaut who returns to earth unknowingly carrying an alien infestation that causes him to mutate into a ever-growing giant-tentacled blob-like creature. The film features the first big-screen appearance of Dr. Bernard Quatermass (played with pushy perfection by Brian Donlevy) in a tense adaptation by director Val Guest and co-screenwriter Richard Landau of Nigel Kneale's first Quatermass BBC teleserial. Not as bleak, and not quite as good as the 1957 sequel, *Quatermass 2,* but still a well acted, well written, sci-fi classic. Known as *The Creeping Unknown* when released in U.S., the just-released videotape is the original "international" version with about three minutes of footage never-before-seen in the states. **AKA:** The Creeping Unknown. ♫ ♫ ♫

1955 78m/B *GB* Brian Donlevy, Margia Dean, Jack Warner, Richard Wordsworth; *D:* Val Guest; *W:* Richard H. Landau, Val Guest; *M:* James Bernard. **VHS** *NOS, SNC*

Queen of Outer Space

Notorious male-chauvinist sci-fi cheapie set in the far-future year of 1985. Space cadet guys crash on Venus, find it ruled by "dolls," like a masked queen who has wicked plans in store for mankind. Starts out slow, but then the unintentional laughs keep coming as the cast plays the hyperdumb material straight—famed scribe Ben Hecht allegedly intended his script outline (rewritten by Charles Beaumont) as satire, but maybe that's just an excuse. Most of the women were recruited from beauty pageants, as in *Abbott & Costello Go to Mars.* Don't be surprised if you've seen the sets and costumes before, either; they were

"Men caused the vruin of dis vorld and it vas time for da vimmen to take over."

—Zsa Zsa Gabor in *Queen of Outer Space.*

borrowed from *Forbidden Planet* and others. **WOOF!**

1958 80m/C Zsa Zsa Gabor, Eric Fleming, Laurie Mitchell, Paul Birch, Barbara Darrow, Dave Willcock, Lisa Davis, Patrick Waltz, Marilyn Buferd, Marjorie Durant, Lynn Cartwright, Gerry Gaylor; **D:** Edward L. Bernds; **W:** Charles Beaumont. **VHS, Beta** *FXV*

Quest for Fire

An interesting attempt to create a serious film set in prehistoric times. During the Ice Age, a small group of proto-men lose their carefully guarded fire during an attack from an enemy tribe, and are forced to wander the land searching for a way to renew the flames. The fire is serious business; without it, they are dangerously vulnerable to the elements. During their journey, they encounter and battle various animals and tribesmen in order to survive. The story is fascinating, and a refreshing change from the usual "Women in Fur Bikinis Threatened by Dinosaurs" story familiar from earlier prehistoric epics. The film also has moments of disturbing violence and a somewhat bleak tone that may make it challenging to some viewers. The characters' language was developed by *A Clockwork Orange* author Anthony Burgess, while the primitive movements were designed by Desmond (*The Naked Ape*) Morris. Ron Perlman went on to play Vincent, the Beast in TV's *Beauty and the Beast*; Rae Dawn Chong is the daughter of Tommy Chong of the comic duo Cheech and Chong. 🎬🎬🎬

1982 (R) 75m/C *FR* Everett McGill, Ron Perlman, Nameer El-Kadi, Rae Dawn Chong; **D:** Jean-Jacques Annaud; **W:** Gerard Brach. Academy Awards '82: Best Makeup; Genie Awards '83: Best Actress (Chong). **VHS, Beta, LV** *FOX, INJ*

Quest for Love

Quirky sci-fi story of a man who passes through a time warp and finds himself able to maintain two parallel lives. Based on John Wyndham's short story. 🎬🎬🎬

1971 90m/C *GB* Joan Collins, Tom Bell, Denholm Elliott, Laurence Naismith; **D:** Ralph Thomas. **VHS, Beta** *NO*

Quest of the Delta Knights

Swashbuckling fantasy about a kingdom suffering under an evil ruler and his equally sinister queen. They are opposed by the heroic Delta Knights whose only chance to defeat the fiendish powers of darkness is by unearthing a legendary storehouse containing technology from the age of Atlantis and all the powers of the Ancients. 🎬🎬🎬

1993 (PG) 97m/C David Warner, Olivia Hussey, Corbin Allred, Brigid Conley Walsh, David Kriegel; **D:** James Dodson. **VHS** *HMD*

The Quiet Earth

For scientist Zac Hobson (Bruno Lawrence, the Gerard Depardieu of New Zealand films), it really is the day the Earth stood still as he awakens one morning to find himself seemingly alone in the world. This part of the film is best, as he desperately searches for survivors, sets up housekeeping in a mansion, and enjoys the run of the city before beginning to go a bit mad. Then, recalling *The World, The Flesh, and the Devil,* he finds two survivors, a woman and a Maori tribesman. Predictable sexual tensions erupt before Lawrence turns to the more pressing issue of trying to restore the damage wrought by a government experiment that disrupted space and time. A film of many dimensions, and a haunting, enigmatic finish. Director Geoff Murphy later directed *Freejack.* 🎬🎬🎬

1985 (R) 91m/C *NZ* Bruno Lawrence, Alison Routledge, Peter Smith; **D:** Geoff Murphy; **W:** Bruno Lawrence, Sam Pillsbury, Bill Baer; **M:** John Charles. **VHS, Beta, LV** *FOX*

Quintet

Many consider this atypical Robert Altman sf effort one of the unpredictable director's

worst films, but the Hound thinks it has...something. Setting is a nuke-inspired second Ice Age, where Paul Newman and wife Brigitte Fossey wander into the last known city. There, peasant-garbed inhabitants, having given up hope for tomorrow, play an assassination game called quintet, which Newman learns quickly. Bizarre frozen production design and heavy symbolism (like ubiquitous carrion black dogs) make this tough sledding, but the hypnotic musical score and general aura of fatalism set it apart from more conventional apocalyptic fare. Main complaint: a buildup to an action climax that just doesn't happen. 🎵🎵🎵

1979 118m/C Paul Newman, Bibi Andersson, Fernando Rey, Vittorio Gassman, David Langton, Nina Van Pallandt, Brigitte Fossey; **D:** Robert Altman; **W:** Lionel Chetwynd, Patricia Resnick, Robert Altman, Frank Barhydt. **VHS, Beta** *FOX*

Radioactive Dreams

Surreal, practically senseless fantasy wherein two men, trapped in a bomb shelter for 15 years with nothing to read but mystery novels, emerge as detectives into a post-holocaust world looking for adventure. 🎵🎵

1986 (R) 94m/C John Stockwell, Michael Dudikoff, Lisa Blount, George Kennedy, Don Murray, Michelle Little; **D:** Albert Pyun; **W:** Albert Pyun. **VHS, Beta, LV** *LIV, VES*

Raiders of Atlantis

The domed continent of Atlantis surfaces in the Caribbean and discharges hordes of armored punk warriors on motorcycles (!!!). Wielding big guns, grenades, and wisecracks, a couple of idle commandoes save the world, but not the viewer's stunned senses. Fantasy-occult-action slop as only low-budget Italian filmmakers could pull off. Or couldn't, as the case may be. Keep sea sickness pills handy for the theme music. **AKA:** The Atlantis Interceptors. **WOOF!**

1983 100m/C *IT* Christopher Connelly; **D:** Roger Franklin. **VHS, Beta** *PSM*

Raiders of the Lost Ark

Classic '30s-style adventure reminiscent of early serials spawned two sequels and numer-

ous rip-offs. Made Harrison Ford a household name as dashing hero and intrepid archeologist Indiana Jones. He battles mean Nazis, decodes hieroglyphics, fights his fear of snakes, and even has time for a little romance in his quest for the biblical Ark of the Covenant. Karen Allen is perfectly cast as his feisty ex-flame, more than a little irritated with the smooth talker who dumped her years earlier. Asks viewers to suspend belief as every chase and stunt tops the last. Unrelated opening sequence does a great job of introducing the character. Followed by *Indiana Jones and the Temple of Doom.* 🎵🎵🎵🎵

1981 (PG) 115m/C Harrison Ford, Karen Allen, Wolf Kahler, Paul Freeman, John Rhys-Davies, Denholm Elliott, Ronald Lacey, Anthony Higgins, Alfred Molina; **D:** Steven Spielberg; **W:** George Lucas, Philip Kaufman; **M:** John Williams. Hugos '82: Dramatic Presentation; Academy Awards '81: Best Art Direction/Set Decoration, Best Film Editing, Best Sound, Best Visual Effects; People's Choice Awards '82: Best Film; Nominations: Academy Awards '81: Best Cinematography, Best Director (Spielberg), Best Picture, Best Original Score. **VHS, Beta, LV, 8mm** *PAR*

Rats

In 2225, the beleaguered survivors of a nuclear holocaust struggle with a mutant rodent problem. 🎵🎵

1983 100m/C Richard Raymond, Richard Cross; **D:** Vincent Dawn. **VHS, Beta** *NO*

Re-Animator

Based on H.P. Lovecraft's serial novella, this grisly Gothic deals with a medical student (Jeffrey Combs) who re-animates the dead and finds that his problems are only beginning. It has become a black-humor cult classic for its numerous excesses and terrific acting. The famous "head" scene is horror/sf's equivalent to the campfire scene in *Blazing Saddles.* Director Stuart Gordon was a Chicago theatre director before directing this entertaining gorefest; Combs has become a familiar character actor specializing in psychosis. Barbara Crampton, who's become a scream-queen favorite, has done several more sci-fi and horror features, and also joined the cast of a daytime soap opera. Available in "R" and un-rated versions, plus a special remastered "10th Anniversary" edition containing extra footage

"Who's going to believe a talking head? Get a job in a sideshow."

—Dr. Herbert West (Jeffery Combs) in *Re-Animator.*

"Quit your whining, you'll only feel a little prick." Jeffrey Combs is *Re-Animator.*

and commentary by director and cast. For true fans, it's required viewing; far and away the best of the three. Followed by the disappointing *Bride of Re-Animator.* 🦴🦴🦴🦴

1984 86m/C Jeffrey Combs, Bruce Abbott, Barbara Crampton, David Gale, Robert Sampson; **D:** Stuart Gordon; **W:** Stuart Gordon, Dennis Paoli, William J. Norris; **M:** Richard Band. **VHS, Beta, LV** *LIV, VES*

Reactor

A low-budget sci-fi film about kidnapped scientists, alien ships, and an activated nuclear reactor. 🦴

1985 90m/C Yanti Somer, Melissa Long, James R. Stuart, Robert Barnes, Nick Jordan. **VHS, Beta** *NO*

Rebel Storm

A group of freedom fighters team up to rescue America from the totalitarian rulers that are in charge in 2099 A.D. 🦴

1990 (R) 99m/C Zach Galligan, Wayne Crawford, June Chadwick, Rod McCary, John Rhys-Davies, Elizabeth Kiefer; **D:** Francis Schaeffer. **VHS, Beta, LV** *ACA*

Red Planet Mars

"The Sermon on the Mount...on Mars!" The ads promised "out of this world excitement and suspense," but this adaptation of the play *Red Planet,* by John L. Balderson and John Hoare, is mostly limited to two laboratory sets. Peter Graves stars as a scientist who picks up radio transmissions from a utopian Mars that plunge our planet into economic and spiritual chaos, especially when later messages appear to be coming from God. Herbert Berghof co-stars as an ex-Nazi (in cahoots with the Russians) who is causing all the static. Not what one would call a good movie, perhaps, but you've never seen anything like it. 🦴🦴

1952 87m/B Peter Graves, Andrea King, Marvin Miller, Herbert Berghof, House Peters Jr., Vince Barnett, Morris Ankrum, Walter Sande; **D:** Harry Horner; **W:** Anthony Veiller, John Balderston; **C:** Joseph Biroc. **VHS** *MGM, FCT*

Remote Control

A circulating videotape of a 1950's sci-fi flick is turning people into murderous zombies, thanks to some entrepreneurial aliens. Silly, but performed by young actors with gusto. 🦴🐾

1988 (R) 88m/C Kevin Dillon, Deborah Goodrich, Christopher Wynne, Jennifer Tilly; **D:** Jeff Lieberman; **M:** Peter Bernstein. **VHS, Beta, LV** *LIV, HHE*

Replikator: Cloned to Kill

In the 21st century, a ruthless criminal gets hold of replication techology that can duplicate anything, including people. So it's up to a cop and two cyberpunks to stop the destruction. 🦴🐾

1994 (R) 96m/C Michael St. Gerard, Brigitte Bako, Ned Beatty; **D:** G. Philip Jackson; **W:** Tony Johnston, Michelle Bellerose, John Dawson. **VHS** *PSM*

Reptilicus

Laughable attempt to get Denmark into the Godzilla business. Nordic miners find the skeleton of a previously unclassified dinosaur with its tail section frozen and intact. The beast's defrosted flesh regenerates into a vast acid-spitting serpent that looks like the dragon of medieval folklore but moves like a puppet from the *Kukla, Fran and Ollie* show. Oh,

TV on Tape: Red Dwarf

As TV sci-fi sitcoms go, *Red Dwarf* is the one to beat.

On the BBC since 1988, this British spoof started off with a premiere episode called "The End," in which a ne'er-do-well crewman aboard the miles-long interstellar mining craft *Red Dwarf* awoke from cryogenic detention to learn that his shipmates succumbed to a radiation leak and three million years have gone by. Mankind is extinct, and his only companions are a sentient hologram of a much-disliked officer, the ship's sarcastic computer, and a natty-dressing humanoid evolved from a pet cat (later a robot joined the ensemble). Coasting through a hostile universe, these pitiful remnants of humanity are constantly threatened by alien interlopers, bizarre phenomena, and their own incompatible personalities, in plotlines conceived by the writing team of Rob Grant and Doug Naylor that are riotously funny yet often sf in the best mind-expanding sense (it helps that *Red Dwarf* has the luxury of spectacular f/x; check out the cosmic zoom that opens the first-season series).

A cult fandom has dedicated 'zines, web pages, and even destructive computer viruses to the program. Two-volume sets of the first five seasons are carried on video in the U.S. (more extensive collections exist overseas). Recent attempts at an American remake of *Red Dwarf* were unsuccessful. Or, in the words of show's far-future slang, all smegged up.

1988-present/C *GB* **Selected cast:** Craig Charles, Chris Barrie, Robert Llewellyn, Danny John-Jules, Norman Lovett, Hattie Hayridge. **VHS** *FOX, FCT*

---

and we get some travelogues of Copenhagen and the song "Tivoli Nights." Reptilicus later justified his limp existence by reappearing in recurrent gag clips on the Monkees' popular TV show, and recent reports from Denmark hint this pic has become a cult item in the tradition of *The Rocky Horror Picture Show,* with revival-house audiences echoing the lame dialogue back at the screen. 🦴

1962 90m/C *DK* Carl Ossosen, Ann Smyrner, Mimi Heinrich, Poul Wildaker, Asbjorn Andersen, Marla Bregens; **D:** Sidney Pink; **W:** Sidney Pink, Ib Melchior. **VHS** *ORI*

Resurrection of Zachary Wheeler

Interesting curio in which a presidential candidate, severely injured in a car crash, is deemed worthy for lifesaving organ transplants at a mysterious clinic in New Mexico. Leslie Nielsen is fun as the nervy reporter who snoops around and discovers the surgeons' secret: grotesque "somas," genetically blank clones whose organs are 100% compatible with recipients. A somewhat open ending lets viewers ponder the morality it all—Operation Rescue take note. 🦴🦴🦴

1971 (G) 100m/C Angie Dickinson, Bradford Dillman, Leslie Nielsen, Jack Carter, James Daly; **D:** Bob Wynn. **VHS, Beta** *NO*

The Return

Jan-Michael Vincent and Cybill Shepherd meet as adults and discover that they had both, as children, been visited by aliens who had given technology to a cattle-mutilating prospector. A mess with no idea of what sort of film it wants to be. **AKA:** The Alien's Return. **WOOF!**

1980 (PG) 91m/C Cybill Shepherd, Raymond Burr, Jan-Michael Vincent, Martin Landau, Vincent Schiavelli, Zachary Vincent, Farah Bunch, Neville Brand, Susan Kiger; **D:** Greydon Clark. **VHS, Beta** *NO*

Return of Captain Invincible

Beloved wartime superguy Captain Invincible was subpoenaed before a McCarthyite panel and blacklisted for wearing a red-colored cape and flying without a license. Now a U.S. presi-

al, features Bela Lugosi as Chandu, a heroic sorcerer who uses his occult powers to conquer a religious sect of cat worshipers on the island of Lemuria. In the process, he fights to save the Princess Nadji, makes himself invisible, and performs all the other actions appropriate to a magician hero. Classic thrills from a past master. *Chandu on Magic Island* incorporated chapters five through 12 into a feature-length movie. Lugosi played arch-villain Roxnor in the inferior 1933 *Chandu the Magician*. 🦴 🦴

1934 156m/B Bela Lugosi, Maria Alba, Clara Kimball Young; *D:* Ray Taylor. **VHS, Beta** *DVT, NOS, SNC*

The Return of Swamp Thing

The DC Comics creature rises again out of the muck to fight mutants and evil scientists. Tongue-in-cheek, and nothing at all like the literate, ecologically oriented comic from which it was derived. 🦴 🦴

1989 (PG-13) 95m/C Louis Jourdan, Heather Locklear, Sarah Douglas, Dick Durock; *D:* Jim Wynorski. **VHS, Beta, LV** *COL*

Return of the Aliens: The Deadly Spawn

Organisms from a meteorite multiply and spread through a small town in the form of toothy tadpoles who grow...and grow. A handful of resourceful young folks (nice to see screen teens smart enough to debate about Velikovsky) notice the threat, but too late to prevent their parents from getting limbs and faces chewed off, in truly loathsome gore scenes. If you can stomach the disgusting stuff, this is an example of a genre pic done well on a 16mm budget. Retitling of *The Deadly Spawn* as its own sequel (!) has caused viewer confusion, abetted by spurious rumors that this is part 2 to Charles Band's *Parasite*. **AKA:** The Deadly Spawn. 🦴 🦴 🦴

1983 (R) 90m/C Charles George Hildebrandt; *D:* Douglas McKeown. **VHS** *NO*

> "I don't mind the giant fly head. It's the stink of rotting flesh on your breath." Vincent Price in the ***Return of the Fly.***

dent decides the country needs its hero again, and puts the now-derelict Legend in Leotards through alcohol rehab and superpower retraining. Australian spoof has great premise, let down too often by slipshod storytelling and weak f/x. Gains altitude with its outlandish musical numbers, some of them written by the Rocky Horror team of Richard Hartley and Richard O'Brien. A singing Christopher Lee plays archvillain Mr. Midnight with lordly gusto. **AKA:** Legend in Leotards. 🦴 🦴

1983 (PG) 90m/C AU Alan Arkin, Christopher Lee, Kate Fitzpatrick, Bill Hunter, Graham Kennedy, Michael Pate, Hayes Gordon, Max Phipps, Noel Ferrier; *D:* Philippe Mora; *W:* Steven E. de Souza. **VHS, Beta, LV** *NO*

Return of Chandu

This film, which combines the 12-chapter seri-

Return of the Fly

Slightly lame sequel to the 1958 classic *The Fly* finds Vincent Price reprising his role as the brother of the doomed inventor in the first film.

Better take this one as an almost-comedy, especially once you get a load of the much larger fly-head designed for the Fly's son Philippe (Brett Halsey) to wear. This time around it's the meddling assistant David Frankham who screws things up, causing the teleported one to become part-man part-fly. The film lacks continuity, and despite Price, lacks the charm of the original. The next sequel, *The Curse of the Fly,* had to wait to 1965 to be made. 🐾🐾

1959 80m/B Vincent Price, Brett Halsey, John Sutton, Dan Seymour, David Frankham; *D:* Edward L. Bernds. **VHS, Beta, LV** FOX, FCT

Return of the Jedi

The third volume in George Lucas' trilogy does everything right. Two memorable villains— Jabba the Hut and the Emperor—are introduced, and the almost-too-cute Ewoks join our heroes as they fight against the forces of the Empire on three fronts. The effects somehow manage to outdo the first two, and the whole story builds to a completely satisfying conclusion. But the scene that sums up the whole trilogy comes near the middle. That's when C-3Po, standing by a campfire, tells what has happened up until then to a crowd of rapt Ewoks in their language. They're every audience that's ever been spellbound by a story. They're us. 🐾🐾🐾🐾

1983 (PG) 132m/C Mark Hamill, Carrie Fisher, Harrison Ford, Billy Dee Williams, David Prowse, James Earl Jones, Alec Guinness, Kenny Baker, Denis Lawson, Anthony Daniels, Peter Mayhew, Ian McDiarmid; *D:* Richard Marquand; *W:* George Lucas, Lawrence Kasdan; *C:* Alan Hume; *M:* John Williams; *V:* Frank Oz. Hugos '84: Dramatic Presentation; Academy Awards '83: Best Visual Effects; People's Choice Awards '84: Best Film; Nominations: Academy Awards '83: Best Art Direction/Set Decoration, Best Sound, Best Original Score. **VHS, Beta, LV** FOX, RDG, HMV

Revenge of the Creature

In this follow up to *The Creature From the Black Lagoon,* the monstrous Gill-man is captured in his Amazon habitat and taken to a Florida marine park. There he is put on display for visitors and cheerfully subjected by John Agar to experiments involving an electric prod. Growing restless in his captive surroundings, the creature breaks free and makes for the ocean. His escape is only a cover for his true intentions, however, which involve stalking and kidnapping pretty grad student Lori Nelson. This rather weak sequel, originally shot in 3-D and based on a story by William Alland, includes screen debut of Clint Eastwood as a lab technician. Between exciting moments, we're treated to endless billing and cooing by Agar and Nelson, and time-killing footage of marine park attractions like "Flippy, the Educated Porpoise." It's available on laserdisc as part of a special "Encore Edition Double Feature" with *The Creature Walks Among Us.* 🐾🐾

1955 82m/B John Agar, Lori Nelson, John Bromfield, Robert Williams, Nestor Paiva, Clint Eastwood; *D:* Jack Arnold; *W:* Martin Berkeley; *C:* Charles S. Welbourne. **VHS, LV** MCA, FCT

Revenge of the Teenage Vixens from Outer Space

A low-budget film about three sex-starved females from another planet who come to Earth to find men. When the ones they meet do not live up to their expectations, the frustrated females turn the disappointing dudes into vegetables (vegetables don't talk back). 🐾🐾

1986 84m/C Lisa Schwedop, Howard Scott; *D:* Jeff Ferrell. **VHS, Beta** NO

Riders of the Storm

A motley crew of Vietnam vets runs a covert television broadcasting station from an in-flight B-29, jamming America's legitimate airwaves. Interesting premise with boring result. **AKA:** The American Way. 🐾🐾

1988 (R) 92m/C Dennis Hopper, Michael J. Pollard, Eugene Lipinski, James Aubrey, Nigel Pegram; *D:* Maurice Phillips; *W:* Scott Roberts. **VHS, Beta, LV** SUE, NLC

Riding with Death

A man who can become invisible, thanks to a military experiment, uses his power to uncover a dastardly plot by a mad scientist. So-so TV pilot. 🐾🐾

1976 97m/C Ben Murphy, Andrew Prine, Katherine Crawford, Richard Dysart; *D:* Alan J. Levi. **VHS, Beta** MCA

The Road Warrior

Incredible photography, terrific stunts, and full-tilt pace make this futuristic sf western one of

"We are not accustomed to see such a beautiful woman connected with science."

—One of the many male chauvinists in *Reptilicus.*

the most influential movies of the early '80s. It's a rare sequel (to *Mad Max*) that surpasses the original on sheer intensity. The action takes place after nuclear war has destroyed Australia. Max (Mel Gibson) helps a colony of oil-drilling survivors defend themselves from the roving murderous outback gangs and escape to the coast. Well-drawn characters and a climactic chase scene that's among the most exciting ever filmed. Worth another look any time; worth owning. 🐾🐾🐾🐾

1982 (R) 95m/C Mel Gibson, Bruce Spence, Emil Minty, Vernon Wells; **D:** George Miller; **W:** George Miller. **VHS, Beta, LV** *WAR*

Robinson Crusoe on Mars

When the orbital ship Mars Gravity Probe 1 is forced to make an emergency landing on the planet's surface, Com. Draper (Paul Mantee) faces the immediate problems of limited supplies of air, water, and food. "Hard" science purists may not approve of the solutions he finds but that's not a problem. This adaptation of Daniel Defoe's novel is more about loneliness anyway. And despite the film's age, it has a remarkably contemporary look. One of the key props is a prototype camcorder, and Draper is often dressed in baggy pants, high-topped boots, T-shirt, and what appears to be a gimme cap. To create a believable alien world, director Byron Haskin combined sets and models with well-chosen Death Valley locations. Some elements are a bit campy now and the title may sound like it belongs on a kidflick, but the film is still a lot of fun to watch. The laserdisc version preserves the original widescreen ratio and contains extra material. 🐾🐾🐾

1964 109m/C Adam West, Vic Lundin, Paul Mantee; **D:** Byron Haskin; **W:** Ib Melchior, John C. Higgins; **C:** Winton C. Hoch; **M:** Nathan Van Cleave. **LV** *IME*

Robo-C.H.I.C.

Producers of *RoboCop* sued over this vulgar spoof—ostensibly for plagiarism (prompting the change of title to *Cyber-Chic*), but the Hound hopes it was more of class action on behalf of the poor souls tricked into watching. A scientist creates a heavy-duty robot woman (pinup model Kathy Shower in a costume apparently fashioned from oven mitts). She joins the hunt for a misunderstood mad bomber (played by Burt Ward, 'Robin' from the '60s *Batman* TV show). Stupid characters, f/x to match. **AKA:** Cyber-Chic. **WOOF!**

1989 90m/C Kathy Shower, Jack Carter, Burt Ward, Lyle Waggoner, Ed Hansen, Phil Proctor, Kip King; **D:** Jeffrey Mandel, Ed Hansen; **W:** Jeffrey Mandel; **C:** Ken Carmack, Mike Wemple. **VHS, Beta** *AIP*

RoboCop

Detroit cop killed in action is used as donor for the face and brain of a crime-fighting cyborg. Trouble begins when RoboCop starts remembering his life as a human and discovers corruption within the giant company that created' him in more ways than one. Not just superhero action; there's a bleak, cynical view of the future (with catastrophes sprightly described by happy-talk newscaster Leeza Gibbons) coupled with an acid satire of corporate values, and an underlying sadness about the dehumanized, strangely forlorn main character, which Peter Weller manages to convey with a minimum of expression—or flesh, for that matter. Terrific special f/x include Rob Bottin's cyborg suit and the slick stop-motion animation by Phil Tippet that brings to life Robocop's deadliest (but dumbest) nemesis, Enforcement Droid 209. Ferocious violence nearly earned this an X-rating; copies of Paul Verhoeven's original cut are sought by collectors. Inspired two sequels and a short-lived TV series, all progressively less interesting. 🐾🐾🐾🐾

1987 (R) 103m/C Peter Weller, Nancy Allen, Ronny Cox, Kurtwood Smith, Ray Wise, Miguel Ferrer, Dan O'Herlihy, Robert DoQui, Felton Perry, Paul McCrane, Del Zamora; **D:** Paul Verhoeven; **W:** Michael Miner, Edward Neumeier; **M:** Basil Poledouris. Nominations: Academy Awards '87: Best Film Editing, Best Sound. **VHS, Beta, LV** *ORI*

RoboCop 2

More cynical, even more violent—is that possible?—sequel to the 1987 pic. 'Nuke,' a new addictive drug, has made streets of future Detroit worse than ever. RoboCop's corporate owners, dissatisfied with his performance and vulnerabilities during a police strike, eventually replace him with a stronger cyborg powered by the brain of a psycho pusher/addict/cult leader

(after a series of other unwilling donors gruesomely self-destruct). RoboCop 2 goes berserk, natch, and the metal beings fight an epic battle, in between enough subplots for three movies. Comic-book elements predominate in a script concocted by graphic novelist Frank Miller (*Batman: The Dark Knight Returns*) and directed kinetically by Irvin Kerschner (*The Empire Strikes Back*), emphasizing bitter sarcasm and graphic savagery at the expense of the original's muted but vital emotion quotient. Definitely worth a look from fans. ⚟⚟

1990 (R) 117m/C Peter Weller, Nancy Allen, Belinda Bauer, Dan O'Herlihy, Tom Noonan, Gabriel Damon, Galyn Gorg, Felton Perry, Patricia Charbonneau; *D:* Irvin Kershner; *W:* Walon Green. **VHS, Beta, LV** *ORI*

RoboCop 3

The third RoboCop flick sat on the studio shelf before belated release in 1993. In a break in continuity, RoboCop's new Japanese owners plan to build an ultra-modern city in place of the decrepit 21st-century Detroit, but first must evict thousands of residents. The rebel cyborg (now played by Robert Burke) joins with common citizen to protect their homes, befriending a tiny waif/computer hacker for maximum kid appeal. There's an agile robot Ninja warrior to do battle with the surprisingly slow-moving hero, an apt metaphor of new models from Tokyo replacing America's lumbering gas-guzzlers, but the plot and action sequences are cheap-looking and rehashed. Watch the opening, at least, for a guest cameo by the well-remembered ED-209. ⚟⚟

1991 (PG-13) 104m/C Robert Burke, Nancy Allen, John Castle, CCH Pounder, Bruce Locke, Rip Torn, Remi Ryan, Felton Perry; *D:* Fred Dekker; *W:* Fred Dekker, Frank Miller; *M:* Basil Poledouris. **VHS, LV** *ORI*

Roboman

American scientist gets in car crash in Soviet Union. When he returns to the States as a

"Where the heck do you put the butane!" Kurtwood Smith and the Zippo-esque Peter Weller in *RoboCop*.

cyborg, his friends seem to notice a change. **AKA:** Who? 🎞🎞🎞

1975 (PG) 91m/C *GB GE* Elliott Gould, Trevor Howard, Joe Bova, Ed Grover, James Noble, John Lehne; *D:* Jack Gold. **VHS** *ACE, MTX*

Robot Carnival

A collection of eight short films from Japan's top animators, each revolving around the theme of artificial life. Many of the films are without dialogue, and most are lyrical evocations of emotion, like "Presence," the tale of an aging inventor haunted by the android girl he created. In the improbable but beautifully animated "Cloud," a little robot-boy trudges through a shifting cloudscape of romantic images. "Starlight Dancer" is a charming love-story featuring two girls, a futuristic amusement park, and a lovesick robot. "Deprive" is a straightforward science-fiction vignette, and "Nightmare" echoes Disney's version of *The Legend of Sleepy Hollow* as a city-dweller is pursued by mechanized monsters. "Franken's Gears" explores the Frankenstein legend with unexpected results and "A Tale of Two Robots" is a delightful satirical fantasy about a group of young people frantically battling a crazed inventor's monster robot in Eighteenth Century Japan. Those looking for straightforward action might want to look elsewhere, but there are wonderful things here. 🎞🎞🎞🎞

1987 90m/C *JP D:* Atsuko Fukushima, Katsuhiro Otomo, Hiroyuki Kitazume, Mao Lamdo, Hidetoshi Ohmori, Kouji Morimoto, Yasuomi Umetsu, Hiroyuki Kitakubo, Takashi Nakamura. **VHS** *WTA, STP, TPV*

Robot Holocaust

Somewhere in the future, the weird-looking robots have rebelled and reduced humanity to barbarian warriors. A small band of heroes and heroines go on perilous expedition to hit the master electronic brain known as The Dark One, though other adjectives might suffice. One critic noted its resemblance to a pile of excrement. Others have said much the same for the film. Made in New York by the creators of the ever-popular *Mutant Hunt*. **WOOF!**

1987 79m/C Norris Culf, Nadine Hart, Joel von Ornsteiner, Jennifer Delora, Andrew Howarth, Angelika Jager, Rick Gianasi; *D:* Tim Kincaid; *W:* Tim Kincaid. **VHS, Beta** *NO*

Robot Jox

In the future, wars between East and West are eliminated, but Cold War competition thrives thanks to officiated gladiator duels between titanic robots, each one piloted by a single human operator. Will brotherhood and goodness prevail? Semi-meaningful, semi-ludicrous sci fi (with uneven quality f/x by David Allen), this hijacked hardware concepts from the role-playing game Battletech, the Japanese sagas *Robotech* and *Gundam,* and others; toy-conscious viewers will also note the fighting machines' suspicious similarity to popular '80s playthings like Transformers and Gobots. At least *Robot Jox* is better than those respective cartoon features, but considering that the script is by Hugo Award-winning sf novelist Joe Haldeman (*The Forever War*), this must be classed as a disappointment. Produced by Charles Band. 🎞🎞

1990 (PG) 84m/C Gary Graham, Anne-Marie Johnson, Paul Koslo, Robert Sampson, Danny Kamekona, Hilary Mason, Michael Alldredge; *D:* Stuart Gordon; *W:* Joe Haldeman. **VHS, LV** *COL*

Robot Monster

This legendary golden turkey gives *Plan 9 from Outer Space* a run for its low budget as the worst movie of all time. The last six people on Earth—a professor, his wife and daughter, assistant, and two children—make their stand against Ro-Man, a ridiculous alien outfitted in a gorilla suit, topped by a deep sea diver's helmet. Ro-Man is instructed by his ruler, the Great One (not Jackie Gleason), to kill the Earthlings, but he is conflicted: "To be like the hu-man. To laugh. Feel. Want. Why are these things not in the plan?" Shot in four days for less than $20,000. Director Phil Tucker (then 26 years old) went on to direct *Dance Hall Racket,* starring Lenny Bruce, and *Cape Canaveral Monsters*. The music is by the venerable Elmer Bernstein, who went on to score such classics as *To Kill a Mockingbird, The Great Escape, The Magnificent Seven,* and, yes, *Cat Women of the Moon*. **AKA:** Monsters from the Moon. 🎞🎞🎞

1953 62m/B George Nader, Claudia Barrett, Gregory Moffett, Selena Royle, George Barrows, John Mylong; *D:* Phil

Tucker; **W:** Wyott Ordung; **C:** Jack Greenhalgh; **M:** Elmer Bernstein. **VHS, Beta, LV** *RHI, FCT, COL*

The Robot Vs. the Aztec Mummy

Grade-Z Mexican horror film pits a jealous mummy who guards a tomb against tomb robbers and the robot they invent. Special effects are laughable today—the robot's ears are lightbulbs—but true mummy movie fans might want to watch this one. Everyone else will probably be better off skipping it. **AKA:** El Robot Humano; La Momia Azteca Contra el Robot Humano. **WOOF!**

1959 65m/**B** *MX* Ramon Gay, Rosita Arenas, Crox Alvarado, Luis Aceves Cantaneda, Emma Rolden; **D:** Rafael Portillo; **W:** Alfredo Salazar. **VHS, Beta** *SNC, AOV, MRV*

Robot Wars

Not exactly a sequel to *Robot Jox,* not even an incredible simulation. A future nation-state's security depends on their scorpion-like MRAS-2 mega-robot. When it falls into enemy hands, the hero unearths the long-lost MRAS-1 and pilots it for a very brief clash of the titans. This Charles Band production (directed by his father Albert) barely lasts an hour; a lengthy featurette fills time with behind-the-scenes details of Band's Full Moon Productions facilities.

1993 (PG) 106m/**C** Don Michael Paul, Barbara Crampton, James Staley, Lisa Rinna, Danny Kamekona, Yuji Okumoto, J. Downing, Peter Haskell; **D:** Albert Band. **VHS, Beta, LV** *PAR*

Rock & Roll Cowboys

A humble roadie wants to become a rock and roll star. A Mephistophelian character called Damien Shard promises him the opportunity with an instrument that taps directly into the brain to transform thought into music. The Psychotronic Alpha Sampler is actually an evil mind-control device, but clear minds were evidently in short supply when this malfunctioning Australian satire with scattered music-videos came together. Cyberbunk, not cyberpunk. **WOOF!**

1992 83m/**C** *AU* Peter Phelps, David Franklin, John Doyle; **D:** Robert Stewart. **VHS** *MOV*

Rock & Rule

An ambitious animated film that manages to rise above a rather hackneyed storyline. After a nuclear war has wiped out humanity, a new race of beings descended from rats and dogs takes over. Mok, a rock star who bears more than a passing resemblance to Mick Jagger, wants to conjure up a demon that will grant him control of this brave new world. However, Mok finds he needs a perfect voice to complete the summoning-spell. He attempts to seduce Angel, a singer in a struggling rock band, into helping him fulfill his evil purpose. Mok spirits Angel away to "Nuke York," and her friends rush to her rescue; will they be too late? This film pushes its rock soundtrack hard; good songs are provided by Deborah Harry, Cheap Trick, Lou Reed, and Iggy Pop. This was Canadian studio Nelvana's last feature. It followed a number of good children's specials, like *The Devil & Daniel Mouse.*

1983 85m/**C** **D:** Clive A. Smith; **M:** Deborah Harry, Lou Reed, Iggy Pop; **V:** Paul LeMat, Susan Roman, Don Francks, Dan Hennessey, Chris Wiggins, Catherine Gallant, Catherine O'Hara. **VHS, Beta, LV** *MGM*

Rocket Attack U.S.A.

Antiquated and ridiculous tale of nuclear warfare about the time of Sputnik, with Russia's first strike blowing up New York City and environs. Mercifully short, with time for a little romance. Everything about this movie is so bad it's good for a laugh. **WOOF!**

1958 70m/**B** Monica Davis, John McKay, Dan Kern, Edward Czerniuk, Art Metrano; **D:** Barry Mahon. **VHS, Beta** *NO*

The Rocketeer

Lightheaded fun. Bill Campbell plays a 1930s stunt pilot who stumbles upon a prototype jet-backpack sought after by the nasty Nazis. Donning the secret weapon and a custom-made mask, he becomes a flying superhero, in the spirit of the '30s matinee serials. Breezy, family entertainment with stupendous special effects and tons of Hollywood references, like a great villain (Timothy Dalton) clearly based on Errol Flynn, and a Rhondo Hatton lump-a-like (the not-so-tiny Tiny Ron with accents by

R

proper pacing and become a monotonously continuous montage of captures, fights, escapes, and rescues. ♫ ♫

1936 ?m/B Buster Crabbe, Jean Rogers, Charles Middleton. **VHS** *LOO, HEG*

Rocketship X-M

Cheaply produced and rushed into theatres to beat out George Pal's much-touted *Destination Moon,* this vintage tale depicts a pioneering lunar mission that goes awry thanks to a pencil-and-paper (!) navigational error and lands instead on Mars, where the Earth explorers discover the portentous remnants of human-like society destroyed by atomic war. Static and melodramatic, but worthy as a historic curio. Considered the first American movie released that took space travel seriously, if not entirely accurately—astronaut garb seems to consist of street clothes or bomber jackets. Scenes on Martian terrain (actually Death Valley, a good guess at the real thing) were tinted red. Some video versions carry additional f/x footage lensed much later, with long-shot doubles for the actors. **AKA:** Expedition Moon. ♫ ♫ ♪

1950 77m/B Lloyd Bridges, Osa Massen, John Emery, Hugh O'Brian, Noah Beery Jr.; **D:** Kurt Neumann. **VHS, Beta, LV** *MED, RXM*

The Rocky Horror Picture Show

Campy, vampy, and anything but subtle, the mother of all cult hits arrived on home video after 15 years of midnight screenings. On tape, of course, the audience participation element is lost. (Or at least lessened; what you and your friends want to do and wear in the privacy of your own place is none of the Hound's business.) So, what about the movie itself? It's not bad. The story isn't too important in this kinky musical send-up of old sci-fi/horror movies. The rock score is loud and energetic; the lyrics surprisingly wiity. Susan Sarandon and Barry Bostwick are fine as the innocent hero and heroine, but the film belongs to Tim Curry's Dr. Frank-N-Furter. He redefines outrageous excess as the mad scientist who favors mascara, high heels, and fishnet hose. Curry wrings every drop of mad humor from the

Riff Raff hopes to catch the garter. Little Nell, Patricia Quinn, Tim Curry, and Richard O'Brien in *The Rocky Horror Picture Show.*

make-up king Rick Baker). Campbell's All-American girlfriend is played by Jennifer Connelly, obviously chosen for her resemblance to '50s' pin-up queen Bettie Page. Dave Stevens, upon whose gorgeous comic this film is based, drew her character as a tribute to the still popular Ms. Page. ♫ ♫ ♫

1991 (PG) 109m/C Bill Campbell, Jennifer Connelly, Alan Arkin, Timothy Dalton, Paul Sorvino, Melora Hardin, Tiny Ron, Terry O'Quinn, Ed Lauter, James Handy; **D:** Joe Johnston; **W:** Danny Bilson, Paul DeMeo; **M:** James Horner. **VHS, Beta, LV** *DIS, CCB, IME*

Rocketship

Based on the popular comic strip of the '30s, Flash Gordon battles sea monsters, ray guns, and robots in this sci-fi adventure, which is an edited version of the first Flash serial. Although cheap looking today, the Flash Gordon serials were really the best ever made, with plenty of action and gadgetry to amuse young viewers. However, they were meant to be viewed one chapter at a time. These edited feature versions have a tendency to sacrifice

role—and there's a lot to wring. In the process, he shows how a talented stage actor can overpower a screen production, either film or video. Followed by the disappointing *Shock Treatment*.

♫ The Time Warp; Science Fiction Double Feature; Wedding Song; Sweet Transvestite; The Sword of Damocles; Charles Atlas Song; Whatever Happened to Saturday Night; Touch-a Touch-a Touch-a Touch Me; Eddie's Teddy. 🗡🗡🗡᭸

1975 (R) 105m/C Tim Curry, Susan Sarandon, Barry Bostwick, Meat Loaf, Little Nell, Richard O'Brien; **D:** Jim Sharman; **W:** Jim Sharman, Richard O'Brien; **M:** John Barry. **VHS, LV** *FOX, FCT, PMS*

Rodan

Rodan, a gigantic pterodactyl, is awakened from his slumbers in a mineshaft by ill-considered H-bomb tests. He breakfasts on some gigantic mutant grubs (good) and then flies around destroying things (bad...very bad). After a while the monster is joined by a mate, and then the fun (and havoc) begins in earnest. Rodan, who would appear in several later monster epics, seems less than impressive in his solo debut. Japanese monster-maniacs will enjoy it, but the uninitiated might want to stick with the better Godzilla flicks. **AKA:** Radon; Radon the Flying Monster. 🗡᭸

1957 74m/C *JP* Kenji Sahara, Yumi Shirakawa, Akihiko Hirata, Akio Kobori; **D:** Inoshiro Honda; **W:** Takeshi Kimura, Takeo Murata; **C:** Isamu Ashida. **VHS, Beta, LV** *PAR, MLB, VES*

Roller Blade

Are you sitting down for this? In a post-holocaust world where the slogan "skate or die" is taken quite literally, a sexy sect of Amazonian nuns on in-line rollerskates worship a "have a nice day" happy face and battle forces of evil (a masked-wrestler type with a gnomelike puppet pal fixed to his hand) using martial arts, mysticism, communal bathing, and hockey sticks. Cheapjack filmed-on-video mutation must truly be seen to be believed. It's good for a few laughs, but once you realize the no-brainer dialogue and schlock production values aren't going to improve the bizarre novelty

turns into an irritant very quickly. Sequellized in *Roller Blade Warriors*; not surprisingly, film-maker Donald Jackson also wrought *Hell Comes to Frogtown*. 🗡᭸

1985 88m/C Suzanne Solari, Jeff Hutchinson, Shaun Mitchelle; **D:** Donald G. Jackson. **VHS, Beta** *NWV*

Roller Blade Warriors: Taken By Force

Roller babes battle evil mutant while balancing on big boots with small wheels. 🗡

1990 90m/C Kathleen Kinmont, Rory Calhoun, Abby Dalton, Elizabeth Kaitan. **VHS** *NO*

Rollerball

James Caan is utterly convincing as a troubled jock in the near-future who can't escape the game. Though the film was meant to be a critique of violent sports and the public's reaction to them, it undercuts that message with its own visceral thrills. Word has it that during breaks in the filming, the crew actually played a version of the game on the sets! Flashy, shocking, sometimes exhilarating. 🗡🗡🗡

1975 (R) 123m/C James Caan, John Houseman, Maud Adams, Moses Gunn, Ralph Richardson, John Beck; **D:** Norman Jewison; **W:** William Harrison; **C:** Douglas Slocombe; **M:** Andre Previn. **VHS, Beta, LV** *MGM*

Roswell: The U.F.O. Cover-Up

Fact-based drama finds intelligence officer Major Jesse Marcel (Kyle McLachlan) investigating the wreckage of a craft near his Roswell, New Mexico, air base in the summer of 1947. Marcel believes the craft is extraterrestrial—as are the strange bodies recovered from the wreckage. An Air Force press release announces a UFO but is quickly retracted and Marcel's suspicions ridiculed. A 30-year reunion still finds him obsessed and seeking to clear his name but this time Marcel's investigations may finally lead to the truth. Made for TV; based on the book *UFO Crash at Roswell* by Kevin D. Randle and Donald R. Schmitt. 🗡🗡᭸

1994 (PG-13) 91m/C Kyle MacLachlan, Dwight Yoakam, Kim Greist, Martin Sheen, Xander Berkeley, J.D. Daniels,

"My, what charming underclothes you both have."
—Dr. Frank-N-Furter (Tim Curry) to Brad and Janet (Barry Bostwick and Susan Sarandon) *in The Rocky Horror Picture Show.*

Runaway

Rogue robots on the loose! Who ya gonna call? 'Bot-busters! But this isn't supposed to be a comedy. Instead, the less-than-top-drawer Michael Crichton effort is a formula near-future thriller with a cop (Tom Selleck) and his new partner (Cynthia Rhodes) tracking down out-of-control machines and being chased by same. Definitely not another *Blade Runner*. Features Gene Simmons of the rock group KISS as the villain. Well-photographed by veteran John Alonzo with some nice mechanical and visual effects. 🦴🦴

1984 (PG-13) 100m/C Tom Selleck, Cynthia Rhodes, Gene Simmons, Stan Shaw, Kirstie Alley, Joey Cramer, G.W. Bailey; **D:** Michael Crichton; **W:** Michael Crichton; **C:** John A. Alonzo; **M:** Jerry Goldsmith. **VHS, Beta, LV** *COL*

Running Against Time

A teacher tries to change history (and erase his brother's Vietnam death) by time-warping back to 1963 and preventing JFK's murder. The made-for-cable-TV movie takes an offhanded gee-whiz approach to a tantalizing premise, as temporal paradoxes multiply in *Back to the Future* style. No Kennedy assassination-conspiracy theories, by the way, but Lyndon Johnson fans may not like his depiction here. Based on the novel *A Time to Remember* by Stanley Shapiro. 🦴🦴🦴

1990 (PG) 93m/C Robert Hays, Catherine Hicks, Sam Wanamaker, James DiStefano, Brian Smiar; **D:** Bruce Seth Green; **W:** Robert Glass. **VHS** *MCA*

Running Delilah

Delilah (Kim Cattrall) is a secret agent who is apparently killed by a vicious arms dealer. Only her fellow agent (Billy Zane) resurrects her and Delilah is transformed into a cybernetic super agent. And her assignment is to go after a terrorist who's building a nuclear weapon with plutonium supplied by Delilah's killer. 🦴🦴🦴

1993 85m/C Kim Cattrall, Billy Zane, Diana Rigg. **VHS** *ABC*

The Running Man

A special effects-laden adaptation of the Stephen King novel (originally published under

Attached at the elbow, James Caan and his Siamese twin overcome the odds to make it to the *Rollerball* finals.

Doug Wert, John M. Jackson, Peter MacNicol, Bob Gunton, Charles Martin Smith; **D:** Jeremy Paul Kagan; **W:** Jeremy Paul Kagan, Arthur Kopit, Paul Davids; **C:** Steven Poster; **M:** Elliot Goldenthal. **VHS, LV** *REP*

R.O.T.O.R.

R.O.T.O.R. (Robotic Officer of Tactical Operations Research) is a beefy, humanoid law enforcement 'droid meant to stop criminals. Instead, R.O.T.O.R. tries to use deadly force on an unwary lady speeder and threatens to wreck the town when it refuses to shut down for reprogramming. Very cheap pilfering of *The Terminator*, shot in Dallas. Few f/x. Poetical quotes from John Milton, though. **WOOF!**

1988 90m/C Richard Gesswein, Margaret Trigg, Jayne Smith; **D:** Cullen Blaine. **VHS, LV** *IMP*

his Richard Bachman pseudonym) about a futuristic television game show. Convicts are given a chance for pardon—all they have to do is survive an ongoing battle with specially trained assassins in the bombed-out sections of Los Angeles. Schwarzenegger is suitably grim, and couch potatoes will enjoy seeing longtime game show host and ex-Hogan's Hero Richard Dawson in a major role. This is sci fi with an attitude—fast-moving, occasionally nasty, and always enjoyable. 🦴🦴ᵛ

1987 (R) 101m/C Arnold Schwarzenegger, Richard Dawson, Maria Conchita Alonso, Yaphet Kotto, Mick Fleetwood, Dweezil Zappa, Jesse Ventura, Mick Fleetwood; **D:** Paul Michael Glaser; **W:** Steven E. de Souza; **C:** Thomas Del Ruth; **M:** Harold Faltermeyer. **VHS, Beta, LV** LIV, VES

Samson in the Wax Museum

Silver-masked Mexican wrestling hero Santo (called Samson in the U.S. version of the film) does battle with a mad scientist who has discovered a way to make wax monsters (including a not-very-convincing Frankenstein creature) come to life. Not one of the best Santos, but still good fun for old and new fans. Viva Santo! **AKA:** Santo en el Museo de Cera; Santo in the Wax Museum. 🦴🦴

1963 92m/B MX Santo, Claudio Brook, Ruben Rojo, Norma Mora, Roxana Bellini, Jose Luis Jimenez; **D:** Alfonso Corona Blake; **W:** Fernando Galiana, Julio Porter; **C:** Jose Ortiz Ramos. **VHS** SNC, HHT

Samson Vs. the Vampire Women

Santo (in U.S. versions of the film his name was converted to the more familiar Samson), the masked hero and athlete, once again battles the forces of darkness. This time a horde of slinky female vampires are trying to make an unsuspecting girl their next queen. One of the most fondly regarded of the Santo/Samson series, and a good place to begin exploring the whole crazy Mexican wrestling super hero genre. Santo began his adventures in El Emmascarado de Plata in 1952 and continued his mat-scrambling in such titles as Santo Contro el Cerebro Diabolico, Santo en el Museo de Cera, and Santo Contra la Hija de Frankenstein. 🦴🦴ᵛ

1961 89m/B MX Santo, Lorena Velasquez, Jaime Fernandez, Maria Duval; **D:** Alfonso Corona Blake; **W:** Alfonso Corona Blake. **VHS, Beta** SNC, HHT

Santa Claus Conquers the Martians

A Martian spaceship comes to Earth and kidnaps Santa Claus and two children. Martian kids, it seems, are jealous that Earth tykes have Christmas. One of those low-budget holiday items that raked in the cash year after year at holiday matinees. Not meant to be taken too seriously even by children, there are quite a few touches of intentional satire aimed at parents in the audience. Features then-child star Pia Zadora. Nicholas Webster's only other directorial credit appears to be his own low-budget production of Gone Are the Days (1963) with Alan Alda and Godfrey Cambridge. **AKA:** Santa Claus Defeats the Aliens. 🦴🦴

1964 80m/C John Call, Pia Zadora, Leonard Hicks, Vincent Beck, Victor Stiles, Donna Conforti, Bill McCutcheon; **D:** Nicholas Webster; **W:** Glenville Mareth; **C:** David Quaid. **VHS, Beta** COL, SNC, SUE

Saturn 3

Funnier than Spaceballs, but this is no joke. Stanley Donen—yes, the Singin' in the Rain, An American in Paris Stanley Donen—directed this nearly incomprehensible black hole of a movie set on the Planet of Cheap Special Effects, where Farrah Fawcett and Kirk Douglas operate an experimental space station ("When they want to give the solar system an enema," goes the joke, "that's where they stick the tube in"). They are visited by Harvey Keitel, whose voice has been dubbed to make him sound like George Sanders. But he's still the same old psycho we know and love here on Earth. Farrah is easily upstaged by Hector, Keitel's killer robot, which develops the hots for her. 🦴

1980 (R) 88m/C GB Farrah Fawcett, Kirk Douglas, Harvey Keitel, Ed Bishop; **D:** Stanley Donen; **W:** Martin Amis; **M:** Elmer Bernstein. **VHS, Beta, LV** FOX

Scanner Cop

When deranged scientist Sigmund Glock escapes from prison, he's determined to take

"Let me tell you the way the world is: nothing works right."
—Tom Selleck in Runaway.

tions for his band of psychic gangsters and goes about eliminating any opposition. David Cronenberg's sketchy script (inspired by the real-life birth-defect epidemic caused by Thalidomide) got attention, for good or ill, from Dick Smith's trendsetting, gruesome makeup f/x—most notoriously, a man's head exploded apart by telekinesis. Carnage aside, its a creepy freakout, low on characterization but with a perpetually pulsing soundtrack that may drive some viewers out of their own skulls. 🎵🎵♭

1981 (R) 102m/C *CA* Stephen Lack, Jennifer O'Neill, Patrick McGoohan, Lawrence Dane; *D:* David Cronenberg; *W:* David Cronenberg; *M:* Howard Shore. **VHS, Beta, LV** COL, SUE

Scanners 2: The New Order

Non-Cronenberg sequel to the 1981 cult classic finds police out to build an effective crime-fighting unit out of the Scanners, but one power-mad official is using the enslaved mutants in his own underground psychic militia. Not as visceral as the first film, but a stronger storyline and special effects make it an agreeable followup, with sympathy quotient for the Scanners actually outstripping the grossout stuff. 🎵🎵♭

1991 (R) 104m/C *CA* David Hewlett, Deborah Raffin, Yvan Ponton, Isabelle Mejias, Valentin Trujillo, Tom Butler, Vlasta Vrana, Dorothee Berryman, Raoul Trujillo; *D:* Christian Duguay; *W:* B.J. Nelson; *M:* Marty Simon. **VHS, Beta, LV** MED, IME, VTR

Scanners 3: The Takeover

Third *Scanners* entry was done by the same team as the second, yet is camped-up schlock that matches neither predecessor in tone. A leather-clad Scanner sexpot plans world domination through a media alliance with evil businessmen. She's opposed by a good-guy Scanner who sets the intellectual level in an early sequence that combines scanning with kickboxing (scan fu?). Much heads exploded, one pigeon exploded. 🎵

1992 (R) 101m/C *CA* Steve Parrish, Liliana Komorowska, Valerie Valois; *D:* Christian Duguay. **VHS, LV** REP

"How many times have I told you! No starch in my underwear!" Stephen Lack in *Scanners.*

revenge on Peter Harrigan, the cop who put him behind bars. With the aid of an evil assistant and a mind-altering drug, Glock kidnaps and programs innocent citizens into cop-killing maniacs. Harrigan's only weapon is a rookie cop with the Scanner power to read minds—and then destroy them. 🎵♭

1994 (R) 94m/C Daniel Quinn, Darlanne Fluegel, Richard Lynch, Mark Rolston, Hilary Shepard, Gary Hudson, Cyndi Pass, Luca Bercovici, Brion James; *D:* Pierce David; *W:* John Bryant, George Saunders. **VHS, LV** REP

Scanners

'Ephemerol,' a sedative administered to pregnant women in the 1940s, has sired a generation of Scanners, mutant telepaths pushed toward madness by their own lethal brain waves. Scanner Ironside harbors Hitler aspira-

Scream and Scream Again

Vincent Price is a sinister doctor who tries to create a super race of people devoid of emotions. Peter Cushing is the mastermind behind the plot. Christopher Lee is the agent investigating a series of murders. Three great horror stars, a psychadelic disco, great '60s fashions; it's all here. 🦴🦴🖤

1970 (PG) 95m/C *GB* Vincent Price, Christopher Lee, Peter Cushing, Judy Huxtable, Alfred Marks, Anthony Newlands, Uta Levka, Judi Bloom, Yutte Stensgaard; *D:* Gordon Hessler. **VHS, Beta** *LIV, VES, ORI*

Screamers

A mad scientist on a desert island gleefully turns a group of escaped convicts into grotesque monstrosities. The video box makes reference to the doc's victims being "turned inside out," which, to put it mildly, isn't strictly accurate. The monsters are actually vaguely fish-like. A gory and gratuitous horror romp, recycled from an obscure Italian release, with little to recommend it. **AKA:** L'Isola Degli Uomini Pesce; Island of the Fishmen; Something Waits in the Dark. 🦴

1980 (R) 83m/C Richard Johnson, Joseph Cotten, Barbara Bach, Charles Cass, Beryl Cunningham, Cameron Mitchell, Mel Ferrer; *D:* Sergio Martino, Dan T. Miller. **VHS, Beta** *SUE*

The Sea Serpent

A young sea captain and a crusty scientist unite to search out a giant sea monster awakened by atomic tests. Not one of Ray Milland's better films. 🦴🖤

1985 92m/C *SP* Timothy Bottoms, Ray Milland, Jared Martin; *D:* Gregory Greens. **VHS, Beta** *LIV*

Search and Destroy

Sci-fi action flick about the capture of a secret biological warfare research station. Lotsa action, that's for sure—but where's the plot? 🦴

1988 (R) 87m/C Stuart Garrison Day, Dan Kuchuck, Peggy Jacobsen; *D:* J. Christian Ingvordsen. **VHS, Beta** *MCG*

The Secret of the Golden Eagle

A boy and his new adventurer friend are on a quest to find the strange "Golden Statue" that causes people to grow old before their time. They must take it from criminals who are using it for evil purposes. A good adventure/fantasy for the entire family. 🦴🦴

1991 90m/C Michael Berryman, Brandon McKay; *D:* Cole McKay. **VHS** *WLA*

The Secret of the Telegian

A rare Japanese sci-fi flick about a soldier who uses a teleportation device to avenge himself on fellow soldiers who tried to kill him. Oddly subdued and disturbing for a '60s Japanese sf film, especially considering that it came from Toho studios, which also produced the Godzilla movies. This was the last of Toho's "transformation" movies, preceded by *The H Man* (1958) and *The Human Vapor* (1960). **AKA:** The Telegian; Denso Ningen. 🦴🦴🖤

1961 85m/C *JP* Koji Tsurata, Yumi Shirakawa, Akihiko Hirata, Tadao Nakamura, Seizaburo Kawazu; *D:* Jun Fukuda; *W:* Shinichi Sekizawa; *C:* Kazuo Yamada. **VHS** *SNC*

Secrets of Dreamland

Another documentary about the activities being conducted in at Area 51 (also known as Dreamland) and the super-secret military operations, world-wide data control systems, mind-control experiments and weaponry, and super aeronautics and avionic programs under way there. This one does have one hell of a twist. Norio Hayakawa, a former director for the Civilian Intelligence Network (a group that evaluates government black projects and covert operations) believes that all of the above are part of a secret government plan to stage a fake alien attack, creating world-wide panic, allow marshall law(s) to be put into effect, and bring about the arch fear of the conspiracy theorist...the New World Order. Lots of photographs and film footage lend support. Followed by *Secrets of Dreamland 2* in which Hayakawa continues on, delving into the Christian myth and how it relates to extraterrestrials, the one-world government, and, of course, Area 51. 🦴🦴🦴

1995 /C VHS *TPV, UFO*

> "10 seconds: the pain begins. 15 seconds: you can't breathe. 20 seconds: your head explodes."
> —*Scanners.*

> "They're men turned inside out! And worse...they're still alive!"
>
> *—Screamers.*

Seedpeople

Originality doesn't exactly blossom in Full Moon Production's variation on *Invasion of the Body Snatchers*. Seeds fall from outer space and germinate in sleepy Comet Valley, creating clone duplicates of rural residents. The seedpeople occasionally morph into monsters, for some so-so f/x. Not very fertile. ♪♪

1992 87m/C Sam Hennings, Andrea Roth, Dane Witherspoon, David Dunard, Holly Fields, Bernard Kates, Anne Betancourt, Sonny Carl Davis; **D:** Peter Manoogian; **W:** Jackson Barr; **M:** Boby Mithoff. **VHS, Beta** *PAR*

Seven Faces of Dr. Lao

The mysterious Dr. Lao (Tony Randall) brings his magical circus into the small western town of Abalone and changes the lives of the residents forever. The circus' attractions include a nearly senile Merlin the Magician, the blind seer Apollonius, an abominable snowman, the god Pan, Medusa, a giant serpent, and a tiny fish which turns out to be the Loch Ness Monster. The line between magic and reality blurs for several Abalonians: shy librarian Barbara Eden sees her secret lover in Pan; a crooked entrepreneur (Arthur O'Connell) finds that he bears an unsettling resemblance to the giant serpent; and the town battleaxe is (temporarily) turned into a statue. Lao closes the show with a none-too-subtle parable about an ancient city that was destroyed by the gods for greed and ingratitude (with footage taken from director Pal's earlier film *The Lost Continent*). Not as ambitious or strange as the novel that inspired it (Charles Finney's 1935 work, *The Circus of Dr. Lao*), this is still a charming family film with marvelous special effects and makeup (Randall plays seven characters). Try watching it right after (or before) an *Odd Couple* marathon. It's fun. ♪♪♪

1963 101m/C Tony Randall, Barbara Eden, Arthur O'Connell, Lee Patrick, Noah Beery Jr., John Qualen, John Ericson, Minerva Urecal; **D:** George Pal; **W:** Charles Beaumont. **VHS, Beta, LV** *MGM*

The Seventh Voyage of Sinbad

Ray Harryhausen works his stop-motion animation magic in what may be the first color film of its type. Sinbad (Kerwin Mathews) decides that his thumb-size girlfriend, Princess Parisa (Kathryn Grant), would be easier to love if normal size. So off he goes to search for the egg of a Roc, which will reverse the spell cast by the evil magician Sokurah (Torin Thatcher). On the Isle of Colossa, the only place them Roc things hang, Parisa frees a genie-of-the-lamp to help on the quest. On the way, Sinbad and crew must battle some of Harryhausen's most memorable and likable creations: a two-headed Roc, a man-eating cyclops, a fire-breathing dragon, and most impressively, a sword-fighting skeleton brought to life by Sokurah. This is the one that really got Harryhausen rolling on his fantasy film career, a career that would go on through his last film *Clash of the Titans*. One of Bernard Herrmann's finest scores; during the duel with the skeleton, if you listen you can hear the bones. ♪♪♪

1958 (G) 94m/C Kerwin Mathews, Kathryn Grant, Torin Thatcher, Richard Eyer; **D:** Nathan (Hertz) Juran; **W:** Kenneth Kolb; **M:** Bernard Herrmann. **VHS, Beta, LV** *COL, MLB, CCB*

The Sex Machine

In the year 2037, a scientist finds two of the world's greatest lovers and unites them so he can transform their reciprocating motion into electricity. It worked on paper. **WOOF!**

1976 (R) 80m/C Agostina Belli. **VHS, Beta** *MED*

The Shadow

Who knows what evil lurks in the hearts of men? Why "The Shadow" of course, as is shown in this highly stylized big screen version of the '30s pulp fiction series and radio show that once starred Orson Welles. Billionaire playboy Lamont Cranston (Alec Baldwin) is a master of illusion and defender of justice thanks to his alter ego and his secret network of operatives. Aided by companion Margo Lane (Penelope Ann Miller), the Shadow battles super-criminal Shiwan Khan (John Lone), the deadliest descendant of Ghenghis Khan. Numerous and elaborate special effects provide icing on the cake for those in the mood for a journey back to the radio past or a quick superhero fix. A bad scripting choice reveals

The Hound Salutes: George Pal

There are fans who say that the Hollywood career of George Pal (1908-1980) parallels that of Walt Disney. But while Uncle Walt went on to become a household name as an entertainment innovator, Pal, who took as many risks with even more way-out material, suffered reversals for every step forward. George Pal's history alternates between fantasy masterpieces and tantalizing sci-fi projects that just missed greatness.

Born in Hungary, Pal worked in Germany, the Netherlands, and France before arrived in Hollywood in the 1940s as an animator. Rather than simple cartooning, Pal perfected three-dimensional stop-motion techniques featuring whimsical figures, and his Oscar-winning "Puppetoon" short subjects, done for Paramount, were unique for the time and preceded works like *The Nightmare Before Christmas* by half a century.

Inevitably Pal moved into mainstream features, soon showing a serious interest in sf and fantasy. Though science-fiction literature was enjoying its Golden Age at the time, Hollywood's genre efforts were marginal, almost nonexistent except for comic-strip adaptations. Pal changed that with his big-budget, carefully researched production *Destination Moon* (based on a Robert Heinlein novella), which brought off-planet exploration to the screen in realistic, almost documentary fashion. Though it may seem a bit stiff by today's standards, back in 1950 there had never been anything like *Destination Moon*.

It's fair to say that in the years before Sputnik, George Pal did more research into space missions than did the U.S. government, and *Destination Moon*'s success propelled a sci-fi boom in the 1950s. Numerous imitators offered low-budget, B-movie genre pics, but Pal (often in conflict with more Earthbound studio moguls who Just Didn't Get It) wielded all the resources of Hollywood f/x magic and design to produce the blockbusters *When Worlds Collide, The War of the Worlds,* and *Destination Moon*'s semi-sequel *Conquest of Space*. This last, however, was a costly failure for Paramount, and no serious space-travel depictions came out of Hollywood studios for 10 years.

Pal was unusual for his era in that he had great respect for writers—David Duncan, scripter of Pal's classic *The Time Machine,* said Pal was the only director who ever consulted with him during a shoot. A true devotee of fantastic literature, Pal was drawn to an unsung giant of sf literature, Olaf Stapledon, whose *Odd John* (1935) is probably the best serious novel on the mutant-superman theme. Unfortunately the script Pal commissioned turned out a mediocrity (complete with a Hollywood happy ending) and was mercifully never shot. Unwilling to relinquish the premise, Pal decided to film a somewhat lesser novel about psychic superhumans, Frank Robinson's *The Power*.

Some critics have described the resulting film as the finest screen sf up to that time, a well-made and intelligent thriller about a scientist (George Hamilton) stalked by an unknown mastermind whose brain waves alter perception and reality. Today it has a cult of admirers, but when *The Power* bombed at the box office in 1967 it caused the most painful reversal in Pal's career and, in effect, ended it.

Pal's final completed project was another audacious adaptation, of the "Doc Savage" series of pulp novels (penned by various authors under the pseudonym Kenneth Robeson since 1933). Pal planned an adventure in the style of a vintage 007, but the studio, fixated on the camp phenom of TV's *Batman,* turned *Doc Savage—The Man of Bronze* into an archaic spoof by the time it staggered onto screens briefly in 1975. Rumor has it Pal's early vision of Doc Savage caught the ears of network TV executives, who reworked the premise into a prime time hit—*Mission: Impossible*.

A feature-length tribute, *The Fantasy Film Worlds of George Pal,* mixing interviews, clips, and tributes from the likes of Ray Bradbury and Charlton Heston, can be found on home video. And a set of original George Pal Puppetoons are compiled in *The Puppetoon Movie*.

interesting premise, but degenerates into typical post-*Alien* monster flick and gore f/x. 🦴🦴

1989 (R) 88m/C Louise Fletcher, David Beecroft, James Hong, Shawn Weatherly, Lu Leonard; **D:** J.S. Cardone; **W:** J.S. Cardone. **VHS, Beta, LV** *PAR*

She

Willis O'Brien's team of f/x wizards assembled for the original *King Kong* worked on many RKO features afterwards. One is *She,* and their handiwork is the film's chief glory. They whip up H. Rider Haggard's lost city of Kor, transferred from Africa to the Arctic and warmed into life by underground volcanoes. Kor is a combination of Egyptian, Greek, Mayan, and Art Deco motifs (including the *King Kong* gates), and at the heart of it all it Ayesha, alias She-Who-Must-Be-Obeyed, a woman over 2,000 years old made young and immortal by stepping into the Flame of Life, a strange phenomenon that burns fitfully in a secret grotto. Three adventurers arrive in Kor; Ayesha is convinced that one of them is her reincarnated lover and urges him to take a pyrological bath. Sumptuous spectacle and a rousing Max Steiner music score make this the best version of the oft-filmed story. Alas, a stop-motion mastodon sequence planned by O'Brien was never filmed. Commercial VHS and laser prints run a few minutes short, inexplicably missing a key scene between Nigel Bruce and the high priests of Kor. 🦴🦴🦴🦴

1935 95m/B Helen Gahagan, Randolph Scott, Nigel Bruce, Helen Mack, Gustav von Seyffertitz; **D:** Irving Pichel, Lansing C. Holden; **W:** Dudley Nichols, Ruth Rose; **C:** J. Roy Hunt; **M:** Max Steiner. **VHS** *KIV*

She

A beautiful female warrior rules over the men in a post-holocaust world "23 years after the Cancellation." A lengthy quest takes She and her friends—Tom, Dick, and Hari—into battle with increasingly bizarre foes, like chainsaw-wielding guys wrapped in bandages and the self-cloning minions of a Darth-Vader type whose mask sports Mickey Mouse ears. If you can forgive the unrecognizable mangling of H. Rider Haggard's original novel (still a spellbinder, well worth reading), this postnuke rub-

The Congeniality Award goes to...Miss Connecticut! *She Demons* have pageants too, you know.

the Shadow's origin from the beginning, ruining the opportunity for much potential suspense and mystery, but this is still a fun and satisfactory adaptation. Plenty of wry humor, but surprisingly, none of it comes from Jonathan Winters, who plays his police chief role straight. 🦴🦴

1994 (PG-13) 112m/C Alec Baldwin, John Lone, Penelope Ann Miller, Peter Boyle, Ian McKellen, Tim Curry, Jonathan Winters; **D:** Russell Mulcahy; **W:** David Koepp; **C:** Stephen Burum. **VHS, LV** *MCA*

Shadowzone

As a result of NASA experiments in dream travel, an interdimensional monster invades our world in search of victims, changing shape to match their thoughts. Begins well, with slightly

bish is good for laughs, several of them intentional.

1983 90m/C Sandahl Bergman, Harrison Muller, Quin Kessler, David Goss; **D:** Avi Nesher. **VHS, Beta** *LIV*

She Demons

This is a really weird one. A pleasure craft loaded with babes crashes into a remote island controlled by a mad ex-Nazi scientist with a really hokey accent. Instead of doing the sensible thing and establishing a private harem, Herr Doktor transforms the lovelies into rubber-faced monsters (who from the neck down are still perfectly normal). Everyone's favorite '50s TV jungle heroine, Irish *Sheena, Queen of the Jungle* McCalla, turns up with Tod Griffin to confront the villains amid luxuriously phoney sets. '50s so-bad-it's-good nonsense at its finest. Don't miss it!

1958 68m/B Irish McCalla, Tod Griffin, Victor Sen Yung, Rudolph Anders, Tod Andrews; **D:** Richard Cunha. **VHS, Beta** *RHI, SNC, MWP*

Short Circuit

Advanced robot designed for the military is hit by lightning and begins to think for itself. The vaguely humanoid tin man is taken in by a spacey animal lover (who initially mistakes her visitor for an alien first contact and exults "I always knew They would pick me!"), then hides from meanies at the weapons lab who want their hardware back. Somewhere in here are Asimovian themes about the nature and rights of artificial sentient life forms, but such deep thoughts are buried under tons of slapstick gags and chase scenes apparently designed for short attention spans. A joke reference to the Three Stooges is no accident; everything happens at hyperspeed, and characters are needlessly obnoxious.

1986 (PG) 98m/C Steve Guttenberg, Ally Sheedy, Austin Pendleton, Fisher Stevens, Brian McNamara, G.W. Bailey; **D:** John Badham; **W:** S.S. Wilson, Brent Maddock; **C:** Nick McClean; **M:** David Shire; **V:** Tim Blaney. **VHS, Beta, LV** *FOX*

Short Circuit 2

Sequel to the adorable-robot-outwits-bad-guys tale is aimed strictly at small fry but counts as an improvement, with better pacing and wittier whimsy. The cheerful metal hero, Number Five, arrives in the city to visit old friends, draws the attention of a greedy toy merchant and a gang of jewel thieves. Downside is you'll probably need to see the first *Short Circuit* to fully appreciate how comparatively cute and painless this one is.

1988 (PG) 95m/C Fisher Stevens, Cynthia Gibb, Michael McKean, Jack Weston, David Hemblen; **D:** Kenneth Johnson; **W:** S.S. Wilson, Brent Maddock; **M:** Charles Fox; **V:** Tim Blaney. **VHS, Beta, LV** *COL*

Shredder Orpheus

Your chance to witness Greek mythology updated/mangled in a post-apocalyptic setting with skateboard-thrash culture sensibilities. Armed with a mind-altering "lyre-axe guitar" that Jimi Hendrix secretly developed, future rocker Orpheus skateboards through hell (actually its closest equivalent, a cable-TV network) to rescue his zombified wife from the Gray Zone underworld. Cluttered with pop-culture parodies, slogans, gratuitous pavement surfing, and miscellaneous weirdness, this holds the attention for about 40 minutes until it just runs out of plot and tries unsuccessfully to coast along on Attitude. For a 20th-century take on Orpheus and Eurydice that doesn't wipe out, see Jean Cocteau's classic *Orphee* instead.

1989 93m/C Jesse Bernstein, Robert McGinley, Vera McCaughan, Megan Murphy, Carlo Scandiuzzi; **D:** Robert McGinley. **VHS, Beta** *AIP*

Silent Running

Astronauts of a future overtechnologized Earth grudgingly care for the last remaining wilderness environments, sent into orbit for eventual reforestation. When authorities instead order the project scrapped and the vegetation destroyed, nature-loving Bruce Dern mutinies and pilots his dome-enclosed woodland into the safety of deep space. Douglas Trumbull's directorial debut; he created special effects for *2001,* but this small-budget, more moralistic effort (filmed largely aboard a disused aircraft carrier) is clearly an eco-product of the '60s, with a Joan Baez theme ballad

> "Never trust a mutant."
> —Sage advice from Amazon Sandahl Bergman in 1983's *She.*

and heavy-handed tree-hugging. If you can
slog through the sentimentality, there's a
haunting closer that one commentator called
the most powerful image in modern sf cinema.
The film's three waddling robots—Huey,
Dewey, and Louie—can be seen as the inspiration for R2D2 and his cutesy brethren. 🦴🦴🦴

1971 (G) 90m/C Bruce Dern, Cliff Potts, Ron Rifkin; *D:*
Douglas Trumbull; *W:* Michael Cimino, Deric Washburn,
Steven Bochco; *M:* Prof. Peter Schickele. **VHS, Beta, LV**
MCA

Sinbad and the Eye of the Tiger

Sinbad (Patrick Wayne replacing John Phillip
Law) sails to Charnak to ask Prince Kassim for
the hand of his sister, Farah (Jane Seymour).
Unfortunately, the prince has been babooni-
fied by their evil stepmother Zenobia (Margaret Whiting). To break the spell, Sinbad must
once again hit the road, er sea, and face a myr-
iad of Ray Harryhausen's stop-motion creatures, including the Minaton, a giant troglodyte

(originally planned to be played by an actor), a
saber-toothed tiger, and a giant walrus. Even
the baboon is animated. The locations are
great—like the rock tombs of ancient Petra or
the glaciers of the Pyrenees. Harryhausen's
second-to-last film. *Eye of the Tiger* was
intended to be *Sinbad at the World's End,* with
Law reprising his Sinbad role, but budget con-
strictions limited the production. 🦴🦴

1977 (G) 113m/C *GB* Patrick Wayne, Jane Seymour, Taryn
Power, Margaret Whiting; *D:* Sam Wanamaker; *W:* Beverley Cross. **VHS, Beta, LV** COL, CCB

Sinbad of the Seven Seas

It's a sin, it's so bad, this Italian muscle epic
claiming to be based on an obscure Edgar
Allen Poe retelling of Arabian Nights legends
(quoth Poe's agent: Nevermore!). Lou Ferrigno, in Hercules mode, plays the famous
adventurer. Can Sinbad find the magic jewels
so a prince will triumph over a sorcerer? "I'll
give it a shot," he says, and wrestles with

latex-and-plywood monsters. Woeful dubbed dialogue also includes the villain's immortal declaration, "My evil gods make me the top of the heap around here." **WOOF!**

1989 90m/C *IT* Lou Ferrigno, John Steiner, Leo Gullotta, Teagan Clive; *D:* Enzo G. Castellari. **VHS, Beta, LV** *WAR, OM*

The Sisterhood

A pair of amazons fight for women's rights in a post-nuclear future. Cheap feminist theme laid over warmed-over sci-fi plot. 🦴

1988 (R) 75m/C Rebecca Holden, Chuck Wagner, Lynn-Holly Johnson, Barbara Hooper; *D:* Cirio H. Santiago. **VHS, Beta, LV** *MED*

Skeeter

Yes, it's the attack of the killer mosquito! Not just any mosquito of course, but a new gigantic species bred on toxic waste. They're invading the quiet desert town of Mesquite—and they're out for blood. There aren't many surprises in this update of the old "giant mutant insect" flick, but it's good for a few laughs. Still, if giant mosquitos are what you crave, you'll probably find 1995's *Mosquito* a bit more amusing. 🦴🦴

1993 (R) 95m/C Tracy Griffith, Jim Youngs, Charles Napier, Michael J. Pollard; *D:* Clark Brandon; *W:* Clark Brandon, Lanny Horn; *M:* David Lawrence. **VHS, LV** *COL*

Sky Pirates

Space epic deals about pieces of ancient stone left by prehistoric extraterrestrials, now lost in a time warp. Bad stunts, bad script, and notably bad acting make it a woofer in any era. **WOOF!**

1987 88m/C *AU* John Hargreaves, Max Phipps, Meredith Phillips; *D:* Colin Eggleston. **VHS, Beta** *FOX*

Slaughterhouse Five

Fine adaptation of Kurt Vonnegut's challenging breakthrough novel has never managed to

"Hey, wait a minute! I thought you said we were going on a picnic!" Billy Pilgrim (Michael Sacks) and fellow prisoners in *Slaughterhouse Five.*

find an audience. Perhaps Vonnegut's quizzical pessimism and director George Roy Hill's straightforward approach to it simply don't mesh for viewers. The story trips back and forth across time and space—never losing its intelligent humor—from the World War II firebombing of Dresden to hero Billy Pilgrim's (Michael Sacks) imprisonment with B-movie queen Montana Wildhack (Valerie Perrine) by extraterrestrials. Considerable philosophizing occurs in between. So it goes. (Fans who have missed this one really should give it a look. It's better than its reputation.) 🦴🦴🦴

1972 (R) 104m/C Michael Sacks, Valerie Perrine, Ron Leibman, Eugene Roche, Perry King, Sharon Gans, Roberts Blossom; *D:* George Roy Hill; *W:* Stephen Geller; *C:* Miroslav Ondricek. Hugos '73: Dramatic Presentation; Cannes Film Festival '72: Special Jury Prize; Nominations: Cannes Film Festival '72: Best Film. **VHS, Beta, LV** *MCA*

Slave Girls from Beyond Infinity

With a title like that, what you see is what you get. And what you get is a sci-fi/exploitation ripoff of "The Most Dangerous Game," with two scantily clad runaway slave girls escaping their intergalactic penal colony only to land on a mysterious planet where the evil Zed hunts wayward humans for sport. Sole redeeming social value is makeup f/x by John Buechler. 🦴

1987 (R) 80m/C Elizabeth Cayton, Cindy Beal, Brinke Stevens; *D:* Ken Dixon. **VHS, Beta, LV** *AFE*

Sleeper

"I can't believe you haven't had sex in 200 years." "204 if you count my marriage." Woody Allen has seen the future, and in it, tobacco, fat, and hot fudge are the healthiest things for you, and watching Howard Cosell is considered cruel and unusual punishment. Allen's most ambitious film to date is as much an homage to silent comedy as it is science fiction. Allen portrays Greenwich Village health food store owner Miles Monroe, who goes to the hospital with a peptic ulcer and is cryogenically frozen. He wakes up "in a bird's-eye wrapper" in the year 2173, where he immediately finds himself on the ten most wanted list as an alien. Diane Keaton costars as ditzy would-be poetess Luna, whom he is forced to take hostage. Great gags involve jet-pack suits, giant vegetables, stereotypically gay and Jewish tailor robots, and a malfunctioning Orgasmatron. Diane gets to do her Marlon Brando imitation. The rebel fight song ("Rebels are we/Born to be free...") was first heard in Allen's *Bananas*. The Dixieland soundtrack features Woody wailing on clarinet. 🦴🦴🦴

1973 (PG) 88m/C Woody Allen, Diane Keaton, John Beck, Howard Cosell, Mary Gregory, Don Keefer; *D:* Woody Allen; *W:* Marshall Brickman, Woody Allen; *C:* David M. Walsh; *M:* Woody Allen. Hugos '74: Dramatic Presentation. **VHS, Beta, LV** *MGM, FOX, FUS*

The Slime People

Huge prehistoric monsters are awakened from long hibernation by atomic testing in Los Angeles. They take over the city, creating the fog they need to live. Thank goodness for scientist Robert Burton, who saves the day. Filmed in a butcher shop in Los Angeles. **WOOF!**

1963 76m/B Robert Hutton, Robert Burton, Susan Hart, William Boyce, Les Tremayne; *D:* Robert Hutton. **VHS, Beta** *NOS, GEM, RHI*

Slipstream

Big-budget, handsomely made sf is set in a future where an ecological disaster has destroyed society as we know it. The climate has been radically changed, creating a strong wind current. Mark Hamill is an ill-tempered cop who flies a wild-looking plane. He and partner Kitty Aldridge capture poetry-spouting murderer Bob Peck, but before they can bring him to justice, he's kidnapped by dim-witted bounty hunter Bill Paxton. The chase is on. Unfortunately, the chase is filled with holes. At first that doesn't matter because director Steven Lisberger captured some stunning aerial footage and much of the Turkish landscape is exotic and fascinating. Whenever the action moves to ground level, it falters. The characters are poorly drawn and the dialogue is amateurish throughout. But when Ben Kingsley shows up in a cameo role, everyone begins to talk in fortune-cookie aphorisms that are apparently meant to pass for wisdom. 🦴🦴

1989 (PG-13) 92m/C *GB* Mark Hamill, Bill Paxton, Bob Peck, Eleanor David, Kitty Aldridge, Robbie Coltrane, F. Murray Abraham; *Cameos:* Ben Kingsley; *D:* Steven Lisberger; *W:* Tony Kayden; *M:* Elmer Bernstein. **VHS, Beta, LV** *VTR*

The Snow Creature

Stupid troop of explorers bring back a snow creature from the Himalayas. Critter escapes in L.A. and terrorizes all in its path before blending in with club crowd. Very bad monster epic (the first about a snow monster) that strains credibility frame by frame. Occasionally, depending upon camera angle, light, and viewer mood, monster appears to be something other than guy in bad suit sweating. Directed by Billy Wilder's brother and another argument against genetic consistency. **WOOF!**

1954 72m/B Paul Langton, Leslie Denison; **D:** W. Lee Wilder. **VHS, Beta** *NOS, SNC*

this futuristic disaster pic, an international co-production with a jumble of plot tangents that testify to much reworking and re-editing that compelled director Richard Sarafian to use the standard industry pseudonym of 'Allen Smithee' in the credits, a sure sign something went awry. Note the talking bomb (voiced by Paul Williams), a bit borrowed from the much cheaper and better-regarded *Dark Star*. Based on a novel by Takeshi Kawata. 🦴🦴

1992 (PG-13) 111m/C Tim Matheson, Charlton Heston, Peter Boyle, Annabel Schofield, Jack Palance, Corin "Corky" Nemec; **D:** Richard Sarafian; **C:** Russell Carpenter; **M:** Maurice Jarre; **V:** Paul Williams. **VHS, LV** *VMK*

Solar Crisis

In 2050 the sun begins throwing off giant solar flares which turn the Earth extra-crispy. A space team is sent to divert the heat waves, but the mission falls prey to corporate sabotage. Eye-popping special effects highlight

Solar Force

Cop (Michael Pare), stationed on the moon, is sent to Earth to find a stolen chemical that is capable of restoring a destroyed environment. But there are secrets behind the assignment which could cost him his life. 🦴🦴

Dr. Hannibal Lector makes his comic debut in Woody Allen's *Sleeper*.

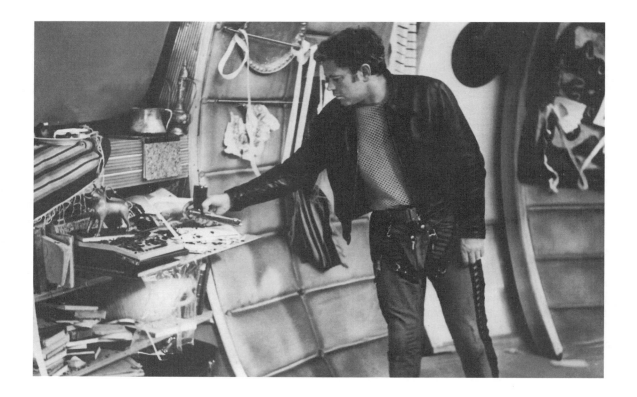

Never point a gun at anyone, especially yourself. Donatas Banionis in *Solaris.*

1994 (R) 91m/C Michael Pare, Billy Drago, Walker Brandt; *D:* Boaz Davidson; *W:* Terrence Pare; *C:* Avi Karpik; *M:* Don Peake. **VHS, LV** *HMK*

Solarbabies

Ridiculous costumes are somehow appropriate to the laughable title, but this isn't an intentional comedy. Rollerskating kids in a drought-stricken future vie for a mysterious power that will replenish the Earth's water. Shades of every sci-fi movie you've ever seen, from *Mad Max* to *Ice Pirates.* Pathetic, despite a cast that's done much, much better. And it was written by the author of *The Wild Bunch*! ♫

1986 (PG-13) 95m/C Richard Jordan, Sarah Douglas, Charles Durning, Lukas Haas, Jami Gertz, Jason Patric; *D:* Alan Johnson; *W:* Walon Green; *M:* Maurice Jarre. **VHS, Beta, LV** *MGM*

Solaris

With this the USSR tried to eclipse *2001: A Space Odyssey* in terms of cerebral science fiction. Some critics thought they succeeded. You may disagree now that the lumbering effort is available on tape. Adapted from a Stanislaw Lem novel, it depicts a dilapidated space lab orbiting the planet Solaris, whose ocean, a vast fluid "brain," materializes the stir-crazy cosmonauts' obsessions—usually morose ex-girlfriends. Talk, talk, talk, minimal special effects. In Russian with English subtitles. In a two-cassette package, with a letterbox format preserving Tarkovsky's widescreen compositions. ♫ ♫

1972 167m/C *RU* Donatas Banionis, Natalya Bondarchuk; *D:* Andrei Tarkovsky; *M:* Eduard Artemyev. Cannes Film Festival '72: Grand Jury Prize; Nominations: Cannes Film Festival '72: Best Film. **VHS, LV** *FXL, FCT, INJ*

Something Wicked This Way Comes

Ray Bradbury wrote the screenplay for this much-anticipated, big-budget adaptation of

his own novel. Darkly magical story told from a young boy's point of view. Mr. Dark's traveling circus comes to town, and while its true nature is revealed a little early, there's still lots of fun, fantasy, and even a few life lessons in store, as the locals flock to the circus, each to be tempted with their own deepest and darkest desires. The usual fine performance by Jason Robards as the boy's father looking for redemption in his son's eyes, the required ham-job by Jonathan Pryce as the sinister Mr. Dark, and good special effects, almost make this a great film. 🦴🦴🦴

1983 (PG) 94m/C Jason Robards Jr., Jonathan Pryce, Diane Ladd, Pam Grier, Richard Davalos, James Stacy; **D:** Jack Clayton; **W:** Ray Bradbury; **C:** Stephen Burum; **M:** James Horner. **VHS, Beta, LV** *DIS*

Son of Blob

A post-*Jeannie,* pre-*Dallas* Larry Hagman directed this exercise in zaniness. A scientist brings home a piece of frozen blob from the North Pole; his wife accidentally revives the dormant gray mass. It begins a rampage of terror by digesting nearly everyone within its reach, including Shelley Berman and Burgess Meredith. One poor guy drinks a blob cocktail and then it...well, sort of drinks *him.* From the inside out. Sequels to classics of *The Blob*'s stature don't usually work, but this one is great fun. **AKA:** Beware! The Blob. 🦴🦴🦴

1971 (PG) 87m/C Robert Walker Jr., Godfrey Cambridge, Carol Lynley, Shelley Berman, Larry Hagman, Burgess Meredith, Gerrit Graham, Dick Van Patten, Gwynne Gilford; **D:** Larry Hagman; **W:** Anthony Harris, Jack Woods; **C:** Al Hamm. **VHS, Beta** *GEM*

Son of Flubber

This thoroughly enjoyable sequel to *The Absent Minded Professor* finds Fred MacMurray still toying with his prodigious invention Flubber, now in a convenient gaseous form. "Flubbergas" causes those who inhale it to float away (which comes in handy during the town's big football game). Fred also monkeys with a weather-changing device and has assorted other problems. High family wackiness from Disney with appearances by Ed Wynn and Paul Lynde. 🦴🦴🦴

1963 96m/B Fred MacMurray, Nancy Olson, Tommy Kirk, Leon Ames, Joanna Moore, Keenan Wynn, Charlie Ruggles, Paul Lynde, Ed Wynn; **D:** Robert Stevenson; **C:** Edward Colman; **M:** George Bruns. **VHS, Beta** *DIS*

Son of Frankenstein

After a reissue double feature of *Frankenstein* and *Dracula* in 1938 became a surprise knockout hit, Universal decided to start making horror movies once again. This is the second sequel (after *The Bride of Frankenstein*) to the 1931 version of the horror classic. The good doctor's skeptical son (Basil Rathbone, in a fine bombastic performance) returns to the family manse and becomes obsessed with his father's work and with reviving the creature, giving us a peek at the Monster's physiology in the process. Full of memorable characters and brooding ambience. Boris Karloff's last appearance as the Monster, but Bela Lugosi's characterization of Ygor, the broken-necked friend of the Monster, steals the show. Originally, Ygor was barely supposed to be in the movie, but director Rowland Lee—who'd thrown out the original script and was making things up as he went along—did Bela a favor by substantially expanding his part. 🦴🦴🦴

1939 99m/C Basil Rathbone, Bela Lugosi, Boris Karloff, Lionel Atwill, Josephine Hutchinson, Donnie Dunagan, Emma Dunn, Edgar Norton, Lawrence Grant, Lionel Belmore; **D:** Rowland V. Lee; **W:** Willis Cooper; **C:** George Robinson. **VHS, Beta, LV** *MCA*

Son of Godzilla

The second of Godzilla's "south seas" pictures (after *Godzilla Vs. the Sea Monster*), this one concerns the adventures of a group of scientists trying to control weather conditions on a tropical island. Their lives are threatened when their experiments hatch the title infant, drawing the unwelcome attention of the adult monster and some gigantic insects as well. It's refreshing to see Godzilla marching among the waving palms instead of smashing cities, and no doubt less expensive for the producers. While Godzilla and his young ward (dubbed "Minya" in Japan) look awful in this entry, and the juvenile aspect of the baby's antics are slightly annoying, this is nevertheless a solidly paced and plotted sci-fi adventure, with good

"When the house is filled with dread, place the beds at head to head."

—Emma Dunn's incantation to ward off evil in *Son of Frankenstein.*

performances, memorable music, and some genuinely touching moments. Minya would return to tug at our heartstrings in *Destroy All Monsters* and *Godzilla's Revenge* before retiring from the screen forever. **AKA:** Gojira no Musuko. 🦴🦴🦴

1966 86m/C *JP* Akira Kubo, Beverly Maeda, Tadao Takashima, Akihiko Hirata, Kenji Sahara; **D:** Jun Fukuda; **W:** Shinichi Sekizawa, Kazue Shiba; **M:** Masaru Sato. **VHS, Beta** *PSM, HHT, DVT*

Son of Kong

Carl Denham (Robert Armstrong) returns to Skull Island, only to discover a younger albino member of Kong's species living there in this often humorous sequel to RKO's immensely popular *King Kong*. Hoping to capitalize on the enormous success of its predecessor, director Ernest Schoedsack quickly threw this together. As a result, its success at the box office did not match the original's, and didn't deserve to, but it's fun. Nifty special effects from Willie O'Brien, the man who brought them to us the first time. Oddly, the understated romance that builds between the ruined Denham and orphaned teenager Mack is one of the sweetest in any fantasy film. 🦴🦴🐾

1933 70m/B Robert Armstrong, Helen Mack, Noble Johnson; **D:** Ernest B. Schoedsack; **W:** Ruth Rose; **M:** Max Steiner. **VHS, Beta, LV** *NOS, MED, FCT*

Soylent Green

The future is... no future. That's the basic message behind this relentlessly dark film that is turned into more than just a grim ecological shocker through excellent performances, including that of Edward G. Robinson in his final role. In the year 2022, New York City is jammed with 40 million people (mostly unemployed), suicide is not only legal—it's encouraged, jam is $150 a jar, and crowd control is done with bulldozers. The most common (and only affordable) food for the masses is the green wafer, Soylent. Policeman Thorn (Chuck Heston) is a worn-out, hard-nosed cop assigned to the murder of a Soylent Company exec. Tab (Chuck Connors) is one of those cleaner types for the company, getting rid of loose ends, one of which is Thorn. Their fight

at the apartment is a doozy. Thorn's researcher (Edward G.) remembers when there were trees, vegetables, democracy, and real sunshine. His demise is the "pretty" part of this film. If you thought things were bad, watch this movie...watch it anyway. Based on the novel *Make Room! Make Room!* by Harry Harrison. 🦴🦴🦴

1973 (PG) 95m/C Charlton Heston, Leigh Taylor-Young, Chuck Connors, Joseph Cotten, Edward G. Robinson, Brock Peters; **D:** Richard Fleischer; **W:** Stanley R. Greenberg; **C:** Richard Kline. **VHS, Beta, LV** *MGM*

Space Monster

Really bad, low-budget flick with a rubber monster and a climactic crash into a "sea of monsters" which is really a fish tank full of crabs. Ultra-cheap production with handed down cast and props. **AKA:** First Woman Into Space; Voyage Beyond the Sun. 🦴🐾

1964 ?m/B VHS *SMW*

Space Mutiny

The giant spaceship Southern Star falls under an attack by mutinous Kalgan, who wants to take everyone to "Pirate World." Direct-to-video pic alternates between cheapo laser battles in what look like boiler rooms to galactic dogfights with expensive f/x—the latter being entire sequences swiped from TV's *Battlestar Galactica* (no wonder the Southern Star looks so familiar) retrofitted with lame-o lines like "Surrender or be blown to astro-dust!" Dig the dorky disco scenes in which space cadets boogie with hula hoops. **WOOF!**

1988 (PG) 93m/C Reb Brown, James Ryan, John Phillip Law, Cameron Mitchell; **D:** David Winters; **W:** Maria Dante. **VHS, Beta** *AIP*

Space Ninja: Sword of the Space Ark

A young fighter pilot returns home to find his planet under siege and his family dead. He vows to seek revenge and sets out to destroy the evil emperor who is wreaking such havoc. 🦴🐾

1981 75m/C D: Bunker Jenkins. **VHS, Beta** *LIV*

Space Rage

A criminal sentenced to life on the prison planet Botany Bay busts out and must be challenged by aging sheriff Richard Farnsworth. The cast does what they can with what amounts to a basic formula western set in outer space. **AKA:** Trackers. 🦴🦴

1986 (R) 78m/C Michael Pare, Richard Farnsworth, John Laughlin, Lee Purcell; **D:** Conrad Palmisano. **VHS, Beta** *LIV*

Space Raiders

A plucky 10-year-old blasts off into a futuristic world of intergalactic desperados, crafty alien mercenaries, starship battles, and cliff-hanging dangers. Recycled special effects (from producer Corman's movie factory) and plot (lifted near-whole from *Star Wars*). **AKA:** Star Child. 🦴🦴

1983 (PG) 84m/C Vince Edwards, David Mendenhall; **D:** Howard R. Cohen; **W:** Howard R. Cohen. **VHS, Beta** *WAR*

Space Soldiers Conquer the Universe

Edited version of the Flash Gordon serial *Flash Gordon Conquers the Universe*. The evil Emperor Ming introduces a horrible plague from outer space called "The Purple Death." Dr. Zarkov, Dale, and Flash Gordon travel from the frozen wastes of Frigia to the palaces of Mongo and must take risk after risk. Twelve chapters at 20 minutes each. 🦴🦴

1940 240m/B Buster Crabbe, Charles Middleton, Carol Hughes. **VHS, Beta** *NOS, CAB*

Spaceballs

The force was not with Mel Brooks, whose spoof of the George Lucas franchise seems light years too late. But why ask for the moon when you have such stars as Rick Moranis as the petulant geek Dark Helmet, John Candy as Barf, who is half-dog/half-man ("I'm my own

"Outta my way!" Charlton Heston pushes his way to the front of the cafeteria line in **Soylent Green.**

It takes a lot of **Spaceballs** to try to imitate *Star Wars*. John Candy, Lorene Yarnell, Daphne Zuniga, and Bill Pullman.

best friend"), Dom DeLuise as the voice of Pizza the Hut, and Brooks, revising his 2,000-Year-Old Man character as the sage Yogurt, whose motto is "May the Schwartz be with you." Chiding the vast *Star Wars* merchandising empire is about as biting as the satire gets. Bidding adieu to our heroes (*Melrose Place*'s Daphne Zuniga as a "Druish Princess," Bill Pullman as space cowboy Lone Starr), Yogurt states, "God willing, we'll all meet again in Spaceballs II—The Search for More Money.'" As can be expected, the gags span the universe from groaner ("What's the matter, Colonel Samdurz, chicken?") to brilliant (a surreal bit in which Helmet's evil forces capture our heroes' stunt doubles by mistake). John Hurt busts a gut reprising his role in *Alien*. 🦴🦴

1987 (PG) 96m/C Mel Brooks, Rick Moranis, John Candy, Bill Pullman, Daphne Zuniga, Dick Van Patten, John Hurt, George Wyner, Lorene Yarnell, Sal Viscuso, Stephen Tobolowsky, Michael Winslow; **D:** Mel Brooks; **W:** Ronny Graham, Thomas Meehan, Mel Brooks; **C:** Nick McLean; **M:** John Morris; **V:** Joan Rivers, Dom DeLuise. **VHS, Beta, LV** *MGM*

Spaced Invaders

Ship full of little green Martians is en route to an alien war but mistakenly lands in rural Illinois (they overhear a rebroadcast of Orson Welles' "War of the Worlds" and assume the target has changed). It's Halloween, and the bumbling would-be conquerors are mistaken for trick-or-treaters. Earth children know the truth: "They're not bad, just stupid." The same may be said for the satire's loud and repetitive bathroom humor. Okay f/x. 🦴

1990 (PG) 102m/C Douglas Barr, Royal Dano, Ariana Richards, Kevin Thompson, Jimmy Briscoe, Tony Cox, Debbie Lee Carrington, Tommy Madden; **D:** Patrick Read Johnson; **W:** Scott Lawrence Alexander. **VHS, Beta, LV** *TOU*

Spacehunter: Adventures in the Forbidden Zone

If the jokes were better this could pass as a comedy. Galactic bounty hunter agrees to rescue three damsels held captive by a cyborg on

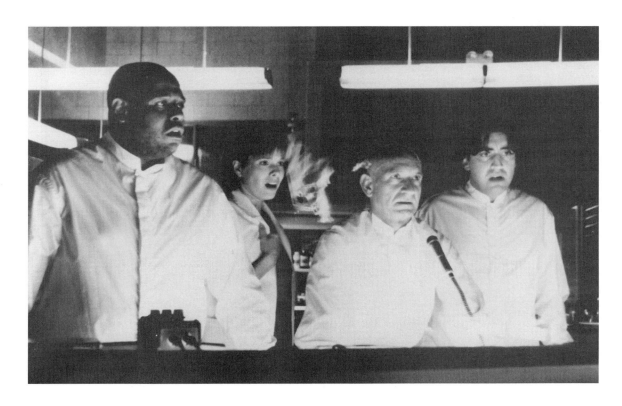

a bizarre rubble-strewn world. Peter Strauss tries, but he ain't no Harrison Ford, and Molly Ringwald won't give Chewbacca much serious competition either. Interesting costumes and set design in this no-brainer, which on video loses its novelty of being lensed in 3-D. 🦴 🦴

1983 (PG) 90m/C *CA* Peter Strauss, Molly Ringwald, Michael Ironside, Ernie Hudson, Andrea Marcovicci; *D:* Lamont Johnson; *W:* Len Blum; *M:* Elmer Bernstein. **VHS, Beta, LV** *COL*

Spaceship

Attempted *Airplane*-style sci-fi spoof that only works in fits and starts. Leslie Nielsen (before he got his comic timing down pat in the *Naked Gun* series) commands a spacecraft that picks up a silly alien—it looks like a load of glop with a single Cyclopean eye-stalk on top—that starts eating the crew. Special f/x are flagrantly cheap. Goofiest scenes are song-and-dance numbers and excerpts from Japanese monster flicks edited in. **AKA:** The Creature Wasn't Nice; Naked Space. 🦴 🦴

1981 (PG) 88m/C Cindy Williams, Bruce Kimmel, Leslie Nielsen, Gerrit Graham, Patrick Macnee, Ron Kurowski; *D:* Bruce Kimmel. **VHS** *LIV*

Species

If the outline for a really good episode of Fox TV's *The X-Files* fell into the wrong hands, the result might have been this crazed chase adventure. At heart, it's a B science fiction flick that's been pumped up with a classy cast, gobs of gore, and lots of morphing effects. The plot revolves around a hot-to-trot blonde babe (model Natasha Henstridge in her debut) who's also a murderous alien monster. Ben Kingsley leads the team that's trying to kill her. For fans, there are lots of laughs, intentional and un-, and some undeniably enjoyable cheap thrills. 🦴 🦴 🦴

1995 (R) 108m/C Ben Kingsley, Michael Madsen, Alfred Molina, Forest Whitaker, Marg Helgenberger, Natasha Henstridge; *D:* Roger Donaldson; *W:* Dennis Feldman; *C:* Andrzej Bartkowiak; *M:* Christopher Young. **VHS, LV** *MGM*

We were going to show a picture of the *Species,* but it was too darn scary....Forest Whitaker, Susan Bartkowiak, Ben Kingsley, and Alfred Molina, however, are getting an eye full.

Split

A vagrant named Starker changes his identity repeatedly to elude detection by the all-seeing "Company Director," who in the course of the narrative replaces his body with cybernetic components and ends up looking like Marvel Comics' Silver Surfer. Way-out surreal tale lends itself to various interpretations, but debuting director Chris Shaw keeps things moving and mildly satirical in tone, interspersing his puzzlers with computer graphics that compensate in creativity for what the pic lacks in budget. Cult discovery awaits. ♫♫♫

1990 85m/C John Flynn, Timothy Dwight, Chris Shaw, Joan Bechtel; **D:** Chris Shaw. **VHS** *AIP*

Split Second

Rutger Hauer is a futuristic cop tracking down a vicious alien serial killer in London in the year 2008. The monster rips out the hearts of his victims and then eats them in what appears to be a satanic ritual in this blood-soaked thriller wanna-be. Hauer gives a listless performance and overall, the action is quite dull. The music soundtrack also manages to annoy with the Moody Blues song "Nights in White Satin" playing at the most inappropriate times. A British/American co-production. ♫♭

1992 (R) 91m/C *GB* Rutger Hauer, Kim Cattrall, Neil Duncan, Michael J. Pollard, Alun Armstrong, Pete Postlethwaite, Ian Dury, Roberta Eaton; **D:** Tony Maylam. **VHS** *HBO*

Sputnik

A Frenchman, amnesiac after a car crash, comes up against Russian scientists, space-bound dogs, and weightlessness. Pleasant and charming family fun though clearly dated. Another fine performance from Mischa Auer. Dubbed. **AKA:** A Dog, a Mouse, and a Sputnik. ♫♫

1961 80m/B *FR* Noelia Noel, Mischa Auer, Denise Grey; **D:** Jean Dreville. **VHS, Beta** *INJ*

Stalker

A meteorite, crashing to Earth, has caused a wasteland area known as the Zone. The Zone is forbidden to anyone except special guides called Stalkers. Three Stalkers enter the region searching for its center, which contains a room that supposedly reveals fantasies. From the Soviet team that made *Solaris*. Filmed with both color and black-and-white sequences. Suspenseful atmosphere due to the director's use of long takes, movement, and color. In Russian with English subtitles. ♫♫♫

1979 160m/C *RU* Alexander Kaidanovsky, Nikolai Grinko, Anatoli Solonitzin, Alice Freindlikh; **D:** Andrei Tarkovsky; **M:** Eduard Artemyev. **VHS** *FXL, FCT*

Star Crash

This spaghetti space opera followed closely on the heels of *Star Wars*. A trio of adventurers (a woman, a man, and a robot) are sent by space-emperor Christopher Plummer to square off against interstellar bad-guy Joe Spinell with wits and high-tech (for the time) wizardry. It's all cheesy but very enjoyable, pulled off with a style and flair way beyond its limited budget. Caroline Munro, as always, makes a sexy and appealing heroine. Beats the heck out of *Battlestar Galactica*. **AKA:** Stella Star. ♫♫♭

1978 (PG) 92m/C *IT* Caroline Munro, Marjoe Gortner, Christopher Plummer, David Hasselhoff, Robert Tessier, Joe Spinell, Nadia Cassini, Judd Hamilton; **D:** Lewis (Luigi Cozzi) Coates; **W:** Lewis (Luigi Cozzi) Coates; **M:** John Barry. **VHS, Beta, LV** *NLC*

Star Crystal

After their space station explodes, survivors in an escape craft realize they're sealed in with a lethal sluglike alien, who only stops killing when he brings up the Holy Bible on the ship's computer and decides that these humans aren't so bad after all. Cheap imitation of *Alien* sure takes a novel twist, but viewers may not find it very heavenly. ♫

1985 (R) 93m/C C. Jutson Campbell, Faye Bolt, John W. Smith; **D:** Lance Lindsay. **VHS, Beta** *NWV, VTR, HHE*

Star Quest

A genetically engineered female warrior uses the hunt for a distant alien relic as a means to free herself from her corporate creators. Interesting, if not thoroughly successful obscurity that attempts do pull off an epic space opera

on 16mm for a paltry $200,000. Some of the visual whammies are the equal of many big-budget Hollywood spectaculars. Filmed in Virginia and the Washington, D.C., area. **AKA:** Beyond the Rising Moon; Space 2074. 🦴 🦴 ⚰️

1989 90m/C Tracy Davis, Hans Bachman, Michael Mack; **D:** Phillip Cook. **VHS, Beta, LV** *NO*

Star Quest

Competently told space tale has a good cast and a nice O. Henry ending. In an opening lifted straight from *Planet of the Apes*, astronauts en route to the planet Trion are awakened from hibernation to find that their captain is dead and someone is after them. As they settle on a chain of command, their numbers dwindle and they're forced to face the question that pops up in so many sf flicks: Which of us is the robot? The tale moves right along with good effects, sets, and characters who have some depth to go along with their funny accents. 🦴 🦴 ⚰️

1994 (R) 95m/C Steven Bauer, Emma Samms, Alan Rachins, Brenda Bakke, Ming-Na Wen, Gregory McKinney, Cliff DeYoung; **D:** Rick Jacobson. **VHS, LV** *NHO*

Star Slammer

A beautiful woman rebel is unjustly sentenced to a brutal intergalactic prison ship. She leads the convicts to escape amid zany situations. Low-budget, unevenly funny sci-fi spoof, divided into chapters like a serial and promising a sequel at the end (the Hound is not holding his breath). Cameos include a guest appearance by the main monster from *Return of the Aliens: The Deadly Spawn*. 🦴 ⚰️

1987 (R) 85m/C Ross Hagen, John Carradine, Sandy Brooke, Aldo Ray; **D:** Fred Olen Ray. **VHS, Beta, LV** *VMK*

Star Trek: The Motion Picture

The crew of the *Enterprise* reassembles to search out and fight a strange alien force that threatens Earth. This was the first film adapta-

"Hey, I didn't do it. Don't look at me." Innocent black dog is *not* the **Stalker.**

Star Trek 2: The Wrath of Khan

"I have hurt you. And I wish to go on...hurting you." Ricardo Montalban picks up where he was left off by Captain Kirk in the 1967 TV episode, "Space Seed" (also available on video). Montalban's galaxy-chewing performance as the vengeful genetically engineered supervillain ("From Hell's heart I stab at thee," he thunders) perhaps single-handedly rescued this fledgling cinematic franchise after the critical debacle of the first *Star Trek* movie. Spock "dies" ("Don't grieve, Admiral," he gasps to Kirk. "It is logical"), but you can't keep a good Vulcan down. Galloping around the cosmos may be a game for the young, as Kirk observes, but there would be five more sequels with the original crew of the Enterprise. Cheers to Kirstie Alley, on board as bald-pated Vulcan. ♫ ♫ ♫

1982 **(PG)** 113m/C William Shatner, Leonard Nimoy, Ricardo Montalban, DeForest Kelley, Nichelle Nichols, James Doohan, George Takei, Walter Koenig, Kirstie Alley, Merritt Butrick, Paul Winfield, Bibi Besch; *D:* Nicholas Meyer; *W:* Jack Sowards; *C:* Gayne Rescher; *M:* James Horner. **VHS, Beta, LV, 8mm** *PAR*

Star Trek 3: The Search for Spock

Captain Kirk hijacks the *USS Enterprise* and commands the crew (who look a little wearier with each picture in the series) to go on a mission to the Genesis Planet, a young world whose environment has been given a jumpstart by a mysterious scientific device. Kirk is determined to find out whether Mr. Spock has somehow survived his death in *The Wrath of Khan*, the previous film. As usual, there are plenty of Klingons to provide danger. Somewhat slower than *Khan*, but still fun for fans. Christopher Lloyd is wonderful as a Klingon commander. Third in the series of *Star Trek* movies. The laserdisc edition carries the film in widescreen format. ♫ ♫ ♪

1984 **(PG)** 105m/C William Shatner, Leonard Nimoy, DeForest Kelley, James Doohan, George Takei, Walter Koenig, Mark Lenard, Robin Curtis, Merritt Butrick, Christopher Lloyd, Judith Anderson, John Larroquette, James B. Sikking, Nichelle Nichols, Cathie Shirriff, Miguel Ferrer, Grace Lee Whitney; *D:* Leonard Nimoy; *W:* Harve Bennett; *M:* James Horner. **VHS, Beta, LV, 8mm** *PAR*

"I'm not going to be the first to apologize this time!" Leonard Nimoy and William Shatner in **Star Trek: The Motion Picture.**

tion of the classic '60s TV series. Director Robert Wise, whose previous credits included noted sf epic *The Day the Earth Stood Still,* gives it his all, but the movie was a disappointment to most Trek fans. Ponderous and slow moving, the movie is ultimately crushed under its legendary source material. The many sequels that followed were much more effective in terms of pacing and story-telling. Twelve additional minutes of previously unseen footage have been added to the home video version. The laserdisc edition offers the film in widescreen format. ♫ ♫

1980 **(G)** 143m/C William Shatner, Leonard Nimoy, DeForest Kelley, James Doohan, Stephen Collins, Persis Khambatta, Nichelle Nichols, Walter Koenig, George Takei; *D:* Robert Wise; *M:* Jerry Goldsmith. Nominations: Academy Awards '79: Best Art Direction/Set Decoration, Best Original Score. **VHS, Beta, LV** *PAR*

TV on Tape: Star Trek

The inescapable fave, the 1966-69 NBC TV series set aboard the giant interstellar science-military exploration vessel *U.S.S. Enterprise* with its multicultural multi-species crew, led by Captain Kirk, Dr. McCoy, the emotionless Mr. Spock, and all those expendable guys in red shirts, matched against galaxies of danger, foes, riddles, and rewards. Many participants, most notoriously William Shatner, profess ignorance as to why *Star Trek* remains so popular.

The Hound knows. Classic *Star Trek* (more so than *The Next Generation* or the angst-ridden *Deep Space Nine*) is the only enduring sf of the post-JFK era to declare that tomorrow will be *better* than today, that mankind can surmount moral imperfections and become a force for good in the universe, instead of spawning technological nightmares (*Blade Runner, The Terminator*) or backsliding into neosavagery (*Mad Max*). With well-conceived characters, sophisticated f/x for the time, and prominent sf writers like Harlan Ellison and Theodore Sturgeon assisting, the program won two Hugos before chronic low ratings forced it off the air. Even before cancellation a subculture of "Trekkie" viewers began to boldly support the show As No Fans Had Done before, in growing numbers as the old episodes went into syndication.

Whilst *Trek* authorities squabble over the contributions and near-messianic status of executive producer Gene Roddenberry (compared to barely remembered original producer Gene L. Coon, who died early on), there's no doubt Roddenberry's campaigns among the faithful helped revive the *Star Trek* franchise, after numerous false starts, with the first *Trek* motion picture in 1979 and the outstandingly successful *Next Generation* series in the 1980s. Now it's virtually impossible to imagine broadcast sf (or American popular culture) without *Star Trek*, and Paramount Home Video makes available all 78 Classic episodes plus "The Cage," Roddenberry's prototype pilot (later incorporated into the two-part episode "The Menagerie") with an excitable Spock, Jeffrey Hunter as a self-doubting captain, and notable variations in f/x, costumes, and production design.

The original *Enterprise* crew (except for Walter "Chekov" Koenig) did re-enlist for an NBC Saturday-morning cartoon continuation that aired from 1973 to 1975 (winning an Emmy in its final year). Though plotlines suffer from being shoehorned into half-hour time slots, presence of some of the classic *Trek* scriptwriters ensured consistency and quality control. True devotees should check out the 11 volumes (2 episodes per tape) carried by Paramount Home Video for such insights as Spock's painful childhood ("Yesteryear," Vol. 2) and the spiny creature that eats tribbles ("More Tribbles, More Troubles," Vol. 1).

1966-69/C *Selected cast:* William Shatner, Leonard Nimoy, DeForest Kelly, James Doohan, Michelle Nichols, George Takei, Walter Koenig. Hugos '67, '68: Dramatic Presentation. **VHS, LV** *PAR, MOV*

Star Trek 4: The Voyage Home

This one makes it official (and *Star Trek 6* only confirms it): the even-numbered *Star Trek* movies are better than the odd-numbered ones. This is a whale of a tale that you don't have to be a Trekker to enjoy. The crew of the *Bounty* (remember, the *Enterprise* was destroyed in *The Search for Spock*) time travels back to '80s San Francisco to retrieve two humpbacks and bring them back to the 23rd Century to save the Earth from a space probe unwittingly wreaking havoc while trying to communicate with the extinct species. The venerable cast hasn't been this funny since "The Trouble with Tribbles," particularly Leonard Nimoy as Spock, whose deadpan delivery and unsteady command of contemporary profanities earn the biggest laughs. The "Director's Series" edition features Leonard

To Boldly Go...

"**S**tar Date: 13-12.4. The impossible has happened. From directly overhead, we're picking up a recorded distress signal. The call letters of a vessel which has been missing for two centuries. Did another Earth ship once probe out of the galaxy as we intend to do? What happened to it out there? Is this some warning they've left behind?"

—Capt. Kirk (William Shatner) in "Where No Man Has Gone Before," episode number one (though not the first episode aired) of TV's *Star Trek*.

"Don't grieve, Admiral. It is logical."

—Spock's (Leonard Nimoy) dying words to Kirk (William Shatner) in *Star Trek 2: The Wrath of Khan*.

Nimoy's take on the Star Trek films and a behind-the-scenes look at how *The Voyage Home*'s special effects were created. 🦴🦴🦴🐾

1986 (PG) 119m/C William Shatner, DeForest Kelley, Catherine Hicks, James Doohan, Nichelle Nichols, George Takei, Walter Koenig, Mark Lenard, Leonard Nimoy; *D:* Leonard Nimoy; *W:* Steve Meerson, Peter Krikes, Nicholas Meyer, Harve Bennett; *C:* Don Peterman. Nominations: Academy Awards '86: Best Cinematography, Best Sound, Best Original Score. **VHS, Beta, LV, 8mm** *PAR*

Star Trek 5: The Final Frontier

A renegade Vulcan kidnaps the *Enterprise* and takes it on a journey to the mythic center of the universe. William Shatner's big-action directorial debut (he also co-wrote the original story) is a poor follow-up to the Nimoy-directed fourth Trek film. The series was getting pretty tired by this time anyway, but this heavy-handed and pretentiously pseudo-theological entry certainly didn't help matters any. Long-time fans, though, will delight in yet another example of Shatner's obsessive bravado. The film is available in widescreen format on laserdisc. 🦴🐾

1989 (PG) 107m/C William Shatner, Leonard Nimoy, DeForest Kelley, James Doohan, Laurence Luckinbill, Walter Koenig, George Takei, Nichelle Nichols, David Warner; *D:* William Shatner; *W:* David Loughery; *C:* Andrew Laszlo; *M:* Jerry Goldsmith. Golden Raspberry Awards '89: Worst Picture, Worst Actor (Shatner), Worst Director (Shatner). **VHS, Beta, LV, 8mm** *PAR*

Star Trek 6: The Undiscovered Country

The original crew of the *Enterprise* exits in grand style in the sixth Star Trek film. Mirroring the fall of the iron curtain, a disaster in the Klingon Empire leads to negotiation of a peace treaty between the Klingons and the Federation. At the request of Spock, and over Kirk's reservations, the intrepid crew of the *Enterprise* are sent to escort the Klingon Chancellor to the talks. When the Klingon ship is attacked, Kirk and the crew of the *Enterprise* are accused of the crime. The search for the real perpetrators leads the crew on another galaxy-saving adventure. A great cast accompanies the regulars, including Christopher Plummer as a Klingon general fond of quoting Shakespeare (though you can't really appreciate Shakespeare until you have heard it in the original Klingon) and David Warner as the forward-looking Klingon Chancellor. Terrific special effects, typical Star Trek humor, and exciting action, make this one of the best Star Trek outings, and a most fitting conclusion to the series. Look for cameos from Christian Slater and Michael Dorn (Worf of *Star Trek: The Next Generation*). Nicholas Meyer also directed *Star Trek 2: The Wrath of Khan* and wrote the screenplay for *Star Trek 4: The Voyage Home*. 🦴🦴🦴🦴

1991 (PG) 110m/C William Shatner, Leonard Nimoy, DeForest Kelley, James Doohan, George Takei, Walter Koenig, Nichelle Nichols, Christopher Plummer, Kim Cattrall, Iman, David Warner, Mark Lenard, Grace Lee Whitney, Brock Peters, Kurtwood Smith, Rosana De Soto, John Schuck, Michael Dorn; *Cameos:* Christian Slater; *D:* Nicholas Meyer; *W:* Nicholas Meyer, Denny Martin Flinn; *M:* Cliff Eidelman. Nominations: Academy Awards '91: Best Makeup. **VHS, Beta, CD-I** *PAR*

Star Trek Generations

The television voyage continues in this first film featuring the *Next Generation* cast, and seventh overall Star Trek film. Bridging the gap between the generations is legendary Captain James T. Kirk (William Shatner). Following an explosion aboard the newly christened *Enterprise B*, Kirk is trapped in a space anomaly known as the Nexus. Anyone who enters the Nexus feels as if they are in a kind of Nirvana, reliving their happiest moments.

Years later, Kirk is rescued by his successor and current captain of the *Enterprise*, Jean-Luc Picard (Patrick Stewart). The two captains join forces to save the galaxy from the evil Dr. Soren (played with villainous glee by Malcolm McDowell), who longs to return to the Nexus at all costs, including destroying a solar system. Meanwhile, the *Enterprise* battles renegade Klingons who have joined Soren's quest. Android Data (Brent Spiner) provides comic relief (and possibly the funniest moment in Star Trek history) after he receives an emotion chip. Great special effects (courtesy of Industrial Light & Magic) and a heroic ending for Captain Kirk are mixed with the traditional Star Trek morality lesson. The result is a rousing-good space adventure. Whoopi Goldberg makes an appearance as the mysterious and enlightened barkeep Guinan, and Scotty (James Doohan) and Chekov (Walter Koenig) from the original cast have cameos. 🎜 🎜 🎜

1994 (PG) 117m/C William Shatner, Patrick Stewart, Malcolm McDowell, Whoopi Goldberg, Jonathon Frakes, Brent Spiner, LeVar Burton, Michael Dorn, Gates McFadden, Marina Sirtis, James Doohan, Walter Koenig, Alan Ruck; *D:* David Carson; *W:* Ronald D. Moore, Brannon Braga; *M:* Dennis McCarthy. **VHS, Beta** *PAR*

Star Wars

"A long time ago in a galaxy far, far away ..." That's how the movie that changed the film industry begins. Even though its special effects may have been eclipsed, it's still one of Hollywood's best, the first chapter of an epic coming-of-age trilogy. Recently remastered, the tape version looks and sounds almost as good as it did in theatres. It's a solidly constructed film with a grand final act. John Williams' stirring score can't be overvalued. In this part of the tale, the characters—a young hero, a captured princess, a hot-shot pilot, cute robots, a vile villain, and a heroic and mysterious Jedi knight—are more archetypes that individuals but that's part of filmmaker George Lucas' point. He makes no secret of the influence of

C3PO suddenly realizes that the funny feeling in his lower quadrant is somehow triggered by Princess Leia (Carrie Fisher). *Star Wars.*

TV on Tape: Star Trek: The Next Generation

Seventy-eight years in the future of the future. Who came up with an idea like that? Somewhere, a thousand voices are shouting out the answer in unison, but let's leave it as a rhetorical question for now.

To revive an old television series, updated for a new audience is not such a new idea—it happened many times before. A series would disappear from the airwaves for a few years, only to return, even on another network. Personalities such as Jack Benny, Bob Newhart, Jackie Gleason, and Lassie would return again and again with different titles, formats, or networks.

But no television show had ever returned as a reincarnation of itself. Of course, *Star Trek* is a unique entity in the entertainment world. It was "the show that would not die." If it hadn't continued in movies and television, surely somewhere there would be a packed house enjoying it as community theatre.

In 1987, there was a demand for *Star Trek* that could not be satisfied by a theatrical motion picture every other year. There was a growing void—an unknown entertainment anomaly—that needed to be filled on a weekly basis. When Captain Jean-Luc Picard stepped out on the bridge of a fresh new (and much larger) starship *Enterprise* to head towards an "Encounter at Farpoint," he was there to "make it so." *The Next Generation* had to be so much the same, but so much different.

The first season was a shake-down cruise. Many episodes were simply retreads from the old series, with the new crew stepping through familiar paces. Maybe they didn't go so far as to have the ship overrun with Tribbles, but it wouldn't have been much of a surprise.

Picard and his crew were often accused of being wimps, tossing daisies at their weekly nemesis when they should have been taking more resolute action. Sometimes, it seemed as though they expected their conflicts to disappear by themselves, while they waited things out over somethingorother ale and whatchamacallit wine in 10 Forward.

Luckily, sometime during the second season, they began to hit their stride. No longer trying to be a kinder, gentler version of the original crew, the characters began to take on a life of their own, and stories began to grow out of the characters. The question was no longer "What new menace will the Enterprise have to face this week?" but "How will Worf deal with the issues of his Klingon heritage as a Starfleet officer?" or "What changes will take place in the political affairs of the Romulan empire?". What was synthetic became organic. Awkward children grew up to become adults. An emotionless android was given the gift of laughter by a cynical god. Themes that would have played false in the first season, took on truth because the people became true.

Gaining speed during the following seasons, it became apparent that *The Next Generation* was no longer merely an outgrowth of a phenomenon. It could stand on its own—surely it would have been a great show, even if there'd never been a previous generation. "Classic" *Trek* merely gave it a legacy that enriched it all the more.

Traveling along at cruising speed, another nameless void began to grow, and *Deep Space Nine* had to come forth to fill it. Certain corners of the galaxy became far too intriguing for an occasional visit, and one such place was this far-off outpost where the Ferengi, Bajoran, Cardassian, and so many other cultures came together, with new friends and foes always ready to leap forth from the wondrous Wormhole.

Another factor was becoming more apparent at about the same time. While the two-part episodes were probably considered a bit of a gamble, they soon proved that not only could the series keep its audience interested for more than an hour's worth per story, but those episodes were very often overwhelming favorites. And so, after 178 episodes, *Star Trek: The Next Generation* left the once-daring, now-cozy nest of syndication for bigger, wider, more expensive adventures on the silver multiplex screen.

Once again, the Trek void was quickly filled with the launch of yet another series, this time with not only a new ship and crew, but a whole new quadrant of space to explore. *Voyager* has survived a shake-down of its own, and is just starting to develop its own place in space.

Who knows, maybe there are more *Trek* series yet to come—after all, it's still a very big universe. But hopefully they won't try to jump another 78 years into the future of the future of the future. They might start a trend. Already, we have a revival of *Kung Fu*, in which a 100-year old David Carradine kicks butt side-by-side with his grandson. What's next, *Bonanza 2000*?

1987-94/C *Selected cast:* Patrick Stewart, Jonathon Frakes, Gates McFadden, Michael Dorn, Marina Siritis, Denise Crosby, Brent Spiner, Wil Wheaton, LeVar Burton Hugos '93: Dramatic Presentation. **VHS** *PAR, MOV*

Joseph Campbell's ideas about myth and story-telling. Followed by *The Empire Strikes Back* (1980) and *Return of the Jedi* (1983). The subtitle "Episode IV: A New Hope" refers to a trilogy of films set before these three, and in production at press time. ✂✂✂✂

1977 (PG) 121m/C Mark Hamill, Carrie Fisher, Harrison Ford, Alec Guinness, Peter Cushing, Kenny Baker, Peter Mayhew, David Prowse, Anthony Daniels; **D:** George Lucas; **W:** George Lucas; **C:** Gilbert Taylor; **M:** John Williams; **V:** James Earl Jones. Hugos '78: Dramatic Presentation; Academy Awards '77: Best Art Direction/Set Decoration, Best Costume Design, Best Film Editing, Best Sound, Best Visual Effects, Best Original Score; Golden Globe Awards '78: Best Score; Los Angeles Film Critics Association Awards '77: Best Film; National Board of Review Awards '77: 10 Best Films of the Year; People's Choice Awards '78: Best Film; Nominations: Academy Awards '77: Best Director (Lucas), Best Original Screenplay, Best Picture, Best Supporting Actor (Guinness). **VHS, Beta, LV** *FOX, RDG, HMV*

Starchaser: The Legend of Orin

This feature cartoon was released on theatre screens in 3-D, and one truly got dizzy watching the sweeps and swoops of spacecraft with an extra dimension thrown in. That factor is gone on videotape but the rollercoaster sensation still lingers in a *Star Wars*-inspired plot about a young boy recruited by a Han Solo-type space pilot (whose cigar and unshaven jowls give him quite a villainous appearance). His instructions see the boy through tests of bravery and courage to eliminate a nasty horde of malevolent robots planning to crush all organic sentient life in the universe. Despite the plundering of George Lucas, it's an exciting sci-fi adventure odyssey suitable for all ages. ✂✂✂

1985 (PG) 107m/C D: Steven Hahn; **M:** Andrew Belling. **VHS, Beta, LV** *PAR*

Starflight One

A space shuttle is called on to save the world's first hypersonic airliner trapped in an orbit above earth. The film features good special effects, but also a predictable "rescue-mission" plot. **AKA:** Starflight: The Plane that Couldn't Land. ✂✂

Don't do it, James. Looks are deceiving. James Spader and Jaye Davidson in **Stargate**.

A Long Time Ago in a Galaxy Far, Far Away...

Episode IV: A NEW HOPE

"It is a period of civil war: Rebel spaceships, striking from a hidden base, have won their first victory against the evil Galactic Empire. During the battle, Rebel spies managed to steal secret plans to the Empire's ultimate weapon, the DEATH STAR, an armored space station with enough power to destroy an entire planet. Pursued by the Empire's sinister agents, Princess Leia races home aboard her starship, custodian of the stolen plans that can save her people and restore freedom to the galaxy...."

—prologue to *Star Wars*.

1983 155m/C Ray Milland, Lee Majors, Hal Linden, Lauren Hutton, Robert Webber, Terry Kiser; **D:** Jerry Jameson. **VHS, Beta** *LIV, VES*

Stargate

Imagine the Cecil B. deSpielberg production of *Close Encounters with the Ten Commandments*. U.S. military probe of a ring-shaped ancient Egyptian artifact (your tax dollars at work) sends he-man colonel Kurt Russell and geeky Egyptologist James Spader into a parallel universe. There they meet the builders of the pyramids who are enslaved by an evil despot (Jaye Davidson) posing as a sun god. Ambitious premise gets an A for effort, but a silly plot jumbles Biblical epic panoramas and "Oh Wow!" special effects with otherworldly mysticism and needless emotional hang-ups. Spader's shaggy scholar is neurotically fun, Russell's jarhead a bore, and Davidson's vampy villain provides some surprises, though none as memorable as the one he provided in *The Crying Game*. Followed by a sequel novel, *Stargate: Rebellion*. 🦴🦴🦴

1994 (PG-13) 119m/C Kurt Russell, James Spader, Jaye Davidson, Viveca Lindfors, Alexis Cruz, Leon Rippy, John Diehl, Erik Avari, Mili Avital; **D:** Roland Emmerich; **W:** Dean Devlin, Roland Emmerich; **C:** Jeff Okun. **VHS, LV** *LIV*

Starman

An alien from an advanced civilization lands in Wisconsin. He hides beneath the guise of a grieving young widow's recently deceased husband. He then makes her drive him across country to rendezvous with his spacecraft so he can return home. Not the *E.T.* rip-off you'd expect from that description. This is a well-acted, interesting twist on the "Stranger in a Strange Land" theme. Jeff Bridges is fun as the likable Starman; Karen Allen is lovely and earthy in her worthy follow-up to *Raiders of the Lost Ark*. A good family sf flick, available in widescreen format on laserdisc. 🦴🦴🦴

1984 (PG) 115m/C Jeff Bridges, Karen Allen, Charles Martin Smith, Richard Jaeckel, Robert Phalen; **D:** John Carpenter; **W:** Bruce A. Evans, Raynold Gideon; **C:** Donald M. Morgan; **M:** Jack Nitzsche. Nominations: Academy Awards '84: Best Actor (Bridges). **VHS, Beta, LV** *COL*

Starship

No-frills *Star Wars* ripoff about human slaves trying to escape a planet run by evil robots. British sci fi has a surface veneer of cool f/x but absolutely nothing underneath—no sense of fun, wonder, or whatever. Half a consolation bone goes to actor Deep Roy, encased in a expressionless robot suit but still the character one roots for the most. **AKA:** Lorca and the Outlaws; 2084. 🦴🦴

1987 (PG) 91m/C *GB* John Tarrant, Cassandra Webb, Donough Rees, Deep Roy, Ralph Cotterill; **D:** Roger Christian. **VHS, Beta** *HHE*

Starship Invasions

Christopher Lee leads a group of bad aliens seeking to take over the Earth. He's thwarted by UFO expert Robert Vaughn, who is aided by a group of good aliens. Cheesy special effects have this one looking like a bad sci-fi serial from the '40s. 🦴

1977 (PG) 89m/C *CA* Christopher Lee, Robert Vaughn, Daniel Pilon, Helen Shaver, Henry Ramer, Victoria (Vicki) Johnson; **D:** Edward Hunt; **W:** Edward Hunt. **VHS** *WAR*

Steel and Lace

Bruce Davison is the scientist brother of a

TV on Tape: Starblazers

In 1979, U.S. sf fans were introduced to a new animated series of unusual depth and complexity. *Starblazers,* titled *Uchuu Senkan Yamato* (*Space Cruiser Yamato*) in its native Japan, came as a surprise in several ways.

First of all, and most obviously, it was anime—Japanese animation, which meant it was done in a very distinctive style, one most American viewers hadn't seen much of outside of *Speed Racer.* Secondly, the three seasons of *Starblazers* each formed one long story, divided into consecutive episodes that had to be seen in order to be understood. This approach had been the norm in U.S. movie-serials like *Flash Gordon,* but since the '60s, producers had increasing-ly opted for the more viewer-friendly convention of independent episodes focused on a set of characters. Finally, whereas most U.S. animated sf had been fairly simple minded, or aimed at young children, *Starblazers* was a serious story of high drama, with complex characters. All of these factors made for classic space-opera adventure.

In the year 2199, Earth has been rendered a radioactive wasteland, thanks to constant bombardment from the hostile planet Gamilon. Humanity has fled to underground cities, and even these are imperiled by steadily mounting levels of radiation. Just as things look hopeless, a message is received from Queen Starsha of the distant planet Iscandar, offering aid to the beleaguered planet. The World War II battleship *Yamato,* recently rediscovered on the now-dry ocean floor, is refitted for space travel, and a group of intrepid heroes, the "Star Force," is assembled to make the journey to Iscandar. But Gamilon's forces are determined to stop Star Force before it can save Earth.

As anime fandom grew through the '80s, a number of fans rediscovered the original Japanese version of the series. Today, *Starblazers,* or *Space Cruiser Yamato* among purists, is still justly regarded as a classic.

1979-82/C *JP* **VHS** *WTA*

---

classical pianist who commits suicide after being raped. After a few years in the lab he revives her as an enticing cyborg, which enacts its revenge on the preppie types who got away with the crime. Well-acted but well-worn vengeance premise, more morbid than entertaining, and the robotics hardware goes on display only briefly. 🦴🦴

1990 (R) 92m/C Bruce Davison, Clare Wren, Stacy Haiduk, David Naughton, David Lander; *D:* Ernest Farino; *W:* Joseph Dougherty, Dave Edison. **VHS, Beta, LV** *FRH*

Steel Dawn

Another monosyllabic post-apocalypse samurai western, *Shane* with a *Mad Max* makeover. After war has turned to the world into a desert (and evidently melted all the guns; everyone wields bladed weapons) leather-clad swords-man Patrick Swayze defends a frontier widow (the star's real-life wife Lisa Niemi) in a dispute over water and territory. Far from the worst of its breed; genre regular Brion James has one of his better expendable roles, and there's one heckuva showdown between Swayze and Christopher Neame. Loses half a bone for the hero's ludicrous method of warrior meditation—he stands on his head. Title was rumored to be an in-joke jab at Columbia Pictures president Dawn Steel. 🦴🦴

1987 (R) 90m/C Patrick Swayze, Lisa Niemi, Christopher Neame, Brett Hool, Brion James, Anthony Zerbe; *D:* Lance Hool; *W:* Doug Lefler; *M:* Brian May. **VHS, Beta, LV** *LIV, VES*

Steel Frontier

Post-apocalypse actioner finds a group of survivors trying to make a life for themselves in a

town they call New Hope. But then a group of bandit soldiers take over—until a lone hero comes along to save the day. Any resemblance between Joe Lara and Clint Eastwood is no coincidence; this direct-to-video sci-fi pic lassoes western motifs galore, by now a pretty stale gimmick, pardner.

1994 (R) 94m/C Joe Lara, Brion James, Bo Svenson, Stacie Foster; **D:** Paul G. Volk, Jacobsen Hart; **W:** Jacobsen Hart. **VHS, LV** *PMH*

Stephen King's Golden Years

Stephen King creates a chilling vision of scientific progress gone awry in this shocking techno-thriller. After being accidentally exposed to exotic chemicals in a lab explosion, an aging janitor undergoes an extraordinary transformation and the government will sacrifice anything to learn more about it. Originally a made-for-television miniseries.

1991 232m/C Keith Szarabajka, Frances Sternhagen, Ed Lauter, R.D. Call. **D:** Josef Anderson. **VHS, LV** *WOV*

Stephen King's The Langoliers

One of the worst Stephen King adaptations in recent memory (and there have been some bad ones). This bloated variation of *Ten Little Indians* finds 10 airline passengers dozing off on their L.A.-to-Boston flight and awakening to find their fellow passengers and the crew have vanished. Of course, one passenger (David Morse) is a pilot and he manages to land the plane in Bangor, Maine (where the miniseries was filmed), only to discover things on the ground are as strange as those in the air. Each of the characters has their own problems, which are slowly (painfully slowly) revealed. In a great feat of cinematic empathy, viewers, like the characters, will feel time has stopped moving as well. The final special effects of the "langoliers" (creatures that look like flying cannonballs with piranha teeth) are embarrassing in this day. **AKA:** The Langoliers.

1995 (PG-13) 180m/C David Morse, Bronson Pinchot, Patricia Wettig, Dean Stockwell, Kate Maberly, Christopher Collet, Kimber Riddle, Mark Lindsay Chapman, Frankie Faison, Baxter Harris; **Cameos:** Stephen King, Tom Holland; **D:** Tom Holland; **W:** Tom Holland; **C:** Paul Maibaum; **M:** Vladimir Horunzhy. **VHS, LV** *REP*

Stephen King's The Stand

Quite good made-for-TV adaptation of the apocalyptic Stephen King epic (King adapted the screenplay himself) should be ghoulish enough for most. Cool opening featuring Blue Oyster Cult's "Don't Fear the Reaper" as the camera reveals death and more death at a top-secret government lab where a killer virus has escaped. Around the world millions die, and confusion and chaos take over. The few survivors have one thing in common...dreams. Some dream of the godly old woman known as Mother Abigail, and the others of the satanic Randall Flagg, the Walkin' Dude. With the good guys holed up in the "Free Zone" of Boulder, Colorado, and the bad-brood headquartered in Las Vegas, it all comes down to a battle of good vs. evil, nuclear weapons and hands of God allowed. Religious allegory will be interesting to some, and tedious to others. For a TV movie this one doesn't pull too many punches. Matt Frewer as the deranged weapon maker Trashcan Man is a scene stealer, even though the rest of the cast does just fine. **AKA:** The Stand.

1994 360m/C Jamey Sheridan, Ruby Dee, Gary Sinise, Molly Ringwald, Miguel Ferrer, Laura San Giacomo, Rob Lowe, Adam Storke, Corin "Corky" Nemec, Ray Walston, Bill Fagerbakke, Ossie Davis, Shawnee Smith, Matt Frewer; **Cameos:** Ed Harris, Kathy Bates, Kareem Abdul-Jabbar, Stephen King; **D:** Mick Garris; **W:** Stephen King; **C:** Eddie Pei. **VHS, LV** *REP*

Stephen King's The Tommyknockers

Another of King's creepy tales adapted for TV. Bobbi (Marg Helgenberger) and Gard (Jimmy Smits) live in the small town of Haven, Maine (actually filmed on New Zealand's North Island). She's an aspiring writer; he's a fading poet with a drinking problem and a metal plate in his head (this is important). Walking in the woods, Bobbi stumbles over a long-buried spaceship. When she starts an obsessive excavation of the object, it begins to take possession of the townspeople—their eyes shine green, their teeth fall out, and they find themselves inspired to invent crazy machines that shouldn't work but somehow do. The only

one in town not affected is Gard. The whole thing climaxes in the ship, when Gard confronts the evil, eponymous aliens. Occasionally silly, seldom frightening, but usually entertaining. **AKA:** The Tommyknockers. 🦴🦴ᵛ

1993 (R) 120m/C Jimmy Smits, Marg Helgenberger, Joanna Cassidy, E.G. Marshall, Traci Lords, John Ashton, Allyce Beasley, Cliff DeYoung, Robert Carradine, Leon Woods, Paul McIver; **D:** John Power; **W:** Lawrence D. Cohen. **VHS, LV** *VMK*

Stranded

A group of aliens escaping interplanetary persecution land on Earth and enlist the aid of an Earth family. Solid characters make it more than sci fi; sort of a parable of intolerance, human (and alien) goodness, etc. 🦴🦴

1987 (PG-13) 80m/C Maureen O'Sullivan, Ione Skye, Cameron Dye; **D:** Tex Fuller; **W:** Alan Castle. **VHS, Beta, LV** *COL*

A Strange Harvest with Linda Moulton Howe

Linda Moulton Howe's documentary on animal (and sometimes human) mutilations around the world is crammed full of photos, film, and interviews. Various angles are explored as to whom the culprit(s) is/are. In all cases, an eye, ear, tongue, teeth, jaw flesh, genitals, and the rectum have been removed. There is never any blood or even tracks around the body. Experts testify that the excisions have been accomplished with technology that we may not have, sometimes cutting literally in between cells. Witnesses interviewed talk of moving lights, silent helicopters, and even non-human entities in the areas of mutilations. This documentary will stun and is not for the squeamish. Updated in *A Strange Harvest 1993*. 🦴🦴🦴ᵛ

1980 60m/C D: Linda Moulton Howe; **W:** Linda Moulton Howe. **VHS** *WSH*

Strange Invaders

Most modern pics that want to recreate the attitude of '50s alien flicks try too hard and tip far into camp silliness, but this one gets the deadpan tone just right. Grotesque space beings conquered the midwest town of Cen-terville in the '50s and body-snatched the locals' appearance and attire. Twenty-five years later, Paul LeMat's ex-wife, a Centerville native, disappears, and when he hunts for her the longtime coverup/conspiracy starts to unravel. Some details, notably the gimmick that supermarket tabloid tall tales about flying saucers turn out to be TRUE! aren't so fresh anymore, but the special f/x are still startling—well, maybe not the spaceship interior that looks like a boiler room. Sort of a companion piece to director Michael Laughlin's earlier mad-science tale *Strange Behavior* with some of the same actors. 🦴🦴🦴

1983 (PG) 94m/C Paul LeMat, Nancy Allen, Diana Scarwid, Michael Lerner, Louise Fletcher, Wallace Shawn, Fiona Lewis, Kenneth Tobey, June Lockhart, Charles Lane, Dey Young, Mark Goddard; **D:** Michael Laughlin; **W:** Michael Laughlin, Bill Condon; **C:** Louis Horvath. **VHS, Beta, LV** *VES*

Strange New World

Three astronauts awake from 188 years in the fridge to find cloning has arrived. Made for TV as a pilot for a hoped-for series that might have been even worse. 🦴ᵛ

1975 100m/C John Saxon, Kathleen Miller, Keene Curtis, Martine Beswick, James Olson, Catherine Bach, Richard Farnsworth, Ford Rainey; **D:** Robert Butler. **VHS** *UNI*

The Stranger

Glen Corbett crashlands on a planet an awful lot like Earth—and must stay on the run. Uneven fugitive thriller in sci-fi drag. Made for TV. 🦴ᵛ

1973 100m/C Cameron Mitchell, Glenn Corbett, Sharon Acker, Lew Ayres, George Coulouris, Dean Jagger; **D:** Lee H. Katzin. **VHS** *NO*

The Stranger from Venus

The Day the Earth Stood Still warmed over. Venusian Helmut Dantine tells Earth lady Patricia Neal he's worried about the future of her planet. Real-ly low budget. Includes previews of coming attractions from classic sci fi to somehow make the rental fee worthwhile. **AKA:** Immediate Disaster; The Venusian. **WOOF!**

1954 78m/C Patricia Neal, Helmut Dantine, Derek Bond. **VHS, Beta** *MED, MLB*

Strangers in Paradise

A scientist who had cryogenically frozen himself to escape the Nazis is thawed out in the present, and his powers are used by a delinquent-obsessed sociopath. 🦴🐾

1986 81m/C D: Ulli Lommel; **W:** Ulli Lommel. **VHS, Beta** *LIV, VES*

Street Asylum

Nobody looks more natural, in a garter belt and stockings, begging a dominatrix to give a little whip, than G. Gordon Liddy. That highlight aside, this film, with Liddy as an evil genius who installs kill-on-demand implants in cops to clean up the gutters and rid the streets of scum, has little to offer other than the usual fun-type exploitation. At least with Liddy in the cast Wings Hauser doesn't look quite as bad as usual. Why watch anything other than the uncut 94-minute version? 🦴

1990 (R) 94m/C Wings Hauser, Alex Cord, Roberta Vasquez, G. Gordon Liddy, Marie Chambers, Sy Richardson, Jesse Doran, Jesse Aragon, Brion James; **D:** Gregory Brown. **VHS, Beta, LV** *NO*

Stryker

The ever-lovin' nuclear holocaust has occurred, and good guys and bad guys battle it out for scarce water. If you liked *Mad Max* or *The Road Warrior* so much, go see those again; don't bother with this made-in-Philippines knockoff. **WOOF!**

1983 (R) 86m/C PH Steve Sandor, Andria Fabio; **D:** Cirio H. Santiago; **W:** Howard R. Cohen. **VHS, Beta** *SUE, VTR*

Sun Ra & His Intergalactic Solar Arkestra: Space Is the Place

Home video rescued from limbo this long-unseen indie production showcasing the cosmology of jazz-improv innovator and self-styled space-age prophet Sun Ra, mythologized as a shaman who descends in a starship that looks like a pair of blazing eyeballs. Accompanied by an entourage of Egyptian gods (who are cooler than their big-budget counterparts in *Stargate*), Sun Ra puts on a few concerts and informs Oakland's skeptical black youth that he can save them from oppression and self-destruction via relocation to a paradise planet. Uptight FBI types watch nervously, certain it's some scheme to launch an African space agency. Strange, surreal, politically simplistic, and more than a little self-indulgent, it's not for all tastes but certainly a trip. 🎵 Watusi; Outer Spaceways Inc.; The Satellites are Spinning. 🦴🦴

1974 63m/C D: John Coney; **W:** Joshua Smith. **VHS** *RHP*

Super Force

When astronaut Zach Stone (Ken Olandt) returns from an assignment on Mars he finds his policeman brother has been murdered. He quits NASA and joins the force to get revenge, battling evil crime boss Tao Satori (G. Gordon Liddy). Stone also moonlights as a vigilante, complete with motorcycle and high-tech armoured suit. It's dumb but there's lots of action. 🦴🦴

1990 92m/C Ken Olandt, G. Gordon Liddy, Larry B. Scott, Lisa Niemi, Marshall Teague; **Cameos:** Patrick Macnee; **D:** Richard Compton. **VHS, LV** *MCA*

Super Fuzz

Rookie policeman develops super powers after being accidentally exposed to radiation. Somewhat ineptly, he uses his abilities to combat crime. Somewhat ineptly acted, written, and directed as well. **AKA:** Supersnooper. 🦴🐾

1981 (PG) 97m/C Terence Hill, Joanne Dru, Ernest Borgnine; **D:** Sergio Corbucci; **W:** Sergio Corbucci. **VHS, Beta** *SUE*

Super Mario Bros.

A $42 million adventure fantasy based on the popular Nintendo video game. It's not half bad either, despite the Luigi character's having been turned into a twenty-something dude to provide the obligatory romantic interest. The brothers are in hot pursuit of Daisy, a paleontology student who's been abducted to an alternate Manhattan whose inhabitants are descended from dinosaurs. It seems Daisy is actually the princess of this weird world, exiled to Earth as a baby. Koopa, the evil

The Hound Salutes:
George Lucas

George Lucas was one of a new breed of filmmaker, part of the first generation to come from formal film training.

He graduated from the prestigious University of Southern California's School of Film. After serving as director of photography on the Rolling Stones' documentary *Gimme Shelter*, Lucas, with the help of friend Francis Ford Coppola, turned his 20-minute student film into his first feature, *THX 1138* in 1971. The film failed at the box office, and Lucas set out to write something with greater mass appeal. He succeeded first with *American Graffiti* (1974). This coming-of-age story set in the early '60s began a wave of nostalgia that permeated the decade, and inspired television's *Happy Days* (which borrowed *Graffiti* star Ron Howard).

"A long time ago, in a galaxy far, far away ..." With these famous words, Lucas surpassed all expectations with the release of *Star Wars* in 1977. A futur-

istic fairy tale of epic proportions, it told the story of a young hero, Luke Skywalker, out to save a princess and destroy the evil Galactic Empire. *Star Wars* became landmark in film history for its grand special effects, engaging story, and shear pop culture influence, as well as the most successful film of its time. The marketing frenzy of toys, T-shirts, lunch boxes, posters—virtually anything that could be stamped with a picture or logo—that followed *Star Wars* continues to this day, as does a loyal following of fans spanning two generations. Lucas followed up with two equally successful sequels, *The Empire Strikes Back* (1980) and *Return of the Jedi* (1983), though he chose not to direct either.

Lucas, along with friend Steven Spielberg, created the character of Indiana

Jones, guiding the archaeologist/adventurer through three screen adventures and the failed television show, *Young Indiana Jones*. This film trilogy, like *Star Wars,* sought to restore the sense of adventure and excitement not seen in film since the days of the serial cliffhanger. It succeeded with the charisma of star Harrison Ford and large-scale action sequences that left viewers breathless.

Despite some disappointments (*Howard the Duck, Willow,* and *Radioland Murders*), Lucas remains a dominant force in Hollywood through licensing of his Star Wars properties and his other ventures. Presently, Lucas is working on the Star Wars prequels, and a restored version of the original to be released for the 20th Anniversary in 1997.

George Lucas has become an industry unto himself. He has founded Lucasfilm Ltd., his film production company, Skywalker Sound, LucasArts Entertainment, devoted to developing computer and video game software, and Industrial Light & Magic, one of Hollywood's premiere special effects houses.

---

tyrant currently in power, wants her necklace so he can merge the two dimensions. Dennis Hopper is wonderful as Koopa, basically doing a reptilian version of Frank Booth from *Blue Velvet*. Bob Hoskins makes a fine Mario, enthusiastically partaking in high-tech wizardry and many gags. Crazed rocker Mojo Nixon has a cameo as a street musician named Toad. The movie will please members of its target audience—elementary and junior high kids—though some diehard Nintendo addicts might have some quibbles about the way the game was adapted. Adults should be

amused by the performances, special effects, and the cheerfully chaotic story. 🦴🦴🦴

1993 (PG) 104m/C Bob Hoskins, John Leguizamo, Samantha Mathis, Fisher Stevens, Richard Edson, Dana Kaminsky, Dennis Hopper, Fiona Shaw, Lance Henriksen; *Cameos:* Mojo Nixon; *D:* Rocky Morton, Annabel Jankel; *W:* Edward Solomon, Parker Bennett, Terry Runte; *M:* Alan Silvestri. **VHS, Beta, LV** *HPH, BTV, TOU*

Supergirl

This attempt at a companion to the *Superman* series was a big-budget bomb. Helen Slater made her debut here and nearly killed off her

career in the process (well, the Kryptonite didn't help). The film tells the story (such as it was) of a young woman with super powers, Superman's cousin or something. She's in pursuit of a magic doo-dad, but naturally an evil sorceress (Faye Dunaway) wants it too. Dunaway makes a pretty good villainess, and Peter O'Toole, as a good sorcerer, is the best thing in the film. The special effects are fairly impressive, but these factors aren't enough to rescue this tiresome turkey. Slater is great to look at, but she's much better in almost any of her other, later films. 🦴 🦴

1984 (PG) 114m/C *GB* Faye Dunaway, Helen Slater, Peter O'Toole, Mia Farrow, Brenda Vaccaro, Marc McClure, Simon Ward, Peter Cook, Hart Bochner, Maureen Teefy, David Healy, Matt Frewer; *D:* Jeannot Szwarc; *W:* David Odell; *C:* Alan Hume; *M:* Jerry Goldsmith. **VHS, Beta, LV** *LIV*

Superman: The Movie

The DC Comics legend comes alive in this slightly overblown but still very entertaining $55 million saga. The film follows Superman's life from his infancy on the doomed planet Krypton to his adult career as Earth's Man of Steel. Gene Hackman and Ned Beatty pair marvelously as super criminal Lex Luthor and his bumbling sidekick. Marlon Brando is suitably imposing as Superman's Kryptonian father, and Margot Kidder makes a fine Lois Lane. Award-winning special effects and a script that doesn't take itself too seriously make this good fun. It was followed by three progressively less interesting sequels. 🦴 🦴 🦴

1978 (PG) 144m/C Christopher Reeve, Margot Kidder, Marlon Brando, Gene Hackman, Glenn Ford, Susannah York, Ned Beatty, Valerie Perrine, Jackie Cooper, Marc McClure, Trevor Howard, Sarah Douglas, Terence Stamp, Jack O'Halloran, Phyllis Thaxter; *D:* Richard Donner; *W:* Leslie Newman, Mario Puzo, Robert Benton, David Newman; *C:* Geoffrey Unsworth; *M:* John Williams. Hugos '79: Dramatic Presentation; Academy Awards '78: Best Visual Effects; National Board of Review Awards '78: 10 Best Films of the Year; Nominations: Academy Awards '78: Best Film Editing, Best Sound, Best Original Score. **VHS, Beta, LV** *WAR*

Superman 2

A sequel to the 1978 blockbuster. This time, Superman has his hands full with three villains from his home planet Krypton, whose imprisonment ironically allowed them to escape its destruction. Inconveniently enough, they now have powers to match Superman's own. The romance between reporter Lois Lane and our superhero is made a tad more believable and the storyline is in many ways livelier than the original film. Now that the breathtaking responsibility of creating *the* Superman movie was discharged, the directors and actors could get down to telling an exciting story. *Superman 2* does that admirably. 🦴 🦴 🦴

1980 (PG) 127m/C Christopher Reeve, Margot Kidder, Gene Hackman, Ned Beatty, Jackie Cooper, Sarah Douglas, Jack O'Halloran, Susannah York, Marc McClure, Terence Stamp, Valerie Perrine, E.G. Marshall; *D:* Richard Lester; *W:* Leslie Newman, Mario Puzo, David Newman; *C:* Bob Paynter, Geoffrey Unsworth; *M:* John Williams. **VHS, Beta, LV** *WAR*

Superman 3

The *Superman* series started going seriously awry with this second sequel. Villainous businessman Robert Vaughn tries to conquer Superman via the expertise of a bumbling computer expert (Richard Pryor) and the judicious use of artificial Kryptonite. The Man in the Cape explores his darker side after undergoing transformation into sleaze-ball. Director Richard Lester tried to take this one in a different direction, utilizing satire and direct, physical comedy in place of the previous films' gentler humor. Unfortunately, that's not really what the *Superman* myth is about, and although Pryor does his best, *3* just doesn't measure up. The downplaying of the Superman/Lois Lane romance didn't help, either. 🦴 🦴

1983 (PG) 123m/C Christopher Reeve, Richard Pryor, Annette O'Toole, Jackie Cooper, Margot Kidder, Marc McClure, Annie Ross, Robert Vaughn, Pamela Stephenson; *D:* Richard Lester; *W:* Leslie Newman, David Newman; *C:* Bob Paynter; *M:* John Williams. **VHS, Beta, LV** *WAR*

Superman 4: The Quest for Peace

The third and quite unnecessary sequel, in which the Man of Steel endeavors to rid the world of nuclear weapons. In the process, he again runs afoul of Lex Luthor (Gene Hackman), who is of course very interested in

nuclear energy. So interested, in fact, that he uses it to create Nuclear Man, a sort of atomic anti-Superman who's cloned in record time from a few of the superhero's stray cells. Special effects are dime-store quality and it appears that someone may have walked off with parts of the plot. Still, Christopher Reeve deserves credit for remaining true to character through four films of very uneven quality. 🎬🎬

1987 (PG) 90m/C Christopher Reeve, Gene Hackman, Jon Cryer, Marc McClure, Margot Kidder, Mariel Hemingway, Sam Wanamaker, Jackie Cooper; **D:** Sidney J. Furie; **W:** Mark Rosenthal; **M:** John Williams; **V:** Susannah York. **VHS, Beta, LV** *WAR, APD*

Superman & the Mole Men

The cast of the popular '50s' television show made this rarely seen feature as a "pilot" for the series. Superman faces the danger threatened by the invasion of radioactive mole-men who make their way to the surface world from the bowels of the Earth through an oil-well shaft. The Man of Steel is given a bit more serious treatment than in the resulting series, and the midget mole men present a serious problem. Later divided into a two-part episode of the series. **AKA:** Superman and the Strange People. 🎬🎬🎬

1951 58m/C George Reeves, Phyllis Coates, Jeff Corey; **D:** Lee Sholem; **W:** Richard (Robert Maxwell) Fielding. **VHS, Beta** *WAR*

Supersonic Man

Incoherent shoestring-budget Superman spoof with a masked hero fighting to save the world from the evil intentions of a mad scientist. **WOOF!**

1978 (PG) 85m/C *SP* Michael Coby, Cameron Mitchell, Diana Polakov; **D:** Piquer Simon. **VHS, Beta** *VCI*

Survival Earth

After civilization collapses, humans begin reverting back to a primitive way of life. A

"Thanks for a good time, Fly Boy." Margot Kidder to Christopher Reeve in *Superman*.

the philosophy-spouting villain (who boasts that he personally killed Moamar Khadafy when it all hit the fan) is watchable, but overall the film remains a wasteland, too, albeit an impressively photographed one. Made in South Africa. 🦴🎬

1987 92m/C Chip Mayer, Richard Moll, Sue Kiel; **D:** Michael Shackleton. **VHS, Beta, LV** *LIV, VES*

Suspect Device

Nonsensical cable thriller finds government computer researcher Dan (C. Thomas Howell) mistakenly accessing a secret file and becoming an immediate assassination target. Then Dan discovers he isn't even human—he's really a genetically engineered cross between a robot and a nuclear bomb! Part *Terminator,* part *Three Days of the Condor,* and all silliness. **AKA:** Roger Corman Presents: Suspect Device. 🦴🎬

1995 (R) 90m/C C. Thomas Howell, Stacy Travis, Jed Allan, John Beck, Marcus Aurelius, Jonathan Fuller; **D:** Rick Jacobson; **W:** Alex Simon; **C:** John Aronson; **M:** Christopher Lennertz. **VHS** *NHO*

Swamp Thing

Overlooked camp drama about scientist accidentally turned into tragic half-vegetable, half-man swamp creature, with government agent Adrienne Barbeau caught in the middle, occasionally while topless. A vegetarian nightmare or ecology propaganda? You be the judge. Adapted from the comic book by Wes Craven. 🦴🦴🎬

1982 (PG) 91m/C Adrienne Barbeau, Louis Jourdan, Ray Wise, Dick Durock; **D:** Wes Craven; **W:** Wes Craven. **VHS, Beta, LV** *COL, SUE*

young couple and a soldier of fortune fight against it, hoping for a better existence. 🦴

19?? 90m/C VHS *NO*

Survival Zone

Nuclear holocaust survivors battle a violent band of marauding motorcyclists on the barren ranches of the 21st century. Advice to director Percival Rubens and cohorts: next time, find a plot that's not growing mold. **WOOF!**

1984 (R) 90m/C Gary Lockwood, Morgan Stevens, Camilla Sparv; **D:** Percival Rubens. **VHS, Beta** *PSM*

Survivor

A lone astronaut returns to Earth to find it a sterile, post-nuclear holocaust wasteland, and battles a megalomaniac ruler. Richard Moll as

The Swarm

Back in the late '70s, in addition to demonic possession, Legionnaire's Disease, and punk rock, everyone was worried about a rumored species of "killer bees" flying up from Mexico to sting everyone to death. Several flicks were rushed into existence to allow filmgoers to vicariously live out their newfound terror of murderous insects (and hopefully make the filmmakers lots of money). *The Swarm* was probably the most ambitious of these "Bee" movies, but despite a cast full of dependables like

Henry Fonda, Slim Pickens, and Fred MacMurray, this would-bee disaster epic is just a disaster. Scientist Michael Caine fends off a swarm of the much-vaunted killer bees when they attack metro Houston. The bees everybody was so scared of are really just black spots painted on the film. What a gyp! Yes, it's better than *The Bees,* but that's not saying a lot... 🦴

1978 (PG) 116m/C Michael Caine, Katharine Ross, Richard Widmark, Lee Grant, Richard Chamberlain, Olivia de Havilland, Henry Fonda, Fred MacMurray, Patty Duke, Ben Johnson, Jose Ferrer, Slim Pickens, Bradford Dillman, Cameron Mitchell; ***D:*** Irwin Allen; ***W:*** Stirling Silliphant; ***C:*** Fred W. Koenekamp; ***M:*** Jerry Goldsmith, John Williams. Nominations: Academy Awards '78: Best Costume Design. **VHS, Beta** *WAR*

Sword & the Sorcerer

Good, and at times gooey, special effects, along with a decent I-wish-I was-Errol-Flynn performance from Lee Horsley make this a worthwhile fantasy swashbuckler. Prince Talon (Horsley) and his band of tough and loyal mercenaries fight to regain his kingdom from King Cromwel, who, along with an evil sorcerer awakened from a thousand-year sleep, had killed his parents eleven years ago. Babes-a-plenty, lots of steel-on-steel action (although the three-bladed sword is more than silly), and an outrageous self rescue from a crucifixion-by-impalement make up for the at times bad dialogue. 🦴🦴

1982 (R) 100m/C Lee Horsley, Kathleen Beller, George Maharis, Simon MacCorkindale, Richard Lynch, Richard Moll, Robert Tessier, Nina Van Pallandt, Anna Bjorn, Jeff Corey; ***D:*** Albert Pyun; ***W:*** Albert Pyun. **VHS, Beta, LV** *MCA*

Synapse

Black-marketeer Andre (Chris Makepeace) is double crossed by a partner and arrested by Life Corp., which runs this futuristic civilization. As an experimental punishment, his mind is implanted into the body of Celeste (Karen Duffy). The plot, screwy as it is, takes precedence over the poorly staged action scenes, and the acting is a cut above average for the genre. Unfortunately, the scene in which a woman performs brain surgery on herself isn't as neat or as gross as it could have been. 🦴🦴

1995 (R) 89m/C Karen Duffy, Saul Rubinek, Matt McCoy, Chris Makepeace; ***D:*** Allan Goldstein. **VHS** *AVE*

Syngenor

Syngenor stands for Synthesized Genetic Organism, to differentiate it from all other organisms. Created by science, it escapes, and a crack team of scientists and gung-ho military types are mobilized to track it down. 🦴

1990 (R) 98m/C Starr Andreeff, Michael Laurence, David Gale, Charles Lucia, Riva Spier, Jeff Doucette, Bill Gratton, Lewis Arquette, Jon Korkes, Melanie Shatner; ***D:*** George Elanjian Jr.; ***M:*** Tom Chase, Steve Rucker. **VHS** *HMD*

T-Force

Title refers to a *Terminator* squad of law enforcement robots in the near future. When these SWATdroids kill some hostages during a terrorist shootout, city authorities order the T-Force disassembled, causing the members to turn renegade and fight their creators instead. Derivative plot rarely gets in the way of hard-hitting action, and there's some compensatory humor from flesh-and-blood cop Jack Scalia. 🦴🦴

1994 (R) 101m/C Jack Scalia, Erin Gray, Evan Lurie, Daron McBee; ***D:*** Richard Pepin. **VHS, LV** *PMH*

Tarantula

I know a spider that swallowed a cow.... In the '50s, movie theatres were infested with movies about giant ants, scorpions, grasshoppers, and mantises. This was the best of these that came after *Them*. Scientist Leo G. Carroll's growth formula literally gets away from him when the spider on which he is experimenting accidentally gets loose. This "crawling terror 100 feet high" wreaks havoc in the Arizona desert, until the Air Force (led by pilot Clint Eastwood) saves the day. Jack Arnold also directed *Creature from the Black Lagoon, The Incredible Shrinking Man,* and *It Came from Outer Space.* 🦴🦴🦴

1955 81m/B Leo G. Carroll, John Agar, Mara Corday, Nestor Paiva, Ross Elliott, Clint Eastwood; ***D:*** Jack Arnold; ***W:*** Robert M. Fresco, Martin Berkeley; ***C:*** George Robinson. **VHS** *MCA*

A Taste for Flesh and Blood

A monster from outer space comes to Earth and is delighted with the easy pickings for his insatiable appetite. A brave boy and girl, and a

TV on Tape:
Tales of Tomorrow

These tales of yesterday were an early and fairly successful sf anthology series that aired on ABC from 1951 to 1956.

Its first episodes, based on Jules Verne's *Twenty Thousand Leagues Under the Sea,* starred Thomas Mitchell with Leslie Nielsen in a supporting role. Other entries were based on magazine stories and original teleplays.

Surviving episodes of this creaky but historical series were issued on tape for the brief presence of James Dean in the first sample, "The Evil Within," a feeble Jekyll-Hyde takeoff with Rod Steiger's method acting out of place in the science lab.

The second tale, "The Spider's Web," about castaways on an island of giant radioactive (and conveniently offscreen) bugs, was scripted by Frank de Felitta, later a bestselling horror author (he adapted the screenplay for *Audrey Rose* from his own novel). Watch and you'll appreciate Rod Serling's innovative *Twilight Zone,* and snigger at archaic ads for the all-important sponsor Kreisler ("the name that makes news in watch bands!").
1951-56/B VHS *DVT*

NASA commander must join forces to take the alien out. This one is billed as a campy salute to '50s B movies. 🦴 🦴
1990 (R) 84m/C Rubin Santiago, Lori Karz, Tim Ferrante. **VHS** *NO*

Teen Alien

On Halloween night some kids explore a spooky old house with the reputation of being haunted. Aliens from the planet Varrow are afoot, rather, and the wrap up turns the thing into a subteen version of *Invasion of the Body Snatchers.* Way dull sci-fi thriller in which the real horrors are the acting and direction. **AKA:** The Varrow Mission. **WOOF!**
1988 (PG) 88m/C Vern Adix; *D:* Peter Senelka. **VHS, Beta** *PSM*

Teenage Caveman

After *I Was a Teenage Werewolf* and *I Was a Teenage Frankenstein,* intrepid American International Pictures further mined the youth market with—what else—*Teenage Caveman.* Robert Vaughn stars as "The Boy" (he would later become "The Man"...from U.N.C.L.E., that

is), who defies his elders by venturing from his clan's desolate terrain into the forbidden land beyond, where he encounters the dreaded God That Gives Death With Its Touches. If you have seen *Planet of the Apes,* you can anticipate the surprise ending. Villain Frank De Kova is more fondly remembered as Chief Wild Eagle of the Hekawi tribe on TV's *F-Troop.* Look for Jonathan Haze (*Little Shop of Horrors*) as one of the tribespeople. Roger Corman directed in ten days on a $70,000 budget. He certainly got his money's worth out of Beach Dickerson, who was utilized for four roles, including that of a bear. Corman even recruited him to play the drum in the funeral scene for one of his characters. Dinosaur footage courtesy of the film, *One Million B.C.* **AKA:** Out of the Darkness; Prehistoric World. 🦴 🦴
1958 66m/B Robert Vaughn, Darrah Marshall, Leslie Bradley, Frank De Kova, Beach Dickerson, Jonathan Haze; *D:* Roger Corman. **VHS** *COL*

Teenage Mutant Ninja Turtles: The Movie

Although a bit more rambunctious, this is a

very close adaptation of Kevin Eastman and Peter Laird's surprise hit self-published comic-book series. Four sewer-dwelling turtles that have turned into warrior ninja mutants due to radiation exposure take it upon themselves to rid the city of crime and pizza. Aided by television reporter April O'Neil and their ninja master, Splinter the Rat, the turtles encounter several obstacles, including the evil warlord Shredder. A most excellent live-action version of the popular comic book characters which will hold the kids' interest. Much head-kicking and rib-crunching action as Leonardo, Donatello, Raphael, and Michelangelo fight for the rights of pre-adolescents everywhere. Since this was a production of Hong Kong's Golden Harvest, much of the martial arts action is far superior to that of most American kung fu features. Elias Koteas stands out as the Turtles' ally Casey Jones, looking like a young Robert DeNiro. Combines real actors with Jim Henson creatures. 🐢🐢🐢

1990 (PG) 95m/C Judith Hoag, Elias Koteas, Michael Turney, James Sato; **D:** Steven Barron; **W:** Todd W. Langen, Bobby Herbeck; **C:** John Fenner; **M:** John Du Prez; **V:** Robbie Rist, Corey Feldman, Brian Tochi, Kevin Clash, David McCharen. **VHS, Beta, LV, 8mm** *FHE, LIV, WTA*

Teenage Mutant Ninja Turtles 2: The Secret of the Ooze

Amphibious pizza-devouring mutants search for the toxic waste that turned them into marketable martial-artist ecologically correct kid idols. Same formula as the first go-round with some new characters tossed in, but much of the fun feels manufactured this time, without the original's attention to character. First screen appearance by lame rapper Vanilla Ice further damages the production. Animatronic characters from the laboratory of Jim Henson. 🐢🐢

1991 (PG) 88m/C Francois Chau, David Warner, Paige Turco, Ernie Reyes Jr., Vanilla Ice; **D:** Michael Pressman; **W:** Todd W. Lagen; **C:** Shelly Johnson. **VHS, Beta** *COL, NLC*

Teenage Mutant Ninja Turtles 3

Check it out dudes; the Teenage Mutant Ninja Turtles hit 17th century Japan to rescue loyal friend, reporter April O'Neil (Paige Turco).

Plenty of smoothly executed, blood-free martial arts moves keep the pace rolling, while the turtles battle an evil lord and English pirates. Meanwhile, old pal Casey Jones (Elias Koteas) babysits the samurais sent to New York in exchange for the Turtles, teaching them the wonders of hockey and beer. Seeing the TMNT's use a little more of their reptilian grey matter, and snarf a little less pizza, should contribute to a relatively high adult tolerance level (considering the genre), and loads of good clean fun for the kiddies. This entry in the series has more heart and a better story than the previous two combined. Beautiful scenery of Washington's national forest areas stand in for Japan. 🐢🐢🐢

1993 (PG) 95m/C Elias Koteas, Paige Turco, Stuart Wilson, Sab Shimono, Vivian Wu; **D:** Stuart Gillard; **W:** Stuart Gillard; **M:** John Du Prez; **V:** Randi Mayem Singer, Matt Hill, Jim Raposa, David Fraser. **VHS, LV** *NLC, COL, IME*

Teenagers from Outer Space

"Thrill-crazed space kids blasting the flesh off humans!" So screamed the ads for this sadly neglected contender in the Golden Turkey sweepstakes. A flying saucer unloads a rowdy pack of aliens who carry disintegrating ray guns (that look suspiciously like Buck Rogers cap pistols) and unleash on the unsuspecting populace a giant Gargon (or, as we call it on this planet, a lobster). An indication of the limited budget writer-producer-director Tom Graeff had to work with is that the Gargon is only seen in shadow. Chock-full of Woodenesque (as in Ed) touches as an unsteady command of day for night (and vice-versa). Dave Love stars as Derek, the more sensitive of the aliens who mutinies and falls in love with a beautiful local. Reportedly, Dave Love is a pseudonym for Graeff. Picked up by Warner Brothers and released with *Gigantis*. *Variety* said, "While Graeff may not have made a good picture, he has made an interesting one that every now and again smacks of brilliance...an artistry that marks Graeff as a filmmaker to be heard from." Apparently, this was his only film. **AKA:** The Gargon Terror. 🐢🐢

1959 86m/B Dave Love, Tom Graeff, Dawn Anderson, Harvey B. Dunn, Bryant Grant, Tom Lockyear; **D:** Tom Graeff; **W:** Tom Graeff; **C:** Tom Graeff. **VHS** *SNC*

"Ancient Japan, 1603. Without a map...without a clue...without a pizza."

—*Teenage Mutant Ninja Turtles 3.*

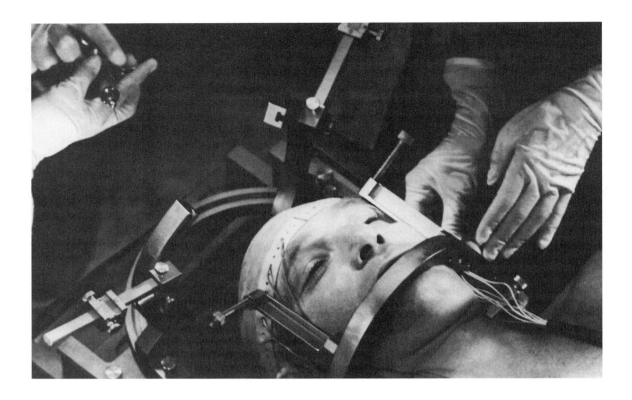

"This won't hurt a bit...." Sadistic orthodontist tightens *The Terminal Man*'s headgear.

TekWar

It's 2044, and society is plagued by "Tek," an illegal, addictive microchip that creates powerful virtual-reality fantasies. Disgraced ex-cop Jake Cardigan (Greg Evigan), sent into cryogenic prison for Tek possession, gets early parole so he can assist the Cosmos Detective Agency in their search for a missing scientist. TV movie based on the first of William Shatner's Tek books (which could have been retitled "Cyberpunk for Dummies"), is more fun to watch than the novels are to read, with some clever set designs, costumes, and f/x abetting a plot that's little more than updated gumshoe cliches. Subsequently a TV series. 🦴🦴🦴

1994 92m/C Greg Evigan, Eugene C. Clark, Torri Higginson, William Shatner; **D:** William Shatner. **VHS** *MCA*

10th Victim

Sci-fi cult film set in the 21st century has Marcello Mastroianni and Ursula Andress pursuing one another in a futuristic society where legalized murder is used as the means of population control. Intriguing movie where Andress kills with a double-barreled bra, the characters hang out at the Club Masoch, and comic books are considered literature. Based on *The Seventh Victim* by Robert Sheckley. **AKA:** La Decima Vittima; La Dixieme Victime. 🦴🦴🦴

1965 92m/C *IT* Ursula Andress, Marcello Mastroianni, Elsa Martinelli, Salvo Randone, Massimo Serato; **D:** Elio Petri; **W:** Tonino Guerra. **VHS, Beta** *SUE, NLC*

Terminal Impact

Two independent federal marshals find themselves battling indestructible, hi-tech soldiers when they investigate the disappearance of a television news reporter. 🦴🦴

1995 (R) 94m/C Bryan Genesse, Frank Zagarino, Jennifer Miller. **VHS, LV** *NLC*

The Terminal Man

A slick, visually compelling adaptation of the

Michael Crichton novel. A scientist plagued by violent mental disorders has a computer-controlled regulator implanted in his brain. The computer malfunctions and he starts a murdering spree. Futuristic vision of man-machine symbiosis gone awry. Well acted, but still falls short of the novel. 🦴🦴🦴

1974 (R) 107m/C George Segal, Joan Hackett, Jill Clayburgh, Richard Dysart, James B. Sikking, Norman Burton; **D:** Mike Hodges; **W:** Mike Hodges. **VHS, Beta** *WAR*

The Terminator

Futuristic cyborg is sent to present-day Earth. His job: kill the woman who will conceive the child destined to become the great liberator and arch-enemy of the Earth's future rulers. The cyborg is also pursued by another futuristic visitor, who falls in love with the intended victim. Director James Cameron's pacing is just right in this exhilarating, explosive thriller which displays Arnie as one cold-blooded villain who utters a now famous line: "I'll be back." Followed by *Terminator 2: Judgment Day.* 🦴🦴🦴

1984 (R) 108m/C Arnold Schwarzenegger, Michael Biehn, Linda Hamilton, Paul Winfield, Lance Henriksen, Bill Paxton, Rick Rossovich, Dick Miller; **D:** James Cameron; **W:** James Cameron; **M:** Brad Fiedel. **VHS, Beta, LV** *NO*

Terminator 2: Judgment Day

He said he'd be back and he is, programmed to protect the boy who will be mankind's post-nuke resistance leader. But the T-1000, a shape-changing, ultimate killing machine, is also on the boy's trail. Twice the mayhem, five times the special effects, ten times the budget of the first, but without Arnold it'd be half the movie. The word hasn't been invented to describe the special effects, particularly THE scariest nuclear holocaust scene yet. Worldwide megahit, but the $100 million budget nearly ruined the studio; Arnold accepted his $12 million in the form of a jet. Laserdisc fea-

Jim Carrey's body double? *Terminator 2.*

tures include pan and scan, widescreen, and a "Making of T-2" short. 🦴🦴🦴🦴

1991 (R) 139m/C Arnold Schwarzenegger, Linda Hamilton, Edward Furlong, Robert Patrick, Earl Boen, Joe Morton; *D:* James Cameron; *W:* James Cameron; *M:* Brad Fiedel. Hugos '92: Dramatic Presentation; Academy Awards '91: Best Makeup, Best Sound, Best Sound Effects Editing, Best Visual Effects; MTV Movie Awards '92: Best Film, Best Male Performance (Schwarzenegger), Best Female Performance (Hamilton), Breakthrough Performance (Furlong), Most Desirable Female (Hamilton), Best Action Sequence; People's Choice Awards '92: Best Film; Nominations: Academy Awards '91: Best Cinematography, Best Sound. **VHS, LV, 8mm** *LIV*

Terror Beneath the Sea

A mad scientist wants to rule the world with his cyborgs. American and Japanese scientists unite to fight him. Fine special effects, especially the transformation from human to monster. **AKA:** Kaitei Daisenso; Water Cyborgs. 🦴🦴🦴

1966 85m/C *JP* Sonny Chiba, Peggy Neal, Franz Gruber, Gunther Braun, Andrew Hughes, Mike Daneen; *D:* Hajime Sato. **VHS, Beta** *DVT*

Terror Is a Man

A mad scientist attempts to turn a panther into a man on a secluded island. Early Filipino horror attempt inspired by H.G. Wells' *The Island of Doctor Moreau*. **AKA:** Blood Creature. 🦴🦴

1959 89m/B *PH* Francis Lederer, Greta Thyssen, Richard Derr, Oscar Keesee; *D:* Gerardo (Gerry) De Leon. **VHS** *SNC*

Terror of Mechagodzilla

It's monster vs. machine in the heavyweight battle of the universe as a huge mechanical Godzilla built by aliens is pitted against the real thing. The last Godzilla movie made until *Godzilla 1985*. **AKA:** Monsters from the Unknown Planet; The Escape of Megagodzilla; Mekagojira No Gyakushu. 🦴🦴

1978 (G) 79m/C *JP* Katsuhiko Sasakai, Tomoko Al. **VHS, Beta** *PAR*

The Terror Within

Reptilian mutants hit the streets searching for human women to breed with. Have the Teenage Mutant Ninja Turtles grown up? 🦴

1988 (R) 90m/C George Kennedy, Andrew Stevens, Starr Andreeff, Terri Treas; *D:* Thierry Notz; *W:* Thomas McKelvey Cleaver; *M:* Rick Conrad. **VHS, Beta** *MGM*

The Terror Within 2

In a world destroyed by biological warfare, a warrior and the woman he rescued traverse the badlands occupied by hideous mutants. What they don't know is that the real terror comes from within. How can they possibly survive? Not without decent dialogue, that's for sure. 🦴🦴

1991 (R) 90m/C Andrew Stevens, Stella Stevens, Chick Vennera, R. Lee Ermey; *D:* Andrew Stevens. **VHS** *VES, LIV*

Terrornauts

When man begins space exploration, Earth is attacked by aliens. The defenders are taken to an outdated fortress where they learn that their forebears were similarly attacked. Juvenile, lackluster, contrived, and really dumb. **WOOF!**

1967 77m/C *GB* Simon Oates, Zena Marshall, Charles Hawtrey, Stanley Meadows; *D:* Montgomery Tully. **VHS, Beta** *NLC*

Test Tube Teens from the Year 2000

This is a throwback to the mid-'60s. The opening titles, presented over the silhouette of a naked dancing woman, could have come straight from that era. The fast-forwardable plot concerns the title characters' efforts to go back in time and stop Camella Swales (Morgan Fairchild) from banning conventional reproduction. Production designers took their cue from the deliberately cheesy sets and props used on television's *Mystery Science Theater 3000*. Don't miss the apple corer that's glued to the front of the time machine and the white "boots" made of cardboard sleeves over tennis shoes. This, folks, is what low-budget video is all about. **AKA:** Virgin Hunters. 🦴🦴

1993 (R) 74m/C Morgan Fairchild, Ian Abercrombie, Brian Bremer, Christopher Wolf, Michelle Matheson, Sara Suzanne Brown, Don Dowe; *D:* Ellen Cabot; *W:* Kenneth J. Hall; *M:* Reg Powell. **VHS, Beta, LV** *PAR*

Tetsuo: The Iron Man

"Your future is metal!" Weird 16mm live-action Japanese "normal-sized monster movie" about an office worker gradually transformed into a walking metal collection of cables, drills, wires, and gears. The mutant creature faces off with an equally bizarre metals fetishist (played by the director) whose rituals somehow spawned him. Graphic violence and mutilation (the Hound, for one, was glad this was in B&W!) mated with near-nonstop stop-motion f/x and nightmare/folklore imagery. Tough going if you're not in the mood. Or even if you are in the mood. Allegedly a metaphor of homosexuality in rigid Japanese society, for what that's worth. Big-budget sequel *Tetsuo II: Body Hammer* is thus far commercially unavailable on American home video. English subtitles. 🗡🗡

1992 67m/B *JP* Tomoroh Taguchi, Kei Fujiwara, Shinya Tsukamoto; **D:** Shinya Tsukamoto; **W:** Shinya Tsukamoto. **VHS** *FXL*

Them!

"A horror horde of crawl-and-crush giants clawing out of the Earth from mile-deep catacombs!" Inspired by the success of *The Beast from 20,000 Fathoms,* this was the first and the best of the giant bug movies (no picnic jokes, please). What hath the atomic age wrought? Radiation-enhanced behemoths—or should we say behe-ants—which terrorize New Mexico before devastating a Navy ship and finally hiding out in the sewers of Los Angeles. Hoping to stomp them out are policeman James Whitmore, FBI agent James (*The Thing*) Arness, scientist Edmund Gwenn (best-loved as Santa Claus in *Miracle on 34th Street*), and his beautiful daughter Joan Weldon. According to Fess Parker, Walt Disney saw his brief bit as a pilot and sought him out to audition for the role that would make him a legend, Davy Crockett. As chilling as *The Fly*'s cries of "Help me" is little Sandy Descher's sudden cry of "Them." Olin Howlin, who

"It's a great plan...once we get past a few bugs." ***Them!***

appears as a drunk, was "The Blob's" first victim. Look quick for Leonard Nimoy. The ants were actual-sized models and were not stop-motion animated (special effects supervisor Ralph Ayres was nominated for an Academy Award). This was Warner Brothers' highest-grossing film of the year. 🦴🦴🦴▷

1954 93m/B James Whitmore, Edmund Gwenn, Fess Parker, James Arness, Onslow Stevens, Jack Perrin, Joan Weldon, Leonard Nimoy, Sandy Descher, Olin Howlin; **D:** Gordon Douglas; **W:** Ted Scherdemann; **C:** Sid Hickox. **VHS, Beta, LV** *WAR*

There's Nothing Out There

Seven teenagers spend Spring Break at a secluded mountain cabin, anticipating sex and wild times. But one boy, who claims to have seen every horror movie on video, knows the signs of a horror plot just waiting to happen. He's the only one prepared when an idiotic-looked alien frog monster attacks and kills. There's one already famous scene in which a potential victim swings out of the danger by grabbing the dangling microphone boom at the top of the frame. That's amusing, but in general this no-budget parody of screen schlock is barely better than the dreck it imitates. 🦴

1990 91m/C Craig Peck, Wendy Bednarz, Mark Collver, Bonnie Bowers, John Carhart III, Claudia Flores, Jeff Dachis; **D:** Rolfe Kanefsky; **W:** Rolfe Kanefsky. **VHS, Beta, LV** *PSM*

They

Guys on a hunting jaunt land their plane in the wilderness to discover that some sort of alien invasion has taken place and they're cut off from humanity. We glimpse a wobbly flying disk, smoke bombs, and a red flashlight beam. Notorious non-ending, in which last two survivors turn into children and scamper off into a Garden of Eden, has caused many a late-show viewer to bold upright and blink in disbelief. Made in Wisconsin by wannabes. **AKA:** Invasion from Inner Earth; Hell Fire. **WOOF!**

1977 88m/C Paul Dentzer, Debbie Pick, Nick Holt; **D:** Ito Rebane. **VHS, Beta** *NO*

They Came from Beyond Space

Aliens invade the Earth and possess the brains of humans. They only want a few slaves to help them repair their ship which crashed on the moon. The only person able to stop them is a scientist with a steel plate in his head. Silly and forgettable. 🦴

1967 86m/C Robert Hutton, Michael Gough; **D:** Freddie Francis. **VHS, Beta** *SUE*

They Came from Within

What do you get when you cross an aphrodisiac with a venereal disease? Well, if you are director David Cronenberg, you get this nasty little parasitic organism, capable of turning the its host human into a raging sex fiend, and then making an exit that would make an *Alien* chest-burster proud. Cronenberg's first nearly mainstream film is set in the sterile, clinical setting of the Starliner high-rise, the perfect contrast to the symbolic spread of the "venereal disease," in this case implanted by a messed-up parasite-research doctor in place of supposed transplant organs. Look for '60s horror queen Barbara Steele in the famous bathtub "entry" scene. Similar in attitude to many zombie films, you can either find meaning in the loads of symbolism, or just sit back and enjoy the shocking, gory, sleazy ride. **AKA:** Shivers; The Parasite Murders. 🦴🦴▷

1975 (R) 87m/C CA Paul Hampton, Joe Silver, Lynn Lowry, Barbara Steele; **D:** David Cronenberg; **W:** David Cronenberg. **VHS, Beta** *LIV, VES*

They Live

A semi-serious science-fiction spoof about a drifter (a surprisingly solid perf from ex-wrestler Roddy Piper) who accidentally discovers an alien conspiracy. They're taking over the country under the guise of Reaganism, capitalism, and yuppiedom. Piper and his homeless pals decide to do something about it. Screenplay written by director John Carpenter under the pseudonym "Frank Armitage." Lots of demented fun, although it devolves a bit into action flick material towards the end. 🦴🦴▷

1988 (R) 88m/C Roddy Piper, Keith David, Meg Foster, George Flower, Peter Jason, Raymond St. Jacques, John Lawrence, Sy Richardson, Jason Robards III, Larry Franco; **D:** John Carpenter; **W:** John Carpenter; **C:** Gary B. Kibbe; **M:** Alan Howarth, John Carpenter. **VHS, Beta, LV** *MCA*

They Saved Hitler's Brain

No, this is not the Pat Buchanan story. Probably must viewing for bad movie connoisseurs, but for those with more sober and rational tastes (and we know you're out there), this infamous golden turkey has little to offer except the ludicrous title and fleeting shots of Der Fuhrer's severed head in a jar and still giving orders ("Mach Schnell!"). The years have not mellowed "Mr. H." (as he is now called). Even in his pickled state, he wants to take over the world by unleashing the deadly "Nerve Gas G." This film was assembled from footage from a '50s espionage melodrama combined with new footage. Nestor Paiva's credits include *Mighty Joe Young, Creature from the Black Lagoon, Tarantula,* and *Jesse James Meets Frankenstein's Daughter.* Incredibly, David Bradley began his career filming stage productions of Shakespeare plays and directed Charlton Heston in his first role in *Peer Gynt* before graduating to *Dragstrip Riot, 12 to the Moon,* and of course, this. **AKA:** Madmen of Mandoras; The Return of Mr. H. **WOOF!**
1964 91m/B Walter Stocker, Audrey Caire, Nestor Paiva, Carlos Rivas, Dani Lynn; *D:* David Bradley. **VHS, Beta, 8mm** *VYY*

The Thing

One of the best of the Cold War allegories and a potent lesson to those who won't eat their vegetables. Sci-fi classic begins with an alien spacecraft embedded in the Artic ice and the creature (Arness as the killer carrot), discovered by a research team. The critter is accidentally thawed and then wreaks havoc, sucking the life from sled dog and scientist alike. It's a giant seed-dispersing vegetable run amuck, unaffected by missing body parts, bullets, or cold. In other words, Big Trouble. Excellent direction—assisted substantially by producer Hawks—and supported by strong performances, sparkling dialogue, and a machine-gun pace. Even more important is the film's

"*The Thing* is...well, we don't know what the heck it is!" T.K. Carter, Kurt Russell, and Donald Moffat.

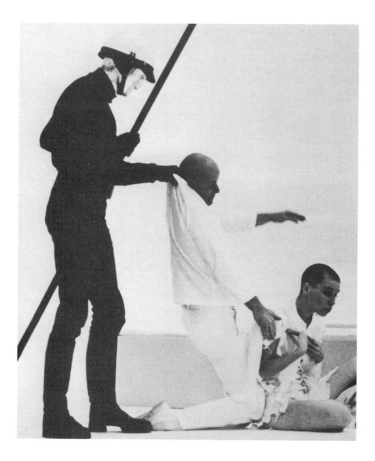

There?," since the seeds/spores take on human shapes. 🦴🦴🦴◁

1982 (R) 127m/C Kurt Russell, Wilford Brimley, T.K. Carter, Richard Masur, Keith David, Richard Dysart, David Clennon, Donald Moffat, Thomas G. Waites, Charles Hallahan; **D:** John Carpenter; **C:** Dean Cundey; **M:** Ennio Morricone. **VHS, Beta, LV** *MCA*

Things to Come

Groundbreaking (and very loose) adaptation of H.G. Wells' prophecies, best viewed today as taking place on an alternate world, an Earth that might have been. Narrative begins in 1940 and runs to 2036 to chronicle the travails of Everytown, where the filmmakers depict fictionally for the first time what would soon be tragically real: innocent civilians bombed, gassed, and infected in a global war that lasts until 1970 (note that when the year "1945" flashes onscreen a puff of smoke shaped like a mushroom cloud appears, an accidental bit of accuracy). Politicians having made a mess of things, a group of scientific airmen take over running the world, and when the dust rolls away, behold Everytown of 2036 in its shining whiteness and glory. Every man is a superman, every woman a superwoman, wearing zoot-suit togas with huge shoulders (original script notes said our descendants will have so many items in their pockets that the shoulders must fortify and hold their clothing up). Scientists decide to build a huge space gun to fire two astronauts to the moon, but a division between the sciences and humanities (like that which plagued real-life universities in the '60s and '70s) rears its ugly head, and a group of artists try to tear the space gun down with their bare hands. Final scene, with Raymond Massey pointing to the stars and declaring "It is this or nothingness. Which shall it be? Which shall it be?" triumphantly sums up the science-fiction dream of man's destiny in space. In the public domain, *Things to Come* is carried on video by numerous labels, and quality varies widely. Look for the U.S.-release prints that include a five-minute montage of titanic machines rebuilding civilization, a sequence designed by director William Cameron Menzies to surpass anything ever seen in Buck Rogers comics. Superb musical score by Arthur Bliss. 🦴🦴🦴◁

Officer Friendly makes computer dating even more painful in *THX 1138*.

atmosphere of frozen claustrophobia and isolation. Available colorized (don't do it). Remade in 1982 and often copied. Loosely based on "Who Goes There?" by John Campbell. **AKA:** The Thing From Another World. 🦴🦴🦴◁

1951 87m/B James Arness, Kenneth Tobey, Margaret Sheridan, Dewey Martin; **D:** Christian Nyby, Howard Hawks; **W:** Charles Lederer; **M:** Dimitri Tiomkin. **VHS, Beta, LV** *MED, TTC, MLB*

The Thing

A team of scientists at a remote Antarctic outpost discover a buried spaceship with an unwelcome alien survivor still alive. Bombastic special effects overwhelm the suspense and the solid cast. Less a remake of the 1951 science-fiction classic than a more faithful version of John Campbell's short story "Who Goes

1936 92m/B *GB* Margaretta Scott, Edward Chapman, Raymond Massey, Ralph Richardson, Cedric Hardwicke, Derrick DeMarney; *D:* William Cameron Menzies; *W:* Lajos Biro, H.G. Wells; *C:* Georges Perinal; *M:* Arthur Bliss. **VHS, Beta** *NOS, PSM, SNC*

This Is Not a Test

When news comes of an impending nuclear attack, a state trooper at a roadblock offers sanctuary to passing travellers. The effectiveness of the film's social commentary is hindered by its small budget. 🦴🦴

1962 72m/B Seamon Glass, Mary Morlass, Thayer Roberts, Aubrey Martin; *D:* Frederic Gadette. **VHS, Beta** *SNC*

This Island Earth

The planet Metaluna is in desperate need of uranium to power its defense against enemy invaders. A nuclear scientist and a nuclear fission expert from Earth are kidnapped to help out. The first serious movie about interplanetary escapades. Bud Westmore created pulsating cranium special effects make-up. 🦴🦴🦴

1955 86m/C Jeff Morrow, Faith Domergue, Rex Reason, Russell Johnson; *D:* Joseph M. Newman; *M:* Herman Stein. **VHS, Beta, LV** *MCA, MLB*

Those Fantastic Flying Fools

A mad race to be the first on the moon brings hilarious results. Loosely based on a Jules Verne story. **AKA:** Blast-Off; Jules Verne's Rocket to the Moon. 🦴🦴🦴

1967 95m/C *GB* Burl Ives, Troy Donahue, Gert Frobe, Terry-Thomas, Hermione Gingold, Daliah Lavi, Lionel Jeffries; *D:* Don Sharp. **VHS** *NO*

Three Stooges in Orbit

Following the release of their classic two-reelers to syndicated television, the Three Stooges enjoyed a resurgence in popularity and were signed for a series of feature films, beginning with *Have Rocket Will Travel*. After taking on Hercules in *The Three Stooges Meet...*, they went into *Orbit,* where they battle a Martian Army that is after nutty inventor Emil Sitka's ultimate invention, a sort of flying submarine/tank/rocket. For die-hard fans and kids only. 🦴🦴

1962 87m/B Moe Howard, Larry Fine, Joe DeRita, Emil Sitka, Carol Christensen, Edson Stroll; *D:* Edward L. Bernds; *W:* Elwood Ullman; *C:* William F. Whitley. **VHS** *COL*

The Three Worlds of Gulliver

Colorful version of the Jonathan Swift classic fits in more of the plot than most adaptations, though it softens the author's corrosive satire. Here, after those well-known tribulations with the small and small-minded Lilliputians, Gulliver and his fiancee drift to another island—Brobdingnag, inhabited by a superstitious and callous race of giants. It's Gulliver's turn to view things from a tiny perspective, and there are close encounters with a squirrel and an alligator, engineered via the stop-motion of Ray Harryhausen. Columbia TriStar markets a Harryhausen boxed set of fantasies, and that particular edition of *The Three Worlds of Gulliver* includes an interview with the f/x maestro. **AKA:** The Worlds of Gulliver. 🦴🦴🦴

1959 100m/C Kerwin Mathews, Jo Morrow, Basil Sydney, Mary Ellis; *D:* Jack Sher; *W:* Arthur Ross, Jack Sher; *M:* Bernard Herrmann. **VHS, Beta, LV** *COL, MLB, CCB*

Thunderbirds Are Go

A feature film version of Anderson's futuristic British TV series featuring rave electronic marionette faves, the Tracy family. In this adventure, the Tracys rescue the disabled Zero X spacecraft. Filled with spectacular gadgets, explosions, and remarkable puppetry. 🦴🦴

1966 92m/C *D:* Gerry Anderson. **VHS, Beta** *MGM*

THX 1138

In the dehumanized world of the future, people live in underground cities run by computer, are force-fed drugs to keep them passive, emotions and sex are forbidden, and people no longer have names—just serial numbers. Robert Duvall is THX 1138. When the computer-matched couple THX 1138 and LUH 3417 discover true love, they attempt to escape their oppressive society in order to be together. The film borrows generously from such classics as George Orwell's *1984,* Aldous Huxley's *Brave*

> "We're gonna draw a bit of everybody's blood, 'cause we're gonna find out who's the thing."
>
> —Macready (Kurt Russell) in *The Thing* (1982).

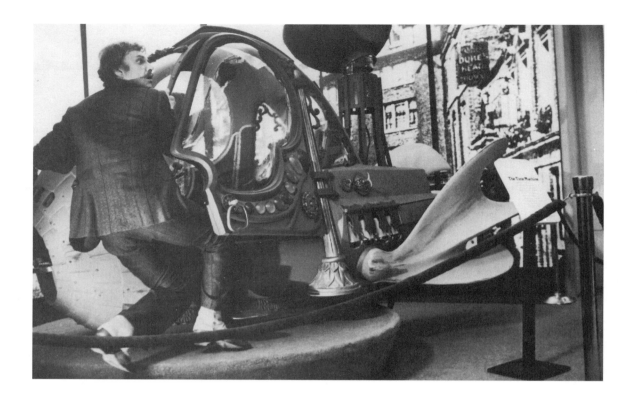

I wouldn't steal *that* car, it's way too conspicuous. What could Malcolm MacDowell be *thinking* in *Time After Time*?

New World, and Stanley Kubrick's *2001: A Space Odyssey.* Director George Lucas tells the story primarily through stunning sound (Walter Murch, the sound editor, co-wrote the screenplay) and visuals (almost everything in this future is gleaming white and everyone has shaved heads), and only sparse, almost catatonic, dialogue. Still, the film is more interesting as a preview of what Lucas would do than what he does here. The film only hints at Lucas' story-telling talent. This was Lucas' first film, inspired by a 20-minute student short he made at USC. The laserdisc version carries the film in widescreen format. 🦴🦴ᵇ

1971 (PG) 88m/C Robert Duvall, Donald Pleasence, Maggie McOmie, Don Pedro Colley, Ian Wolfe, Marshall Efron; **D:** George Lucas; **W:** George Lucas, Walter Murch; **C:** Dave Meyers, Albert Kihn; **M:** Lalo Schifrin. **VHS, Beta, LV** WAR, FUS

Ticks

Killer mutant arachnids terrorize a Northern California campground! A bunch of not-terribly bright backwoods marijuana farmers dump some nasty chemicals into the local water supply. This results in a plague of grapefruit-sized parasites who attack first them and then the usual troop of unwary teen campers. And if that's not enough environmental bad karma for you, a forest fire breaks out, trapping the teens. There are some fine squirm-inducing moments in this flick, which was produced by *Re-Animator*'s Brian Yuzna. Those with weak stomachs, however, might want to stick to similar films from the '50s, which don't include graphic shots of monster bugs burrowing under hapless characters' skins. **AKA:** Infested. 🦴🦴

1993 (R) 85m/C Ami Dolenz, Rosalind Allen, Alfonso Ribeiro, Peter Scolari; **D:** Tony Randel. **VHS, LV** REP

Time After Time

In Victorian London, circa 1893, H. G. Wells (whom filmmakers love to portray as an eccentric inventor, rather than the novelist and

historian he was in real life) is experimenting with his time machine. He discovers the machine has been used by an associate (who turns out to be Jack the Ripper) to travel to San Francisco and wreck havoc in 1979. Wells follows to stop any further murders and the ensuing battle of wits is both entertaining and imaginative. Malcolm McDowell is charming as Wells and Mary Steenburgen is equally fine as Wells' modern American love interest. Several years later, Steenburgen would play the heroine of another time-travel romance, *Back to the Future, Part 3.* 🦴🦴🦴

1979 (PG) 112m/C Malcolm McDowell, David Warner, Mary Steenburgen, Patti D'Arbanville, Charles Cioffi, Kent Williams, Andonia Katsaros; *D:* Nicholas Meyer; *W:* Nicholas Meyer; *C:* Paul Lohmann; *M:* Miklos Rozsa. National Board of Review Awards '79: 10 Best Films of the Year. **VHS, Beta, LV** *WAR*

Time Bandits

Director Terry Gilliam's first non-Monty Python film still features several Python alumni. Mad

dwarves, being pursued by the Supreme Being (Ralph Richardson), lead a young boy (Craig Warnock) on a journey through time and space with the likes of Robin Hood (John Cleese), Napoleon (Ian Holm), King Agamemnon (Sean Connery), and other time-warp pals. David Warner is a natural Evil Incarnate. As in Gilliam's later film, *The Adventures of Baron Munchausen,* a lot of this film plays like a cartoon, as reality shatters into one dreamworld after another. A fantasy epic, funny and imaginative. 🦴🦴🦴

1981 (PG) 110m/C *GB* John Cleese, Sean Connery, Shelley Duvall, Katherine Helmond, Ian Holm, Michael Palin, Ralph Richardson, Kenny Baker, Peter Vaughan, Craig Warnock, David Warner; *D:* Terry Gilliam; *W:* Terry Gilliam, Michael Palin. **VHS, Beta, LV** *PAR*

Time Fighters

A time machine has the ability to travel at the speed of light from prehistoric times to the

"We lost Sneezy along the way, but the six of us are ready for a little time traveling." Mike Edwards, Kenny Baker, Malcolm Dixon, Tiny Ross, Jack Purvis, David Rappaport, and Snow White (not pictured) in *Time Bandits.*

distant future. This is a great help to the Time fighters. 🦴 🦴

1985 60m/C VHS, Beta *SUE*

The Time Guardian

A time-traveling city from the 40th century arrives in the Australian desert in 1988, pursued by killer cyborgs (looking a lot like *Star Trek*'s fave menace, the Borg). Muddled and confusing melange of borrowed sci-fi elements with no clear identity of its own. Some good f/x. What's a nice girl like Princess Leia doing in an also-ran like this? 🦴 🦴

1987 (PG) 89m/C Tom Burlinson, Carrie Fisher, Dean Stockwell, Nikki Coghill; *D:* Brian Hannant; *W:* Brian Hannant, John Baxter. **VHS, Beta, LV, 8mm** *COL, SUE, NLC*

The Time Machine

Film version of H.G. Wells' seminal sf novel has aged poorly. It's slow, talky, and not particularly well acted. Still, the Morlocks are spooky dudes, and even at its worst moments, the production's sets and Oscar-winning special effects look good. Remade in 1978. 🦴 🦴 🦴

1960 103m/C Rod Taylor, Alan Young, Yvette Mimieux, Whit Bissell, Sebastian Cabot, Tom Helmore; *D:* George Pal; *W:* David Duncan; *C:* Paul Vogel. Academy Awards '60: Best Special Effects. **VHS, Beta, LV** *MGM, MLB*

Time Machine

Sunn Classics, the company that did all those UFO and Noah's Ark documentaries in the '70s, was responsible for this inferior adaptation of the H.G. Wells classic. The story's setting was unwisely moved to the '70s, keeping down costuming costs but also losing the charm of the original's Victorian milieu. John Beck is the Time Traveller, whose adventures in history incorporate a lot of economical stock footage. Blonde Priscilla Barnes is the ingenuous Weena. Do yourself a favor and stick to the George Pal version. 🦴 🦴

1978 (G) 99m/C John Beck, Priscilla Barnes, Andrew Duggan; **D:** Henning Schellerup. **VHS, Beta** *NO*

Time Runner

It's 2022, and the Earth is being used as target practice by alien invaders. Space captain Mark Hamill falls through an unexplained time warp back to 1992 where he can battle the secret alien vanguard of humanlike infiltrators and change the planet's destiny. Canadian sci-fi washout lacks logic. Great Moments in Low-Budget Aliens: their devastating, incomprehensible battle machine turns out to be a bulldozer with a fog lights. 🦶

1992 (R) 90m/C *CA* Mark Hamill, Brion James, Rae Dawn Chong; **D:** Michael Mazo. **VHS, LV** *NLC, COL*

Time Trackers

A Roger Corman cheapie about a race through time, from present-day New York to medieval England, to recover a time machine before it alters the course of history. 🦶🦶

1988 (PG) 87m/C Kathleen Beller, Ned Beatty, Will Shriner; **D:** Howard R. Cohen. **VHS, Beta** *MGM*

The Time Travelers

A group of scientists discover and pass through a porthole leading to Earth's post-Armageddon future where they encounter tribes of nasty mutants. The last remnants of humanity use androids (who with their featureless, noseless faces look faintly menacing in their own right) as slave labor to build a spaceship to escape the dying planet. Sensing (correctly) that there's not much fun to be had the future, the time travelers make a serious effort to return to their past. This is a serious, thoughtful science-fiction film with an accent on ideas as opposed to phoney-looking monsters. Some viewers might find it a bit too bleak for casual viewing. Professional sf-movie maven Forrest J. Ackerman has a bit role. It was remade several years later as *Journey to the Center of Time*. **AKA:** Time Trap. 🦶🦶

1964 82m/C Preston Foster, Phil Carey, Merry Anders, John Hoyt, Joan Woodbury, Dolores Wells, Dennis Patrick, Forrest J. Ackerman, Carol White; **D:** Ib Melchior; **W:** Ib Melchior; **C:** William Zsigmond. **VHS, Beta** *NO*

Time Troopers

Austrian-made tale set in another one of those post-nuke societies, where special police must execute anyone who has used up their allotted energy ration, whether they're ready to die or not. Small-scale sci fi, similar to *Logan's Run* in concept, but without the eye candy f/x to fall back upon. Nothing whatsoever to do with time travel, despite the anglicized title. **AKA:** Morgen Grauen; Morning Terror. 🦶🦶

1989 (R) 90m/C *AT* Albert Fortell, Hannelore Elsner; **D:** L.E. Neiman. **VHS, Beta** *PSM*

Time Walker

An archaeologist unearths King Tut's coffin in California. An alien living inside is unleashed and terrorizes the public. 🦶

1982 (PG) 86m/C Ben Murphy; **D:** Tom Kennedy; **M:** Richard Band. **VHS, Beta** *NLC*

Timecop

Terminator rip-off is fodder for Van Damme followers with lots of action and good special effects (you weren't expecting acting too). In 2004, time travel has been perfected (despite gaping logical inconsistencies far too numerous to mention or care about). Due to the potential for misuse, a special Time Enforcement police unit has been established to prevent evil doers from changing the past to improve their fortunes in the present. Of course someone does. Evil Senator McComb (Ron Silver), who also happens to oversee the Timecop force, has been altering the past to insure his election to the presidency. Timecop Max Walker (Van Damme) must travel back in time to prevent this from occurring. It's also Walker's chance to alter his personal history since his wife Melissa (Mia Sara) was killed in an explosion he can now prevent. If only someone could travel back in time and prevent this film from having been made. Van Damme and director Peter Hyams re-teamed for the Die-Hard-in-a-Hockey-Arena flick, *Sudden Death*. The film is based on a *Dark Horse* comic. 🦶

> "If that machine can do what you say it can do, destroy it, George! Destroy it before it destroys you!"
>
> —Filby (Alan Young) in
> *The Time Machine.*

We're pretty sure we've seen Arnold Schwarzenegger in this nasty predicament before, but we don't have **Total Recall.**

1994 (R) 98m/C Jean-Claude Van Damme, Ron Silver, Mia Sara, Bruce McGill, Scott Lawrence, Kenneth Welsh, Gabrielle Rose, Duncan Fraser, Ian Tracey, Gloria Reuben, Scott Bellis, Jason Schombing, Kevin McNulty, Sean O'Byrne, Malcolm Stewart, Alfonso Quijada, Glen Roald, Theodore Thomas; **D:** Peter Hyams; **W:** Mark Verheiden, Gary De Vore; **C:** Peter Hyams. **VHS, LV** *MCA*

Timemaster

Orphaned 12-year-old Jesse (Jesse Cameron-Glickenhaus, the director's son, to nobody's surprise) knows his parents are alive in another time. They're all fighting battles throughout history for the amusement of advanced aliens on a distant world, and kindly extraterrestrial Isaiah (Pat Morita) sends the boy on a rescue mission bouncing around time and space. Scrap-heap of genre cliches, pasted together and semi-coherent. Shocking thing is it doesn't look cheap at all; someone armed with a real script could have made a decent flick with this budget. Your chance to see Michael Dorn out from under his *Star Trek* Klingon forehead as the main villain. **WOOF!**

1995 (PG-13) 100m/C Jesse Cameron-Glickenhaus, Noriyuki "Pat" Morita, Joanna Pacula, Michael Dorn, Duncan Regehr, Michelle Williams; **D:** James Glickenhaus; **W:** James Glickenhaus. **VHS, LV** *MCA*

Timerider

Your basic dirtbike/sf/western finds an intellectually challenged motorcycle rider stuck in 1877 (he never quite figures out why he gets blank stares when he asks to use the phone). As always, Fred Ward is excellent. He gets fine support from Belinda Bauer and bad guy Peter Coyote. Co-written and co-produced by Michael Nesmith, best known for his days with the rock group "The Monkees." A wry sense of humor has earned this one a solid cult status. **AKA:** The Adventure of Lyle Swan. 🎬🎬

1983 (PG) 93m/C Fred Ward, Belinda Bauer, Peter Coyote, Richard Masur, Ed Lauter, L.Q. Jones, Tracey Walter; **D:** William Dear; **W:** Michael Nesmith, William Dear; **C:** Larry Pizer. **VHS, Beta, LV** *NO*

Timestalkers

A college professor's infatuation with a young woman is complicated by their pursuit of a criminal from the 26th century into the past. Mildly entertaining made-for-TV adventure. Forrest Tucker's last film. 🎬🎬

1987 100m/C William Devane, Lauren Hutton, Klaus Kinski, John Ratzenberger, Forrest Tucker, Gail Youngs; **D:** Michael A. Schultz. **VHS** *FRH*

Tobor the Great

Silly, overly juvenile vintage sci fi about a boy, his inventor grandfather, and their pride and joy, Tobor the Robot. Villainous commie spies try to misuse Tobor, only to be thwarted in the end. Apparently aimed at viewers too young to figure out where the name 'Tobor' came from. 🎬

1954 77m/B Charles Drake, Billy Chapin, Karin Booth, Taylor Holmes, Joan Gerber, Steve Geray; **D:** Lee Sholem. **VHS, LV** *REP*

Total Recall

Mind-bending sci-fi adventure set in the 21st century, when Earth's citizens have fictionalized memories implanted to grant them

adventures they couldn't afford to experience. Restless construction worker Quaid (Arnold Schwarzenegger) undergoes the procedure to exorcize his fixation with the Mars mining colony, but something goes wrong. It seems he really was a secret agent on Mars and had a false memory implant to wipe his true identity out. Or did he? Dodging assassins at every turn, Quaid heads for Mars for answers. Elaborate expansion of Philip K. Dick's short tale "We Can Remember It for You Wholesale" is an entertaining but problematic puzzler, rewritten to fit Schwarzenegger's Conan-scale persona; whenever the mazelike plot becomes too much, Quaid can just punch his way out, though the storyline's logic grows progressively tortured—until the hero can't even exist if everything is taken literally. Add half a bone is you're an unquestioning action fan, since spectacular f/x and graphic violence are rife throughout. Grotesque mutant makeup by Rob Bottin. 🦴🦴🦴

1990 (R) 113m/C Arnold Schwarzenegger, Rachel Ticotin, Sharon Stone, Michael Ironside, Ronny Cox, Roy Brocksmith, Marshall Bell, Mel Johnson Jr.; **D:** Paul Verhoeven; **W:** Gary Goldman, Dan O'Bannon; **M:** Jerry Goldsmith. Academy Awards '90: Best Visual Effects; Nominations: Academy Awards '90: Best Sound. **VHS, Beta, LV, 8mm** *IME, FUS, LIV*

Toward the Terra

In the distant future mankind is forced to evacuate Earth and settles on the planet Atarakusha. Society ruthlessly suppresses anything which could destabilize it in an effort to prevent the mistakes which destroyed the Earth. The most destablizing presence is the MU, a new race with incredible mental powers, who are ruthlessly hunted and eliminated. But the leader of the MU reaches out to a human with his own inexplicable powers to aid in establishing a new world. In Japanese with subtitles. 🦴🦴

1980 112m/C *JP* **VHS** *CPM*

Trancers

A psycho zombie cult of the future goes back in time to 1985 to meddle with fate. Only Jack Deth, a longtime Trancer terminator, can save mankind. Low-budget *Blade Runner* imitation,

with widely scattered clever touches. One is the gimmick of time-travel via a drug that injects one's consciousness down "the genetic bridge" to the bodies of distant ancestors (hence Jack Deth's tough-talking superior officer shows up in the Reagan era as a tough-talking little girl). Followed by four sequels. **AKA:** Future Cop. 🦴🦴

1984 (PG-13) 76m/C Tim Thomerson, Michael Stefoni, Helen Hunt, Art LaFleur, Telma Hopkins, Richard Herd, Anne Seymour; **D:** Charles Band; **W:** Danny Bilson, Paul DeMeo, Phil Davies; **C:** Mac Ahlberg. **VHS, Beta, LV** *LIV, VES*

Trancers 2: The Return of Jack Deth

Fatigued followup sees Jack Deth, stranded in 20th-century L.A., in action again when another outbreak of Trancers occurs (inadequately explained, of course). Meanwhile the intricacies of time travel leave him henpecked by two wives from different eras. Weak pacing undermines whatever suspense there might have been. 🦴

1990 (R) 85m/C Tim Thomerson, Helen Hunt, Megan Ward, Biff Manard, Martine Beswick, Jeffrey Combs, Barbara Crampton, Richard Lynch, Alyson Croft, Telma Hopkins, Art LaFleur; **D:** Charles Band; **W:** Jackson Barr; **C:** Adolfo Bartoli. **VHS, Beta, LV** *PAR*

Trancers 3: Deth Lives

Third film of the *Trancers* series actually explains what Trancers are in the first place. How's that for procrastination? Mild diversion has Jack Deth, aided by a monstrous cyborg, materializing (via conventional time machine now) in Los Angeles of 2005 to stamp out the Trancers at their origin, as lab-mutated U.S. Marines. Semper fi, yeah right. Followed by *Trancers 4: Jack of Swords* and *Trancers 5: Sudden Death.* 🦴🦴

1992 (R) 83m/C Tim Thomerson, Melanie Smith, Andrew (Andy) Robinson, Tony Pierce, Dawn Ann Billings, Helen Hunt, Megan Ward, Stephen Macht, Telma Hopkins; **D:** C. Courtney Joyner; **W:** C. Courtney Joyner; **C:** Adolfo Bartoli; **M:** Richard Band. **VHS, Beta, LV** *PAR*

Trancers 4: Jack of Swords

Crazily inconsistent series on time-traveling cop Jack Deth now thrusts its hapless hero into

"Step through 'The Time Portal' beyond the crack in Space and Time where the fantastic world of the Future will freeze your blood with its weird horrors!"
—*The Time Travelers.*

a medieval dimension (reflecting more than anything else producer Charles Band moving his outfit to Romania) where Trancers rule, literally, as vampiric nobles feeding on the peasantry. Thanks to Tim Thomerson's expert talents as at mixing the hardboiled tough-guy pose with slapstick comedy, this has the funniest intentional jokes of the cycle. 🦴🦴🦴

1993 (R) 74m/C Tim Thomerson, Stacie Randall, Ty Miller, Terri Ivens, Mark Arnold, Clare Hartley, Alan Oppenheimer, Stephen Macht, David Nutter; **W:** Peter David; **M:** Gary Fry. **VHS, Beta** *PAR*

Trancers 5: Sudden Deth

Filmed simultaneously with *Trancers 4*, this is supposedly the final chapter of Jack Deth's saga. Underwhelming swashbuckler has future cop Deth helping rebels occupy the castle of Caliban (names were borrowed from Shakespeare's *The Tempest*). But the evil Lord Caliban is resurrected, and Sherwood Forest heroics continue rather listlessly in a talky opus that spends much time arguing, rather belatedly, for Trancer rights. Typically for a Full Moon tape, the short running time is padded out with lengthy featurettes devoted to the making of *Trancers 5* and other imponderables. 🦴🦴

1994 (R) 73m/C Tim Thomerson, Stacie Randall, Ty Miller, Terri Ivens, Mark Arnold, Clare Hartley, Alan Oppenheimer, Jeff Moldovan, Lochlyn Munro, Stephen Macht; **D:** David Nutter; **W:** Peter David; **M:** Gary Fry. **VHS, Beta** *PAR*

Transatlantic Tunnel

Semi-wishful 1930s prophecy, set after 1950, about engineer Richard Dix spearheading the construction of a giant undersea tunnel from England to America—that, among other things, will guarantee world peace. More ironic when you consider this was a remake of a 1933 German epic *Der Tunnel* (from a 1913 novel by Bernard Kellerman), which critics generally hold to be superior. The English film suffers distracting subplots about financial trickery and Dix's family problems that take the camera off the impressive futuristic designs and f/x. All versions of *The Tunnel* were banned among the Allies when WWII began. **AKA:** The Tunnel. 🦴🦴

1935 94m/B *GB* Richard Dix, Leslie Banks, Madge Evans, Helen Vinson, Sir C. Aubrey Smith, George Arliss, Walter Huston; **D:** Maurice Elvey. **VHS, Beta** *VYY, SNC, HHT*

Transformations

An interplanetary pilot battles a deadly virus that threatens life throughout the universe. Obscure space jetsam. 🦴🦴

1988 (R) 84m/C Rex Smith, Patrick Macnee, Lisa Langlois, Christopher Neame; **D:** Jay Kamen. **VHS, LV** *VTR*

Trapped in Space

Space freighter on a preprogrammed course for Venus collides with a meteor, depleting the oxygen supply. No-frills fight for survival ensues among the crew members. Low-budget production for cable TV, based on the short story "Breaking Strain" by Arthur C. Clarke, is a fairly ordinary yarn of cosmic jeopardy with just-adequate special effects. 🦴🦴

1994 (PG-13) 87m/C Jack Wagner, Jack Coleman, Craig Wasson, Sigrid Thornton, Kay Lenz; **D:** Arthur Seidelman; **W:** John Vincent Curtis, Melinda M. Snodgrass; **M:** Jay Gruska. **VHS, Beta** *PAR*

Tremors

Comic sci-fi creature feature has a tiny desert town being attacked by giant man-eating worm-type "Graboids." Luckily handymen Kevin Bacon and Fred Ward are on the scene to accidentally save the day with the help of guns-R-us couple Michael Gross and Reba McEntire. Not your average *Jaws*-on-dry-land ripoff. Just the right mixture of scares and the funny stuff as people and even entire cars are sucked under and devoured. Collector's edition laserdisc has deleted scenes, the making of, interviews, audio commentary, and is, of course, letterboxed. 🦴🦴🦴

1989 (PG-13) 96m/C Kevin Bacon, Fred Ward, Finn Carter, Michael Gross, Reba McEntire, Bibi Besch, Bobby Jacoby, Charlotte Stewart, Victor Wong, Tony Genaros; **D:** Ron Underwood; **W:** S.S. Wilson, Brent Maddock; **M:** Ernest Troost. **VHS, Beta, LV** *MCA*

Tremors 2: Aftershocks

The Graboids have resurfaced and are eating their way through Mexican oil fields. Earl Bas-

sett (Fred Ward) is back in demand as the man who can put a stop to the toothy worms' carnage (good thing, too, because all his profits from even the Graboid video game have been eaten up by dumb decisions). Joined by my-gun-is-bigger-than-your-gun Burt Gummer (Michael Gross), he sets out to once again put an end to the wriggly rampage before the damn things vomit up (a new reproductive twist) too many more wormkids. More tongue-in-cheek humor, even messier special effects, and larger quantities of worm guts than the first film. Almost as much fun. The laserdisc offers a letterboxed version. 🦴🦴🐾

1996 (PG-13) 100m/C Fred Ward, Michael Gross, Helen Shaver, Christopher Gartin, Marcelo Tubert; **D:** S.S. Wilson; **W:** S.S. Wilson, Brent Maddock. **VHS, LV** *MCA*

The Trial of the Incredible Hulk

The Hulk returns to battle organized crime and is aided by his blind superhero/lawyer friend Daredevil. Followed by *The Death of the Incredible Hulk*. Made for television. 🦴🦴

1989 96m/C Bill Bixby, Lou Ferrigno, Rex Smith, John Rhys-Davies, Marta DuBois, Nancy Everhard, Nicholas Hormann; **D:** Bill Bixby. **VHS** *VTR*

A Trip to the Moon

Primitive, but pioneering; this is perhaps the first science-fiction film. Up to this time, audiences had been thrilled by photographed events such as a train arriving at a station. Frenchman George Melies, a professional magician, opened up a whole new world of imagination with stop-motion photography, multiple exposure, and other ingenious camera tricks that gave birth to the art of special effects. This film is perhaps best known for the bit in which a rocket is launched into the eye of the Man in the Moon. Based on Jules Verne's *From the Earth to the Moon* and H. G. Wells' *First Men in the Moon*. **AKA:** A Trip to Mars; Le Voyage dans la Lune. 🦴🦴🦴🐾

When the moon hits your eye, like a.... No, when the moon's eye is hit with a big.... Anyway, that's amore. *A Trip to the Moon.*

It's going to be a long wait for that shoeshine. Bruce Willis in *12 Monkeys.*

lization running parallel to the outside world. Wielding never-defined superpowers, the bewildered hero fights video-game battles against a rogue artificial intelligence seeking to dominate mankind. The sketchy plot of this much-anticipated Disney sci fi sounds better than it plays, with more attention paid to ground-breaking computer graphics f/x than the script, which isn't halfway as clever as any given episode of the superficially similar '90s TV show *ReBoot.* Some designs by famed sf illustrator Jean "Moebius" Girard. Music by Wendy Carlos. 🎵🎵♪

1982 (PG) 96m/C Jeff Bridges, Bruce Boxleitner, David Warner, Cindy Morgan, Barnard Hughes, Dan Shor; *D:* Steven Lisberger. Nominations: Academy Awards '82: Best Costume Design, Best Sound. **VHS, Beta, LV** *DIS*

The Trouble with Dick

There's plenty of trouble with this adolescent would-be comedy. An ambitious young science-fiction writer's personal troubles (which include being involved with several over-sexed women) begin to appear in his writing. Basically a genre-movie reworking of *The Secret Life of Walter Mitty,* but nowhere near as charming as that description might suggest. The box cover displays a "Festival Winner" announcement, but don't be fooled! The story (what there is of it) gets very tedious after first five minutes. Former *Partridge Family* member Susan Dey appears as one of Dick's women. 🎵

1988 (R) 86m/C Tom Villard, Susan Dey; *D:* Gary Walkow; *M:* Roger Bourland. Sundance Film Festival '87: Grand Jury Prize. **VHS, Beta** *ACA*

12 Monkeys

Forty years after a plague wipes out 99 percent of the human population and sends the survivors underground, scientists send prisoner James Cole (Bruce Willis) to the 1990s to investigate the connection between the virus and seriously deranged fanatic Jeffrey Goines (Brad Pitt), whose father happens to be a renowned virologist. Director Terry Gilliam's demented vision is a bit tougher and less capricious than usual, and the convoluted plot and accumulated detail require a keen atten-

1902 21m/B *FR* Victor Andre, Bleuette Bernon, Georges Melies; *D:* Georges Melies. **VHS, 8mm** *GVV*

Tripods: The White Mountains

Sci-fi thriller about the takeover of Earth by alien tripods. The conquerors start controlling human minds, but not until after they are sixteen years old. Two boys seek to end the terror. 🎵♪

1984 150m/C John Shackley, Jim Baker, Cari Seel; *D:* Graham Theakston. **VHS, Beta, LV** *IME*

Tron

Computer programmer Jeff Bridges is sucked into the memory banks of a giant mainframe and exists as a warrior in a virtual-reality civi-

tion span, but as each piece of the puzzle falls into place the story becomes a fascinating sci-fi spectacle. Pitt drops the pretty-boy image with a nutzoid performance that'll make revelers stop swooning in a heartbeat. Inspired by the 1962 French short *La Jetee*. 🦴🦴🦴

1995 (R) 131m/C Bruce Willis, Madeleine Stowe, Brad Pitt, Christopher Plummer, David Morse, Frank Gorshin, John Seda; **D:** Terry Gilliam; **W:** David Peoples, Janet Peoples; **M:** Paul Buckmaster. Golden Globe Awards '96: Best Supporting Actor (Pitt); Nominations: Academy Awards '95: Best Costume Design, Best Supporting Actor (Pitt). **VHS** *MCA*

12:01

It's the *Groundhog Day* premise played for thrills. Barry Thompson (Jonathan Silverman) is an employee at a scientific research firm who finds himself reliving the same twenty-four hour period over and over again. And what a day it is—he discovers a secret project is causing the mysterious time warp, falls in love with beauteous scientist Lisa (Helen Slater) and watches as she gets murdered. Can Barry figure out how to stop what's going on and change things enough to save her? Adaptation of the short story "12:01" by Richard Lupoff, which was previously made into a short film. Made for television. 🦴🦴🦴

1993 (PG-13) 92m/C Jonathan Silverman, Helen Slater, Martin Landau, Nicolas Surovy, Jeremy Piven; **D:** Jack Sholder. **VHS, LV** *NLC, IME*

20 Million Miles to Earth

A spaceship returning from an expedition to Venus crashes on Earth, releasing a fast-growing reptilian beast that rampages throughout Athens. Another entertaining example of stop-motion animation master Ray Harryhausen's work, offering a classic battle between the monster and an elephant. 🦴🦴🦴

1957 82m/B William Hopper, Joan Taylor, Frank Puglia, John Zaremba; **D:** Nathan (Hertz) Juran. **LV** *COL*

Kirk Douglas, poised to pounce and spear the giant underwater vacuum cleaner hose (the deadliest kind) in ***20,000 Leagues Under the Sea.***

The Fifth Dimension

"**Y**ou're traveling through another dimension. A dimension not only of sight and sound, but of mind. A journey into a wondrous land whose boundaries are that of imagination. That's the signpost up ahead...your next stop: the Twilight Zone."

"Up there, up there in the vastness of space and the void that is sky. Up there is an enemy known as isolation. It sits there in the stars waiting, waiting with a patience of eons. Forever waiting...in the Twilight Zone."

—Rod Serling's opening and closing narration in "Where Is Everybody?" the October 2, 1959, pilot episode of *The Twilight Zone*.

20,000 Leagues Under the Sea

From a futuristic submarine, Captain Nemo wages war on the surface world. A shipwrecked scientist and sailor do their best to thwart Nemo's dastardly schemes. Buoyant Disney version of the Jules Verne fantasy led to a fresh crop of Verne movies, but only *Journey to the Center of the Earth* came close to this one in quality. Outstanding special effects and a lively cast, with only Paul Lukas failing to make a strong impression. A big hit, it firmly established Disney as a live-action feature studio. 🦴🦴🦴🐾

1954 127m/C Kirk Douglas, James Mason, Peter Lorre, Paul Lukas, Robert J. Wilke, Carleton Young; **D:** Richard Fleischer; **W:** Earl Fenton; **C:** Franz Planer. Academy Awards '54: Best Art Direction/Set Decoration (Color), Best Special Effects; National Board of Review Awards '54: 10 Best Films of the Year; Nominations: Academy Awards '54: Best Film Editing. **VHS, Beta, LV** *DIS*

The 27th Day

Despite some outdated philosophy and all-too-obvious preaching about the good and bad guys of the Cold War, this extremely literate film should have most viewers thinking along with the onscreen characters. An alien, piloting one of the spaceships from *Earth Vs. the Flying Saucers,* gives five mysterious capsules to five Earthlings from five different countries. Only the mind of each human can open his/her capsule. Once open, however, anyone can order the three contained radiation pellets anywhere on Earth to instantly vaporize all humans within a 1500 mile radius. Dogs, cats, and anything not human will be totally unharmed. Twenty-seven days or the death of the holder will render the capsules harmless. All five, even the "English Bathing Beauty" (as Valerie French's character was called in the press kits), want to save the world, but of course some of the evil governments involved have other ideas. Despite flaws, an intelligent film adaptation of the John Mantley novel, still to be published when Columbia Pictures purchased the rights. Mantley is credited for the screenplay. 🦴🦴🐾

1957 75m/B Gene Barry, Valerie French, George Voskovec, Arnold Moss, Stefan Schnabel, Ralph Clanton, Friedrich Ledebur, Mari Tsien, Azenath Jani; **D:** William Asher; **W:** John Mantley; **C:** Henry Freulich. **VHS** *MOV, MLB*

Twilight Zone: The Movie

Four horrific tales are anthologized in this film as a tribute to Rod Sterling and his popular television series. Three of the episodes are based on classic *Twilight Zone* scripts. "Nightmare at 20,000 Feet" is the most genuinely chilling of the group, effectively reworking the original tale of a monster glimpsed on the wing of a plane. "It's a Good Life," the story of a malevolent little boy gifted with supernatural powers, gets a bit too cartoony in places (but does feature an amusing cameo by Billy Mumy, who played the little boy in the original TV episode). "Kick the Can" is an icky-sweet tale of senior citizens who briefly regain their lost childhoods. The fourth story is a well-meaning but rather predictable blast at racism. Actor Vic Morrow was killed in a helicopter crash during filming of this episode. All in all, this *Zone* is somewhat uneven, but still a strong effort, thanks to some fine actors and directors. 🦴🦴🐾

1983 (PG) 101m/C Dan Aykroyd, Albert Brooks, Vic Morrow, Kathleen Quinlan, John Lithgow, Scatman Crothers, Kevin McCarthy, Bill Quinn, Selma Diamond, Abbe Lane, John Larroquette, Jeremy Licht, Patricia Barry, William Schallert,

TV on Tape:
The Twilight Zone

Americans first entered *The Twilight Zone* on October 2, 1959. Nearly four decades later, this "wondrous land whose boundaries are that of the imagination" still haunts us. The series attracted the best writers (Richard Matheson, Charles Beaumont) and a roster of stars (Burgess Meredith, Agnes Moorhead, Lee Marvin) and future stars (Robert Redford, Jack Klugman, William Shatner). The instantly recognizable theme music is the universal symbol of something eerie.

The Twilight Zone was created by Rod Serling, the distinguished playwright who in the golden age of live television, set the standard of excellence with such scripts as "Patterns," "Requiem for a Heavyweight," and "The Comedian." Mike Wallace was among those who thought his new series was a comedown: "For the time being and for the foreseeable future, you've given up on writing anything important for television, right?," he asked during an interview at the time.

Anything important? Some of the most memorable *The Twilight Zone* episodes were morality plays that addressed such topics as racism, the folly of war, and the wages of sin. Some of the most enduring *Zones* are not the shockers, but such nostalgic reveries as "Kick the Can" (which Steven Spielberg remade in the ill-conceived feature film) and "Walking Distance," in which harried businessman Gig Young yearns to return to "the parks and merry go rounds" of his youth. Both are available on videocassette on "Volume 5."

Still, when aficionados talk *Twilight*, they remember the episodes with the jolting O'Henry twists, such as "Time Enough at Last" (on "Volume 2"), in which bookworm Burgess Meredith chooses the wrong time to break his glasses; "Nightmare at 20,000 Ft." ("Volume 3") starring William Shatner as a mentally unstable plane passenger who doesn't really see a monster on the wing, does he?; and "To Serve Man" ("Volume 17"), about the unappetizing double meaning of a visiting extraterrestrial's book.

There are, at present, more than 20 volumes of *The Twilight Zone* available on videocassette. Each contains two episodes, with the notable exception of "Treasures of the Twilight Zone" which contains six rare episodes, including the unnerving pilot, "Where is Everybody," and two episodes not televised in more than two decades, "The Encounter" and the French short, "An Occurrence at Owl Creek Bridge," which went on to win the Academy Award. The video also contains episode promos and an interview with Serling.

Well, we could go on like this for hours. Everybody has a favorite episode. Ours, unfortunately not yet available on video, is "Living Doll," in which Telly Savalas is menaced by his stepdaughter's doll: "My name is Talky Tina, and I'm going to kill you!" Oh yes, and "Will the Real Martian Please Stand Up." And "The After Hours" with the mannequins who come to life....

1959-64/B Hugos '61, '62, '63: Dramatic Presentation. **VHS, LV** *FXV, FOX, MOV*

Burgess Meredith, Cherie Currie; *Cameos:* Billy Mumy; *D:* John Landis, Steven Spielberg, George Miller, Joe Dante; *W:* John Landis; *M:* Jerry Goldsmith. **VHS, Beta, LV** *WAR*

Two Lost Worlds

A young hero battles monstrous dinosaurs, pirates, and more in this cheapy when he and his shipmates are shipwrecked on an uncharted island. Don't miss the footage from *Captain Fury, One Billion B.C.,* and *Captain Caution,* and James Arness long before his Sheriff Dillon fame and his "big" role in *The Thing.* **WOOF!**

1950 63m/B James Arness, Laura Elliott, Bill Kennedy; *D:* Norman Dawn. **VHS, Beta** *NO*

"Hi HAL, I'm home!" Keir Dullea in *2001: A Space Odyssey.*

2001: A Space Odyssey

Director Stanley Kubrick and writer Arthur C. Clarke redefined cinematic science fiction with this masterpiece. Dispensing with many conventional narrative techniques, they told the centuries-spanning story through startling (though sometimes opaque) images. Kubrick succeeded in making space travel seem absolutely real and believable. Who cares if the plot makes no sense? The stately pace, the combination of effects and music, and the core conflict between man and machine have made the film a cultural milestone. Martin Balsam originally recorded the voice of HAL, but was replaced by Douglas Rain. Arthur C. Clarke adapted the script from his novel *The Sentinel.* Followed by a sequel, *2010: The Year We Make Contact.* Laserdisc edition is presented in letterbox format and features a special supplementary section on the making of *2001,* a montage of images from the film, production documents, memos, and photos. Also included on the disc is a NASA film entitled *Art and Reality,* which offers footage from the Voyager I and II flybys of Jupiter. 𝄢𝄢𝄢𝄢

1968 (G) 139m/C *GB* Keir Dullea, Gary Lockwood, William Sylvester, Dan Richter, Leonard Rossiter; *D:* Stanley Kubrick; *W:* Stanley Kubrick, Arthur C. Clarke; *C:* Geoffrey Unsworth; *V:* Douglas Rain. Hugos '69: Dramatic Presentation; Academy Awards '68: Best Visual Effects; National Board of Review Awards '68: 10 Best Films of the Year; Nominations: Academy Awards '68: Best Art Direction/Set Decoration, Best Director (Kubrick), Best Story & Screenplay. **VHS, Beta, LV** *MGM, CRC, FCT*

2010: The Year We Make Contact

Even though the sequel doesn't come close to the first film in style or originality, it's still fun if viewed simply as a good potboiler. The plot inventively answers most of the questions left hanging by Kubrick and Clarke. Americans and Russians unite to investigate the abandoned starship *Discovery's* decaying orbit around Jupiter and try to determine why the HAL 9000 computer sabotaged its mission years before, while signs of cosmic change are detected on and around the giant planet. 𝄢𝄢𝄢

1984 (PG) 116m/C Roy Scheider, John Lithgow, Helen Mirren, Bob Balaban, Keir Dullea, Madolyn Smith, Mary Jo Deschanel; *D:* Peter Hyams; *W:* Peter Hyams; *C:* Peter Hyams; *M:* David Shire; *V:* Douglas Rain. Hugos '85: Dramatic Presentation; Nominations: Academy Awards '84: Best Art Direction/Set Decoration, Best Makeup, Best Sound. **VHS, Beta, LV** *MGM*

UFO Secret: The Roswell Crash

The alleged crash of an alien spacecraft in Roswell, New Mexico, is probably the most famous incident in the annals of UFOlogy. Tales of the cover-up have persisted for years; many documentaries and even a movie was made on the 1947 occurrence. The research of Kevin Randle and Don Schmidt, considered by many to be the most knowledgeable about Roswell, provides lots of information, and interviews with more than a few witnesses make this in-depth report more than interesting. 1995's *Alien Autopsy: Fact or Fiction* featured the supposed body of an extraterrestrial removed from the site. 𝄢𝄢𝄢𝄒

1993 50m/C **D:** Mark Wolfe; **W:** Mark Wolfe; **M:** Gertrude Houston. **VHS** *UFO*

UFO Secrets of the Third Reich

This video uses film footage, photos, charts, and documents to explore the occult connections of Hitler's Third Reich. Tracing what Adolph felt was his heritage, from the Knights Templar through Uranus 13, a basic history of several secret societies is given. Claiming that the Reich had the knowledge and technology to build "flying discs" is one thing, but showing film footage of a BMW saucer flying around is another. That footage alone, not to mention the documentation of a raid on the secret Nazi sub/saucer base in Antarctica by Admiral Byrd, make this a not-to-be-missed free-thinker's video. 🦴🦴🦴

19?? 60m/C **D:** Thomas L. Fink; **W:** Jurgen Rathofer, Ralf Ettl. **VHS** *UFO*

UFO: Target Earth

Scientist attempts to fish flying saucer out of lake and costs studio $70,000. 🦴

1974 (G) 80m/C Nick Plakias, Cynthia Cline, Phil Erickson; **D:** Michael de Gaetano. **VHS** *MOV*

Uforia

Good ol' boy Fred Ward meets up with a UFO-obsessed girl named Arlene (Cindy Williams). Their budding romance is threatened by Ward's friend, a crooked evangelist (Harry Dean Stanton) who sees Arlene's UFO-babble as a potential money-making scheme. Stanton intends to use Arlene's prophecies of impending extraterrestrial contact to bilk his revivalist audiences. The humor is sometimes clumsy, but works often enough to make for fun viewing. Versatile Fred Ward also played writer Henry Miller in *Henry and June* and fought killer worms in the two *Tremors* movies. 🦴🦴🕊

1981 92m/C Cindy Williams, Harry Dean Stanton, Fred Ward, Hank Worden; **D:** John Binder; **W:** John Binder; **M:** Richard Baskin. **VHS, Beta** *MCA*

UFOs: Secrets of the Black World

Covering the same subject as Norio Hayakawa's *Secrets of Dreamland* tapes, this video offers even more information on Area 51, the famous site of many UFO sightings and alleged storehouse of "alien" knowledge, craft, E.T.s, and a possible cloning site. The German film crew gives us interviews with top scientists, engineers, and security personnel who claim to have seen the "goods" (including the aliens, who are in cahoots with the government). Good footage of the rather remarkable maneuvers of craft, whether they are alien or Earthmade. 🦴🦴🦴

19?? 135m/C **VHS** *UFO*

The Ultimate Warrior

Yul Brynner must defend the plants and seeds of a pioneer scientist to help replenish the world's food supply in this thriller set in 2012. 🦴🦴🕊

1975 (R) 92m/C Yul Brynner, Max von Sydow, Joanna Miles, Richard Kelton, Lane Bradbury, William Smith; **D:** Robert Clouse; **W:** Robert Clouse. **VHS, Beta** *WAR*

Ultra Warrior

Slash-and-paste job by Roger Corman's company incorporates a dizzying quantity of stock footage from earlier Corman releases (*Lords of the Deep, Battle Beyond the Stars, The Unborn,* and other gems) sluiced together into basic post-apocalyptic filler about an adventurer in radioactive 2058 who joins with friendly mutants to overthrow a bad guy whose secret weapon is a flame thrower mounted atop a giant Santa Claus. Oh, for the glory days of *Attack of the Crab Monsters*. **AKA:** Welcome to Oblivion. **WOOF!**

1992 (R) 80m/C Dack Rambo, Meshach Taylor, Clare Beresford. **VHS** *NHO*

The Unearthly Stranger

Earth scientist marries woman and decides she's from another planet. Not a '90s-style gender drama; seems she's part of an invading alien force, but really does love her Earth man. Surprisingly good low-budget sci fi. 🦴🦴🕊

1964 75m/B *GB* John Neville, Gabriella Licudi, Philip Stone, Patrick Newell, Jean Marsh, Warren Mitchell; **D:** John Krish. **VHS** *MOV*

Universal Soldier

A reporter (Ally Walker) discovers a secret government project to design perfect robo-soldiers by using the bodies of dead GIs, including tough guys Dolph Lundgren and Jean-Claude Van Damme who were killed in Vietnam. But the knowledge is going to get her killed until Van Damme has flashbacks of his past (the soldier's memories have supposedly been erased) and agrees to help her. Lundgren, not quite cured of the psychosis he had when alive, doesn't have the same compassion and goes after them both. Big-budget thriller with some good action sequences and a lot of violence. Lundgren (*Masters of the Universe*) is surprisingly good in a few over-the-top scenes. Roland Emmerich took his taste for science fiction even further with *Stargate* and *Independence Day*. 🐾🐾

1992 (R) 98m/C Jean-Claude Van Damme, Dolph Lundgren, Ally Walker, Ed O'Ross, Jerry Orbach; **D:** Roland Emmerich. **VHS, LV** *LIV*

Unknown World

A group of scientists tunnel to the center of the Earth to find a refuge from the dangers of the atomic world. Big start winds down fast. Director Terry Morse is sometimes credited as Terrell O. Morse. 🐾

1951 73m/B Bruce Kellogg, Marilyn Nash, Victor Kilian, Jim Bannon; **D:** Terry Morse; **M:** Ernest Gold. **VHS, Beta** *NOS, PSM, SNC*

Unnatural

A mad scientist creates a soulless child from the genes of a murderer and a prostitute. The child grows up to be the beautiful Hildegarde Neff, who makes a habit of seducing and destroying men. Dark, arresting film from a very popular German story. 🐾🐾🐾

1952 90m/B Hildegarde Neff, Erich von Stroheim, Karl-Heinz Boehm, Harry Meyen, Harry Helm, Denise Vernac, Julia Koschka; **D:** Arthur Maria Rabenalt. **VHS** *SNC*

Until the End of the World

Confusing but fascinating Wim Wenders road movie works best when viewed at least twice, and it's well worth the effort. It's 1999 and Sam Farber (William Hurt) needs to take some snapshots, and quick. His mom is blind, and dying. His dad (Max von Sydow) is one super-brain inventor, and has come up with a camera capable of recording images that can than be played back in a device that will allow mom to view them. A beautiful jetsetter (Solveig Dommartin), her lover (Sam Neill), a bounty hunter, a private dick, and a couple of bank robbers are all on his trail after the camera, stolen money, Hurt, or one of the other trackers. The route covers 15 cities worldwide, and ends up in the Australian outback at dad's secret lab. An about-to-explode nuclear satellite adds tension and leads to a dreamy aboriginal climax. Cinematically stunning. Wenders' humor and life philosophies are apparent throughout and every performance from the international cast is top notch. Use of high-definition video (HDTV) is a first and the soundtrack is noisily hip. **AKA:** Bis ans Ende der Welt. 🐾🐾🐾🐾

1991 (R) 158m/C William Hurt, Solveig Dommartin, Sam Neill, Max von Sydow, Ruediger Vogler, Ernie Dingo, Jeanne Moreau; **D:** Wim Wenders; **W:** Wim Wenders, Peter Carey; **M:** Graeme Revell. **VHS, Beta, LV** *WAR*

Urusei Yatsura Movie 1: Only You

Lum is a Princess of the Oni, an alien race who have come to repossess Earth. The planet's one chance is for an Earthling to beat Lum in the Oni's national sport—tag. When unlucky teenager Ataru Moroboshi is chosen he actually beats Lum. Which means he has to marry her. In Japanese with English subtitles. 🐾🐾🐾

198? 100m/C *JP* **VHS** *ANI*

Urusei Yatsura Movie 2: Beautiful Dreamer

The second full-length film based on the popular Japanimation series. The perpetually unlucky teenager Ataru Moroboshi and his classmates at Tomobiki High School find themselves reliving the day before the School Festival over and over again. It's up to Ataru's alien girlfriend Lum to solve the puzzle, which involves a magician who specializes in dreams. Funny and surreal, and more complex than you'd think from the more slapstick TV

series; the film contains some surprising references to classic science fiction like *Planet of the Apes* and *Frankenstein*. In Japanese with English subtitles, but don't let that stop you from checking this out. Great fun and beautifully animated. 🦴🦴🦴
1992 90m/C *JP* **D:** Oshii Mamoru. **VHS, LV** *CPM, INJ, ANI*

Urusei Yatsura Movie 3: Remember My Love

A magician family friend of Princess Lum put a curse on her at birth when she wasn't invited to Lum's christening (shades of "Sleeping Beauty")—that Lum would never be happy with her true love. But Ataru is the real victim. When the magician happens upon him in the new amusement park she turns him into a pink hippopotamus to spite Lum. In Japanese with English subtitles. 🦴🦴🦴
1985 93m/C *JP* **VHS, LV** *ANI*

Urusei Yatsura Movie 4: Lum the Forever

When a great cherry tree is cut down near where Lum and friends are making a movie, she mysteriously loses her horns, and with them her powers. In Japanese with English subtitles. 🦴🦴🦴
1986 94m/C *JP* **VHS, LV** *ANI, WTA, ING*

Urusei Yatsura Movie 5: The Final Chapter

Boy meets girl with Japanimation twist. Lum's fiance, Lupa, is introduced and the fate of the Earth is in Ataru's hands. Japanese with English subtitles. 🦴🦴🦴
1988 90m/C *JP* **VHS, LV** *WTA*

Urusei Yatsura Movie 6: Always My Darling

Space princess Lupica abducts Aturu in order to get the greatest love potion in the galaxy.

Lum wants him back. In Japanese with English subtitles. 🦴🦴🦴
1991 77m/C *JP* **VHS** *ANI, ING*

V

Creepy and surprisingly smart sci-fi miniseries. Advanced aliens, known as Visitors, land their saucers on Earth in the spirit of friendship, or so they claim. But their human-like appearance is a facade; hiding their reptilian faces behind fake skin masks, the Visitors basically want to consume Earth's resources, including fillet of *Homo sapiens*. The first half of this two-parter is sf in the best *Twilight Zone* tradition, comparing alien invasion to U.S. foreign policy in Central America and savaging the nation's media brainwash and pop-culture attitudes (a high-school band welcomes the Visitors with the *Star Wars* theme). Once hero newsman Marc Singer learns the Visitors' true intentions, a resistance movement is born, and the saga rather disappointingly turns into a standard blow-up-the-bad-guys action/adventure. Robert Englund, later to be enshrined as Freddy in the *Nightmare on Elm Street* movies, is a cast standout as a benign Visitor. Sequelled by miniseries conclusion *V: The Final Battle,* and a short-lived TV series. 🦴🦴🦴
1983 190m/C Marc Singer, Jane Badler, Faye Grant, Robert Englund, Michael Durrell, Peter Nelson, Neva Patterson, Andrew Prine, Richard Herd, Rafael Campos; **D:** Kenneth Johnson; **W:** Kenneth Johnson. **VHS** *WAR, MOV*

V: The Final Battle

Followup to the popular miniseries *V,* centering on the intrigue among the human underground resistance fighting those man-eating lizards from outer space, who have effectively conquered humanity through economic and cultural imperialism more so than death rays. Unfortunately, the interplanetary intrigue leans heavily toward the prime-time soap operatics of *Dynasty* (complete with a Brit-accented space-bitch clone of Joan Collins). Climax—in which one character simply uses the Force or something to save the world—is so lame even the lowly paperback novelization didn't dare replicate it. While the Visitors are

"Torture, murder, mutilation! Brilliant! Absolutely brilliant!"

—James Woods marvels over foreign TV programming in *Videodrome.*

indeed driven off, they returned to further torment mankind, though not for very long, in a subsequent, short-lived TV series. 🎬🎬

1984 285m/C Marc Singer, Robert Englund, Michael Ironside, Jane Badler; **D:** Richard T. Heffron. **VHS** *WAR*

The Valley of Gwangi

The genesis of this idea—cowboys vs. dinosaurs—goes back to a 1942 unproduced project by Willis O'Brien, the man who created King Kong. But it took Ray Harryhausen's stop-motion effects to bring it finally to the screen. The climactic fight between an allosaurus and an elephant is some of his best work, and the whole film stands up well. If it lacks the magic and poetry of *Jason and the Argonauts,* it's still grand stuff for kids. 🎬🎬🎬

1969 (G) 95m/C James Franciscus, Gila Golan, Richard Carlson, Laurence Naismith, Freda Jackson; **D:** James O'Connolly; **W:** William Bast. **VHS, Beta, LV** *WAR*

Vampire Vixens from Venus

Loads of cheap but juicy special effects and enough boobs for the most demanding T&A aficionado. Three ultra-ugly aliens grow breasts and transform themselves into gorgeous babes in order to perpetrate an intergalactic drug smuggling caper. The drug they need is a derivative of the "life" essence of men, giving the three (Theresa Lynn, Leslie Glass, and "60 Foot Centerfold" J.J. North) reason to shed their threads before draining every last drop from their previously happy-as-hell victims, turning them into quivering, gooey, emaciated husks. Naturally, the outer-space DEA, as well as local uniforms, are hot on the trail. Features guest appearances by recently retired scream queen Michelle Bauer and loopy comic Charlie Callas. 🎬

1994 90m/C Leon Head, Theresa Lynn, J.J. North, Leslie Glass, John Knox, Michelle (McClellan) Bauer, Charlie Callas; **D:** Tewd A. Bohus; **W:** Tewd A. Bohus; **C:** Curtis Mattikow; **M:** Ariel Shallit. **VHS** *SHR*

Varan the Unbelievable

A chemical experiment near a small island in the Japanese archipelago disturbs a prehistoric monster beneath the water. The awakened monster spreads terror on the island. Most difficult part of this movie is deciding what the rubber monster model is supposed to represent. **AKA:** Daikaiju Baran; The Monster Baran. 🎬

1961 70m/B *JP* Myron Healey, Tsuruko Kobayashi; **D:** Inoshiro Honda. **VHS, Beta** *NOS, VCI*

The Vengeance of Fu Manchu

In this, the third film featuring Christopher Lee as the evil Fu Manchu, the evil doctor is back in his native China, where he forms an alliance with the Mafia. In addition, just to keep things interesting, Fu abducts a surgeon and forces him to turn a prisoner into the exact double of the intrepid Sir Nayland Smith of Scotland Yard. The series was getting a bit predictable by now, but *Vengeance* still retains some of that old Manchu charm. 🎬🎬🎬

1967 m/C *GB* Christopher Lee, Tsai Chin, Douglas Wilmer, H. Marion Crawford, Horst Frank, Maria Rohm, Tony Ferrer; **D:** Jeremy Summers; **W:** Peter Welbeck; **C:** John von Kotze. **VHS** *NO*

Venus Rising

After a rocky start, this one wobbles along for 90 minutes and collapses at a weak conclusion. Although it's technically sf, the film lacks special effects or a strong vision of the near future (in this case Hawaii). It also lacks a decent plot and interesting characters. Toss in continuity mistakes, a non-exploitative approach to what might have been pure exploitation, and you've got a real mess. In the early 21st century, Eve (Audie England) escapes from a prison island and tries to make a place for herself in an amorphously authoritarian society. Billy Wirth is the ex-con who's hired to capture her. Another escapee, a murder, a suicide, and some cliched virtual reality stuff fill out the running time. Be forewarned—Morgan Fairchild's role is very small. 🎬

1995 (R) 91m/C Audie England, Costas Mandylor, Billy Wirth, Morgan Fairchild; **D:** Leora Barish; **W:** Leora Barish. **VHS** *COL*

The Venus Wars

When the planet Venus collides with an ice asteroid the resulting transformation makes

the planet capable of sustaining human life. But when a group from Earth arrives to colonize Venus they bring all the worst traits of humanity with them. Animated; in Japanese with English subtitles. 🦴🦴🦴

1989 104m/C *JP* **VHS, LV** *INJ, CPM, WTA*

Videodrome

Director David Cronenberg continues his exploration of both the evolution and the deterioration of the flesh. Cable programmer (James Woods) becomes hooked on the pirate TV show *Videodrome,* which delivers loads of real sex, real torture, and real murder. Along with the fun, the show is having an effect on his love life (with Deborah "Blondie" Harry), genetically altering his body (turning him into a human VCR) and blurring his view of reality. With his newly formed stomach orifice, he is easily programmed by organic videocassettes. While another director's use of such disgust-

ing images might be off putting, Cronenberg's particularly sick fantasies tend to fascinate and demand further viewing. Special effects by Rick Baker. Stick around for the last scene, it may be the most perfect one you'll ever see. All hail the new flesh! 🦴🦴🦴

1983 87m/C *CA* James Woods, Deborah Harry, Sonja Smits, Peter Dvorsky; *D:* David Cronenberg; *W:* David Cronenberg; *M:* Howard Shore. Genie Awards '84: Best Director (Cronenberg). **VHS, Beta, LV** *MCA*

Village of the Damned

In some ways, this British production is another take on the *Invasion of the Body Snatchers* theme—infiltration by aliens who are like us but not like us. It can also be seen an early example of post-World War II generational conflicts. But forget interpretations. This is simply one of the best sf thrillers ever made. When an English village is subjected to a mysterious event, several unusual children are conceived. Later, they demonstrate remark-

" Wait a minute...I always keep it right here in my left breast pocket." James Woods searches for his pen in *Videodrome.*

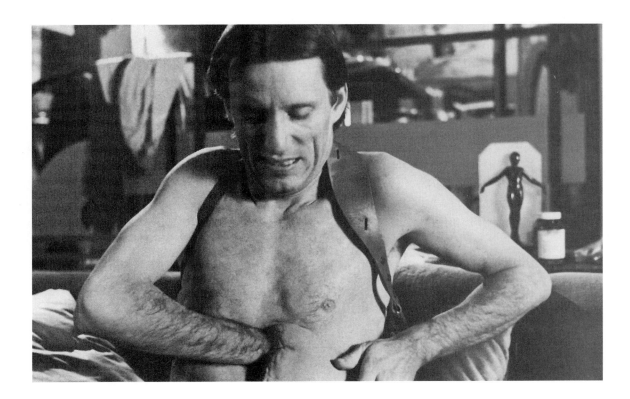

able, threatening powers. Casting the urbane George Sanders in the lead is unusual but effective. This is one of his best roles, and he brings a restrained emotional power to the story's conclusion. Pay no attention to the dated soundtrack. From the novel *The Midwich Cuckoos* by John Wyndham. Followed by a sequel, *The Children of the Damned,* in 1964 and an atrocious 1995 remake. 🦴🦴🦴🦴

1960 78m/B *GB* George Sanders, Barbara Shelley, Martin Stephens, Laurence Naismith, Michael C. Goetz, Michael C. Gwynne; *D:* Wolf Rilla; *W:* Wolf Rilla, Stirling Silliphant, George Barclay; *C:* Geoffrey Faithfull. **VHS, Beta, LV** *MGM, MLB*

Village of the Damned

What a yawner! The quiet town of Midwich, California, has been enveloped by a strange force that impregnates the local women. The albino children born of this incident have disturbing telepathic powers that they display through their bright orange and red eyes—

supposedly precipitating a plot to take control. The characters have no personalities, the dialogue is sloppy and stilted, the plot comes to a slapdash conclusion, and the pedestrian special effects appear to have been tailored for the small screen. Pale remake of the 1960 British horror classic, which was based on John Wyndham's novel *The Midwich Cuckoos,* fails to capture the eeriness of its predecessor. The children's glowing eyes make them look about as threatening as Nintendo addicts. 🦴

1995 (R) 98m/C Christopher Reeve, Kirstie Alley, Linda Kozlowski, Mark Hamill, Meredith Salenger, Michael Pare, Peter Jason, Constance Forslund; *D:* John Carpenter; *W:* John Carpenter, David Himmelstein; *C:* Gary B. Kibbe; *M:* John Carpenter, Dave Davies. **VHS, LV** *MCA*

Village of the Giants

"Hey, those are my ducks!" You can't blame Tommy Kirk for getting so excited. These web-footed behemoths shaking their tail-feathers on the dance floor have ingested size-enhanc-

ing "goop." Beau Bridges and some bad teens looking for kicks steal the stuff, "zoom to supersize" (scream the ads) and take over the town, imposing curfew on the adults. Ronny Howard, a long way from Mayberry, costars as Genius, who invented the formula, with Johnny Crawford, son of "The Rifleman," as one of the good teens who try to cut Bridges down to size. With music by the Beau Brummels, who were more believable as animated characters on *The Flintstones.* Based on H.G. Wells' *The Food of the Gods.* Forget the smartass *Mystery Science Theater 3000* treatment this received. It's a lot of fun on its own. 🦴 🦴 🦴

1965 82m/C Ron Howard, Johnny Crawford, Tommy Kirk, Beau Bridges, Freddy Cannon, Beara Bridge, Robert Random; *D:* Bert I. Gordon; *W:* Alan Cailou; *C:* Paul Vogel; *M:* Jack Nitzsche. **VHS, Beta** *NLC, MLB, SUE*

The Vindicator

This Canadian pic seems like a prototype for the *Robocop* series, right down to an elaborate cyborg costume designed by Stan Winston's studio. Researcher's colleagues arrange for him to roast in a lab explosion (apparently for the offense of being the only scientist around who isn't a junkie, pervert, sadist, or corporate swine), then encase his mangled body in an exoskeleton intended for Mars astronauts, a suit with built-in life support, super-strength and crush-kill-destroy automated defense mode. 'Frankenstein' (as the credits list him) isn't happy about the lifestyle change and escapes, hunted by female mercenary Pam Grier. Plot is violent and comic-bookish, but good for its breed, with slam-bang action and satisfying f/x. **AKA:** Frankenstein '88. 🦴 🦴 🦴

1985 (R) 92m/C *CA* Terri Austin, Richard Cox, David McIlwraith, Pam Grier; *D:* Jean-Claude Lord. **VHS, Beta** *FOX*

VIP, My Brother Superman

The Vips are modern-day descendants of superbeings about to become legends in their own times. SuperVip is broad of chest and pure in spirit while his brother MiniVip possesses only limited powers. From the creator of *Allegro Non Troppo* comes this enticing, amusing piece of animation. 🦴 🦴 🦴

1990 90m/C *D:* Bruno Bozzetto. **VHS** *EXP, TPV*

Virtual Assassin

If the *Project Shadowchaser* series leaves you hungry for yet more Canadian sci-fi *Die Hard* ripoffs, you are welcome to this mongrel, sort of a *Die Hard Drive* in which a ham villain leads his multicultural gang (they look like the Village People with guns) to take over a research lab and steal a 'biological' computer virus. Naturally, the drunken janitor (Michael Dudikoff) just happens to be an ex-cop with a score to settle. Inanity wastes some decent f/x and cool gadgets, include a police robot who's a neat riff on *Robocop*'s ED-209. **AKA:** Cyberjack. 🦴 🦴 🦴

1995 (R) 99m/C *CA JP* Michael Dudikoff, Brion James, Jon Cuthbert, Suki Kaiser, James Thom; *D:* Robert Lee; *W:* Eric Poppen. **VHS, LV** *TTC*

Virtuosity

Parker Barnes, an ex-cop with a tragic past, is sprung from his unjust imprisonment when he agrees to help capture computer-generated killer Sid 6.7. Sid has escaped from cyberspace with the help of his mad-scientist creator, and goes on a murderous rampage in 1997 Los Angeles. This virtual-reality bad guy has a personality composed of some 200 serial killers and criminal minds (including the murderer of Parker's wife), so Parker's got his work cut out for him. Conveniently, criminal-behavior psychologist Madison Carter (Kelly Lynch) is around to lend her expert advice. Sid taunts Parker with recollections of his wife's murder and tries to frame him for additional crimes. Sid enjoys the game and especially likes Parker as an adversary. The silly plot is somewhat overcome by strong performances from Russell Crowe as the deliciously evil Sid (his symphony of screams is truly sadistic), and Washington as the unflinchingly noble hero. Director Brett Leonard is a cyberspace veteran, previously helming *The Lawnmower Man.* 🦴 🦴 🦴

1995 (R) 105m/C Denzel Washington, Russell Crowe, Kelly Lynch, Stephen Spinella, William Forsythe, Louise Fletcher, William Fichtner, Costas Mandylor, Kevin J. O'Connor; *D:* Brett Leonard; *W:* Eric Bernt; *C:* Gale Tattersall; *M:* Christopher Young. **VHS, Beta** *PAR*

"Teenagers zoom to supersize! See them burst out of their clothes and bust up a town!"

—*Village of the Giants.*

Exeter (hardy har har) are malevolent aliens in human form. Impoverished production values even manage to exclude any sight of their saucer. 🎵

1987 93m/C Marcus Vaughter, Johanna Grika, Joel Hile, Nicole Rio; *D:* Rick Sloane. **VHS, Beta** *TWE*

Voyage of the Rock Aliens

The extravagantly talentless Pia Zadora is Dee-Dee, a small-town girl who yearns to be a singer. Her town ("Speelburgh"—get it? Get it?) is visited by rock-musician aliens who give her her big break. This truly awful film wants to be a heartwarming musical fantasy, but ends up falling on its face. Jermaine Jackson does a tiresome dance-number with Pia, Pia can't act, the few decent actors (like Michael Berryman of *The Hills Have Eyes*) are wasted as stereotypical small-town "eccentrics," Pia can't act, and...well, she can't sing either, frankly. Avoid. **WOOF!**

1987 97m/C Pia Zadora, Tom Nolan, Craig Sheffer, Rhema, Ruth Gordon, Michael Berryman, Jermaine Jackson; *D:* James Fargo; *W:* S. James Guidotti, Edward Gold, Charles Hairston; *C:* Gilbert Taylor; *M:* Jack White. **VHS, Beta** *PSM*

Voyage to the Bottom of the Sea

Before he capsized the Poseidon and lit the *Towering Inferno*, Irwin Allen, the master of disaster, made his very best film. Take the plunge with the intrepid crew of the Seaview, an experimental atomic submarine that is put to the ultimate test when the Earth is endangered by a burning radiation belt. Walter Pidgeon stars as Admiral Harriman Nelson, whom the crew comes to doubt his sanity when he wants to launch a missile into the belt. On board are Peter Lorre as a trustworthy marine biologist, Joan Fontaine as a not-so-trustworthy scientist, Michael Ansara as a religious fanatic who believes the blazing sky is God's will. We dream of a fetchingly uniformed Barbara "Jeannie" Eden dancing on the mess hall tabletops. Frankie Avalon is also on board to sing the title tune. Much better than the TV series that ran this movie's good name aground. 🎵🎵🎵

1961 106m/C Walter Pidgeon, Joan Fontaine, Barbara Eden, Peter Lorre, Robert Sterling, Michael Ansara,

Stop playing with those electrical wires or you'll put your *other* eye out, Big Guy! Dean Parkin in *The War of the Colossal Beast*.

Virus

After nuclear war and plague destroy civilization, a small group of people gather in Antarctica and struggle with determination to carry on life. A look at man's genius for self-destruction and his endless hope. **AKA:** Fukkatsu no Hi. 🎵🎵

1982 (PG) 102m/C *JP* George Kennedy, Sonny Chiba, Glenn Ford, Robert Vaughn, Stuart Gillard, Stephanie Faulkner, Ken Ogata, Bo Svenson, Olivia Hussey, Chuck Connors, Edward James Olmos; *D:* Kinji Fukasaku. **VHS, Beta** *VTR, MED*

Visitants

Cheap, chintzy spoof in which a stupid '50s teenager discovers that his neighbors, an uptight married couple named Lubbock and

Frankie Avalon; **D:** Irwin Allen; **W:** Irwin Allen, Charles Bennett; **C:** Winton C. Hoch. **VHS, Beta, LV** *FOX, FCT*

Voyage to the Planet of Prehistoric Women

Astronauts journey to Venus, where they discover a race of gorgeous, telepathic women led by Mamie Van Doren who wear sea-shell bikinis and worship a pterodactyl. This was the third film to incorporate footage from the (much better) Russian science-fiction film *Planeta Burg (Planet of Storms)*, and the second one by Roger Corman (his 1965 *Voyage to the Prehistoric Planet* cannibalized the Russian flick as well). As you might expect, it's pretty much incomprehensible, but fans of "prehistoric women" movies (and Mamie Van Doren) will probably enjoy it. The film was directed (and narrated) by Peter Bogdanovich—his directorial debut—under the pseudonym Derek Thomas. This retread is no relation to the 1966 cheapie *Women of the Prehistoric Planet*. **AKA:** Gill Woman; Gill Women of Venus. 🎵 🎵

1968 78m/C Mamie Van Doren, Mary Mark, Paige Lee, Aldo Roman; **D:** Peter Bogdanovich; **W:** Henry Ney. **VHS** *SNC*

Voyage to the Prehistoric Planet

In the year 2020, an expedition to Venus is forced to deal with dinosaurs and other perils. This was the first of two hatchet-job remakes of the Russian sf film *Planeta Burg* (the second was Peter Bogdanovich's 1968 *Voyage to the Planet of the Prehistoric Women*). For this go-round, executive producer Roger Corman edited in some new scenes featuring Basil Rathbone (best known for his portrayal of Sherlock Holmes) and Faith Domergue, as well as a few from his own *Queen of Blood,* which coincidentally also starred Rathbone and also was based on an acquired Russian sf film. **AKA:** Voyage to a Prehistoric Planet. 🎵 🎵

1965 80m/C Basil Rathbone, Faith Domergue, Marc Shannon, Christopher Brand; **D:** John Sebastian. **VHS** *NOS, SNC*

War in Space

Powerful U.N. Space Bureau Starships and UFOs band together to battle alien invaders among the volcanoes and deserts of Venus. 🎵

1977 91m/C *JP* Kensaku Marita, Yuko Asano, Ryo Ikebe. **VHS, Beta** *VDA*

The War of the Colossal Beast

This sequel to *The Amazing Colossal Man* finds the seventy-foot Colonel Manning even angrier at the attempts to kill him than he was in the first film. So he wreaks more havoc until scolded by his sister into committing suicide for being such a troublemaker. Cheesy special effects but good for a laugh. **AKA:** The Terror Strikes. 🎵 🎵

1958 68m/B Dean Parkin, Sally Fraser, Russ Bender, Roger Pace, Charles Stewart; **D:** Bert I. Gordon. **VHS** *COL*

War of the Gargantuas

Tokyo is once again the boxing ring for giant monsters. This time, instead of pseudo-dinosaurs, we have a not-so-jolly green giant called the gargantua. The green meanie emerges from the ocean to save a ship from a rubbery giant octopus before eating the crew (and spitting out their clothes afterwards). Suave American scientist-type Russ Tamblyn speculates on whether the beast is the adult version of a young ape-like critter he and his colleagues had found and lost some years before. When a gentle "brown gargantua" appears, Tamblyn decides that it's his original subject, who "may have scraped off some flesh on a rock" during his escape from the lab and thus engendered a clone of itself (?!). When the green gargantua won't mend its people-eating ways, its brother engages it in an apocalyptic, building-busting battle. This is fairly strange even for a Japanese monster flick. One scene in a nightclub features an incredible, jaw-droppingly awful song called "The Words Get Stuck in My Throat," which is alone worth the rental price. This is the sequel to *Frankenstein Conquers the World*. **AKA:** Furankenshutain No Kaiju Sanda Tai Gailah; Sanda Tai Gailah; Duel of the Gargantuas; Frankenstein Monsters: Sanda Vs. Gairath. 🎵 🎵

1970 (G) 92m/C *JP* Russ Tamblyn, Kumi Mizuno, Kenji Sahara, Jun Tazaki, Kenji Sahara, Jun Tazaki; **D:** Inoshiro Honda; **W:** Inoshiro Honda, Kaoru Mabuchi; **C:** Hajime Koizumi; **M:** Akira Ifukube. **VHS, LV** *PAR*

"If they're mortal, they have mortal weaknesses. They'll be stopped somehow."

—Forrester (Gene Barry) in
The War of the Worlds.

E.T.'s *first* visit was nothing to phone home about. There's no Elliott among this hostile group. *War of the Worlds.*

War of the Robots

A dying alien civilization kidnaps two brilliant Earth scientists in the hope that they'll help it survive. 🎵

1978 99m/C Antonio Sabato, Melissa Long, James R. Stuart. **VHS, Beta, LV** *VCI*

War of the Wizards

Low-budget sci-fi thriller about an alien woman with supernatural powers who comes to take over the Earth. But, lucky for all Earthlings, she's challenged by a hero-type just in the nick of time. **AKA:** The Phoenix. 🎵🎵

1981 (PG) 90m/C Richard Kiel; **D:** Richard Caan. **VHS, Beta** *NO*

The War of the Worlds

H.G. Wells' classic novel of the invasion of Earth by Martians, updated to 1950s California, with spectacular special effects of destruction caused by the Martian war machines. Pretty scary and tense; based more on Orson Welles' radio broadcast than on the book. Still very popular; hit the top 20 in sales when released on video. Classic thriller later made into a TV series. Produced by George Pal, who brought the world much sci fi, including *The Time Machine, Destination Moon,* and *When Worlds Collide,* and who appears here as a street person. 🎵🎵🎵

1953 85m/C Gene Barry, Ann Robinson, Les Tremayne, Lewis Martin, Robert Cornthwaite, Sandro Giglio, **Cameo:** George Pal; **D:** Byron Haskin. Academy Awards '53: Best Special Effects; Nominations: Academy Awards '53: Best Film Editing, Best Sound. **VHS, Beta, LV** *PAR*

WarGames

Teen computer hacker, thinking that he's sneaking an advance look at a new line of video games, breaks into the U.S. missile-defense system and challenges it to a bout of Global Thermonuclear Warfare. The game

might just turn out to be the real thing if the boy can't stop it. Though heavily grounded in the Reagan Cold-War years, this remains one of the first and best of the cyberflicks; oft-imitated formula of high-tech whiz kids getting into trouble comes on like gangbusters, though the plot slackens near the end. John Badham signed on late in the project, taking the directorial reins from Martin Brest. 🎝🎝🎝
1983 (PG) 110m/C Matthew Broderick, Dabney Coleman, John Wood, Ally Sheedy, Barry Corbin; **D:** John Badham; **W:** Walter F. Parkes, Lawrence Lasker; **C:** William A. Fraker. Nominations: Academy Awards '83: Best Cinematography, Best Original Screenplay, Best Sound. **VHS, Beta, LV** FOX

Warlords

Clone soldier David Carradine and his organic computer (an ugly jive-talking head) join with a scrappy girl and battle mutant hordes in a post-apocalyptic desert. Filmmaker Fred Olen Ray maintains a sense of humor throughout this amateurish action drivel, but most viewers may conclude that the joke's on them. 🎝
1988 (R) 87m/C David Carradine, Sid Haig, Ross Hagen, Fox Harris, Robert Quarry, Victoria Sellers, Brinke Stevens, Dawn Wildsmith; **D:** Fred Olen Ray. **VHS, Beta, LV** VMK

Warlords of the 21st Century

Bandit gang speed around the galaxy in an indestructible battle cruiser. Then the boys are challenged by a space lawman. Gratuitously violent action pic lacking real action. Filmed on planet New Zealand. **AKA:** Battletruck. 🎝♭
1982 91m/C Michael Beck, Annie McEnroe, James Wainwright; **D:** Harley Cokliss; **W:** Harley Cokliss, Irving Austin, John Beech. **VHS, Beta** SUE

Warlords 3000

In the future, Earth is a barren wasteland ravaged by raging electrical storms. Deadly cancers are rampant and the few people who have survived take their comfort in a hallucinogenic drug that provides a temporary pleasure and a permanent madness. Drug lords control the planet but one man is out to eliminate the scum and save the future. 🎝♭
1993 (R) 92m/C Jay Roberts Jr., Denise Marie Duff, Steve Blanchard, Wayne Duvall; **D:** Faruque Ahmed; **W:** Ron Herbst, Faruque Ahmed. **VHS** COL

Warning from Space

Aliens visit Earth to warn of impending cosmic doom. When it becomes apparent that the one-eyed starfish look is off-putting, they assume human form. Japanese sci fi. **AKA:** The Mysterious Satellite; The Cosmic Man Appears in Tokyo; Space Men Appear in Tokyo; Unknown Satellite Over Tokyo; Uchujin Tokyo Ni Arawaru. 🎝♭
1956 87m/B JP Toyomi Karita, Keizo Kawasaki, Isao Yamagata, Shozo Nanbu, Buntaro Miake, Mieko Nagai, Kiyoko Hirai; **D:** Koji Shima. **VHS** NOS, SMW, SNC

Warrior of the Lost World

Ginty and his talking motorcycle must destroy the evil Omega Force, who tyrannically rule the world of the postnuke future et cetera, et cetera. One-size-fits-all premise, horrible f/x, miserable direction. And those are its good points. Only for really hard-core Donald Pleasence fans or those trying to trace Persis Khambatta's career after the first *Star Trek* movie. **WOOF!**
1984 90m/C Robert Ginty, Persis Khambatta, Donald Pleasence; **D:** David Worth. **VHS, Beta** NO

The Wasp Woman

Director Roger Corman is at it again, this time dishing up the tale of a female cosmetics mogul (Susan Cabot) who unwisely tests a beauty-potion made of wasp enzymes on herself. As a result, she starts moonlighting as a hokey-looking wasp-headed fiend. That'll teach her! Anthony Eisley is her prospective boyfriend, who unfortunately seems to prefer her assistant Barboura Morris. Not what you'd call blindingly original, it's still good schlocky fun. Interestingly, the monster in the film was a reversal of the one depicted on the movie's poster, which showed a sultry woman's face attached to a humongous wasp. Extant prints have added footage shot to fill television time slots. *Evil Spawn* (1987) was an unofficial remake. 🎝♭
1959 84m/B Susan Cabot, Anthony Eisley, Barboura Morris, Michael Marks, William Roerick, Frank Gerstle, Bruno Ve Sota, Frank Wolff; **D:** Roger Corman; **W:** Leo Gordon; **C:** Harry Newman. **VHS** NOS, RHI, SNC

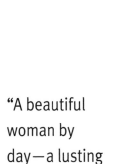

"A beautiful woman by day—a lusting queen wasp by night."

—The Wasp Woman.

for the mythical Dryland, unknown since the polar ice caps melted, flooding the Earth. Forming an uneasy alliance with Helen (Jeanne Tripplehorne) and her young adopted daughter Enola (Tina Majorino), who has the map to Dryland tattooed on her back, the Mariner searches the oceans for Dryland. The bad guys are the Smokers, led by the evil Deacon played by Dennis Hopper, who can do these roles in his sleep. They too want to find Dryland, and want the map (and hence the girl) in order to find it. Of course, Mariner grows found of Helen and the girl, and ultimately must rescue them from the Smokers. The action, sets, and effects are stunning, but a poor script ultimately sinks this fish story. 🐟🐟

1995 (PG-13) 135m/C Kevin Costner, Dennis Hopper, Jeanne Tripplehorn, Tina Majorino, Michael Jeter, R.D. Call, Robert Joy; *D:* Kevin Reynolds; *W:* Peter Rader, Marc Norman, David N. Twohy; *C:* Dean Semler; *M:* James Newton Howard. Nominations: Academy Awards '95: Best Sound; Golden Raspberry Awards '95: Worst Picture, Worst Actor (Costner). **VHS, LV** *MCA*

Wavelength

Predating all the 'Alien Autopsy' tomfoolery by a good decade, this has rocker Robert Carradine's psychic girlfriend picking up hypersonic distress signals—sounds like whales—from childlike aliens, recovered from a UFO crash site and kept on ice in a secret government base beneath the Hollywood hills (script takes pains to make that geographic novelty quite plausible). Fun, enthusiastically cheap sci fi. Compare the ending of this with *Starman*...separated at birth? Soundtrack by Tangerine Dream. 🐟🐟🐟

1983 (PG) 87m/C Robert Carradine, Cherie Currie, Keenan Wynn; *D:* Mike Gray; *W:* Mike Gray; *M:* Tangerine Dream. **VHS, Beta, LV** *SUE, VTR*

Waxwork 2: Lost in Time

Sequel to the ostensibly non-sf *Waxwork*, in which monsters in an infamous waxworks museum turned out to be real. On trial for the fiends' crimes, a heroic young couple must travel through a bizarre time machine and enter other universes ("God's Nintendo game") where horror and sci-fi movie charac-

"We spent $150 million on this?" Kevin Costner should have cut bait on **Waterworld.**

Waterworld

The Man From Atlantis meets *Mad Max.* Industry knives sharpened with glee before release, with some insiders calling this luck-impaired project "Fishtar" and "Kevin's Gate." With an estimated $150 million budget, the film must look to overseas sales and secondary markets to make any money. Most of the budget does seem to have ended up on screen, which makes for a visually striking, and at times daunting, film. The ocean vistas and action scenes on water are spectacular. Costner, who did just about everything but cater the meals, stars as Mariner, a mutant who has developed the ability to breathe underwater via gills in order to survive in this water-covered world. He reluctantly helps human survivors search

ters actually do exist. It's a pretext to recreate scenes from past genre flicks, from the gothic horror of *Frankenstein* to the high-tech gore of *Alien,* and it all hangs together like an explosion in a cliche factory. An end title boasts "Filmed entirely in the fourth dimension." 🦴

1991 (R) 104m/C Zach Galligan, Alexander Godunov, Bruce Campbell, Michael Des Barres, Monika Schnarre; *D:* Anthony Hickox. **VHS** *LIV*

into a toadlike creature and basically solves all their problems in a zany kind of way. Oingo Boingo did the amusing theme song. Rather puzzlingly, the film inspired a cable series that didn't get off the ground until the '90s. 🦴🦴🦴

1985 (PG-13) 94m/C Kelly Le Brock, Anthony Michael Hall, Ilan Mitchell-Smith, Robert Downey Jr., Bill Paxton, Suzanne Snyder, Judie Aronson; *D:* John Hughes; *W:* John Hughes; *C:* Matthew F. Leonetti; *M:* Ira Newborn. **VHS, Beta, LV** *MCA*

Weird Science

One of the stranger and more amusing of John Hughes' '80s teen comedies. Anthony Michael Hall and his fellow nerd Ilan Mitchell-Smith use a very special kind of software to create the ideal woman, in the person of Kelly Le Brock. The leering implications of these two junior Frankensteins "making a woman" are thankfully glossed over; Le Brock is a wise and mature being who proves to be a dweeb's best friend. She turns Hall's bullying older brother

Welcome Back Mr. Fox

An award-winning science-fiction short wherein an obnoxious movie producer cheats death by being cryogenically frozen, and then wakes up years later no wiser for the experience. Suitably, he receives his comeuppance. 🦴🦴🦴

1983 21m/C E.D. Phillips, Gustav Vintas; *D:* Walter W. Pitt III. **VHS, Beta** *NO*

Anthony Michael Hall and Ilan Mitchell-Smith haven't *quite* figured out the appeal of push-up bras—but they sense that it's good. *Weird Science.*

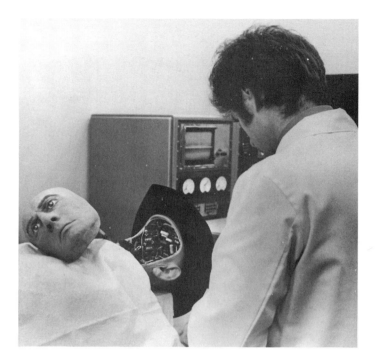

The ULTIMATE face-off. A mechanical Yul Brynner in *Westworld*.

Wes Craven Presents Mind Ripper

Yet another *Alien*-type rip-off in which a secret government experiment to produce self-healing super soldiers goes awry. The mad scientists who created the beast become trapped in an abandoned nuclear site, and must kill the creature. The scientists are picked off one by one with the usual gross special effects. Lance Henriksen (once again in material far below his worth) plays the good-hearted lead scientist who left the experiment when he discovered its violent purpose, but is forced to return now that the creature has run amok. The film does an adequate job of retreading very familiar ground. The problem is it is so predictable (right down to the 'it must be dead this time' ending), why bother to watch it (or film it) again. You may be enticed by horror maven Wes Craven's name on the film (and you may wonder how it got there). Craven executive produced a script by his son, Jonathan Craven.

There is definitely some nepotism involved here. **AKA:** Mind Ripper. 🦴 ᵛ
1995 (R) 90m/C Lance Henriksen, John Diehl, Natasha Gregson Wagner, Dan Blom, Claire Stansfield; **D:** Joe Gayton; **W:** Jonathan Craven, Phil Mittleman; **C:** Fernando Arguelles; **M:** J. Peter Robinson. **VHS** *AVE*

Westworld

Michael Crichton wrote and directed this story of Delos, an adult vacation resort of the future which offers the opportunity to live in various fantasy worlds where guests' every need and fantasy are serviced by lifelike robots. James Brolin and Richard Benjamin are businessmen who choose the western fantasy world. When an electrical malfunction occurs, the robots begin to go berserk, and the vacation turns deadly. Despite low-end special effects, the taut script and good performances make this a solid thriller. The film was an early attempt at the technology-runs-amok story that Crichton would make famous in *Jurassic Park*. Yul Brynner is perfect as the menacing western gunslinger whose skills become all too real. Followed by a sequel, *Futureworld* (1976). 🦴🦴🦴 ᵛ
1973 (PG) 90m/C Yul Brynner, Richard Benjamin, James Brolin, Dick Van Patten, Majel Barrett, Norman Bartold, Alan Oppenheimer; **D:** Michael Crichton; **W:** Michael Crichton; **C:** Gene Polito. **VHS, Beta, LV** *MGM*

What Waits Below

A scientific expedition encounters a lost race living in caves in South America. Good cast, bad acting, and lousy script. Might have been much better. 🦴 ᵛ
1983 (PG) 88m/C Timothy Bottoms, Robert Powell, Lisa Blount; **D:** Don Sharp. **VHS, Beta** *LIV*

When Dinosaurs Ruled the Earth

When *One Million Years B.C.* ruled the box office, the Brits cranked out a few additional lively prehistoric fantasies. A sexy cavegirl, exiled because of her blond hair convinces superstitious tribe that she's bad luck, acquires a cave-beau and a dinosaur guardian. This gets a clever plug at the climax of *Jurassic Park*, but its scientific, uh, accuracy puts in more in the league of *The Flintstones*.

Stop-motion animation from Jim Danforth, story by eminent author J.G. Ballard. Under the name Angela Dorian, Vetri was Playmate of the Year in 1968 (A.D.). 𝄞𝄞

1970 (G) 96m/C *GB* Victoria Vetri, Robin Hawdon, Patrick Allen, Drewe Henley, Sean Caffrey, Magda Konopka, Imogen Hassall, Patrick Holt, Jan Rossini; *D:* Val Guest; *W:* Val Guest. **VHS, Beta, LV** *WAR, FCT, MLB*

When Worlds Collide

Another planet is found to be rushing inevitably towards Earth. Luckily, a companion planet will likely arrive in time to take Earth's place. A select group of people attempt to escape in a spaceship; others try to maneuver their way on board. Oscar-quality special effects and plot make up for some cheesy acting and bad writing. The only movie spaceship to be launched from a ramp rather than the traditional launch pad. The new planet is disappointingly represented only by a poor landscape painting—apparently an elaborate model of the scenery was planned, but time ran out on the production. Followed by a sequel novel, *After Worlds Collide,* by Philip Wylie and Edwin Balmer. 𝄞𝄞𝄞

1951 (G) 81m/C Richard Derr, Barbara Rush, Larry Keating, Peter Hanson, John Hoyt, Judith Ames; *D:* Rudolph Mate; *W:* Sydney Boehm; *C:* John Seitz, William Howard Greene. Academy Awards '51: Best Special Effects; Nominations: Academy Awards '51: Best Color Cinematography. **VHS, Beta, LV** *PAR*

Where Time Began

The discovery of a strange manuscript of a scientist's journey to the center of the Earth leads to the decision to recreate the dangerous mission. Based on Jules Verne's classic novel *Journey to the Center of the Earth,* but not anywhere near as fun or stirring. 𝄞𝄞

1977 (G) 87m/C Kenneth More, Pep Munne, Jack Taylor; *D:* J. Piquer Simon. **VHS, Beta** *SUE*

White Dwarf

Confusing made-for-TV sci-fi/fantasy adventure finds edgy Manhattan internist Driscoll Rampart (Neal McDonough) serving his residency on Rusta, a war-torn planet located in a white-dwarf star system. The planet is divided into two hemispheres, one in perpetual darkness and the other in constant light. Rampart learns the ropes from mystical doc Akada (Paul Winfield), who's also involved in a peace accord between Rusta's warring leaders. Other characters include an immortal princess, her fish-monster guardian, and a boy afflicted with a strange disease that gives him the ability to change into various animals. Visually striking but overly ambiguous—the film never quite resolves its science-fiction and fantasy elements. Some of the problems can probably be traced to the fact that it was intended as the pilot for a never-launched weekly series. 𝄞𝄞

1995 91m/C Paul Winfield, Neal McDonough, CCH Pounder, Ele Keats, Michael McGrady, Katy Boyer; *D:* Peter Markle; *W:* Bruce Wagner; *M:* Stewart Copeland. **VHS** *CAF*

Who Framed Roger Rabbit

Technically marvelous, cinematically hilarious, eye-popping combination of cartoon and live action create a Hollywood of the 1940s where cartoon characters are real and a repressed minority working in films. A 'toon-hating detective (Bob Hoskins) is hired to uncover the unfaithful wife of 2-D star Roger, and instead uncovers a conspiracy to wipe out all 'toons. Kathleen Turner notably lent her seductive tones to the va-va-voom appeal of Jessica Rabbit, who, after all, wasn't bad—just drawn that way. Special appearances by many cartoon characters from the past. Coproduced by Touchstone (Disney) and Amblin (Spielberg). Adapted from *Who Censored Roger Rabbit?* by Gary K. Wold. 𝄞𝄞𝄞

1988 (PG) 104m/C Bob Hoskins, Christopher Lloyd, Joanna Cassidy, Alan Tilvern, Stubby Kaye; *D:* Robert Zemeckis; *W:* Jeffrey Price, Peter S. Seaman; *C:* Dean Cundey; *M:* Alan Silvestri; *V:* Charles Fleischer, Mae Questel, Kathleen Turner, Amy Irving, Mel Blanc, June Foray, Frank Sinatra. Hugos '89: Dramatic Presentation; Academy Awards '88: Best Film Editing, Best Visual Effects; National Board of Review Awards '88: 10 Best Films of the Year; Nominations: Academy Awards '88: Best Art Direction/Set Decoration, Best Cinematography, Best Sound. **VHS, Beta, LV** *TOU, WTA*

Wicked City

Based on the Japanese comic strip by Hideyuki Kikuchi, but looking more like a remake of the anime of the same name, *Wicked City* delivers the now-expected doses of over-the-

"...Where nothing can possibly go worng."
—*Westworld.*

rebellion. Christopher Jones stars as rock idol Max Frost, who uses his influence with the young (not to mention L.S.D. dumped in Washington, D.C.'s water supply) to get the voting age lowered to 14 and himself elected president. His first act is to incarcerate all citizens over the age of 30 in "retirement homes." Richard Pryor co-stars as Stanley X, drummer and author of *The Aborigine Cookbook*. Shelley Winters goes over the top as Max's groovy-impaired mother ("Senator," she rebukes Hal Holbrook, "I'm sure my son has a very good reason for paralyzing the country"). The soundtrack scored a hit, "Shape of Things to Come." The chilling last line is a knockout: "Everybody over 10 ought to be put out of business." 🎵🎵♭

1968 97m/C Shelley Winters, Christopher Jones, Hal Holbrook, Richard Pryor, Diane Varsi, Millie Perkins, Ed Begley Sr.; **D:** Barry Shear; **W:** Robert Thom; **C:** Richard Moore; **M:** Les Baxter. Nominations: Academy Awards '68: Best Film Editing. **VHS, Beta, LV** *HBO*

Wild Palms

No, the plot makes virtually no sense, but a series of striking images—none more surprising than the rhino in the swimming pool—make up for a lot. In 2007 Los Angeles, Harry (James Belushi) takes a job at a TV station that offers virtual reality programming to viewers, but this isn't benign technology. And what is the resistance up to? Dana Delany is stuck in a thankless role as his wife, Kim Cattrall is his former lover, but Angie Dickinson, cutting loose with everything she's got, has the most fun as Harry's power-mad mother-in-law who's also a sadistic co-conspirator of a nasty senator (Robert Loggia). Based on the comic strip by writer Wagner, this exercise in weird style over substance has been compared to *Twin Peaks*, but at least it has an ending. Executive producer Oliver Stone has a cameo which concerns the JFK conspiracy. In two parts. Look for lots of familiar faces in supporting roles. 🎵🎵♭

1993 300m/C James Belushi, Robert Loggia, Dana Delany, Kim Cattrall, Angie Dickinson, Ernie Hudson, Bebe Neuwirth, Nick Mancuso, Charles Hallahan, Robert Morse, David Warner, Ben Savage, Bob Gunton, Brad Dourif, Charles Rocket; **Cameos:** Oliver Stone; **D:** Phil Joanou, Kathryn Bigelow, Keith Gordon, Pete Hewitt; **W:**

Hey, Cave Boys! Before you go exiling someone just because she's a blond, maybe you should take a good look at those wigs you're wearing. There was no such thing as a good hair day **When Dinosaurs Ruled the Earth.**

top Hong Kong-style action, special effects, and outrageous stunts. Hey, the atmosphere is cool too, with lush cinematography capturing a futuristic Hong Kong with both its neon-lit color and the dark, *Blade Runner*esque feel necessary to convey the uncomfortable feelings of the humans forced to co-exist with the sinister reptoids, shape-shifting disguised-as-human creatures intent on ruling the world. Luckily for humankind, the monster-police are more than happy to do a little reptoid-bashing. A little like John Carpenter's *They Live,* but without the glasses and a whole lot more intense. Produced and co-written by Tsui Hark, who has directed some fine kick-butt demon-kung-fu action flicks himself. 🎵🎵

1992 88m/C *HK* Jacky Cheung, Leon Lai, Michelle Li; **D:** Peter Mak; **W:** Tsui Hark. **VHS** *FXL*

Wild in the Streets

"If you're over 30, you'd better forget it...." So goes the theme song to this chilling black comedy that puts a paranoid spin on youthful

The Hound Salutes:
Claude Rains

Claude Rains will always be remembered for one brilliant role, the "poor corrupt official" Capt. Louis Renault in *Casablanca*. But in his long and distinguished career as one of Hollywood's best character actors (and leading men) he also played key roles in science-fiction, horror, and fantasy films.

His screen debut was in one of the all-time sf greats, *The Invisible Man*. In the title role, Rains couldn't use a film actor's most important tool—his face. He's either masked or off-camera for virtually the entire movie. Instead, Rains made full use of an equally effective talent, his voice, an instrument that could be authoritative, sly, funny, plaintive. On screen, he could convey just about any emotion or action except clumsiness.

He went on to play the gentle angelic guide in *Here Comes Mr. Jordan*, Lon Chaney Jr.'s unbelieving father in *The Wolfman*, and the title role in the 1943 *The Phantom of the Opera*. Like most people who have worked in the field, his career has been checkered. He was Arthur Conan Doyle's Prof. Challenger in the 1960 *The Lost World* (unavailable on home video), and then made the rarely seen Italian *Battle of the Worlds* in 1963.

But Rains was a product of the Hollywood studio system, and that was a world which, for all its unfairness, created a host of brilliant actors—both men and women—who had the screen presence to carry a film in the lead, but also had the talent and training to shine in important character roles. Claude Rains could do that. He brought a feeling of grace to any role he played.

In the book *Horror Films* (Simon & Schuster, Monarch Film Studies), author R.H.W. Dillard makes a point of Rains' "rigidly controlled performance" in *The Wolfman*. In analyzing the film's structure, Dillard notes that the moral focus of the action shifts to Rains' character at the conclusion, and that transfer lessens the film's emotional and intellectual power. It's a valid point, but at the same time, it demonstrates how effective Rains could be with flawed material. And with the right stuff—even when he was invisible—Claude Rains was one of the best. His limited contribution to screen science-fiction is still significant.

Bruce Wagner; **C:** Phedon Papamichael; **M:** Ryuichi Sakamoto. **VHS** *ABC, FCT*

Wild, Wild Planet

2015: A spaced idiocy. When the market for "sword and sandals" epics declined, the Italians simply turned their gladiators into scientists and jumped aboard the sci-fi bandwagon. Tony Russell stars as our hero, Mike Halstead, who leads the charge against the mad scientist who has dispatched female agents in tight leather pants to miniaturize us. More brawn than brains, but lots of fun. Followed up by *War of the Planets* that same year. 🦴🐾

1965 93m/C *IT* Tony Russell, Lisa Gastoni, Massimo Serato, Franco Nero, Charles Justin; **D:** Anthony (Antonio

Margheriti) Dawson; **W:** Ivan Reiner; **C:** Riccardo Pallton Pallottini. **VHS** *SMW*

The Wild World of Batwoman

A campy cult film in which Batwoman (Katherine Victor, who earlier starred in director Jerry Warren's truly wretched *Teenage Zombies*) and a bevy of Bat Girls are pitted against an evil doctor in order to find the prototype of an atomic hearing aid/nuclear bomb. Out-camps the campy *Batman* TV series. Most of the entertainment value comes from the fact that you can't believe you're actually watching this. Also released theatrically as *She Was a Hippy Vampire* due to legal pressure. **AKA:** She Was a Hippy Vampire. 🦴

1966 70m/C Katherine Victor, George Andre, Steve Brodie, Lloyd Nelson; **D:** Jerry Warren. **VHS, Beta** *RHI, SNC, DVT*

Willow

A blockbuster fantasy epic which seems intent on cramming together everything from the story of Moses in the Rushes to "Snow White," complete with dwarves. Willow is the little Nelwyn (sort of like a hobbit, but even shorter) who finds the lost baby Daikini and is assigned the task of returning her safely to her people. It seems the girl is actually a sacred infant who is destined to overthrow the evil queen Bavmorda and rule the land. As you might expect from executive producer George Lucas, there is much action and plenty of clever, high-quality special effects. But the story (by Lucas) is strangely predictable, and so aggressively packed with action and glitzy effects that the story itself seems to get lost. 🦴🦴⚬

1988 (PG) 118m/C Warwick Davis, Val Kilmer, Jean Marsh, Joanne Whalley, Billy Barty, Pat Roach, Ruth Greenfield, Patricia Hayes, Gavan O'Herlihy, Kevin Pollak; **D:** Ron Howard; **W:** Bob Dolman; **M:** James Horner. **VHS, Beta, LV, 8mm** *COL*

A Wind Named Amnesia

A strange amnesia wind sweeps away all of mankind's knowledge and human civilization vanishes. Humanity is ignorant, innocent, and brutal. Then a mysterious young man is miraculously re-educated and searches for those who destroyed man's memories. He wanders a mostly deserted landscape searching for anyone else who might have retained or regained intelligence. He finds a woman who can speak, and a lethal robot, reminiscent of the Walkers in *Return of the Jedi,* that seems driven to attack him. While that could be the basis for any number of B-movies, writer Hideyuki Kikuchi, animator Satoru Nakamura, and director Kazuo Yamazaki take time to speculate on the larger questions raised by the story: the philosophical implications of pure innocence, the nature of men and women, and the evolution of religion. In Japanese with English subtitles. 🦴🦴🦴

1993 80m/C JP **D:** Kazuo Yakmazaki; **W:** Hideyuki Kikuchi. **VHS** *CPM*

Wired to Kill

In a wrecked future world (what, again?), two whiz-kid teens seek justice for their parents' murder by building a remote-controlled erector set programmed for revenge. Shot in South Africa, this formula revenge flick gains a few shreds of interest if you know writer/director Franky Schaeffer is a prominent evangelical activist who turned to sleaze filmmaking to try to break into the secular movie industry. Thus there's a stronger sense of moral doom than usual in its dystopian society where nothing seems to work except automated 800 numbers. Otherwise, no revelation. 🦴⚬

1986 (R) 96m/C Merritt Butrick, Emily Longstreth, Devin Hoelscher, Frank Collison; **D:** Franky Schaeffer; **W:** Franky Schaeffer. **VHS, Beta** *LIV*

Witch Hunt

Dennis Hopper takes over for Fred Ward as private dick H. Phillip Lovecraft in this sequel to 1991's *Cast a Deadly Spell.* Once again our hero is just about the only person in the alternate-universe 1953 Hollywood who refuses to use magic. Lovecraft is hired by Kim Hudson (Penelope Ann Miller) to tail her two-timin' husband. Suddenly hubby is corpsified and it's a case of murder. Great special effects, but not the usual crisp plot that director Paul Schrader helms. Eric Bogosian is fine as a blowhard senator trying to ban magic. Music by Angelo Badalamenti. Fans of the first one will love the fantasy-noir feel. 🦴🦴⚬

1994 (R) 101m/C Dennis Hopper, Penelope Ann Miller, Eric Bogosian, Sheryl Lee Ralph, Julian Sands, Alan Rosenberg, Valerie Mahaffey, Debi Mazar; **D:** Paul Schrader; **W:** Joseph Dougherty; **M:** Angelo Badalamenti. **VHS** *HBO*

The Wizard of Speed and Time

Ambitious, self-taught young movie f/x master is hired by a greedy producer to jazz up a TV show with his gags and gadgets. But he doesn't know the same exec has vowed to stop

Mexican Wrestling Superheroes

There are those who will tell you that professional wrestling and cinematic fantasy aren't that far apart. Aside from the issue of how "real" pro-wrestling is, both it and fantasy films involve the viewer in a larger-than-life world, where conflicts are at once both simpler and vastly more complex than they are in day-to-day life.

Both are about heroes and villains. Of course, of the two, it's the movies that involve themselves with the threat of alien invasion, rampaging monsters, and evil geniuses...that sort of thing has no place in the wrestling ring. Or does it?

In the '60s and '70s, the Mexican film industry created a new kind of superhero, a wrestling star who is also a man of valor and unimpeachable morals (this alone would qualify as a fantasy, according to many fans). This mighty defender of justice would go a few rounds against a ringside adversary, sign fans' auto-graphs, and then, heeding an urgent plea for help from a super-scientist or govern-ment official, zoom off to battle threats from another world. Never seen without his mask, but not infrequently shirtless (the better to show off his muscles), the wrestling superhero used not only his martial skills but an arsenal of gadgets that usually resembled something from a kids' toy-chest. Villains mocked these devices at their peril, however; those light-bulb rayguns were *deadly*!

The archetypal Mexican wrestling hero was unquestionably El Santo.

Immediately recognizable by his silver and blue mask, Santo waged a one-man war of justice against a veritable army of werewolves, bat-people, female vam-pires, robots, zombies, and other crea-tures of evil (including a giant amoeba that looked like an over-filled, out-of-con-trol trash bag). There were over thirty Santos movies made up to 1982—*Santo Vs. the Television Assassin* was the last one, but like all the best heroes, Santo's legend lives on in the hearts of his fans.

There were other wrestling heroes, of course, just as there were U.S. super-heroes other than Superman. Neutron, Blue Demon, and Mil Mascaras. Lest any-one think this brand of heroics was strict-ly for the men-folk, there was also a brief but highly regarded series of *Wrestling Women* movies. The best known are *Wrestling Women Vs. the Aztec Mummy* and *Wrestling Women Vs. the Killer Robot*, which featured one of the strangest robots in cinematic history.

So what are you waiting for? Grab a couple of these tapes and hit the mat!

him at all costs to win a backstage bet. Mike Jittlov, a true special-effects expert, plays him-self in this personally financed all-ages come-dy that brims with inside jokes, soapbox satire, self-indulgence, and the sunniest portrayal of Hollywood fringies this side of *Ed Wood*. Its zippy, joyous style evokes a Pee Wee Herman-esque vision of life and a sincere plea for dreamers everywhere to persevere despite the odds (and unions). Constant visual trickery incorporates footage from Jittlov's many stop-motion and collage short subjects; be quick with the "freeze" and "rewind" buttons to catch it all, right down to subliminals. Plot is reportedly based on Jittlov's own fraught expe-rience working on a prime-time special in 1979. As for the long-gestated "WoSaT," its aborted theatrical release and videosocassette debut on a B-movie label set Jittlov and his estranged producer to trading accusations over what went wrong. The filmmaker subsequently took his case to cyberspace, presiding over comput-er bulletin boards patronized by a growing cult of WoSaT fans. 🦴🦴🦴

1988 (PG) 95m/C Mike Jittlov, Richard Kaye, Page Moore, David Conrad, Steve Brodie, John Massari, Frank Laloggia, Philip Michael Thomas, Angelique Pettyjohn, Arnetia Walk-er, Paulette Breen; **D:** Mike Jittlov; **W:** Mike Jittlov, Richard Kaye, Deven Chierighino; **M:** John Massari. **VHS, LV** *WTA*

Wizards

After a nuclear war, Earth has turned into a medieval fantasy world full of fairies and monsters. The good but bumbling sorcerer Avatar teams up with a shell-shocked battle-android and a couple of elves to battle his evil brother Blackwolf, who seeks to take over the world from the ruined land of Scortch. In a rather startling touch, Blackwolf uses old Nazi propaganda films to inspire his army of bloodthirsty mutants. Alternately funny and bleak, silly and thought-provoking. A profane, crude, and typically Bakshian animated fantasy with great graphics. Seventies comics fans will note a similarity between Bakshi's character-designs and those of cartoonist Vaughn Bode. 🎬🎬🎬
1977 (PG) 81m/C D: Ralph Bakshi; **W:** Ralph Bakshi; **M:** Andrew Belling; **V:** Bob Holt, Richard Romanus, Jesse Wells, David Proval. **VHS, Beta, LV** *FOX, WTA*

Woman in the Moon

Assorted people embark on a trip to the moon and discover water, and an atmosphere, as well as gold. Fritz Lang's last silent outing is nothing next to *Metropolis,* with a rather lame plot (greedy trip bashers seek gold), but interesting as a vision of the future. Lang's predictions about space travel often hit the mark. Silent with music. **AKA:** By Rocket to the Moon; Girl in the Moon. 🎬🎬📼
1929 115m/B *GE* Klaus Pohl, Willy Fritsch, Gustav von Wagenheim, Gerda Maurus; **D:** Fritz Lang. **VHS, Beta** *VYY, IHF, LSV*

Women of the Prehistoric Planet

The members of a space rescue mission face the usual deadly perils on a strange planet, including a "giant" spider and lizards, and very unrealistic man-eating plants. During their stay, the astronauts manage to bring together a native couple, Linda and Tang. As far as the title is concerned, get this: Linda is the only woman, and she's not "of" the planet in question. See if you can last long enough to catch the "amazing" plot twist at the end. 🎬
1966 87m/C Wendell Corey, Irene Tsu, Robert Ito, Stuart Margolin, Lyle Waggoner, Adam Roarke, Merry Anders, John Agar, Paul Gilbert; **D:** Arthur C. Pierce; **W:** Arthur C. Pierce; **C:** Arch R. Dalzell. **VHS, Beta** *NO*

World Gone Wild

Action yarn about a post-apocalyptic world of the future where an evil cult leader brainwashes his disciples. Together they battle a small band of eccentrics for the world's last water source. Stale rehash (with ineffective satiric elements) of the Mad Max genre, served with Adam Ant for campy appeal. 🎬📼
1988 (R) 95m/C Bruce Dern, Michael Pare, Adam Ant, Catherine Mary Stewart, Rick Podell; **D:** Lee H. Katzin. **VHS, Beta, LV** *MED, VTR*

Wrestling Women Vs. the Aztec Ape

An unclassifiable epic of brawny beauties versus a brawnier beast. The Golden Rubi and her sister Gloria Venus (Elizabeth Campbell and Lorena Velasquez) battle a mad doctor and his Aztec robot gorilla. Dubbed badly, of course, but are you going to let that bother you? This flick was the much anticipated follow-up to the classic *Wrestling Women Vs. the Aztec Mummy.* **AKA:** Doctor of Doom. 🎬🎬
1962 75m/C *MX* Elizabeth Campbell, Lorena Velasquez, Armando Silvestre, Roberto Canedo; **D:** Rene Cardona Sr. **VHS, Beta** *RHI, HHT, SNC*

Wrestling Women Vs. the Aztec Mummy

The Golden Rubi and her sister, two Mexican female wrestlers, go up against Xochitl, an ancient Aztec wrestler who has inconveniently returned to life. They also have to contend with an army of Asian female wrestlers. It may not make much sense, but its no-holds barred, shoulder-to-the-mat fun. The long-haired Aztec Mummy, who can change into a snake or bat, started back in 1957 in a series of adventures including *Curse of the Aztec Mummy* and *The Robot Vs. the Aztec Mummy.* Rhino Video's print is the "Rock 'n' Roll" version and replaces the original creepy orchestral soundtrack with pseudo-rockabilly tunes. 🎬🎬📼
1959 88m/C *MX* Lorena Velasquez, Armando Silvestre, Elizabeth Campbell, Eugenia Saint Martin; **D:** Rene Cardona Sr. **VHS, Beta** *SNC, RHI, HHT*

TV on Tape: The X-Files

The X-Files surprised everyone by becoming a cult hit for Fox TV, and then growing into a solid ratings winner with a larger audience. The network that had been known for comedy, both good and trashy, suddenly had a science-fiction hit on its hands.

The show's premise is simple but inventive, and loose enough to give writers a wide range of subjects. Fox Mulder (David Duchovny) is an FBI agent who never met a conspiracy theory he didn't like. He believes every La-la fantasy that waltzes down the lane from alien abductions—they got his sister when he was a boy—to lake monsters. His partner, pathologist Dana Scully (Gillian Anderson), is a level-headed skeptic who demands hard evidence for everything. Surrounding them is a supporting cast that ranges from shadowy bureaucrats to circus freaks and the usual supernatural suspects—vampires, werewolves, zombies, etc.

Though the plots cover the full spectrum of supernatural phenomena, the series has been developing one primary set of villains: unidentified but presumably wealthy and powerful conspirators who have infiltrated the federal government and are involved in "The Project." They have ties to Mulder's family and were somehow involved with Scully's insufficiently explained abduction. The show's creator and producer Chris Carter has been carefully coy about their motives and objectives. Why is the show so successful? Here are a few reasons:

Casting. Anderson and Duchovny work well together, and the relationship between their characters is intellectual, not sexual. They respect each other as friends and professional equals. Though they're bound together by strong emotions, particularly paranoia, any romance would detract from their effectiveness as protagonists.

Spooky atmosphere. Suspenseful situations are often created with nothing more than smoke, flashlights and extreme camera angles. Other effects—notably a menagerie of creatures—are seldom revealed fully. They appear quickly and are gone.

Humor, often self-deprecating. If the series ever takes itself and its conspiratorial mindset completely seriously, it will lose its charm.

Imitation. The producers are quick to pick up on the latest hot pop culture touchstones, from *Silence of the Lambs* to Navajo code talkers, and then to weave them into the storylines.

The X-Files has been remarkably long-lived for a science-fiction/supernatural series. The producers have managed to maintain the integrity of their central idea while making it consistently fresh, inventive and often funny.

1994-present/C *Selected cast:* David Duchovny, Gillian Anderson. **VHS** *FXV, MOV*

X from Outer Space

A space voyage to Mars brings back a giant rampaging creature. Badly dubbed. 🦴

1967 (PG) 85m/C *JP* Eiji Okada, Peggy Neal, Toshiya Wazaki, Itoko Harada, Shinichi Yanagisawa, Franz Gruber, Keisuke Sonoi, Mike Daning, Torahiko Hamada; *D:* Nazui Nihonmatsu. **VHS, Beta** *ORI*

X: The Man with X-Ray Eyes

One of Roger Corman's best science-fiction films, an existential horror story about a doctor (Ray Milland) who fools around with experimental eye-drops that give him X-ray vision. The idea of being able to see through solid objects (like...for example...*clothes*?) was run into the ground in early "nudie" pictures, but Corman bypasses such sophomoric pleasures in favor of a slowly mounting feeling of unease. Although Milland has fun with his powers at first, things go awry when he accidentally offs a colleague. Now on the lam, he begins to realize his enhanced sight is slowly

Sci-Fi Experience

"How come he made the hundred most beautiful people list and I didn't?!" A pouty Gillian Anderson and a smug David Duchovny in *The X-Files.*

tle son doing the *Carrie* routine with telekinesis. Emphasis on slime, sex, disease, and splatter, much of it inventively nightmarish, most of it offensive—like a raped woman gestating in a matter of minutes and giving birth to a full-grown man. By way of contrast, the same British producer did 1977's *The Glitterball* (available on video in the U.K.), a children's feature that strongly prefigured Steven Spielberg's *E.T.* 🎞

1983 (R) 80m/C *GB* Philip Sayer, Bernice Stegers, Danny Brainin, Simon Nash, Maryam D'Abo, David Cardy, Anna Wing, Peter Mandell, Robert Fyfe; **D:** Harry Bromley Davenport; **W:** Iain Cassle, Robert Smith; **C:** John Metcalfe. **VHS, Beta, LV** *NLC*

Xtro 2: The Second Encounter

Second encounter was only between *Xtro* director Harry Bromley Davenport and a camera; this has no story relation to the 1983 sleazefest and is instead your basic *Alien* ripoff. Research facility transfers people to a parallel dimension. One traveler returns playing host to a spiny H.R. Giger knockoff that escapes into the air shafts and threatens to kill everyone in the building. Impressive photography and set design considering the sub-$1 million budget, but creature f/x are inert. 🎞🎞

1991 (R) 92m/C *CA* Jan-Michael Vincent, Paul Koslo, Tara Buckman, Jano Frandsen, Nicholas Lea, W.F. Wadden, Rolf Reynolds, Nic Amoroso, Tracy Westerholm; **D:** Harry Bromley Davenport. **VHS, LV** *NLC*

Yongkari Monster of the Deep

A giant burrowing creature is causing earthquakes and generally ruining scores of Japanese models. Dubbed. **AKA:** Dai Koesu Yongkari; Monster Yongkari; Great Monster Yongkari. 🎞

1967 (PG) 79m/C Oh Young Il, Nam Chung-Im; **D:** Kim Ki-dak. **VHS, Beta** *ORI*

Young Frankenstein

Gene Wilder plays Dr. Frankenstein ("It's pronounced 'Frahnkenschteen'," he corrects), a brain surgeon who inherits the family castle back in Transylvania. He's skittish about the

getting stronger. Finally he sees through eternity itself, going mad in the process. A powerful, disturbing story; too bad Corman didn't make more films like it. Don Rickles has a small part as a carny owner. **AKA:** The Man with the X-Ray Eyes; X. 🎞🎞🎞🎞

1963 79m/C Ray Milland, Diana Van Der Vlis, Harold J. Stone, John Hoyt, Don Rickles, Dick Miller, Jonathan Haze, Lorie Summers, Vicki Lee; **D:** Roger Corman; **W:** Robert Russell, Robert Dillon; **C:** Floyd Crosby; **M:** Les Baxter. **VHS, Beta, LV** *WAR*

Xtro

English chap abducted by aliens years before returns to his family as a fast-metamorphosing mutant "bearing black magic from outer space," as the original ads helpfully explained a pointless subplot about the man's nasty lit-

family business, but when he learns his grandfather's secrets, he becomes obsessed with making his own monster, aided by Marty Feldman as Igor ("It's pronounced 'Eyegor'," he returns). Wilder and monster Peter Boyle make a memorable song-and-dance team to Irving Berlin's "Puttin' on the Ritz," and Gene Hackman's cameo as a blind man is inspired. Teri Garr ("What knockers!" "Oh, sank you!") is adorable as a fraulein, and Cloris Leachman ("He's vass my—boyfriend!") is wonderfully scary. Wilder saves the creature with a switcheroo, in which the doctor ends up with a certain monster-sized body part. Hilarious parody (written by Mel Brooks and Wilder himself) that pays an accurate and witty homage to the original. 🎞🎞🎞🎞

1974 (PG) 108m/B Peter Boyle, Gene Wilder, Marty Feldman, Madeline Kahn, Cloris Leachman, Teri Garr, Kenneth Mars, Richard Haydn; *Cameos:* Gene Hackman; *D:* Mel Brooks; *W:* Gene Wilder, Mel Brooks; *M:* John Morris. Hugos '75: Dramatic Presentation; Nominations: Academy Awards '74: Best Adapted Screenplay, Best Sound. **VHS, Beta, LV** *FOX, HMV*

Zardoz

Thanks to more than a decade of witless *Road Warrior* retreads, John Boorman's controversial parable of the far future has never looked better. In 2293 Earth society is broken into strict and segregated classes: a society of bored, detached intellectuals burdened with eternal life; a horde of primitives who have the privilege of breeding as long as they're slain regularly; and an elite unit of killers who do the job. Sean Connery (in a role first offered to Burt Reynolds) is one of the latter, a clever barbarian who destroys the old order of things by stowing away in the floating monolithic head of the god Zardoz (as in Wiz*ard* of *Oz*) to penetrate the immortals' stronghold. Pretentious it may be, but you could do a lot worse than Boorman's splendid visuals and weighty metaphysical meditations. 🎞🎞🎞

1973 105m/C Sean Connery, Charlotte Rampling, John Alderton, Sara Kestelman, Sally Anne Newton, Niall Buggy; *D:* John Boorman; *W:* John Boorman; *C:* Geoffrey Unsworth. **VHS, Beta, LV** *FOX*

Stop right there! And don't *ever* let me catch you ordering the chicken nuggets again! *Xtro.*

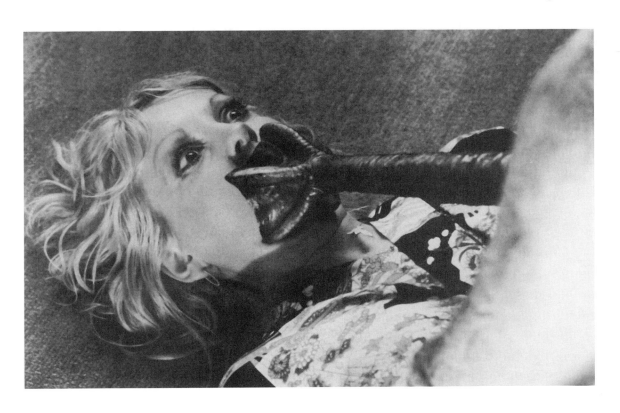

"Half of me thinks making this movie was a good career move, but ..." Sean Connery and his alter ego in *Zardoz*.

sent to be executed. Can they escape? Maudlin and simplistic. **AKA:** Z.P.G. 🦴🦴

1972 95m/C Oliver Reed, Geraldine Chaplin, Diane Cilento, Don Gordon; **D:** Michael Campus; **W:** Frank de Felitta, Max Ehrlich. **VHS** *PAR*

Zombies of the Stratosphere

Republic's third Martian-invasion serial showed denizens of the red planet at their very worst. This time three Martians (i.e. "zombies") practice their skullduggery against Earth and one of them is played by a young Leonard Nimoy (the eyebrows look Vulcan but unfortunately we are never permitted to see any ears under his hood). The extraterrestrials hope to plant an H-bomb to blow Earth out of orbit and upgrade their dying world to being third from the sun. Luckily for humanity, opposing them is Judd Holdren (whose rewritten role was originally the Commander Cody character he played in *Radar Men from the Moon*). Six months after Republic finished this, the USA detonated its own H-bomb for the first time, so perhaps we are not so lucky after all. On video in 12 chapters; also available in a 93 minute, colorized condensation. **AKA:** Satan's Satellites. 🦴🦴🦴

1952 152m/B Judd Holdren, Aline Towne, Leonard Nimoy, John Crawford, Ray Boyle; **D:** Fred Brannon. **VHS, Beta, LV** *REP, VCN, MLB*

Zeram

Zeram is a giant renegade space alien lured to Earth by a female bounty hunter. How does she expect to capture it? Why, with a warp machine, space bazooka, electric shield, and a computer named Bob, of course. Dubbed. Followed by *Zeram 2*. 🦴🦴

1991 92m/C *JP* Yuko Moriyama, Yukihiro Hotaru, Kunihiko Ida; **D:** Keita Amemiya; **W:** Hajime Matsumoto. **VHS** *FXL, FCT*

Zero Population Growth

In the 21st century the government has decreed that no babies may be born for a 30-year span in order to control the population. But Geraldine Chaplin and Oliver Reed secretly have a child and when they are discovered are

Zone Troopers

Five American GIs in WWII-ravaged Europe stumble upon a wrecked alien spacecraft. The pilot is dead, but the co-pilot manages to get away, and soon the boys find themselves confronted by an alien rescue party—an intergalactic posse known as the "Zone Troopers"—who have come to save their injured comrade. The historical setting gives this flick an interesting twist. 🦴🦴

1985 (PG) 86m/C Timothy Van Patten, Tim Thomerson, Art LaFleur, Biff Manard; **D:** Danny Bilson; **W:** Danny Bilson, Paul DeMeo; **C:** Mac Ahlberg; **M:** Richard Band. **VHS, Beta** *LIV*

Zontar, the Thing from Venus

A scientist is contacted by an alien intelligence from Venus and begins doing its bidding, con-

vinced that its intentions are benevolent. Surprise! "Zontar" turns out to be a giant batlike critter who hides in a cave and he's far from friendly; he takes over people's wills with smaller replicas of itself, which implant control-devices in their victims' necks. This hokey but fun movie is a remake of the noted 1956 Roger Corman epic *It Conquered the World.*

Some might argue that a remake of Corman's rather routine monster film was hardly necessary, but *Zontar* actually manages to top the original for sheer overacted corny amusement.

1966 68m/C John Agar, Anthony Huston, Warren Hammack, Pat Delaney, Susan Bjorman; **D:** Larry Buchanan; **W:** Larry Buchanan. **VHS** *SNC, VDM*

"Red Hot Rock and Roll Wrestling Women with Rebel Rousin' Robot Gorilla Girls and Hell Raisin' Horror together in One Amazing Film!"

—*Wrestling Women Vs. the Aztec Ape.*

Sci-Fi Connections

If watching the movies just isn't enough for you... the following listings offer sci-fi related Web pages, 'zines and newsletters, fan clubs, conventions, and selected books. We do recommend, however, that you get some fresh air at some point.

WEB PAGES

The Adventures of Buckaroo Banzai Across the Eighth Dimension
http://www.towson.edu/~flynn/banzai.html
http://www.teleport.com/~amichan/
http://www.xnet.com/~mcollins/banzai.html
http://bbs.annex.com/relayer/bbanzai.html
http://members.aol.com/STScience/index.html
   The Adventures of Buckaroo Banzai (sound bites)
http://www.acm.uiuc.edu/rml/Sounds/Buck_Banzai/

Air & Space Magazine
http://airspacemag.com/

Alien Empire
http://www.umd.umich.edu/~mszlaga/alien/alien-empire.html

Alien Saga
http://found.cs.nyu.edu/michael/alien/

AnimEigo
http://www.wilmington.net/modular/animeigo/a_home.html

Isaac Asimov
http://www.clark.net/pub/wmcbrine/html/Asimov.html

Babylon 5
http://www.hyperion.com/lurk/lurker.html

Back to the Future
http://www.hsv.tis.net/~bttf/

Barbarella
http://www.gem.valpo.edu/~cnavta/Barbarella/

Batman Forever
http://www.inch.com/~jeffz/bat.html
http://www.batmanforever.com

Battlestar Galactica
http://mcmfh.acns.carleton.edu/BG/
http://src.doc.ic.ac.uk/public/media/tv/collections/tardis/us/sci-fi/BattlestarGalactica/index.

Birmingham Science Fiction Club
http://members.aol.com/rbsfco/index.html

Blade Runner
http://dingo.cc.uq.oz.au/~csmchapm/bladerunner/trivia.html
http://kzsu.stanford.edu/uwi/br/off-world.html
http://madison.tdsnet.com/bladerunner/
http://www.cis.ohio-state.edu/hypertext/faq/usenet/movies/bladerunner-faq/faq.html

Blakes' 7
http://www.ee.surrey.ac.uk/Contrib/SciFi/Blakes7/

Bradley University's Science Fiction Club Psi Phi
http://www.bradley.edu/campusorg/psiphi/

Brazil
http://www.cis.ohio-state.edu/hypertext/faq/usenet/movies/brazil-faq/faq.html
http://poppy.kaist.ac.kr/cinema/brazil/

Bubonicon 28
http://www.unm.edu/~lundgren/Bubonicon.html

Canadian SF&F Resource Guide
http://www.magi.com/~gonzo/cansfrg.html

Century Magazine
http://www.supranet.com/century/

C.J. Cherryh
http://ea.ethz.ch:80/cherryh/

Arthur C. Clarke Unauthorized Homepage
http://www.lsi.usp.br/%7Erbianchi/clarke/

ConNotation—The Magician's SF Convention Listing
http://www.compulink.co.uk/~magician/conlist.htm Societies

Dagobah System
http://www.li.net/~yoda/dagobah.html

Dark Carnival
http://www.darkcarnival.com/

The Dark Crystal
http://www.fairfield.net/wyvern/darkcrys/

Dark Dimension British SciFi Club
http://expert.cc.purdue.edu/~drwho/text.html

Dark Planet
http://biotech.chem.indiana.edu/~lusnyde/cover.html

Definition of Science Fiction
http://www.metu.edu.tr/~www69/users/gokce/sf_defn.html

Del Rey Books
http://www.randomhouse.com/delrey/

Philip K. Dick
http://www.users.interport.net/~regulus/pkd/pkd-int.html

Dr. Who
http://www.bris.ac.uk/Depts/Union/BTS/
http://www.pipex.net/people/chuck/sf/drwho/dwas/

http://www.nl2k.edmonton.ab.ca/~doctor/clubslist.html
http://www.ee.surrey.ac.uk/Contrib/SciFi/DrWho/

Dune
http://daemon.apana.org.au/~isikeli/dune.html
http://home.earthlink.net/~gregszcz/
http://www.princeton.edu/~cgilmore/dune/faq/index.html

Enigma
http://gsa.asucla.ucla.edu/~enigma/index.html

Fan Tek's Newsletter The Castle
http://www.cfar.umd.edu/~waksman/fantek/

Folklore Guilds
http://www.apci.net/~galadon/

The Forbidden Planet
http://www.tizeta.it/home/duo/fbhome.htm

Fourth Foundation: Occidental Science Fiction and Fantasy Club
http://www.oxy.edu/~4thfound/index.html

The Fright Page
http://www.fright.com/

Future Fantasy Bookstore
http://futfan.com/home-text.html

Future Mall of 2050
http://www.waterw.com/~scott/index.html

Gamera Page
http://tswww.cc.emory.edu/~kgowen/gamera.html

The Gathering: Highlander WWW
http://www.seachange.com/highlander
http://www.highlander-official.com

Generation War
http://www.webmovie.com/ffwd.htm

Genie Science Fiction and Fantasy Roundtables
http://www.sfrt.com/sfrt/

William Gibson
http://www.vkool.com/gibson/index.html

Godzilla
http://www.ama.caltech.edu/users/mrm/godzilla.html

Head Together Video Catalogue— Science Fiction
http://www.ibp.com/pit/heads-together/cat_Science-Fiction.html

Hour of the Wolf
http://www.users.interport.net/~jfreund/hotw/
index.html

House of Speculative Fiction
http://cyberus.ca/specific/

Hugo Awards
http://www.lm.com/~lmann/awards/hugos
/hugos.html

Independence Day
http://www.id4.com/

Invaders (TV Show)
http://www.ee.surrey.ac.uk/Contrib/SciFi/
invaders/

Irish Science Fiction Association
http://arrogant.itc.icl.ie/ISFA.html

Jordon's Time Killing Sci-Fi
http://pomo.nbn.com/people/biscuit/

Jurassic Park
http://infolane.com/infolane/apunix/sci-jur.html

Katsucon 2
http://elfie.bevc.blacksburg.va.us/katsucon/
katsuni.html

KingCon Society
http://dragon.acadiau.ca/~860473m/kingcon.
html

The Klingon Language Institute
http://www.kli.org/

LaJetee
http://www.favela.org/frenzy/lajette/lajette1.
html

Libertarian Futurist Society
http://www.libertarian.com/LFS/

H.P. Lovecraft Page
http://www.primenet.com/~dloucks/hplpage.
html

**Marshall Space Flight Center (MSFC)
Liftoff**
http://liftoff.msfc.nasa.gov/

Metropolis
http://members.aol.com/PolisHome/metropolis.
html

Michael Hill's Sci Fi
http://www.seanet.com/~jghill/

Milieux
http://ddi.digital.net/~milieux/index.html

Minnesota Science Fiction Society
http://www.mnstf.org/mnstf/

MSC Cepheid Variable
http://wwwmsc.tamu.edu/MSC/CepheidVariable
/CepheidVariable.html

Mystery Science Theater 3000
http://www.mst3000.com/
http://www.reellife.com/PFE/mystery/mystery-
home.html
http://www.missouri.edu/~c638278/mst3k/
mst3k.html
http://www.slinknet.com/~wmorgan/mst3k.
html
http://www.ssc.com/~roland/mst3k/mst3k.
html
http://www.cris.com/~outlawyr/mst3k.shtml
http://www.comcentral.com/mst/mstsched.
shtml

National Space Science Data Center
http://nssdc.gsfc.nasa.gov/

National Space Society (NSS)
http://spacelink.msfc.nasa.gov/

Nebula Awards (1965-1995)
http://www.lm.com/~lmann/awards/nebulas/
nebulas.html

**The New England Science Fiction
Association**
http://www.panix.com/NESFA/home.html

New Jersey Science Fiction Society
http://www.mordor.com/kat/njsfs.html

Northwest Science Fiction Society
http://www.seanet.com/Users/warlock/nwsfs.
html

**Old Dominion University Science Fiction
and Fantasy Club**
http://www.cs.odu.edu/~berto_s/scifi_dir/scifi.
html

Omni Magazine
http://www.omnimag.com/

The Other *Worlds* Cafe
http://www.suba.com/~janice/

Plan 9 from Outer Space
http://www.conxtion.com/admin/Jeff_Renzi/
Movies/Plan9/Plan9.html

Planet of the Apes
http://members.aol.com/thespleen/index.html
http://members.aol.com/rogerapple/
forbiddenzone.html

Planet Earth
http://www.demon.co.uk/elpasso/planet-earth/
general.htm

The Planetary Society
http://planetary.org/tps/

Polaris—The St. Albans Science Fiction Society
http://www.scom.com/polaris/

Quanta
http://www.etext.org/Zines/Quanta/

Quantum Leap
http://www-usacs.rutgers.edu/fun-stuff/tv/quantum-leap/

Quark's Sci Fi Page
http://www.algonet.se/~quark/index.html

Realm of Shadows
http://www.pacificnet.net/~mrnobody/vampyre/

Rocky Horror Picture Show
http://www.cybercomm.net/~doble/rhps.html
http://www.wintermute.ch/~wintermute/rhps.htm
http://www.vnet.net/users/banshee/RHPS.html
http://net-gate.com/~smw/rhps.html

SciFi Channel
http://www.scifi.com/

Sci-Fi Entertainment
http://www.geocities.com/Hollywood/3382/index.html

Sci-Fi WEBsite
http://www.sci-fi-mag.com/

Sci-Web
http://www.scifiweb.com/

Science Fiction Continuum (S & J Video)
http://www.webcreations.com/sjvideo/

Science Fiction and Fantasy Links
http://www.ee.ucg.ie/science_fiction.html

Science Fiction and Fantasy Writers of America
http://www.sfwa.org/

The Science Fiction Gallery
http://www.onestep.com/

Science Fiction Resource Guide
ftp://sflovers.rutgers.edu/pub/sf-lovers/Web/sf-resource.guide.html

The Science Fiction Shop
http://www.tagonline.com/Ads/SciFiShop/

Science Fiction TV Episode Guides
http://www.nova.edu/Inter-Links/scifi.html

Science Fiction Weekly
http://www.scifi.com/sfw/

Ridley Scott
http://www.uq.oz.au/~csmchapm/bladerunner/

Screamers
http://www.spe.sony.com/Pictures/SonyMovies/Screamers/index.html

SF Fantasy Cardiff
http://www.cf.ac.uk/ccin/main/ents/sffc/sffc.html

Something Is Out There
http://www.ee.surrey.ac.uk/Contrib/SciFi/Something/

Space Dog
http://www.spacedog.org/

Space Rangers
http://www.ee.surrey.ac.uk/Contrib/SciFi/Space Rangers/

Speed Fighters
http://www.buildup.co.jp/new/english/speedfighter.html

Star One Delta
http://www.premier.net/~smengrs/sod.htm

Star Trek
http://www.mcs.net/~forbes/trek-reviews/
http://www.quintnet.com/~cobra/
http://www.shore.net/~treks/
http://wwwedu.cs.utwente.nl/~schudel/stb.html
http://www.ny.frontiercomm.net/~freeprny/sttng.html
http://www.ee.surrey.ac.uk/Contrib/SciFi/StarTrek/FAQ.html
http://www.ee.surrey.ac.uk/Contrib/SciFi/StarTrek/STTNG/
http://www.cosy.sbg.ac.at/rec/startrek/star_trek_resources.html
http://www.netshop.net/Startrek/web/

Star Wars
http://www.wpi.edu/ftp/starwars/
http://www.maddog.ctstateu.edu/darkjedi/index.html
http://www.dom.net/wrd/new/ref/sw/
http://www.angelfire.com/pg1/alderaan/index.html
http://www.columbia.edu/~gan3/swars.html
http://www.wp.com/Fox/mj.html
http://maple.lemoyne.edu/~shannowh/starwars.html
http://www.ozemail.com.au/~beard/Dark_Side.html

http://alpha.wcoil.com/~mmurray/StarWars/Index.html

Stargate
http://www.foresight.co.uk/stargate/

Starman
http://www.calweb.com/~smccrory/starman.html

Strange Days
http://www.strangedays.com/

Tardis
http://www.primenet.com/~jgeorge/tardis.html

Terminator/Terminator 2
http://www.cis.ohio-state.edu/hypertext/faq/usenet/movies/terminator-faq/faq.html
http://bell.maths.tcd.ie/pub/films/terminator/

J.R.R. Tolkien
http://www.lights.com/tolkien/

Tor Science Fiction & Fantasy
http://www.tor.com/

Troma
http://www.troma.com/home/

Tron
http://www.aquila.com/guy.gordon/tron/tron.htm

Twelve Monkeys
http://www.mca.com/universal_pictures/12/faq.html

2001: A Space Odyssey
http://www.lehigh.edu/~pjl2/films/2001.html

UK Science Fiction Fandom Archives
http://www.dcs.gla.ac.uk/SF-Archives/

The Unio-Mystica Fantasy Page
http://www.best.com/~wooldri/awooldri/fantasy.html

University of Michigan Fantasy & Science Fiction Pages
http://www.umich.edu/~umfandsf/

VideoHound
www.thomson.com/videohound.html

Wargames
http://www-public.rz.uni-duesseldorf.de/~ritterd/wargames/logon.htm

Waterworld
http://www.mca.com/unicity/waterworld/

The World Fantasy Convention
http://www.farrsite.com/wfc/index.htm

The X-Files
http://www.rutgers.edu/x-files.html
http://www.thex-files.com/

Zinescope
http://www.uta.fi/~tlakja/index.html

˙ZINES/NEWSLETTERS

Analog Science Fiction & Fact
1540 Broadway
New York NY 10036
(212)698-1313
(212)782-8338 (fax)
1-800-333-4561
Monthly. $39.97/year. Covers the gamut of sci fi in film and television.

Animerica
Viz Communications, Inc.
PO Box 77010
San Francisco CA 94107
*Monthly. $4.95/issue ($6.50 in Canada);
$58/year ($70 in Canada, $158 elsewhere).
Combines anime and manga information.*

Asimov's Science Fiction
1540 Broadway
New York NY 10036
(212)698-1313
1-800-333-4108
Monthly. $39.97/year. Publishes sci-fi and horror short stories.

Bits and Pieces
John Clayton
10354 Windstream Dr.
Columbia MD 21044
$3.50/issue. Printed vehicle for the Horror and Fantasy Film Society of Baltimore.

Center for the Study of Science Fiction Newsletter
University of Kansas—Center for the Study of Science Fiction
English Department
Lawrence KS 66045
(913)864-3380
(913)864-4298
Annual. Free.

Cinefantastique
7240 W. Roosevelt Rd.
Forest Park IL 60130
(708)366-5566
(708)366-1441 (fax)
1-800-798-6515
Bimonthly. $27/year ($32 outside the U.S.).

Cinescape
Cinescape Group, Inc.
1920 Highland Ave., Ste. 222
Lombard IL 60148
(708)268-2498
Monthly. $4.99/issue ($6.50 Canada); $24.95/year ($36.95 in Canada and Mexico; $100 elsewhere). Highlights hi-tech action films as well as science fiction.

Clarion Science Fiction and Fantasy Writers' Workshop Newsletter
c/o Mary Sheridan
Lyman Briggs School, E-185 Holmes
Michigan State University
East Lansing MI 48825
(517)355-9598
(517)353-4765 (fax)
$10 contribution. Offers news of the Clarion Science Fiction workshop, their graduates, and other news related to science fiction.

The Drive-In Theater Newsletter
Nathan Miner
225 W. 1st St.
Frostburg MD 21532
$1.50/issue.

Ejecto-Pod
Jan Johnson
29 Darling St., No. 2
Boston MA 02120

Famous Monsters of Filmland
Dynacomm
Subscription Dept.
PO Box 9669
North Hollywood CA 91609
$24.95/year ($40 in Canada and Mexico; $50 elsewhere).

Fangoria
475 Park Ave. S.
New York NY 10016
(212)689-2830
(212)889-7933 (fax)
$37.97/year ($46.97 outside the U.S.). Covers horror and sci-fi films.

Fantasy Commentor
48 Highland Cir.
Bronxville NY 10708-5909
(914)961-6799
Semiannual. $10 contribution. Publishes articles, reviews, and prose on sci fi and fantasy.

Femme Fatales
7240 W. Roosevelt Rd.
Forest Park IL 60130

(708)366-5566
$18/year ($21 in Canada and elsewhere).

G-Fan
Daikaiju Enterprises
Box 3468
Steinbach MB Canada R0A 2A0
$20/year. Official fanzine of G-Force, the Godzilla Society of North America.

Heavy Metal
Metal Mammoth
584 Broadway, Ste. 608
New York NY 10012
(212)274-8462
(212)274-8969 (fax)
Bimonthly. $12.95/year. Presents illustrations and articles for fantasy enthusiasts.

It's Only a Movie!
Michael Flores
PO Box 14683
Chicago IL 60614-0683
$12/12 issues. Official organ of the Chicago Psychotronic Film Society.

The Joe Bob Report
PO Box 2002
Dallas TX 75221
(214)985-7448 (fax)
Biweekly. $65/26 issues ($100 outside the U.S.).

Lovecraft Studies
Necronomicon Press
PO Box 1304
West Warwick RI 02893
(401)828-7161
(401)738-6125 (fax)
$12/year ($15 outside the U.S.). Studies the life and writings of horror and sci-fi pioneer H.P. Lovecraft.

The Magazine of Fantasy & Science Fiction
Mercury Press, Inc.
143 Cream Hill Rd.
West Cornwall CT 06796
(203)672-6376
(203)672-2643 (fax)
Monthly. $2.95/issue; $29.90/year ($34.90 outside U.S.).

Magical Blend
PO Box 600
Chico CA 95927-9883
(916)893-9037
(916)893-9076 (fax)
Quarterly. $5.95/issue ($6.95 outside the U.S.); $19.95/year ($21.95 outside U.S.).

Manga Vizion
Viz Communications, Inc.
PO Box 77010
San Francisco CA 94107
*Monthly. $4.95/issue ($6.50 in Canada);
$58/year ($70 in Canada). "North America's only
monthly manga anthology."*

Monster! International
Kronos Productions
MPO Box 67
Oberlin OH 44074-0067

Monsterscene
Gorgo Entertainment Group
1036 S. Ahrens Ave.
Lombard IL 60148
*Quarterly. $5.95/issue; $24/year. Covers horror
and sci-fi movie history, actors, directors, and
videos.*

Movie Club
Don Dohler
12 Moray Ct.
Baltimore MD 21236
*$15.80/6 issues. Covers B-movies, classic
horror, and sci fi.*

New Lovecraft Collector
Necronomicon Press
PO Box 1304
West Warwick RI 02893
(401)828-7161
(401)738-6125 (fax)
*Quarterly. $5/issue ($6 outside U.S.). Covers
upcoming publications or film adaptions of H.P.
Lovecraft's work.*

Nippon Rando No Yumei Kaiju
Montag Enterprises
1151 Raymond Ave., No. 205
Glendale CA 91201-1850
*$12/year. "Showcases famous monsters of
Japanland."*

Oracle Science Fiction and Fantasy Magazine
Science Fiction and Fantasy Productions, Inc.
21111 Mapleridge
Southfield MI 48075
(810)355-9827
Quarterly. $7.20/issue.

Other Dimensions
Necronomicon Press
PO Box 1304
West Warwick RI 02893
(404)828-7161
(404)738-1625 (fax)

*$5/issue. Examines the influences of sci fi and
horror in the various mediums.*

Other Worlds
PO Box 209
Brooklyn NY 11228-0209
Annual. $9.95/issue.

Outre: The World of Ultra Media
1320 Oakton St.
Evanston IL 60202
(847)866-7155
(847)866-7554 (fax)
*Quarterly. $20/year ($30 in Canada; $50
elsewhere).*

Parts
Friday Jones
451 Moody St., No. 134
Waltham MA 02154-0442
*$3/issue ($5 outside the U.S.). Fanzine of all
things connected with the film* Re-Animator.

Planet B
Basement Productions
728 James St., Apt. 4
Pittsburgh PA 15212
SASE. Two-page B-movie newsletter.

Planet X
Scott Moon
PO Box 161221
Sacramento CA 95816
*$3.95/issue. "An SF/pop culture escape from the
world gone mad!"*

Protoculture Addicts
Ianus Publications
5000 Iberville St. #332
Montreal PQ Canada H2H 256
(514)523-8680
*Bimonthly. $4.95/issue; $25/year ($26.75 in
Canada; $40 overseas). Showcases both manga
and anime.*

PRSFS Newsletter (Potomac River Science Fiction Society)
12315 Judson Rd.
Wheaton MD 20906
Monthly. $2.50/issue.

Psychotronic Video
Michael J. Weldon
3309 Rte. 97
Narrowsburg NY 12764-6126
*Bimonthly. $22/year ($24 outside U.S.). Covers
unusual film and video releases.*

Satellite News
Mystery Science Theater 3000 Information Club

Sci Fi Connections

Best Brains, Inc.
PO Box 5325
Hopkins MN 55343
Included in membership.

Sci-Fi Entertainment
Sovereign Media
457 Carlisle Dr.
Herndon VA 22070
(703)471-1556
(703)471-1559 (fax)
*Bimonthly. $14.95/year ($18.95 outside U.S.).
Covers programming for the Sci-Fi Channel and
includes news and interviews.*

Sci Fi Universe
H.G. Publications, Inc.
9171 Wilshire Blvd., Ste. 300
Beverly Hills CA 90210
(310)858-7100
(310)275-3857
1-800-217-9306
*Bimonthly. $4.95/issue; $29.95/year. "The
magazine for science fiction fans with a life!"*

Science-Fantasy Correspondent
c/o Carrollton Clark
9122 Rosslyn
Arlington VA 22209
3/year. $25/year.

Science Fiction Chronicle
PO Box 022730
Brooklyn NY 11202-0056
(718)643-9011
(718)643-9011 (fax)
*Monthly. $30/year ($36 in Canada; $41
overseas). Offers the latest science-fiction and
fantasy news.*

Science Fiction Convention Register
101 S. Whiting, Ste. 700
Alexandria VA 22304
(703)461-8645
*3/year. $12/year. Lists all yearly sci-fi
conventions.*

Science Fiction Eye
PO Box 18539
Asheville NC 28814
(704)684-5575
(704)684-5779
*Biannual. $5/issue. Includes critical analyses
and commentary on the science-fiction field.*

Science-Fiction Studies
c/o Prof. Arthur B. Evans
DePauw University
Greencastle IN 46135-0037
(317)658-4758

(317)658-4177 (fax)
*3/year. $15/issue ($17 in Canada; $18
elsewhere); $22 for institutions ($25 in Canada;
$26 elsewhere).*

Scream Factory
Deadline Press
PO Box 2808
Apache Junction AZ 85217
(408)353-4450
*Quarterly. $24/year ($34 outside U.S.). Features
articles and reviews of sci-fi and horror films.*

Screem Magazine
490 S. Franklin St.
Wilkes-Barre PA 18702-3765
*Quarterly. $15/year ($20 in Canada; $40
elsewhere). Covers horror, sci-fi, and
exploitation film from all eras.*

Society for the Furtherance and Study of Fantasy and Science Fiction, Inc.
PO Box 1624
Madison WI 53701-1624
Publishes articles and prose on fantasy and sci fi.

Star Trek: Deep Space Nine
Starlog Press
475 Park Ave. S.
New York NY 10016
*$25/year ($35 outside U.S.). Chronicles episodes
of the popular sci-fi series and behind the
scenes information.*

Star Trek: The Official Fan Club Magazine
Official Fan Club
PO Box 111000
Aurora CO 80011
(303)341-1813
(303)341-1401 (fax)
*Bimonthly. $14.95/year ($21.95 outside U.S.).
Covers everything related to the Star Trek series,
films and fans.*

Star Wars Insider
Official Star Wars Fan Club
PO Box 111000
Aurora CO 80042
*Quarterly. $9.95 (includes membership). Covers
everything related to the science-fiction trilogy.*

Starbase-Superstar Facts & Pix
Sterling-Macfadden Partnership
233 Park Ave. S.
New York NY 10003
(212)780-3500
(212) 780-3555 (fax)
*Quarterly. $3.95/issue; $15.80/year. Presents
interviews with science-fiction actors and
personalities.*

Starburst
Visual Imagination
PO Box 156
Manorville NY 11949
(011)44 181 875 1520
(011)44 181 875 1588 (fax)
$4.99/issue ($6.25 in Canada).

Starlog
475 Park Ave. S. 8th Fl.
New York NY 10016
(212)689-2830
(212)689-7933
Monthly. $39.97/year. Reports on sci fi in television and films.

Warp Four
c/o John R. Racano
113 Cleveland Ave.
Colonia NJ 07067
(201)679-7756
Quarterly. $4/issue. Covers science fiction, fantasy, and horror in any medium.

World SF Newsletter
World SF International Science Fiction
    Association of Professionals
855 S. Harvard Dr.
Palatine IL 60067-7026
Quarterly. $15/year.

Weird City
Dave Szurek
1206 Wheeler Ave., Apt. 2
Hoquiam WA 98550-1901
$2.50/issue.

Zontar, the Magazine from Venus
Jan Johnson
29 Darling St., No.2
Boston MA 02120

FAN CLUBS

A.U.R.O.R.A.
PO Box 1204
Upper Marlboro MD 20773

Air, Sea, and Space Club
19205 Seneca Ridge Ct.
Gaithersburg MD 20879
(301)869-1755
John Samorjczyk Jr., Contact

Back to the Future Fan Club
11101 Cardinal Dr.
Madison AL 35758-5803
(205)230-6288
Stephen M. Clark, Contact

Barbara Bain International
c/o Ms. Terry S. Bowers
603 N. Clark St.
River Falls WI 54022-1044
(715)425-5172
Terry S. Bowers, Contact

Boston Star Trek Association
PO Box 1108
Boston MA 02103-1108
(617)894-BSTA
Lora Haines, Contact

Elvira Fan Club
14755 Ventura Blvd., 1-710
Sherman Oaks CA 91403

Fans of Leonard Nimoy and Deforest Kelley
PO Box 620503
Littleton CO 80123
(303)972-8966
Laura Guyer, Contact

Federation Council
5970 Independence Hwy.
Albany OR 97321
(503)928-9261
Nancy Hoven, Contact

Flight Patrol Fan Club
19205 Seneca Ridge Ct.
Gaithersburg MD 20879
(301)869-1755
John Samorjczyk, Jr., Contact

Friends of the Doctor
PO Box 17665
Portland OR 97217
(503 236-8710
Victoria Selander, Contact

G-Force, the Godzilla Society of North America
Daikaiju Enterprises
Box 3468
Steinbach MB Canada RoA 2Ao

Galaxy Patrol Fan Club
c/o Dale L. Ames
22 Colton St.
Worcester MA 01610
(508)799-2078
Dale L. Ames, Contact

The Hamill Exchange
PO Box 526177
Salt Lake City UT 84152-6177
Nacolle Parsons, Contact

Sci Fi Connections

International Network of Somewhere in Time Enthusiasts
PO Box 1556
Covina CA 91722
(818)810-1203
Bill Shepard, Contact

International Space: 1999 Alliance
86 1st St.
New London OH 44851-1196
(419)929-3351
John Von Kamp, Contact

Klingon Empire
9 Avis Dr.
Latham NY 12110
Toran Zantai K'dai, Contact

Klingon Strike Force
12601 22nd Ave. S.
Seattle WA 98168-2323
(206)433-6203
Keel Epetai K'ta-ri, Contact

Leonard Nimoy Fan Club
17 Gateway Dr.
Batavia NY 14020
(716)343-6605
Barbara Walker, Contact

Lost in Space Fannish Alliance
7331 Terri Robyn
St. Louis MO 63129
(314)846-2846
Flint Mitchell, Contact

LucasFilm Fan Club
PO Box 111000
Aurora CO 80042
(303)341-1813
Daniel H. Madsen, Contact

Martin Landau Aficionados
c/o Ms. Terry S. Bowers
603 N. Clark St.
River Falls WI 54022-1044
(715)425-5172
Terry S. Bowers, Contact

Mystery Science Theater 3000 Information Club
Best Brains, Inc.
PO Box 5325
Hopkins MN 55343

Niatrek International
30 E. Packard Ct.
Niagara Fall NY 14301-2821
Dave Jeffery, Contact

Quantum League
22 Chalkfarm Dr.
Toronto ON Canada M3L lL2
(416)241-1386
Michelle Sauve, Contact

The Rocky Horror Picture Show Fan Club
220 W. 19th, Ste. 2-A
New York NY 10011

Sci-Fi Society of Long Island
400 Collington Dr.
Ronkonkoma NY 11779
(516)737-2171
Gregory Jones, Contact

Star Trek: The Official Fan Club
PO Box 111000
Aurora CO 80042
(303)341-1813
Daniel H. Madsen, Contact

Star Trek Welcommittee
PO Drawer 12
Saranac MI 48881
(413)247-5339
Shirley S. Maiewski, Contact

Star Wars Fan Club
PO Box 111000
Aurora CO 80042
(303)341-1813
Daniel H. Madsen, Contact

Starfleet
PO Box 980008
West Sacramento CA
(916)348-0726
Rob Lerman, Contact

Trekville U.S.A.
c/o Jay S. Hastings
1021 S. 9th Ave.
Scranton PA 18504
(717)343-7806
Jay S. Hastings

Turtle Force—The Official Fan Club of the Teenage Mutant Ninja Turtles
PO Box 3974
Schaumburg IL 60168-3974
(708)351-6565
A.J. Marsiglia, Contact

Walter Koenig International
PO Box 15546
North Hollywood CA 91615-5546
Carolyn Atkinson, Contact

William Shatner Connection
7059 Atoll Ave.

North Hollywood CA 91605
(818)764-5499
Joyce Mason, Contact

United Federation of Planets
6201 Revere St.
Philadelphia PA 19149
(215)537-TREK
Michael R. Marinelli, Contact

United Trekkers of Planet Earth
PO Box 470
Winona TX 75792
Maxine Harris, Contact

V Fan Club
8048 Norwich Ave.
Van Nuys CA 91402-5616
(818)901-1466
Kathy R. Pillsbury, Contact

CONVENTIONS

Accelerate
78 Sterry Rd.
Dagenham, Essex RM10 8NT England
For fans of the Quantum Leap *series.*

Albacon
10 Atlas Rd.
Springburn, Glasgow G21 4TE Scotland

AlbaCon
PO Box 2085
Albany NY 1220-0085
(518)456-5242

Arcana
PO Box 8036
Minneapolis MN 55408
For fans of horror, dark fantasy, sf, and games.

Archon
PO Box 483
Chesterfield MO 63006-0483
(314)FAN-3026
A gathering for science-fiction writers.

**The Atlanta StarCon & Comics
    Convention**
Michael Allgood
(770)934-7400
For fans of sci fi and comics.

Bubonicon
NMSF Conference
PO Box 37257
Albuquerque NM 87176
(502)266-8905

Bouchereon
PO Box 8296
Minneapolis MN 55408-0296
For fans of sci fi and mystery.

Conference
PARSEC
Box 3681
Pittsburgh PA 15230
(412)344-0236

Contagion
PO Box 867
Rutherglen, Glasgow G73 4HR Scotland
For Star Trek *fans.*

Contradiction
Box 100, Bridge Sta.
Niagara Falls NY 14305

Conversion
PO Box 1088, Station M
Calgary AB T2P 2K9 Canada
(403)259-3938

Darkover Grand Council Meeting
c/o Armida Council
Box 7203
Silver Spring MD 20907
(202)737-4609
For fans of the "Darkover" book series.

Def Con
47 Marsham
Orton Goldhay, Peterborough PE2 5RN England
For fans of Star Trek/Red Dwarf *TV programs.*

Delecon
PO Box 1313
Shawnee Mission KS 66222
A Star Trek *convention.*

Diversicon
PO Box 8036
Minneapolis MN 55408-8036
(612)822-8303

Evolution
13 Lindfield Gardens
Hampstead, London NW3 6PX England

Fantasticon UK
38 Planetree Ave.
Fenham, Newcastle NE4 9TH England
For fans of Star Wars, Star Trek, B5, *and* The X-Files.

Farpoint
Steve Wilson
(410)799-2869

**Sci Fi
Connections**

GaylaxiCon
PO Box 176
Somerville MA 02143
(617)321-9292
Sci-fi convention for gay and lesbian fans.

Gen Con
Gen Con HQ
201 Sheridan Springs Rd.
Lake Geneva WI 53147

Generations
4 Aspenwood House, Ipsley St.
Redditch, Worcestershire B98 7AR England
For fans of the Star Trek: The Next Generation *TV series.*

Icon
PO Box 525
Iowa City IA 52244
(319)351-4374

In Con
Deborah Fredericks
1217 E. Empire
Spokane WA 99207
(509)482-5288

Inconjunction
PO Box 19776
Indianapolis IN 46219
(317)839-5519

Katsucon
Katsu Productions
PO Box 11582
Blacksburg VA 24062-1582
For fans of anime.

LosCon
LASFS
11513 Burbank Blvd.
North Hollywood CA 91601
(818)760-9234

Menopticon
22 Seven Acres Ln., Norden, Rochdale
Lancanster, England OL127R1
For fans of the Dr. Who *TV series.*

Moscon
PO Box 9622
Moscow ID 83843
(509)334-4434

Nexus
26 Milner Rd.
Horfield, Bristol BS7 9PQ England
For fans of the Star Trek *series.*

NovaCon
14 Park St., Lye
Stourbridge, W. Midlands, BY9 8SS England

NovaCon
One Trek Mind, Inc.
PO Box 3363
Merrifield VA 22116
(703)280-5373
For fans of the Star Trek *series.*

OryCon
PO Box 5703
Portland OR 97228-5703
(503)283-0802

Panopticon
PO Box 7831
London, England SW15 6YD
For fans of the Dr. Who *series.*

RavenCon
Michael Pederson
PO Box 17338
Richmond VA 23226
(804)750-1902
For sci-fi, fantasy, comics, and games enthusiasts.

ReaderCon
PO Box 381246
Cambridge MA 02238
(617)625-6507

RebelCon
Stephen Sandberg
(508)587-1223

Rising Star
Dr. Fred R. Eichelman
545 Howard Dr.
Salem VA 24153
(540)389-9400
For fans of the Star Trek *series.*

RiverCon
Box 58009
Louisville KY 40268
(502)448-6562

San Diego Comic-Con International
PO Box 128458
San Diego CA 92112
(619)491-2475
For comic book fans.

Sci-Con
c/o HaRoSFA
PO Box 9434
Hampton VA 23670

(804)865-1407
For fans of Star Wars *and magic.*

Shore Leave
PO Box 6809
Lowson MD 21285
(410)785-7000
For fans of the Star Trek *series.*

Shorecon
Multigenre, Inc.
266 Spruce Dr.
Brick NJ 08723-6528
(908)262-9249

Starcon
Mike Stannard
PO Box 2037
San Bernardino CA 92406
(909)880-8558
For fans of sci fi and horror.

Starcon
PO Box 24590
Denver CO 80224
(303)671-8735
For fans of Star Trek *and fantasy.*

UnConvention
Institute of Education, Bedford Street, London
PO Box 146
Glasgow, England G1 5RN
For those interested in government, UFOs, and conspiracies.

Unification
8 Ennerdale Close
Oadby, Leicester, England LE2 4TN
Covers Star Trek.

Voyage
15 Fullers Ct.
Exeter, Devon, England EX2 4DZ
For fans of Voyage to the Bottom of the Sea.

Warp Two
David Simons
69 Merlin Crescent
Edgeware, Middx, England HA8 6JB
For fans of the Star Trek *series.*

Weekend in Sherwood
Spirit of Sherwood
1276 W. Marshall St.
Ferndale MI 48220
(313)544-0608
For fans of BBC's Robin of Sherwood *series.*

WesterCon/ConDiablo
PO Box 3177
El Paso TX 79923

(800)585-8754
For fans of western fantasies.

William Campbell's Fantasticon
(305)388-2890

WishCon
500 Monroe Tpk.
Monroe CT 06468
(617)986-9952
For fans of Star Trek, Dr. Who, *and comics.*

WorldCon/L.A. Con
c/o SCIFI
PO Box 8442
Van Nuys CA 91409

World Fantasy Con
PO Box 473
Oak Forest IL 60452

BOOKS

Alien Encounters: Anatomy of Science Fiction
Mark Rose. 1981. Harvard University Press. $16.

Alien to Femininity: Speculative Fiction & Feminist Theory
Marleen S. Barr. 1987. Greenwood Publishing Group, Inc. $45.

Aliens & Alien Societies
Stanley Schmidt. 1996. Writer's Digest Books. $17.99.

Aliens, Robots, and Spaceships
Jeff Rovin. 1995. Facts on File. $35.

Androids, Humanoids, & Other Folklore Monsters: Science & Soul in Science Fiction Films
Schelde Per. 1993. New York University Press. $40.

The Apollo Adventure: The Making of the Apollo Space Program and the Movie Apollo 13
Jeffery Kluger. 1995. Pocketbooks. $12 (paper).

Classic Science Fiction Films
Jeff Rovin. 1993. Carol Publishing. $16.95 (paper).

Cult Science Fiction Films: From the Amazing Colossal Man to Yog: The Monster from Space
Welch Everman. 1995. Carol Publishing. $17.95 (paper).

Sci Fi Connections

The Encyclopedia of Science Fiction
John Clute and Peter Nicholls. 2nd ed., 1995. St. Martin's Griffin. $29.95 (paper).

Fantastic Cinema Subject Guide
Bryan Senn and John Johnson. 1992. McFarland & Co. $49.95.

Future Noir: The Making of Blade Runner
Paul M. Sammon. 1996. Harper Prism. $14 (paper).

George Lucas: The Creative Impulse
Charles Champlin. 1992. Abrams. $39.95.

Godzilla—King of the Movie Monsters: An Illustrated Guide to Japanese Monster Movies
Robert Marrero. 1996. Fantasma Books. $15.95 (paper).

History of Science Fiction Movies
Adam Knee. 1996. Diderot Publisher. $12 (paper).

I Am Spock
Leonard Nimoy. 1995. Hyperion. $24.95.

The Illustrated Star Wars Universe
Kevin J. Anderson. 1995. Bantam. $35.

Interviews with B Science Fiction and Horror Movie Makers
Tom Weaver. 1988. McFarland & Co. $38.50.

It Came from the Drive-In
Norman Partridge, ed. 1996. DAW Books, Inc. $5.50 (paper).

It Came from Weaver Five: Interviews with 20 Zany, Glib & Earnest Moviemakers in the SF & Horror Traditions of the Forties & Fifties
Tom Weaver. 1996. McFarland & Co. $38.50.

Japanese Science Fiction, Fantasy & Horror Films: A Critical Analysis & Filmography of 103 Features Released in the United States, 1950-1992
Stuart Galbraith. 1994. McFarland & Co. $45.

Monsters & Aliens from George Lucas
Bob Carrau. 1993. Harry N. Abrams, Inc. $19.95.

The Mystery Science Theater 3000 Colossal Episode Guide
1996. Bantam Books. $16.95 (paper).

New Sci-Fi Movies 1995: From Stargate to Waterworld
Van Hise-Schuster. 1996. Movie Publisher Services, Inc. $16.95 (paper).

Nightmare of Ecstasy: The Life and Art of Edward D. Wood, Jr.
Rudolph Grey. 1992. Feral House. $14.95 (paper).

The Overlook Film Encyclopedia: Science Fiction
Phil Hardy, ed. 1994. Overlook Press. $50; $40 (paper).

Replications: A Robotic History of the Science Fiction Film
J.P. Telotte. 1995. University of Illinois Press. $29.95.

S-F 2: A Pictorial History of Science Fiction Films from Rollerball to Return of the Jedi
Richard Meyers. 1984. Carol Publishing. $19.95.

The Science Fiction and Fantasy Film Handbook
Alan Frank. 1982. Barnes & Noble Books—Imports. $41.50.

Science Fiction Filmmaking in the 1980's: Interviews with Actors, Directors, Producers & Writers
Lee Goldberg. 1995. McFarland & Co. $37.50.

Star Trek Concordance
Bjo Trimble. Carol Publishing. $19.95 (paper).

Star Trek Interview Book
Allan Asherman. Pocketbooks. $7.95 (paper).

Star Trek: The Klingon Way: A Warrior's Guide
Marc Okrand. 1996. Pocketbooks. $12 (paper). In both English and Klingon.

Star Trek Movie Memories
William Shatner. 1995. HarperCollins. $6.99 (paper).

Them or Us: Archetypal Interpretations of Fifties Alien Invasion Films
Patrick Lucanio. 1988. Indiana University Press. $29.95.

3D Studio Sci-Fi Effects
Jon Bell. 1996. New Riders Publishing. $50. Book and CD-ROM combo.

A Trekker's Guide to Collectibles
Jeffery Synder. 1996. Schiffer Publishing. $29.95 (paper).

Yesterday's Tomorrows: The Golden Age of Science Fiction Movie Posters
Bruce L. Wright. 1993. Taylor Publishing Co. $19.95 (paper)

Alternate Titles Index

Before you panic because you think the Hound didn't include the video you're looking for, check out this index to see if it may be hiding under an assumed name. If you still can't find it, then write the Hound and let 'em know that he should include the title in the next edition (God willing) of this exquisite science-fiction reference.

The Cave Dwellers *See* One Million B.C. (1940)

Cave Man *See* One Million B.C. (1940)

The Chief Wants No Survivors *See* No Survivors, Please (1963)

Chikyu Boelgun *See* The Mysterians (1958)

Circuitry Man 2 *See* Plughead Rewired: Circuitry Man 2 (1994)

Code Name: Trixie *See* The Crazies (1973)

Collision Course *See* The Bamboo Saucer (1968)

Contamination *See* Alien Contamination (1981)

The Cosmic Man Appears in Tokyo *See* Warning from Space (1956)

Cosmo 2000: Planet Without a Name *See* Cosmos: War of the Planets (1980)

Cosmonauts on Venus *See* Planeta Burg (1962)

The Crawling Terror *See* The Cosmic Monsters (1958)

Created to Kill *See* Embryo (1976)

The Creature from Another World *See* The Crawling Eye (1958)

Creature from Galaxy 27 *See* Night of the Blood Beast (1958)

The Creature Wasn't Nice *See* Spaceship (1981)

Creatures of the Prehistoric Planet *See* Horror of the Blood Monsters (1970)

Creatures of the Red Planet *See* Horror of the Blood Monsters (1970)

The Creepers *See* Island of Terror (1966)

The Creeping Unknown *See* The Quatermass Experiment (1955)

Curse of the Mushroom People *See* Attack of the Mushroom People (1963)

Cyber-Chic *See* Robo-C.H.I.C. (1989)

Cyberjack *See* Virtual Assassin (1995)

Cyborg Cop 2 *See* Cyborg Soldier (1994)

Dagora *See* Dagora, the Space Monster (1965)

Dai Koesu Yongkari *See* Yongkari Monster of the Deep (1967)

Daikaiju Baran *See* Varan the Unbelievable (1961)

Daikaiju Gamera *See* Gamera, the Invincible (1966)

Daikyoju Gappa *See* Gappa the Trifibian Monster (1967)

Dallos *See* Battle for Moon Station Dallos (1986)

Dark Angel *See* I Come in Peace (1990)

Deadlocked: Escape from Zone 14 *See* Deadlock 2 (1994)

The Deadly Rays from Mars *See* Flash Gordon: Mars Attacks the World (1938)

The Deadly Spawn *See* Return of the Aliens: The Deadly Spawn (1983)

Deadly Sting *See* Evil Spawn (1987)

Death and the Green Slime *See* The Green Slime (1968)

Death from Outer Space *See* The Day the Sky Exploded (1957)

Demon *See* God Told Me To (1976)

The Demon Planet *See* Planet of the Vampires (1965)

Demons of the Swamp *See* Attack of the Giant Leeches (1959)

Denso Ningen *See* The Secret of the Telegian (1961)

Der Chef Wuenscht Keine Zeugen *See* No Survivors, Please (1963)

Der Schweigende Stern *See* First Spaceship on Venus (1960)

Deranged *See* Idaho Transfer (1973)

Diabolik *See* Danger: Diabolik (1968)

Die Folterkammer des Dr. Fu Manchu *See* The Castle of Fu Manchu (1968)

Digital Dreams *See* Dungeonmaster (1983)

Disaster in Time *See* Grand Tour: Disaster in Time (1992)

Docteur M. *See* Club Extinction (1989)

Doctor of Doom *See* Wrestling Women Vs. the Aztec Ape (1962)

A Dog, a Mouse, and a Sputnik *See* Sputnik (1961)

The Doomsday Machine *See* Escape from Planet Earth (1967)

Doppelganger *See* Journey to the Far Side of the Sun (1969)

Duel of the Gargantuas *See* War of the Gargantuas (1970)

Duel of the Space Monsters *See* Frankenstein Meets the Space Monster (1965)

Earth Defense Forces *See* The Mysterians (1958)

Ebirah, Terror of the Deep *See* Godzilla Vs. the Sea Monster (1966)

El Robot Humano *See* The Robot Vs. the Aztec Mummy (1959)

The Electric Monster *See* The Electronic Monster (1957)

End of the World *See* Panic in the Year Zero! (1962)

Enemy from Space *See* Quatermass 2 (1957)

Ercole al Centro Della Terra *See* Hercules in the Haunted World (1964)

Ercole alla Conquista di Atlantide *See* Hercules and the Captive Women (1963)

Ercole e la Regina de Lidia *See* Hercules Unchained (1959)

The Escape of Megagodzilla *See* Terror of Mechagodzilla (1978)

Escapement *See* The Electronic Monster (1957)

Evil Dead 3 *See* Army of Darkness (1992)

Expedition Moon *See* Rocketship X-M (1950)

The Fabulous Baron Munchausen *See* The Original Fabulous Adventures of Baron Munchausen (1961)

First Woman Into Space *See* Space Monster (1964)

Flash Gordon's Trip to Mars *See* Flash Gordon: Mars Attacks the World (1938)

The Flesh Creatures *See* Horror of the Blood Monsters (1970)

Flesh Creatures of the Red Planet *See* Horror of the Blood Monsters (1970)

The Forbin Project *See* Colossus: The Forbin Project (1970)

Forbrydelsens Element *See* The Element of Crime (1984)

4...3...2...1...Morte *See* Mission Stardust (1968)

Frankenstein '88 *See* The Vindicator (1985)

Frankenstein Meets the Spacemen *See* Frankenstein Meets the Space Monster (1965)

Frankenstein Monsters: Sanda Vs. Gairath *See* War of the Gargantuas (1970)

Fu Manchu and the Kiss of Death *See* Kiss and Kill (1968)

Fukkatsu no Hi *See* Virus (1982)

Fungus of Terror *See* Attack of the Mushroom People (1963)

Furankenshutain No Kaiju Sanda Tai Gailah *See* War of the Gargantuas (1970)

Future Cop *See* Trancers (1984)

Gambara Vs. Barugon *See* Gamera Vs. Barugon (1966)

Gamera *See* Gamera, the Invincible (1966)

Gamera Tai Barugon *See* Gamera Vs. Barugon (1966)

Gamera Tai Gaos *See* Gamera Vs. Gaos (1967)

Gamera Tai Guiron *See* Gamera Vs. Guiron (1969)

Gamera Tai Shinkai Kaiju Jigara *See* Gamera Vs. Zigra (1971)

Gamera Vs. Gyaos *See* Gamera Vs. Gaos (1967)

Gamera Vs. the Deep Sea Monster Zigra *See* Gamera Vs. Zigra (1971)

Gamma Sango Uchu Daisakusen *See* The Green Slime (1968)

Gammera *See* Gamera, the Invincible (1966)

The Gargon Terror *See* Teenagers from Outer Space (1959)

Ghidora, the Three-Headed Monster *See* Ghidrah the Three Headed Monster (1965)

Ghidorah Sandai Kaiju Chikyu Saidai No Kessan *See* Ghidrah the Three Headed Monster (1965)

Ghidrah *See* Ghidrah the Three Headed Monster (1965)

The Giant Leeches *See* Attack of the Giant Leeches (1959)

Gigantis, the Fire Monster *See* Godzilla Raids Again (1955)

Gill Woman *See* Voyage to the Planet of Prehistoric Women (1968)

Gill Women of Venus *See* Voyage to the Planet of Prehistoric Women (1968)

Girl in the Moon *See* Woman in the Moon (1929)

Gladiatorerna *See* The Gladiators (1970)

Gnaw: Food of the Gods 2 *See* Food of the Gods: Part 2 (1988)

Godzilla Fights the Giant Moth *See* Godzilla Vs. Mothra (1964)

Godzilla Tai Mosura *See* Godzilla Vs. Mothra (1964)

Godzilla Vs. Gigan *See* Godzilla on Monster Island (1972)

Godzilla Vs. Hedora *See* Godzilla Vs. the Smog Monster (1972)

Godzilla Vs. Mechagodzilla *See* Godzilla Vs. the Cosmic Monster (1974)

Godzilla Vs. the Bionic Monster *See* Godzilla Vs. the Cosmic Monster (1974)

Godzilla Vs. the Giant Moth *See* Godzilla Vs. Mothra (1964)

Godzilla Vs. the Thing *See* Godzilla Vs. Mothra (1964)

Godzilla's Counter Attack *See* Godzilla Raids Again (1955)

Gojira *See* Godzilla, King of the Monsters (1954)

Gojira no Musuko *See* Son of Godzilla (1966)

Gojira Tai Hedora *See* Godzilla Vs. the Smog Monster (1972)

Gojira Tai Megalon *See* Godzilla Vs. Megalon (1973)

Gojira Tai Meka-Gojira *See* Godzilla Vs. the Cosmic Monster (1974)

Gomar the Human Gorilla *See* Night of the Bloody Apes (1968)

Grave Robbers from Outer Space *See* Plan 9 from Outer Space (1956)

Graveyard Tramps *See* Invasion of the Bee Girls (1973)

Great Monster Yongkari *See* Yongkari Monster of the Deep (1967)

The Greatest Battle on Earth *See* Ghidrah the Three Headed Monster (1965)

Green Monkey *See* Blue Monkey (1987)

Hands of a Killer *See* Planets Against Us (1961)

The Happiness Cage *See* Mind Snatchers (1972)

Harrison Bergeron *See* Kurt Vonnegut's Harrison Bergeron (1995)

The Head That Wouldn't Die *See* The Brain that Wouldn't Die (1963)

Hector Servadac's Ark *See* On the Comet (1968)

Hell Fire *See* They (1977)

Hellfire *See* Primal Scream (1987)

Hercules and the Conquest of Atlantis *See* Hercules and the Captive Women (1963)

Hercules and the Haunted Women *See* Hercules and the Captive Women (1963)

Hercules Goes Bananas *See* Hercules in New York (1970)

Hercules: The Movie *See* Hercules in New York (1970)

H.G. Wells' New Invisible Man *See* The New Invisible Man (1958)

Alternate Titles

Mind Ripper *See* Wes Craven Presents Mind Ripper (1995)

Mindwarp: An Infinity of Terror *See* Galaxy of Terror (1981)

A Modern Bluebeard *See* Boom in the Moon (1946)

The Monster Baran *See* Varan the Unbelievable (1961)

Monster from a Prehistoric Planet *See* Gappa the Trifibian Monster (1967)

Monster Maker *See* Monster from the Ocean Floor (1954)

Monster of Monsters *See* Ghidrah the Three Headed Monster (1965)

Monster of Terror *See* Die, Monster, Die! (1965)

The Monster with Green Eyes *See* Planets Against Us (1961)

Monster Yongkari *See* Yongkari Monster of the Deep (1967)

Monster Zero *See* Godzilla Vs. Monster Zero (1965)

Monsters from the Moon *See* Robot Monster (1953)

Monsters from the Unknown Planet *See* Terror of Mechagodzilla (1978)

Monstrosity *See* The Atomic Brain (1964)

Morgen Grauen *See* Time Troopers (1989)

Morning Terror *See* Time Troopers (1989)

Mosura *See* Mothra (1961)

Mosura Tai Gojira *See* Godzilla Vs. Mothra (1964)

Mothra Vs. Godzilla *See* Godzilla Vs. Mothra (1964)

Mutant *See* Forbidden World (1982)

The Mutilator *See* The Dark (1979)

Mysterious Invader *See* The Astounding She-Monster (1958)

The Mysterious Satellite *See* Warning from Space (1956)

Na Komete *See* On the Comet (1968)

Naked Space *See* Spaceship (1981)

Nankai No Daiketto *See* Godzilla Vs. the Sea Monster (1966)

The Night Caller *See* Night Caller from Outer Space (1966)

The Night Crawlers *See* Navy Vs. the Night Monsters (1966)

Night of the Big Heat *See* Island of the Burning Doomed (1967)

Night of the Silicates *See* Island of Terror (1966)

Nostradamus No Daiyogen *See* Last Days of Planet Earth (1974)

Oblivion 2 *See* Backlash: Oblivion 2 (1995)

Operation Monsterland *See* Destroy All Monsters (1968)

Oru Kaiju Daishingeki *See* Godzilla's Revenge (1969)

Out of the Darkness *See* Teenage Caveman (1958)

The Parasite Murders *See* They Came from Within (1975)

Parts: The Clonus Horror *See* The Clonus Horror (1979)

The Peace Game *See* The Gladiators (1970)

Perils from Planet Mongo *See* Flash Gordon: Rocketship (1936)

The Phoenix *See* War of the Wizards (1981)

Planet of Horrors *See* Galaxy of Terror (1981)

Planet of Storms *See* Planeta Burg (1962)

Planet of the Lifeless Men *See* Battle of the Worlds (1961)

The Plants Are Watching *See* The Kirlian Witness (1978)

Prehistoric World *See* Teenage Caveman (1958)

Prey *See* Alien Prey (1983)

Project Shadowchaser 2 *See* Night Siege Project: Shadowchaser 2 (1994)

Prophecies of Nostradamus *See* Last Days of Planet Earth (1974)

Purple Death from Outer Space *See* Flash Gordon Conquers the Universe (1940)

Queen of Blood *See* Planet of Blood (1966)

Radio Ranch *See* The Phantom Empire (1935)

Radon *See* Rodan (1957)

Radon the Flying Monster *See* Rodan (1957)

Ragewar *See* Dungeonmaster (1983)

Retaliator *See* Programmed to Kill (1986)

The Return of Mr. H. *See* They Saved Hitler's Brain (1964)

The Return of the Giant Monsters *See* Gamera Vs. Gaos (1967)

Robert A. Heinlein's The Puppet Masters *See* The Puppet Masters (1994)

Rocket to the Moon *See* Cat Women of the Moon (1953)

Roger Corman Presents: Suspect Device *See* Suspect Device (1995)

Roger Corman's Frankenstein Unbound *See* Frankenstein Unbound (1990)

The Salute of the Jugger *See* The Blood of Heroes (1989)

Sanda Tai Gailah *See* War of the Gargantuas (1970)

Santa Claus Defeats the Aliens *See* Santa Claus Conquers the Martians (1964)

Santo en el Museo de Cera *See* Samson in the Wax Museum (1963)

Santo in the Wax Museum *See* Samson in the Wax Museum (1963)

Satan's Satellites *See* Zombies of the Stratosphere (1952)

Satellite of Blood *See* First Man into Space (1959)

She Was a Hippy Vampire *See* The Wild World of Batwoman (1966)

Shivers *See* They Came from Within (1975)

Alternate Titles

Slave Girls *See* Prehistoric Women (1950)

Something Waits in the Dark *See* Screamers (1980)

Space Avenger *See* Alien Space Avenger (1991)

Space Invasion from Lapland *See* Invasion of the Animal People (1962)

Space Invasion of Lapland *See* Invasion of the Animal People (1962)

Space Men *See* Assignment Outer Space (1961)

Space Men Appear in Tokyo *See* Warning from Space (1956)

Space Mission of the Lost Planet *See* Horror of the Blood Monsters (1970)

Space Monster Dagora *See* Dagora, the Space Monster (1965)

Space Mutants *See* Planet of the Vampires (1965)

Space Soldiers *See* Flash Gordon: Rocketship (1936)

Space 2074 *See* Star Quest (1989)

Spaceship to the Unknown *See* Flash Gordon: Rocketship (1936)

Spaziale K.1 *See* The Human Duplicators (1964)

The Spider *See* Earth Vs. the Spider (1958)

Spider-Man *See* The Amazing Spider-Man (1977)

Spirit of the Dead *See* The Asphyx (1972)

The Split *See* The Manster (1959)

The Stand *See* Stephen King's The Stand (1994)

Star Child *See* Space Raiders (1983)

Starflight: The Plane that Couldn't Land *See* Starflight One (1983)

Stella Star *See* Star Crash (1978)

Storm Planet *See* Planeta Burg (1962)

Strange Journey *See* Fantastic Voyage (1966)

The Strange World of Planet X *See* The Cosmic Monsters (1958)

The Sun Demon *See* Hideous Sun Demon (1959)

The Super Inframan *See* Infra-Man (1976)

Superman and the Strange People *See* Superman & the Mole Men (1951)

Supersnooper *See* Super Fuzz (1981)

Teenage Monster *See* Meteor Monster (1957)

The Telegian *See* The Secret of the Telegian (1961)

Terreur dans l'Espace *See* Planet of the Vampires (1965)

Terror from the Sun *See* Hideous Sun Demon (1959)

Terror in Space *See* Planet of the Vampires (1965)

Terror in the Midnight Sun *See* Invasion of the Animal People (1962)

The Terror Strikes *See* The War of the Colossal Beast (1958)

Terrore nello Spazio *See* Planet of the Vampires (1965)

Thin Air *See* Invasion of the Body Stealers (1969)

The Thing From Another World *See* The Thing (1951)

Three Tornadoes *See* Blue Tornado (1992)

Time of the Beast *See* Mutator (1990)

Time Trap *See* The Time Travelers (1964)

Timeslip *See* The Atomic Man (1956)

Timewarp *See* Day Time Ended (1978)

Titan Find *See* Creature (1985)

Tomb of the Living Dead *See* Mad Doctor of Blood Island (1969)

The Tommyknockers *See* Stephen King's The Tommyknockers (1993)

The Tomorrow Man *See* 984: Prisoner of the Future (1984)

Trackers *See* Space Rage (1986)

A Trip to Mars *See* A Trip to the Moon (1902)

The Trollenberg Terror *See* The Crawling Eye (1958)

The Tunnel *See* Transatlantic Tunnel (1935)

2084 *See* Starship (1987)

2002: The Rape of Eden *See* Bounty Hunter 2002 (1994)

Uchu Daikaiju Dogora *See* Dagora, the Space Monster (1965)

Uchudai Dogora *See* Dagora, the Space Monster (1965)

Uchujin Tokyo Ni Arawaru *See* Warning from Space (1956)

Unknown Satellite Over Tokyo *See* Warning from Space (1956)

Vampire Men of the Lost Planet *See* Horror of the Blood Monsters (1970)

The Varrow Mission *See* Teen Alien (1988)

The Venusian *See* The Stranger from Venus (1954)

Virgin Hunters *See* Test Tube Teens from the Year 2000 (1993)

Vortex *See* Day Time Ended (1978)

Voyage Beyond the Sun *See* Space Monster (1964)

Voyage to a Prehistoric Planet *See* Voyage to the Prehistoric Planet (1965)

War Between the Planets *See* Planet on the Prowl (1965)

The War of the Monsters *See* Gamera Vs. Barugon (1966)

War of the Planets *See* Cosmos: War of the Planets (1980)

Water Cyborgs *See* Terror Beneath the Sea (1966)

Welcome to Oblivion *See* Ultra Warrior (1992)

Who? *See* Roboman (1975)

The Wizard of Mars *See* Horrors of the Red Planet (1964)

The Worlds of Gulliver *See* The Three Worlds of Gulliver (1959)

X *See* X: The Man with X-Ray Eyes (1963)

Yosei Gorasu *See* Gorath (1964)

Zeta One *See* Alien Women (1969)

Z.P.G. *See* Zero Population Growth (1972)

Cast Index

The following index lists all actors credited in the main review section (including cameos and voiceovers), alphabetically by said actors' last names. Don't be fooled because they are presented here in first name/last name format. Alphabetizing by first names would be foolish, and you expect more of us than that. If you keep flipping pages, eventually you'll find the "Director Index," which is pretty much the same thing but for directors. Get it?

Michael Aldredge
Incredible Melting Man '77
Robot Jox '90

Kitty Aldridge
Slipstream '89

Julio Aleman
Neutron and the Black
    Mask '61
Neutron Vs. the Amazing
    Dr. Caronte '61
Neutron Vs. the Death
    Robots '62

Jason Alexander
Coneheads '93

Jeff Alexander
Curse of the Swamp
    Creature '66

Suzanne Alexander
Cat Women of the Moon
    '53

Marta Alicia
Mindwarp '91

Jed Allan
Suspect Device '95

Ginger Lynn Allen
Hollywood Boulevard 2 '89

Karen Allen
Raiders of the Lost Ark '81
Starman '84

Nancy Allen
The Philadelphia
    Experiment '84
RoboCop '87
RoboCop 2 '90
RoboCop 3 '91
Strange Invaders '83

Patrick Allen
Invasion of the Body
    Stealers '69
Island of the Burning
    Doomed '67
When Dinosaurs Ruled the
    Earth '70

Rosalind Allen
Ticks '93

Sheila Allen
Children of the Damned
    '63

Valerie Allen
I Married a Monster from
    Outer Space '58

Woody Allen
Sleeper '73

Kirstie Alley
Runaway '84
Star Trek 2: The Wrath of
    Khan '82
Village of the Damned '95

Corbin Allred
Quest of the Delta Knights
    '93

**Maria Conchita
Alonso**
Predator 2 '90
The Running Man '87

Walter George Alton
The Puma Man '80

Crox Alvarado
The Robot Vs. the Aztec
    Mummy '59

Lyle Alzado
Neon City '91

Bin Amatsu
Magic Serpent '66

Don Ameche
Cocoon '85
Cocoon: The Return '88

Judith Ames
When Worlds Collide '51

Leon Ames
The Absent-Minded
    Professor '61
Son of Flubber '63

Nic Amoroso
Xtro 2: The Second
    Encounter '91

John Amos
Beastmaster '82
Hologram Man '95

Morey Amsterdam
It Came from Outer Space
    '53

Merry Anders
The Time Travelers '64
Women of the Prehistoric
    Planet '66

Rudolph Anders
Phantom from Space '53
She Demons '58

Asbjorn Andersen
Reptilicus '62

Gotha Andersen
The Element of Crime '84

Angry Anderson
Mad Max: Beyond
    Thunderdome '85

Dawn Anderson
Teenagers from Outer
    Space '59

Donna Anderson
On the Beach '59

Ingrid Anderson
Hercules '83

Judith Anderson
Star Trek 3: The Search for
    Spock '84

Melody Anderson
Flash Gordon '80

Richard Anderson
Forbidden Planet '56

Warner Anderson
Destination Moon '50

Bibi Andersson
Quintet '79

Gaby Andre
The Cosmic Monsters '58

George Andre
The Wild World of
    Batwoman '66

Victor Andre
A Trip to the Moon '02

Andre the Giant
The Princess Bride '87

Starr Andreeff
Nightfall '88
Syngenor '90
The Terror Within '88

Ursula Andress
Clash of the Titans '81
10th Victim '65

David Andrews
Cherry 2000 '88

Harry Andrews
The Final Programme '73

Tod Andrews
She Demons '58

William Andrews
Geisha Girl '52

Pier Angeli
Octaman '71

Angelyne
Earth Girls Are Easy '89

Evelyn Ankers
The Invisible Man's
    Revenge '44

Morris Ankrum
Beginning of the End '57
Earth Vs. the Flying
    Saucers '56
From the Earth to the
    Moon '58
The Giant Claw '57
Half Human '58
Invaders from Mars '53
Kronos '57
Red Planet Mars '52

Anna-Lisa
Have Rocket Will Travel '59

Francesca Annis
Dune '84

Krull '83

Michael Ansara
Access Code '84
It's Alive '74
Voyage to the Bottom of
    the Sea '61

Susan Anspach
Blue Monkey '87

Adam Ant
Cyber Bandits '94
World Gone Wild '88

Lysette Anthony
Krull '83

Susan Anton
Making Mr. Right '86

Gabrielle Anwar
Body Snatchers '93

Kazuya Aoyama
Godzilla Vs. the Cosmic
    Monster '74

John Aprea
Cyber-Tracker '93

Jesse Aragon
Street Asylum '90

Angel Aranda
Planet of the Vampires '65

Michael Aranda
Creepozoids '87

John Archer
Destination Moon '50

Arianne Arden
Beyond the Time Barrier
    '60

George Ardisson
Hercules in the Haunted
    World '64

Rosita Arenas
Neutron and the Black
    Mask '61
Neutron Vs. the Amazing
    Dr. Caronte '61
Neutron Vs. the Death
    Robots '62
The Robot Vs. the Aztec
    Mummy '59

Alan Arkin
Edward Scissorhands '90
Return of Captain
    Invincible '83
The Rocketeer '91

Richard Arlen
The Crawling Hand '63
The Human Duplicators
    '64
Island of Lost Souls '32

George Arliss
Transatlantic Tunnel '35

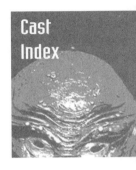

Cast Index

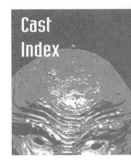

Cast
Index

Sidney Blackmer
Deluge '33

Taurean Blacque
Deepstar Six '89

Steven Blade
Alien Seed '89

Ruben Blades
Predator 2 '90

Vivian Blaine
The Dark '79
Parasite '82

Paul Blaisdell
It Conquered the World '56

Geoffrey Blake
Philadelphia Experiment 2 '93

Susan Blakely
Intruders '92

Mari Blanchard
Abbott and Costello Go to Mars '53

Steve Blanchard
Warlords 3000 '93

Karen Blanguernon
No Survivors, Please '63

William Bledsoe
Dark Side of the Moon '90

Brian Blessed
Flash Gordon '80

Dan Blom
Wes Craven Presents Mind Ripper '95

Claire Bloom
Charly '68
Clash of the Titans '81
The Illustrated Man '69

Judi Bloom
Scream and Scream Again '70

Roberts Blossom
Slaughterhouse Five '72

Lisa Blount
Nightflyers '87
Radioactive Dreams '86
What Waits Below '83

Ralph Bluemke
Invader '91

Alan Blumenfeld
Dark Side of the Moon '90

Hart Bochner
Making Mr. Right '86
Supergirl '84

Lloyd Bochner
Millenium '89

Karl-Heinz Boehm
Unnatural '52

Earl Boen
Terminator 2: Judgment Day '91

Beatrice Boepple
Quarantine '89

Eric Bogosian
Witch Hunt '94

Kelley Bohanan
Idaho Transfer '73

John Boles
Frankenstein '31

Faye Bolt
Star Crystal '85

Derek Bond
The Stranger from Venus '54

Natalya Bondarchuk
Solaris '72

Beulah Bondi
The Invisible Ray '36

Lisa Bonet
New Eden '94

Frank Bonner
Equinox '71

Tony Bonner
Creatures the World Forgot '70

Pat Boone
Journey to the Center of the Earth '59

Charley Boorman
Excalibur '81

James Booth
Deep Space '87
Programmed to Kill '86

Karin Booth
Tobor the Great '54

Powers Boothe
Mutant Species '95

Ernest Borgnine
The Black Hole '79
Escape from New York '81
Super Fuzz '81

Carroll Borland
Bio Hazard '85

Barbara Bosson
The Last Starfighter '84

Barry Bostwick
Megaforce '82
Project Metalbeast: DNA Overload '94
The Rocky Horror Picture Show '75

Joseph Bottoms
The Black Hole '79
Intruder Within '81

Sam Bottoms
Project Shadowchaser 3000 '95

Timothy Bottoms
Invaders from Mars '86
The Sea Serpent '85
What Waits Below '83

Joy Boushel
The Fly '86

Dennis Boutsikaris
*batteries not included '87

Joe Bova
Roboman '75

Michael Bowen
New Eden '94
Night of the Comet '84

Bonnie Bowers
There's Nothing Out There '90

David Bowie
The Man Who Fell to Earth '76

Judi Bowker
Clash of the Titans '81

Bruce Boxleitner
Tron '82

William Boyce
The Slime People '63

Blake Boyd
Dune Warriors '91

Stephen Boyd
Fantastic Voyage '66

Katy Boyer
White Dwarf '95

Sully Boyer
The Manhattan Project '85

William Boyett
The Hidden '87

Lara Flynn Boyle
The Dark Backward '91

Peter Boyle
Disaster at Silo 7 '88
Outland '81
The Shadow '94
Solar Crisis '92
Young Frankenstein '74

Ray Boyle
Zombies of the Stratosphere '52

Lorraine Bracco
Hackers '95

Lane Bradbury
The Ultimate Warrior '75

Bernard Braden
The Day the Earth Caught Fire '61

Jesse Bradford
Hackers '95

David Bradley
Cyborg Cop '93
Cyborg Soldier '94

Kellee Bradley
Fortress of Amerikka '89

Leslie Bradley
Teenage Caveman '58

Bob Brady
Liquid Sky '83

Janelle Brady
Class of Nuke 'Em High '86

Scott Brady
The China Syndrome '79

Eric (Hans Gudegast) Braeden
Aliens Are Coming '80
Colossus: The Forbin Project '70
Escape from the Planet of the Apes '71
The Power Within '79

Danny Brainin
Xtro '83

Christopher Brand
Voyage to the Prehistoric Planet '65

Neville Brand
The Return '80

Marlon Brando
Superman: The Movie '78

Henry Brandon
The Land Unknown '57

Walker Brandt
Solar Force '94

Marjorie Bransfield
Abraxas: Guardian of the Universe '90

Betsy Brantley
I Come in Peace '90

Benjamin Bratt
Demolition Man '93

Gunther Braun
Terror Beneath the Sea '66

Pinkas Braun
Mission Stardust '68

Bart Braverman
Alligator '80

Peter Breck
The Crawling Hand '63

Paulette Breen
The Clonus Horror '79
The Wizard of Speed and Time '88

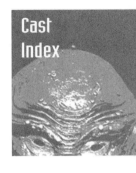

**Cast
Index**

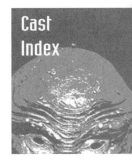

Cast Index

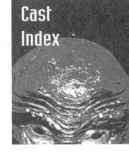

**Cast
Index**

Ralph Cotterill
Starship '87

Paul Coufos
Dragonfight '92
Food of the Gods: Part 2
'88
The Lost Empire '83

Paul Coulj
Prototype X29A '92

George Coulouris
The Stranger '73

Keith Coulouris
Beastmaster 3: The Eye of
Braxus '95

Richard Council
The Manhattan Project '85

Hazel Court
The Curse of Frankenstein
'57
Devil Girl from Mars '54

Chuck Courtney
Meteor Monster '57

Brian Cousins
Invisible: The Chronicles of
Benjamin Knight '93
Mandroid '93

Jerome Cowan
Have Rocket Will Travel '59

Nicola Cowper
Journey to the Center of
the Earth '88

Brian Cox
Murder by Moonlight '91

Courteney Cox
Cocoon: The Return '88
Masters of the Universe
'87
Misfits of Science '85

Mitchell Cox
A.P.E.X. '94
Prototype X29A '92

Richard Cox
The Vindicator '85

Ronny Cox
Captain America '89
Martians Go Home! '90
Mind Snatchers '72
RoboCop '87
Total Recall '90

Tony Cox
Spaced Invaders '90

Peter Coyote
E.T.: The Extra-Terrestrial
'82
Timerider '83

Buster Crabbe
Alien Dead '85

Buck Rogers Conquers the
Universe '39
Destination Saturn '39
Flash Gordon Conquers
the Universe '40
Flash Gordon: Mars
Attacks the World '38
Flash Gordon: Rocketship
'36
Rocketship '36
Space Soldiers Conquer
the Universe '40

Michael Craig
Mysterious Island '61

Yvonne Craig
Mars Needs Women '66

Joey Cramer
Flight of the Navigator '86
Runaway '84

Barbara Crampton
From Beyond '86
Re-Animator '84
Robot Wars '93
Trancers 2: The Return of
Jack Deth '90

Carl Crane
Destroy All Planets '68

Kenneth Cranham
Monkey Boy '90

Bryan Cranston
The Companion '94
Dead Space '90

Nick Cravat
Island of Dr. Moreau '77

H. Marion Crawford
The Brides of Fu Manchu
'66
The Castle of Fu Manchu
'68
The Face of Fu Manchu '65
Kiss and Kill '68
The Vengeance of Fu
Manchu '67

John Crawford
Zombies of the
Stratosphere '52

Johnny Crawford
Village of the Giants '65

Katherine Crawford
Riding with Death '76

Wayne Crawford
Rebel Storm '90

Richard Crenna
Intruders '92
Leviathan '89
Marooned '69

Bernard Cribbins
Daleks—Invasion Earth
2150 A.D. '66

Ed Crick
Future Hunters '88

Alyson Croft
Trancers 2: The Return of
Jack Deth '90

Hume Cronyn
*batteries not included '87
Cocoon '85
Cocoon: The Return '88

Leland Crooke
Dead Man Walking '88

Cathy Lee Crosby
The Dark '79

Denise Crosby
The Eliminators '86
Mutant Species '95

Mary Crosby
Ice Pirates '84

Harley Cross
The Fly 2 '89

Richard Cross
Rats '83

Scatman Crothers
Twilight Zone: The Movie
'83

Lindsay Crouse
Communion '89
Iceman '84

Emilia Crow
Grand Tour: Disaster in
Time '92

Rick Crowe
I Was a Zombie for the FBI
'82

Russell Crowe
Virtuosity '95

Tom Cruise
Legend '86

Rosalie Crutchley
Creatures the World Forgot
'70

Alexis Cruz
Stargate '94

Jon Cryer
Superman 4: The Quest for
Peace '87

Billy Crystal
The Princess Bride '87

Norris Culf
Robot Holocaust '87

Joseph Culp
The Arrival '90

Beryl Cunningham
Screamers '80

Robert Cunningham
No Survivors, Please '63

Cherie Currie
Parasite '82
Twilight Zone: The Movie
'83
Wavelength '83

Michael Currie
The Philadelphia
Experiment '84

Steven Curry
Glen and Randa '71

Tim Curry
Legend '86
The Rocky Horror Picture
Show '75
The Shadow '94

Jane Curtin
Coneheads '93

Alan Curtis
The Invisible Man's
Revenge '44

Donald Curtis
Earth Vs. the Flying
Saucers '56
It Came from Beneath the
Sea '55

Jamie Lee Curtis
The Adventures of
Buckaroo Banzai Across
the Eighth Dimension
'84
Forever Young '92

Keene Curtis
Strange New World '75

Ken Curtis
The Killer Shrews '59

Liane Curtis
Critters 2: The Main
Course '88

Robin Curtis
Star Trek 3: The Search for
Spock '84

Tony Curtis
Brainwaves '82
Lobster Man from Mars '89

Wanda Curtis
King Dinosaur '55

Jacqueline Curtiss
Fire Maidens from Outer
Space '56

Jill Curzon
Daleks—Invasion Earth
2150 A.D. '66

Cyril Cusack
Fahrenheit 451 '66
1984 '84

Peter Cushing
At the Earth's Core '76
Biggles '86

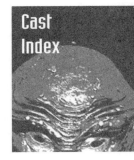

**Cast
Index**

Ruby Dee
Stephen King's The Stand '94

Kevin Dees
Jet Benny Show '86

Eddie Deezen
Hollywood Boulevard 2 '89

Khigh Deigh
The Manchurian Candidate '62

Albert Dekker
Dr. Cyclops '40
Gamera, the Invincible '66
Kiss Me Deadly '55

Kim Delaney
Darkman 2: The Return of Durant '94
Project Metalbeast: DNA Overload '94

Pat Delaney
Zontar, the Thing from Venus '66

Dana Delany
Wild Palms '93

Michael DellaFemina
Invisible: The Chronicles of Benjamin Knight '93
Mandroid '93

Nathalie Delon
Eyes Behind the Stars '72

Jennifer Delora
Robot Holocaust '87

Gerald Delsol
Children of the Damned '63

Dom DeLuise
Fail-Safe '64

Derrick DeMarney
Things to Come '36

Patrick Dempsey
Outbreak '94

Jeffrey DeMunn
The Blob '88

Jake Dengel
Prayer of the Rollerboys '91

Maurice Denham
Night Caller from Outer Space '66

Leslie Denison
The Snow Creature '54

Brian Dennehy
Cocoon '85
Cocoon: The Return '88

Richard Denning
The Black Scorpion '57

Creature from the Black Lagoon '54
Day the World Ended '55

Sandy Dennis
God Told Me To '76

Paul Dentzer
They '77

Johnny Depp
Edward Scissorhands '90

Joe DeRita
Have Rocket Will Travel '59
Three Stooges in Orbit '62

Bruce Dern
Silent Running '71
World Gone Wild '88

Laura Dern
Jurassic Park '93

Richard Derr
Terror Is a Man '59
When Worlds Collide '51

Jacqueline Derval
Battle of the Worlds '61

Michael Des Barres
Nightflyers '87
Waxwork 2: Lost in Time '91

Mary Jo Deschanel
2010: The Year We Make Contact '84

Sandy Descher
Them! '54

William Devane
The Dark '79
Timestalkers '87

Joanna DeVarona
A*P*E* '76

Danny DeVito
Batman Returns '92

Dean Devlin
Moon 44 '90

Gordon Devol
Killings at Outpost Zeta '80

George DeVries
Mission Mars '67

Colleen Dewhurst
Dead Zone '83

Johana DeWinter
Planet Earth '74

Anthony Dexter
Fire Maidens from Outer Space '56

Tony Dexter
The Phantom Planet '61

Susan Dey
Looker '81

The Trouble with Dick '88

Cliff DeYoung
Carnosaur 2 '94
Flight of the Navigator '86
Pulse '88
Star Quest '94
Stephen King's The Tommyknockers '93

Selma Diamond
Twilight Zone: The Movie '83

Leonardo DiCaprio
Critters 3 '91

George DiCenzo
Back to the Future '85

Bobby DiCicco
The Philadelphia Experiment '84

Danny Dick
Dungeonmaster '83

Angie Dickinson
Resurrection of Zachary Wheeler '71
Wild Palms '93

Sandra Dickinson
The Hitchhiker's Guide to the Galaxy '81

Lance Dickson
Project: Nightmare '85

Neil Dickson
Biggles '86

Robert Diedermann
Invader '91

John Diehl
City Limits '85
Dark Side of the Moon '90
Stargate '94
Wes Craven Presents Mind Ripper '95

Anton Diffring
Fahrenheit 451 '66

Dudley Digges
The Invisible Man '33

Alan Dijon
Assignment Outer Space '61

Bradford Dillman
Bug '75
Escape from the Planet of the Apes '71
Lords of the Deep '89
Resurrection of Zachary Wheeler '71
The Swarm '78

Kevin Dillon
The Blob '88
No Escape '94
Remote Control '88

Melinda Dillon
Captain America '89
Close Encounters of the Third Kind '77

Ernie Dingo
Until the End of the World '91

James DiStefano
Running Against Time '90

Andrew Divoff
Backlash: Oblivion 2 '95
Oblivion '94

Richard Dix
Transatlantic Tunnel '35

Robert Dix
Horror of the Blood Monsters '70

David Dixon
The Hitchhiker's Guide to the Galaxy '81

James Dixon
It's Alive '74

Steve Dixon
The Carrier '87
Mosquito '95

Rainbow Dolan
In the Aftermath: Angels Never Sleep '87

Guy Doleman
On the Beach '59

Ami Dolenz
Ticks '93

Faith Domergue
The Atomic Man '56
It Came from Beneath the Sea '55
This Island Earth '55
Voyage to the Prehistoric Planet '65

Arturo Dominici
Hercules '58

Solveig Dommartin
Until the End of the World '91

Troy Donahue
Dr. Alien '88
Monster on the Campus '59
Omega Cop '90
Those Fantastic Flying Fools '67

James Donald
Quatermass and the Pit '68

Peter Donat
The China Syndrome '79

Brian Donlevy
Gamera, the Invincible '66

**Cast
Index**

Ian Dury
Split Second '92

Dan Duryea
The Bamboo Saucer '68

Todd Dutson
Force on Thunder
Mountain '77

Charles S. Dutton
Alien 3 '92

Maria Duval
Samson Vs. the Vampire
Women '61

Robert Duvall
The Handmaid's Tale '90
THX 1138 '71

Shelley Duvall
Time Bandits '81

Wayne Duvall
Final Approach '91
Warlords 3000 '93

Peter Dvorsky
Videodrome '83

Timothy Dwight
Split '90

William Dwyer
Charly '68

Cameron Dye
The Last Starfighter '84
Stranded '87

Peter Dyneley
The Manster '59

Richard Dysart
Back to the Future, Part 3
'90
Meteor '79
Riding with Death '76
The Terminal Man '74
The Thing '82

Dick Dyszel
The Alien Factor '78
Night Beast '83

Marilee Earle
The Lost Missile '58

George Eastman
After the Fall of New York
'85
Hands of Steel '86

Rodney Eastman
Deadly Weapon '88

Robert Easton
The Giant Spider Invasion
'75

Clint Eastwood
Revenge of the Creature
'55
Tarantula '55

Marjorie Eaton
The Atomic Brain '64

Roberta Eaton
Split Second '92

Shirley Eaton
Around the World Under
the Sea '65
Kiss and Kill '68

Christine Ebersole
Mac and Me '88

Aimee Eccles
Humanoid Defender '85

Barbara Eden
Seven Faces of Dr. Lao '63
Voyage to the Bottom of
the Sea '61

Beatie Edney
Highlander '86

Richard Edson
Attack of the 50 Ft. Woman
'93
Super Mario Bros. '93

Bill Edwards
First Man into Space '59

Elizabeth Edwards
The Pink Chiquitas '86

Lance Edwards
Peacemaker '90

Meredith Edwards
The Electronic Monster '57

Rick Edwards
Hearts & Armour '83

Vince Edwards
Andy and the Airwave
Rangers '89
Space Raiders '83

Marshall Efron
THX 1138 '71

Julie Ege
Creatures the World Forgot
'70

Samantha Eggar
The Brood '79

Nicole Eggert
Amanda and the Alien '95

Lisa Eichhorn
Moon 44 '90

Jill Eikenberry
The Manhattan Project '85

Lisa Eilbacher
The Amazing Spider-Man
'77
Leviathan '89

Anthony Eisley
Deep Space '87
Navy Vs. the Night
Monsters '66

The Wasp Woman '59

Anita Ekberg
Abbott and Costello Go to
Mars '53

Nameer El-Kadi
Quest for Fire '82

Jack Elam
The Aurora Encounter '85
Kiss Me Deadly '55

John Eldridge
I Married a Monster from
Outer Space '58

John Elerick
Embryo '76

Sandor Eles
The Evil of Frankenstein
'64

Danny Elfman
Forbidden Zone '80

Hector Elizondo
Final Approach '91
Leviathan '89

Kay Elkhardt
Dr. Goldfoot and the Bikini
Machine '65

Biff Elliot
The Dark '79

Erica Elliot
The Creation of the
Humanoids '62

Chris Elliott
The Abyss '89

Denholm Elliott
The Boys from Brazil '78
Indiana Jones and the Last
Crusade '89
Quest for Love '71
Raiders of the Lost Ark '81

Laura Elliott
Two Lost Worlds '50

Ross Elliott
Tarantula '55

Mary Ellis
The Three Worlds of
Gulliver '59

Michael Elphick
The Element of Crime '84

Hannelore Elsner
Time Troopers '89

Cary Elwes
The Princess Bride '87

Ron Ely
Doc Savage '75

Jonathon Emerson
Nightfall '88

Karrie Emerson
Chopping Mall '86

James H. Emery
Phoenix the Warrior '88

John Emery
Kronos '57
Rocketship X-M '50

Daniel Emilfork
The City of Lost Children
'95

Michael Emmet
Attack of the Giant
Leeches '59
Night of the Blood Beast
'58

Kyoko Enami
Gamera Vs. Barugon '66

Alicia Encinas
The Bees '78

Audie England
Venus Rising '95

Robert Englund
Mysterious Two '82
V '83
V: The Final Battle '84

Dieter Eppler
The Head '59

Catharine Erhardt
Cinderella 2000 '78

Leif Erickson
Invaders from Mars '53

Phil Erickson
UFO: Target Earth '74

John Ericson
The Bamboo Saucer '68
Seven Faces of Dr. Lao '63

R. Lee Ermey
Body Snatchers '93
Endless Descent '90
The Terror Within 2 '91

Leon Errol
The Invisible Man's
Revenge '44

Patrick Ersgard
Mandroid '93

David Essex
Octaman '71

Emilio Estevez
Freejack '92

Joe Estevez
Dark Universe '93

Erik Estrada
Alien Seed '89
Andy and the Airwave
Rangers '89

Gene Evans
Donovan's Brain '53

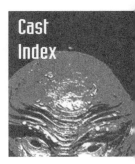

**Cast
Index**

Frances Fisher
Attack of the 50 Ft. Woman
'93

Gregory Fisher
1984 '84

Joely Fisher
The Companion '94

Shug Fisher
The Giant Gila Monster '59

Peter Fitz
Club Extinction '89

Kate Fitzpatrick
Return of Captain
Invincible '83

Joe Flaherty
Back to the Future, Part 2
'89
Blue Monkey '87

James Flavin
King Kong '33

Flea
Back to the Future, Part 2
'89

John Fleck
Mutant on the Bounty '89

Mick Fleetwood
The Running Man '87

Charles Fleischer
Back to the Future, Part 2
'89

Eric Fleming
Conquest of Space '55
Queen of Outer Space '58

Louise Fletcher
Brainstorm '83
Firestarter '84
Invaders from Mars '86
Shadowzone '89
Strange Invaders '83
Virtuosity '95

Claudia Flores
There's Nothing Out There
'90

Don Flourney
The Giant Gila Monster '59

George Flower
They Live '88

Darlanne Fluegel
Battle Beyond the Stars
'80
Darkman 3: Die Darkman
Die '95
Project: Alien '89
Scanner Cop '94

Joe Flynn
The Computer Wore Tennis
Shoes '69

Now You See Him, Now
You Don't '72

John Flynn
Split '90

Kick Fairbanks Fogg
Alien Space Avenger '91

Michael Foley
Prison Planet '92

Bridget Fonda
Frankenstein Unbound '90

Henry Fonda
Fail-Safe '64
Meteor '79
The Swarm '78

Jane Fonda
Barbarella '68
The China Syndrome '79

Peter Fonda
Futureworld '76

Benson Fong
Conquest of Space '55

Joan Fontaine
Voyage to the Bottom of
the Sea '61

Dick Foran
Atomic Submarine '59

Bryan Forbes
Quatermass 2 '57

Anitra Ford
Invasion of the Bee Girls
'73

Ann Ford
Logan's Run '76

Glenn Ford
Superman: The Movie '78
Virus '82

Harrison Ford
Blade Runner '82
The Empire Strikes Back
'80
From "Star Wars" to
"Jedi": The Making of a
Saga '83
Indiana Jones and the Last
Crusade '89
Indiana Jones and the
Temple of Doom '84
Raiders of the Lost Ark '81
Return of the Jedi '83
Star Wars '77

Wallace Ford
The Ape Man '43

Ken Foree
From Beyond '86

Deborah Foreman
Lobster Man from Mars '89

Steve Forrest
Captain America '79

Constance Forslund
Village of the Damned '95

Robert Forster
Alligator '80
The Black Hole '79
Peacemaker '90

John Forsythe
Mysterious Two '82

William Forsythe
Virtuosity '95

Albert Fortell
Time Troopers '89

Gregory Fortescue
The Carrier '87

Brigitte Fossey
Quintet '79

Meg Foster
Backlash: Oblivion 2 '95
Futurekick '91
Leviathan '89
Masters of the Universe
'87
Oblivion '94
They Live '88

Phil Foster
Conquest of Space '55

Preston Foster
Doctor X '32
The Time Travelers '64

Stacie Foster
Cyber-Tracker 2 '95
Steel Frontier '94

Rich Foucheux
Invader '91

Frank Fowler
The Atomic Brain '64

Harry Fowler
Fire Maidens from Outer
Space '56

Douglas Fowley
Cat Women of the Moon
'53

Colin Fox
Food of the Gods: Part 2
'88

Jerry Fox
Evil Spawn '87

Michael J. Fox
Back to the Future '85
Back to the Future, Part 2
'89
Back to the Future, Part 3
'90

Robert Foxworth
Beyond the Stars '89

Jonathon Frakes
Star Trek Generations '94

Anne Francis
Forbidden Planet '56

Barbara Francis
The Beast of Yucca Flats
'61

James Franciscus
Beneath the Planet of the
Apes '69
Marooned '69
The Valley of Gwangi '69

Don Francks
984: Prisoner of the Future
'84

Larry Franco
They Live '88

Jano Frandsen
Xtro 2: The Second
Encounter '91

Gary Frank
Deadly Weapon '88

Horst Frank
The Head '59
The Vengeance of Fu
Manchu '67

David Frankham
Return of the Fly '59

David Franklin
Rock & Roll Cowboys '92

Pamela Franklin
Food of the Gods '76

William Franklyn
Quatermass 2 '57

Arthur Franz
Abbott and Costello Meet
the Invisible Man '51
Atomic Submarine '59
Flight to Mars '51
Invaders from Mars '53
Monster on the Campus
'59

Duncan Fraser
Timecop '94

Sally Fraser
It Conquered the World '56
The War of the Colossal
Beast '58

Stuart Fratkin
Dr. Alien '88

William Frawley
Abbott and Costello Meet
the Invisible Man '51

Lynne Frederick
Phase 4 '74

Dean Fredericks
The Phantom Planet '61

Joan Freeman
Panic in the Year Zero! '62

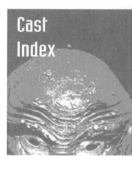

Cast
Index

Steve Geray
Tobor the Great '54

Joan Gerber
Tobor the Great '54

Frank Gerstle
The Atomic Brain '64
Killers from Space '54
The Wasp Woman '59

Jami Gertz
Solarbabies '86

Richard Gesswein
R.O.T.O.R. '88

John Getz
The Fly '86
The Fly 2 '89

Rick Gianasi
Escape from Safehaven '88
Mutant Hunt '87
Robot Holocaust '87

Cynthia Gibb
Short Circuit 2 '88

Marla Gibbs
The Meteor Man '93

Henry Gibson
The Incredible Shrinking Woman '81
Innerspace '87

Mel Gibson
Forever Young '92
Mad Max '80
Mad Max: Beyond Thunderdome '85
The Road Warrior '82

Mimi Gibson
The Monster that Challenged the World '57

Pamela Gidley
Cherry 2000 '88

Stefan Gierasch
Megaville '91

Alan Gifford
Phase 4 '74

Sandro Giglio
The War of the Worlds '53

Vincent Gil
Body Melt '93

Marcus Gilbert
Army of Darkness '92
Biggles '86

Paul Gilbert
Women of the Prehistoric Planet '66

Gwynne Gilford
Son of Blob '71

Jack Gilford
Cocoon '85
Cocoon: The Return '88

Stuart Gillard
Virus '82

Dana Gillespie
The People that Time Forgot '77

John Gillick
I Was a Zombie for the FBI '82

Richard Gilliland
Bug '75

Hugh Gillin
Doin' Time on Planet Earth '88

James Gillis
Alien Space Avenger '91

Hermione Gingold
Those Fantastic Flying Fools '67

Bob Ginnaven
The Day It Came to Earth '77

Robert Ginty
Programmed to Kill '86
Warrior of the Lost World '84

Sheila Gish
Highlander '86

Robert Gist
Jack the Giant Killer '62

Leslie Glass
Vampire Vixens from Venus '94

Ron Glass
Deep Space '87

Seamon Glass
This Is Not a Test '62

Isabel Glasser
Forever Young '92

Bob Glaudini
Parasite '82

Paul Gleason
Digital Man '94
Doc Savage '75

Brian Glover
Alien 3 '92

Crispin Glover
Back to the Future '85
Back to the Future, Part 2 '89

Danny Glover
Iceman '84
Predator 2 '90

John Glover
Automatic '94

Gremlins 2: The New Batch '90
Meet the Hollowheads '89

Julian Glover
The Empire Strikes Back '80
Indiana Jones and the Last Crusade '89
Quatermass and the Pit '68

Boy Gobert
Kamikaze '89 '83

Mark Goddard
Strange Invaders '83

Drew Godderis
Evil Spawn '87

Miguel Godreau
Altered States '80

Alexander Godunov
Waxwork 2: Lost in Time '91

Michael C. Goetz
Village of the Damned '60

Peter Michael Goetz
King Kong Lives '86

John Goff
The Alpha Incident '76

Gila Golan
The Valley of Gwangi '69

Eleanor Gold
The New Gladiators '87

Whoopi Goldberg
Star Trek Generations '94

Harold Goldblatt
Children of the Damned '63

Jeff Goldblum
The Adventures of Buckaroo Banzai Across the Eighth Dimension '84
Earth Girls Are Easy '89
The Fly '86
Invasion of the Body Snatchers '78
Jurassic Park '93

Ricky Paull Goldin
Hyper-Sapien: People from Another Star '86

Jenette Goldstein
Aliens '86

Bob(cat) Goldthwait
Out There '95

Arlene Golonka
Dr. Alien '88

Cuba Gooding, Jr.
Outbreak '94

Michael Goodliffe
The Day the Earth Caught Fire '61

Deborah Goodrich
Remote Control '88

Allen Goorwitz *See* **Allen Garfield**

Don Gordon
The Borrower '89
Zero Population Growth '72

Gavin Gordon
The Bride of Frankenstein '35

Hayes Gordon
Return of Captain Invincible '83

Leo Gordon
Alienator '89
Bog '84

Roy Gordon
Attack of the 50 Foot Woman '58

Ruth Gordon
Voyage of the Rock Aliens '87

Galyn Gorg
RoboCop 2 '90

Gabriel Gori
The Bronx Executioner '86

Frank Gorshin
Invasion of the Saucer Men '57
The Meteor Man '93
12 Monkeys '95

Marjoe Gortner
Food of the Gods '76
Star Crash '78

David Goss
She '83

Louis Gossett, Jr.
Enemy Mine '85
Monolith '93
The Punisher '90

Michael Gothard
Lifeforce '85

Ingrid Goude
The Killer Shrews '59

Michael Gough
Batman '89
Batman Forever '95
Batman Returns '92
They Came from Beyond Space '67

Elliott Gould
Capricorn One '78
Roboman '75

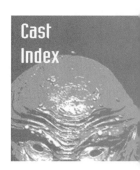

Cast Index

Cast
Index

Judy Huxtable
Scream and Scream Again '70

Leila Hyams
Island of Lost Souls '32

Jacquelyn Hyde
The Dark '79

Alex Hyde-White
Biggles '86
Indiana Jones and the Last Crusade '89

Martha Hyer
Abbott and Costello Go to Mars '53
First Men in the Moon '64
Geisha Girl '52
Mistress of the World '59

Diana Hyland
Hercules and the Princess of Troy '65

Jane Hylton
The Manster '59

Ice-T
Johnny Mnemonic '95

Hiroshi Ichikawa
Godzilla on Monster Island '72

Hiroki Ida
Cyber Ninja '94

Kunihiko Ida
Zeram '91

Eric Idle
The Adventures of Baron Munchausen '89
Jabberwocky '77
Mom and Dad Save the World '92

Kyunna Ignatova
Planeta Burg '62

Ryo Ikebe
Gorath '64
War in Space '77

Oh Young Il
Yongkari Monster of the Deep '67

Peter Illing
The Electronic Monster '57

Igor Illinski
Aelita: Queen of Mars '24

Iman
Star Trek 6: The Undiscovered Country '91

Barrie Ingham
Invasion '65

Aharon Ipale
Invisible: The Chronicles of Benjamin Knight '93

Kathy Ireland
Alien from L.A. '87
Mom and Dad Save the World '92

Michael Ironside
Highlander 2: The Quickening '91
Murder in Space '85
Neon City '91
Spacehunter: Adventures in the Forbidden Zone '83
Total Recall '90
V: The Final Battle '84

Anthony Isbell
I Was a Zombie for the FBI '82

Emi Ito
Destroy All Monsters '68
Ghidrah the Three Headed Monster '65
Godzilla Vs. Mothra '64
Mothra '61

Robert Ito
The Adventures of Buckaroo Banzai Across the Eighth Dimension '84
Women of the Prehistoric Planet '66

Yumi Ito
Destroy All Monsters '68
Ghidrah the Three Headed Monster '65
Godzilla Vs. Mothra '64
Mothra '61

Stan Ivar
Creature '85

Terri Ivens
Trancers 4: Jack of Swords '93
Trancers 5: Sudden Deth '94

Burl Ives
Those Fantastic Flying Fools '67

Dana Ivey
Explorers '85

Dan Jackson
Mysterious Island '61

Freda Jackson
The Valley of Gwangi '69

Jermaine Jackson
Voyage of the Rock Aliens '87

John M. Jackson
Roswell: The U.F.O. Cover-Up '94

Leonard Jackson
The Brother from Another Planet '84

Peter Jackson
Bad Taste '88

Samuel L. Jackson
Jurassic Park '93

Peggy Jacobsen
Search and Destroy '88

Billy Jacoby
Beastmaster '82
Dr. Alien '88

Bobby Jacoby
Tremors '89

Richard Jaeckel
The Dark '79
The Green Slime '68
Starman '84

Carl Jaffe
First Man into Space '59

Sam Jaffe
Battle Beyond the Stars '80
The Day the Earth Stood Still '51

Angelika Jager
Robot Holocaust '87

Dean Jagger
Alligator '80
End of the World '76
The Stranger '73

Mick Jagger
Freejack '92

Brion James
Blade Runner '82
Cherry 2000 '88
The Companion '94
Dead Man Walking '88
Enemy Mine '85
Future Shock '93
Mutator '90
Nemesis '93
Scanner Cop '94
Steel Dawn '87
Steel Frontier '94
Street Asylum '90
Time Runner '92
Virtual Assassin '95

Godfrey James
At the Earth's Core '76

Sidney James
Quatermass 2 '57

Steve James
The Brother from Another Planet '84

Azenath Jani
The 27th Day '57

Leon Janney
Charly '68

Robert Jannucci
Exterminators of the Year 3000 '83

David Janssen
Marooned '69

Chona Jason
Dragon Fury '95

Peter Jason
Alien Nation '88
Hyper-Sapien: People from Another Star '86
They Live '88
Village of the Damned '95

Jennifer Jayne
The Crawling Eye '58

Peter Jeffrey
The Adventures of Baron Munchausen '89

Chuck Jeffreys
Aftershock '88

Lang Jeffries
Mission Stardust '68

Lionel Jeffries
First Men in the Moon '64
Those Fantastic Flying Fools '67

Rudolph Jelinek
The Original Fabulous Adventures of Baron Munchausen '61

Claudia Jennings
Death Sport '78

Todd Jensen
Armageddon: The Final Challenge '94
Cyborg Cop '93

Adele Jergens
Abbott and Costello Meet the Invisible Man '51
Day the World Ended '55

Michael Jeter
Waterworld '95

Penn Jillette
Hackers '95

Chrysti Jimenez
Omega Cop '90

Jose Luis Jimenez
Samson in the Wax Museum '63

Mike Jittlov
The Wizard of Speed and Time '88

David Johansen
Freejack '92

Robert John
Creatures the World Forgot '70

Mervyn Johns
Day of the Triffids '63

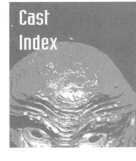

Cast
Index

Andy Kaufman
God Told Me To '76
Heartbeeps '81

David Kaufman
Invisible: The Chronicles of
Benjamin Knight '93

Gunther Kaufman
Kamikaze '89 '83

Christine Kavanagh
Monkey Boy '90

Hanbel Kawai
Cyber Ninja '94

Tamio Kawaji
Gappa the Trifibian
Monster '67

Keizo Kawasaki
Warning from Space '56

Hiroyuki Kawase
Godzilla Vs. Megalon '73
Godzilla Vs. the Smog
Monster '72

Seizaburo Kawazu
The Secret of the Telegian
'61

Dianne Kay
Andy and the Airwave
Rangers '89

Richard Kaye
The Wizard of Speed and
Time '88

Stubby Kaye
Who Framed Roger Rabbit
'88

Stacy Keach
Amanda and the Alien '95
Class of 1999 '90
New Crime City: Los
Angeles 2020 '94

Larry Keating
When Worlds Collide '51

Buster Keaton
Boom in the Moon '46

Diane Keaton
Sleeper '73

Michael Keaton
Batman '89
Batman Returns '92

Ele Keats
White Dwarf '95

Richard Keats
A.P.E.X. '94

Hugh Keays-Byrne
Mad Max '80

Don Keefer
Sleeper '73

Howard Keel
Day of the Triffids '63

Tom Keene
Plan 9 from Outer Space
'56

Oscar Keesee
Terror Is a Man '59

Andrew Keir
Daleks—Invasion Earth
2150 A.D. '66

Harvey Keitel
Death Watch '80
Saturn 3 '80

Brian Keith
Meteor '79
Moon Pilot '62

David Keith
Firestarter '84

Ian Keith
It Came from Beneath the
Sea '55

Michael Keith
King Kong Vs. Godzilla '63

Cecil Kellaway
The Beast from 20,000
Fathoms '53

Barbara Kellerman
Quatermass Conclusion
'79

Barry Kelley
Jack the Giant Killer '62

DeForest Kelley
Star Trek: The Motion
Picture '80
Star Trek 2: The Wrath of
Khan '82
Star Trek 3: The Search for
Spock '84
Star Trek 4: The Voyage
Home '86
Star Trek 5: The Final
Frontier '89
Star Trek 6: The
Undiscovered Country
'91

Bruce Kellogg
Unknown World '51

Brian Kelly
Around the World Under
the Sea '65

David Patrick Kelly
Dreamscape '84

Jack Kelly
Forbidden Planet '56

Paula Kelly
The Andromeda Strain '71

Robyn Kelly
Flesh Gordon 2: Flesh
Gordon Meets the
Cosmic Cheerleaders '90

Richard Kelton
The Ultimate Warrior '75

Edward Kemmer
Earth Vs. the Spider '58

Warren Kemmerling
The Dark '79

Martin Kemp
Cyber Bandits '94

Terry Kemper
People Who Own the Dark
'75

Tony Kendall
People Who Own the Dark
'75

Arthur Kennedy
Fantastic Voyage '66

Bill Kennedy
Two Lost Worlds '50

Douglas Kennedy
The Amazing Transparent
Man '60
The Land Unknown '57

George Kennedy
Radioactive Dreams '86
The Terror Within '88
Virus '82

Gerard Kennedy
Body Melt '93

Graham Kennedy
Return of Captain
Invincible '83

June Kennedy
Earth Vs. the Spider '58

Merele Kennedy
Nemesis '93

Patsy Kensit
Blue Tornado '92

April Kent
The Incredible Shrinking
Man '57

Elizabeth Kent
Mindwarp '91

Robert Kent
The Phantom Creeps '39

Edith Ker
Delicatessen '92

David Kerman
Frankenstein Meets the
Space Monster '65

Dan Kern
Rocket Attack U.S.A. '58

Karin Kernke
The Head '59

Frederick Kerr
Frankenstein '31

Larry Kerr
The Lost Missile '58

Linda Kerridge
Alien from L.A. '87

Brian Kerwin
It Came from Outer Space
2 '95
King Kong Lives '86

Lance Kerwin
Enemy Mine '85

Quin Kessler
She '83

Sara Kestelman
Zardoz '73

Evelyn Keyes
Before I Hang '40

Irwin Keyes
Backlash: Oblivion 2 '95

Persis Khambatta
Megaforce '82
Phoenix the Warrior '88
Star Trek: The Motion
Picture '80
Warrior of the Lost World
'84

Margot Kidder
Superman: The Movie '78
Superman 2 '80
Superman 3 '83
Superman 4: The Quest for
Peace '87

Nicole Kidman
Batman Forever '95

Elizabeth Kiefer
Rebel Storm '90

Richard Kiel
The Human Duplicators
'64
The Phantom Planet '61
War of the Wizards '81

Sue Kiel
Survivor '87

Udo Kier
Johnny Mnemonic '95

Susan Kiger
The Return '80

Terence Kilburn
Fiend Without a Face '58

Melanie Kilgour
Maniac Warriors '90s

Victor Kilian
Dr. Cyclops '40
Unknown World '51

Val Kilmer
Batman Forever '95
Willow '88

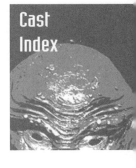

Cast
Index

Cal Kuniholm
Dark Star '74

Robert Kurcz
Moontrap '89

Ron Kurowski
Spaceship '81

Shishir Kurup
Coneheads '93

Clyde Kusatsu
Dr. Strange '78

Burt Kwouk
The Brides of Fu Manchu '66

Sam Kydd
Island of Terror '66

Matthew Laborteaux
Aliens Are Coming '80

Ronald Lacey
Raiders of the Lost Ark '81

Stephen Lack
Scanners '81

Cheryl Ladd
Millenium '89

Diane Ladd
Carnosaur '93
Embryo '76
Something Wicked This Way Comes '83

Patricia Laffan
Devil Girl from Mars '54

Marcey Lafferty
Day Time Ended '78

Art LaFleur
Forever Young '92
Trancers '84
Trancers 2: The Return of Jack Deth '90
Zone Troopers '85

Christine Lahti
The Henderson Monster '80

Leon Lai
Wicked City '92

Frank Laloggia
The Wizard of Speed and Time '88

Christopher Lambert
Fortress '93
Highlander '86
Highlander 2: The Quickening '91
Highlander: The Final Dimension '94

Adele Lamont
The Brain that Wouldn't Die '63

Duncan Lamont
The Evil of Frankenstein '64

Burt Lancaster
Island of Dr. Moreau '77

Elsa Lanchester
The Bride of Frankenstein '35

Rodolfo Landa
Neutron Vs. the Amazing Dr. Caronte '61

Juliet Landau
Neon City '91

Martin Landau
Access Code '84
Destination Moonbase Alpha '75
Meteor '79
The Return '80
12:01 '93

David Lander
Steel and Lace '90

Harry Landers
Phantom from Space '53

Judy Landers
Dr. Alien '88

Sonny Landham
Predator '87

Marla Landi
First Man into Space '59

D.W. Landingham
Omega Cop '90

Carole Landis
One Million B.C. '40

Hal Landon, Jr.
Bill & Ted's Bogus Journey '91

Judy Landon
Prehistoric Women '50

Abbe Lane
Twilight Zone: The Movie '83

Charles Lane
The Invisible Woman '40
Strange Invaders '83

Diane Lane
Judge Dredd '95

Stephen Lang
Project X '87

Glenn Langan
The Amazing Colossal Man '57

Jessica Lange
King Kong '76

Frank Langella
Masters of the Universe '87

Lisa Langlois
The Nest '88
Transformations '88

David Langton
Quintet '79

Paul Langton
The Cosmic Man '59
The Incredible Shrinking Man '57
It! The Terror from Beyond Space '58
The Snow Creature '54

Angela Lansbury
The Manchurian Candidate '62

Joi Lansing
Atomic Submarine '59

Robert Lansing
Empire of the Ants '77
The 4D Man '59
The Nest '88

Francine Lapensee
Bounty Hunter 2002 '94

Jane Lapotaire
The Asphyx '72
Murder by Moonlight '91

Joe Lara
American Cyborg: Steel Warrior '94
Hologram Man '95
Steel Frontier '94

John Larroquette
Star Trek 3: The Search for Spock '84
Twilight Zone: The Movie '83

Darrell Larson
City Limits '85

Jay B. Larson
Cinderella 2000 '78

Eva LaRue
Crash and Burn '90

Larry Latham
Aftermath '85

Louise Latham
The Philadelphia Experiment '84

Hugh Latimer
The Cosmic Monsters '58

John Laughlin
Space Rage '86

Charles Laughton
Island of Lost Souls '32

Rod Lauren
The Crawling Hand '63

Michael Laurence
Syngenor '90

John Laurie
Devil Girl from Mars '54

Ed Lauter
Digital Man '94
King Kong '76
The Rocketeer '91
Stephen King's Golden Years '91
Timerider '83

Daliah Lavi
Those Fantastic Flying Fools '67

John Phillip Law
Alienator '89
Barbarella '68
Danger: Diabolik '68
Golden Voyage of Sinbad '73
Space Mutiny '88

Barbara Lawrence
Kronos '57

Bruno Lawrence
The Quiet Earth '85

Delphi Lawrence
Frozen Alive '64

Joey Lawrence
Pulse '88

John Lawrence
The Asphyx '72
They Live '88

Scott Lawrence
Timecop '94

Dean Lawrie
Bad Taste '88

Adam Lawson
A.P.E.X. '94

Denis Lawson
Return of the Jedi '83

Priscilla Lawson
Flash Gordon: Rocketship '36

Sarah Lawson
Island of the Burning Doomed '67

Frank Lawton
The Invisible Ray '36

Norma Lazarendo
Night of the Bloody Apes '68

Gene Le Brock
Fortress of Amerikka '89
Metamorphosis '90

Kelly Le Brock
Weird Science '85

John Le Mesurier
Jabberwocky '77

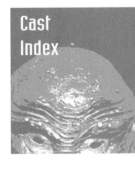

**Cast
Index**

Jason Lively
Night of the Creeps '86

Christopher Lloyd
The Adventures of
   Buckaroo Banzai Across
   the Eighth Dimension
   '84
Back to the Future '85
Back to the Future, Part 2
   '89
Back to the Future, Part 3
   '90
Star Trek 3: The Search for
   Spock '84
Who Framed Roger Rabbit
   '88

Doris Lloyd
The Invisible Man's
   Revenge '44

Tony LoBianco
God Told Me To '76

Bruce Locke
RoboCop 3 '91

Calvin Lockhart
Predator 2 '90

June Lockhart
Out There '95
Strange Invaders '83

Heather Locklear
Firestarter '84
The Return of Swamp
   Thing '89

Loryn Locklin
Fortress '93

Gary Lockwood
Survival Zone '84
2001: A Space Odyssey '68

Tom Lockyear
Teenagers from Outer
   Space '59

John Loder
Non-Stop New York '37

Roger Lodge
Not of this Earth '88

Janice Logan
Dr. Cyclops '40

Ricky Dean Logan
Back to the Future, Part 2
   '89
Back to the Future, Part 3
   '90

Robert Loggia
Lifepod '93
The Lost Missile '58
Wild Palms '93

Rachel Loiselle
Mosquito '95

Herbert Lom
Dead Zone '83

Journey to the Far Side of
   the Sun '69
Mysterious Island '61

Leigh Lombardi
Moontrap '89

John Lone
Iceman '84
The Shadow '94

Kathy Long
Knights '93

Melissa Long
Reactor '85
War of the Robots '78

John Longden
Quatermass 2 '57

Emily Longstreth
Wired to Kill '86

Deborah Loomis
Hercules in New York '70

Rod Loomis
Bill & Ted's Excellent
   Adventure '89

Silvia Lopel
Hercules Unchained '59

Sal Lopez
The Fire Next Time '93

Byron Lord
Mars Needs Women '66

Traci Lords
Not of this Earth '88
Plughead Rewired:
   Circuitry Man 2 '94
Stephen King's The
   Tommyknockers '93

Lynn Loring
Journey to the Far Side of
   the Sun '69

Peter Lorre
20,000 Leagues Under the
   Sea '54
Voyage to the Bottom of
   the Sea '61

Eb Lottimer
Futurekick '91
Lords of the Deep '89

Bessie Love
The Lost World '25

Dave Love
Teenagers from Outer
   Space '59

Suzanna Love
Brainwaves '82

Tim Loveface
Mosquito '95

Jon Lovitz
Mom and Dad Save the
   World '92

My Stepmother Is an Alien
   '88

Rob Lowe
The Dark Backward '91
Stephen King's The Stand
   '94

Curt Lowens
Invisible: The Chronicles of
   Benjamin Knight '93
Mandroid '93

Lynn Lowry
The Crazies '73
They Came from Within '75

Myrna Loy
The Mask of Fu Manchu
   '32

Lisa Lu
Demon Seed '77

Charles Lucia
Syngenor '90

Joseph Lucien
The City of Lost Children
   '95

Laurence Luckinbill
Star Trek 5: The Final
   Frontier '89

William Lucking
Doc Savage '75
Duplicates '92
Humanoid Defender '85

Pamela Ludwig
Dead Man Walking '88

Ted Luedemann
Jet Benny Show '86

Laurette Luez
Prehistoric Women '50

Bela Lugosi
The Ape Man '43
Bride of the Monster '56
The Invisible Ray '36
Island of Lost Souls '32
The Phantom Creeps '39
Plan 9 from Outer Space
   '56
Return of Chandu '34
Son of Frankenstein '39

Paul Lukas
20,000 Leagues Under the
   Sea '54

Paul Lukather
Dinosaurus! '60

Keye Luke
Gremlins '84

Oldrich Lukes
First Spaceship on Venus
   '60

Wolfgang Lukschy
Frozen Alive '64

Baruch Lumet
The Killer Shrews '59

Deanna Lund
Dr. Goldfoot and the Bikini
   Machine '65

Dolph Lundgren
I Come in Peace '90
Johnny Mnemonic '95
Masters of the Universe
   '87
The Punisher '90
Universal Soldier '92

Vic Lundin
Robinson Crusoe on Mars
   '64

Cherie Lunghi
Excalibur '81

Ida Lupino
Food of the Gods '76

Evan Lurie
Hologram Man '95
T-Force '94

Aaron Lustig
Bad Channels '92

Franc Luz
The Nest '88

Maria Pia Luzi
Planets Against Us '61

John Lynch
Hardware '90
Monkey Boy '90

Kate Lynch
Def-Con 4 '85

Kelly Lynch
Virtuosity '95

Ken Lynch
I Married a Monster from
   Outer Space '58

Richard Lynch
Aftershock '88
Death Sport '78
Dragon Fury '95
God Told Me To '76
Scanner Cop '94
Sword & the Sorcerer '82
Trancers 2: The Return of
   Jack Deth '90

Paul Lynde
Son of Flubber '63

Carol Lynley
Son of Blob '71

Dani Lynn
They Saved Hitler's Brain
   '64

Mara Lynn
Prehistoric Women '50

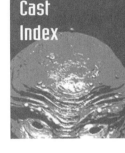

Cast Index

Stephen Markle
984: Prisoner of the Future '84

Alfred Marks
Scream and Scream Again '70

Michael Marks
The Wasp Woman '59

Hugh Marlowe
The Day the Earth Stood Still '51
Earth Vs. the Flying Saucers '56

Florence Marly
Planet of Blood '66

Percy Marmont
Four Sided Triangle '53

Kelli Maroney
Chopping Mall '86
Night of the Comet '84

Kenneth Mars
Misfits of Science '85
Young Frankenstein '74

Jean Marsh
The Unearthly Stranger '64
Willow '88

Darrah Marshall
Teenage Caveman '58

E.G. Marshall
Stephen King's The Tommyknockers '93
Superman 2 '80

Herbert Marshall
The Fly '58

Ken Marshall
Krull '83

Nancy Marshall
Frankenstein Meets the Space Monster '65

Steve Marshall
Night of the Creeps '86

Zena Marshall
Terrornauts '67

K.C. Martel
E.T.: The Extra-Terrestrial '82

Donna Martell
Project Moon Base '53

Gregg Martell
Dinosaurus! '60

Peter Martell
Planet on the Prowl '65

Ian Marter
Doctor Faustus '68

Andrea Martin
Kurt Vonnegut's Harrison Bergeron '95

Aubrey Martin
This Is Not a Test '62

Dean Paul Martin
Misfits of Science '85

Dewey Martin
The Thing '51

Jared Martin
The New Gladiators '87
The Sea Serpent '85

Lewis Martin
The War of the Worlds '53

Lock Martin
The Day the Earth Stood Still '51

Ross Martin
Conquest of Space '55

Strother Martin
Kiss Me Deadly '55

Tommy Martin
PSI Factor '80

Elsa Martinelli
10th Victim '65

Paul Marvel
The Psychotronic Man '91

Martin Mase
Alien Contamination '81

Nelson Mashita
Darkman '90

Ace Mask
Not of this Earth '88

Hilary Mason
Robot Jox '90

James Mason
The Boys from Brazil '78
Journey to the Center of the Earth '59
20,000 Leagues Under the Sea '54

Laurence Mason
Hackers '95

Pamela Mason
Navy Vs. the Night Monsters '66

Sharon Mason
Primal Scream '87

Tom Mason
Aliens Are Coming '80

John Massari
The Wizard of Speed and Time '88

Osa Massen
Rocketship X-M '50

Raymond Massey
Things to Come '36

Ben Masters
Making Mr. Right '86

Mary Elizabeth Mastrantonio
The Abyss '89

Gina Mastrogiacomo
Alien Space Avenger '91

Marcello Mastroianni
10th Victim '65

Richard Masur
The Thing '82
Timerider '83

Christine Matchet
The Illustrated Man '69

Mahdu Mathen
Children of the Damned '63

Michelle Matheson
Test Tube Teens from the Year 2000 '93

Tim Matheson
Solar Crisis '92

Kerwin Mathews
Battle Beneath the Earth '68
Jack the Giant Killer '62
Octaman '71
The Seventh Voyage of Sinbad '58
The Three Worlds of Gulliver '59

Thom Mathews
Alien from L.A. '87
Heatseeker '95

Samantha Mathis
Super Mario Bros. '93

Kyalo Mativo
Baby … Secret of the Lost Legend '85

John Matshikiza
Dust Devil '93

Hiroki Matsukata
Magic Serpent '66

Walter Matthau
Fail-Safe '64

Lester Matthews
The Invisible Man's Revenge '44

Robin Mattson
Captain America '79

Victor Mature
One Million B.C. '40

John Matuszak
Ice Pirates '84

Nicole Maurey
Day of the Triffids '63

Jon Maurice
Primal Scream '87

Gerda Maurus
Woman in the Moon '29

Mathilda May
Lifeforce '85

Christiane Maybach
The Head '59

Chip Mayer
Survivor '87

Peter Mayhew
The Empire Strikes Back '80
Return of the Jedi '83
Star Wars '77

John Maynard
Biohazard: The Alien Force '95
Dark Universe '93

Melanie Mayron
Heartbeeps '81

Debi Mazar
Batman Forever '95
Witch Hunt '94

Joseph Mazzello
Jurassic Park '93

Daron McBee
T-Force '94

Chi McBride
Cosmic Slop '94

Frances Lee McCain
Gremlins '84

Irish McCalla
She Demons '58

Holt McCallany
Alien 3 '92

David McCallum
Around the World Under the Sea '65

Frances McCann
The Creation of the Humanoids '62

Andrew McCarthy
Club Extinction '89

Annette McCarthy
Creature '85

Kevin McCarthy
Duplicates '92
Eve of Destruction '90
Final Approach '91
Innerspace '87
Invasion of the Body Snatchers '56
Invasion of the Body Snatchers '78
Twilight Zone: The Movie '83

Rod McCary
Rebel Storm '90

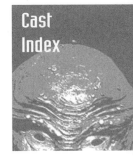

Cast Index

3 7 1

Sci-Fi Experience

Meat Loaf
The Rocky Horror Picture
Show '75

Ralph Meeker
The Alpha Incident '76
Food of the Gods '76
Kiss Me Deadly '55
Mind Snatchers '72

Don Megowan
The Creation of the
Humanoids '62
The Creature Walks Among
Us '56

Isabelle Mejias
Scanners 2: The New
Order '91

Georges Melies
A Trip to the Moon '02

Marisa Mell
Danger: Diabolik '68

Douglas Mellor
The Beast of Yucca Flats
'61

Sid Melton
The Lost Continent '51

David Mendenhall
Space Raiders '83

Alex Meneses
Amanda and the Alien '95

Heather Menzies
Captain America '79

Burgess Meredith
Clash of the Titans '81
Last Chase '81
Son of Blob '71
Twilight Zone: The Movie
'83

Judi Meredith
Jack the Giant Killer '62
Planet of Blood '66

Lee Meriwether
The 4D Man '59

John Merrick
Killers from Space '54

Dina Merrill
Anna to the Infinite Power
'84

Gary Merrill
Around the World Under
the Sea '65
Mysterious Island '61

Louis D. Merrill
The Giant Claw '57

Jane Merrow
Island of the Burning
Doomed '67

Mary Mertens
The Alien Factor '78

Laurie Metcalf
Making Mr. Right '86

Art Metrano
Rocket Attack U.S.A. '58

Nancy Mette
Meet the Hollowheads '89

Jim Metzler
Circuitry Man '90
Plughead Rewired:
Circuitry Man 2 '94

Harry Meyen
Unnatural '52

Dina Meyer
Johnny Mnemonic '95

Buntaro Miake
Warning from Space '56

Christopher Michael
Guyver 2: Dark Hero '94

Dario Michaelis
The Day the Sky Exploded
'57

Jordan Michaels
Lifepod '80

Charles Middleton
Flash Gordon Conquers
the Universe '40
Flash Gordon: Mars
Attacks the World '38
Flash Gordon: Rocketship
'36
Rocketship '36
Space Soldiers Conquer
the Universe '40

Joanna Miles
Bug '75
The Ultimate Warrior '75

Vera Miles
Brainwaves '82

Kim Milford
Laserblast '78

Ray Milland
Panic in the Year Zero! '62
The Sea Serpent '85
Starflight One '83
X: The Man with X-Ray
Eyes '63

Dennis Miller
The Net '95

Dick Miller
Explorers '85
Gremlins '84
Innerspace '87
It Conquered the World '56
Night of the Creeps '86
Project X '87
The Terminator '84
X: The Man with X-Ray
Eyes '63

Jason Miller
The Henderson Monster
'80

Jennifer Miller
Terminal Impact '95

Jonny Lee Miller
Hackers '95

Joshua Miller
Class of 1999 '90

Julie Miller
Primal Scream '87

Kathleen Miller
Strange New World '75

Mark Thomas Miller
Misfits of Science '85

Marvin Miller
Red Planet Mars '52

Penelope Ann Miller
The Shadow '94
Witch Hunt '94

Roosevelt Miller, Jr.
Game of Survival '89

Ty Miller
Trancers 4: Jack of Swords
'93
Trancers 5: Sudden Deth
'94

Walter Miller
Ghost Patrol '36

Andra Millian
Nightfall '88

Donna Mills
Beyond the Bermuda
Triangle '75

John Mills
Dr. Strange '78
Quatermass Conclusion
'79

Josh Milrad
Beastmaster '82

James Milton
Escape from Galaxy Three
'76

Yvette Mimieux
The Black Hole '79
The Time Machine '60

Sal Mineo
Escape from the Planet of
the Apes '71

Mike Minett
Bad Taste '88

Emil Minty
The Road Warrior '82

Fabrizio Mioni
Hercules '58

Helen Mirren
Excalibur '81
The Fiendish Plot of Dr. Fu
Manchu '80
2010: The Year We Make
Contact '84

Kunihiko Mitamura
Godzilla Vs. Biollante '89

Cameron Mitchell
Flight to Mars '51
Screamers '80
Space Mutiny '88
The Stranger '73
Supersonic Man '78
The Swarm '78

Francis Mitchell
Abraxas: Guardian of the
Universe '90

George Mitchell
The Andromeda Strain '71

Laurie Mitchell
Missile to the Moon '59
Queen of Outer Space '58

Mary Mitchell
Panic in the Year Zero! '62

Sasha Mitchell
Class of 1999 2: The
Substitute '93

Warren Mitchell
The Crawling Eye '58
The Unearthly Stranger '64

Ilan Mitchell-Smith
Journey to the Center of
the Earth '88
Weird Science '85

Shaun Mitchelle
Roller Blade '85

Chris Mitchum
Aftershock '88
Biohazard: The Alien Force
'95
Day Time Ended '78

John Mitchum
Escapes '86

Kim Miyori
The Punisher '90

Kumi Mizuno
Attack of the Mushroom
People '63
Godzilla Vs. Monster Zero
'65
Godzilla Vs. the Sea
Monster '66
Gorath '64
War of the Gargantuas '70

Roger Mobley
Jack the Giant Killer '62

Donald Moffat
The Thing '82

Cast Index

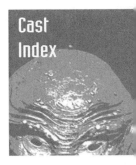

**Cast
Index**

Nancy Olson
The Absent-Minded
  Professor '61
Son of Flubber '63

Mollie O'Mara
Escape from Safehaven
  '88

Ron O'Neal
The Final Countdown '80

Amy O'Neill
Honey, I Shrunk the Kids
  '89

Dick O'Neill
Gamera, the Invincible '66

Jennifer O'Neill
Scanners '81

Julius Ongewe
First Spaceship on Venus
  '60

Alan Oppenheimer
The Groundstar
  Conspiracy '72
Invisible: The Chronicles of
  Benjamin Knight '93
Trancers 4: Jack of Swords
  '93
Trancers 5: Sudden Deth
  '94
Westworld '73

Don Opper
Android '82
Critters '86
Critters 2: The Main
  Course '88
Critters 3 '91
Critters 4 '91

Terry O'Quinn
The Rocketeer '91

Jerry Orbach
Universal Soldier '92

Wyott Ordung
Monster from the Ocean
  Floor '54

Cyril O'Reilly
Philadelphia Experiment 2
  '93

Vera Orlova
Aelita: Queen of Mars '24

Ed O'Ross
The Hidden '87
Universal Soldier '92

Marina Orsini
Battle of the Worlds '61

Dyana Ortelli
Alienator '89

Humberto Ortiz
Arcade '93

Lyn Osborn
The Amazing Colossal Man
  '57
Invasion of the Saucer
  Men '57

Milo O'Shea
Barbarella '68

Cliff Osmond
Hangar 18 '80
Invasion of the Bee Girls
  '73

Carl Ossosen
Reptilicus '62

Maureen O'Sullivan
Stranded '87

Ryutaro Otomo
Magic Serpent '66

Annette O'Toole
Superman 3 '83

Peter O'Toole
Supergirl '84

Nobuko Otowa
Last War '68

Carl Ottosen
Journey to the Seventh
  Planet '61

Peter Outerbridge
The Android Affair '95

Rick Overton
Earth Girls Are Easy '89

Patricia Owens
The Fly '58

Frank Oz
The Empire Strikes Back
  '80

Roger Pace
The War of the Colossal
  Beast '58

Tom Pace
The Astro-Zombies '67

Joanna Pacula
Deep Red '94
Timemaster '95

Harrison Page
Carnosaur '93

Debra Paget
From the Earth to the
  Moon '58

Drew Pahich
Dark Star '74

Robert Paige
Abbott and Costello Go to
  Mars '53

Debbie Paine
The Computer Wore Tennis
  Shoes '69

Heidi Paine
Alien Seed '89

Nestor Paiva
Creature from the Black
  Lagoon '54
The Mole People '56
Revenge of the Creature
  '55
Tarantula '55
They Saved Hitler's Brain
  '64

Jack Palance
Batman '89
Cyborg 2 '93
Solar Crisis '92

Michael Palin
Brazil '85
Jabberwocky '77
Time Bandits '81

Anita Pallenberg
Barbarella '68

Gregg Palmer
The Creature Walks Among
  Us '56

Lilli Palmer
The Boys from Brazil '78

Luciana Paluzzi
The Green Slime '68

Michael Pare
Dragonfight '92
Moon 44 '90
The Philadelphia
  Experiment '84
Solar Force '94
Space Rage '86
Village of the Damned '95
World Gone Wild '88

Reg Park
Hercules and the Captive
  Women '63
Hercules in the Haunted
  World '64
Hercules, Prisoner of Evil
  '64

Ellen Parker
The Lost Missile '58

Fess Parker
Them! '54

Kim Parker
Fiend Without a Face '58
Fire Maidens from Outer
  Space '56

Paula Jai Parker
Cosmic Slop '94

Sarah Jessica Parker
Flight of the Navigator '86

Dean Parkin
The War of the Colossal
  Beast '58

Patrick Paroux
Delicatessen '92

Leslie Parrish
The Giant Spider Invasion
  '75
The Manchurian Candidate
  '62

Steve Parrish
Scanners 3: The Takeover
  '92

Cyndi Pass
Scanner Cop '94

Michael Pataki
The Amazing Spider-Man
  '77

Michael Pate
Return of Captain
  Invincible '83

Bill Paterson
The Adventures of Baron
  Munchausen '89

Mandy Patinkin
Alien Nation '88
The Princess Bride '87

Jason Patric
Frankenstein Unbound '90
Solarbabies '86

Cynthia Patrick
The Mole People '56

Dennis Patrick
The Time Travelers '64

Joan Patrick
The Astro-Zombies '67

Lee Patrick
Seven Faces of Dr. Lao '63

Robert Patrick
Fire in the Sky '93
Future Hunters '88
Terminator 2: Judgment
  Day '91

Neva Patterson
V '83

Scott Patterson
Alien Nation: Dark Horizon
  '94

Mark Patton
Anna to the Infinite Power
  '84

Will Patton
The Puppet Masters '94

Alexandra Paul
Cyber Bandits '94

Don Michael Paul
Alien from L.A. '87
Robot Wars '93

Nancy Paul
Lifeforce '85

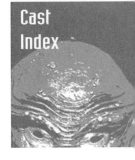

Cast
Index

Roddy Piper
Hell Comes to Frogtown
'87
They Live '88

Bruce Pirrie
The Pink Chiquitas '86

Anne Marie Pisani
Delicatessen '92

Joe Piscopo
King Kong '76

Brad Pitt
12 Monkeys '95

Jeremy Piven
12:01 '93

Mary Kay Place
Explorers '85
Modern Problems '81

Nick Plakias
UFO: Target Earth '74

Dana Plato
Beyond the Bermuda
Triangle '75

Oliver Platt
Flatliners '90

Alice Playten
Legend '86

Donald Pleasence
Escape from New York '81
Fantastic Voyage '66
The Puma Man '80
THX 1138 '71
Warrior of the Lost World
'84

Suzanne Pleshette
The Birds '63

Shelley Plimpton
Glen and Randa '71

Amanda Plummer
Freejack '92

Christopher Plummer
Dreamscape '84
Kurt Vonnegut's Harrison
Bergeron '95
Prototype '83
Star Crash '78
Star Trek 6: The
Undiscovered Country
'91
12 Monkeys '95

Rick Podell
World Gone Wild '88

Klaus Pohl
Woman in the Moon '29

Priscilla Pointer
Mysterious Two '82

Diana Polakov
Supersonic Man '78

Anna Maria Polani
Hercules Against the Moon
Men '65

Jon Polito
Highlander '86

Kevin Pollak
Willow '88

Michael J. Pollard
The Arrival '90
I Come in Peace '90
Riders of the Storm '88
Skeeter '93
Split Second '92

Sarah Polley
The Adventures of Baron
Munchausen '89

Yvan Ponton
Scanners 2: The New
Order '91

Richard Portnow
Meet the Hollowheads '89

Pete Postlethwaite
Split Second '92

Michal Postnikow
First Spaceship on Venus
'60

Terry Potter
Bad Taste '88

Cliff Potts
The Groundstar
Conspiracy '72
Silent Running '71

Ely Pouget
Death Machine '95
Endless Descent '90
Lawnmower Man 2: Jobe's
War '95

CCH Pounder
Lifepod '93
RoboCop 3 '91
White Dwarf '95

Arla Powell
Battle Beyond the Sun '63

Clive Powell
Children of the Damned
'63

Robert Powell
The Asphyx '72
What Waits Below '83

Taryn Power
Sinbad and the Eye of the
Tiger '77

Tyrone Power, Jr.
Cocoon '85

Alexandra Powers
Cast a Deadly Spell '91

Bruce Powers
Horror of the Blood
Monsters '70

Mala Powers
Escape from Planet Earth
'67

Tom Powers
Destination Moon '50

Michael Praed
Nightflyers '87

Judson Pratt
Monster on the Campus
'59

Wolfgang Preiss
Club Extinction '89
Mistress of the World '59

Luis Prendes
Alien Predators '80

Micheline Presle
Mistress of the World '59

Jason Presson
Explorers '85

Cyndy Preston
The Brain '88

Kelly Preston
Metalstorm: The
Destruction of Jared Syn
'83

Mike Preston
Metalstorm: The
Destruction of Jared Syn
'83

Robert Preston
The Last Starfighter '84

Sue Price
Nemesis 2: Nebula '94

Vincent Price
The Abominable Dr. Phibes
'71
Dr. Goldfoot and the Bikini
Machine '65
Edward Scissorhands '90
Escapes '86
The Fly '58
The Invisible Man Returns
'40
The Last Man on Earth '64
Master of the World '61
Return of the Fly '59
Scream and Scream Again
'70

Robert Prichard
Alien Space Avenger '91
Class of Nuke 'Em High '86

Andrew Prine
The Eliminators '86
Riding with Death '76
V '83

Ted Prior
Future Zone '90
Mutant Species '95

Juergen Prochnow
Dune '84
The Fire Next Time '93
Judge Dredd '95

Phil Proctor
Lobster Man from Mars '89
Robo-C.H.I.C. '89

Olga Prokhorova
Project: Genesis '93

Robert Prosky
Gremlins 2: The New Batch
'90

David Prowse
A Clockwork Orange '71
The Empire Strikes Back
'80
From "Star Wars" to
"Jedi": The Making of a
Saga '83
Return of the Jedi '83
Star Wars '77

Jonathan Pryce
The Adventures of Baron
Munchausen '89
Brazil '85
Something Wicked This
Way Comes '83

Richard Pryor
Superman 3 '83
Wild in the Streets '68

Roger Pryor
The Man They Could Not
Hang '39

Frank Puglia
20 Million Miles to Earth
'57

Bill Pullman
Spaceballs '87

Lee Purcell
The Incredible Hulk
Returns '88
Space Rage '86

Edmund Purdom
After the Fall of New York
'85

**Carolyn Purdy-
Gordon**
From Beyond '86

Amrish Puri
Indiana Jones and the
Temple of Doom '84

Jack Purvis
The Adventures of Baron
Munchausen '89

Jessica Puscas
Andy and the Airwave
Rangers '89

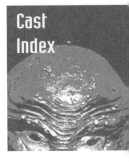

**Cast
Index**

Gloria Reuben
Timecop '94

Paul (Pee Wee Herman) Reubens
Batman Returns '92

Clive Revill
The Empire Strikes Back '80

Roberta Rex
Children of the Damned '63

Fernando Rey
Quintet '79

Ernie Reyes, Jr.
Teenage Mutant Ninja Turtles 2: The Secret of the Ooze '91

Patrick Reynolds
The Eliminators '86

Peter Reynolds
Devil Girl from Mars '54

Rolf Reynolds
Xtro 2: The Second Encounter '91

William Reynolds
The Land Unknown '57

Rhema
Voyage of the Rock Aliens '87

Christopher Rhodes
Gorgo '61

Cynthia Rhodes
Runaway '84

Hari Rhodes
Conquest of the Planet of the Apes '72

John Rhys-Davies
Cyborg Cop '93
Indiana Jones and the Last Crusade '89
The Lost World '92
Raiders of the Lost Ark '81
Rebel Storm '90
The Trial of the Incredible Hulk '89

Alfonso Ribeiro
Ticks '93

Ariana Richards
Grand Tour: Disaster in Time '92
Jurassic Park '93
Spaced Invaders '90

Michael Richards
Coneheads '93

Ian Richardson
Brazil '85

Jay Richardson
Alienator '89

Bad Girls from Mars '90

John Richardson
Cosmos: War of the Planets '80

Lee Richardson
The Fly 2 '89

Natasha Richardson
The Handmaid's Tale '90

Ralph Richardson
Dragonslayer '81
Rollerball '75
Things to Come '36
Time Bandits '81

Sy Richardson
Dead Man Walking '88
Street Asylum '90
They Live '88

Peter Mark Richman
PSI Factor '80

Anthony Richmond
Devil Girl from Mars '54

Dan Richter
2001: A Space Odyssey '68

Deborah Richter
Cyborg '89

Don Rickles
X: The Man with X-Ray Eyes '63

Kimber Riddle
Stephen King's The Langoliers '95

Ron Rifkin
Silent Running '71

Diana Rigg
Running Delilah '93

John Riggs
Invasion of the Space Preachers '90

Robin Riker
Alligator '80

Jack Riley
Attack of the Killer Tomatoes '77

Walter Rilla
The Face of Fu Manchu '65
Frozen Alive '64
The Gamma People '56

Shane Rimmer
The People that Time Forgot '77

Fred Rinaldo
Abbott and Costello Meet the Invisible Man '51

Molly Ringwald
Spacehunter: Adventures in the Forbidden Zone '83

Stephen King's The Stand '94

Lisa Rinna
Robot Wars '93

Nicole Rio
Visitants '87

Michael Ripper
Quatermass 2 '57

Leon Rippy
Moon 44 '90
Stargate '94

Carlos Rivas
The Black Scorpion '57
They Saved Hitler's Brain '64

George Riviere
Journey Beneath the Desert '61

Gianni Rizzo
Mission Stardust '68

Pat Roach
Willow '88

Glen Roald
Timecop '94

Adam Roarke
Women of the Prehistoric Planet '66

John Roarke
Mutant on the Bounty '89

Jason Robards, Jr.
A Boy and His Dog '75
The Day After '83
Something Wicked This Way Comes '83

Jason Robards, III
They Live '88

Gale Robbins
Parasite '82

Tim Robbins
Howard the Duck '86

Alan Roberts
Dinosaurus! '60

Arthur Roberts
Not of this Earth '88

Cheri Roberts
It's Dead—Let's Touch It! '92

Ewan Roberts
Day of the Triffids '63

Gary Roberts
Alien Intruder '93

Jay Roberts, Jr.
Aftershock '88
Warlords 3000 '93

Julia Roberts
Flatliners '90

Marty Roberts
Alien Space Avenger '91

Michael D. Roberts
Ice Pirates '84

Perry Roberts
Lock 'n' Load '90

Ray Roberts
Alien Dead '85

Tanya Roberts
Beastmaster '82
Hearts & Armour '83

Thayer Roberts
This Is Not a Test '62

Wink Roberts
The Day It Came to Earth '77

Cliff Robertson
Brainstorm '83
Charly '68

Andrew (Andy) Robinson
Trancers 3: Deth Lives '92

Ann Robinson
Midnight Movie Massacre '88
The War of the Worlds '53

Bumper Robinson
Enemy Mine '85

Edward G. Robinson
Soylent Green '73

McKinlay Robinson
The Pink Chiquitas '86

Rob Robinson
The Bronx Executioner '86

Rafael H. Robledo
Darkman '90

Eugene Roche
Slaughterhouse Five '72

Chris Rock
Coneheads '93

Charles Rocket
Earth Girls Are Easy '89
Wild Palms '93

William Roerick
The Wasp Woman '59

Beth Rogan
Mysterious Island '61

Jean Rogers
Flash Gordon: Mars Attacks the World '38
Flash Gordon: Rocketship '36
Rocketship '36

Mimi Rogers
Deadlock '91

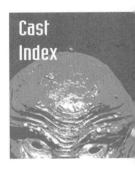

**Cast
Index**

Cast Index

Armin Shimerman
Arena '89

Sab Shimono
Teenage Mutant Ninja
Turtles 3 '93

Takashi Shimura
Ghidrah the Three Headed
Monster '65
Godzilla, King of the
Monsters '54
Gorath '64
Last Days of Planet Earth
'74
The Mysterians '58

Yumi Shirakawa
Gorath '64
H-Man '59
Last War '68
The Mysterians '58
Rodan '57
The Secret of the Telegian
'61

Talia Shire
Hyper-Sapien: People from
Another Star '86

Cathie Shirriff
Star Trek 3: The Search for
Spock '84

Joe Shishido
Fugitive Alien '86

Dan Shor
Bill & Ted's Excellent
Adventure '89
Tron '82

Martin Short
Innerspace '87

Kathy Shower
Robo-C.H.I.C. '89

Will Shriner
Time Trackers '88

Tsen Shu-yi
Infra-Man '76

Elisabeth Shue
Back to the Future, Part 2
'89
Back to the Future, Part 3
'90
Link '86

Sylvia Sidney
God Told Me To '76

Donald Siegel
Invasion of the Body
Snatchers '56

Casey Siemaszko
Back to the Future '85
Back to the Future, Part 2
'89

Gregory Sierra
The Clones '73

Honey, I Blew Up the Kid
'92

James B. Sikking
Final Approach '91
Outland '81
Star Trek 3: The Search for
Spock '84
The Terminal Man '74

Henry Silva
Alligator '80
Buck Rogers in the 25th
Century '79
The Manchurian Candidate
'62
Megaforce '82

Joe Silver
They Came from Within '75

Ron Silver
Lifepod '93
Timecop '94

Jonathan Silverman
12:01 '93

Paul Silverman
The Carrier '87

Armando Silvestre
Neutron and the Black
Mask '61
Neutron Vs. the Amazing
Dr. Caronte '61
Neutron Vs. the Death
Robots '62
Night of the Bloody Apes
'68
Wrestling Women Vs. the
Aztec Ape '62
Wrestling Women Vs. the
Aztec Mummy '59

Gene Simmons
Runaway '84

Pat Simmons
The Giant Gila Monster '59

Gunther Simon
First Spaceship on Venus
'60

Michel Simon
The Head '59

Robert F. Simon
Chinese Web '78

Lisa Simone
The Giant Gila Monster '59

O.J. Simpson
Capricorn One '78

Frank Sinatra
The Manchurian Candidate
'62

Sinbad
Coneheads '93

Charles Sinclair
The Green Slime '68

Marc Singer
Beastmaster '82
Beastmaster 2: Through
the Portal of Time '91
Beastmaster 3: The Eye of
Braxus '95
Dead Space '90
High Desert Kill '90
In the Cold of the Night '89
V '83
V: The Final Battle '84

Ritchie Singer
Encounter at Raven's Gate
'88

Gary Sinise
Stephen King's The Stand
'94

Marina Sirtis
Star Trek Generations '94

Emil Sitka
Three Stooges in Orbit '62

Sean Six
Alien Nation: Dark Horizon
'94

George Skaff
The Incredible Petrified
World '58

Jimmie F. Skaggs
Backlash: Oblivion 2 '95

Lilia Skala
Charly '68

Brigitte Skay
Alien Women '69

Tom Skerritt
Alien '79
Dead Zone '83

Ione Skye
Stranded '87

Jeremy Slate
The Lawnmower Man '92

Christian Slater
Beyond the Stars '89

Helen Slater
Supergirl '84
12:01 '93

Suzee Slater
Chopping Mall '86

Tommy Sledge
Lobster Man from Mars '89

Leo Slezak
Baron Munchausen '43

Everett Sloane
Hercules and the Princess
of Troy '65

Jean Smart
Project X '87

Brian Smiar
Running Against Time '90

Yakov Smirnoff
The Adventures of
Buckaroo Banzai Across
the Eighth Dimension
'84

A. Thomas Smith
Invader '91

Sir C. Aubrey Smith
Transatlantic Tunnel '35

Charles Martin Smith
Roswell: The U.F.O. Cover-
Up '94
Starman '84

**Cheryl "Rainbeaux"
Smith**
Incredible Melting Man '77
Laserblast '78
Parasite '82

Craig Smith
Bad Taste '88

Ian Smith
Body Melt '93

Jayne Smith
R.O.T.O.R. '88

Jeffrey Smith
Lock 'n' Load '90

John W. Smith
Star Crystal '85

Kent Smith
Moon Pilot '62

Kurtwood Smith
Fortress '93
RoboCop '87
Star Trek 6: The
Undiscovered Country
'91

Lane Smith
Duplicates '92

Lewis Smith
The Adventures of
Buckaroo Banzai Across
the Eighth Dimension
'84

Madolyn Smith
Final Approach '91
2010: The Year We Make
Contact '84

Maggie Smith
Clash of the Titans '81

Mel Smith
The Princess Bride '87

Melanie Smith
Trancers 3: Deth Lives '92

Paul Smith
Dune '84

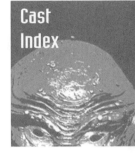

Cast
Index

**Cast
Index**

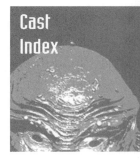

Cast
Index

Peter Vaughan
Brazil '85
Time Bandits '81

Robert Vaughn
Battle Beyond the Stars
'80
Hangar 18 '80
The Lucifer Complex '78
Starship Invasions '77
Superman 3 '83
Teenage Caveman '58
Virus '82

Marcus Vaughter
Visitants '87

Bruno Ve Sota
Attack of the Giant
Leeches '59
The Wasp Woman '59

Lorena Velasquez
Samson Vs. the Vampire
Women '61
Wrestling Women Vs. the
Aztec Ape '62
Wrestling Women Vs. the
Aztec Mummy '59

Chick Vennera
The Terror Within 2 '91

Jesse Ventura
Abraxas: Guardian of the
Universe '90
Predator '87
The Running Man '87

Lino Ventura
Mistress of the World '59

Viviane Ventura
Battle Beneath the Earth
'68

Gwen Verdon
Cocoon '85
Cocoon: The Return '88

Ben Vereen
Intruders '92

Denise Vernac
Unnatural '52

Howard Vernon
Alphaville '65

John Vernon
Blue Monkey '87

Gennadi Vernov
Planeta Burg '62

Cec Verrell
Hell Comes to Frogtown
'87

Marie Versini
The Brides of Fu Manchu
'66

Victoria Vetri
Invasion of the Bee Girls
'73

When Dinosaurs Ruled the
Earth '70

Karin Viard
Delicatessen '92

Yvette Vickers
Attack of the 50 Foot
Woman '58
Attack of the Giant
Leeches '59

Katherine Victor
Mesa of Lost Women '52
The Wild World of
Batwoman '66

Steven Vidler
Encounter at Raven's Gate
'88

Tom Villard
The Trouble with Dick '88

Herve Villechaize
Forbidden Zone '80

Fernando Villena
Planet of the Vampires '65

Jan-Michael Vincent
Alienator '89
Damnation Alley '77
The Return '80
Xtro 2: The Second
Encounter '91

Zachary Vincent
The Return '80

Melanie Vincz
The Lost Empire '83

Steve Vinovich
Hollywood Boulevard 2 '89

Helen Vinson
Transatlantic Tunnel '35

Jesse Vint
Bug '75
Death Sport '78
Forbidden World '82
I Come in Peace '90

Gustav Vintas
Welcome Back Mr. Fox '83

M. Virzinskaya
The Amphibian Man '61

Sal Viscuso
Spaceballs '87

Giovanni Visentin
Hearts & Armour '83

Judith Vittet
The City of Lost Children
'95

Viva
Forbidden Zone '80

Sonia Viviani
Hercules 2 '85

Darlene Vogel
Back to the Future, Part 2
'89

Jack Vogel
Lock 'n' Load '90

Ruediger Vogler
Until the End of the World
'91

Vicki Volante
Horror of the Blood
Monsters '70

Gian Marie Volonte
Journey Beneath the
Desert '61

Lenny Von Dohlen
Electric Dreams '84

Loni von Friedl
Journey to the Far Side of
the Sun '69

Rik von Nutter
Assignment Outer Space
'61

Joel von Ornsteiner
Robot Holocaust '87

**Gustav von
Seyffertitz**
She '35

Erich von Stroheim
Unnatural '52

Max von Sydow
Conan the Barbarian '82
Death Watch '80
Dreamscape '84
Dune '84
Flash Gordon '80
Judge Dredd '95
The Ultimate Warrior '75
Until the End of the World
'91

Hanz von Teuffen
The Flying Saucer '50

**Gustav von
Wagenheim**
Woman in the Moon '29

Otto von Wernherr
Liquid Sky '83

George Voskovec
The 27th Day '57

Arnold Vosloo
Darkman 2: The Return of
Durant '94
Darkman 3: Die Darkman
Die '95

Vlasta Vrana
Scanners 2: The New
Order '91

Koji Wada
Gappa the Trifibian
Monster '67

W.F. Wadden
Xtro 2: The Second
Encounter '91

Stuart Wade
Meteor Monster '57
Monster from the Ocean
Floor '54

Lyle Waggoner
Robo-C.H.I.C. '89
Women of the Prehistoric
Planet '66

Chuck Wagner
The Sisterhood '88

Jack Wagner
Trapped in Space '94

**Natasha Gregson
Wagner**
Wes Craven Presents Mind
Ripper '95

Corinne Wahl
Equalizer 2000 '86

Edward Wain
The Last Woman on Earth
'61

James Wainwright
Warlords of the 21st
Century '82

Ralph Waite
Crash and Burn '90

Thomas G. Waites
The Thing '82

Akiko Wakabayashi
Dagora, the Space
Monster '65
Ghidrah the Three Headed
Monster '65

Setsuko Wakayama
Godzilla Raids Again '55

Gregory Walcott
Plan 9 from Outer Space
'56

Christopher Walken
Batman Returns '92
Brainstorm '83
Communion '89
Dead Zone '83
Mind Snatchers '72

Ally Walker
Universal Soldier '92

Arnetia Walker
The Wizard of Speed and
Time '88

Clint Walker
Deadly Harvest '72

Cast Index

The Road Warrior '82

Kenneth Welsh
Timecop '94

Ming-Na Wen
Star Quest '94

George Wendt
Dreamscape '84
Forever Young '92

Jan Werich
The Original Fabulous
Adventures of Baron
Munchausen '61

Karen Werner
Mysterious Two '82

Oskar Werner
Fahrenheit 451 '66

Doug Wert
Roswell: The U.F.O. Cover-
Up '94

Dick Wesson
Destination Moon '50

Adam West
Doin' Time on Planet Earth
'88
Omega Cop '90
Robinson Crusoe on Mars
'64

Dottie West
The Aurora Encounter '85

Gregory West
Class of 1999 2: The
Substitute '93

Tracy Westerholm
Xtro 2: The Second
Encounter '91

Jack Weston
Short Circuit 2 '88

Patricia Wettig
Stephen King's The
Langoliers '95

Paul Wexler
Doc Savage '75

Marius Weyers
Deepstar Six '89

Tom Weyland
People Who Own the Dark
'75

Michael Whalen
Missile to the Moon '59
The Phantom from 10,000
Leagues '56

Justin Whalin
The Fire Next Time '93

Joanne Whalley
Willow '88

Wil Wheaton
The Last Starfighter '84

**Dana Wheeler-
Nicholson**
Circuitry Man '90

Forest Whitaker
Body Snatchers '93
Species '95

Carol White
The Time Travelers '64

David White
The Amazing Spider-Man
'77

Earl White
Nemesis 2: Nebula '94

Peter Whitford
Dead End Drive-In '86

Margaret Whiting
Sinbad and the Eye of the
Tiger '77

Jill Whitlow
Night of the Creeps '86

Stuart Whitman
Omega Cop '90

James Whitmore
Planet of the Apes '68
Them! '54

Grace Lee Whitney
Star Trek 3: The Search for
Spock '84
Star Trek 6: The
Undiscovered Country
'91

Paul Whitthorne
Critters 4 '91

James Whitworth
Planet of Dinosaurs '80

Susanne Widl
Invisible Adversaries '77

Richard Widmark
The Swarm '78

Bud Widom
The Green Slime '68

Dianne Wiest
Edward Scissorhands '90

Ralph Wilcox
Megaforce '82

Robert Wilcox
Doctor Satan's Robot '40
The Man They Could Not
Hang '39
Mysterious Doctor Satan
'40

Henry Wilcoxon
Escape from Planet Earth
'67

Katy Wild
The Evil of Frankenstein
'64

Poul Wildaker
Reptilicus '62

Andrew Wilde
1984 '84

Gene Wilder
Young Frankenstein '74

Valerie Wildman
Neon City '91

Dawn Wildsmith
Alienator '89
Evil Spawn '87
Warlords '88

Kathleen Wilhoite
Fire in the Sky '93

Robert J. Wilke
20,000 Leagues Under the
Sea '54

Barbara Wilkin
The Flesh Eaters '64

Charles Wilkinson
Quarantine '89

Dave Willcock
Queen of Outer Space '58

Jack Willcox
Prison Planet '92

Jean Willes
Invasion of the Body
Snatchers '56

Bill Williams
The Giant Spider Invasion
'75

Billy Dee Williams
Alien Intruder '93
Batman '89
The Empire Strikes Back
'80
From "Star Wars" to
"Jedi": The Making of a
Saga '83
Return of the Jedi '83

Cindy Williams
Spaceship '81
Uforia '81

**Dick Anthony
Williams**
Edward Scissorhands '90

Edy Williams
Bad Girls from Mars '90

Grant Williams
Escape from Planet Earth
'67
The Incredible Shrinking
Man '57
The Monolith Monsters '57

Ian Patrick Williams
Bad Channels '92

Jason Williams
Flesh Gordon '72

JoBeth Williams
The Day After '83

Kelli Williams
Lifepod '93

Kent Williams
Time After Time '79

Michelle Williams
Timemaster '95

Paul Williams
Battle for the Planet of the
Apes '73

Peter Williams
Destroy All Planets '68

Robert Williams
Revenge of the Creature
'55

Simon Williams
The Fiendish Plot of Dr. Fu
Manchu '80

Fred Williamson
The New Gladiators '87

Nicol Williamson
Excalibur '81

Noble Willingham
Fire in the Sky '93

Bruce Willis
12 Monkeys '95

Douglas Wilmer
The Brides of Fu Manchu
'66
Golden Voyage of Sinbad
'73
The Vengeance of Fu
Manchu '67

Barbara Wilson
Invasion of the Animal
People '62

**Don "The Dragon"
Wilson**
Cyber-Tracker '93
Cyber-Tracker 2 '95
Futurekick '91

Elizabeth Wilson
The Incredible Shrinking
Woman '81

George Wilson
Attack of the Killer
Tomatoes '77

Ian Wilson
Day of the Triffids '63

Joi Wilson
Creepozoids '87

Lisle Wilson
Incredible Melting Man '77

Rita Wilson
The Day It Came to Earth
'77

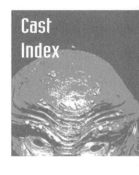

Cast Index

Dwight Yoakam
Roswell: The U.F.O. Cover-Up '94

Kekao Yokoo
Geisha Girl '52

Francine York
Curse of the Swamp Creature '66

Michael York
Island of Dr. Moreau '77
Logan's Run '76

Susannah York
Superman: The Movie '78
Superman 2 '80

Alan Young
The Time Machine '60

Carleton Young
20,000 Leagues Under the Sea '54

Clara Kimball Young
Return of Chandu '34

Dey Young
Strange Invaders '83

Richard Young
Assassin '86

Sean Young
Baby ... Secret of the Lost Legend '85
Blade Runner '82
Dune '84

Gail Youngs
Timestalkers '87

Jim Youngs
Skeeter '93

Victor Sen Yung
She Demons '58

Grace Zabriskie
Galaxy of Terror '81
Megaville '91

Pia Zadora
Santa Claus Conquers the Martians '64
Voyage of the Rock Aliens '87

Frank Zagarino
Night Siege Project: Shadowchaser 2 '94
Project Shadowchaser 3000 '95
Terminal Impact '95

Halina Zalewska
Planet on the Prowl '65

Del Zamora
RoboCop '87

Billy Zane
Back to the Future '85
Back to the Future, Part 2 '89
Critters '86
Megaville '91
Running Delilah '93

Lenore Zann
Def-Con 4 '85

Dweezil Zappa
The Running Man '87

John Zaremba
20 Million Miles to Earth '57

Robert Z'Dar
Beastmaster 2: Through the Portal of Time '91
Dragonfight '92

Jaimie Zemarel
Night Beast '83

Gerard Zepeda
Night of the Bloody Apes '68

Anthony Zerbe
Dead Zone '83

The Omega Man '71
Steel Dawn '87

Georgi Zhonov
Planeta Burg '62

Howard Zieff
Flesh Gordon '72

Terri Zimmern
The Manster '59

William Zipp
Future Force '89

Hanns Zischler
Club Extinction '89

Arlene Zoellner
Gamera Vs. Zigra '71

Gloria Zoellner
Gamera Vs. Zigra '71

Rod Zuanic
Mad Max: Beyond Thunderdome '85

Daphne Zuniga
The Fly 2 '89
Spaceballs '87

Steve Zurk
Biohazard: The Alien Force '95

Director Index

This index lists all directors credited in the main review section, alphabetically by their last names. If you've got time to kill, you might look up a director's name in the "Cast Index," just to see if s/he may have had a cameo in a movie reviewed in this book. But that's up to you.

Director Index

**Director
Index**

Ron Howard
Cocoon '85
Willow '88

Linda Moulton Howe
A Strange Harvest with
Linda Moulton Howe '80

Harry Hoyt
The Lost World '25

Hua-Shan
Infra-Man '76

Reginald Hudlin
Cosmic Slop '94

Warrington Hudlin
Cosmic Slop '94

Gene Huff
Bob Lazar: Excerpts from
the Government Bible
'94

John Hughes
Weird Science '85

Ken Hughes
The Atomic Man '56

Edward Hunt
Alien Warrior '85
The Brain '88
Starship Invasions '77

Paul Hunt
The Clones '73

Peter Hunt
Hyper-Sapien: People from
Another Star '86

Waris Hussein
The Henderson Monster
'80

Robert Hutton
The Slime People '63

Willard Huyck
Howard the Duck '86

Peter Hyams
Capricorn One '78
Outland '81
Timecop '94
2010: The Year We Make
Contact '84

**J. Christian
Ingvordsen**
Search and Destroy '88

Sam Irvin
Backlash: Oblivion 2 '95
Oblivion '94
Out There '95

Donald G. Jackson
Hell Comes to Frogtown
'87
Roller Blade '85

G. Philip Jackson
Replikator: Cloned to Kill
'94

Peter Jackson
Bad Taste '88

Philip Jackson
Project: Genesis '93

Rick Jacobson
Star Quest '94
Suspect Device '95

Bob James
Alien Seed '89

Jerry Jameson
Starflight One '83

Annabel Jankel
Super Mario Bros. '93

Bunker Jenkins
Space Ninja: Sword of the
Space Ark '81

Jean-Marie Jeunet
The City of Lost Children
'95
Delicatessen '92

Norman Jewison
Rollerball '75

Mike Jittlov
The Wizard of Speed and
Time '88

Phil Joanou
Wild Palms '93

Alan Johnson
Solarbabies '86

Kenneth Johnson
Alien Nation: Dark Horizon
'94
The Incredible Hulk '77
Short Circuit 2 '88
V '83

Lamont Johnson
The Groundstar
Conspiracy '72
Spacehunter: Adventures
in the Forbidden Zone
'83

Patrick Read Johnson
Spaced Invaders '90

Joe Johnston
Honey, I Shrunk the Kids
'89
The Rocketeer '91

Brian Thomas Jones
Escape from Safehaven
'88

Donald M. Jones
Project: Nightmare '85

Gary Jones
Mosquito '95

L.Q. Jones
A Boy and His Dog '75

C. Courtney Joyner
Trancers 3: Deth Lives '92

Nathan (Hertz) Juran
Attack of the 50 Foot
Woman '58
The Brain from Planet
Arous '57
The Deadly Mantis '57
First Men in the Moon '64
Jack the Giant Killer '62
The Seventh Voyage of
Sinbad '58
20 Million Miles to Earth
'57

Jeremy Paul Kagan
Roswell: The U.F.O. Cover-
Up '94

Jay Kamen
Transformations '88

Piotr Kamler
Chronopolis '82

Minoru Kanaya
Fugitive Alien '86

Rolfe Kanefsky
There's Nothing Out There
'90

Jonathan Kaplan
Project X '87

Y. Kasancki
The Amphibian Man '61

Lee H. Katzin
The Man from Atlantis '77
The Stranger '73
World Gone Wild '88

**Lloyd (Samuel Weil)
Kaufman**
Class of Nuke 'Em High '86

Philip Kaufman
Invasion of the Body
Snatchers '78

Yoshiaki Kawajiri
Neo-Tokyo '86

Don Keeslar
Bog '84

Ray Kellogg
The Giant Gila Monster '59
The Killer Shrews '59

Tom Kennedy
Time Walker '82

Erle C. Kenton
Island of Lost Souls '32

Irvin Kershner
The Empire Strikes Back
'80
RoboCop 2 '90

Kim Ki-dak
Yongkari Monster of the
Deep '67

Bruce Kimmel
Spaceship '81

Tim Kincaid
Mutant Hunt '87
Robot Holocaust '87

Rick King
Prayer of the Rollerboys
'91

Hiroyuki Kitakubo
Robot Carnival '87

Hiroyuki Kitazume
Robot Carnival '87

Robert J. Kizer
Godzilla 1985 '85
Hell Comes to Frogtown
'87

Damian Klaus
Futurekick '91

Randal Kleiser
Flight of the Navigator '86
Honey, I Blew Up the Kid
'92

Richard Kletter
The Android Affair '95

Pavel Klushantsev
Planeta Burg '62

Bernard Knowles
Frozen Alive '64

John Korty
The People '71

Bernard L. Kowalski
Attack of the Giant
Leeches '59
Night of the Blood Beast
'58

Stanley Kramer
On the Beach '59

Lee Kresel
Mothra '61

John Krish
The Unearthly Stranger '64

Jon Kroll
Amanda and the Alien '95

Stanley Kubrick
A Clockwork Orange '71
Dr. Strangelove, or: How I
Learned to Stop
Worrying and Love the
Bomb '64
2001: A Space Odyssey '68

Kiyosumi Kukazawa
Fugitive Alien '86

Paul Kyriazi
Omega Cop '90

Rene Laloux
Fantastic Planet '73

Director
Index

Tom McGough
Alien Autopsy: Fact or Fiction? '95

Cole McKay
The Secret of the Golden Eagle '91

Douglas McKeown
Return of the Aliens: The Deadly Spawn '83

Tom McLoughlin
The Fire Next Time '93

John McNaughton
The Borrower '89

John McTiernan
Predator '87

Ib Melchior
The Angry Red Planet '59
The Time Travelers '64

Georges Melies
A Trip to the Moon '02

William Cameron Menzies
Invaders from Mars '53
Things to Come '36

William Mesa
Galaxis '95

Alan Metzger
New Eden '94

Nicholas Meyer
The Day After '83
Star Trek 2: The Wrath of Khan '82
Star Trek 6: The Undiscovered Country '91
Time After Time '79

Ted V. Mikels
Aftermath '85
The Astro-Zombies '67

John Milius
Conan the Barbarian '82

Ray Milland
Panic in the Year Zero! '62

Dan T. Miller
Screamers '80

George Miller
Mad Max '80
Mad Max: Beyond Thunderdome '85
The Road Warrior '82
Twilight Zone: The Movie '83

Dan Milner
The Phantom from 10,000 Leagues '56

Michael Miner
Deadly Weapon '88

Steve Miner
Forever Young '92

Rob Minkoff
Honey, I Shrunk the Kids '89

Philippe Mora
Communion '89
Return of Captain Invincible '83

Andrew Morahan
Highlander: The Final Dimension '94

Kouji Morimoto
Robot Carnival '87

Louis Morneau
Carnosaur 2 '94

Terry Morse
Godzilla, King of the Monsters '54
Unknown World '51

Rocky Morton
Super Mario Bros. '93

John Llewellyn Moxey
The Power Within '79

Russell Mulcahy
Highlander '86
Highlander 2: The Quickening '91
The Shadow '94

Jimmy T. Murakami
Battle Beyond the Stars '80

John Murlowski
Automatic '94

Geoff Murphy
Freejack '92
The Quiet Earth '85

William Murray
Primal Scream '87

Ivan Nagy
Captain America 2: Death Too Soon '79

Takashi Nakamura
Robot Carnival '87

Ronald Neame
Meteor '79

Hal Needham
Megaforce '82

James Neilson
Moon Pilot '62

L.E. Neiman
Time Troopers '89

Alvin J. Neitz
The Puma Man '80

Gary Nelson
The Black Hole '79

Ralph Nelson
Charly '68
Embryo '76

Avi Nesher
She '83

Kurt Neumann
The Fly '58
Kronos '57
Rocketship X-M '50

Peter Newbrook
The Asphyx '72

Sam Newfield
Ghost Patrol '36
The Lost Continent '51
The Monster Maker '44

Joseph M. Newman
This Island Earth '55

Ted Nicolaou
Bad Channels '92
Dungeonmaster '83

Nazui Nihonmatsu
X from Outer Space '67

Leonard Nimoy
Star Trek 3: The Search for Spock '84
Star Trek 4: The Voyage Home '86

Stephen Norrington
Death Machine '95

Bill W.L. Norton
Baby ... Secret of the Lost Legend '85

Thierry Notz
The Terror Within '88

David Nutter
Trancers 5: Sudden Deth '94

Christian Nyby
The Thing '51

James O'Connolly
The Valley of Gwangi '69

Motoyoshi Oda
Godzilla Raids Again '55

David Odell
Martians Go Home! '90

George Ogilvie
Mad Max: Beyond Thunderdome '85

Hidetoshi Ohmori
Robot Carnival '87

Kazuki Ohmori
Godzilla Vs. Biollante '89

Wyott Ordung
Monster from the Ocean Floor '54

Stuart Orme
The Puppet Masters '94

Ron Ormond
Mesa of Lost Women '52

Mamoru Oshii
Battle for Moon Station Dallos '86

Katsuhiro Otomo
Akira '89
Neo-Tokyo '86
Robot Carnival '87

Frank Oz
The Dark Crystal '82

George Pal
Seven Faces of Dr. Lao '63
The Time Machine '60
sidebar p. 347

Conrad Palmisano
Space Rage '86

Eric Parkinson
Future Shock '93

Robert Parrish
Journey to the Far Side of the Sun '69

Maurice Penczner
I Was a Zombie for the FBI '82

David Peoples
The Blood of Heroes '89

Richard Pepin
Cyber-Tracker '93
Cyber-Tracker 2 '95
Hologram Man '95
T-Force '94

Wolfgang Petersen
Enemy Mine '85
Outbreak '94

Kristine Peterson
Critters 3 '91

Elio Petri
10th Victim '65

Daniel Petrie
Cocoon: The Return '88

Maurice Phillips
Riders of the Storm '88

Irving Pichel
Destination Moon '50
She '35

Arthur C. Pierce
Women of the Prehistoric Planet '66

Sidney Pink
Journey to the Seventh Planet '61
Reptilicus '62

Seth Pinsker
The Hidden 2 '94

Walter W. Pitt, III
Welcome Back Mr. Fox '83

Director Index

Lesley Selander
Flight to Mars '51

Jack M. Sell
The Psychotronic Man '91

Peter Senelka
Teen Alien '88

Michael Shackleton
Survivor '87

Ken Shapiro
Modern Problems '81

Jim Sharman
The Rocky Horror Picture Show '75

Don Sharp
The Brides of Fu Manchu '66
The Face of Fu Manchu '65
Those Fantastic Flying Fools '67
What Waits Below '83

William Shatner
Star Trek 5: The Final Frontier '89
TekWar '94

Chris Shaw
Split '90

Linda Shayne
Purple People Eater '88

James K. Shea
Planet of Dinosaurs '80

Barry Shear
Wild in the Streets '68

Jack Sher
The Three Worlds of Gulliver '59

Gary Sherman
Mysterious Two '82

John Sherwood
The Creature Walks Among Us '56
The Monolith Monsters '57

Frank Shields
Project: Alien '89

Stanley Shiff
Lobster Man from Mars '89

Koji Shima
Warning from Space '56

Takeshi Shirado
Odin: Photon Space Sailor Starlight '85

Jack Sholder
The Hidden '87
12:01 '93

Lee Sholem
Escape from Planet Earth '67

Superman & the Mole Men '51
Tobor the Great '54

Lindsay Shonteff
The Killing Edge '86

Donald Siegel
Invasion of the Body Snatchers '56

Ron Silver
Lifepod '93

Adam Simon
Carnosaur '93

Juan Piquer Simon
Endless Descent '90
Supersonic Man '78
Where Time Began '77

Rick Sloane
Visitants '87

Jack Smight
Damnation Alley '77
The Illustrated Man '69

Clive A. Smith
Rock & Rule '83

Alan Smithee
The Birds 2: Land's End '94

Mark Sobel
Access Code '84

Iain Softley
Hackers '95

Steven Spielberg
Close Encounters of the Third Kind '77
E.T.: The Extra-Terrestrial '82
Indiana Jones and the Last Crusade '89
Indiana Jones and the Temple of Doom '84
Jurassic Park '93
Raiders of the Lost Ark '81
Twilight Zone: The Movie '83

C. Ray Stahl
Geisha Girl '52

Eric Steven Stahl
Final Approach '91

Richard Stanley
Dust Devil '93
Hardware '90

David Steensland
Escapes '86

Frederick Stephani
Flash Gordon: Rocketship '36

Sandor Stern
Assassin '86
Duplicates '92

Steven Hilliard Stern
Murder in Space '85

Andrew Stevens
The Terror Within 2 '91

Robert Stevenson
The Absent-Minded Professor '61
Non-Stop New York '37
Son of Flubber '63

Robert Stewart
Rock & Roll Cowboys '92

Mark Stock
Midnight Movie Massacre '88

Herbert L. Strock
The Crawling Hand '63

John Sturges
Marooned '69

Kevin Sullivan
Cosmic Slop '94

Jeremy Summers
The Vengeance of Fu Manchu '67

Henry Suso
Death Sport '78

Edward Sutherland
The Invisible Woman '40

E.W. Swackhamer
The Amazing Spider-Man '77

Jeannot Szwarc
Bug '75
Supergirl '84

Sylvio Tabet
Beastmaster 2: Through the Portal of Time '91

Tibor Takacs
984: Prisoner of the Future '84

Greg Tallas
Prehistoric Women '50

Richard Talmadge
Project Moon Base '53

Shigeo Tanaka
Gamera Vs. Barugon '66

Andrei Tarkovsky
Solaris '72
Stalker '79

Rin Taro
Neo-Tokyo '86

Norman Taurog
Dr. Goldfoot and the Bikini Machine '65

Bertrand Tavernier
Death Watch '80

Don Taylor
Escape from the Planet of the Apes '71
The Final Countdown '80
Island of Dr. Moreau '77

Ray Taylor
Flash Gordon Conquers the Universe '40
Return of Chandu '34

Lewis Teague
Alligator '80
Deadlock '91

Frank Telford
The Bamboo Saucer '68

Julien Temple
Earth Girls Are Easy '89

Kevin S. Tenney
Peacemaker '90

Herbert Tevos
Mesa of Lost Women '52

Graham Theakston
Tripods: The White Mountains '84

Ralph Thomas
Quest for Love '71

Harry Z. Thomason
The Day It Came to Earth '77

J. Lee Thompson
Battle for the Planet of the Apes '73
Conquest of the Planet of the Apes '72

Norman Tokar
The Cat from Outer Space '78

Robert Torrance
Mutant on the Bounty '89

Robert Townsend
The Meteor Man '93

Brian Trenchard-Smith
Dead End Drive-In '86
Official Denial '93

Victor Trivas
The Head '59

Bryan Trizers
PSI Factor '80

Francois Truffaut
Fahrenheit 451 '66

Douglas Trumbull
Brainstorm '83
Silent Running '71

Shinya Tsukamoto
Tetsuo: The Iron Man '92

Slava Tsukerman
Liquid Sky '83

**Director
Index**

Category List

Listed below are way too many subjects by which we categorize the videos reviewed in this book, with definitions for these sometimes bizarre classifications, because—go figure—not everyone thinks like the Hound. For this reason, we invite you, the reader, to submit your own ingenious categories (which are really only helpful if you also provide the movies that fall into said categories) and they may show up when we all meet again in *VideoHound's Sci-Fi Experience—The Sequel*, God willing. Following this "Category List" is, appropriately enough, a "Category Index," which puts all these categories to good use.

Abbott & Costello They show up in the craziest places with the craziest people.

Adam & Eve Allegories Movies in which even your little brother could see where the "two last people on Earth" plot is headed.

Adapted from a Book Movies that borrowed their plots from real writers and actually gave them credit for it. You might be surprised at some on the list—run right out to the library. See also *Books to Film*.

Adapted from a Cartoon Movies that borrowed their plots from real cartoonists.

Adapted from a Comic Strip Same thing but in print media.

Adapted from a Game Same thing but usually sillier.

Adapted from a Play or Musical Same thing, originally live.

Adapted from a Story Same thing but usually shorter.

Adapted from Television Same thing but often less creative.

Adapted from the Radio Same thing but with added visuals.

Adolescence see *Hell High School; Teen Angst*

Aircraft Might land safely, but that flight insurance *is* only a buck.... See also *It's a Bird...It's a Plane...It's....*

Alien Abduction Stories of people who've watched too many episodes of *The X-Files*.

Alien & Ripoffs If something works, stick with it.

Alien Beings—Benign Friendly well-meaning space visitors, including Kathy Ireland. See also *Alien Beings—Vicious*.

Alien Beings—Vicious Not-so-friendly, and, well, *mean* space visitors, often bent on world domination (but not including Microsoft). See also *Alien Beings—Benign*.

Amusement Parks And you thought the "Hall of Presidents" was scary. See also *Carnivals & Circuses*.

Animals see *Cats; Dogs; Killer Apes; Killer Birds; Killer Cats; Monkeying Around*

Animation see *Japanimation; 'Toons*

Anime see *Japanimation*

Anthology When the plot wasn't long enough to allow the film to last even an hour and a half. See also *Serials*.

Archaeology see *Big Digs*

Area 51 see *Conspiracies Involving Unexplained Phenomena*

Assassinations Murder rationalized by politics. See also *I Spy.*

At the Movies *Dead End Drive-In, Midnight Movie Massacre,* etc.

Automobiles see *Killer Cars; Motor Vehicle Dept.*

Babies see *That's a Baby?*

BBC TV Productions British couch-potato imports.

Behind Bars see *Great Escapes; Men in Prison; Women in Prison*

Big Battles Big-budget (or least the illusion of it) clash of large, opposing military forces on Earth and other locales.

Big Budget Stinkers Pathetic wastes of money; think *Waterworld,* or *Ishtar* (which isn't in this book but we wanted to make that connection anyway).

Big Digs Movies featuring archaeologists—there were more than just Indiana Jones.

Bigfoot/Yeti What is a bigfoot anyway? Is it an ape? Is it a bear? Will someone please tell us?

Bikers Often groups of men compensating for physical shortcomings by riding motorcycles.

Birds see *Killer Birds*

Black Comedy Movies featuring biting or despairing humor that makes you feel guilty for laughing. See also *Comedy; Satire & Parody.*

Blindness Loss of sight figures prominently.

Bloody Mayhem Expanded scenes of arterial explosions of both human and non-human blood.

Books to Film: Isaac Asimov This guy actually understands the science behind his fiction.

Books to Film: Ray Bradbury Very prolific, very scary.

Books to Film: Edgar Rice Burroughs He wrote things other than *Tarzan.*

Books to Film: Arthur C. Clarke HAL's dad.

Books to Film: Michael Crichton *Jurassic Park* wasn't his first, you know.

Books to Film: Phillip K. Dick Pessimistic views of the future.

Books to Film: Stephen King What's the deal with *The Lawnmower Man?*

Books to Film: H.P. Lovecraft Pulp fiction writer turned demi-god.

Books to Film: Mary Shelley You know, Frankenstein.

Books to Film: Jules Verne All the way From the Center of the Earth to 20,000 Leagues under the Sea to the Moon.

Books to Film: Kurt Vonnegut There should be more of these.

Books to Film: H.G. Wells War of the Island of the Village of the Time Machines to Come.

Buddies Abbott & Costello, Bill & Ted, Don Johnson and Tiger...

Bugs see *Killer Bugs & Slugs*

Burial at Space You gotta put 'em somewhere....

Campus Capers School spirit tends to lose its positive connotations. See also *Hell High School.*

Cannibalism "It's peeeeeeople!" and other non-vegetarian scenarios.

Carnivals & Circuses There's a reason kids are scared of clowns. See also *Amusement Parks.*

Cartoons see *Japanimation; 'Toons*

Cats The Hound only grudgingly approves of these movies. See also *Killer Cats.*

Cave People Scantily clad folks living in primitive conditions, Hollywood style. See also *Dinosaurs.*

Chases Like a road trip but faster. See also *Road Trip.*

Childhood Visions Stories dominated by the kid point of view. Can you say child psychologist?

Circuses see *Carnivals & Circuses*

Classic Horror Boris Karloff, Vincent Price, piercing screams. See also *Horror; Supernatural Horror.*

Cloning see *Genetics & Cloning*

Cold Spots Frostbite isn't the only thing to fear.

Cold War see *Red Scare*

Comedy Funny stuff generally lacking in drama. See also *Black Comedy; Genre Spoofs; Horror Comedy; Satire & Parody.*

Comets see *Meteors & Comets*

Communism see *Red Scare*

Computers All hail HAL. See also *Rampant Technology; Robots & Androids; Virtual Reality.*

Cops Robotic, cyborgoise, and even human. See also *Detectives.*

Corporate Shenanigans Profit-hunting honchos wreak havoc on the world. World usually wreaks back.

Cosmic Cowboys Ridin' on the star range.

Crime & Criminals Superheroes often figure prominently. See also *Fugitives.*

Cryogenics see *Suspended Animation*

Cyperpunk Streetwise aggression with a techno edge.

Cyborgs Like robots but with human components; what Data and the Tin Man emulate. See also *Robots & Androids.*

Death & the Afterlife Dead people, undead people, walking dead people, and other dead issues.

Deep Blue *The Abyss* to *Waterworld.* See also *Sea Disasters; Shipwrecked; Submarines.*

Deserts It's not the heat so much as the giant nuclear cactus that gets ya.

Detectives Clue-happy but often grizzled and cynical— *Alphaville,* or *Witch Hunt.* See also *Cops; Feds.*

Dinosaurs Great big prehistoric clunkers (but not C-64s). See also *Cave People; Godzilla and Friends; Killer Reptiles.*

Disaster Flicks Natural and man-made. See also *Meltdown; Sea Disasters.*

Diseases, Viruses & Plagues That's a nasty cough you've got...urk!

Documentary Typically a serious examination of an issue or idea, but these generally cover UFOs.

Dogs There is just not enough darn canine sci fi.

Dragons Fire-breathing lizards, usually from the Middle Ages.

Dream Girls Devils Girls, Vampire Vixens, Fire Maidens, and other male fantasies.

Drugs see *Pill Poppin'*

Eco-Vengeance! Mother Nature always said...don't play ball in her house! See also *Killer Birds; Killer Bugs & Slugs; Killer Plants.*

Ever'body Was Kung Fu Fighting Fists of aluminum foil; much head-kicking, rib-crunching, chop-socky action.

Extraordinary Pairings One of these things is not like the other...*King Kong Vs. Godzilla,* for example.

Eyeballs! Unnerving scenes involving eyeballs.

Fantasy Kind of like sci fi, but this stuff couldn't *really* happen. See also *Japanimation; 'Toons.*

Feds Men and women of the Bureau, the Agency, the Shop, or any national police organization with an acronym and a dress code. See also *Detectives; I Spy.*

Femme Fatale She done him and him and him wrong. See also *Wonder Women.*

Fires In sci-fi land they tend to happen early, in order to

properly disfigure the designated villain.

Flash Gordon The comic strip turned radio serial *cum* pulp magazine *nee* film serial (also novels and TV series) to feature-length films (and parodies).

Flying Saucers see *Alien Beings—Benign; Alien Beings—Vicious; UFOs/UFOlogy*

4 Bones Yep! Here it is! Our picks!

Frankenstein Well known guy with bolts in his neck.

Friendship see *Buddies*

Fu Manchu-aroo The supervillain as portrayed by Christopher Lee, Boris Karloff, and even Peter Sellers.

Fugitives On the lam.

Gangs Roaming groups of people with evil intent. See also *Crime & Criminals.*

Genetics & Cloning Fooling with—and photocopying—the double helix. See also *Mad Doctors & Scientists.*

Genre Spoofs Serious looks at film genres—not! See also *Comedy; Satire & Parody.*

Giants *The Amazing Colossal Man* visits *The Village of the Giants.* See also *Shrinkage.*

Godzilla & Friends Big battling reptiles and insects, usually poorly dubbed.

Great Escapes Men and women break out. See also *Men in Prison; Women in Prison.*

Growin' Old For the most part, people avoiding the situation.

Hell High School Isn't that redundant? See also *Campus Capers; Teen Angst.*

Hercules A demi-god's labors are never done.

Horror Just plain scary stuff that isn't classic or overtly funny or other worldly or relying heavily on a proliferation

of blood. See also *Bloody Mayhem; Classic Horror; Horror Comedy; Supernatural Horror*

Horror Comedy Laughing all the way to the grave. See also *Black Comedy; Comedy; Genre Spoofs; Satire & Parody.*

Hunted! Prey for a day. See also *Survival.*

I Spy Trench coats, fedoras, dark glasses, and often martinis (shaken, not stirred).

Identity Who am I? Who are you? Who are we? Why do you ask so many questions?

Insects see *Killer Bugs & Slugs*

Invisibility Some outta sight guys and gals.

Island Fare Generally inhabited by mutants or mad scientists.

It's a Bird...It's a Plane...It's... People and humanoids flying with minimum or no apparati.

Japanimation Animated action from the land of Godzilla. See also *'Toons.*

Killer Apes They think they're King Kong on the Planet of the Apes. See also *Monkeying Around.*

Killer Birds *The Birds, The Giant Claw,* and other instances of death swooping down from the trees.

Killer Brains Literally, they have a mind of their own. See also *Renegade Body Parts.*

Killer Bugs & Slugs *Attack of the Giant Leeches* to *The Wasp Woman.*

Killer Cars Recalls would be futile. See also *Motor Vehicle Dept.*

Killer Cats In this Hound's opinion, the dastardliest of all villains. See also *Cats.*

Killer Dreams Not all occur on Elm Street.

Killer Plants Including foliage, fruits, and fungi.

Killer Reptiles Alligators, frogs, gila monsters, and whatever the hell Godzilla is.

Killer Rodents Mickey's evil twins.

Killer Sea Critters Wet and squishy deadly things from the deep. See also *Deep Blue; Sea Disasters.*

"Klaatu Barada Nikto" Movies that contain this classic quote.

Lost Worlds Usually places forgotten by Time and/or People. See also *Parallel Universes.*

Mad Doctors & Scientists Sin in the name of science. See also *Science & Scientists.*

Made for Television see *TV Movies; TV Pilot Movies; TV Series*

Magic Hocus pocus, often with an evil intent. See also *Sword & Sorcery.*

Mars & Martians To and from the Red Planet.

Martial Arts see *Ever'body Was Kung Fu Fighting*

Medieval Romps Dirty peasants, deodorized kings and queens, and knights in shining armor.

Meltdown Or, how I learned to stop worrying and love the bomb. See also *Disaster Flicks.*

Men in Prison Macho guys behind bars. See also *Fugitives; Great Escapes; Women in Prison.*

Meteors & Comets Way better spectacles than Khahoutek.

Mexican Wrestling Superheroes Need we say more?

Monkeying Around Here they come, walking down...oops, wrong monkeys. See also *Killer Apes.*

Monsters see *Alien Beings—Vicious; Frankenstein; Giants; Godzilla & Friends; Killer Apes; Killer Brains; Killer Bugs & Slugs; Killer Cats; Killer Plants; Killer Reptiles; Killer Rodents; Killer Sea Critters; Mummies; Vampires; Werewolves; Zombies*

Monty Python British comedy troupe whose talents are often not appreciated by the uptight.

Motor Vehicle Dept. DeLoreans, Firebirds, and other cars o' the future. See also *Bikers; Killer Cars.*

MST3K Movies Movies immortalized by three 'bots and a boob on *Mystery Science Theater 3000.*

Mummies Withered folks wrapped in toilet paper.

Mystery Science Theater 3000 see *MST3K Movies*

Mythology & Folklore Clash of the Golden Voyage of the Argonauts. See also *Fantasy.*

Nazi Zombies The fascist undead. See also *Nazis & Other Paramilitary Slugs; Zombies.*

Nazis & Other Paramilitary Slugs The real jack-booted government thugs. See also *Nazi Zombies; World War II.*

Negative Utopia Things seemed so perfect until... See also *Post Apocalypse; Rampant Technology.*

Niebo Zowiet Recycled Movies that cannibalized this Soviet sf. See also *Planeta Burg Recycled.*

Nuclear Disaster see *Meltdown*

Parallel Universes Same time, same place, different channel. See also *Lost Worlds.*

Parenthood see *That's a Baby?*

Pill Poppin' Consumption of drugs, mostly illegal or in extra-large doses.

The Planet of the Apes Because the Hound himself keeps forgetting that there wasn't one titled *Revenge of the Planet of the Apes*... or *Return to the Planet of the Apes*... or *Bride of the....*

Planeta Burg Recycled Movies that cannibalized this Soviet sf. See also *Niebo Zowiet Recycled.*

Post Apocalypse No more convenience stores. See also *Negative Utopia; Rampant Technology.*

Pregnant Men Ow!

Presidents We're still plagued by them in the future.

Prison see *Great Escapes; Men in Prison; Women in Prison*

Producers: Charles Band/Full Moon The *Trancer*-man just keeps cranking 'em out.

Producers: Roger Corman/New World It might be easier to list what wasn't produced by Mr. Corman.

Producers: Hammer It's Hammer time!

Producers: George Lucas Well, *Star Wars* for one....

Producers: George Pal Puppetoonimation put to good use.

Producers: Steven Spielberg Did you know he made his first sf flick at age 16?

Producers: Toho Big Japanese monsters following in Godzilla's footsteps.

Producers: Troma Tromatic takes on the sci-fi genre.

Producers: Universal Studios Ahhh...the classics.

Psychiatry see *Shrinks*

Pure Ego Vehicles Why? Because they can.

Race Against Time The fate of humankind (or at least Springfield IL) is pitted against the clock.

Raiders of the Lost Ark Because its sequels aren't RLA2 and RLA3.

Rampant Technology Machines that wreak havoc. See also *Computers; Cyborgs; Robots & Androids; Virtual Reality.*

Rebel With a Cause Bucking the establishment for a reason.

Rebel Without a Cause Bucking the establishment just because it's the establishment.

Red Scare Cold war and communism (not the cancer-causing M 'n' Ms).

Renegade Body Parts Hands, fingers, eyes, brains, and other appendages with a life of their own. See also *Killer Brains.*

Rescue Missions Goin' to great lengths to save. See also *Rescue Missions Involving Time Travel.*

Rescue Missions Involving Time Travel Goin' to even greater lengths to save. See also *Rescue Missions; Time Travel.*

Restored Footage Recouped scenes that were originally too violent, too shocking, too poorly transferred...or just to sell more laserdiscs.

Revenge Is Sweet Generally of the bloody variety.

Road Trip Escapism courtesy two- and four-wheeled vehicles. See also *Bikers; Chases; Motor Vehicle Dept.*

Road Warrior & Rip-Offs They're all mad about Max.

Robots & Androids Danger, Will Robinson! See also *Cyborgs; Rampant Technology.*

Rock Stars on Film But can they act?

Romance Love among the stars.

Roswell see *Conspiracies Involving Unexplained Phenomena; UFOs/UFOlogy*

Sanity Check Inmates running the asylum; also deviant states of mind. See also *Shrinks.*

Satire & Parody Biting social comment or genre spoofs.

See also *Black Comedy; Comedy; Genre Spoofs; Horror Comedy.*

Science & Scientists If they could have only left well enough alone... See also *Mad Doctors & Scientists.*

Sea Disasters Not just *Waterworld.* See also *Deep Blue; Disaster Flicks; Killer Sea Critters; Shipwrecked.*

Serials Like TV only in movie theatres. Designed to make your parents come back every week.

Sex & Sexuality Focus is on lust, for better or worse.

Sexploitation Softcore epics usually lacking in plot but not skin.

Shipwrecked Gilligan!! See also *Sea Disasters.*

Shrinkage Not just of concern to men...Lily Tomlin shrunk, too.

Shrinks As in head shrinkers (psychiatrists, not witch doctors). See also *Sanity Check.*

Silent Films Often employing a very rudimentary means of subtitling.

Snakes Slithery critters with a bad rap.

Space Operas Going where no spam has gone before.

Special F/X Extravaganzas The spaceships in these films don't have strings attached.

Special F/X Extravaganzas: Make-Up Faces only a mother could love.

Special F/X Wizards: Rick Baker He went from *Octaman* to *Star Wars.*

Special F/X Wizards: Rob Bottin Did you know he designed the giant mouse in *Rock 'n' Roll High School*?

Special F/X Wizards: Anton Furst Responsible for the slimy creature in *Alien.*

Special F/X Wizards: Ray Harryhausen Heart-stopping

stop-motion animation at its best.

Special F/X Wizards: Douglas Trumbull He went from *Star Trek: The Motion Picture* to designing theme park rides—does that scare anyone?

Spies & Espionage see *I Spy*

Star Wars Just in case anyone can't remember all three titles.

Submarines *The Abyss* to *Voyage to the Bottom of the Sea.* See also *Deep Blue.*

Superheroes Men and women of extraordinary strength and/or abilities wearing silly-looking costumes. See also *Mexican Wrestling Superheroes.*

Supernatural Horror Forces from beyond terrorize those who are here. See also *Classic Horror; Horror.*

Survival Nobody said it was going to be easy. See also *Hunted!; Negative Utopia; Post Apocalypse.*

Suspended Animation I'll explain it later. Not to be confused with suspended disbelief, although both are a big part of these movies.

Sword & Sorcery see *Arnold Schwarzenegger's Early Career*

Teen Angst Adolescent anxieties become even more angst-ridden in the sci-fi universe. See also *Hell High School.*

Television see *TV Movies; TV Pilot Movies; TV Series*

Terrorism Torture with a political purpose (like presidential election campaigns). See also *Crime & Criminals; I Spy.*

That's a Baby? Faces even a mother can't love. See also *Pregnant Men.*

3-D Flicks Movies requiring special glasses that often cause headaches (watching the movies without the glass-

es can sometimes cause headaches as well).

3 Stooges Why, I oughta....

Time Travel Fast forward or reverse. See also *Rescue Missions Involving Time Travel.*

'Toons Animated features—they're not just for kids anymore. See also *Japanimation.*

True Stories? Approximations of real-life events, often significantly fictionalized for the screen.

TV Movies First shown on broadcast, cable, or foreign television before hitting your VCR. See also *BBC TV Productions.*

TV Pilot Movies Some made it to the small screen on a weekly basis; some did not.

TV Series A selection of our favorite sci-fi shows that are available on video.

20 Highest-Grossing Films of All Time *Waterworld* didn't make the list.

UFOs/UFOlogy Apparently, all alien species use the same design team. See also *Alien Abduction; Alien Beings— Benign; Alien Beings— Vicious.*

Unexplained Phenomena Ummm, it's hard to define.... See also *Conspiracies Involving Unexplained Phenomena.*

Unicorns Pointy-headed horses, usually considered good luck.

Vampires Generally night people, they prefer red.

Venus & Venusians On and around the Blue Planet.

Virtual Reality The ultimate in interactive TV. See also *Computers; Rampant Technology.*

Wedding Hell Marriages that don't start off on the right foot. Or claw. Or whatever.

Werewolves Full-moon wonders (not to be confused with Charles Band).

Westerns, Sci-Fi Style They don't even have indoor plumbing, and you want 'em to deal with the supernatural?

Women Impressive women and less-than-impressive women. See also *Dream Girls; Femme Fatale; Women in Prison; Wonder Women.*

Women in Prison But featuring no flicks starring Linda Blair.

Wonder Women *Alien, Attack of the 50 Foot Woman, Attack of the 60 Foot Centerfold,* etc. See also *Dream Girls.*

Woofs! Those pics not even rating a half a bone.

World War I The first big one.

World War II The next big one.

World War III The last big one. See *Post Apocalypse.*

Wrestling And you thought Hulk Hogan was weird.

You Lose, You Die Sports taken to the extreme, where only the winner survives. See also *Post Apocalypse.*

Zombies Astro zombies, government zombies (same diff), Nazi zombies, teenage zombies—we got all kinds.

Category Index

Categories. Movies that fall under the categories. I think you know the drill. Flip back to page 407 for a list of the categories with some sublime definitions if you need help. Thanks for playing.

Abbott & Costello
Abbott and Costello Go to Mars
Abbott and Costello Meet the Invisible Man

Adam & Eve Allegories
Beyond the Time Barrier
Escape from Galaxy Three
The Last Woman on Earth
They
Women of the Prehistoric Planet

Adapted from a Book
See also Books to Film
Altered States
The Andromeda Strain
Anna to the Infinite Power
At the Earth's Core
The Atomic Man
The Bamboo Saucer
Battle Beyond the Stars
Beastmaster
Biggles
Blade Runner
The Boys from Brazil
The Bride of Frankenstein
Buck Rogers Conquers the Universe
Bug
Charly
Children of the Damned
A Clockwork Orange
Colossus: The Forbin Project
Communion
The Curse of Frankenstein
Damnation Alley
Day of the Triffids
Dead Zone

Death Race 2000
Die, Monster, Die!
Doc Savage
Doctor Faustus
Dr. Strangelove, or: How I Learned to Stop Worrying and Love the Bomb
Donovan's Brain
Dune
Empire of the Ants
The Face of Fu Manchu
Fahrenheit 451
Fail-Safe
Firestarter
Food of the Gods
Food of the Gods: Part 2
Frankenstein
Frankenstein Unbound
Freejack
From Beyond
The Groundstar Conspiracy
The Handmaid's Tale
Hearts & Armour
The Hitchhiker's Guide to the Galaxy
The Illustrated Man
The Incredible Shrinking Man
Invasion of the Body Snatchers
The Invisible Man
Island of Dr. Moreau
Island of Lost Souls
It Came from Outer Space
Journey to the Center of the Earth
Journey to the Center of the Earth
Jurassic Park
Kiss and Kill
The Land that Time Forgot

Lathe of Heaven
Light Years
Logan's Run
The Lost World
The Lost World
The Man Who Fell to Earth
The Manchurian Candidate
The Martian Chronicles: Part 1
The Martian Chronicles: Part 2
The Martian Chronicles: Part 3
The Mask of Fu Manchu
Master of the World
Memoirs of an Invisible Man
Millenium
Mission Stardust
Monkey Boy
Mysterious Island
The New Invisible Man
Nightflyers
1984
No Escape
The Omega Man
On the Beach
On the Comet
Outbreak
The People
The People that Time Forgot
The Philadelphia Experiment
Planet of the Apes
The Princess Bride
The Puppet Masters
Quest for Fire
Roswell: The U.F.O. Cover-Up
Running Against Time
The Running Man
Scream and Scream Again
Seven Faces of Dr. Lao

She
She
Slaughterhouse Five
Solar Crisis
Solaris
Something Wicked This Way Comes
Soylent Green
Stephen King's The Langoliers
Stephen King's The Stand
Stephen King's The Tommyknockers
TekWar
10th Victim
The Terminal Man
Terror Is a Man
They Came from Beyond Space
The Thing
Things to Come
The Three Worlds of Gulliver
The Time Machine
Time Machine
Total Recall
Transatlantic Tunnel
A Trip to the Moon
20,000 Leagues Under the Sea
The 27th Day
2001: A Space Odyssey
2010: The Year We Make Contact
Village of the Damned
Village of the Damned
Village of the Giants
The War of the Worlds
Where Time Began
Who Framed Roger Rabbit

Adapted from a Cartoon
Flash Gordon
The Guyver
Guyver 2: Dark Hero
Masters of the Universe
Wicked City
Zeram

Adapted from a Comic
The Amazing Spider-Man
Barbarella
Batman
Batman Forever
Batman Returns
Captain America
Dr. Strange
Flash Gordon
Hardware
Heavy Metal
Howard the Duck
The Incredible Hulk
Judge Dredd
The Punisher
The Return of Swamp Thing
Rocketship
Supergirl
Superman: The Movie
Superman 2
Superman 3
Superman 4: The Quest for Peace
Swamp Thing
Teenage Mutant Ninja Turtles: The Movie
Teenage Mutant Ninja Turtles 2: The Secret of the Ooze

Teenage Mutant Ninja Turtles 3
Timecop
The Trial of the Incredible Hulk

Adapted from a Game
Super Mario Bros.
Tron

Adapted from a Play or Musical
Devil Girl from Mars
Forbidden Planet
Red Planet Mars
The Rocky Horror Picture Show

Adapted from a Story
Amanda and the Alien
The Android Affair
The Beast from 20,000 Fathoms
The Birds
A Boy and His Dog
Cinderella 2000
Cosmic Slop
Creature from the Black Lagoon
The Day the Earth Stood Still
The Final Programme
The Fly
The Invisible Boy
The Invisible Woman
Johnny Mnemonic
Kurt Vonnegut's Harrison Bergeron
La Jetee
The Land Unknown
The Lawnmower Man
The Monolith Monsters
Mothra
Nightfall
Overdrawn at the Memory Bank
Quest for Love
Re-Animator
Revenge of the Creature
Rollerball
The Thing
Trapped in Space
12:01
Unnatural

Adapted from Television
Alien Nation: Dark Horizon
Buck Rogers in the 25th Century
Coneheads
The Crawling Eye
Daleks—Invasion Earth 2150 A.D.
Doctor Who and the Daleks
Dr. Who: Cybermen—The Early Years
Fugitive Alien
Quatermass and the Pit
The Quatermass Experiment
Quatermass 2
Star Trek: The Motion Picture
Star Trek 2: The Wrath of Khan
Star Trek 3: The Search for Spock
Star Trek 4: The Voyage Home
Star Trek 5: The Final Frontier
Star Trek 6: The Undiscovered Country
Star Trek Generations

Thunderbirds Are Go
Twilight Zone: The Movie

Adapted from the Radio
The Shadow
The War of the Worlds

Aircraft
Bamboo Saucer
Beyond the Time Barrier
Biggles
Blue Thunder
Blue Tornado
Capricorn One
Final Approach
The Final Countdown
Invader
Millenium
No Survivors, Please
Starflight One
Stephen King's The Langoliers
Things to Come
Thunderbirds Are Go

Alien Abduction
Alien Seed
Communion
Earth Vs. the Flying Saucers
Eyes Behind the Stars
Fire in the Sky
Lost Was the Key
Official Denial
Out There
Project: Alien
Slaughterhouse Five
Starship Invasions
Strange Invaders
V
Xtro

Alien & Rip-Offs
Alien
Alien 3
Alien Contamination
Alien Prey
Alien Seed
Aliens
Blue Monkey
Creature
Creepozoids
Dark Universe
Deep Space
Deepstar Six
Forbidden World
Galaxy of Terror
Horror Planet
Leviathan
Nightflyers
Predator
Star Crystal
Wes Craven Presents Mind Ripper
Xtro 2: The Second Encounter

Alien Beings — Benign
See also Alien Beings—Vicious
The Abyss
Aftershock
Alien Autopsy: Fact or Fiction?

Alien from L.A.
Alien Nation
Alien Nation: Dark Horizon
Alien Private Eye
Alien Warrior
Alien Women
Amanda and the Alien
The Aurora Encounter
*batteries not included
The Brain from Planet Arous
The Brother from Another Planet
The Cat from Outer Space
Close Encounters of the Third Kind
Cocoon
Cocoon: The Return
Communion
Coneheads
The Cosmic Man
The Cosmic Monsters
The Day the Earth Stood Still
Day Time Ended
Dead Weekend
Doin' Time on Planet Earth
Earth Girls Are Easy
The Empire Strikes Back
Enemy Mine
E.T.: The Extra-Terrestrial
Explorers
Fire in the Sky
Flight of the Navigator
Gremlins
Gremlins 2: The New Batch
The Hidden
Howard the Duck
Hyper-Sapien: People from Another
   Star
Intruders
It Came from Outer Space
It's Dead—Let's Touch It!
The Last Starfighter
Lords of the Deep
Mac and Me
The Man from Atlantis
The Man Who Fell to Earth
The Martian Chronicles: Part 2
The Martian Chronicles: Part 3
Martians Go Home!
Missile to the Moon
Mission Stardust
Moon Pilot
My Stepmother Is an Alien
Mysterious Two
Official Denial
The Phantom Planet
Project: Genesis
PSI Factor
Purple People Eater
Return of the Jedi
Solarbabies
Spaced Invaders
Star Trek 4: The Voyage Home
Star Wars
Starman
Starship Invasions
Stranded
The Stranger from Venus
Super Mario Bros.
Supergirl
Superman: The Movie

Superman 2
Superman 3
Superman 4: The Quest for Peace
Teenage Mutant Ninja Turtles 2: The
   Secret of the Ooze
Terrornauts
This Island Earth
The 27th Day
UFO: Target Earth
Voyage of the Rock Aliens
War of the Robots
Warning from Space
Wavelength
Zone Troopers

Alien Beings—Vicious
See also Alien Beings—Benign
The Adventures of Buckaroo Banzai
   Across the Eighth Dimension
Alien
Alien 3
Alien Contamination
Alien Dead
The Alien Factor
Alien Nation: Dark Horizon
Alien Predators
Alien Prey
Alien Seed
Alien Space Avenger
Alienator
Aliens
Aliens Are Coming
The Alpha Incident
The Angry Red Planet
The Arrival
The Astounding She-Monster
The Astro-Zombies
Atomic Submarine
Backlash: Oblivion 2
Bad Channels
Bad Taste
Battle Beyond the Stars
Battle of the Worlds
Bio Hazard
The Blob
The Blob
Blue Flame
Body Snatchers
The Borrower
The Brain
The Brain Eaters
The Brain from Planet Arous
Cat Women of the Moon
Class of Nuke 'Em High 3: The
   Good, the Bad and the Subhu-
   manoid
The Cosmic Monsters
Creature
Creepozoids
Critters
Critters 2: The Main Course
Critters 3
Critters 4
The Dark
Dark Star
Dark Universe
Day the World Ended
Day Time Ended
Dead Space

Deep Space
Destroy All Monsters
Destroy All Planets
Devil Girl from Mars
Dr. Alien
Doctor Who and the Daleks
Doctor Who: Cybermen—The Early
   Years
Earth Vs. the Flying Saucers
The Empire Strikes Back
Encounter at Raven's Gate
End of the World
Escape from Galaxy Three
Escapes
The Eye Creatures
Eyes Behind the Stars
First Man into Space
Flight to Mars
Flying Discman from Mars
Forbidden World
Frankenstein Meets the Space Mon-
   ster
From Beyond
Fugitive Alien
Galaxy Invader
Galaxy of Terror
Gamera Vs. Guiron
Gamera Vs. Zigra
Ghidrah the Three Headed Monster
The Giant Claw
The Giant Spider Invasion
God Told Me To
Godzilla Vs. the Cosmic Monster
Grampa's Sci-Fi Hits
Grand Tour: Disaster in Time
The Green Slime
Gremlins
Gremlins 2: The New Batch
The Guyver
Guyver 2: Dark Hero
Hands of Steel
The Hidden
The Hidden 2
High Desert Kill
Horror of the Blood Monsters
Horror Planet
The Human Duplicators
I Come in Peace
I Married a Monster from Outer
   Space
I Was a Zombie for the FBI
Invader
Invaders from Mars
Invasion
Invasion Earth: The Aliens Are Here!
Invasion of the Animal People
Invasion of the Bee Girls
Invasion of the Body Snatchers
Invasion of the Body Stealers
Invasion of the Saucer Men
Invasion of the Space Preachers
Invisible Adversaries
Invisible Invaders
Island of the Burning Doomed
It Came from Outer Space 2
It Conquered the World
It! The Terror from Beyond Space
Journey to the Seventh Planet
Killers from Space

Category
Index

4 1 5
Sci-Fi Experience

Category Index

Category
Index

Superman: The Movie
Superman 3
TekWar
Time After Time
Time Bandits
Timestalkers
The Vengeance of Fu Manchu
Virtual Assassin
Virtuosity
Warlords of the 21st Century

Cryogenics
See Suspended Animation

Cyberpunk
Arcade
Blade Runner
Bubblegum Crisis
Cyborg 2
Cyborg Cop
Cyborg Soldier
Demolition Man
Freejack
Futurekick
Hackers
Hardware
Johnny Mnemonic
The Lawnmower Man
Lawnmower Man 2: Jobe's War
Liquid Dreams
Megaville
Nemesis
Nemesis 2: Nebula
Overdrawn at the Memory Bank
Replikator: Cloned to Kill
RoboCop
RoboCop 2
RoboCop 3
Rock & Roll Cowboys
TekWar
The Terminator
Terminator 2: Judgment Day
Tetsuo: The Iron Man
THX 1138
Total Recall
Tron
Universal Soldier
Virtuosity
Wild Palms

Cyborgs
See also Robots & Androids
The Abominable Dr. Phibes
Alienator
American Cyborg: Steel Warrior
Assassin
Cyborg
Cyborg 2
Cyborg Cop
Cyborg Soldier
Digital Man
The Eliminators
Futurekick
Godzilla on Monster Island
Godzilla Vs. Megalon
Hands of Steel
Heatseeker
Knights

Mutant Hunt
Nemesis
Nemesis 2: Nebula
Programmed to Kill
Prototype X29A
Robo-C.H.I.C.
RoboCop
RoboCop 2
RoboCop 3
Roboman
Spacehunter: Adventures in the
    Forbidden Zone
Steel and Lace
The Terminator
Terminator 2: Judgment Day
Terror Beneath the Sea
Tetsuo: The Iron Man
The Time Guardian
Trancers 3: Deth Lives
The Vindicator

Death & the Afterlife
The Asphyx
Bill & Ted's Bogus Journey
Brainstorm
The Day It Came to Earth
Donovan's Brain
Flatliners
Future Shock
The Indestructible Man
Making Contact
Star Trek 3: The Search for Spock
Unnatural
Welcome Back Mr. Fox

Deep Blue
See also Sea Disasters; Ship-
    wrecked; Submarines
The Abyss
Around the World Under the Sea
Beyond the Bermuda Triangle
Deepstar Six
Endless Descent
The Final Countdown
Gorgo
The Incredible Petrified World
It Came from Beneath the Sea
Leviathan
Lords of the Deep
The Man from Atlantis
The Sea Serpent
20,000 Leagues Under the Sea
Terror Beneath the Sea
Waterworld

Deserts
Capricorn One
Dune
Dune Warriors
Equalizer 2000
Indiana Jones and the Last Crusade
Mad Max
Mad Max: Beyond Thunderdome
New Eden
Roswell: The UFO Cover Up
Star Wars
Stargate
Steel Dawn

Stryker
Tarantula
Tremors
Tremors 2: Aftershocks
Warlords

Detectives
See also Cops; Feds
Abbott and Costello Meet the Invisi-
    ble Man
Alphaville
Blade Runner
Cast a Deadly Spell
The Element of Crime
Kiss Me Deadly
The Pink Chiquitas
Primal Scream
Radioactive Dreams
TekWar
Who Framed Roger Rabbit
Witch Hunt

Dinosaurs
See also Cave People; Godzilla and
    Friends; Killer Reptiles
At the Earth's Core
Baby ... Secret of the Lost Legend
The Beast from 20,000 Fathoms
Carnosaur
Carnosaur 2
Dinosaur Island
Dinosaurus!
Gorgo
Journey to the Center of the Earth
Jurassic Park
King Dinosaur
The Land that Time Forgot
The Land Unknown
The Lost Continent
The Lost World
The Lost World
On the Comet
One Million B.C.
The People that Time Forgot
Planet of Dinosaurs
Reptilicus
Robot Monster
Son of Kong
Super Mario Bros.
Teenage Caveman
Two Lost Worlds
The Valley of Gwangi
Voyage to the Prehistoric Planet
When Dinosaurs Ruled the Earth

Disaster Flicks
See also Meltdown; Sea Disasters
Assignment Outer Space
The China Syndrome
The Day the Earth Caught Fire
The Day the Sky Exploded
Deluge
Gorath
Last Days of Planet Earth
The Last Woman on Earth
The Lost Missile
Meteor
Planet on the Prowl

The Swarm
When Worlds Collide

Diseases, Viruses & Plagues
Alien Nation: Dark Horizon
The Andromeda Strain
The Beast from 20,000 Fathoms
Blue Monkey
Bounty Hunter 2002
The Carrier
The Crazies
Cyborg
Dead Man Walking
Dead Space
Incredible Melting Man
The Last Man on Earth
The Omega Man
Outbreak
Project: Alien
Quarantine
Stephen King's The Stand
They Came from Within
Transformations
12 Monkeys
Virus
Xtro

Documentary
Alien Autopsy: Fact or Fiction?
Bob Lazar: Excerpts from the Government Bible
Contact: An Investigation into the Extraterrestrial Experiences of Eduard Meier
Lost Was the Key
Messengers of Destiny
Secrets of Dreamland
A Strange Harvest with Linda Moulton Howe
UFO Secret: The Roswell Crash
UFO Secrets of the Third Reich
UFOs: Secrets of the Black World

Dogs
Battle for Moon Station Dallos
The Borrower
A Boy and His Dog
The Brain from Planet Arous
Dr. Cyclops
Lawnmover Man 2: Jobe's War
Night of the Creeps
Quintet
Sputnik
The Thing

Dragons
Dragonslayer
Excalibur
Jack the Giant Killer
The Magic Serpent
Q (The Winged Serpent)
Seventh Voyage of Sinbad
Willow

Dream Girls
Abbott & Costello Go to Mars
Alien from L.A.

Alien Intruder
Alien Women
Barbarella
Creatures the World Forgot
Dead Weekend
Devil Girl from Mars
Dinosaur Island
Dr. Alien
Dr. Goldfoot and the Bikini Machine
Fire Maidens from Outer Space
Forbidden Planet
Four Sided Triangle
Galaxina
Gamera Vs. Guiron
Hercules and the Princess of Troy
Hollywood Boulevard 2
Journey to the Seventh Planet
Kiss and Kill
Looker
Missile to the Moon
My Stepmother Is an Alien
Prehistoric Women
Queen of Outer Space
Star Crash
Vampire Vixens from Venus
Voyage to the Planet of Prehistoric Women
When Dinosaurs Ruled the Earth

Drugs
See Pill Poppin'

Eco-Vengeance!
See also Killer Birds; Killer Bugs & Slugs; Killer Plants
Alligator
The Birds
Deadly Harvest
The Fire Next Time
Food of the Gods
Idaho Transfer
Jurassic Park
Last Days of Planet Earth
The Swarm
Ticks

Ever'body Was Kung Fu Fighting
Aftershock
The Bronx Executioner
Cyber Ninja
Cyborg
Cyborg 2
Dragon Fury
The Eliminators
Futurekick
Heatseeker
Knights
Nemesis
Omega Cop
Roller Blade
Scanners 3: The Takover
Space Ninja: Sword of the Space Ark
Timecop
Trancers 3: Deth Lives

Extraordinary Pairings
Frankenstein Meets the Space Monster
King Kong Vs. Godzilla
Santa Claus Conquers the Martians
Superman & the Mole Men
Wrestling Women Vs. the Aztec Ape
Wrestling Women Vs. the Aztec Mummy

Eyeballs!
Atomic Submarine
Beastmaster 3: The Eye of Braxus
The Birds
The Birds 2: Land's End
Children of the Damned
The City of Lost Children
A Clockwork Orange
The Crawling Eye
The Dark
Demolition Man
The Eye Creatures
The Golden Voyage of Sinbad
Metamorphosis
Saturn 3
Scanners
The Seventh Voyage of Sinbad
Spaceship
A Trip to the Moon
Village of the Damned
Village of the Damned
Waterworld
X: The Man with X-Ray Eyes

Fantasy
See also Japanimation; 'Toons
The Adventures of Baron Munchausen
Alien from L.A.
The Amazing Spider-Man
Andy and the Airwave Rangers
Barbarella
Baron Munchausen
Beastmaster
Beastmaster 2: Through the Portal of Time
Beastmaster 3: The Eye of Braxus
Biggles
Bill & Ted's Bogus Journey
Bill & Ted's Excellent Adventure
Cast a Deadly Spell
Chronopolis
Cinderella 2000
The City of Lost Children
Clash of the Titans
Conan the Barbarian
Conan the Destroyer
The Dark Crystal
Doc Savage
Doctor Faustus
Dragonslayer
Dreamscape
Dungeonmaster
Edward Scissorhands
Escapes
Excalibur
Golden Voyage of Sinbad
Hearts & Armour

Category Index

The Brain
The Brain that Wouldn't Die
The Brood
Carnosaur
Carnosaur 2
The Carrier
Chopping Mall
The Crawling Eye
The Crawling Hand
Creepozoids
Dark Side of the Moon
Darkman
Day the World Ended
The Evil of Frankenstein
Food of the Gods
Food of the Gods: Part 2
Frankenstein Unbound
Future Shock
Invasion of the Saucer Men
The Invisible Man's Revenge
It's Alive
The Killer Shrews
Last Days of Planet Earth
Link
Mad Doctor of Blood Island
Man Made Monster
Night of the Bloody Apes
The Robot Vs. the Aztec Mummy
Rodan
Samson in the Wax Museum
Samson Vs. the Vampire Women
Scanners
Scanners 2: The New Order
Scanners 3: The Takeover
Screamers
Seedpeople
She Demons
The Slime People
Stephen King's Golden Years
Stephen King's The Stand
Stephen King's The Tommyknockers
The Swarm
They Came from Within
They Saved Hitler's Brain
Twilight Zone: The Movie
Varan the Unbelievable
Videodrome
Village of the Damned
The Vindicator
The Wasp Woman
Wrestling Women Vs. the Aztec Ape
Wrestling Women Vs. the Aztec
    Mummy

Horror Comedy
See also Black Comedy; Comedy;
    Genre Spoofs; Satire & Parody
Army of Darkness
Attack of the Killer Tomatoes
Bad Channels
Bad Taste
Critters
Critters 2: The Main Course
Critters 3
Critters 4
Evil Spawn
From Beyond
Gremlins
Gremlins 2: The New Batch

Night of the Creeps
Q (The Winged Serpent)
Re-Animator
There's Nothing Out There
Tremors
Tremors 2: Aftershocks

Hunted!
See also Survival
Battle for Moon Station Dallos
Bounty Hunter 2002
Cyborg 2
Freejack
Project Shadowchaser 3000
Slave Girls from Beyond Infinity
Split

I Spy
See also Feds; Terrorism
Access Code
Alien Women
Dog Soldier: Shadows of the Past
The Groundstar Conspiracy
Roboman
Running Delilah

Identity
See also Buddies; Post Apocalypse
Blade Runner
The Borrower
Brainwaves
Darkman
Duplicates
Final Approach
The Groundstar Conspiracy
The Human Duplicators
I Married a Monster from Outer
    Space
Journey to the Far Side of the Sun
Megaville
Next One
The Nutty Professor
Seedpeople
Teen Alien
The Thing
Total Recall
Trancers
Trancers 2: The Return of Jack Deth

Insects
See Killer Bugs & Slugs

Invisibility
Abbott and Costello Meet the Invisi-
    ble Man
The Amazing Transparent Man
Clash of the Titans
Doctor Faustus
The Golden Voyage of Sinbad
Invisible Invaders
The Invisible Man
The Invisible Man Returns
The Invisible Man's Revenge
The Invisible Terror
Invisible: The Chronicles of Ben-
    jamin Knight
The Invisible Woman
Memoirs of an Invisible Man

The New Invisible Man
Now You See Him, Now You Don't
The Phantom Creeps
Phantom from Space
Return of Chandu
Riding with Death

Island Fare
Attack of the Crab Monsters
Attack of the Mushroom People
Cyber Bandits
Dinosaur Island
Food of the Gods
Island of Dr. Moreau
Island of Lost Souls
Jurassic Park
King Kong
Mad Doctor of Blood Island
Mysterious Island
No Escape
Return of Chandu
Son of Kong
Terror Is a Man

It's a Bird...It's a Plane...It's
    a....
Clash of the Titans
Flying Disc Man from Mars
Invasion of the Body Stealers
King of the Rocketmen
Lawnmower Man 2: Jobe's War
Lost Planet Airmen
Meteor Man
The Puma Man
RoboCop 3
The Rocketeer
Supergirl
Superman: The Movie
Superman 2
Superman 3
Superman 4: The Quest for Peace
Superman and the Mole Men
Zombies of the Stratosphere

Japanimation
See also 'Toons
Akira
Battle for Moon Station Dallos
Bubblegum Crisis
Demon City Shinjuku
Dog Soldier: Shadows of the Past
GUY: Awakening of the Devil
Neo-Tokyo
Odin: Photon Space Sailer Starlight
Project A-ko
Robot Carnival
Toward the Terra
Urusei Yatsura Movie 1: Only You
Urusei Yatsura Movie 2: Beautiful
    Dreamer
Urusei Yatsura Movie 3: Remember
    My Love
Urusei Yatsura Movie 4: Lum the
    Forever
Urusei Yatsura Movie 5: The Final
    Chapter
Urusei Yatsura Movie 6: Always My
    Darling

The Venus Wars
A Wind Named Amnesia

Killer Apes
See also Monkeying Around
A*P*E*
The Ape Man
Battle for the Planet of the Apes
Beneath the Planet of the Apes
Conquest of the Planet of the Apes
Escape from the Planet of the Apes
King Kong
King Kong Lives
King Kong Vs. Godzilla
Link
Mighty Joe Young
Planet of the Apes
Son of Kong
Wrestling Women Vs. the Aztec Ape

Killer Birds
Batman Returns
The Birds
The Birds 2: Land's End
Ghidrah the Three Headed Monster
The Giant Claw
Rodan
The Seventh Voyage of Sinbad

Killer Brains
See also Renegade Body Parts
The Brain
The Brain from Planet Arous
The Brain that Wouldn't Die
Donovan's Brain
Fiend Without a Face
Journey to the Seventh Planet
Neutron Vs. the Death Robots

Killer Bugs & Slugs
The Abominable Dr. Phibes
Attack of the Giant Leeches
The Bees
Beginning of the End
The Black Scorpion
Blue Monkey
The Borrower
Bug
Cat Women of the Moon
Clash of the Titans
The Cosmic Monsters
Damnation Alley
The Deadly Mantis
Destroy All Monsters
Dune
Earth Vs. the Spider
Empire of the Ants
Evil Spawn
The Fly
The Fly
The Fly 2
Food of the Gods
Food of the Gods: Part 2
Galaxy of Terror
The Giant Spider Invasion
Godzilla Vs. Megalon
Godzilla Vs. Mothra
The Incredible Shrinking Man

Invasion of the Bee Girls
Journey to the Seventh Planet
Killers from Space
Last Days of Planet Earth
The Lost Continent
Mesa of Lost Women
Missile to the Moon
Monster from Green Hell
The Monster that Challenged the
    World
Mosquito
Mothra
Mysterious Island
The Nest
Night of the Creeps
Parasite
Phase 4
Return of the Fly
Rodan
Sinbad and the Eye of the Tiger
Skeeter
Something Wicked This Way Comes
Son of Godzilla
The Swarm
Tarantula
Them!
They Came from Within
Ticks
Tremors
Tremors 2: Aftershocks
The Wasp Woman

Killer Cars
See also Motor Vehicle Dept.
Death Race 2000
Death Sport
Equinox
Mad Max
Mad Max: Beyond Thunderdome
The Road Warrior

Killer Cats
See also Cats
The Atomic Man
Batman Returns
Cat Women of the Moon
Dr. Cyclops
The Incredible Shrinking Man
Mutator

Killer Dreams
Dreamscape
Lathe of Heaven
Shadowzone
Until the End of the World

Killer Plants
The Angry Red Planet
Attack of the Killer Tomatoes
Attack of the Mushroom People
Body Snatchers
Day of the Triffids
Godzilla Vs. Biollante
Invasion of the Body Snatchers
It Conquered the World
The Land Unknown
The Lost Continent
Navy Vs. the Night Monsters

Revenge of the Teenage Vixens from
    Outer Space
Seedpeople
Swamp Thing
The Thing

Killer Reptiles
Alligator
Creature from the Black Lagoon
The Creature Walks Among Us
Destroy All Monsters
Gamera, the Invincible
Gamera Vs. Barugon
Gamera Vs. Gaos
Ghidrah the Three Headed Monster
The Giant Gila Monster
Godzilla, King of the Monsters
Godzilla 1985
Godzilla on Monster Island
Godzilla Raids Again
Godzilla Vs. Biollante
Godzilla Vs. Megalon
Godzilla Vs. Monster Zero
Godzilla Vs. Mothra
Godzilla Vs. the Cosmic Monster
Godzilla Vs. the Sea Monster
Godzilla Vs. the Smog Monster
Godzilla's Revenge
Jason and the Argonauts
King Kong Vs. Godzilla
Metamorphosis
Mothra
Q (The Winged Serpent)
Reptilicus
Revenge of the Creature
Son of Godzilla
The Three Worlds of Gulliver
20 Million Miles to Earth
V
V: The Final Battle

Killer Rodents
The Abominable Dr. Phibes
Food of the Gods
Food of the Gods: Part 2
The Killer Shrews
The Mole People
The Princess Bride
Radioactive Dreams
Rats

Killer Sea Critters
See also Deep Blue; Sea Disasters
Alligator
Around the World Under the Sea
Attack of the Giant Leeches
The Beast from 20,000 Fathoms
Bride of the Monster
Clash of the Titans
Creature from the Black Lagoon
The Creature Walks Among Us
Curse of the Swamp Creature
Dagora, the Space Monster
Deepstar Six
Demon of Paradise
Endless Descent
The Flesh Eaters
Godzilla Vs. the Sea Monster

**Category
Index**

Gorgo
It Came from Beneath the Sea
Jason and the Argonauts
Leviathan
Lords of the Deep
The Lost Continent
Monster from the Ocean Floor
The Monster of Piedras Blancas
The Monster that Challenged the World
Mysterious Island
Octaman
The Phantom from 10,000 Leagues
Revenge of the Creature
The Sea Serpent
Seven Faces of Dr. Lao
Swamp Thing
20,000 Leagues Under the Sea
Voyage to the Bottom of the Sea
War of the Gargantuas

"Klaatu Barada Nikto"
Army of Darkness
The Day the Earth Stood Still
Invasion of the Space Preachers

Lost Worlds
See also Parallel Universes
Alien from L.A.
At the Earth's Core
Creatures the World Forgot
Dinosaur Island
Journey to the Center of the Earth
King Dinosaur
King Kong
The Land that Time Forgot
The Land Unknown
The Lost Continent
The Lost World
The Mole People
Mysterious Island
On the Comet
The People that Time Forgot
The Phantom Empire
Planet of Dinosaurs
Son of Kong
Two Lost Worlds
What Waits Below
When Dinosaurs Ruled the Earth
Where Time Began

Mad Doctors & Scientists
See also Science & Scientists
The Abominable Dr. Phibes
The Amazing Transparent Man
The Ape Man
The Astro-Zombies
The Beast of Yucca Flats
Before I Hang
Body Melt
The Brain that Wouldn't Die
Bride of the Monster
The Brides of Fu Manchu
The Brood
Carnosaur
The Castle of Fu Manchu
The City of Lost Children
Curse of the Swamp Creature

Cyborg Cop
Darkman
Darkman 2: The Return of Durant
Darkman 3: Die Darkman Die
Deep Red
Deep Space
Dr. Alien
Dr. Cyclops
Dr. Goldfoot and the Bikini Machine
Doctor Satan's Robot
Doctor X
Donovan's Brain
Embryo
The Face of Fu Manchu
The Fiendish Plot of Dr. Fu Manchu
The Flesh Eaters
Four Sided Triangle
The 4D Man
Frankenstein
Frankenstein Unbound
From Beyond
The Gamma People
Geisha Girl
The Giant Spider Invasion
The Head
Hideous Sun Demon
The Indestructible Man
The Invisible Man
The Invisible Ray
The Invisible Terror
Island of Dr. Moreau
Island of Lost Souls
Island of Terror
Jurassic Park
Kiss and Kill
The Lawnmower Man
Lawnmower Man 2: Jobe's War
Mad Doctor of Blood Island
Man Made Monster
The Man They Could Not Hang
Mandroid
The Manster
The Mask of Fu Manchu
Master of the World
Metamorphosis
The Monster Maker
Mysterious Doctor Satan
Night of the Bloody Apes
The Phantom Creeps
Philadelphia Experiment 2
Re-Animator
Samson in the Wax Museum
Scanner Cop
Screamers
She Demons
Star Trek Generations
Supersonic Man
Terror Is a Man
Unnatural
The Vengeance of Fu Manchu
Wes Craven Presents Mind Ripper
X: The Man with X-Ray Eyes

Made for Television
See TV Movies; TV Series

Magic
See also Sword & Sorcery
Beastmaster

Cast a Deadly Spell
Doctor Mordrid: Master of the Unknown
Hearts & Armour
Highlander: The Final Dimension
Krull
Legend
Magic Serpent
Metalstorm: The Destruction of Jared Syn
Neutron Vs. the Amazing Dr. Caronte
Return of Chandu
Seven Faces of Dr. Lao
The Seventh Voyage of Sinbad
Sinbad of the Seven Seas
Sword & the Sorcerer
Urusei Yatsura Movie 2: Beautiful Dreamer
Urusei Yatsura Movie 3: Remember My Love
Witch Hunt

Mars & Martians
Aelita: Queen of Mars
Alien Contamination
The Angry Red Planet
Capricorn One
Conquest of Space
Devil Girl from Mars
Flash Gordon: Mars Attacks the World
Flight to Mars
Flying Discman from Mars
Horrors of the Red Planet
Invaders from Mars
It! The Terror from Beyond Space
Mars Needs Women
The Martian Chronicles: Part 1
The Martian Chronicles: Part 2
The Martian Chronicles: Part 3
Martians Go Home!
Mission Mars
Planet of Blood
The Purple Monster Strikes
Quatermass and the Pit
Red Planet Mars
Robinson Crusoe on Mars
Rocketship X-M
Santa Claus Conquers the Martians
Spaced Invaders
Total Recall
The War of the Worlds
X from Outer Space
Zombies of the Stratosphere

Martial Arts
See Ever'body Was Kung Fu Fighting

Medieval Romps
Army of Darkness
Dragonslayer
Excalibur
Jabberwocky
Jack the Giant Killer
Legend
Magic Serpent

Wrestling Women Vs. the Aztec
   Mummy

Mystery Science Theater 3000
See MST3K Movies

Mythology & Folklore
See also Fantasy
Clash of the Titans
Force on Thunder Mountain
Golden Voyage of Sinbad
Hercules
Hercules 2
Hercules Against the Moon Men
Hercules and the Captive Women
Hercules and the Princess of Troy
Hercules in New York
Hercules in the Haunted World
Hercules, Prisoner of Evil
Hercules Unchained
Jason and the Argonauts
Seven Faces of Dr. Lao

Nazi Zombies
See also Nazis & Other Paramilitary
   Slugs; Zombies
Scream and Scream Again
She Demons
They Saved Hitler's Brain

Nazis & Other Paramilitary Slugs
See also Nazi Zombies; World War II
The Boys from Brazil
Captain America
Dr. Strangelove, or: How I Learned
   to Stop Worrying and Love the
   Bomb
Equalizer 2000
The Flesh Eaters
Indiana Jones and the Last Crusade
Indiana Jones and the Temple of
   Doom
The Lucifer Complex
Philadelphia Experiment 2
Prayer of the Rollerboys
Raiders of the Lost Ark
Red Planet Mars
The Rocketeer
Scream and Scream Again
She Demons
Strangers in Paradise
They Saved Hitler's Brain
UFO Secrets of the Third Reich
Wizards
Zone Troopers

Negative Utopia
See also Post Apocalypse; Rampant
   Technology
Alphaville
Brazil
Fahrenheit 451
Logan's Run
Metropolis
Mindwarp
984: Prisoner of the Future

1984
Philadelphia Experiment 2
Rollerball
Soylent Green
10th Victim
THX 1138
Time Troopers
Zardoz

Niebo Zowiet Recycled
See also Planeta Burg Recycled
Battle Beyond the Sun
Planet of Blood

Nuclear Disaster
See Meltdown

Parallel Universes
See also Lost Worlds
Blue Flame
Heavy Metal
Journey to the Far Side of the Sun
Masters of the Universe
Prisoners of the Lost Universe
Quest for Love
Shadowzone
Star Trek: Generations
Stargate
Super Mario Bros.
Tron
Who Framed Roger Rabbit
Xtro 2: The Second Encounter

Parenthood
See That's a Baby?

Pill Poppin'
Altered States
The Brother from Another Planet
I Come in Peace
Liquid Sky
Outland
RoboCop 2
Scanners
Scanners 2: The New Order
Scanners 3: The Takeover
TekWar
THX 1138
Warlords 3000
Wild in the Streets

The Planet of the Apes
Battle for the Planet of the Apes
Beneath the Planet of the Apes
Conquest of the Planet of the Apes
Escape from the Planet of the Apes
Planet of the Apes

Planeta Burg Recycled
See also Niebo Zowiet Recycled
Voyage to the Planet of Prehistoric
   Women
Voyage to the Prehistoric Planet

Post Apocalypse
See also Negative Utopia; Rampant
   Technology
After the Fall of New York

Aftermath
Aftershock
Armageddon: The Final Challenge
Battle for the Planet of the Apes
Beneath the Planet of the Apes
The Blood of Heroes
A Boy and His Dog
Circuitry Man
City Limits
Crash and Burn
The Creation of the Humanoids
Creepozoids
Crime Zone
Cyborg
Damnation Alley
Day the World Ended
Dead Man Walking
Def-Con 4
Dragon Fury
Dune Warriors
The Element of Crime
Equalizer 2000
Escape from Safehaven
Exterminators of the Year 3000
The Final Combat
The Final Executioner
First Spaceship on Venus
Fortress of Amerikka
Future Hunters
Glen and Randa
The Handmaid's Tale
Hardware
Hell Comes to Frogtown
In the Aftermath: Angels Never
   Sleep
Interzone
Judge Dredd
The Killing Edge
Knights
Land of Doom
The Last Man on Earth
The Lawless Land
Mad Max
Mad Max: Beyond Thunderdome
A Man Called Rage
Maniac Warriors
Mindwarp
Nemesis
Neon City
Night of the Comet
984: Prisoner of the Future
Omega Cop
The Omega Man
On the Beach
Panic in the Year Zero!
People Who Own the Dark
Phoenix the Warrior
Planet Earth
Planet of the Apes
Plughead Rewired: Circuitry Man 2
Prayer of the Rollerboys
Prison Planet
The Quiet Earth
Quintet
Radioactive Dreams
Rats
Rebel Storm
The Road Warrior
Robot Holocaust

**Category
Index**

Frankenstein
The Invisible Man
The Invisible Man Returns
The Invisible Woman
Island of Lost Souls
Revenge of the Creature
Son of Frankenstein

Psychiatry
See Shrinks

Pure Ego Vehicles
Conan the Destroyer
Sun Ra & His Intergalactic Solar
   Arkestra: Space Is the Place
Waterworld
The Wizard of Speed and Time

Race Against Time
Alien
Alien Space Avenger
Aliens
The Andromeda Strain
The China Syndrome
Dr. Strangelove, or: How I Learned
   to Stop Worrying and Love the
   Bomb
Fail-Safe
Grand Tour: Disaster in Time
Star Trek IV: The Voyage Home
Stargate
Outbreak
Voyage to the Bottom of the Sea
WarGames

Raiders of the Lost Ark
Indiana Jones and the Last Crusade
Indiana Jones and the Temple of
   Doom
Raiders of the Lost Ark

Rampant Technology
See also Computers; Cyborgs;
   Robots & Androids; Virtual Reali-
   ty
The Android Affair
Armageddon: The Final Challenge
Assassin
Back to the Future
The Black Hole
Blade Runner
Brainstorm
Charly
Chopping Mall
Circuitry Man
Colossus: The Forbin Project
The Companion
Crash and Burn
The Creation of the Humanoids
Cyber Bandits
Cyber-Tracker 2
Demon Seed
Digital Man
Dr. Goldfoot and the Bikini Machine
Dungeonmaster
Duplicates
Electric Dreams
The Eliminators

Eve of Destruction
Fail-Safe
The Final Programme
The Fly
The Fly
The Fly 2
Futureworld
The Gamma People
Hackers
Hologram Man
Johnny Mnemonic
Judge Dredd
Lawnmower Man 2: Jobe's War
Metropolis
Mutant Hunt
Mutant Species
The Net
New Crime City: Los Angeles 2020
Nightflyers
The Phantom Empire
The Philadelphia Experiment
Plughead Rewired: Circuitry Man 2
The Power Within
Project: Nightmare
Pulse
The Quiet Earth
Replikator: Cloned to Kill
RoboCop
RoboCop 2
RoboCop 3
Robot Holocaust
Robot Jox
Rock & Roll Cowboys
R.O.T.O.R.
Runaway
Search and Destroy
Shadowzone
Short Circuit
Short Circuit 2
Steel and Lace
Terminal Impact
The Terminal Man
The Terminator
Things to Come
Transatlantic Tunnel
Tron
12:01
2001: A Space Odyssey
The Vindicator
Virtuosity
WarGames
Weird Science
Westworld
Wild Palms
Wired to Kill
Wrestling Women Vs. the Aztec Ape
Zardoz

Rebel With a Cause
See also Rebel Without a Cause
Armageddon: The Final Challenge
The Blob
Brazil
The China Syndrome
Dragon Fury
Fahrenheit 451
Game of Survival
The Manhattan Project
Megaville

1984
Outbreak
Overdrawn at the Memory Bank
Philadelphia Experiment 2
Project X
Quarantine
Split
Steel Frontier
THX 1137
Total Recall
V: The Final Battle
WarGames

Rebel Without a Cause
See also Rebel With a Cause
A Boy and His Dog
A Clockwork Orange
Doin' Time on Planet Earth
The Man Who Fell to Earth
Sleeper

Red Scare
The Bamboo Saucer
Battle Beneath the Earth
Dr. Strangelove, or: How I Learned
   to Stop Worrying and Love the
   Bomb
The Gamma People
Invasion of the Body Snatchers
The Manchurian Candidate
The Professor
Tobor the Great
2010: The Year We Make Contact

Renegade Body Parts
See also Killer Brains
The Adventures of Baron Mun-
   chausen
The Brain that Wouldn't Die
The Crawling Eye
The Crawling Hand
Galaxy of Terror
The Head
Jack the Giant Killer
Re-Animator
Reptilicus
Waxwork 2: Lost in Time

Rescue Missions
See also Rescue Missions Involving
   Time Travel
The City of Lost Children
Dead Man Walking
Escape from New York
Galaxy of Terror
Marooned
Outbreak
Planeta Burg
Project Shadowchaser 3000
Return of Chandu
Return of the Jedi
Shredder Orpheus
Spaceballs
Spacehunter: Adventures in the
   Forbidden Zone
Star Trek 3: The Search for Spock
Star Wars
Starflight One

Category
Index

Johnny Mnemonic
The Man Who Fell to Earth
Runaway
The Running Man
Super Mario Bros.
World Gone Wild

Romance
The Amphibian Man
The Android Affair
Assignment Outer Space
Captain America 2: Death Too Soon
A Chinese Ghost Story
The Companion
Dinosaurus!
Edward Scissorhands
The Empire Strikes Back
Excalibur
Forever Young
Four Sided Triangle
Heartbeeps
King Kong
Making Mr. Right
Millenium
New Eden
The Princess Bride
Quest for Love
Return of the Jedi
The Rocketeer
Star Wars
Starman
THX 1138
Time After Time
12:01
The Unearthly Stranger

Roswell
See Conspiracies Involving Unexplained Phenomena; UFOs/UFOlogy

Sanity Check
See also Shrinks
Communion
Dark Star
Dr. Strangelove, or: How I Learned to Stop Worrying and Love the Bomb
Doctor X
Dreamscape
Scanners
Solaris
Street Asylum
Terminator 2: Judgment Day
12 Monkeys
Until the End of the World

Satire & Parody
See also Black Comedy; Comedy; Genre Spoofs; Horror Comedy
Abbott and Costello Go to Mars
Alien Space Avenger
Alien Women
Bill & Ted's Bogus Journey
Bill & Ted's Excellent Adventure
A Clockwork Orange
Dark Star

Dr. Strangelove, or: How I Learned to Stop Worrying and Love the Bomb
The Fiendish Plot of Dr. Fu Manchu
Flesh Gordon
Galactic Gigolo
Galaxina
Hardware Wars and Other Film Farces
Hell Comes to Frogtown
I Was a Zombie for the FBI
The Incredible Shrinking Woman
Invasion Earth: The Aliens Are Here!
Jabberwocky
Jet Benny Show
Kurt Vonnegut's Harrison Bergeron
The Meteor Man
Mutant on the Bounty
The Nutty Professor
Overdrawn at the Memory Bank
The Pink Chiquitas
The Princess Bride
Return of Captain Invincible
The Rocky Horror Picture Show
Sleeper
Spaceship
Strange Invaders
A Taste for Flesh and Blood
They Live
Uforia
Voyage of the Rock Aliens
World Gone Wild
Young Frankenstein

Science & Scientists
See also Mad Doctors & Scientists
Alien Autopsy: Fact or Fiction?
Altered States
Android
The Andromeda Strain
Around the World Under the Sea
Assassin
The Atomic Man
The Brides of Fu Manchu
Children of the Damned
Creature Walks Among Us
Demon Seed
Die, Monster, Die!
Dr. Alien
The Eliminators
Fantastic Voyage
The Fly
The Fly
The Fly 2
Forbidden World
Four Sided Triangle
The 4D Man
From the Earth to the Moon
The Henderson Monster
Humanoid Defender
The Incredible Hulk Returns
The Invisible Man Returns
Jurassic Park
Link
The Lost World
Monkey Boy
My Stepmother Is an Alien
Outbreak
The Professor

Project X
Prototype X29A
The Quiet Earth
Return of the Fly
The Rocky Horror Picture Show
The Secret of the Telegian
The Sex Machine
Son of Flubber
Species
Stephen King's Golden Years
Swamp Thing
The Thing
Things to Come
This Island Earth
Time Trackers
The Time Travelers
12:01
Unknown World
Where Time Began

Sea Disasters
See also Deep Blue; Disaster Flicks; Killer Sea Critters; Shipwrecked
The Abyss
Deepstar Six
Deluge
Leviathan
Transatlantic Tunnel
Waterworld

Serials
Blake of Scotland Yard
Destination Saturn
Doctor Satan's Robot
Flash Gordon Conquers the Universe
Flash Gordon: Mars Attacks the World
Flash Gordon: Rocketship
Flying Discman from Mars
King of the Rocketmen
Lost Planet Airmen
Manhunt of Mystery Island
Mysterious Doctor Satan
The Phantom Creeps
The Phantom Empire
The Purple Monster Strikes
Return of Chandu
Space Soldiers Conquer the Universe
Zombies of the Stratosphere

Sex & Sexuality
See also Sexploitation
Alien Prey
Bad Girls from Mars
Barbarella
A Boy and His Dog
Cherry 2000
Cinderella 2000
The Companion
Dead Weekend
Demon Seed
Dr. Alien
Frankenstein Unbound
Galactic Gigolo
The Handmaid's Tale
Hell Comes to Frogtown

Category Index

Sleeper
Son of Blob
Strange New World
Strangers in Paradise
2001: A Space Odyssey
Welcome Back Mr. Fox

Sword & Sorcery
Beastmaster
Beastmaster 2: Through the Portal of Time
Beastmaster 3: The Eye of Braxus
Clash of the Titans
Conan the Barbarian
Conan the Destroyer
Dragonslayer
Dungeonmaster
Excalibur
The Golden Voyage of Sinbad
Hearts & Armour
Hercules
Hercules Against the Moon Men
Hercules and the Captive Women
Hercules and the Princess of Troy
Hercules in the Haunted World
Hercules, Prisoner of Evil
Hercules Unchained
Highlander
Jack the Giant Killer
Jason and the Argonauts
Krull
Legend
The Magic Serpent
Masters of the Universe
The Princess Bride
The Seventh Voyage of Sinbad
Sinbad and the Eye of the Tiger
Sinbad of the Seven Seas
Willow

Teen Angst
See also Hell High School
Bill & Ted's Excellent Adventure
Body Snatchers
Coneheads
Deadly Weapon
Doin' Time on Planet Earth
E.T.: The Extra-Terrestrial
The Fly 2
Hackers
The Manhattan Project
Misfits of Science
Prayer of the Rollerboys
Solarbabies
Starchaser: The Legend of Orin
Teenage Caveman
Teenage Mutant Ninja Turtles 2: The Secret of the Ooze
Teenagers from Outer Space
Urusei Yatsura Movie 1: Only You
Urusei Yatsura Movie 2: Beautiful Dreamer
Urusei Yatsura Movie 3: Remember My Love
Village of the Giants
Weird Science
Wild in the Streets

Television
See TV Movies; TV Series; TV Pilot Movies

Terrorism
See also Crime & Criminals; Spies & Espionage
Brazil
Captain America 2: Death Too Soon
Crash and Burn
Death of the Incredible Hulk
Fortress of Amerikka
Hologram Man
Kamikaze '89
Night Siege: Project Shadowchaser 2
Programmed to Kill
Project Shadowchaser 3000
Running Delilah
T-Force
Virtual Assassin

That's a Baby?
See also Pregnant Men
Alien 3
Baby ... Secret of the Lost Legend
The Brood
Demon Seed
Enemy Mine
Gappa the Trifibian Monster
Gorgo
Horror Planet
It's Alive
Son of Godzilla
2001: A Space Odyssey
20 Million Miles to Earth
Unnatural

3-D Flicks
A*P*E*
Cat Women of the Moon
Creature from the Black Lagoon
The Creature Walks Among Us
Invaders from Mars
It Came from Outer Space
Metalstorm: The Destruction of Jared Syn
Parasite
Revenge of the Creature
Robot Monster
Spacehunter: Adventures in the Forbidden Zone
Starchaser: The Legend of Orin

3 Stooges
Army of Darkness
Have Rocket Will Travel
Short Circuit
Three Stooges in Orbit

Time Travel
See also Rescue Missions Involving Time Travel
A.P.E.X.
Army of Darkness
The Atomic Man
Back to the Future
Back to the Future, Part 2

Back to the Future, Part 3
Battle for the Planet of the Apes
Beastmaster 2: Through the Portal of Time
Beneath the Planet of the Apes
Beyond the Time Barrier
Biggles
Bill & Ted's Bogus Journey
Bill & Ted's Excellent Adventure
Blue Flame
Buck Rogers in the 25th Century
Chronopolis
Conquest of the Planet of the Apes
Daleks—Invasion Earth 2150 A.D.
Day Time Ended
Doctor Mordrid: Master of the Unknown
Doctor Who and the Daleks
Doctor Who: Cybermen—The Early Years
The Eliminators
Escape from the Planet of the Apes
Escapes
The Final Countdown
Frankenstein Unbound
Freejack
Future Zone
Galaxis
Grand Tour: Disaster in Time
Hercules in New York
Idaho Transfer
Millenium
Nemesis 2: Nebula
Next One
The Philadelphia Experiment
Philadelphia Experiment 2
Planet of the Apes
Running Against Time
Slaughterhouse Five
Star Trek 4: The Voyage Home
Superman: The Movie
Teenage Mutant Ninja Turtles 3
The Terminator
Terminator 2: Judgment Day
Test Tube Teens from the Year 2000
Time After Time
Time Bandits
Time Fighters
The Time Guardian
The Time Machine
Time Machine
Time Runner
Time Trackers
The Time Travelers
Timecop
Timemaster
Timerider
Timestalkers
Trancers
Trancers 2: The Return of Jack Deth
Trancers 3: Deth Lives
Trancers 4: Jack of Swords
Trancers 5: Sudden Deth
12 Monkeys
12:01
Waxwork 2: Lost in Time

'Toons
See also Japanimation

Lathe of Heaven
Out There
The Psychotronic Man
Roswell: The U.F.O. Cover-Up
A Strange Harvest with Linda Moulton Howe
The Stranger
X: The Man with X-Ray Eyes

Unicorns
Blade Runner
Have Rocket Will Travel
Legend
Seven Faces of Dr. Lao

Vampires
Horror of the Blood Monsters
It! The Terror from Beyond Space
The Last Man on Earth
Lifeforce
Not of this Earth
Plan 9 from Outer Space
Planet of Blood
Planet of the Vampires
Samson Vs. the Vampire Women
Trancers 4: Jack of Swords
Vampire Vixens from Venus

Venus & Venusians
Abbott and Costello Go to Mars
Escape from Planet Earth
First Spaceship on Venus
The Green Slime
Have Rocket Will Travel
The Illustrated Man
It Conquered the World
Planeta Burg
Queen of Outer Space
The Stranger from Venus
20 Million Miles to Earth
Vampire Vixens from Venus
The Venus Wars
Voyage to the Planet of Prehistoric Women
Voyage to the Prehistoric Planet
War in Space
Zontar, the Thing from Venus

Virtual Reality
See also Computers; Rampant Technology
Arcade
Brainstorm
Cyber Bandits
Future Shock
Hologram Man
The Lawnmower Man
Lawnmower Man 2: Jobe's War
Looker
Megaville
TekWar
Venus Rising
Virtual Assassin
Virtuosity
Wild Palms

Wedding Hell
The Bride of Frankenstein

Bride of the Monster
I Married a Monster from Outer Space
Project Moonbase

Werewolves
Hercules, Prisoner of Evil
The Professor
Project Metalbeast: DNA Overload

Westerns, Sci-Fi Style
Back to the Future, Part 3
Backlash: Oblivion 2
Battle Beyond the Stars
Ghost Patrol
Meteor Monster
Neon City
Oblivion
Outland
The Phantom Empire
The Road Warrior
Space Rage
Steel Dawn
Steel Frontier
Timerider
Westworld

Women
See also Dream Girls; Femme Fatale; Women in Prison; Wonder Women
Aelita: Queen of Mars
The Astounding She-Monster
Mars Needs Women
Mesa of Lost Women
Prehistoric Women
Queen of Outer Space
Revenge of the Teenage Vixens from Outer Space
Samson Vs. the Vampire Women
She
She
The Sisterhood
Star Quest
Steel and Lace
Unnatural

Women in Prison
See also Men in Prison
Alien 3
Deadlock
Deadlock 2
Star Slammer

Wonder Women
See also Dream Girls
Alien
Alien 3
Alienator
Aliens
Attack of the 50 Foot Woman
Attack of the 50 Ft. Woman
Batman Returns
Battle Beyond the Stars
Conan the Destroyer
Galaxis
Heavy Metal
Hell Comes to Frogtown

The Lost Empire
Phoenix the Warrior
Prehistoric Women
Robo-C.H.I.C.
Roller Blade
Running Delilah
Star Quest
Supergirl
The Vindicator
The Wild World of Batwoman
Willow
Wrestling Women Vs. the Aztec Ape
Wrestling Women Vs. the Aztec Mummy
Zeram

Woofs!
After the Fall of New York
Aftermath
Alien Predators
Alien Warrior
Andy and the Airwave Rangers
A*P*E*
Biohazard: The Alien Force
The Birds 2: Land's End
Bog
Boom in the Moon
Bounty Hunter 2002
The Brain
Cosmos: War of the Planets
The Crawling Hand
The Creation of the Humanoids
The Day It Came to Earth
Dead Weekend
Demon of Paradise
Dinosaur Island
Dr. Alien
End of the World
Escape from Galaxy Three
Escape from Planet Earth
Evil Spawn
Exterminators of the Year 3000
Galactic Gigolo
Galaxy Invader
Game of Survival
Highlander 2: The Quickening
Horror Planet
The Incredible Petrified World
Interzone
Invasion of the Animal People
Invasion of the Body Stealers
Journey to the Center of the Earth
The Last Woman on Earth
A Man Called Rage
Megaforce
Modern Problems
The Monster of Piedras Blancas
Mutant Hunt
The New Gladiators
Night Beast
Nightfall
Nude on the Moon
People Who Own the Dark
Phoenix the Warrior
The Pink Chiquitas
Plan 9 from Outer Space
Prehistoric Women
Prison Planet
The Puma Man

Distributor List

The following explains what those three-letter codes at the end of each review stand for. They stand for distributor names. Flip one more page and you'll find the "Distributor Guide," which offers addresses, phone numbers, and yes, sometimes even fax numbers, for each company listed in the "Distributor List." All this info for one low price. What a deal.

ABC—ABC Videoon Home Video, Inc.
ACA—Academy Entertainment
ACE—Ace Video
AFE—Amazing Fantasy Entertainment
AHV—Active Home Video
AIP—A.I.P. Home Video, Inc.
ANI—AnimEigo Inc.
AOV—Admit One Video
APD—Applause Productions, Inc.
AVE—WarnerVision
BAR—Barr Films
BFV—Best Film & Video Corporation
BTV—Baker & Taylor Video
CAB—Cable Films & Video
CAF—Cabin Fever Entertainment
CAN—Cannon Video
CCB—Critics' Choice Video, Inc.
CDV—Television International
CEL—Celebrity Home Entertainment
CNG—Congress Entertainment, Ltd.
CNM—Cinemacabre Video
COL—Columbia Tristar Home Video
CPM—Central Park Media/U.S. Manga Corps
CRC—Criterion Collection
CTH—Corinth Video

CVC—Connoisseur Video Collection
DIS—Walt Disney Home Video
DVT—Discount Video Tapes, Inc.
EXP—Expanded Entertainment
FCT—Facets Multimedia, Inc.
FHE—Family Home Entertainment
FLI—Films Inc. Video
FLL—Full Moon Home Video
FOX—CBS/Fox Video
FRG—Fright Video
FRH—Fries Home Video
FUS—Fusion Video
FXL—Fox/Lorber Home Video
FXV—FoxVideo
GEM—Video Gems
GHV—Genesis Home Video
GKK—Goodtimes Entertainment
GLV—German Language Video Center
GPV—Grapevine Video
GVV—Glenn Video Vistas, Ltd.
HBO—HBO Home Video
HEG—Horizon Entertainment
HHE—Hollywood Home Entertainment
HHT—Hollywood Home Theatre
HMD—Hemdale Home Video
HMK—Hallmark Home Entertainment
HMV—Home Vision Cinema

HPH—Hollywood Pictures Home Video
HTV—Hen's Tooth Video
HVL—Home Video Library
ICA—First Run Features/Icarus Films
IHF—International Historic Films, Inc. (IHF)
IME—Image Entertainment
IMP—Imperial Entertainment Corp.
INC—Increase/SilverMine Video
ING—Ingram Entertainment
INJ—Ingram International Films
JEF—JEF Films, Inc.
JFK—Just for Kids Home Video
KAR—Karol Video
KIV—Kino on Video
LIV—Live Entertainment
LOO—Loonic Video
LSV—LSVideo, Inc.
LUM—Lumivision Corporation
MCA—MCA/Universal Home Video
MCG—Management Company Entertainment Group (MCEG), Inc.
MED—Media Home Entertainment
MGM—MGM/UA Home Entertainment
MIL—Milestone Film & Video
MLB—Mike LeBell's Video

MNC—Monarch Home Video
MOV—Movies Unlimited
MPI—MPI Home Video
MRV—Moore Video
MTX—MNTEX Entertainment, Inc.
MWP—Wade Williams Productions, Inc.
NHO—New Horizons Home Video
NLC—New Line Home Video
NOS—Nostalgia Family Video
NWV—New World Entertainment
ORI—Orion Home Video
PAR—Paramount Home Video
PMH—PM Entertainment Group, Inc.
PMS—Professional Media Service Corp.
PSM—Prism Entertainment
PYR—Pyramid Film & Video
RDG—Reader's Digest Home Video
REP—Republic Pictures Home Video
RHI—Rhino Home Video

RHP—Rhapsody Films
RXM—Rex Miller
SHR—Shanachie Entertainment
SMW—Something Weird Video
SNC—Sinister Cinema
STP—Streamline Pictures
SUE—Sultan Entertainment
SUN—Sun Video
TLF—Time-Life Video and Television
TOU—Buena Vista Home Video
TPV—Tapeworm Video Distributors
TRI—Triboro Entertainment Group
TTC—Turner Home Entertainment Company
TTV—Troma Team Video
TVC—The Video Catalog
TWE—Trans-World Entertainment
UFO—UFO Central
UND—Uni Distribution
UNI—Unicorn Video, Inc.

VCD—Video City Productions/Distributing
VCI—Video Communications, Inc. (VCI)
VCN—Video Connection
VDA—Video Action
VDC—Vidcrest
VDM—Video Dimensions
VEC—Valencia Entertainment Corp.
VES—Vestron Video
VHE—VCII Home Entertainment, Inc.
VMK—Vidmark Entertainment
VTR—Anchor Bay
VYY—Video Yesteryear
WAR—Warner Home Video, Inc.
WLA—Western L.A. Film Productions, Inc.
WNE—WNET/Thirteen Non-Broadcast
WOV—Worldvision Home Video, Inc.
WSH—Wishing Well Distributing
WTA—Whole Toon Catalogue

Distributor Guide

The following listings offer the addresses, phone numbers, and fax numbers for distributors cited in the main review section. Those listings with the code **OM** are on moratorium (distributed at one time, though not currently). The good news is, a copy of the video may still be lurking at your video store. If the video is not being distributed at all, the code **NO** appears. Of course, new titles are being made available on video every day, so don't give up hope yet.

ABC VIDEO *(ABC)*
Capital Cities/ABC Video Enterprises
1200 High Ridge Rd.
Stamford, CT 06905
(203)968-9100
Fax: (203)329-6464

ACADEMY ENTERTAINMENT *(ACA)*
9250 Wilshire Blvd., Ste. 400
Beverly Hills, CA 90212
Fax: (310)275-2195

ACE VIDEO *(ACE)*
19749 Dearborn St.
Chatsworth, CA 91311
(818)718-1116
1-800-727-2229
Fax: (818)718-9109

ACTIVE HOME VIDEO *(AHV)*
12121 Wilshire Blvd., No. 401
Los Angeles, CA 90025
(310)447-6131
1-800-824-6109
Fax: (310)207-0411

ADMIT ONE VIDEO *(AOV)*
PO Box 66, Sta. O
Toronto, ON, Canada M4A 2M8
(416)463-5714
Fax: (416)463-5714

A.I.P. HOME VIDEO, INC. *(AIP)*
10726 McCune Ave.
Los Angeles, CA 90034
Fax: (213)559-8849

AMAZING FANTASY ENTERTAINMENT *(AFE)*
3061 Fletcher Dr.
Los Angeles, CA 90065
(213)550-4530

ANCHOR BAY *(VTR)*
500 Kirts Blvd.
Troy, MI 48084
(810)362-9660
1-800-786-8777
Fax: (810)362-4454

ANIMEIGO INC. *(ANI)*
PO Box 989
Wilmington, NC 28402-0989
(910)251-1850
1-800-242-6463
Fax: (910)763-2376

APPLAUSE PRODUCTIONS, INC. *(APD)*
85 Longview Rd.
Port Washington, NY 11050
(516)883-2825
1-800-278-7326
Fax: (516)883-7460

BAKER & TAYLOR VIDEO *(BTV)*
501 S. Gladiolus
Momence, IL 60954
(815)472-2444
1-800-775-2300
Fax: 1-800-775-3500

BARR FILMS *(BAR)*
12801 Schabarum
Irwindale, CA 91706
(818)338-7878

1-800-234-7878
Fax: (818)814-2672

BEST FILM & VIDEO CORPORATION *(BFV)*
108 New South Rd.
Hicksville, NY 11801-5223
(516)931-6969
1-800-527-2189
Fax: (516)931-5959

BUENA VISTA HOME VIDEO *(TOU)*
350 S. Buena Vista St.
Burbank, CA 91521-7145
(818)562-3568

CABIN FEVER ENTERTAINMENT *(CAF)*
100 W. Putnam Ave.
Greenwich, CT 06830
(203)661-1100
Fax: (203)863-5258

CABLE FILMS & VIDEO *(CAB)*
PO Box 7171, Country Club Sta.
Kansas City, MO 64113
(816)362-2804
1-800-514-2804
Fax: (816)341-7365

CANNON VIDEO *(CAN)*
PO Box 17198
Beverly Hills, CA 90290
(310)772-7765

CBS/FOX VIDEO *(FOX)*
PO Box 900
Beverly Hills, CA 90213

(562)-373-4800
1-800-800-2369
Fax: (562)373-4803

**CELEBRITY HOME ENTERTAIN-
MENT** *(CEL)*
22025 Ventura Blvd., Ste. 200
PO Box 4112
Woodland Hills, CA 91365-4112
(818)595-0666
Fax: (818)716-0168

**CENTRAL PARK MEDIA/U.S.
MANGA CORPS** *(CPM)*
250 W. 57th St., Ste. 317
New York, NY 10107
(212)977-7456
1-800-833-7456
Fax: (212)977-8709

CINEMACABRE VIDEO *(CNM)*
PO Box 10005-D
Baltimore, MD 21285-0005

**COLUMBIA TRISTAR HOME
VIDEO** *(COL)*
Sony Pictures Plz.
10202 W. Washington Blvd.
Culver City, CA 90232
(310)280-8000
Fax: (310)280-2485

**CONGRESS ENTERTAINMENT,
LTD.** *(CNG)*
Learn Plz., Ste. 6
PO Box 845
Tannersville, PA 18372-0845
(717)620-9001
1-800-847-8273
Fax: (717)620-9278

**CONNOISSEUR VIDEO COLLEC-
TION** *(CVC)*
1575 Westwood Blvd., Ste. 305
Los Angeles, CA 90024
(310)231-1350
1-800-529-2300
Fax: (310)231-1359

CORINTH VIDEO *(CTH)*
34 Gansevoort St.
New York, NY 10014
(212)463-0305
1-800-221-4720
Fax: (212)929-0010

CRITERION COLLECTION *(CRC)*
c/o The Voyager Company
1 Bridge St.
Irvington, NY 10533-1543

CRITICS' CHOICE VIDEO, INC.
(CCB)
PO Box 749
Itasca, IL 60143-0749
(708)775-3300
1-800-367-7765
Fax: (708)775-3355

DISCOUNT VIDEO TAPES, INC.
(DVT)
PO Box 7122
Burbank, CA 91510
(818)843-3366
Fax: (818)843-3821

EXPANDED ENTERTAINMENT
(EXP)
28024 Dorothy Dr.
Agoura Hills, CA 91301-2635
(818)991-2884
1-800-996-TOON
Fax: (818)991-3773

FACETS MULTIMEDIA, INC. *(FCT)*
1517 W. Fullerton Ave.
Chicago, IL 60614
(312)281-9075
1-800-331-6197
Fax: (312)929-5437

FAMILY HOME ENTERTAINMENT
(FHE)
c/o Live Home Video
15400 Sherman Way
PO Box 10124
Van Nuys, CA 91410-0124
(818)908-0303
1-800-677-0789
Fax: (818)778-3259

FILMS INC. VIDEO *(FLI)*
5547 N. Ravenswood Ave.
Chicago, IL 60640-1199
(312)878-2600
1-800-323-4222
Fax: (312)878-0416

**FIRST RUN FEATURES/ICARUS
FILMS** *(ICA)*
153 Waverly Pl.
New York, NY 10014
(212)727-1711
1-800-876-1710
Fax: (212)989-7649

FOX/LORBER HOME VIDEO *(FXL)*
419 Park Ave. S., 20th Fl.
New York, NY 10016
(212)532-3392
Fax: (212)685-2625

FOXVIDEO *(FXV)*
2121 Avenue of the Stars, 25th Fl.
Los Angeles, CA 90067
(310)369-3900
1-800-800-2FOX
Fax: (310)369-5811

FRIES HOME VIDEO *(FRH)*
6922 Hollywood Blvd., 12th Fl.
Hollywood, CA 90028
(213)466-2266
Fax: (213)466-2126

FRIGHT VIDEO *(FRG)*
16 Kenmar Dr., Ste. 141
Billerica, MA 01821-4788

FULL MOON HOME VIDEO *(FLL)*
8721 Santa Monica Blvd., Ste.
526
West Hollywood, CA 90069
(213)341-5959

FUSION VIDEO *(FUS)*
100 Fusion Way
Country Club Hills, IL 60478
(708)799-2073
Fax: (708)799-8375

GENESIS HOME VIDEO *(GHV)*
15820 Arminta St.
Van Nuys, CA 91406

**GERMAN LANGUAGE VIDEO
CENTER** *(GLV)*
7625 Pendleton Pike
Indianapolis, IN 46226-5298
(317)547-1257
1-800-252-1957
Fax: (317)547-1263

GLENN VIDEO VISTAS, LTD.
(GVV)
6924 Canby Ave., Ste. 103
Reseda, CA 91335
(818)881-8110
Fax: (818)981-5506

GOODTIMES ENTERTAINMENT
(GKK)
16 E. 40th St., 8th Fl.
New York, NY 10016-0113
(212)951-3000
Fax: (212)213-9319

GRAPEVINE VIDEO *(GPV)*
PO Box 46161
Phoenix, AZ 85063
(602)973-3661
Fax: (602)973-0060

**HALLMARK HOME ENTERTAIN-
MENT** *(HMK)*
6100 Wilshire Blvd., Ste. 1400
Los Angeles, CA 90048
(213)549-3790
Fax: (213)549-3760

HBO HOME VIDEO *(HBO)*
1100 6th Ave.
New York, NY 10036
(212)512-7400
Fax: (212)512-7498

HEMDALE HOME VIDEO *(HMD)*
7966 Beverly Blvd.
Los Angeles, CA 90048
(213)966-3700
Fax: (213)653-5452

HEN'S TOOTH VIDEO *(HTV)*
2805 E. State Blvd.
Fort Wayne, IN 46805
(219)471-4332
Fax: (219)471-4449

**HOLLYWOOD HOME ENTERTAIN-
MENT** *(HHE)*
6165 Crooked Creek Rd., Ste. B
Norcross, GA 30092-3105

HOLLYWOOD HOME THEATRE
(HHT)
1540 N. Highland Ave., Ste. 110
Hollywood, CA 90028
(213)466-0127

**HOLLYWOOD PICTURES HOME
VIDEO** *(HPH)*
Fairmont Bldg. 526
500 S. Buena Vista St.
Burbank, CA 91505-9842

HOME VIDEO LIBRARY *(HVL)*
Better Homes & Gardens Books
PO Box 10670
Des Moines, IA 50336
1-800-678-2665
Fax: (515)237-4765

HOME VISION CINEMA *(HMV)*
5547 N. Ravenswood Ave.
Chicago, IL 60640-1199
(312)878-2600
1-800-826-3456
Fax: (312)878-8648

HORIZON ENTERTAINMENT
(HEG)
45030 Trevor Ave.
Lancaster, CA 93534
(805)940-1040
1-800-323-2061
Fax: (805)940-8511

IMAGE ENTERTAINMENT *(IME)*
9333 Oso Ave.
Chatsworth, CA 91311
(818)407-9100
1-800-473-3475
Fax: (818)407-9111

**IMPERIAL ENTERTAINMENT
CORP.** *(IMP)*
4640 Lankershim Blvd., Ste. 201
North Hollywood, CA 91602
(818)762-0005
1-800-888-5826
Fax: (818)762-0006

INCREASE/SILVERMINE VIDEO
(INC)
6860 Canby Ave., Ste. 118
Reseda, CA 91335
(818)342-2880
1-800-233-2880
Fax: (818)342-4029

INGRAM ENTERTAINMENT *(ING)*
2 Ingram Blvd.
La Vergne, TN 37086-7006
(615)287-4000
1-800-759-5000
Fax: (615)287-4992

INGRAM INTERNATIONAL FILMS
(INJ)
7900 Hickman Rd.
Des Moines, IA 50322
(515)254-7000
1-800-621-1333
Fax: (515)254-7021

**INTERNATIONAL HISTORIC
FILMS, INC. (IHF)** *(IHF)*
PO Box 29035
Chicago, IL 60629
(312)927-2900
Fax: (312)927-9211

JEF FILMS, INC. *(JEF)*
Film House
143 Hickory Hill Cir.
Osterville, MA 02655-1322
(508)428-7198
Fax: (508)428-7198

JUST FOR KIDS HOME VIDEO
(JFK)
6320 Canoga Ave., Penthouse
Ste.
PO Box 4112
Woodland Hills, CA 91365-4112
(818)715-1980
1-800-445-8210
Fax: (818)716-0168

KAROL VIDEO *(KAR)*
PO Box 7600
Wilkes Barre, PA 18773
(717)822-8899
Fax: (717)822-8226

KINO ON VIDEO *(KIV)*
333 W. 39th St., Ste. 503
New York, NY 10018
(212)629-6880
1-800-562-3330
Fax: (212)714-0871

LIVE ENTERTAINMENT *(LIV)*
15400 Sherman Way
PO Box 10124
Van Nuys, CA 91410-0124
(818)988-5060

LOONIC VIDEO *(LOO)*
2022 Taraval St., Ste. 6427
San Francisco, CA 94116
(510)526-5681

LSVIDEO, INC. *(LSV)*
PO Box 415
Carmel, IN 46032

LUMIVISION CORPORATION
(LUM)
877 Federal Blvd.
Denver, CO 80204-3212
(303)446-0400
1-800-776-LUMI
Fax: (303)446-0101

**MANAGEMENT COMPANY
ENTERTAINMENT GROUP
(MCEG), INC.** *(MCG)*
1888 Century Park E., Ste. 1777
Los Angeles, CA 90067-1721
(310)282-0871
Fax: (310)282-8303

MCA/UNIVERSAL HOME VIDEO
(MCA)
100 Universal City Plz.
Universal City, CA 91608-9955
(818)777-1000
Fax: (818)733-1483

MEDIA HOME ENTERTAINMENT
(MED)
510 W. 6th St., Ste. 1032
Los Angeles, CA 90014
(213)236-1336
Fax: (213)236-1346

**MGM/UA HOME ENTERTAIN-
MENT** *(MGM)*
2500 Broadway
Santa Monica, CA 90404-6061
(310)449-3000
Fax: (310)449-3100

MIKE LEBELL'S VIDEO *(MLB)*
75 Freemont Pl.
Los Angeles, CA 90005
(213)938-3333
Fax: (213)938-3334

MILESTONE FILM & VIDEO *(MIL)*
275 W. 96th St., Ste 28C
New York, NY 10025
(212)865-7449
Fax: (212)222-8952

REX MILLER *(RXM)*
Rte. 1, Box 457-D
East Prairie, MO 63845
(314)649-5048

MNTEX ENTERTAINMENT, INC.
(MTX)
500 Kirts Dr.
Troy, MI 48084-5225

MONARCH HOME VIDEO *(MNC)*
2 Ingram Blvd.
La Vergne, TN 37086-7006
(615)287-4632
Fax: (615)287-4992

MOORE VIDEO *(MRV)*
PO Box 5703
Richmond, VA 23220
(804)745-9785
Fax: (804)745-9785

MOVIES UNLIMITED *(MOV)*
6736 Castor Ave.
Philadelphia, PA 19149
(215)722-8298
1-800-466-8437
Fax: (215)725-3683

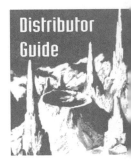

Distributor
Guide

MPI HOME VIDEO *(MPI)*
16101 S. 108th Ave.
Orland Park, IL 60462
(708)460-0555
Fax: (708)873-3177

NEW HORIZONS HOME VIDEO
(NHO)
2951 Flowers Rd. S., Ste. 237
Atlanta, GA 30341
(404)458-3488
1-800-854-3323
Fax: (404)458-2679

NEW LINE HOME VIDEO *(NLC)*
116 N. Robertson Blvd.
Los Angeles, CA 90048
(310)967-6670
Fax: (310)854-0602

NEW WORLD ENTERTAINMENT
(NWV)
1440 S. Sepulveda Blvd.
Los Angeles, CA 90025
(310)444-8100
Fax: (310)444-8101

NOSTALGIA FAMILY VIDEO *(NOS)*
PO Box 606
Baker City, OR 97814
(503)523-9034
1-800-784-8362
Fax: (503)523-7115

ORION HOME VIDEO *(ORI)*
1888 Century Park E.
Los Angeles, CA 90067
(310)282-0550
Fax: (310)282-9902

PARAMOUNT HOME VIDEO
(PAR)
Bluhdorn Bldg.
5555 Melrose Ave.
Los Angeles, CA 90038
(213)956-8090
Fax: (213)862-1100

PM ENTERTAINMENT GROUP,
INC. *(PMH)*
9450 Chivers Ave.
Sun Valley, CA 91352
(818)504-6332
1-800-934-2111
Fax: (818)504-6380

PRISM ENTERTAINMENT *(PSM)*
1888 Century Park, E., Ste. 350
Los Angeles, CA 90067
(310)277-3270
Fax: (310)203-8036

PROFESSIONAL MEDIA SERVICE
CORP. *(PMS)*
19122 S. Vermont Ave.
Gardena, CA 90248
(310)532-9024
1-800-223-7672
Fax: 1-800-253-8853

PYRAMID FILM & VIDEO *(PYR)*
2801 Colorado Ave.
Santa Monica, CA 90404
(310)828-7577
1-800-421-2304
Fax: (310)453-9083

READER'S DIGEST HOME VIDEO
(RDG)
Reader's Digest Rd.
Pleasantville, NY 10570

REPUBLIC PICTURES HOME
VIDEO *(REP)*
5700 Wilshire Blvd., Ste. 525
Los Angeles, CA 90036
(213)965-6900
Fax: (213)965-6963

RHAPSODY FILMS *(RHP)*
PO Box 179
New York, NY 10014
(212)243-0152
Fax: (212)645-9250

RHINO HOME VIDEO *(RHI)*
10635 Santa Monica Blvd., 2nd
Fl.
Los Angeles, CA 90025-4900
(310)828-1980
1-800-843-3670
Fax: (310)453-5529

SHANACHIE ENTERTAINMENT
(SHR)
13 Laight St.
New York, NY 10013
(212)334-0284
Fax: (212)334-5207

SINISTER CINEMA *(SNC)*
PO Box 4369
Medford, OR 97501-0168
(503)773-6860
Fax: (503)779-8650

SOMETHING WEIRD VIDEO
(SMW)
c/o Mike Vraney
PO Box 33664
Seattle, WA 98133
(206)361-3759
Fax: (206)364-7526

STREAMLINE PICTURES *(STP)*
PO Box 691418
West Hollywood, CA 90069
(310)998-0070
Fax: (310)998-1145

SULTAN ENTERTAINMENT *(SUE)*
116 N. Robertson Blvd.
Los Angeles, CA 90048
(213)976-6700

SUN VIDEO *(SUN)*
15 Donnybrook
Demarest, NJ 07627
(201)784-0662
Fax: (201)784-0665

TAPEWORM VIDEO DISTRIBU-
TORS *(TPV)*
27833 Hopkins Ave., Unit 6
Valencia, CA 91355
(805)257-4904
Fax: (805)257-4820

TELEVISION INTERNATIONAL
(CDV)
c/o Jason Films
2825 Wilcrest, Ste. 407
Houston, TX 77042
(713)266-3097
Fax: (713)266-3148

TIME-LIFE VIDEO AND TELEVI-
SION *(TLF)*
1450 E. Parham Rd.
Richmond, VA 23280
(804)266-6330
1-800-621-7026

TRANS-WORLD ENTERTAIN-
MENT *(TWE)*
8899 Beverly Blvd., 8th Fl.
Los Angeles, CA 90048-2412

TRIBORO ENTERTAINMENT
GROUP *(TRI)*
12 W. 27th St., 15th Fl.
New York, NY 10001
(212)686-6116
Fax: (212)686-6178

TROMA TEAM VIDEO *(TTV)*
1501 Broadway, Ste. 2605
New York, NY 10036
(212)997-0595
Fax: (212)997-0968

TURNER HOME ENTERTAIN-
MENT COMPANY *(TTC)*
Box 105366
Atlanta, GA 35366
(404)827-3066
1-800-523-0823
Fax: (404)827-3266

UFO CENTRAL *(UFO)*
2321 Abbott Kinney Blvd.
Venice, CA 90291
1-800-350-4639

UNI DISTRIBUTION *(UND)*
60 Universal City Plz.
Universal City, CA 91608
(818)777-4400
Fax: (818)766-5740

UNICORN VIDEO, INC. *(UNI)*
9025 Eton Ave., Ste. D.
Canoga Park, CA 91304
(818)407-1333
1-800-528-4336
Fax: (818)407-8246

VALENCIA ENTERTAINMENT
CORP. *(VEC)*
45030 Trevor Ave.
Lancaster, CA 93534-2648
(805)940-1040

1-800-323-2061
Fax: (805)940-8511

VCII HOME ENTERTAINMENT, INC. *(VHE)*
13418 Wyandotte St.
North Hollywood, CA 91605
(818)764-1777
1-800-350-1931
Fax: (818)764-0231

VESTRON VIDEO *(VES)*
c/o Live Home Video
15400 Sherman Way
PO Box 10124
Van Nuys, CA 91410-0124
(818)988-5060
1-800-367-7765
Fax: (818)778-3125

VIDCREST *(VDC)*
PO Box 69642
Los Angeles, CA 90069
(213)650-7310
Fax: (213)654-4810

VIDEO ACTION *(VDA)*
708 W. 1st St.
Los Angeles, CA 90012
(213)687-8262
1-800-422-2241
Fax: (213)687-8425

THE VIDEO CATALOG *(TVC)*
PO Box 64267
Saint Paul, MN 55164-0267
(612)659-4312
1-800-733-6656
Fax: (612)659-4320

VIDEO CITY PRODUCTIONS/DISTRIBUTING *(VCD)*
4266 Broadway
Oakland, CA 94611
(510)428-0202
Fax: (510)654-7802

VIDEO COMMUNICATIONS, INC. (VCI) *(VCI)*
11333 E. 60th Pl.
Tulsa, OK 74146
(918)254-6337
1-800-331-4077
Fax: (918)254-6117

VIDEO CONNECTION *(VCN)*
3123 W. Sylvania Ave.
Toledo, OH 43613
(419)472-7727
1-800-365-0449
Fax: (419)472-2655

VIDEO DIMENSIONS *(VDM)*
322 8th Ave., 4th Fl.
New York, NY 10001
(212)929-6135
Fax: (212)929-6135

VIDEO GEMS *(GEM)*
12228 Venice Blvd., No. 504
Los Angeles, CA 90066

VIDEO YESTERYEAR *(VYY)*
Box C
Sandy Hook, CT 06482
(203)426-2574
1-800-243-0987
Fax: (203)797-0819

VIDMARK ENTERTAINMENT *(VMK)*
2644 30th St.
Santa Monica, CA 90405-3009
(310)314-2000
Fax: (310)392-0252

WADE WILLIAMS PRODUCTIONS, INC. *(MWP)*
13001 Wornall Rd.
Kansas City, MO 64145-1211
Fax: (816)941-7055

WALT DISNEY HOME VIDEO *(DIS)*
500 S. Buena Vista St.
Burbank, CA 91521
(818)562-3560

WARNER HOME VIDEO, INC. *(WAR)*
4000 Warner Blvd.
Burbank, CA 91522
(818)954-6000

WARNERVISION *(AVE)*
A Time Warner Company
75 Rockefeller Plz.
New York, NY 10019
(212)275-2900
1-800-95-WARNER
Fax: (212)765-0899

WESTERN L.A. FILM PRODUCTIONS, INC. *(WLA)*
7425 Clinton St.
Los Angeles, CA 90036-5703

WHOLE TOON CATALOGUE *(WTA)*
PO Box 369
Issaquah, WA 98027-0369
(206)391-8747

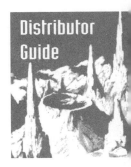

Distributor
Guide